OTHON DE GRANDSON

OTHON DE GRANDSON

EDWARD I'S LOYAL KNIGHT OF RENOWN

JOHN MARSHALL

First published in Great Britain in 2025 by
PEN AND SWORD HISTORY
An imprint of
Pen & Sword Books Ltd
Yorkshire – Philadelphia

ISBN 978 1 39903 962 8

A CIP catalogue record for this book is available from the British Library.

Typeset in Times New Roman 9.5/11.5 by SJmagic DESIGN SERVICES, India.
Printed and bound in the UK by CPI Group (UK) Ltd.

The Publisher's authorised representative in the EU for product safety is
Authorised Rep Compliance Ltd., Ground Floor, 71 Lower Baggot Street,
Dublin D02 P593, Ireland.
www.arccompliance.com

For a complete list of Pen & Sword titles please contact
PEN & SWORD BOOKS LIMITED
George House, Units 12 & 13, Beevor Street, Off Pontefract Road,
Barnsley, South Yorkshire, S71 1HN, England
E-mail: enquiries@pen-and-sword.co.uk
Website: www.pen-and-sword.co.uk

or

PEN AND SWORD BOOKS
1950 Lawrence Rd, Havertown, PA 19083, USA
E-mail: uspen-and-sword@casematepublishers.com
Website: www.penandswordbooks.com

CONTENTS

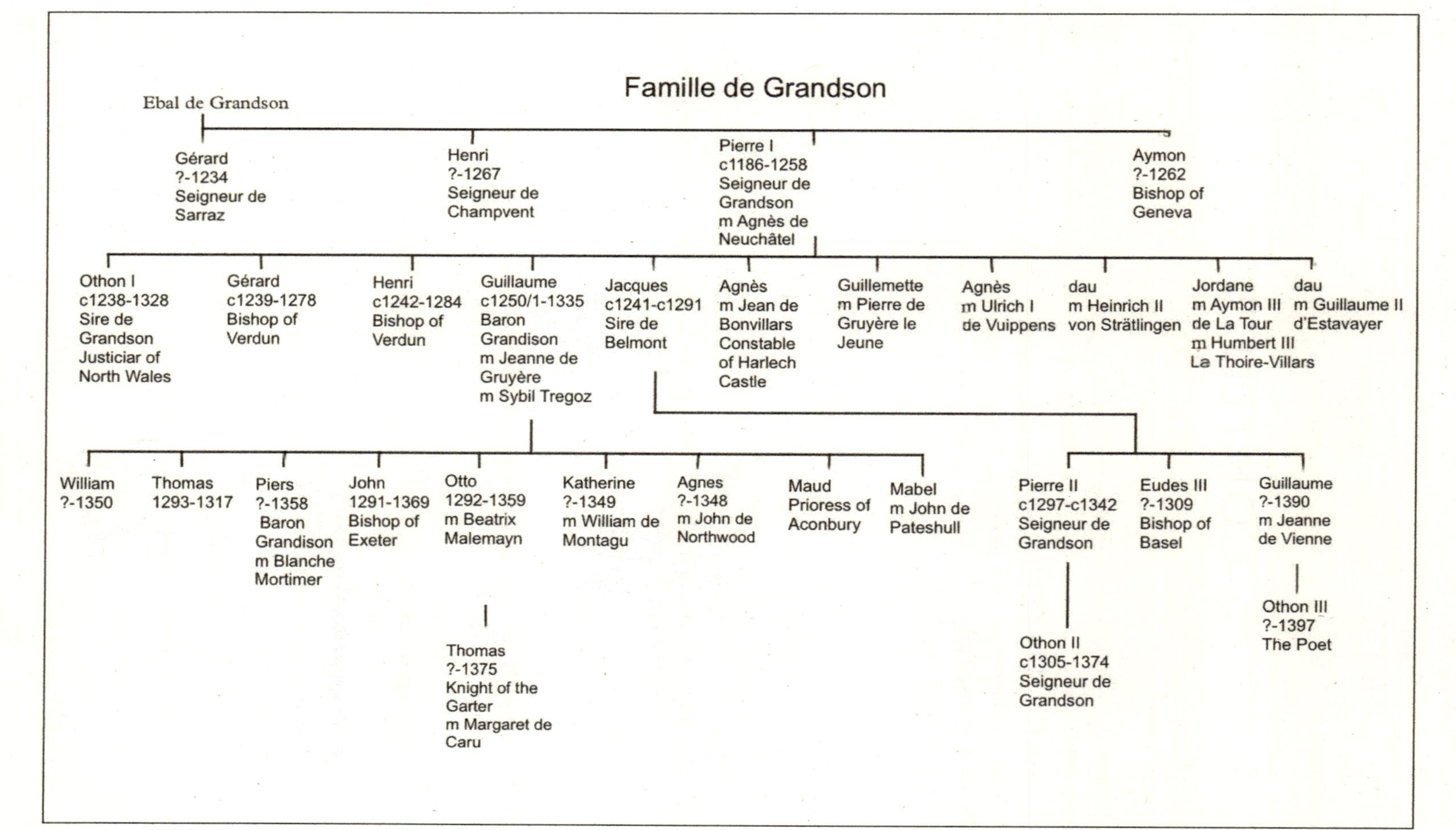

Famille de Grandson
Ebal de Grandson
Gérard ?-1234 Seigneur de Sarraz
Henri ?-1267 Seigneur de Champvent
Pierre I c1186-1258 Seigneur de Grandson m Agnès de Neuchâtel
Aymon ?-1262 Bishop of Geneva
Othon I c1238-1328 Sire de Grandson Justiciar of North Wales
Gérard c1239-1278 Bishop of Verdun
Henri c1242-1284 Bishop of Verdun
Guillaume c1250/1-1335 Baron Grandison m Jeanne de Gruyère m Sybil Tregoz
Jacques c1241-c1291 Sire de Belmont
Agnès m Jean de Bonvillars Constable of Harlech Castle
Guillemette m Pierre de Gruyère le Jeune
Agnès m Ulrich I de Vuippens
dau m Heinrich II von Strätlingen
Jordane m Aymon III de La Tour m Humbert III La Thoire-Villars
dau m Guillaume II d'Estavayer
William ?-1350
Thomas 1293-1317
Piers ?-1358 Baron Grandison m Blanche Mortimer
John 1291-1369 Bishop of Exeter
Otto 1292-1359 m Beatrix Malemayn
Katherine ?-1349 m William de Montagu
Agnes ?-1348 m John de Northwood
Maud Prioress of Aconbury
Mabel m John de Pateshull
Pierre II c1297-c1342 Seigneur de Grandson
Eudes III ?-1309 Bishop of Basel
Guillaume ?-1390 m Jeanne de Vienne
Thomas ?-1375 Knight of the Garter m Margaret de Caru
Othon II c1305-1374 Seigneur de Grandson
Othon III ?-1397 The Poet

MAPS

40 km
20 mi
© d-maps.com
Tyre
Acre
Hattin
Nazareth
Qaqun
Arsuf
Jerusalem
Holy Land - Outremer

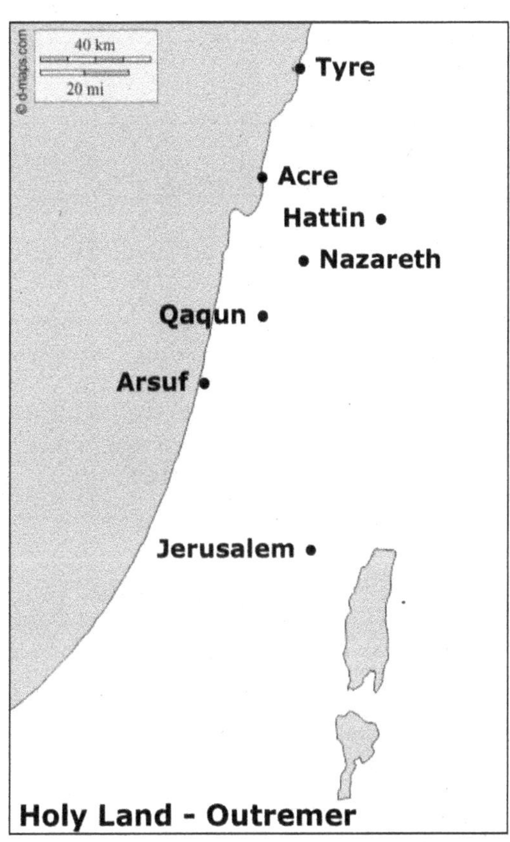

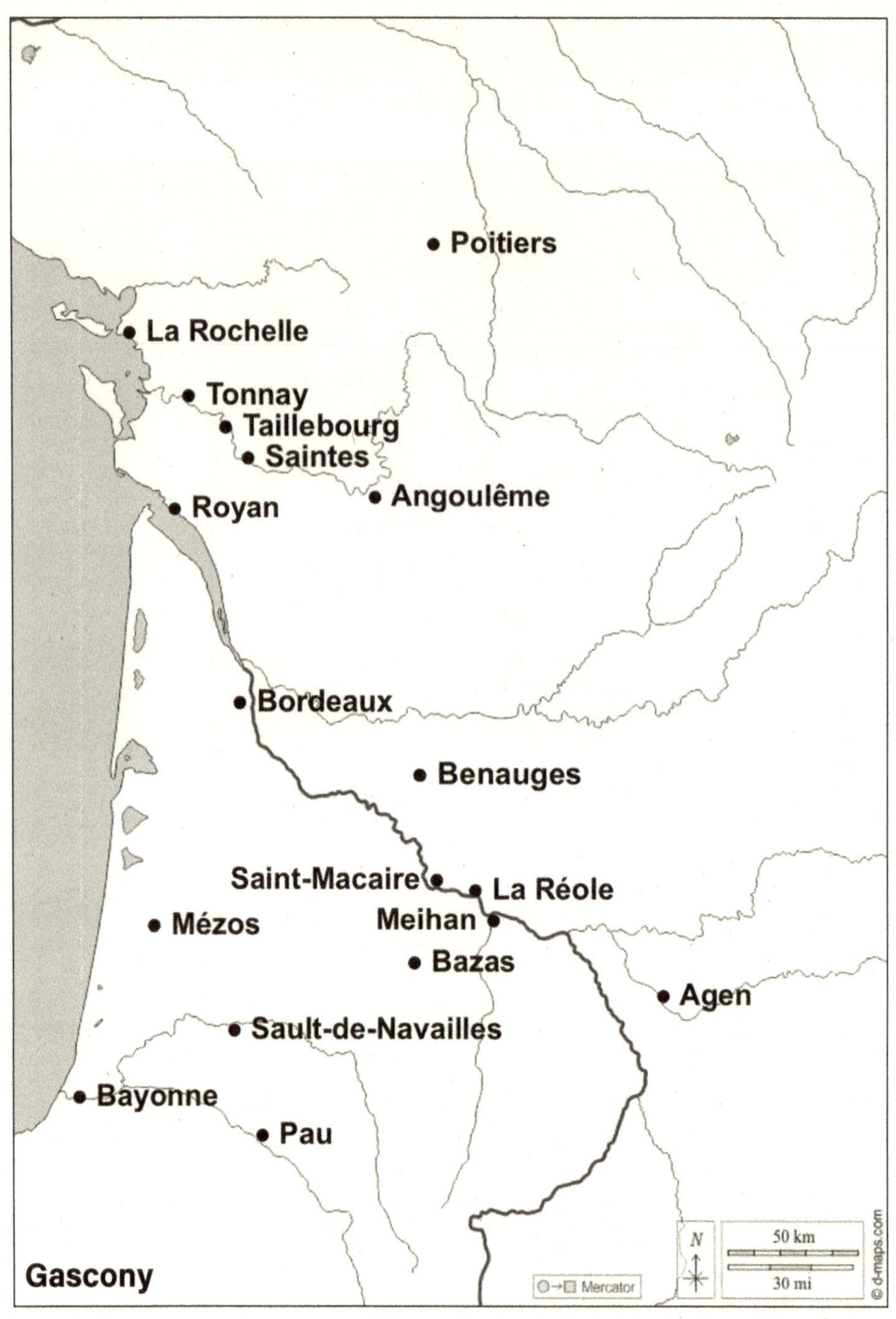
Poitiers
La Rochelle
Tonnay
Taillebourg
Saintes
Angoulême
Royan
Bordeaux
Benauges
Saint-Macaire
La Réole
Meihan
Mézos
Bazas
Agen
Sault-de-Navailles
Bayonne
Pau
Gascony
Mercator
N
50 km
30 mi
© d-maps.com

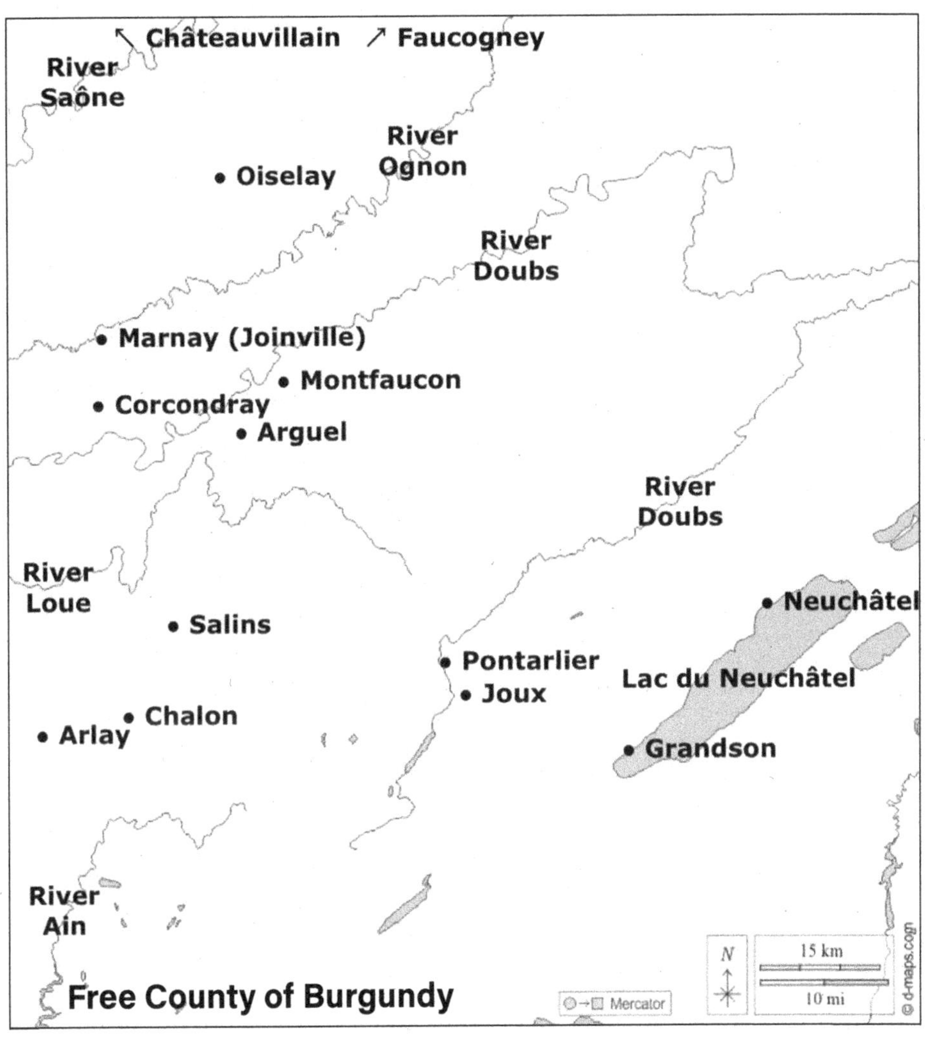
↖ Châteauvillain
↗ Faucogney
River Saône
River Ognon
Oiselay
River Doubs
Marnay (Joinville)
Montfaucon
Corcondray
Arguel
River Doubs
River Loue
Salins
Neuchâtel
Pontarlier
Joux
Lac du Neuchâtel
Chalon
Arlay
Grandson
River Ain
Free County of Burgundy
Mercator
N
15 km
10 mi
© d-maps.com

Mercator
N
80 km
40 mi
© d-maps.com
Carlisle
Newcastle
Bowes
Darlington
Brough
Richmond
Lancaster
York
Deganwy
Dyserth
Chester
Lincoln
Boston
Shrewsbury
Norwich
Montgomery
Ludlow
Kenilworth
Worcester
Evesham
Hereford
Northampton
Gloucester
Oxford
Caerffili
Westminster
Windsor
Canterbury
Salisbury
Dover
Lewes
Hastings
Portsmouth
Pevensey
England and Wales

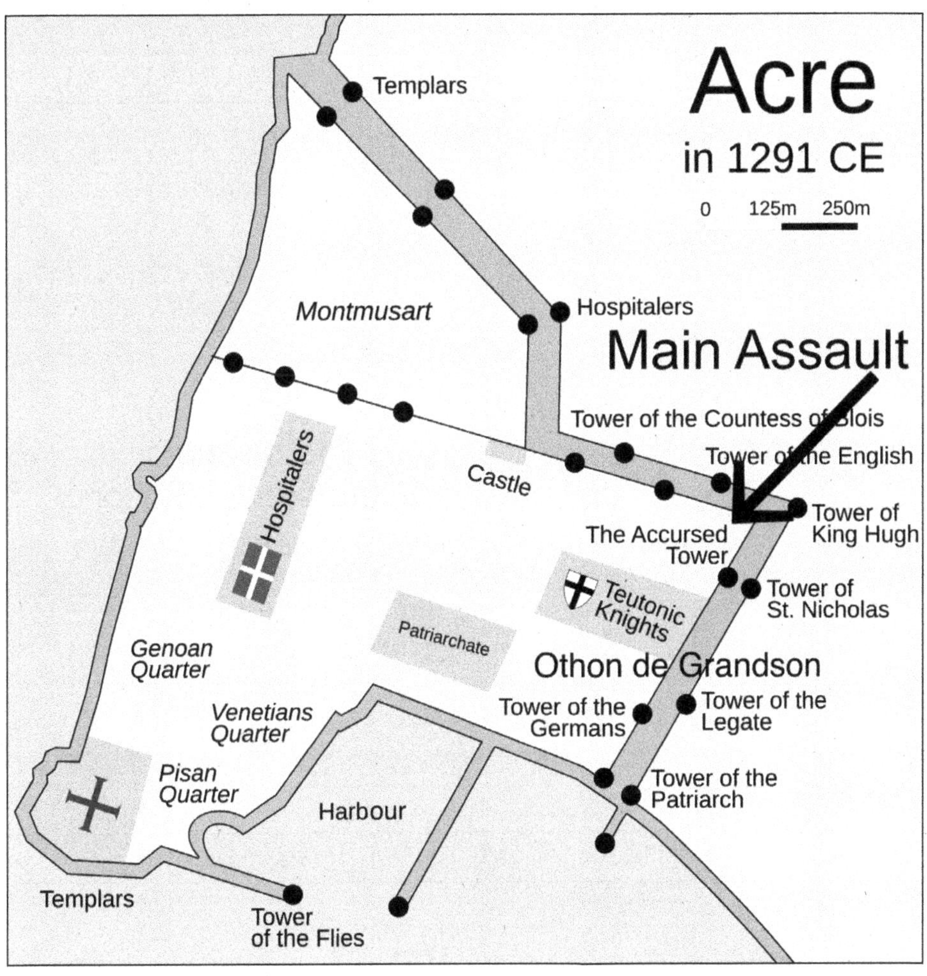
Acre
in 1291 CE
0 125m 250m
Templars
Hospitalers
Main Assault
Montmusart
Tower of the Countess of Blois
Tower of the English
Castle
Hospitalers
Tower of King Hugh
The Accursed Tower
Tower of St. Nicholas
Teutonic Knights
Patriarchate
Genoan Quarter
Othon de Grandson
Venetians Quarter
Tower of the Germans
Tower of the Legate
Pisan Quarter
Tower of the Patriarch
Harbour
Templars
Tower of the Flies

The travels of
Othon de Grandson
500 km
300 mi
© d-maps.com
Roxburgh
Lanercost
Berwick
Anglesey
Conwy
London
Dover
Channel Islands
Cambrai
Paris
Poitiers
Epailly
Grandson
Lausanne
Bordeaux
Lyon
Bayonne
Avignon
Turin
Zaragoza
Florence
Viterbo
Rome
Trapani
Palermo
Lajazzo (Ayas)
Kolossi
Acre
Nazareth
Equidistant conic

ABBREVIATIONS

Archives

ACV	Archives cantonales vaudoises, Lausanne, Switzerland
ADI	Archives départementales de l'Isère, Grenoble, France
ADS	Archives départementales de la Savoie, Chambéry, France
ANF	Archives nationales de France, Paris, France
AST	Archivio di Stato di Torino, Italy
BNF	Bibliothèque Nationale de France, Paris
CAC	Calendar of Ancient Correspondence Concerning Wales
CFR	Calendar of Fine Rolls
CPR	Calendar of Patent Rolls
CCR	Calendar of Close Rolls
CChR	Calendar of Charter Rolls
CChW	Calendar of Chancery Warrants
CLR	Calendar of Liberate Rolls
CRRS	Calendar of Rolls Related to Scotland
CWR	Calendar of Welsh Rolls.
LF	Liber Feodorum (Book of Fees (Fiefs))
RG	Rôles Gascons
TNA	The National Archives of the UK (TNA)

Collected and Published Primary Sources

Cartulaire de Jersey	*Société Jersiaise*. 1919. *Cartulaire de Jersey, Guernsey, et les autres Isles Normandes.* Jersey: The Beresford Library.
Fœdera	Thomas Rymer. 1816. *Fœdera, Conventiones, Litteræ, et Cujuscunque Generis Acta Publica Inter Reges Angliæ et alios quosvis Imperatores, Reges, Pontifices, bel Communitates. Tom* 1, *Pars* 1 *et* 2, London.
Gascon Rolls 1322	G. P. Cuttino. 1949. The Gascon Rolls of 1322, Vol 1. London. Offices of the Royal Historical Society.
La Finanza Sabauda	Mario Chiaudano. 1933–37. La Finanza Sabauda nel XIII sec. 3 Vols Turin. Biblioteca Della Società Storica Subalpina.
Ridgeway	Huw Ridgeway. 2023. An English Cartulary Roll of Peter of Savoy, Lord of Richmond (1240–68): Archives, Interests and Servants

	of an Alien Favourite of Henry III publication of TNA C47/9/1 in English Medieval Government and Administration: Essays in Honour of J.R. Maddicott edited by Nigel Saul & Nicholas Vincent, Woodbridge: The Boydell Press.
Wurstemberger	Johann Ludwig Wurstemberger. 1856–59. Peter der Zweite, Graf von Savoyen, Markgraf in Italien, Sein Haus und Seine Lande. Vols 1–4. Bern: Stæmpfle.

Papal Letters and Registers

Let. Jean XXII	G. Mollat & G de Lesquen. 1905. Lettres Secretes, et Curiales de Pape Jean XXII (1316-1334). Tome II. Paris. Albert Fontemoing.
Reg. Boniface VIII	Georges Digard, Maurice Faucon, Antoine Thomas. 1884. Les Registres de Boniface VIII. Paris. Ernest Thorin.
Reg. Clement V	Monks of St. Benedict. Ed. 1885–1888. Regestum Clementis Papae V. Rome. 9 vols.
Reg. Honorius IV	Maurice Prou. 1888. Les Registres d'Honorius IV. Paris. Ernest Thorin.
Reg. Nicholas IV	Ernest Langlois. 1886. Les Registres de Nicholas IV. Paris. Ernest Thorin.

Archiepiscopal and Episcopal Letters and Registers

Reg. John Grandison	Rev. F. C. Hingeston- Randolph. Ed. 1899. The Register of John de Grandisson, Bishop of Exeter. 3 Vols. London. George Bell and Sons.
Reg. John Peckham	Charles Trice Martin. Ed. 1882-5. Registrum epistolarum fratris Johannis Peckham, Archiepiscopi Cantuariensis. 3 Vols. Cambridge: Cambridge University Press.

Chronicles

Ann. Cestrienses	Richard Copley Christie. 1887. Annales Cestrienses: or Chronicle of the Abbey of St. Werburg at Chester. The Record Society.
Ann. Dunstable	Henry Richards Luard. 1864. Annales Monastici Vol III. London: Longmans, Green, Reader & Dye.
Ann. Gandenses	Hilda Johnstone (Ed.). 1985. Annales Gandenses Annals of Ghent. Oxford: Clarendon Press.
Ann. Londonsienses	Chronicles of the Reigns of Edward I and Edward II, pp. 3–252 DOI: https://doi.org/10.1017/CBO9781139343510.005. Cambridge:

	Cambridge University Press. Print publication year 2012. First published in 1882.
Ann. Osney	Henry Richards Luard, 1869. Annales Monastici Vol IV. London: Longmans, Green, Reader & Dye.
Ann. Tewkesbury	Henry Richards Luard. 1864. Annales Monastici vol I. London: Longmans, Green, Reader and Dye.
Ann. Thomas Wykes	Henry Richards Luard. 1869. Annales Monastici, Vol IV Chronicon vulgo dictum chronicon Thomae Wykes (1066–1289). London: Longmans, Green, Reader & Dye.
Ann. Trevet	Thomas Hog. 1845. F. Nicholai Triveti, de ordine frat. Praedicatorum, Annales. English Historical Society.
Ann. Waverley	Henry Richards Luard. 1865. Annales Monastici Vol II Annales Monasterii de Waverleia. London: Longman, Green, Longman, Roberts & Green.
Brut	Brut y Tywysogion, or the Chronicle of the Princes: 1955. Red Book of Hergest version, edited and translated by T. Jones, History and Law Series 16, Cardiff: University of Wales Press.
Cart. Lausanne	La Société d'Histoire de la Suisse Romande, 1851. Conon d'Estavayer. Cartulaire du chapitre de Notre-Dame de Lausanne. Chronique des Évêques, Librairie de Georges Bridel. Lausanne.
Chron. Albani	Henry Thomas Riley. Ed. 1866. *Chronica Monasterii S Albani,* vol iii. Longman, Green, Reader and Dyer : London.
Chron. Bertini	O. Holder-Egger. Ed. 1880. Chronica monasterii Sancti Bertini auctore Johanne de Ypra. Monumental Germaniæ historical Scriptores series. Hannover Hahn. Vol 25.
Chron. Edward I	William Stubbs. 1882–83. Chronicles of the Reigns of Edward I and Edward II, Vol 2. London: Longman.
Chron. Flores	Henry Richards Luard. 1890. Flores Historiarum 3 vols. London: HMSO.
Chron. Gloucester	William Alldis Wright, 1887. The Metrical Chronicle of Robert of Gloucester, Part II. London : HMSO.
Chron. Godefroy de Paris	J-A Buchon. 1846. Chronique Metrique de Godefroy de Paris. Paris: Verdière.
Chron. Guisborough	Walter of Guisborough. 1848. Chronicon domini Walteri de Hemingburgh, Vols 1 & 2. London.
Chron. Johannes de Oxenedes	Johannes de Oxenedes. Henry Ellis (Ed.). 1859. Chronica Johannes de Oxenedes. Cambridge: Cambridge University Press.
Chron. Lanercost	Herbert Maxwell. 1913. The Chronicle of Lanercost, 1272–1346.
Chron. Langtoft	Thomas Wright. 1868. The Chronicle of Pierre de Langtoft: In French Verse from the Earliest Period to the Death of King Edward I, Vol 2.
Chron. Majora Eng	John Allen Giles English translation. 1852–3. Matthew Paris's English History, Vols 1–3. London: Henry G. Bohn.
Chron. Majora Lat	Latin text. Matthæi Parisiensis. 1880. Chronica Majora, Vols 1–5. Henry Richards Luard (Ed.). London: Longmans, Green, Reader & Dye.

Chron. Nangis	Guillaume de Nangis. 1825. Collection des mémoires relatifs à l'histoire de France de Guizot. chez J. L. J. Brière.
Chron. Rishanger	James Orchard Halliwell. 1840. The Chronicle of William de Rishanger, Of the Barons' Wars. The Miracles of Simon de Montfort. London: The Camden Society.
Excidium Acconis	R. B. C. Huygens. 2004. Excidii Aconis. Turnhout: Brepols Publishers.
Gestes des Chiprois	Gaston Raynaud. 1887. Les Gestes des Chiprois. Recueil de chroniques françaises écrites en Orient au 13e & 14e siècles. Philippe de Navarre & Gérard de Montréal publié pour la première fois pour la Société de l'Orient latin.
Giraldus Cambrensis	Giraldus Cambrensis, 1146? –1223? George Frederic Warner, James Francis Dimock & John Sherren Brewer. Giraldi Cambrensis Opera. London: Longman & co.; [etc., etc.], 1861–91.
Hist. Anglicana	Chronicles and Memorials of Great Britain and Ireland, 1859, Bartholomæi de Cotton, Monachi Norwicensus, *Historia Anglicana*.
Magister Thadeus	R. B. C. Huygens. 2004. Magister Thadeus. Brepols Publishers. Turnhout.
Scalacronica	Sir Thomas Gray. Translated Sir Herbert Maxwell. 1907. Glasgow: J. Maclehose.

OTHON DE GRANDSON TIMELINE

c.1238	Born, County of Savoy, now Canton de Vaud, Switzerland.
1240-1	Pierre de Savoie enters English court.
1245	Pierre de Grandson receiving payments from English court.
c.1257	Death of Pierre de Grandson.
1260	Baibars defeats the Mongols at the Battle of Ayn-Jālūt.
1264	Second Baronial War, Battle of Lewes.
1265	Second Baronial War, Battle of Evesham.
	Grandson and his cousin Pierre de Champvent granted property in London.
c.1267	Othon de Grandson knighted.
1267	Grandson made Sheriff of Tipperary.
1268	Antioch falls to Baibars, end of Principality of Antioch.
1271	Accompanied the Lord Edward on the Ninth Crusade.
	Fall of Hospitaller castle of Krak des Chevaliers to Baibars.
1272	Death of King Henry III.
	Truce agreed between Acre and Baibars.
	Assassination attempt on the Lord Edward in Acre.
1273	Meeting at Saint-Georges-d'Esperanche in the Viennois.
1274	Coronation of King Edward I.
1275.	Grandson granted custody of the Channel Islands.
1276	Grandson sent to Gascony to negotiate Gascon–French commercial relations.
	Beginning of the First Welsh War against Llywelyn ap Gruffydd.
	Grandson recalled to Britain.
1277	Along with Henri de Lacy besieges Dolforwyn Castle in Mid Wales, First Welsh War.
	Grandson involved in ordering the early works of Flint Castle.
	Negotiates Treaty of Aberconwy which brings an end to the First Welsh War.
	Grandson granted the Chanel islands outright.
1278	Grandson dispatched once more to France and Gascony.
1279	Treaty of Amiens returns the Agenais per 1259 Treaty of Paris.
1280	Grandson granted the manor of Sheen in Surrey.
1282	Narrowly survives the Battle of Moel-y-Don, Second Welsh War.
	Sicilian Vespers revolt against French rule.
1284	Grandson Justiciar of North Wales.
1286	Grandson dispatched to France; Treaty of Paris returns Saintonge per 1259 treaty.
1288	Grandson held in Zaragoza as a hostage in relation to Sicilian Vespers solution.
1289	Fall of Tripoli, end of County of Tripoli.

1290	Journeys to the Holy Land and lands in Acre.
1291	Commands the English knights at the Fall of Acre, flees to Cyprus.
1292	Grandson involved in election of Jacques de Molay as Grand Master of the Templars.
	King Edward I adjudicates Scottish succession crisis in favour of John Balliol.
	John Balliol crowned King of Scotland.
c.1294	Grandson in Cillician Armenia.
1294	France confiscates Gascony, beginning of Anglo-French War.
	Madog ap Llywelyn and Welsh in revolt.
1295	Suppression of Madog ap Llywelyn revolt.
	John Balliol allies Scotland with France, the 'auld alliance.'
1296	Grandson returns to England from the Middle East.
	Grandson and Amédée V de Savoie treat with the French at Cambrai.
	King Edward I invades Scotland and deposes John Balliol.
	Grandson meets Jacques de Molay in Paris, likely origin of Templar payments to Grandson follows c. 1296–97.
1297	Engages Burgundian nobility in an alliance with England against France.
	Anglo-French truce extended by Grandson among others until 1298.
1298	Robert de Brus and John Comyn appointed Guardians of Scotland.
	Anglo-French truce extended by Grandson among others until 1300.
1299	Summoned to Parliament, becomes Baron Grandison.
	Treaty of Montreuil negotiated by Grandson among others betroths King Edward I to Margaret, half-sister of King Philippe IV of France.
1301	Grandson among others dispatched to Rome regarding Anglo-French peace.
1302	Grandson among those sent by King Edward I to negotiate an end to the Anglo-French War.
1303	Treaty of Paris brings Anglo-French War to a conclusion.
	Grandson and Amédée V de Savoie sent to take repossession of Gascony.
	French attack on Rome, death of Pope Boniface VIII.
1305	The Gascon Clement V elected Pope; Grandson accompanies him to coronation in Lyon.
1306	Robert de Brus murders John Comyn and becomes King of Scotland.
1307	Death of King Edward I, Grandson leaves England for the last time.
	Arrest of the Templars in France.
1308	Coronation of King Edward II.
	Grandson granted former Templar *commanderies* in lieu of former Templar payments.
1314	Execution of Jacques de Molay, Grand Master of the Templars.
	Tour de Nesle scandal in Paris.
	Battle of Bannockburn, Robert de Brus defeats King Edward II.
	Deaths of King Philippe IV of France and Pope Clement V.
1323	Othon de Grandson makes his likely only visit to the Channel Islands.
1328	Died, Aigle, County of Savoy, now Canton de Vaud, Switzerland.

A NOTE ON MONEY

The main money in use in Savoy, France, and the British Isles, and so the substance of this book, were *Livre*, *Sol* and *Denari*, varying in value by the issuing mints' silver content. In Latin this would be expressed as *Libra*, *Solidus* and *Denarius*, rendered in French as *Livre*, *Sou* and *Denier* and lastly rendered into English as Pounds, Shillings, and Pence – shortened in all three languages as L, s and d. No *Libra*, *Livre*, Pound or *Solidus*, *Sou* or Shilling coins were ever issued: they were simply a convenient accounting form.

There were twelve (12) *Denarius, Denier,* or Pence in one (1) *Solidus, Sou,* or Shilling. There were twenty (20) *Solidus*, *Sou,* or Shillings in one (1) *Libra*, *Livre* or Pound. And so, there were two hundred and forty (240) *Denarius*, *Denier,* or Pence in one (1) *Libra*, *Livre* or Pound.

A further accounting form in use in England was the Mark which represented two-thirds of a pound, and so thirteen (13) shillings and four (4) pence or one hundred and sixty (160) pence.

These coins would all be minted in silver, the silver content determining the value of one mint to another, for example *livres Lausannois* to *Livres Tournois* or English *Livres.* An exception from 1252 is the mint in Florence, Italy which began minting in gold. These coins known as *fiorino d'oro* or florins gained enormously in popularity and international usage because of their high intrinsic value.

To help, on occasion, to give some meaning to quoted numbers, we have used the UK National Archives Currency converter. This has been done as a helpful guide and is in no way intended to be a statement of fact. The converter can be found online at www.nationalarchives.gov.uk/currency-converter/ that is hereinafter abbreviated as TNA currency converter.

WITHOUT WHOSE HELP ...

I am indebted to the help of many in the preparation of this book. In no particular order: Jean-Luc Rosset whose patient explanation of Medieval Latin, of its origins and difference from Classical Latin was quite simply invaluable.

Thanks to my son Sean for spending his holiday time in Switzerland delving deep into the byways to seek out long-gone castles in the undergrowth, and for adding his own insight to the developing story; particularly at Épailly.

Thanks to my friend and colleague Michael Ray, author of his own journal article 'The Savoyard Cousins: A Comparison of the Careers and Relative Success of the Grandson (Grandison) and Champvent (Chavent) Families in England'.[1] Michael's support and advice was invaluable in the preparation of this book, particularly sharing his unpublished research into the lives of the *famille de Grandson.* Thanks also to my other fellow contributors to the Henry III roundtable podcasts, distinguished historians Darren Baker and Huw Ridgeway.

I would also very much like to thank Mrs. Élisabeth Hiller van Gaertringen owner of the Épailly estate for her time and tour of the Épailly *Commanderie.* Also, many thanks to renowned Templar historian Alain Demurger for supplying copies of his detailed work on Épailly, in particular.

And lastly, and mostly, thanks as always to my partner, Mary-Claude Dennler, without whose many hours of patience and fortitude trekking the wilds of Burgundy, the archives in Lausanne, Chambéry, Grenoble and Kew, and castles too numerous to mention, this book would simply not have been possible. Her help in trying to make sense of Old French texts should be noted.

NOTABLE GRANDSONS

Jacques de Belmont (c. 1241–c. 1290), Seigneur de Belmont
Founder of the Seigneury de Belmont upon the split of the Grandson lands among the sons of Ebal IV de Grandson therefore uncle to Othon de Grandson. Father of Pierre II de Belmont, the inheritor of the Seigneurie de Grandson from Othon de Grandson.

Guillaume de Bonvillars (unknown), Canon of Lausanne
A nephew of Otho de Grandison, canon of Lausanne in 1308 and prebendary of Corringham, Lincoln, 1324–26.

Henri de Bonvillars (unknown), Prior of Wenlock
Possibly a brother of Jean and Guillaume. He was a Cluniac monk, and for a brief time

Prior of Bermondsey, before his appointment as Henry de Bono Villar to be Prior of Wenlock on 10 September 1284. He was one of Othon de Grandson's attorneys in 1290 and 1294 and received delivery of the Channel Islands on Othon's behalf from Nicholas de Cheny in 1298. In the following year he was Othon's lieutenant in the islands, and a justice itinerant for the King.

Jean de Bonvillars (unknown–1287), Constable of Harlech Castle
Likely son of Sir Henri de Bonvillars, châtelain for Pierre II de Savoie at the Château de Rue. He was brother-in-law to Othon de Grandson. On 2 April 1277 he was bearer of a letter to Othon de Grandson who was besieging Dolforwyn Castle. Was at Chester in September 1277. Revisited Savoy in 1278, was at Evian on 22 March 1279. With Othon de Grandson in Wales in 1282 when latter was commanding forces based on Montgomery. In 1283 was sent to Wales, in 1284 he was described as Othon de Grandson's Knight Companion. Oversaw the construction of Conwy Castle. First Constable of Harlech Castle from 1285 to his death by drowning (probably during siege of Dryslwyn in South Wales) between July and November 1287. Married to Agnès de Bevillard (likely sister of Othon de Grandson) who held on to the Constable of Harlech role until succeeded by Master James of Savoy in 1290.

Othon de Bonvillars (unknown), Justice in the Channel Islands
Justice in the Channel Islands under Otho de Grandison in 1278.

Gérard de Champvent (c. 1264–1285), Canon of Lincoln, Geneva, and Lausanne
Son of Henri de Champvent and Helviz, brother of Guillaume, Othon and Pierre de Champvent, cousin of Othon de Grandson, he was a canon at Geneva, Lausanne, and Lincoln.

Guillaume de Champvent (c. 1239 -1301), Bishop of Lausanne

Son of Henri de Champvent and Helviz, brother of Pierre de Champvent, cousin of Othon de Grandson, in the household of both King Henry III and Edward I of England, also brother of Othon de Champvent, also Bishop of Lausanne. Rector of Filgrave before becoming Dean of St. Martin's le Grand in London. Bishop of Lausanne from 1273 until his death in 1301.

Henri de Champvent (unknown–1251), Seigneur de Champvent

Founder of the Seigneury de Champvent upon the split of the Grandson lands among the sons of Ebal IV de Grandson, therefore uncle to Othon de Grandson.

Jean de Champvent (c. 1285–c. 1333), Banneret

Son of Pierre de Champvent and Agnès, Banneret knight.

Othon de Champvent (c. 1259–1312), Bishop of Lausanne

Son of Henri de Champvent and Helviz, brother of Guillaume and Pierre de Champvent, cousin of Othon de Grandson. Rector of Hursley, Terrington and Havant before becoming Bishop of Lausanne in 1309 until his death in 1312.

Pierre de Champvent (unknown– c. 1303), Steward to King Henry III and Chamberlain of the Royal Household to Edward I

Son of Henri de Champvent and Helviz, brother of Guillaume and Othon de Champvent, both Bishops of Lausanne, cousin of Othon de Grandson. Steward to King Henry III, knighted in 1259, he served as knight of the royal household, then in 1269 Sheriff of Gloucestershire and Constable of Gloucester Castle. Later under Edward I he was again a Steward before becoming a Chamberlain of the Royal Household to King Edward I. Fought in the Welsh Wars, and later in Scotland.

Guillaume d'Estavayer (unknown–c. 1326). Archdeacon of Lincoln

Brother of Pierre. He first appears as one of the Edward I's clerks on 16 February 16, 1283, when the king gave him a prebend at St. Wolfram, Abbeville. In 1289 Othon de Grandson obtained for him the reservation of a canonry at Lincoln, though he already held canonries and prebends at Wells and St. Maurice, Llangadok, and the churches of Grinstead, Sussex, and of Llanpadarn Fawr. He accordingly held the prebend of Corringham, Lincoln, from 1291 to 1324. In 1290 Nicholas IV made him Archdeacon of Lincoln, an office which he exchanged on 13 September 1319, with John de Stratford for the Rectory of Stratford-upon-Avon. He was abroad in June 1306, and from that time had periodical letters of protection as beyond seas down to 1323. He probably died in 1324, for in that year Guillaume de Bonvillars received the prebend of Corringham.

Pierre II d'Estavayer (unknown–c.1322), Lord of Tipperary

Son of Guillaume II d'Estavayer, nephew of Othon de Grandson, he went into the service of King Edward I as a household knight. Given the Lordship of Okonagh and Tipperary for life in 1290 by his uncle Othon, with whom he served at Acre in 1291. His brother Guillaume d'Estavayer became Archdeacon of Lincoln in 1290. In 1298 Peter de Stratelinges, and in 1303 Perrotus de Staniaco and William de Gyes were noted as attorneys for him.

Agnès de Grandson (c. 1240–c. 1313)
Married Ulrich de Vuippens, who was Pierre de Savoie's bailiff in Bern, the couple's son Gérard de Vuippens is discussed below. Sister of Othon de Grandson.

Aymon de Grandson (unknown–1262), Bishop of Geneva
Son of Ebal IV de Grandson, Canon of Lausanne from 1209, also a Canon of the Archdiocese of Besançon in the Free County of Burgundy. Bishop of Geneva from 1215. Uncle to Othon de Grandson.

Gérard de Grandson (c. 1243–1278), Prince Bishop of Verdun
Son of Pierre I de Grandson and Agnès daughter of Count Uhlric III de Neuchâtel and Yolande d'Urach. Brother of Othon, Guillaume and Henri de Grandson. Chaplain in the service of Pierre de Savoie, witnessing his will whilst with the Flanders Army in 1264. Bishop of Verdun from 1275 until his death in 1278. Succeeded at Verdun by his brother Henri.

Guillaume de Grandson/Grandison (c1250/1–1335), Deputy Justiciar of North Wales
Son of Pierre I de Grandson and Agnès daughter of Count Uhlric III de Neuchâtel and Yolande d'Urach. Brother of Gérard, Othon and Henri de Grandson and founder of the English branch of the Grandson family, known as the Grandison family. He served as a knight in the household of Edmund, Earl of Lancaster. He was active in the wars in Gascony, Scotland, and Wales. He served as a Deputy Warden of the Channel Islands from 1294 until 1296. William first married Jeanette de Gruyère, daughter of Pierre de Gruyère and Ambrosie, his second marriage was to Sybil, daughter of John de Tregoz and Mabel FitzWarin. Created Baron Grandison in 1299.

Henri de Grandson (c. 1242–1286), Prince Bishop of Verdun
Son of Pierre I de Grandson and Agnès daughter of Count Uhlric III de Neuchâtel and Yolande d'Urach. Brother of Gérard, Othon, Guillaume de Grandson. He was briefly parson of Greystoke, Cumberland, from 1276 until 1278. He was at the Roman Curia in June 1282, when he sent Edward I news of the Sicilian Vespers. Henri de Grandson held a canonry at Wells in 1284. In 1278 he succeeded his brother Gérard as Bishop of Verdun until his death in 1286.

Pierre I de Grandson (c. 1200–1258), Seigneur de Grandson
Founder of the continuation of the Seigneury de Grandson upon the split of the Grandson lands among the sons of Ebal IV de Grandson, which split away the seignuries of Sarraz and Champvent. Married Agnès daughter of Count Uhlric III de Neuchâtel and Yolande d'Urach. Father of Othon de Grandson.

Katherine de Grandison (1304–1349), Countess of Salisbury
Daughter of Guillaume de Grandison and Sybille de Tregoz, brother of Jean de Grandison, and niece of Othon de Grandson. Katherine married William Montacute, 1st Earl of Salisbury, in about 1320. In around 1348, the Order of the Garter was founded by Edward III, and it is recorded by Jean Froissart that he did so after an incident at a ball when the 'Countess of Salisbury' dropped a garter, and the king picked it up. It is assumed that Froissart is referring either to Catherine or to her daughter-in-law Joan of Kent. Katherine, and so the *famille de Grandson* genes would find their way into the English royal family by way of the Yorkist line. Katherine and William had a daughter Philippa. Philippa was married to Roger Mortimer, 2nd

Earl of March. Philippa and Roger had a son, Edmund 3rd Earl de la Marche, who in turn was followed by Roger, 4th Earl. His daughter was Ann Mortimer, the originator of the Yorkist claim to the English throne.

Mabilia de Grandison (1294–1350)
Daughter of Guillaume de Grandison and Sybille de Tregoz, brother of Jean de Grandison, niece of Othon de Grandson. Mabilia or Mabel married John de Pateshull. They had a son, Roger Beauchamp, 1st Baron Beauchamp whose grandson, another Roger was the grandfather of Margaret Beauchamp.

Margaret Beauchamp was herself the grandmother of King Henry VII and thus the Tudor kings are descended from Mabel.

Jean de Grandison (1292–1369), Bishop of Exeter
Son of Guillaume de Grandison and Sybille de Tregoz, nephew of Othon de Grandson. He studied at Oxford in 1306, then from 1313 to 1317 he studied theology at the University of Paris under Jacques Fournier, who later became Pope Benedict XII. He returned to study at Oxford 1326–27. Later in Avignon he became the chaplain and friend of Pope John XXII, who mentored him and sent him on diplomatic missions. The Pope rewarded Grandisson by making him prebendary at York, Wells and Lincoln, and, in October 1310, Archdeacon of Nottingham.

Theobald de Grandson (unknown), Canon of Lincoln
Son of Jacques de Belmont, brother of Pierre II de Belmont, Othon de Grandson's heir, and so a nephew of Sir Otho de Grandson. He received a Bursal prebend at Wells in June 1299. By his uncle's influence provided a canonry at Lincoln on 4 March 1301, though he held canonries at Geneva and Wells, and the church of Eckington, Sussex. Resigned Eckington and went overseas in 1303. He acquired the manor of Morton, Devon, from Gérard d'Oron and sold it in 1310 to Hugh de Courtenay. Attorney for Otho de Grandson in Ireland in 1325.

Gérard d'Oron (unknown)
Nephew of Otho de Grandson, and may be the Gérard, son of Rudolph, Seigneur de Oron, who sold Concise to him in 1282. Another of Othon's nephews, Pierre d'Oron was treasurer of Lausanne in 1305 and Bishop of Lausanne from 1313 to 1323. The first mention of Gérard in England is in July 1290, when Othon de Grandson gave his nephew Gérard de Oron the reversion of Estremoye and Otheny on his Irish estate. This interest Gérard in 1304 exchanged with Richard de Burgo, Earl of Ulster, for the manor of Morton, Devon. Then and for many years afterwards he was a yeoman in the royal household; on 5 June 1317, Edward II granted him in reward for his good service to himself and to his father the reversion for life of Ditton Camoys, and Shenley, of which Otho de Grandson had a life tenure. Gérard's name occurs frequently in connection with those of his countrymen, Jean de Champvent, Gérard de Cusancia and Gérard and Eudric de Vuippens. He was deputy for his uncle in the Channel Islands in 1321–23, and 1324–25.

Gérard de Sarraz (unknown–c. 1233), Seigneur de Sarraz
Founder of the Seigneury de Sarraz upon the split of the Grandson lands among the sons of Ebal IV de Grandson therefore uncle to Othon de Grandson.

Eudric de Vuippens (unknown)
Son of Ulrich de Vuippens and Agnès de Grandson, sister of Othon de Grandson, he was accordingly his nephew. Brother of Gérard and Pierre. Attorney in England for Aymo de Quarto, provost of Lausanne in 1294; parson of 'Wyrkyngton' in 1303. Eudric is last mentioned in 1312, when he was beyond seas.

Gérard de Vuippens (c. 1260/5–17 March 1325), Bishop of Lausanne
Son of Ulrich de Vuippens and Agnès de Grandson, sister of Othon de Grandson, he was accordingly his nephew. Moved to England to become firstly a sub deacon at the Priory of St. Leonard in Stamford, then a pastor at Greystoke in Cumberland. He went on to become a sub deacon in Richmond and Canon at York before taking on a key diplomatic role with King Edward I during the difficult negotiations with King Philippe IV of France over Gascony. Left England to become firstly Bishop of Lausanne from 1301 until 1309 when he moved on to become the Bishop of Basel until his death in 1325.

Pierre de Vuippens (unknown–1291)
Son of Ulrich de Vuippens and Agnès de Grandson, sister of Othon de Grandson he was accordingly his nephew. Brother of Eudric and Gérard. Othon granted him Estremoye in Ireland. In 1290. Went with Othon to Acre, and probably died there.

FOREWORD

Othon de Grandson was one of the most significant men during the reign of Edward I. Edward's mother, Eleanor of Provence, arrived in England in 1236 to marry Edward's father, Henry III. Eleanor's arrival in England was also marked by the arrival in England of her uncles, William, Peter, and Boniface, who were the sons of the Count of Savoy, Eleanor's maternal family. The harbinger of these was William of Savoy, the Bishop of Vienne, who made an immediate, favourable impression on King Henry and became one of his principal advisers. However, he died in 1239, and it was his brothers, Boniface, and Peter, who had a more lasting impact. Boniface became Archbishop of Canterbury and Peter was granted the lordships of Richmond and Pevensey. But these men did not come alone and well over one hundred other Savoyards came to England at the same time to reap rich rewards for excellent service.

Othon was one of those encouraged to come. His presence was first noted in England in 1265, but he was probably here earlier. He was the lord of Grandson whose castle still adds to the beauty of Lake Neuchâtel in the Pays de Vaud, now in Switzerland.

Although many historians mention Othon, only two authors have studied him in detail. In 1909, C. L. Kingsford wrote a paper about his career in the *Transactions of the Royal Historical Society* (third series, volume 3), after which it was not until 1961 that Esther Rowland Clifford completed a full study entitled *A Knight of Great Renown, The Life and Times of Othon de Grandson* (Chicago).

My interest in Othon dates to 1963 when I began a thesis for the Academic Diploma in Town Planning of the University of London. I discovered, when studying the planned towns of North Wales, that a major figure in their development was Othon de Grandson. My interest was stimulated by the fact that my paternal grandfather's family came from Villars Burquin which is situated on the slopes of the Jura near Grandson and his family was living in Othon's lordship as early as the fifteenth century; so, they could have been Othon's tenants in the fourteenth century.

Othon was one of Edward I's most significant and trusted men and could be described as one of his best friends. He worked closely with (another) Robert Burnell, the Chancellor and Bishop of Bath and Wells. On Burnell's death, Othon stood out as the King's most trusted servant. Othon went on crusade twice and was a major player in the Welsh Wars and the post-conquest government of the principality. He governed the Channel Islands for over fifty years. Othon was a friend of the Queen too and he is depicted on Eleanor of Castile's tomb in Westminster Abbey. Even after the death of Edward I, Othon remained useful in promoting English interests abroad in France, Savoy and at the Papal curia. He was on a journey to Rome when he died at the astonishing age of 90 in 1328.

Apart from my paper concentrating on Othon's wider family and that of his cousin, Peter de Champvent, 'The Savoyard cousins: a comparison of the careers and relative success of the Grandson (Grandison) and Champvent (Chavent) families in England' in *The Antiquaries Journal*, Volume 86 (2006), 148–78, nothing has been written in detail (has been written) on Othon for over sixty years. He was missing from the *Dictionary of National Biography* (1885–1900) but, in the 1990s, a call went out for missing persons in the Dictionary. I suggested Othon and so was pleased to see (the fine historian) John Maddicott's entry in the follow-up volume and it is now in the *Oxford Dictionary of National Biography*.

So, it is a very great pleasure to welcome John Marshall's book on Othon de Grandson. John has already won plaudits for his study in depth of the Welsh castles of Edward I (*Welsh Castle Builders: the Savoyard Style* (2023) and of *Peter of Savoy: The Little Charlemagne* (2024). This book is bound to bring a greater understanding to the life and times of Othon de Grandson.

Michael Ray, 2024

PROLOGUE

Writing in the middle decades of the fourteenth century Jean d'Ypres, Jean V le Long, the abbot of the Benedictine monastery of Saint Bertin in Saint-Omer, Flanders, added lines of history to the chronicle of his abbey. He was a great translator of Latin travellers' tales into French, tales of those who had journeyed across to Outremer, the Crusader States. As such he took it upon himself to record the life of a great knight who had died decades earlier, perhaps the greatest knight of the Middle Ages. The last of the great crusading knights, one described as the last man to set foot upon the last boat leaving Acre at its fall in 1291.[1] Jean wrote:

> And I have heard that I am writing, from certain men of Savoy who are honest and trustworthy, but who have not seen what was told. for they said that a certain Lord de Grandson had been in Savoy for some time, to whom a son had been born. Astronomers were called to observe, calculate, or judge the birth of a child, who said that the child born, if he lived, would be great, powerful, and victorious. A superstitious person, or perhaps a divine one, was present, who, taking a torch from the fire, said that this child would last as long as the torch that was present. The father locked the torch he had taken in the walls, so that it would last longer. This boy lived, grew up, and lived to an old age and an old age, always increasing in honour, until he was too old and tired of living, and caused the aforesaid torch to be taken out of the wall and thrown into the fire. after which the knight, the log being completely consumed in the fire, soon expired. They said further that this fatal Lord de Grandson, being at that time with others beyond the sea, when he heard the son of the king of England, so strong a man, so poisoned, he alone dared to suggest his wounds thus poisoned, perhaps trusting in his fate foretold of the fire; He therefore sucked, and thus Edward was cured. And according to this lord of Grandson, and his subjects, the kings of England were exalted and honoured, and are still to this day esteemed great and powerful throughout England.[2]

The knight was Othon de Grandson. Jean le Long was referencing Grandson's longevity – he lived some ninety years – to explain the tale from Acre of sucking the poison from the stricken Lord Edward, future King Edward I. However, he might as well have been able to tell of many near-death experiences that the knight experienced during his long life. He might have mentioned the Bridge of Boats across the Menai in north Wales and following its crossing the ambush by the men of Gwynedd from which he barely escaped. He might have mentioned the Fall of Acre in 1291 where the knight fought valiantly on the city walls until they fell and a rush through the streets of the doomed last crusader outpost when he was last to leave carrying his friend Jean de Grailly with him. Indeed, he might have mentioned the thousands of miles travelled on behalf of Edward to Spain, Italy, Cyprus, Armenia, Wales, and Scotland, where he met with the countless hazards of medieval travel. That Lord Othon de Grandson lived until 90 was remarkable enough for myths to surround him to explain his longevity, the myth of the fire and the log.

The earlier books in this series, *Welsh Castle Builders* and *Peter of Savoy*, explored the lives of Maître Jacques de Saint George and his fellow builders of Edward's castles in North Wales, explored the lives of Peter of Savoy and his brothers who began the migration from Savoy to England that brought these builders and indeed Othon de Grandson. These tales are indeed heavily interwoven: without Peter of Savoy there would have been no Welsh castle builders, without Peter of Savoy similarly no Othon de Grandson. It was Peter of Savoy who brought the young Othon to England. Peter in effect was the most influential envoy on the European stage for King Henry III. Othon de Grandson would be the most influential envoy on the European stage for his son, King Edward I. As we shall see Othon de Grandson played a key role too in the Welsh castles.

The third book in this Savoyard trilogy will tell the tale of the deeds of two boys who came together when young, Edward and Othon, who had all the adventures available to boys and men of the Middle Ages. Through the pages that follow we will follow the life of one of the greatest knights to have lived, Edward's 'beloved and faithful' Othon.[3]

French historian Charles-Victor Langlois wrote of Edward:

> *On ne saurait trop admirer l'activité du roi anglais; il était à la fois sur la brèche du côté de la vallée du Rhône et du pays de Galles; les fils de toutes les intrigues européennes, en Castille, en Aragon, en Italie, se raccordaient entre ses mains; et il trouvait encore le loisir de veiller, sur le continent, à ses intérêts comme duc d'Aquitaine.*
>
> or
>
> We cannot admire the activity of the English king too much; he was both in the breach on the side of the Rhône valley and of Wales; the threads of all European intrigues, in Castile, in Aragon, in Italy, were connected in his hands; and he still found the leisure to watch over his interests on the continent as Duke of Aquitaine.

How did Edward achieve this reach? He had an Othon.

In the early years of the eighteenth century, there is a story that while Vaud was still under the authority of the Bernese, in the person of the bailiff Gabriel Gros, men gathered in the great cathedral of Lausanne, the one-time Notre-Dame de Lausanne. Workmen heaved at the white marble of the tomb of a great knight, thought by the observers to be the fabled poet Othon III de Grandson, a valorous knight who had achieved some notoriety by losing a duel.[4]

Decades later, in 1796, the romantic poet Marie-Louise Françoise de Pont-Wullyamoz wrote of their discovery:

> *Les tombeaux de la cathédrale ayant été ouverts sous la préfecture de Monsieur de Gross, baillif de Lausanne, on trouva dans le cercueil de Grandson, le fquelette du bon chevalier, revétu de son armure complette, casque en tête, éperons dores aux talons; et près de lui, sa lance et son ecu.*[5]
> The tombs of the cathedral having been opened under the prefecture of Monsieur de Gross, bailiff of Lausanne, we found in Grandson's coffin, the skeleton of the good knight, clad in his full armour, helmet on his head, golden spurs on his heels; and near him, his lance, and his shield.

But Madame de Pont-Wullyamoz had allowed her romantic delusions to mislead her; she waxed lyrical on the opening of the tomb of Othon III de Grandson. The tomb opened: the great knight beneath, in full armour, helmet with lance and shield was not the local noble, for those glinting golden spurs had been given at his ennobling by none other than King Edward, the first of that name, King of England, Duke of Aquitaine, Lord of Ireland. This was the tomb of Othon I de Grandson who had bestrode the European stage and walked with the kings of England and France, popes, and emperors; he was Justiciar of North Wales, a knight of two crusades, indeed the last crusader. This was Othon de Grandson, and this is his story.

CHAPTER 1

Savoy is a land of lakes, glaciers, and tall mountains, towering peaks and glistening blue waters. Set amid the high alpine passes, it sits astride the ancient routes from the balmy Mediterranean lands of the classical world of the South, to the colder, darker world of the North. The name Savoy, in French Savoie, in Italian Savoia, in the local Arpitan Savouè, comes from the Latin Sapaudia (or Sabaudia) – it came from a Celtic name for the Pays de Sapins – Land of the Fir Trees.[1] Mountain passes were the raison d'etre of Savoy, the source of its wealth and therefore the very essence of its being. The Col du Mons Jovis or Grand Saint-Bernard, the Colonne de Jovis or Petit Saint-Bernard, the Mont Cenis – these were the routes of pilgrims to Rome since classical antiquity, including the Via Francigena. If we follow the Via Francigena northward from the Grand Saint-Bernard we come to Lausanne and the Pays de Vaud, the modern Swiss canton of Vaud by Lake Geneva known locally as *lac Léman.* Taking the *Francigena* further northward we pass the Lac du Neuchâtel and on through the Jura into Burgundy. In doing so we pass through the lands of the *famille de Grandson.*

During the time of the failing Kingdom of Arles, or Second Kingdom of Burgundy as it is otherwise called, the Grand Saint-Bernard Pass had been held for a time by Saracens.[2] A Christian leader, Bernard of Aosta,[3] was given the task of restoring the sacked monastery at Bourg-Saint-Pierre but chose to found a new hospice at the summit of the pass still given the Roman name of Mons Jovis around 1050.[4] A century later the pass, and much later the rescue dogs which were trained there, were named after him. The mountain passes lead quite literally to heaven – not so much passes as cracks in the mountain wall that separates Italy from Europe. If you needed to travel between where men spoke French and where men spoke Italian, then you needed to travel through the lands of the Savoyard.

Savoy stretched across the Western Alps in an arc from the Mediterranean to the Gotthard central massif of what is now Switzerland. Spilling down from the high mountains to stretch tentacles of power and influence to Turin and Piedmont in latter-day Italy, down to Provence and the blue-green waters of the Mediterranean, west through the Dauphiné and Bresse on the valley of the river Rhône now France, north down the Grand Saint-Bernard to the valley of the Rhône in modern Switzerland along Lake Geneva (hereinafter referred to by the local French name Lac Léman) to the fertile Pays de Vaud and Burgundy – a fief bounded by the territorially expansive kingdom of France to the west and northwest, by the quarrel between Holy Roman emperors and popes to the north, south and east. There was contrast between the fertile lands of Provence, the Rhône valley, the Pays de Vaud, and the high mountain passes covered for much of the year in snow and ice. Whatever the fertility of the land, it is noted throughout for its stunning natural beauty, vineyards producing the most wonderful wines and pasture supporting livestock in abundance. It might be said of Savoy that it encompassed a garden of Eden.

The County of Savoy had grown from the wreckage of several post-Western Roman Empire kingdoms that had established their rule of the lands of the Jura and Alps. Originally the Franks had dominated, conquering the First Kingdom of Burgundy[5] in 534 only to see what had become by then the Carolingian Empire divided into three by the Treaty of Verdun in 843. The westernmost kingdom would become West Francia and later still France, the easternmost kingdom ultimately the German lands of the Holy Roman Empire. But the Middle Kingdom would be Lotharingia, named after its founder. There would be a temporary reuniting of the Frankish lands, but in 888 the last Carolingian, Charles the Fat, fell and with him the Carolingian Empire was finally laid to rest. At the abbey of Saint-Maurice, the last margrave of Transjurane Burgundy, Rudolf I, was elected king of one of the successor states, Upper Burgundy, centred on the lands of the Jura mountains and alpine foothills, the former Carolingian Margraviate of Transjurane Burgundy. His son, Rudolf II, extended the kingdom, reuniting it in 933 with the lands of Cisjurania and Provence. The united kingdom of upper and lower Burgundy has been known by a number of names: the Kingdom of Arles, the Kingdom of Arles and Vienne, the Arelat and lastly the name we shall use, the Second Kingdom of Burgundy. Geographically it encompassed mostly the course of the river Rhône, ethnically it was a Romance kingdom, linguistically it spoke what we now call Arpitan in the mountains and a form of Occitan farther south.[6] This Second Kingdom of Burgundy remained independent until 1033 when it was absorbed into the empire. The dying last king of Burgundy, Rudolf III, sent his crown and regalia to Holy Roman Emperor, Konrad II. Rudolf had been forced to sign a succession treaty with Henry II, the future Emperor, in 1006 which granted his lands to the empire. Although Henry II did not see this come to fruition, reigning until 1024, his successor Konrad did. It was henceforth generally accepted that the emperor was king of three kingdoms of Germany, of Italy and of Burgundy.[7] Frederick I, known to history as Frederick Barbarossa, went so far as to have himself crowned king of Burgundy at Arles in 1178. However, the independent Burgundian kingdom failed ultimately for want of a centralised state, Saracen incursion[8] and the failure of Rudolf III to provide an heir.[9]

Charles Previté-Orton found little to challenge the conclusions of the chroniclers, that the last king of Burgundy was a 'sluggard'.[10] He had earlier highlighted this failure of centralised state control, and power taken assumed by counts, noting that 'the expulsion of the Saracens, was accomplished not by the king, but by the local barons'.[11] The Saracens based in Provence had made war upon the Jura and Alpine regions for over eighty years in the ninth and tenth centuries, sacking the great monastery at Saint-Maurice, holding the key alpine passes such as the Grand Saint-Bernard, Petit Saint-Bernard and Mont Cenis and laying waste to valleys such as that of the Susa. Their power base had been the fortress Fraxinetum on the heights overlooking the current village of Garde-Freinet, about 12 miles (20 kilometres) northwest of St. Tropez. From this impregnable fortress, the Saracens raided the Rhône valley, the Jura, and the Alps until 973 when Count Guillaume de Provence, the Liberator, defeated and expelled them. The effect upon the region may be said to be analogous to that of the Vikings upon England. Still today the people of the Tarentaise describe dangerous weather as '*temps de Sarrasins*'. That it was not the king but the barons that liberated the region is vital to understanding the end of the Second Kingdom of Burgundy and the emergence of Savoy. Nature, they say, abhors a vacuum and so into the power vacuum of the failed Second Kingdom of Burgundy strode the Savoyards. They also say 'to the victor go the spoils'; the origins of the successor powers in the region to the failed Burgundian Kingdom, that is the counties of Albon, Provence and of Savoy, lay in the extirpation of the Saracen pest.[12]

By the thirteenth century the County of Savoy was a fief of the Holy Roman Empire – it was not to become a duchy until 1416[13] – the empire that, in the view of Voltaire, was neither holy, nor Roman, nor an empire[14] – therefore the Count of Savoy was a vassal of the Holy Roman Emperor, but as Voltaire might have understood, that gave the Count a high degree of latitude for movement and independence. This means, for example, a Count of Savoy would be able to develop his own international foreign policy and alliances independent largely of imperial policy. So, within the titular Kingdom of Burgundy, itself now within the empire, the County of Savoy enjoyed considerable freedom; as an example, Provence to the southwest went as far as to leave the empire in 1246 when acquired by the Angevins.[15] As we shall see, the Counts of Savoy were more than free to conduct their own foreign relations outside of any imperial relations, such as those they developed with the Plantagenet lands which will form a key part of this story.

Set amid this general political background of the decaying Second Kingdom of Burgundy and the beginnings of the County of Savoy lay the castle at Grandson situated at the southernmost point of Lac de Neuchâtel, on the Neuchâtel side in the shadow of the Jura. The lands that would become those of the *famille de Grandson* sat on the Plain of Orbe in the north of what is now the Swiss Canton of Vaud, set between the Gros de Vaud hills to the east and the Jura massif to the north and west, around the plateau lands where the Thielle empties into Lac de Neuchâtel on its way to the Rhine.

In Roman times the fertile land had been steadily farmed, giving rise to several villas, of which notable mosaics remain to this day.[16] The region had seen the decay of the Roman centres of Aventicum (now Avenches) and Eburodunum (now Yverdon). But there was the significant local monastery of Romainmôtier founded in the late fifth century as a part of the Roman diocese of Aventicum, rebuilt by 642 under the rule of Saint Columbanus, the Irish monk who had evangelised much of the region and not to be confused with the Saint Columba known to Scots. By the ninth century the abbey had become a possession of the Burgundian royal family before passing in stages to the supervision of the great monastery at Cluny. Mention is made of Romainmôtier since it introduces us properly to the *famille de Grandson* with whom the Cluniac monks fought for much of the tenth and eleventh centuries for the lands around the southern end of Lac de Neuchâtel. We first meet the *famille de Grandson* in the person of one Lambert I de Grandson, probable founder of the dynasty, who is mentioned in 994 alongside the Archbishop of Lyon, Bishops of Lausanne and Geneva and Rudolf III of the kingdom of Burgundy.[17] Interestingly Lambert is styled '*comes*' or count; whether this title was honorific or referred to Vaud is lost to us, but it is at least possible the Grandsons may have held comital rank and been demoted later by Rudolf. Rudolf would then offer Romainmôtier lands in Ferreyres near La Sarraz and others in Vaud.[18] Adalbert II de Grandson disputed this clerical expansion by building a tower at La Sarraz from where he looted Ferreyres, a complaint of which in 1049 brings us to the first mention of the castle and name of Grandson,[19] Adalbert is named as *Adalbertus, princeps castri Grantionensis.* Adalbert, it seems, had been making war upon Romainmôtier, also attacking their possessions at Champvent a few kilometres from Grandson and at Agiez[20]. Pope Leo IX came to hear the complaints and threatened to excommunicate Adalbert should he not cease and desist his attacks upon the church.[21] The eldest son of the excommunicated Adalbert II was an Othon, perhaps the first use of the Christian name by the family but Adalbert would be succeeded by another Adalbert (the third) who would be followed by Conon the Falcon. Later, in 1195, it would be alleged that Count Thomas I of Savoy kidnapped and then married Marguerite de Genève, but it seems kidnap and marriage were not new bedfellows in the mountain passes. Around 1075 the Falcon swooped from the Jura to kidnap Hilduin IV de Ramerupt, Count of Montdidier and Roucy, with a view to the hand of his daughter, Aélis. Poor Hilduin agreed to the marriage and Conon had his lady. Hilduin's fief in Champagne close by Reims, would bring much advantage to the Grandsons in terms of prestige by association. The story would come to us from Herman of Laon perhaps better known as Herman of Tournai.[22] One must take care, it seems, crossing the mountains.

The Falcon would number Barthélémy de Jura as his eldest son, treasurer of Reims, then Bishop of Laon in Picardy, and so the source of the tale of his parents' marriage. His mother's familial association with Reims, assisted in his career in Champagne and Picardy, through his maternal great-uncle Manassés II de Châtillon. Manassés was a cousin of the reigning Pope Urban II; the once nearly excommunicated Grandsons were indeed going up in the world. Barthélémy, a kinsman, through his mother, of Bernard of Clairvaux, would later retire as a monk to the Cistercian abbey he helped found at Foigny. Barthélémy was at the 1128 Council of Troyes, chaired by Bernard of Clairvaux which ratified the rule of the The Poor Fellow-Soldiers of Christ and of the Temple of Solomon, the Templars. The Templars would establish a commandery at Laon in the same year as a result. And so, the *famille de Grandson* were in at the foundation of the Knights Templar, their association with the order will become a major theme later in our story. With help from his brother Ebal, Barthélémy also took part in the foundation of the Premonstratensian abbey at Lac de Joux in 1126.[23] The Grandsons, so often finding themselves in dispute with Romainmôtier, had founded their own abbey.

Thus, in generations of Grandsons we meet the warlike and the pious – a typical medieval noble family. Conon would be succeeded by Ebal I, Barthélémy's younger brother; given his elder brother's ecclesiastical career, he in turn would be succeeded by another Barthélémy in whom we meet the first crusading Grandson – he will not be the last. The colleague of his grandfather Bishop Barthélémy, Bernard of Clairvaux had preached crusade in 1147 in response to the Fall of Edessa and the young Barthélémy had taken up the cross and joined the Second Crusade. He is reported to have departed this life in Jerusalem in 1158. Barthélémy would be accompanied on crusade by his neighbour from the expanding County of Savoy, Count Amédée III de Savoie, also taking part following the persuasive preaching of Bernard of Clairvaux. Amédée would not see the Holy Land, falling ill and expiring in Cyprus in 1148. No doubt the crusading tales would be passed to succeeding generations of Grandsons. Ebal III followed his crusading father, a charter of 1158–60 is notably witnessed by a Willermus de Cicoin, the *famille de Cicon* being a Burgundian family from the Franche-Comté who would follow the Grandsons in crusading and to north Wales in the next century.[24] In turn Ebal III would be followed by Ebal IV – although it has been recently suggested that III and IV are likely to be the same person.[25]

Grandson castle itself (Fig 1.0) had been constructed on a rectangular ridge of glacial moraine overlooking the lake. Ebal IV de Grandson had been Lord of Grandson until his death in 1235, his fief also including Belmont and La Sarraz. He had been granted the lands by Emperor Frederick Barbarossa to '*construire dans le territoire des Noires-Joux, maisons, villages, bourgs et châteaux, sans autre réserve que celle de suzeraineté immédiate de l'empire*' or 'to build in the territory of the Noires-Joux, houses, villages, villages and castles, without any other reserve than that of immediate suzerainty of the empire'.

In the years 1225–26 Ebal III or IV would like the King Lear of legend divide his lands into three but pass them to three sons not daughters. Henri received Champvent (only 5 miles from Grandson), Girard got La Sarraz and finally Pierre held Grandson itself once Ebal had passed himself, ten years later around 1235–36.[26] It had been on 18 June 1226 that we find Girard first styled '*Girardus de Sarata*' while his father remained '*Yeblo de Granzon*';[27] Henri is first described as the Lord of Champvent in 1231. David Williams has plausibly drawn up a list of the children of Ebal as Ebal (c. 1178?), Girard (c. 1179?), Hugues (c. 1180?), Henri c.1182?), Aymon (c. 1183?), Guillaume (c. 1184?), Othon (c. 1185?) and Pierre (c. 1186?)', noting that these dates are 'very approximate'.[28] Ebal would become Bishop of Lacedaemon (Sparta) in Latin Greece, Hugues, the Prior of Payerne, Guillaume, Treasurer of Lausanne, and lastly Othon, Archdeacon of Rougemont, the others, as we saw, inheriting the lands split by La Sarraz, Champvent and Grandson. A fifth clerical son, Aymon, would follow an ecclesiastical career as Bishop of Geneva from 1215 until 1260, which placed him at the centre of the coming conflict between Pierre de Savoie and the Counts of Geneva, thus bringing the wider family into the conflict and choosing sides. The Grandsons would become loyal lieutenants of the Savoyard, witnessing many charters in his name during his long absences in England.

The mother of this brood of Grandsons was almost certainly Béatrice de Genève, the daughter of Count Amédée I de Genève. Béatrice was the half-sister of Amédée's successor Count Guillaume I de Genève whose daughter Marguerite de Genève would marry Count Thomas I de Savoie who would in turn father Pierre de Savoie – in other words Pierre de Grandson and Pierre de Savoie were kinsmen.

There has been much debate as to whether the Grandsons, and Pierre de Grandson, were by now, vassals of Pierre de Savoie or merely kinsmen. Swiss architectural historian Daniel de Raemy sees no vassal relationship citing the lack of a primary source to this effect, but absence of evidence is not evidence of absence. Maxime Reymond described Grandson as Pierre de Savoie's chargé d'affairs in Vaud.[29] Eugene Cox was certain of the vassal nature of the relationship between Grandson, Belmont and La Sarraz.[30] Undeniably, the Grandson fiefs of Belmont and La Sarraz were enfeoffed in 1251.[31] Whether Grandson was in actuality a vassal or merely an ally we can assuredly say his actions were those of a vassal, and the vassal nature of the other branches of the *famille de Grandson* is highly suggestive. Williams more recently saw the subtle hand of creative ambiguity in the 1251 documents that might leave both Savoy and Grandson room for manoeuvre, writing: 'By insinuating himself between the lord of La Sarraz and the sovereign, Pierre de Savoie could claim to be the Grandsons' overlord; but the Grandsons, while being conciliatory, could be evasive over what that meant.'[32] Pierre de Savoie's biographer Wurstemberger wrote: 'There is no document of enfeoffment from Peter of Grandson, but he himself appears so often in Peter of Savoy's entourage that his feudal relationship is evident.'[33] We should also note Bernard Demotz who wrote 'many vassals have undoubtedly paid homage without a written record.'[34] Perhaps if it walks like a duck and quacks like a duck, then it may well be a duck.

Perhaps a piece of telling evidence does exist, but in England not Savoy; it is contained within the Calendar of Close Rolls for King Henry III and dates from 1252, the year following the enfeoffment of Belmont and La Sarraz to Pierre de Savoie. On the same membrane as an item relating to Pierre de Savoie's Honour of Richmond it is recorded: 'that Peter the Lord of Grandson shall have, without delay, his annual fee twenty pounds'.[35] It is difficult to see the fee paid to Pierre de Grandson as not related to Pierre de Savoie, or indeed also related to young Othon now being at the English court. Indeed the payment to Othon's father Pierre goes back at least until June 1245, just four years after Pierre de Savoie's entry to the English court.[36] As readers of my last book, *Peter of Savoy: The Little Charlemagne*, will be more than aware, this debate surrounding the nature of Pierre de Grandson's relationship with Pierre de Savoie matters given the overwhelming number of members of the wider *famille de Grandson* who will find their way to England. Pierre de Savoie had two motives always to the fore in his political dealings: first, to protect the position of his niece Alianor de Provence and her prized asset, the Lord Edward. Second, the promotion of his feudal position in Savoy and Vaud in particular. That Othon and his brother Guillaume will find positions close to the Lord Edward and that in return he will come to rely upon Pierre de Grandson and Henri de Champvent in Vaud during his time in England, thus satisfying the little Charlemagne's *modus operandi*, is highly suggestive of a quid pro quo.

But is it suggestive of a vassal relationship betwixt the Savoyard and the Grandsons? Perhaps or perhaps not. We know that Pierre especially favoured three families in terms of finding positions at court in England: the *famille de Genève*, that is the disinherited sons of Humbert de Genève, Pierre and Ebal de Genève; the *famille de Joinville*, that is his half-brothers-in-law, Gefferoi and Simon de Geneville/Joinville; last the *famille de Grandson*, the sons of his kinsmen Pierre de Grandson and Henri de Champvent, that is Othon, Guillaume, Gérard de Grandson and Pierre, Gérard, Guillaume de Champvent. Now some of these listed beneficiaries were vassals, others may not have been, but all were family, and it is the importance of family that is the deciding factor.

Pierre de Grandson would marry Agnès de Neuchâtel,[37] likely the daughter of Count Ulrich III de Neuchâtel, they would have a son, Othon; Henri de Champvent would marry a Helvie, and they would have a son, Pierre – both would be taken up by Pierre de Savoie to England to go into the service of the English monarchy.[38] Pierre de Grandson had been a friend of Pierre de Savoie's since at least 1234 and acted on his behalf in the region.[39] Indeed, Pierre and Agnès would have many children: Othon, Gérard who would become Prince Bishop of Verdun, Jacques, Henri another Prince Bishop of Verdun, Pierre, Guillaume, Agnès, Guillemette, Jordane, Marguerite, and others (see family tree).

And so, we come to the birth of the subject of this book, the knight and envoy Sir Othon de Grandson. If his death will be marked by great ceremony amid the splendour of the newly completed Lausanne Cathedral, then his birth is lost in the mists of time – it is simply unknown to us. Charles L. Kingsford in 1909, in the UK, subsequently supported in 1911 by Auguste Burnand in Switzerland, settled upon the year of 1238 as most likely[40] – making him around the same age as England's Prince Edward.[41] We should, however, sound the note of caution, that although this date has subsequently been picked up by *Oxford Dictionary of National Biography*, it is entirely without anything like a primary source, hence Oxford attaching the circa to 1238. Kingsford in a letter to Burnand wrote, '*J'ajoute aussi des raisons qui me font croire que la naissance d'Otton doit remonter à 1238.*' Or 'I also add reasons which make me believe that the birth of Otto must date back to 1238.' These reasons are summarised as a charter of 31st August 1263 which granted the peage or toll of Grandson to Pierre de Savoie, listing the family, which is suggestive of Othon having reached his majority by this time (see appendix).[42] He arrives at 1238 by Henri de Grandson's age of 21 in 1263, thus being born in 1242, also Pierre and Guillaume being underage and the knowledge that Othon was their elder brother.[43] The order in which the sons of Pierre de Grandson were born is not confirmed by the 1263 charter, but that Othon was the eldest is likely indicated by his title Seigneur de Grandson upon the death of his father in 1258. Williams who had plausibly dated the births of the sons of Ebal has subsequently equally plausibly dated the births of three sons of Pierre de Grandson – 'Othon c. 1238, Girard c. 1239, and Guillaume c. 1250'.[44] The dates of birth for the other known brothers, Jacques, and Henri, are lost to us. The daughters of Pierre and Agnès are only partly known and their dates of birth equally lost. Their identity is mostly known or implied by marriage; indeed, as with the daughters of Count Thomas I de Savoie, it is by daughters that the family extended its influence.

The death of Pierre de Grandson is apparent by the 1263 charter being in the name of his wife, Agnès, but also his obit being recorded in the necrology of the Cathedrale de Lausanne, as '*Visitatio beate Marie virg. Obiit Petrus dns Grandissono*'.[45] As eldest boy the young Othon, although likely absent in England, became the 'Lord of Grandson' later romanced in the story by Jean d'Ypres.[46] He inherited his father's lands at the southern tip of the Lac de Neuchâtel, both on the western and eastern shores.

Of the daughters, Agnès would become the second wife of Ulrich I de Vuippens, of their sons Gérard and Pierre de Vuippens much more later. Guillemette would become the wife of Pierre le Jeune, Co-Count of Gruyère. Jordane would become the presumed second wife of Aymon de la Tour. Last, we come to the assumed or implied wives of Pierre II d'Oron, Othon de Bonvillars, whose sons Guillaume and Jean much of later, Guillaume II d'Estavayer, Guillaume de Cicon of which also much more later and others. Sadly, for such an influential family surprisingly little is known of Othon's sisters, despite several of their husbands and sons playing such a leading role in the story.[47]

We also know nothing of the childhood of our protagonist, Othon de Grandson; the only reference we have to his childhood would come from his lifelong friend, Edward I of England. King Edward in later years, referring back to Othon de Grandson's arrival in England, when later bestowing Lordship of the Channel Islands upon him on 25 January 1277, had written of 'Otonis ... on account of his intimacy with the King, and his long and faithful service, from an early age'.[48] The Latin original for the translated text is '*et ut acquietet debita quibus indebitus est in servicio nostra, tempore predicto, et insuper propter specialitatem quam erga ipsum intime gerimus a primeva etate nostra et sua*'. Edward's use of the words '*intime*' and '*nostra et sua*' are important as they describe an intimate relationship of two men from their boyhood (see appendix).[49] Edward's suggestion that Othon's service to the crown had been 'from an early age' when taken with the aforementioned listing of the brothers by his mother Agnès in 1263 suggests Ottonin was elsewhere at this point and strongly implies a move to England by Othon de Grandson while still a child.[50] The impression is only strengthened by the 1281 grant of lands in Ireland to Othon by Edward as having been 'for his homage, and for the service rendered by him from his and the king's youth'.[51]

We know that Pierre de Savoie had surrounded Edward's mother Alianor de Provence and her young boys, the Lord Edward and Edmund, with a protective net of Savoyards at court. Bernard de Savoie and Pierre's kinsman Pierre de Genève had served as constables of Windsor Castle during the boys' childhoods from 1242 until 1249.[52] As we saw earlier Othon's father Pierre being in receipt of payments from the English court from at least June 1245 means that these proceeds fit perfectly within this timeline. Kingsford's suggestion of a move to England by Othon in 1258 is very likely to be off by at least a decade, an arrival in 1244-5 as suggested very plausibly by Williams is better supported by the available evidence. [53]That Pierre de Savoie might add the eldest son of his loyal lieutenant Pierre de Grandson to this protective web is entirely consistent with the Savoyard's actions. The ledger of advantage or otherwise to the English crown attributable to Pierre de Savoie has long been challenged in England, but as we shall see the introduction to Edward of the boy who would perhaps serve him most loyally his entire life must surely be placed highly and firmly on the credit side. It is tempting to see the two boys playing together from what Edward himself suggested as an 'early age'; we know from the toys that Edward would give his own sons that knights and castles played a central role. If we can place, as is then likely, the young Ottonin, the diminutive of Othon, alongside the young Edward at court then the two boys who played together would go on to experience all the adventures that might be offered to medieval boys as men (Fig 1.1).[54]

Pierre de Savoie was then the godfather of the relationship that will be central to this story, that between the Lord Edward and the young Ottonin. How then did Pierre de Savoie gain such a significant role in English life?

CHAPTER 2

In 1120, 1174 and 1220 there had been moves to create an alliance between England and Savoy, but the idea was finally realised in the 1236 marriage of King Henry III and Alianor de Provence. Alianor was the second daughter of Ramon Berenguer, Count of Provence, and Béatrice de Savoie.[1] Béatrice was herself the daughter of Count Thomas I de Savoie and Marguerite de Genève and therefore the sister of a whole host of brothers who, to Matthew Paris's chagrin, would find their way to court in London alongside their niece. First to come was the author of the marriage, Guillaume de Savoie, Bishop elect of Valence. Guillaume became a key counsellor of Henry's but was murdered at Viterbo while on papal business for the crown. His death brought to England his younger brother Pierre de Savoie who was soon rewarded by Henry with the Honours of Richmond, the Eagle and Eu, thus making him one of England's leading landowners.

The reason for the alliance can be seen almost entirely through the prism of the key concern of the Plantagenet kings of England, francophone politics. Henry's father John had lost the family's lands in Normandy, Maine, Poitou, and Anjou – and Henry wanted them back. With the aid of the diplomacy of Pierre de Savoie he tried to construct a 'southern alliance' of Savoy, Provence, and Toulouse to bolster his position in Aquitaine and attempt the return of at least Poitou and Anjou. This was in effect an alliance of francophones who would prefer not to be subjects of the Capetian kings of France if they could help it. It was, however, an alliance that would fail in its goal, but at least in the Treaty of Paris of 1259, much the work again of Pierre de Savoie, the Capetians recognised formally the Plantagenet claim to Gascony for the first time.[2]

However, Henry's preferment of his wife's Savoyard family and his own Lusignan half-brothers would in time destabilise his realm to the point of bringing about the Second Baronial War in England. While the conflict between barons and king had many nuances and should not been seen entirely, as it has been, in terms of being simply anti-foreigner, it marked the early years of the young Othon de Grandson's time in England. In 1258, by what became known as the Provisions of Oxford, a council was imposed upon Henry to rule the kingdom; the so-called Revolution of 1258 had seen Pierre de Savoie side with Simon de Montfort with the aim of removing the Lusignan faction from court. However, the ruling council fell apart, Montfort removing Pierre de Savoie during an absence from England. The Savoyard would side with the king in attempt to recover royal authority, and despite the attempts by King Louis IX of France to arbitrate, a civil war ensued.[3]

The chief battles of the war, that at Lewes in 1264 and Evesham in 1265 which saw the final denouement of the troublesome Earl of Leicester, Simon de Montfort, saw the Lord Edward centre stage. First, at Lewes, Montfort was triumphant, taking both Henry and Edward into what amounted to house arrest. However, in the spring of 1265 Edward escaped, possibly with the connivance of his mother Alianor and uncle Pierre in Flanders, and the slaughter of the Montfortians at Evesham followed.[4] No account from this time mentions his household knight Othon de Grandson, or indeed Henry's steward, his cousin Pierre de Champvent. However, as Kingsford first surmised, it is difficult not to imagine that the young Othon saw his first battles at Lewes and Evesham.

That Othon de Grandson was most probably with Edward, as part of his household knights, is likely suggested by the events following Evesham.[5] Immediately Henry gave orders for land held by the rebels, deceased or otherwise, to be forfeit to the crown.[6] The Savoyard beneficiaries of the postwar land resettlement were the cousins from Lac de Neuchâtel, Pierre de Champvent and Othon de Grandson, both obtaining much property in London.

Firstly, Champvent was granted the London houses of Robert de Muntpelers, lately an enemy of the king and of the rent accruing from a house in Westcheap, London paid by the aforementioned Robert de Muntpelers to one Thomas de Exeporte, also lately an enemy of the king.[7] Secondly, Grandson himself was granted houses at Queenhithe that had belonged to the rebel Simon de Hadestok.[8] Together Champvent and Grandson were granted the lands of Guillaume le Blund, who had fallen fighting on the Montfortian side at Lewes.[9] The ways in which the cousins acted in concert from their first mentions in English accounts is evidenced by an agreement related to the Blund lands. A 1268 agreement made in the dual names of Pierre and Othon relates to the recovery of monies due from the heirs of Guillaume le Blund – 'the agreement made between Peter de Chaumpvent and Otto de Granzun, of the one part, and William son of William de Criketot, one of the heirs of William le Blunt'.[10]

Bustling, noisy Queenhithe, not far from the newly completed St. Paul's Cathedral[11] was where all cargoes of corn and wool entering the city of London were unloaded. A century earlier William FitzStephen had given us a little of the colour of the London Grandson now called home.

> Moreover, there is in London upon the river's bank, amid the wine that is sold from ships and wine-cellars, a public cook-shop. There daily, according to the season, you may find viands, dishes roast, fried, and boiled, fish great and small, the coarser flesh for the poor, the more delicate for the rich, such as venison and birds both big and small. If friends, weary with travel, should of a sudden come to any of the citizens, and it is not their pleasure to wait fasting till fresh food is bought and cooked.[12]

After describing his favourite eatery FitzStephen, obviously proud of his city, went on to describe the beating heart of London:

> To this city, from every nation that is under heaven,
> merchants rejoice to bring their trade in ships.
> Gold from Arabia, from Sabaea spice
> And incense; from the Scythians arms of steel Well-tempered; oil from the rich groves of palm
> That spring from the fat lands of Babylon;
> Fine gems from Nile, from China crimson silks; French wines; and sable, vair and miniver
> From the far lands where Russ and Norsemen dwell.[13]

The London house of Othon de Grandson was a long way from the quiet of his birthplace by Lac de Neuchâtel; he was now one of the 'infinitude of knights or foreigners' that FitzStephen described as treading the streets of a 'city older than Rome'.[14]

Such grants of property by the victorious Henry and Edward were, of course, for services rendered – and given the proximity of such services rendered to Evesham and Lewes it is hard not to conclude Pierre and Othon's participation.[15] We might also see the work of Pierre de Savoie in these grants, who himself of course held the Savoy Palace between the Thames and the Strand. Amongst the grants we also a grant of the houses of William, son of Benedict to Gefferoi de Geneville.[16] The *famille de Geneville*, better known perhaps as the *famille de Joinville* were related to Pierre de Savoie by marriage. He had been instrumental, as he had been for Champvent and Grandson, in Geneville's move to England. Gefferoi became Baron Geneville in England, a close ally of the crown and perhaps instrumental in Edward's escape from Montfortian custody.[17] Gefferoi's brother Simon, the *Seigneur de Gex et Marnay* was Pierre de Savoie's man in Burgundy and had been instrumental in recruiting knights there to serve the English crown in Gascony and England.[18] When the time came for Othon to fill Pierre de Savoie's shoes as envoy and alliance builder in the region for England it would be once more to the *Seigneurie de Gex et Marnay* that he would turn as we shall see later. All of this is illustrative of the family connections which lie at the heart of the Savoyard story in England and the employment of which by the English crown to the reward of both the Plantagenets and the Savoyards.

There is perhaps one more piece of evidence, or more accurately lack thereof that we should think of regarding Grandson's whereabouts during the baronial war. In September 1264, after Lewes and before Evesham, Pierre de Savoie along with Queen Alianor prepared an invasion army in Flanders to rescue Henry and Edward from the Montfortians. In the end the invasion never came, and Edward was freed by other means, but in September 1264 the intention was clear enough that Pierre de Savoie wrote a last will and testament. It is signed by someone of the *famille de Grandson,* but not Othon. The testament was witnessed by Othon's brother, Girard de Grandson, provost of the chapter of Chapelle Saint-Thomas de Canttorbery at Lyon, but also a chaplain in Pierre de Savoie's service.[19] Now of course it is possible that Othon was in Flanders having fled Lewes by way of Pevensey, but his proximity to Edward, the rewards later in London, and his absence from the witness list are strongly suggestive that Kingsford was right, Othon was ar Lewes and possibly Evesham too. Ultimately, we may never know for sure, since the household knight did not trouble the English chroniclers, but the suggestion that the baronial war saw Othon de Grandson see his first battles remains.

More than a year later Othon de Grandson would become Sir Othon de Grandson. It seems likely that his father Pierre de Grandson had died years earlier, in 1258,[20] making Othon the Lord of Grandson, but he did not return to Savoy, and would only pay fleeting visits to his home for the next fifty years, each time while business for Edward meant he could call in en route.[21] Also at Evesham was fellow Savoyard Jean de Grailly, who had brought a Gascon contingent to the battle – his reward from Edward, with Alianor's consent, becoming the Viscount of Benauges and the city of Natz, both in Gascony.[22] It seems therefore certain that, although the Savoyard invasion in support of Henry was not to materialise, the victors of

Evesham had Savoyards in their midst. Jean de Grailly went on to be Edward's sénéchal in Gascony, signing treaties in the king's name with Navarre and France.

We have at least one record of the *famille de Grandson* being involved militarily in the aftermath of the baronial war and indeed perhaps the longest castle siege in English history at that point – it would be Othon's cousin Pierre de Champvent. One of the two main remaining rebel forces (the other in the Isle of Ely) was holed up in the great Montfortian castle of Kenilworth. What followed was one of the few full-scale medieval sieges on English soil, trebuchets, and all. The summons to surrender the castle had come in December 1265, but it was not until 21 June 1266 that the great siege began. There were some 1,200 Montfortians within the castle, protected to the south by the great artificial lake or mere, but on all sides by thick curtain walls. The siege would last some 172 days or six months until final surrender in December 1266, the besieged when they came out looking gaunt and pale. The original siege engines had proven inadequate for the work, the weapons on the inside having greater range than those on the outside, Henry had to call up for replacements from London. Trebuchets were hurling stone balls weighing over 300 lb (140 kg) into the walls of the defenders. Additional artillery for the siege were brought to Kenilworth from Nottingham Castle by Pierre de Champvent, '*one ballistam de trullio and four balistas ad duas pedes*'.[23] Henry brought a papal legate and two bishops to Kenilworth to excommunicate the defenders, who promptly dressed one of their own as a legate and excommunicated the attackers in turn. Two months into the siege Henry celebrated the Assumption of the Virgin Mary with a lavish feast in plain sight of the defenders – psychological warfare designed to drive the starving garrison to surrender. Henry even summoned barges for a waterborne assault across the mere – it failed. Plans to undermine the walls also failed. Archaeologists found a missile thrown some 350 yards (320 metres) by those assaulting the castle –this was a siege in the grand medieval style. Once the siege was finally over Henry called a parliament, which ended with the Dictum of Kenilworth.[24]

The papal legate at Kenilworth was Ottobuono Fieschi, who would later reach the throne of Peter as Pope Adrian V. Fieschi had his own connections with Savoy, his sister Béatrice having been the second wife of Thomas II de Savoie. It seemed to many then that the tentacles of the comital family of Savoy reached far and wide, and indeed this influential network is what first attracted England to an alliance with the Savoyards. The crown had employed both Guillaume and Pierre de Savoie as envoys and the Savoyard Bishop of Hereford, Pierre d'Aigueblanche, it would be no surprise then that they would soon call upon the *famille de Grandson*. It seems that the crown began employing the *famille de Grandson* in a diplomatic role before Othon. In March 1266 Pierre de Champvent's brother, Othon's cousin Guillaume, Dean of Saint Martin Le Grand[25] in London, was entrusted by Henry to travel to Rome to explain events in England to Pope Clement IV. Guillaume was to 'lay before him the damages, injuries, oppressions and grievances inflicted upon the king by occasion of the late disturbance in the realm'.[26] Guillaume de Champvent would go on to become Bishop of Lausanne while keeping a role as envoy and diplomat for the crown in Edward's reign, a role performed also and to a far greater extent by his cousin Othon.

One last story of the Montfortian era relates to Jean de Vesci, the onetime ward of Pierre de Savoie and husband of Savoyard Agnès de Saluzzo. Jean had sided with Simon de Montfort during the recent war and had been injured at the Battle of Evesham. During 1267 he had retired to his family castle at Alnwick, in Northumbria, there to begin a revolt of the northern barons. Edward led an army to the northeast and forced Jean de Vesci into submission, but what happened next is a little at odds with the traditional image of Edward. The chronicler Thomas Wykes describes his mercy to the onetime rebel.[27] In return, as we shall see, Jean de Vesci became a lifelong servant of the future king, trusted alongside Edward's lifelong friend Othon de Grandson. Jean de Vesci would also be one a lifelong friend, and brother in arms of Grandson, they would go on to share many horse miles together. The ability of Edward to show clemency and reward enemies with lifelong service thereafter is something often overlooked in his character.

It is also in this time that Othon acquired land holdings and title in Ireland, an island of which Edward had been Lord since the granting of his appanage in 1254. From 1267 until 1269 Grandson served as Sheriff of Tipperary,[28] although whether this was anything more than a title and he was more than an absentee landlord is difficult to assess as no surviving document places him on the island of Ireland. However, Sheriff he was, and he had been granted two castles in Tipperary, at Kilfeacle and Coonagh. Following the Norman acquisition of Ireland, the former kingdom of Munster had become the Honour of Limerick, from which Tipperary had been lately sprung, and into the hands of Guillaume de Burgh. Guillaume was the brother of Hubert, Earl of Kent, who had come to prominence earlier in Henry III's reign, serving as Chief Justiciar of England and Ireland until 1232. Guillaume's son Richard had died en route to France serving Henry in 1243. Having acquired the lands, Edward passed the de Burgh territory along the river Suir to Othon for safekeeping. Mark Hennessy talks of 'an impressive motte and bailey castle at Kilfeacle … adjacent to uplands in West Tipperary'.[29] Described as a manor, but in possession of a Norman motte also came Kilsylan Manor, now Kilsheelan Manor, some 8 miles (13 kilometres) north of Clonmel. The towns of Tipperary and Clonmel were also granted to Othon, the latter today's county town of Tipperary. Grandson is credited at Clonmel with the building of the town walls and foundation of Greyfriars, a Franciscan friary, in 1269. The grant for murage (a tax for building or rebuilding town walls) is dated to April 1268 and presents a slice of colonial life in mid-thirteenth-century Ireland.

> The K. grants at the instance of Otho de Grandison to the bailiffs and good men of Clommele [Clonmel] for ten years out of intrinsic and foreign merchandise, and for the greater security of adjacent parts, the following customs, namely: – From each hogshead of wine on sale, 2d .; each dicker of hides 1d .; each crannock of any kind of corn, d .; each crannock of salt, d .; each crannock of flour, 4d .; each dicker of goat skins, d .; each band of iron, d .; mark's worth of worked iron, d .; each sack of wool, 2d .; each cow, 1d .; each ox, 1d .; each horse or mare, 1d .; each hog, d .; eight 2 years old, 1d .; each piece of Irish cloth, d .; each cart - load of lead, 2d .; each hundred of wax, 14d .; each crannock of woad, 2d .; 100 lbs . of alum, 1d .; 200 boards, d .; mark's worth of mercery and bateria, id .; each load of worked iron, d .; each French mill - stone, 1d .; each English mill - stone, d .; each piece of foreign cloth, 1d .; each piece of linen cloth from beyond the seas, d .; each hundred of canvas, d .; each weigh of fat, d .; each ship of the cargo of 400 hogsheads of wine, laden with any kind of merchandise, 16d; each ship called farecost, 8d .; and skins

> worth 58., d . At the end of the term of ten years the customs shall cease and be abolished. By the K. himself.[30]

All this sounds like significant work for a newly ennobled minor noble from the Jura, but his period as Sheriff of Tipperary is marked by his witnessing of charters in England and so any visits, if they came to pass at all, can only have been fleeting. The subsequent grant in 1281 of these lands in hereditary right do not seem to have brought and increased interest in lands where even today the name of Grandson is often cited as foundational.[31]

During the period immediately after the Second Baronial War Othon moves from being a squire who did not merit a mention in connection with the battles of Lewes and Evesham to joining witness lists, not of charters in the name of King Henry III but of two charters in the name of his son, the Lord Edward. In the *inspeximuses* of these July and September 1267 charters we learn that the young Othon has now been knighted, he is recorded witnessing these charters, alongside fellow Savoyard Sir Jean de Grailly as 'Sir Otho de Graunzon'.[32] Edward's boyhood friend has now been raised to the exalted rank of knight and joined the household knights of the Lord Edward. Unlike his kinsman Pierre de Savoie, who died as Count of Savoy in May 1268, we do not know where, when and by whom Othon de Grandson became Sir Othon de Grandson. Pierre had been knighted by his nephew King Henry III, the man whom he would serve as counsellor and envoy for nearly thirty years. It seems likely then that Othon would have been knighted by the Lord Edward, the man whom Othon would similarly serve for nearly forty years. If Henry would have a Pierre de Savoie, then Edward would have an Othon de Grandson. That both Savoyards would serve as envoys for kings of England from the 1240s until well into the fourteenth century is remarkable. It would go too far, whatever Matthew Paris might think, to suggest that England outsourced the medieval equivalent of its foreign office to Savoyards for nearly a century, but it came distinctly close to doing so. Much ink has been spilled in considering the wisdom of King Henry III in offering preferment to his Savoyard family by marriage, but for good or ill they served the crown of England as diplomats, ambassadors, and envoys throughout a turbulent and formative time in English affairs.

So, as the young Othon knelt before the Lord Edward, can we imagine the scene not recorded by history? The ceremony of enablement, of dubbing Othon de Grandson a knight, was a very prescribed affair and rich in ceremony. An explanation of the language is helpful, the word we find in sources, '*addobatorum*', was a latinised rendering of the Old French '*adober*' which meant to dress with armour or adorn. The act of dubbing would also be known by its Old French origin of '*adoubement*'. This confirms that the origins of knighthood and chivalry lay deeply rooted in Othon's francophone culture. The ceremony itself later gave rise to the English word 'accolade' which gives us a graphic picture of the ceremony from its Occitan origin '*acolada*', literally 'to the neck' which in Occitan meant 'embrace'. It had been thought for a time by some historians that thirteenth-century English knighting ceremonies did not include the ritual bathing; the archive in Turin for a subsequent enabling of Savoyards in Darlington decades later confirms that it very much did.[33]

Geoffroi de Charny[34] described the ceremony of ennoblement as:

1. The day before the ceremony the knights to be would bathe for some time, the idea being not to physically cleanse but to spiritually cleanse.
2. The night would have been spent in a new bed with clean linen.

3. The following morning the squires would have been dressed by knights, a red tunic to show a willingness to shed blood for the faith, black stockings as a symbol of mortality, a white belt symbolising purity and chastity and finally a red cloak to show humility.
4. The squires would then go to church to hold a vigil.
5. Finally, the ceremony itself saw the affixing of golden spurs, the belt of knighthood, followed by the Lord Edward (as is likely in this case) passing the sword of knighthood along with either a blow (across the cheek) or a tap with the sword (as today). Othon's golden spurs would be with him in this life and the next, as those later opening his tomb in the eighteenth century cast eyes upon their glinting lustre. Sadly, they appear to have subsequently been the subject of grave robbing and are no longer known to us.[35]

The papal legate at Kenilworth, Ottobuono Fieschi, had been sent to England in the summer of 1265 even as the Baronial War reached its climax at Evesham, on a threefold mission: first, to establish peace in the troubled realm of England; second, to reform the church and most importantly, since peace could facilitate the third, to preach crusade. Pope Urban IV had declared a crusade in 1263 but in England the Baronial War had strangled plans, now Urban's successor Clement IV had sent Fieschi to preach crusade once more. A letter from Clement IV to the Patriarch of Jerusalem in August 1266 reports that crusade was being preached in England.[36]

Meanwhile, Llywelyn ap Gruffydd, Prince of Gwynedd, had been expanding his power base in Wales and had sought an alliance with Simon de Montfort to take advantage of the English crown's weakness. Alas for Llywelyn the defeat of Montfort meant a return to the negotiating table and the good offices of Fieschi. In late September 1267 Fieschi accompanied Henry III to the Welsh marches; after four days of negotiations the resulting Treaty of Montgomery not only granted Llywelyn title as Prince of Wales,[37] but also accorded him suzerainty over all other Welsh rulers and robbed Edward personally of his appanage land in Wales. What is more, it had created dangerous sources of conflict, for the native Welsh princes now owed allegiance to the Prince of Wales. But the native Welsh princes were not the only rulers of Wales – there were the marcher lords for all to contend with. The marcher lords occupied Welsh land outside the Kingdom of England, and owed allegiance not to the Prince of Wales, but to the king of England. The marcher lords held lands along much of the Welsh border with England, but also most of South Wales, Glamorgan, and Pembroke. Llywelyn himself held Gwynedd, now extending from the Llyn peninsula all the way to Deeside and down the western coast, as far as the Dovey estuary. His vassals held Powys and Ceredigion, meaning that a cocktail of warring interests held Wales, with ultimately the Prince of Wales and the marcher lords subject to Edward. The Treaty of Montgomery would not provide the basis for a peaceful settlement of Wales.

Nonetheless, when Fieschi finally left an apparently pacified kingdom for Rome in July 1268; he did so with the required commitments to crusade[38] from the English monarchy – on behalf of Henry's sons – for the Lord Edward this was the chance of glory in the Holy Land.

In 1099 following the First Crusade and the fall of Jerusalem the Crusader States had consisted of, north to south, the County of Edessa centred on Edessa itself on what would now be the

Turkish-Syrian border, the Principality of Antioch, today Antakya in the Hatay Province of Turkey, the County of Tripoli centred on Tripoli itself in northern Lebanon, and lastly the Kingdom of Jerusalem which comprised much of modern-day Israel and southern Lebanon. The crusader kingdoms were known in contemporary Western Europe by the francophone '*terre sainte*' or 'Holy Land' or commonly as '*outremer*' that is the land 'over the sea' – these French names being a reminder that for the native inhabitants of the Levant the western newcomers, whether from England, France or elsewhere were '*al-ifranji*' that is 'the franks'.[39]

But by the mid-thirteenth century, following the fall of Edessa to Imad al-din Zengi and his son Nur ad-din and Jerusalem to Salah ad-din, the Crusader kingdoms consisted solely of the rump of the Kingdom of Jerusalem, then only in possession of Acre, plus the County of Tripoli and Principality of Antioch – Outremer was withering upon the vine. The County of Edessa had gone in 1150 to Nur ad-Din and had not been recovered. The great prize Jerusalem was lost to Salah ad-Din in 1187 after the disaster at Hattin. Acre itself, though strongly fortified, remained a vulnerable Christian outpost set amid a hostile sea of Islam. King Louis IX of France had failed in his crusade to recover Jerusalem and indeed his seventh crusade (1248–54) had been an unmitigated disaster; along with England he was eager to make amends. What followed is, depending on how you count your crusades, the eighth or ninth crusade.[40] One of the unfortunate side effects of Louis' failed seventh crusade was the overthrow of the Ayyubid dynasty then ruling Egypt by the hostile Mamluks and in particular Sultan Baibars. The Mamluks were former slaves, made up mostly of enslaved Turks, Copts, Georgians, Slavs, Circassians and Abkhazians – they had one thing in common: they fought ferociously. The thirteenth century offers a salutary lesson for those subsequently seeking regime change in the Middle East – beware what you wish for, you might actually get it.

Al-Malik al-Zahir Rukn al-Din Baibars al-Bunduqdari or Baibars, meaning Great Panther in Turkic, had been a fearsome foe and scourge of the crusaders; he had united Egypt and Syria against the Christians (Fig 1.2). He had been one of the commanders of the Egyptian forces that had inflicted the humiliating defeats on Louis at Mansurah and Fariskur in 1250.[41] Like Europe the Middle East was threatened by the Golden Horde pouring westward across the steppes. In 1258 the Mongols had sacked Baghdad, overthrown the Abbasids there and founded the Il-khanate which would continue to offer alliances to the Frankish west. However, on 3 September 1260 Baibars had defeated an army of Mongols led by Kitbuga at one of history's pivotal battles, Ayn Jālūt. The fourth Mamluk sultan, Qutuz, employed Baibars to meet the Mongol threat but was assassinated by him on their way back to Egypt. In 1261 Baibars installed a caliph to legitimise his sultanate, a caliph being supreme religious leader to a sultan's political power. The Muslim world had lacked a caliph since the sacking of Baghdad. Baibars's installation as a replacement puppet caliph in al-Mustansir II and then al-Hakim I united the Muslim world behind Baibars. The new sultan is described by definitive Crusade historian Steven Runciman as 'a huge man with brown skin, blue eyes and a loud resonant voice' and 'unimpeded by any scruple of honour, gratitude or mercy'.[42]

Once safer from the Mongol threat and having united the Muslim world behind him, he could turn his attention to the remaining Latin thorns in his side. After earlier (1263) sacking the symbolic Nazareth, he had one by one taken their strongholds along the Levantine coast (1265), reducing and massacring all at both Caesarea (only recently refortified by Louis IX) and Haifa before taking the great Hospitaller stronghold of Arsuf.[43] At Arsuf, Baibars had offered terms to the 270 defending Hospitaller knights that they might go free if they surrendered the citadel; they did but Baibars reneged on his deal and enslaved them all. In

1266 the formidable Templar castle at Safed, on the road from Acre to Damascus, fared worse when Baibars induced its surrender before decapitating the yielding knights.[44] In 1267 when the Franks in Acre sought to negotiate with Baibars, at Safed, Runciman recounted that 'the whole castle was encircled with the skulls of murdered Christian prisoners.'[45] Baibars then clearly was not a man to be negotiated with; he began the 1268 fighting season by attacking Jaffa, slaughtering its inhabitants but this time letting the garrison retreat to Acre – this season Acre would be spared. Following the capture of the Templar castle at Beaufort his target would be Antioch.

Antioch had been in Christian hands for 170 years when Baibars arrived at its great walls. On 18 May 1268 he made a breach of the walls, and the defenders were slaughtered in the streets or sold into slavery. Bohemond VI, Antioch's ruler, had not been in the city (he was at Tripoli), prompting Baibars's secretary to record:

> Death came among the besieged from all sides and by all roads: we killed all that thou hadst appointed to guard the city or defend its approaches. If thou hadst seen thy knights trampled under the feet of the horses, thy provinces given up to pillage, thy riches distributed by measures full, the wives of thy subjects put to public sale; if thou hadst seen the pulpits and crosses overturned, the leaves of the Gospel torn and cast to the winds, and the sepulchres of thy patriarchs profaned; if thou hadst seen thy enemies, the Mussulmans trampling upon the tabernacle, and immolating in the sanctuary, monk, priest and deacon; in short, if thou hadst seen thy palaces given up to the flames, the dead devoured by the fire of this world, the Church of St. Paul and that of St. Peter completely and entirely destroyed, certes, thou wouldst have cried out 'Would to Heaven that I were become dust!'[46]

When news of the slaughter and fall of Antioch reached Europe that summer of 1268, to save Acre, Edward, a conventionally pious man, pledged to take the cross and crusade in the Holy Land.[47] Papal Legate Ottobuono dei Fieschi preached at Northampton on Sunday, 24 June 1268; the call to arms was answered not only by Edward, but his brother Edmund and half-brother Guillaume de Valence too – and since Othon de Grandson was with Edward that summer he too took the cross.[48] By the thirteenth century there was a service, developed from that of blessings pilgrims, by which *Cruce Signati*, received the sign of the cross, almost certainly by the actual sewing of a cross to their clothes. Several forms of service survive but most include psalms, the *Kyrie* and *Pater Noster* and words such as '*Accipe signaculum sanctae Crucis*' or 'Receive the sign of the holy cross'.[49] The contemporary song gave their reasons for becoming crusaders: '*Mox crucis assumpsit, cupiens exsolvere dignum Obsequium Christo*' or 'He [Edward] soon took up the cross, desiring to be worthy to be redeemed by Obedience to Christ.' It's easy in our more secular age to be dismissive of those that took up the cross, but perhaps we should also remember the writer of this song had preceded these words with '*Impiger Eaduuardus devitans otia*' or 'Edward the impetuous shunned idleness' for which we might read 'Edward the victor of Evesham was impatient for some martial action.'[50] This was the age-old apparent contradiction of the crusades, piety, and martial action riding side by side. Northampton was not a choice of happenstance, the Church of the Holy Sepulchre there being a replica of the one in Jerusalem and built by a knight who had returned from the First Crusade. Ottobuono and the church would be able to offer two promises to those taking up the cross: first, the remission of sins, no small matter in a time when Edward and Othon would already have run their sword through many opponents, and second, and importantly given the recent civil war, the protection of their lands and property while away doing 'God's will'. Battle remained a mouthwatering prospect for Edward, now nearing 30, and with a continuing thirst for chivalric glory. So, the heir to the English throne, together with his young Castilian wife Leonor and loyal Savoyard Othon de Grandson joined with the saint-to-be Louis in preparing to crusade.

In March 1267 King Louis IX of France had decided once more to take up the cross, to begin again the task that had failed so spectacularly nearly twenty years earlier. Louis' advisers all tried to persuade him that the venture was ill advised, and that losing one army of Frenchmen in the Levant was quite enough for one lifetime. Pointedly, the great French chronicler of the seventh crusade, Jean de Joinville, refused to join his king on what he considered to be a new foolish enterprise:

> I considered that all those who had advised the king to go this expedition committed mortal sin … seeing that he was physically so weak that he could neither bear to be drawn in a coach, nor to ride – so weak, in fact, that he let me carry him in my arms from the Conte d'Auxerre's house, where I went to take leave of him, to the abbey of the Franciscans.[51]

Which is perhaps odd because his brother Gefferoi did, or at least his brother Gefferoi went on crusade, just not with Louis but with Edward. The *famille de Joinville* hailed from the Champagne region of France; Jean de Joinville was Louis' seneschal there. However, his brother Gefferoi had sought another master; links of kin through his mother to Pierre de Savoie had taken him to England where Pierre had arranged an advantageous marriage, following which Gefferoi de Joinville (known in England as Geoffrey de Geneville) had gone into the service of the Lord Edward. Unlike his brother who had decided, this time, not to crusade with Louis, Gefferoi would go on crusade with Edward. Along with Gefferoi would also go his younger brother Guillaume as a cleric, the latter, upon his return had returned to the continent as an archdeacon at Besançon in Burgundy.[52]

It was one thing, however, to take up the cross, but it was another thing to amass the funds to fulfil the vow, and the late Baronial War had once more beggared England and its nobility. Henry had at first wanted to go, but wiser counsel prevailed, the pope preferring that Edmund lead the crusade, but once Edward had taken up the cross, he was not to be dissuaded. But how to finance the expedition? The answer lay in Gascony, already from 1254 a part of Edward's appanage. What is more since the 1259 Treaty of Paris he held Gascony from Louis as his vassal.f Following a meeting in Paris in August 1269, Louis lent his nephew and vassal Edward some 70,000 *Livres Tournois* set against Edward's revenues from Bordeaux.[53] Perhaps there was some method after all in Pierre de Savoie's madness in 1259 of Aquitaine becoming a vassal duchy of Paris. Louis agreed to coordinate and rendezvous with Edward at Aigues-Mortes,[54] the fortified port he had constructed for the seventh crusade as a non-Italian jumping-off point for the Holy Land on the Mediterranean coast – an embarkation date was fixed for May 1270.

In the early summer of 1270 King Louis IV, Saint Louis as he would become, set forth for Outremer once more, not waiting for Edward as agreed. He would not arrive in the Holy Land, since his brother Charles d'Anjou, now the king of Sicily, had other ideas. The Khalif of Tunis was a thorn in Charles' side: 'couldn't you pop by en route,' Charles might have said, 'sort him out for me, I think he wants to convert anyway'. When Louis arrived in Tunisia, Emir of Tunis, Mustansir,[55] didn't want to convert, or indeed submit himself in any way – a siege ensued. Louis set himself up on the ruins of Carthage, but unlike the Romans he was not to conquer. The Tunisian summer brought pestilence, Louis became ill with dysentery and passed from this life on 25 August 1270. Nancy Goldstone, biographer of Marguerite de Provence, his queen, tells us of his last words before adding a little perspective to the future saint's career.

> His last words were 'I will come into thy house … I will worship in the holy temple O Jerusalem! O Jerusalem!' Well should Louis IX king of sigh for Jerusalem. That saintly man led thousands of his countrymen to their deaths and bankrupted his kingdom, and he never even got to set foot in the city.'[56]

While the French faltered among the flies of Tunisia, Esther Rowland Clifford describes what she imagined to be the scene at Portsmouth, England:

> The fleet moved off, a blaze of colour under the August sun, with the lions of England and Leon and the castles of Castile flying above the brilliant line of shields hung from the quarterdeck, where the golden cockleshells of Grandson sparkled between the scarlet chevrons of Clare, the cross sable of Vescy, the checky gold and azure of Clifford, and the arms of half the noble families of England.[57]

It is a nice picture, except it was more likely to have been Dover not Portsmouth.[58] The reason for the likely error comes from the Winchester chronicler who suggests Edward turned back from Portsmouth and sailed from Dover, having made in the interim for Canterbury upon hearing news of his Great-Uncle Boniface trying to have Robert Burnell installed as a replacement.[59] Edward's departure was it seems delayed as news came to England from France that Archbishop Boniface de Savoie had died on 18 July 1270. He was laid to rest alongside his brothers, including Pierre who had died in 1268, at the beautiful abbey of a Hautecombe set beside Lac Bourget in the Savoy. With his death Queen Alianor was now without both her uncles for guidance, Pierre de Savoie having died in 1268. Henry and Alianor without their son, going away to Crusade.

So, from Dover in August sailed the full panoply of English heraldry at its finest heading off on crusade, some 225 knights leading perhaps an army over a thousand strong.[60] Along with Edward and his young wife Leonor de Castille was of course his intimate friend and adviser Othon de Grandson. Othon was not the only family member travelling; he was accompanied by his younger brother Gérard, a cleric and Provost of the Chapter of Saint Thomas de Cantorbery in Lyon. Gérard is listed as receiving the king's protection 'going beyond seas in aid of the Holy Land'.[61] Curiously Othon is nowhere listed as in need of such protection, his participation in the crusade confirmed by his witnessing a charter in January 1271 while in Sicily en route to Acre and of course the account from Jean d'Ypres[62] – one can only assume a close member of Edward's personal entourage was not considered in need of protection. Upon Gérard's return from the Holy Land, Edward was influential in obtaining for him the Bishopric of Verdun, thus placing an ally in an important see of the empire on the frontiers with France.

Other Savoyard knights riding alongside Edward included Jean de Grailly and Gérard de Saint Laurent.[63] Both would return with Edward from crusade to take part in the ensuing Welsh

Wars, Jean de Grailly later becoming seneschal again in Gascony (he'd held the post until 1268), Gérard de Saint Laurent becoming the first Constable of Flint Castle. Two young Scottish knights also on crusade were Roberts V and VI de Brus, grandfather and father of the latterly famed Robert the Bruce.[64] With Edward was one Teobaldo Visconti, a cleric who had come to England with Ottobuono dei Fieschi. He and the prince had become good friends. Visconti would stay with Edward and Othon throughout the coming crusade; upon their return to Europe he would become Pope Gregory X – one opportunity provided by crusade was networking, it didn't hurt the future king of England to be best friends with the future pope, nor the man who would become one of his chief papal curia envoys, Othon de Grandson. Edward was following in the illustrious footsteps of his grand-uncle Richard Cœur de Lion.

In September, as we saw, as the English summer wound to its conclusion they likely left Dover for France. When they eventually arrived at Aigues-Mortes around Michaelmas they found that there was no Louis to meet them: Louis had sailed for Tunis in support of his brother and not the Holy Land. No doubt surprised, Edward sailed for Tunis in the wake of the French king, and en route he may have called in at Sardinia where if he had not learned in France, he now learned that his erstwhile crusading partner, Louis, was no more.[65] Worse still the French had signed a treaty with the Khalif of Tunis, reluctantly Edward accepted Charles d'Anjou's offer of winter quarters upon the island of Sicily. Edward was not best pleased by the treaty, his reputed Plantagenet fury given voice by the chronicler:

> What is all this, my dearest lords? Did we not come against the enemies of Christ, and not to make peace with them? This I will never do, for here is only the beginning, and the highway shall be made plain before us that we may go on to the holy city of Jerusalem![66]

Edward had clearly taken up the cross and meant to see it through until the end, but reluctantly he made his way to Palermo. Charles put the Castello della Zisa at Edward's disposal while they wintered in Sicily. The castle had been built for the Norman king of Sicily, William I, by Arabic builders. While in Sicily and having seen much of his fleet dashed on the rocks, the new King Philippe III decided that enough was enough and walked back to France through Italy. But Edward, despite hearing news in February 1271 of a grave illness having befallen his father Henry, in May 1271 sailed from Trapani bound for Acre. Before leaving Sicily, he had despatched his nephew Henri d'Almayne back to England to see to his affairs, but he would not, as we shall see, make it home. Meanwhile, following a short layover in Cyprus, following a storm at sea, it would be on 9 May 1271 that the Lord Edward and his retinue of some thirteen ships finally reached safe harbour in the Holy Land. The choice of a route by way of Cyprus and a landfall in Outremer at Acre is something that Othon would later return to, writing that an autumn arrival in the Middle East in Cilician Armenia would be preferable. Such an arrival would allow time to winter the horses and prepare for a march on Jerusalem, whereas a spring arrival would bring the onset of a Levantine summer with all its oppressive heat. Othon would later be the possible writer of a treatise offering suggestions for a successful crusade, the writer having learned from bitter experience.[67] The Templar of Tyre describes the English arrival following the short voyage from Cyprus as suffering the ill effects of a '*tempest de mer*' Othon and Edward witnessing a waterspout no less.[68]

As Othon arrived, blinking in the bright sunlight at Acre for the first time, with Edward he would not have been the first Grandson to set foot upon its shore, he was following in the footsteps of his great-grandfather Barthélemy and indeed Gaucher de Châtillon who'd distinguished himself during the siege of 1189–91 when the crusaders had retaken the city. Along with them they had brought John II, Duke of Brittany, who had set forth with Louis IX on his ill-fated diversion to Tunis. John was also Earl of Richmond; Henry had passed the Honour of Richmond to him upon the death of Pierre de Savoie in 1268. They ensconced themselves in the palace found in the northwestern part of Acre built by the Knights Hospitallers nearly two centuries earlier, known as the Knights' Halls. However, though they were few, no doubt to the defenders of Acre, with Baibars again threatening them, they were a welcome addition to the defence as they greeted the English with terrible news.

Upon hearing of Louis' death before Tunis the previous summer, Baibars now considered the threat of crusade ended, and thus his hand freed to deal finally with Acre. In February 1271, the sultan[69] moved first against the Knights Templar at the Chastel Blanc or White Castle of Safita.[70] The castle dominated the routes to Tripoli and Acre, and from its donjon Baibars could see his next prize: the mighty crusader fortress of Krak de Chevaliers, defended by around 300 of The Order of Knights of the Hospital of Saint John of Jerusalem – the Hospitallers.[71] The Krak commanded a narrow valley leading from the coast to the Syrian plain, being the key to the County of Tripoli – or as a Muslim said a 'bone in the throat'. He arrived there on 3 March, but heavy rain meant that he could only begin his assault in earnest on 15 March. The seemingly impregnable castle, perhaps the finest ever constructed and one that had withheld the might of Salah a-Din fell to Baibars on 8 April 1271[72] Taking the Krak, Baibars had attempted to do as little damage as he could in reducing its defenders, inducing them to surrender rather than undue use of mighty trebuchets – this time he did allow safe passage to Tripoli on the coast for the submitting knights. He had in late March breached the outer defences by the feat of tunnelling for weeks through solid rock and undermining the walls, which had crashed to the ground with a mighty roar. The Sultan intended to transform Krak des Chevaliers from a bone in the throat of the Mamluks into a knife at the throat of the crusader kingdoms, especially Tripoli. But in May 1271 Baibars aborted his campaign toward Tripoli and offered a truce to Prince Bohemond, a truce for ten years. But why had Baibars turned back from Tripoli? Crusade historian Runciman is in no doubt: 'The sultan's forbearance towards Bohemond was due to the arrival of a new Crusade.'[73] Indeed, Baibars turning back from Tripoli when he had warned Bohemond that he would ready chains for his captivity was certainly due to the wary sultan being unaware of the meagre force Edward had brought to Acre.

However, likely upon hearing of Edward's numbers, Baibars returned to devouring crusader lands, and Edward was powerless to prevent the fall, on 12 June, of Montfort Castle,[74] held by the Teutonic Order who were allowed to leave with their possessions on the short 15 miles to Acre – Montfort itself was erased from the map. The shockwaves of the fall of the Hospitallers at Krak and the Teutonic Order at Montfort spread everywhere: Arsuf had gone, Antioch had gone, Chastel Blanc had gone, Krak de Chevaliers had gone and now Montfort – the foundation stones of Outremer were falling one by one, the crusaders now holding no castles inland.

There are many contemporary chronicles that tell Othon's story in Outremer, but perhaps the most reliable, and unlike most, an eyewitness is the scribe we know as the Templar of Tyre, author of the French text *Gestes des Chiprois,* that is the Deeds of the Cypriots. Like Runciman and Clifford I have sourced much of Grandson's exploits in the east from the *Gestes des Chiprois* as it is undoubtedly the most reliable, and not because it portrays his actions more favourably. Within the main body of the text is Paul Crawford's excellent English translation, the endnotes have the original Old French. The Templar of Tyre is anonymous, but we know that he was almost certainly neither a Templar nor from Tyre. The scant biographical knowledge we can surmise is that he was a Cypriot nobleman, once a page in the service of Marguerite de Antioch-Lusignan, sister of King Hugh III of Cyprus. His name Templar of Tyre arrives from his close association with the Templars, an association he shared with Grandson and one that placed him close by as eyewitness to the actions of both. The chronicler recounts Edward's arrival at Acre amid the fall of the mighty Krak des Chevaliers:

> 376. In the year 1271 of the Incarnation of Christ, on the eighteenth of February, Baibars, sultan of Babylon, besieged the castle of Krak des Chevaliers, which was held by the Hospital of St. John of Jerusalem. He took it on terms on the eighth of April, sparing their lives. On the ninth of May in the same year the Lord Edward, son of the king of England, arrived in Acre. He encountered a great storm at sea on the voyage out, so much so that a waterspout hit his ship, so that it nearly foundered. He brought his wife with him, and the count of Brittany came along. In September Sir Edmund, brother of the Lord Edward, also came to Acre. And in this same year Baibars, sultan of Babylon, besieged Gibelcar, which belonged to the prince of Antioch, and took it on terms.[75]
>
> 378. In this year the sultan besieged Montfort of the Germans, a castle very near Acre, and took it on the twelfth of June, on terms and sparing their lives. On the sixteenth of July, he conducted the men to Acre and let them go. On this day the men of Acre were all in arms, ready to defend their lands. Then the Lord Edward saw the sultan's host and his great power and knew too well that he did not have the men to fight the sultan with. So, none of the Christians dared go out against him, and the next day the sultan left, and went back to Babylon.[76]

Before we turn to the Templar's last remark, he then told of Edward gathering with him Templar knights and Knights Hospitaller and first venturing out from the walls of Acre:

> 379. And then the Lord Edward mounted a raid and went to attack a rich village called St. George which is about three leagues from Acre. The Templars and Hospitallers went with him, as did the other men of Acre. This was at the end of July, when it was extremely hot. They destroyed the village and slew a great many Saracens and won much loot. But a number of our men died there, on account of honey from bees and other things which they ate, as footmen were accustomed to do, so that they died on the road, from heat and from exhaustion and from the hot food which they had eaten.[77]

In the notes to his translation of the Templar, Paul Crawford, identifies the raided village as 'Probably St. George of La Baene, about twelve miles east of Acre'.[78] Ibn al-Fatur dates the St. George raid to July 1271, writing:

> Early in the morning of 'Id al-Adha in this year [21 July], the Franks made a raid towards al-Shaghur [Seisor] and al-Bi'na [St. George de Lebeyne] with more than fifteen hundred cavalry and a large force of infantry. They seized

> grain and ravaged and burned crops before returning, but a number of them perished through heat and thirst.[79]

From these oriental accounts we can see that little was achieved in the summer of 1271, both accounts speaking of heat and exhaustion – indeed the Levant in full armour in the heat of July was for mad dogs and Englishmen.

Exhaustion is unsurprising. If we want to picture the Othon de Grandson that will have accompanied the Lord Edward on his raid to Saint George de la Baene then we can look to three depictions of Othon clad in thirteenth-century armour that are with us to this day. First, his tomb within Lausanne Cathedral and second with his depiction on the altar cloth from the same cathedral now held by the History Museum in Bern, and last by the depiction on the tomb of his friend Leonor de Castille in Westminster Abbey – these latter images are also likely of him in the Holy Land since they portray him praying at the Church of the Holy Sepulchre in Jerusalem. The armoured Othon at Edward's flank atop his destrier or warhorse, would above his underclothes have been wearing three pieces of chain mail. Two mail chausses (stockings) would have protected his legs and feet, weighing around six kilos each that tied to a stout belt around the waist. His body would have been clad in a gambeson, a padded long shirt that covered his arms and torso. Above the gambeson, Othon would have worn a mail hauberk, made of chain mail his principal protection for arms and torso. Last, above gambeson and hauberk he would have worn a tabard or sleeveless jerkin that would have proudly displayed the arms of the *famille de Grandson.* Upon his head would have been a mail coif. No wonder knights were exhausted in an average high temperature for Acre of 30°C (nearly 90°F).

But then hope rose a little in September 1271, when Edward's younger brother Edmund arrived at the beleaguered Acre from Cyprus along with the king of Cyprus (and Jerusalem) Hugh III.[80] We know of Edmund's alternate route to the Holy Land from his being in Savoy on 16 August 1271.[81] Edmund apparently received the name that would be attached to him thereafter, Crouchback or Crossback from the cross he wore on his back as he arrived in the Holy Land. Hugh III of Cyprus was of the Lusignan clan, related to Edward's half-brother Guillaume de Valence who was with Edward at Acre. But also, Hugh, like Edward, was descended from the Dukes of Aquitaine – Hugh was family. How much in the way of knights Hugh brought with him is debatable since in the summer of 1271 his knights in Cyprus refused their king's call to arms.[82] In June 1271 Baibars had attempted a naval action against Cyprus to distract Hugh; although a failure in military terms,[83] it seems it had achieved its purpose in persuading the knights of Cyprus their interests lay firstly with defending their island.[84] The Cypriot knights had refused to join their king in Acre, eventually Edward arbitrating the dispute, thus enabling them to join Hugh.

Edmund's arrival may well have brought another Grandson to Acre, Othon's younger brother Guillaume, as young Guillaume would be later noted long in Edmund's service. However, his presence in Outremer is unrecorded, and we are not certain of the year in which the young Guillaume joined Edmund's service. His name does not appear on Simon Lloyd's long list of crusade participants,[85] but then Guillaume would have been a young squire of some 20 years and may not have merited a mention, much as his older brother is not mentioned in connection with Lewes or Evesham five years earlier – such was the lowly lot of a squire. We should note however, that given Othon's move to England at a young age, a move by Guillaume to England at some point between 1263 and 1270 cannot be ruled out.

The Templar's account, aforementioned, doesn't explain why Baibars left the Acre region for 'Babylon'. In actuality, immediately upon arrival in Acre, Edward had seen that his position was hopeless without allies. We have seen Acre's king, Hugh, had arrived without much in the way of Cypriot knights; the commune of Acre was less than happy to have an active king of Jerusalem once more, as indeed Hugh was – in short, the crusader kingdom was divided.

So, Edward sent an embassy to the Mongols, Reginald Russell, Godfrey Welles and John Parker, seeking help.[86] Whether by design or coincidence in the autumn of 1271 Abagha Khan who was fighting in Turkestan obliged and sent horsemen toward Aleppo. Ten thousand horsemen under Samagar threatened Baibars's flank to the northeast. This was enough for the lion Baibars to pause devouring Outremer and turn northeast to meet the Mongol threat. But Arabic sources also suggest that it was indeed also the arrival of Edward that gave Baibars cause to withdraw from threatening Acre.

> news reached him [Baibars] that the King of England (the Lord Edward) (Malik al-Inkitar) had arrived at Acre towards the end of Ramadan (c. 12 May), with three hundred horsemen and eight vessels, together with galleys and ships to a total of thirty, apart from those which had arrived in advance with the master of his household, his object was to make the pilgrimage. The Sultan's resolution weakened somewhat.[87]

As high summer turned to autumn and winter Edward was learning, with the arrival of Edmund and Hugh and with Baibars departure from the region, that greater operations were possible. In November he launched a raid across Mount Carmel into the Plain of Sharon, together with the support of Templar, Hospitaller and Teutonic knights on the town of Caco or in Arabic, Qaqun. The castle there had been taken by Baibars back in 1265.[88] Reports of the raid are not entirely reliable; however, the chronicler of Guisborough's account is a little confusing, his dating almost certainly in error, and writing from distance he later wrote:

> Again, around Midsummer, when Edward Muslims assembled at Kakehowe[89] [Caco], which differed from Acre as fifteen miles, he went out in the same place, and rushing in, as it were, into them, with the greatest of them, and smote a thousand men, early in the morning, others turned and were in the hasty flight, and they took abundance of spoils.[90]

The Templar's account, based on most likely eyewitnesses, of this second raid is probably more accurate:

> 381. On the twenty-fourth of November of that year the Lord Edward and King Hugh and the chivalry of Cyprus and Acre, along with the Templars and Hospitallers, went out to attack a fortification called Qaqun, which is in the land of Caesarea twelve leagues or more distant from Acre. They did a good deal of damage to the Saracens and took two Turcoman[91] encampments; they slew many Saracens and captured animals, great and small, about 12,000 of them, and they besieged some Saracens within a tower at Caco. It was very strong, surrounded with ditches filled with water. They came near to taking

> it, but our men were afraid to linger too long while the alarm went out across the land, since the Saracens would then assemble from all parts. So, our men departed and returned to Acre with all their loot, safe and sound.[92]

The summer dating of the Guisborough account differs from oriental chroniclers and is certainly in error, and he incorrectly reports the distance from Acre to Qaqun; the Templar's and Ibn al-Furat's accounts are the more accurate. Nonetheless all accounts give the essence of the story that Edward (and almost certainly Edmund, Othon de Grandson and others) surprised a large force of Turcomans, killing over a thousand and taking over five thousand animals as plunder. These Turcomans were most likely relatively new additions to Baibars's army, being integrated in 1268 and given horses, titles and lands in return for military service. Muslim sources list one emir as killed and one as wounded during this raid. On top of that, the Muslim commander of the castle was forced to abandon his command. Ibn al-Furat wrote:

> At the end of the month of Rabi' II, the month already mentioned [4 December 1271], the Sultan learnt that the Franks had attacked Qaqun [Caco]; the emir Husam al-Din, the ustadh-dar, had been killed and the emir Rukn al-Din al-Jaliq wounded; while the governor of the place had had to leave.[93]

However, Edward did not take the castle itself, and retreated before Baibars could respond in kind. Nonetheless this raiding on Edward's part was as fleas buzzing around the rear of the lion while his attention was elsewhere – at some point soon the lion would turn and devour Acre.

It is possible that on their way to Qaqun they visited Nazareth, at least that is how the writer of the Flores has it, Guisborough had it raided before Saint George de la Baene, but as mentioned earlier his account is perhaps muddled.[94] Certainly, Nazareth at just over 30 miles (50 kilometres) from Acre represented a day's horse ride, almost half the way from Acre to Qaqun. In doing so Edward would be following in the footsteps of his Uncle Louis, king of France, in 1251, although what Edward and Othon may have found is open to question as Baibars had destroyed Christian buildings in the town in 1263. For the devout Othon a visit, however brief, to the grotto of the Annunciation where the angel Gabriel reputedly told Mary of the coming of Jesus, must have been a profound interlude. Assuredly the knights would have offered up a prayer for deliverance that day and in the coming weeks.

Notwithstanding these sorties from Acre the strategic position of the English crusaders and Acre looked hopeless in the face of Baibars and his overwhelming force. In December 1271 Baibars, having dealt with Samagar and his Mongols who had retreated from Aleppo, turned his attention once more toward Acre, and marched on the road to it in the miserable rains of a Levantine winter. The lion might now have his prey at last.

In many ways Edward had achieved more by his mere arrival in the Holy Land than ever he could by raising his sword. Edward's biographer Michael Prestwich agrees, writing: 'had Edward not arrived when he did, Acre would have surrendered to Baibars' Mamluk troops. It does seem that the news of Edward's arrival caused him to change his plans, and to negotiate a ten-year truce with the ruler of Tripoli.'[95] Edward now found himself with a very small force of English knights on the tip of a hostile continent, in a tip whose defences were in a parlous state. Edward had been shocked to discover that the Venetians were in fact trading with the enemy; worse that the Genoese were attempting to muscle into this trade, how could he defend an Outremer that was its own worst enemy? Jerusalem lay a mirage just over the horizon. He had set stall in hopes of the alliance with the Abagha Khan and his Mongols threatening Baibars, but this had been to no avail. In the words of Runciman: 'By the spring of 1272 Prince Edward realised that he was wasting his time.'[96]

But, the lion Baibars, still wary of Abaqa Khan to his rear – a far greater threat than Acre to his front – decided that for now the Mamluk conquest of the Frankish lands could wait a while. Baibars was also conscious of the need to keep Charles d'Anjou, who had designs upon Acre himself, out of the Levant. Charles, for his part, who had greater designs for now upon Constantinople was conscious of the need to retain Acre as a foothold in Outremer. And so it was that on 22 May 1272 a peace treaty was signed at Caesarea by the government of Acre with Sultan Baibars that guaranteed its existence for ten years, ten months, ten days and ten hours – the nearest Edward had come to Jerusalem is likely to have been the visit to Nazareth. No doubt Edward and Othon would have sought some solace after their likely visit to Nazareth that the right of pilgrims to venture there had been restored by the treaty with Baibars. However, it is not clear whether Edward was entirely happy with the truce, as some say he persuaded Acre to sign in the face of the futility of their position, others that he responded angrily to its signature. The latter is perhaps more likely in the light of events following the arrangements made at Caesarea, which suggest that Edward was known to harbour thoughts of one day restoring the Kingdom of Jerusalem to its city.

The Order of Assassins had been formed in the late eleventh century just prior to the First Crusade, the Grand Master calling his disciples Asāsīyūn – meaning people who were faithful to the foundation (of the faith). Within the sect a small group of warriors carried out espionage and assassinations for the cause – and so a word reached Europe: the assassin. Over time two caliphs and many sultans, viziers and crusaders met their ends at the hands of an assassin – another was nearly the Lord Edward himself. The threat was very real; the Lord of Tyre, Philippe de Montfort, was himself killed by an assassin likely in the employ of Baibars on 17 March 1270, Philippe being a distant relative to Edward, being the nephew of the ill-starred Earl of Leicester, himself the husband of Edward's aunt Eleanor.

William of Tyre, in the twelfth century, wrote of the sect in his *Historia rerum in partibus transmarinis gestarum*:

> the chief [the old man] places a dagger in the hand of one or several of his followers; those thus designated hasten away at once, regardless of the consequences of the deed or the probability of personal escape. Zealously they labour for as long as may be necessary, until at last the favourable chance comes which enables them to carry out the mandate of the chief. Neither Christians nor Saracens know whence this name, the Assassins, is derived.[97]

The Templar of Tyre gives us the nearest account in terms of distance in time and place from events that next overtook Edward:

> 382. Now I will tell you what happened to the Lord Edward. It happened that a Saracen man-at-arms came to be baptised at Acre and the Lord Edward had him made into a Christian and retained him in his own quarters. This fellow served the Lord Edward in such a capacity that he would go to spy on the Saracens to find out where one might do them harm, and he performed this

> service many times. It was by his offices that our men went to St. George and Qaqun, and as a result the Lord Edward trusted him so much that he gave orders that he was to be allowed to speak to him at any time of the day or night. So, it happened one night that he came Edward was sleeping with the queen, 'and brought the translator with him, the chambers where the Lord and let it be known that he had just come from spying and that he wanted to speak to the Lord Edward, so that the Lord himself opened his chamber to him, dressed only in an undershirt and braie.[98] The Saracen met him and stabbed him on the hip with a dagger, making a deep, dangerous wound. The Lord Edward felt himself struck, and he struck the Saracen a blow with his fist, on the temple, which knocked him senseless to the ground for a moment. Then the Lord Edward caught up a dagger from the table, which was in the chamber, and stabbed the Saracen in the head and killed him. The alarm was raised throughout the household, and they saw that their lord was injured, and the cry went out through the city of Acre. Thereupon the lords gathered together there and summoned all the doctors and slaves, who sutured his wound and drew out the poison. He made a good recovery, by the grace of God, and he left on the twenty-second of September, and went to his own land across the sea. (Fig 1.4)[99]

The Templar of Tyre raises the idea that the assassin may have been, in effect, a 'double agent', able to move freely between the Mamluk and Christian lands. Such a man may have, according to the Templar, won Edward's trust by supplying the intelligence that led to the attacks on Saint George and Qaqun. The Templar mistakenly refers to Leonor as 'Queen' but as who exactly drew the poison from the wound is a point of variance for chroniclers, all of which were written many years after the events described thus far. Arab sources suggest that they may have believed they'd killed Edward, Ibn al-Furat[100] later wrote:

> An account of the attack made by Sultan Baibars' *fedawis* on King Edward (Ward), and of his murder. King Edward (Ward), who was one of the Frankish kings, had made raids against Qaqun [Caco] and other places, as we have already described. He was not pleased when peace was made between the Sultan and the Franks, and he did not become a party to it. So, the Sultan got the governor of al-Ramla [Rames[, Ibn Shawar, to carry out a plot against him. Ibn Shawar sent messages to try to win favour with the King and to give him to understand that he could provide him with information. He made presents to him, to his wife [Eleanor of Castile] and to his whole entourage, these being brought by one of the fedawis whom he sent to him. These men stayed with the King for a while, and then one of them went into his presence to give him some news about the Sultan. There was no one with him except the interpreter, and so the *fedawi* leaped at him and struck him in five places.[101]

A *fedawi* being a *feda* or as we saw earlier a member of an Ismaili order of assassins known for their willingness to offer up their lives to carry out delegated assignments of murdering appointed victims. Ibn al-Furat is certain that the attack came on behalf of Baibars. Jean d'Ypres wrote decades later:

> My informants told me further that this fateful lord of Grandson was beyond the sea in the company of the son of the King of England; and that when he heard how the prince had been poisoned, he alone, trusting, as I suppose, in the fate that had been foretold for him, dared to suck the venom from the wound; and thus through his aid was Edward healed. Afterwards this lord of Grandson and his kinsfolk rose to high honour with the Kings of England, and unto this day have they great repute in that country. But of this can I avouch no more than was told to me.[102]

Alan Forey seized upon that final line from Jean d'Ypres and concluded that 'it was unlikely there was any substance in the claim' that Othon was responsible for saving Edward's life.[103] Yet all that Jean d'Ypres was saying, unlike many chroniclers, was that he was simply recording what others had told him – one might wish that chroniclers were all so honest. It is impossible to discern from Jean's account the accuracy of the account from the 'men from Savoy' other than to add that Jean found them 'honourable and trustworthy'.

Nonetheless, Ptolemy of Lucca disagreed with Jean's account by having Leonor sucking out the poison in Othon de Grandson's place – certainly, both were equally loyal and committed to Edward. There are three chroniclers who relate to us the events of 16 June 1272, Guisborough (the fullest account),[104] Ptolemy of Lucca and Jean d'Ypres.[105] A problem with Guisborough's account is that he places Edmund Crouchback alongside his stricken brother, except that Edmund had already left for home a month earlier.[106] In the way that stories can be embellished with time later chroniclers such as Rodrigo de Arevalo in Spain (subsequently repeated in England by Robert Le Bel) were writing at some distance in time from events, in the fifteenth and sixteenth centuries, i.e. more than two centuries later and reported as fact what Ptolemy of Lucca had merely recorded as rumour. Almost certainly shocked by the assassination attempt, Edward made a will on 18 June 1272, the list of executors of said last will and testament being Guillaume de Valence, Roger de Clifford, Jean de Bretagne, Robert de Tibetot, Payn de Chaworth, Robert Burnell, Antony Bek and Othon de Grandson – this band of brothers will repeat themselves over and over during Edward's reign.[107] The will also confirms the growing closeness of the relationship between Edward and Othon, one now forged in battle as well as childhood. Opinion in recent years has differed on the likelihood of Othon saving Edward's life. Crusade specialist Forey, as we saw, wrote in 2017 of it being 'unlikely',[108] whereas Edward's biographer Prestwich writing in 2020 suggested that 'the fact that after the attack Othon was named as one of Edward's executors lends some support to the story that it was, he who saved the future king's life.'[109] Ultimately, we can never know who actually sucked out the poison, Leonor or Othon, the certainty being that Edward survived his near-death experience. The accounts are not necessarily mutually exclusive; perhaps it was both who sought to aid the stricken Edward in turn. Given what we know of Othon's relationship with Edward the tale related by 'men of Savoy' to Jean d'Ypres does seem more likely than unlikely. The dagger by which the assassin came within an inch of ending aforesaid reign before it had even really begun was brought home to London and kept safely as a relic by the monks at Westminster Abbey.[110]

The drama of Edward's near murder at the hands of (literally) an assassin, was played out to against the backdrop of Leonor having given birth in April to a baby girl, having fallen pregnant in the summer of 1271 as they arrived in Acre. The young girl would become known as Joan of Acre. The knight who had tried to calm the distraught Leonor was Jean de Vesci;

we get this from Walter of Guisborough's account – '*domino Johanni de Vescy*'[111] – a recent convert to Edward's cause, having sided with Simon de Montfort and fought by his side at Evesham. He had been married to Savoyard Agnès de Saluzzo, the sister of Alésia de Saluzzo who was married to Edmund de Lacy. The knights these ladies of Savoy married, Jean de Vesci and Henri de Lacy, alongside Savoyard Sir Othon de Grandson, would become loyal lieutenants in Edward's coming struggles. We know that Edward's servant and likely saviour at Acre had now been knighted from the aforementioned confirmations of 1267 charters in August 1270 and November 1271 that lists amongst the original witnesses to the charter as 'Sir Otho de Grandisono' – it is the first source we have that raises from 'Ottonin' to 'Sir Otho'.[112] This means Grandson had been knighted in the few years following Evesham, where he most likely took part as we saw earlier.

Meanwhile Runciman had no doubt as to who had set the assassin on his way to Acre, none other than Sultan Baibars, writing, 'Baibars decided to eliminate him.'[113] Put simply, the Sultan was almost certainly aware of Edward's dissatisfaction with the truce of Caesarea and had no intention of allowing the Englishman to return home and come back one day with a much larger force and make good his intention to retake Jerusalem. On 22 September 1272 Edward and Othon embarked from Acre bound once more for England, his health still not fully recovered, his father dying and his dream of seeing Jerusalem and returning it to Christian hands unfulfilled.

Edward left a small group of soldiers at Acre under the command of Othon's fellow countryman, Jean de Grailly, who would soon after be named by Hugh, Seneschal of Jerusalem. The Chronography of the Kingdom of the Franks erroneously had Edward leaving Othon in Acre, the author mistaking Grandson for Grailly – a reminder not to rely too heavily on chroniclers who weren't there.[114] But Jean like Edward would not see Jerusalem, although Jean and Othon would fight the Mamluks again. For now, as they returned home, no doubt Edward and Othon ruminated on the hard reality he'd come face to face within Outremer, that Baibars and his Mamluk army could draw upon seemingly endless reserves of strength, whereas the Christian West could not, and despite heroics the days of the crusader kingdoms were numbered, and the future belonged to Baibars[115] and his successors. Like his great-uncle Richard, Edward had fallen short of Jerusalem, just the 70 miles from Acre short.

Before we leave Acre with Edward and Othon we must mention that it is more than likely that both met a young man who had become well known to future generations, a Venetian by the name of Marco Polo. With Edward on crusade had been Teobaldo Visconti; as Archdeacon of Liège, he'd been an assistant to the papal legate Ottobono Fieschi who had been in England following the baronial war and peached crusade there. During this time, he had become an important friend of the Lord Edward's. Visconti had travelled to Acre with Edward and Othon, where he had heard that in the summer of 1271 he had been elected as Pope Gregory X to replace the now deceased Clément IV. While in Acre, in 1271, Visconti received a letter from the Mongol Great Khan Kublai, the letter brought to him by Niccolò and Maffeo Polo, Marco's father and uncle. The letter requested missionaries be sent east, and accordingly Niccolò, Maffeo and Marco ventured from Acre to the court of Kublai Khan in the autumn of 1271. All this of course came to pass during Edward's and Othon's first six months in Acre, and that given the proximity of Visconti to the English, the Polos did not encounter the Lord Edward and his household knights including Othon is difficult to believe.

Before Visconti left Acre for Rome to become Pope Gregory X, he preached a sermon that was later reported in a crusader treatise, likely written in the early fourteenth century,

Incipit Memoria Terre Sancte, a copy of which exists along with a 'sister' French text *Via Terram Sanctam* in the Bodleian Library in Oxford.[116] The author of the text had heard the sermon first hand, and it is one of the reasons that many have attributed the texts to Othon de Grandson. This attribution by Köhler, accepted by Clifford, has been contested more recently by Forey; we will return to the possibility of *Terram Sanctam* being the words of Grandson later.[117] We can certainly say at this point that someone who heard Gregory's sermon first hand later wrote of it in the document now held in Oxford, and that the possibility that the writer was Sir Othon de Grandson cannot be discounted.

Meanwhile, just before or during his return Edward would have learned of the passing of his Uncle Richard, King of the Romans and erstwhile 'Bad Miller' of Lewes. Richard, Earl of Cornwall, perhaps the richest man in all Europe had died at Berkhamsted on 2 April 1272, and was buried alongside his wife Sanchia de Provence at the beautiful Hailes Abbey in the Cotswold hills.[118]

A generation was passing away. Richard was followed, as King of the Germans, by a Rudolf von Habsburg, of a family who would come to dominate European history for centuries. Like Richard, Rudolf would not be crowned emperor, but his coming to the throne in Aachen began the ascendancy of the House of Habsburg. Their upcoming coveting of the Gotthard Pass between the German and Italian lands of the empire would lead to the growth from 1291 onward of a new polity to the north and east of the Savoyard, the Old Swiss Confederation.

Meanwhile in England, that autumn of 1272, King Henry III, who had been gravely ill in February 1271, grew weaker yet. On 16 November 1272 Henry, confined to his chamber for a fortnight, called Gilbert de Clare to his bedside and charged him with the good care of the realm until the return of his son. The great and the good gathered around him, including his wife of thirty-six years Alianor de Provence. Henry passed away from the kingdom he had kept together for fifty-six years later that day. *Le Roi est mort, longue vie au Roi*, and so passed the days of King Henry the Third of that name. He bequeathed his son a more secure kingdom than his father had given to him – and surely that is the ultimate test of any monarch. Henry had been born into the chaos of his father John's reign, he had been crowned at the tender age of just 10 in Gloucester, not Westminster, and yet it would be the great beautiful soaring Westminster Abbey that he had lavished so much devotion upon that he would leave his nation. His last resting place was indeed the abbey that became his epitaph in stone, his burial there on 20 November 1272. He had lately transferred his idol, Edward the Confessor, to a new tomb. Henry was laid to rest in Edward's original tomb. The chronicler Wykes wrote more glowingly of the funeral itself than his reign, '*ampliori splendore decoris effulgebat mortuum, quam prius dum vixerat appa reret*',[119] that he had shone in death with a splendour more amply than had been seen with the eye when he had lived. Wykes remained critical of Henry, but at least he gives us something of the beauty of the funeral that day in the abbey. Over the coming centuries his decedents would join him in the abbey, but for now Henry lay alone in his tomb, in full coronation regalia. *Le Roi est mort, longue vie au Roi* would have echoed around the abbey, except none present would have then known if the new Roi had survived his crusade, was among the living or the dead. He had outlived his onetime rival and later friend, Louis of France, he had outlived his Savoyard in-laws and loyal advisers; Guillaume and Pierre, he had outlived Archbishop Boniface, his brother Richard, the disapproving Mathew Paris, the upstart Simon de Montfort – Henry was the great survivor. As he passed that afternoon, no doubt his mind went back to his boyhood coronation, to his wedding and young beautiful bride from exotic Provence, to Oxford, to Lewes and Evesham – he had outlasted them all.

The chronicler Walter of Guisborough wrote of Henry, 'he was an ingenuous man, of peaceful not warlike ways;' certainly he'd not been able to recover his father's lands in France as he had dearly wished.[120] His latter-day biographer Darren Baker wrote, 'Henry never outgrew the innocence of the boy who became king.'[121] Henry's reputation suffered over the years in comparison to his Uncle Richard and his distant descendants like his namesake Henry V, also in comparison to his rival Simon de Montfort. But this is largely because those that have judged Henry have done so unfairly, and often, as with Simon de Montfort because they're judging thirteenth-century men with latter-day eyes. A twenty-first-century reader can do no more to reach Henry the King or Henry the man, by going to Westminster to visit his spectacular abbey, a building that has subsequently become part of the very fabric of England – something of which Henry would have been singularly proud. His widow Alianor failed where her sister Marguerite succeeded, Henry was not to be Saint Henry as his friend Louis would become Saint Louis. It is perhaps one of history's unfairnesses that the hapless crusader Louis would be sanctified whereas the equally pious Henry, no warrior himself, would not. I think his recent biographer Baker chose the most suitable epitaph for Henry in the title of his book, *The Great King England Never Knew It Had.*

Henry had also, without knowing it, laid the foundation stones for our story, because through his beloved Queen Alianor, and despite the excesses of his Lusignan half-brothers, he'd not been afraid to call upon advisers and counsellors from beyond the shores of 'Little England' – what Victorian historian James Birchall disparaged as 'herds of foreigners'.[122] Henry had brought to England the talents of men like Guillaume de Savoie, Boniface de Savoie and of course Pierre II de Savoie. Despite the unpopularity it had courted at the time, and in posterity, they brought others in their wake, the loyal Othon de Grandson and Jean de Grailly who would loyally serve his son Edward and of course as we shall soon see, Maître Jacques de Saint-Georges-d'Espéranche – the man who would build for Edward the most magnificent castles in all of Europe. Perhaps if our redoubtable chronicler Matthew Paris could have seen Caernarfon or Conwy or Harlech then maybe he might have judged Henry less harshly – perhaps.

Perhaps, because the necessity for the great castles in Wales that were to follow were only a necessity because Henry had not acted more decisively in Wales during the years 1241–47. He had stopped short of extinguishing the House of Gwynedd, despite having just cause, opportunity and resources. Action then may have saved his son and his kingdom much time and treasure. But that is speculative; he chose to attempt to come to terms with Gwynedd, indeed an agreement short of outright conquest would also be the first preference of his son. The pious Henry had stopped short of a war he did not want and sought to be the peacemaker; sadly, it was a rejected peace not of his doing and so we cannot entirely reproach him.

For all his love of England and its patron saint, Henry was of the Maison Plantagenet: his body lay at Westminster in the abbey he had lovingly rebuilt, but his heart was taken across the sea to the lands he had longed so much to recover, to the ancestral lands of the Loire, and the abbey at Fontevraud.[123] The long days of King Henry were now passed, now would come the days of King Edward I of that name.

CHAPTER 3

It was as Edward was sailing back from Acre to Sicily that he became king, inheriting from his dying father the throne of England – upon landing at Trapani he learned of his father's death. It was a double blow for Edward because he also learned of the death of his son, John. Edward's return to England would be a long and circuitous journey; he did not make at once for London, indicating that he was secure in his succession, a luxury not afforded earlier in the century to his father.

Edward first made his way toward the new pope at Orvieto, for a ghost from the recent past had appeared from the gloom to take the life of his cousin Henri d'Almayne, son of Uncle Richard, erstwhile king of the Romans – he'd been murdered, on 13 March 1271, by Montforts as revenge for the death of Simon at Evesham. He had been slain at Viterbo by his cousins Guy and Simon de Montfort the younger, both sons of the late Simon, and the murder had been quite vicious too, carried out while Henri was in the sanctuary of the Chiesa di San Silvestro. Guy and Simon murdered Henri while he clutched the altar, begging for mercy. 'You had no mercy for my father and brothers,' was Guy's reply. This murder was carried out in the presence of the cardinals (who were conducting a papal election) of King Philippe III of France and of King Charles of Sicily. The deed had shocked Christendom so much that Dante Alighieri found Guy de Montfort a place in the seventh circle of hell in his Divine Comedy.[1] Henri's body was brought back to England and buried at Hailes Abbey. This was very personal for Edward, as Henri had been with him at Windsor from 1240, when he was but a baby. Perhaps Edward may have regretted his clemency toward Guy, as he had taken the seriously injured Montfort to Beeston Castle following the Battle of Evesham in 1265, and later at Windsor in 1266 before the latter-day assassin had escaped.

Edward wanted his former crusading ally and friend, Theobaldo Visconti, the new Pope Gregory X, to bring Guy to justice. Edward met with Gregory on 14 February 1273 at Orvieto, Guy was excommunicated accordingly, but Edward had wanted stronger action. Simon had died later in 1271 at Siena, 'cursed by God, a wanderer and a fugitive' so his punishment had become a moot point.[2] But Guy was stripped of his titles and took service with Charles d'Anjou but was captured off the coast of Sicily in 1287 by the Aragonese; he died in a Sicilian prison before going to that seventh circle of hell, that reserved for men of violence, ending immersed in a river of boiling blood.

The Monfortian punishment dealt with, Edward, Othon and party then travelled northeast from Rome across the never-ending Apennines until they came across the *Via Emilia*, the former Roman road that cut straight across Italy in a northwesterly direction from Rimini toward the Alps. They were recorded as having been entertained at the episcopal palace of Reggio Emilia on 20 May. Their route continued through Emilia Romagna to Parma and then the great city of Milan – leaving Milan, and on to Turin and behind it the wall around Italy, that is the Alps, which would have grown ever higher in their eyes as they made for the

Mont Cenis. The reason for the Mont Cenis route is that it was a mountain pass controlled by his Savoyard great-uncle Philippe and led to Savoy. In 1246,[3] the English crown had come to the overlordship of a number of Savoyard castles: Avigliana and Bard, the margravial palace at Susa, and town of Saint-Maurice d'Agaune – Edward would receive homage from Philippe for them on his way home to England. The treaty of 1246, criticised then and since by Englishmen was about to set in train events that would transform the lives of Edward and Othon as we shall soon see. When he arrived at Rivoli, on the road to Susa, he entered Savoyard territory. The lofty castle, at Rivoli, afforded majestic views across Turin to its front and the Alps they would need to cross to its rear. The Savoyard castellan at Rivoli sent two messengers to meet the English party, who were presented with gifts of wine and food. Philippe's bailiff at Montmélian brought ten oxen, fifty-nine lambs and twenty-nine geese, ready for a royal feast and escorted them on into Savoy.[4]

Savoy encompassed much of the current French departments of Ain and Isère, and all Haute Savoie and Savoie, much of the Swiss canton of Valais, all of Vaud, and the Italian regions of the Valle d'Aosta and Piedmont. But we should note, Savoy had no large urban centres at this time, Geneva and Annecy were the fief of the Count de Geneva. Meanwhile, Lausanne was the fief of the Bishop of Lausanne, and Lyon its Archbishop. But what the Savoyards did control was not only access to these urban centres, their trade routes, but also, vitally, the frighteningly high passes between France and Italy which were the key artery of Europe.

Once along the narrowing Val di Susa they began to climb the Mont Cenis Pass. Beforehand they would have rested at the Castello di San Giorio di Susa, dominating the valley at midway point toward the pass, and noted its unusual merlons each topped by three finials, a striking design later replicated in North Wales at Conwy.[5] Susa had been the birthplace of Edward's great-uncle Pierre de Savoie some seventy years earlier; he would be conscious of now entering the lands of his mother's family. The party including Leonor of Castile and their baby daughter Joan of Acre, crested the mountains into Savoy. A young Edward had married Leonor in her father's kingdom at Burgos back on 1 November 1254, and she had gone with him on crusade. Along with the royal couple, and of course Grandson came Othon's brother Guillaume, Othon's chief household knight Jean de Bonvillars. The remainder of the escorting knights included Jean de Vesci, Robert de Tibetot (future justiciar of west Wales), Payn de Chaworth, Roger de Clifford[6] and household knights including Richard de Brus.

The royal party came down the Mont Cenis Pass[7] on 7 June,[8] their route taking them by the Maurienne valley by way of Aiguebelle, Montmélian and Chambéry.[9] Their destination was the castle of Saint-Georges-d'Espéranche, then under construction for Count Philippe as a new palatial residence.[10] They arrived at Saint-Georges d'Espéranche on 18 June 1273. Edward was no doubt impressed by its polygonal towered grandeur – it left an impression.[11] Saint-Georges-d'Espéranche lies in the rolling hill country above the plain of the river Rhône, some twenty kilometres southeast of Lyon, but fifteen kilometres northeast of Vienne. The hilly uplands above the Rhône, very much like England, were rich in woodland, which made them rich in game – ideally suited to a thirteenth-century count and ideally suited to a young would-be king in search of some good hunting after the hot deserts of the Levant. For Edward and the English in his entourage, they provided a first taste of home.

Philippe had lived pretty much all his life in and around Lyon and had no intention of moving to Chillon by Lac Léman as his late brother Pierre had done. So, at Saint-Georges-d'Espéranche he had decided to build a new palace for himself and his new bride, Alix de Bourgogne. He had acquired the seigneurial rights while Archbishop of Lyon in 1242, but we have no record of a castle earlier than 1270.[12] There was a visit by Edmund Crouchback from England, in early August 1271, en route to the Holy Land.[13] Virtually nothing remains of the castle today, just the lower parts of one tower, but we can thank a Citizen Chabord[14] for a colour-wash plan made of the castle in 1794 and preserved in the Archives de l'Isère, which gives us some idea of its former grandeur. Saint-Georges was of a square outline, a *Carré Savoyard*,[15] with a curtain wall surrounded by a revetted moat, with towers at each corner, of apparently the same size, largely aesthetic and octagonal in shape.[16] An accompanying report by Chabord adds that the curtain walls were some five feet thick and surrounded a great courtyard. He describes the building as 'vaste', and that towards the top of the four octagonal towers were some embrasures.[17] The chief architect for Philippe was a Magistro Jacobo lathomo, or Maître Jacques the builder. The English would later know him as Master James of Saint George.

So, at Saint-Georges-d'Espéranche on 25 June 1273, Philippe did his homage to the yet uncrowned king of England for the aforementioned alpine real estate.[18] and entertained his great-nephew to a tremendous feast – at which we are almost certain Edward and Othon would have been introduced to the onetime master mason for Pierre de Savoie now in the employ of Philippe de Savoie, Maître Jacques. This meeting has been rightly identified as pivotal in Edward's life, and in the history of England and Wales: here the young Edward came face to face with the man who would build castles for him. It is tempting to imagine the conversation might have been. Edward had on his travels, seen Louis IX's magnificent crusader port of Aigues Mortes with its great circular tower, he had seen the complex and state-of-the-art crusader castles in Outremer; now here he was with the master mason constructing a new palace castle for his great-uncle Philippe, Count of Savoy. Edward was certainly impressed by the scale of Jacques's work, that he was embarking upon the simultaneous construction of no less than four castles for Philippe – Voiron, La-Cote-St.-André, St.-Laurent-du-Pont as well as at Saint-Georges.[19] In the coming years, Edward would be in great need of a supervisory master mason who could deliver multiple castles in double-quick time. An interesting echo of the works found by Edward in the Vienneois that summer of 1273 would later be found in Wales. The castles of Voiron, La-Cote-St.-André and St.-Laurent-du-Pont would all have, as was the fashion, round towers while Saint-Georges, as the palace, had octagonal towers – can we see in the ruins in France the prototype for Caernarfon? (Fig 1.5) It is an intriguing thought that the genesis of one of history's most spectacular castles may well have been formed in the minds of Edward and Jacques on 25 June 1273 in the sun of a Viennois afternoon.[20]

While at the Chastel Seint George Philippe took the homage of a recalcitrant local lord, Guillaume I de Tournon, whose castle sat between Vienne and Valence, at a key position on the Rhône, now Tournon-sur-Rhône. Philippe took advantage of Edward's presence to have him, and his knights, witness the homage: perhaps a touch of medieval 'name-dropping' to include the illustrious grandson of his sister Béatrice de Savoie, the '*Roy d'Engleterre*'. Listed among the witnesses are, of course, the ever-present Jean de Vesci and Othon de Grandson.[21] Once more we should note that in the thirteenth-century francophone world, there was nothing unusual in the witnessing, by a knight from Northumbria, a knight from Vaud, of the homage of a knight from the Viennois to the Count of Savoy and Burgundy. Ominously, as Edward indulged in the medieval spectacle of a homage to Philippe by Guillaume, on the same page of the *Fœdera* there is noted a restraint, issued in Edward's name in London to a recalcitrant vassal in Britain, Llywelyn ap Gruffydd, not to build a castle near Montgomery.[22] Storm clouds were gathering, even if those in the Viennois did not quite yet know it.

However, for Edward, Jacques and Othon, Caernarfon lay in the future. Following the feast, Othon de Grandson took his leave of Edward for a while, returning to his home by Lac de Neuchâtel for the first time in many years, whilst Edward continued with the main party through France toward Paris. Grandson had been given leave of Edward for a while and made his way toward Lac de Neuchâtel. His route back to Grandson took him over the Col de la Faucille and along the Vallée de Joux, then as now remote from the lands around Lac Léman. As the onetime crusader knight made his way alongside Lac de Joux, he may well have contemplated his life since leaving for England as a boy. He was returning this way to visit the Abbaye de Joux and its abbot, Jean de Bretigny. One can easily imagine thanks for his safe deliverance from the Holy Land were offered to his ancestors entombed within the walls of the great familial abbey. His return to Vaud was to attend, in particular, a likely upcoming vacancy of the see of Lausanne. The aged incumbent Jean de Cossonay, and Othon's cousin Guillaume de Champvent brought from London, met along with Othon and Count Philippe. The discussions no doubt related to the bishopric since the very next year Guillaume de Champvent would be appointed Bishop of Lausanne. We might pause at this moment to see the status and whereabouts of the *famille de Grandson*, already taken with English affairs:

Othon de Grandson	With the Lord Edward, future Justiciar of North Wales.
Guillaume de Grandson	With the Lord Edward, future Deputy Justiciar.
Henri de Grandson	Future Pastor of Greystoke.
Jacques de Grandson	Lord of Belmont.
Agnès de Grandson	Widowed wife of Ulrich de Vuippens, bailiff of Pierre de Savoie.
Gérard de Vuippens	Son of Agnès, future Pastor of Greystoke, Bishop of Lausanne and English envoy.
Pierre de Champvent	With Henry III as Steward, future King's Chamberlain.
Guillaume de Champvent	Dean of St. Martins-le-Grand in London, future Bishop of Lausanne.

We might usefully add Edward's detachment of Othon to Vaud also suited his purpose, a Grandson bishop ensconced midway along the important English pilgrim route, the Via Francigena, suited the English too. We should remember that Edward's father had been enfeoffed the town of Saint Maurice and castle at Bard and Edward would be enfeoffed the town of Pontarlier and Château de Joux soon after. The new bishop would indeed be Guillaume de Champvent, brother of Pierre de Champvent, the same Champvent that had for many years until the king's recent demise been a loyal steward to Henry III in London. Guillaume de Champvent was also Othon's first cousin, as the Grandson family had separated a generation earlier into the Lords of Grandson and of Champvent. Since the bishopric was the greatest landowner in Vaud, the see had been the cause of past struggles and indeed trebuchets firing toward the bishop's palace. The new Bishop of Lausanne had previously spent much time in England, being a dean of St. Martin Le Grand in London from 1262 until his elevation to the bishopric; he had also been a sub-dean at York Minster.[23] His influence at court in 1262 is evidenced by his joining the Savoyard witness list for a charter relating to Alianor's dowry.[24] Upon his move to Lausanne, Edward would appoint Louis, the son of Thomas II and future Baron de Vaud, to the vacant dean's position at St. Martin, lately occupied by Champvent.[25]

His '*cathedra*' or seat would be the great cathedral at Lausanne, the work of Jean Cotereel and his anonymous father, Cotereel being the man believed to be the late father of Maître Jacques. Grandson had been joined on this family business by his cousin Pierre de Champvent from England in April 1274.[26] While Pierre stayed awhile in Vaud, attending the consecration of Lausanne Cathedral on 20 October 1275,[27] in the presence of Othon's former crusade comrade Pope Gregory X and Rudolph of Habsburg, Othon returned to England to be with Edward not long after his coming coronation in August 1274; we know they were at Northampton together in November 1274.[28] The need to be in Vaud, attending to family business, and balancing that with the need to be in England, illustrates the difficult choices made by Savoyards. Indeed, the visit to Northampton saw the renewal, following his homage of June 1273, of Philippe's pension for what has been described as the 'English Savoyard lands.'[29] Grandson returned to Savoy, and the Viennois to spend Christmas of 1274 at Saint-Georges-d'Espéranche, no doubt with Philipe on Edward's business.

Going back to 1273, the royal party, meanwhile, arrived in the French capital on 17 July 1273,[30] so that he could pay homage to the new French king, Philippe III, for Gascony.[31] It would then be to Gascony, not England, that Edward would first turn his horse toward. The complex interweaving of feudal relationships between French kings, the French nobility, English kings who were also themselves French nobles and lastly Princes of Wales would give rise to continual dispute and warfare in the coming centuries.

It was only in April 1274 that Edward and Leonor finally set out once more for England but, even then, by the overland route through France, not the quicker sea voyage. On the way they took the opportunity to visit Leonor's mother Jeanne in Ponthieu. For those that imagine, in the light of events that will come in Britain, that Edward on becoming king immediately set out upon the conquest of Wales and Scotland, a satisfactory explanation needs to be found of the nearly two years that Edward and Leonor spent in returning to London. Papal affairs, family affairs with the Montforts, family affairs with the Savoyards, paying homage for and suppressing a revolt in Gascony, family affairs in Ponthieu, all seem to have taken a precedence over English affairs. It was a slow passage through Rome, Padua, Bologna, Milan, Turin, the Viennois, Paris, Orleans, Limoges, Saintes, Bordeaux, Bayonne, Bordeaux, Limoges and Paris before ever reaching the English Channel and setting eyes upon England once more, an England they'd last seen as a Dover receded into the distance that late August nearly four years earlier, an England where Henry was still king.

Edward and Leonor returned to a kingdom where the question of the loyalty of the House of Gwynedd was again in doubt. Contravening the express wishes of the government in London, Edward arrived in England, eventually, in the summer of 1274, having made his way from Savoy via Paris but also by way of Gascony, there to put the affairs of the troubled duchy to rights. His slow voyage home from the Holy Land is strongly indicative that, unlike his fathers, and despite the recent baronial war, his succession to the throne was secure and uncontested. By now Edward was 33 years of age; a kingdom lay before him as he landed at Dover on 2 August 1274 and surveyed the great castle before him. Things had changed a good deal since he'd last seen it, four years earlier. Edward had left England a prince he now returned a king.

Edward and his party made their way to London, where on 19 August 1274 he was crowned King of England. Contemporary historian Nicholas Trivet paints a word picture of

Edward for us: 'In build he was handsome and of great stature, towering head and shoulders above the average ... his brow was broad, and the rest of his face regular, though a drooping of the left eyelid recalled his father's expression.'[32]

Sadly, unlike the crowning of his mother Alianor de Provence, we do not have a richly embroidered chronicle of the coronation. Edward processed from the Palace of Westminster to the Abbey by way of a specially built covered walkway. He would have processed into the Abbey behind the sword Curtana, first used at his mother's coronation in 1236.[33] His brother Edmund had wanted to carry the sword, but by his absence from the coronation this was not apparently to be.[34] The essential elements of the coronation service used for Edward could be traced back to the crowning of King Edgar, who had become the first King of All England at Bath in AD 973. At Edward's coronation there would have been the aforesaid procession, an oath or promise, anointing and investiture followed by the Mass.[35] At the time of unction, anointing with holy oil, we can assume the words of Zadok the Priest were said or sung, since they have been used at every coronation since Edgar's:

> Zadok the Priest, and Nathan the Prophet anointed Solomon King.
> And all the people rejoiced and said:
> God save the King! Long live the King!
> May the King live for ever,
> Amen, Alleluia.

The most sacred part of the ceremony was, and still is, the anointing of the king with holy oil, the unction, carried out as suggested by Zadok the Priest and Nathan the Prophet on Solomon himself. This was God turning Edward from a mere mortal into God's anointed ruler of England, in the words given by Shakespeare to Richard II: 'Not all the water in the rough rude sea Can wash the balm off an anointed king' – and so it was firmly believed in 1274.

Along with the acclamations, as with his father and mother of the Laudes Regiæ, '*Christus vincit! Christus regnat! Christus imperat! Christus vincit! Christus regnat! Christus imperat!*' or 'Christ conquers! Christ reigns! Christ commands! Christ conquers! Christ reigns! Christ commands!'[36]

The Coronation Feast, or at least some of what was on the menu, has survived, there were '60 oxen and cows, 60 swine, 2 fat boars, 60 live sheep, 3,000 capons and hens and 40 bacon pigs'.[37] For Edward, the battles of Lewes, Evesham and Acre might be behind him, but far greater tests awaited.

We also know of one salient point in the abbey ceremony itself, apparently when the Archbishop of Canterbury, Robert Kilwardby,[38] placed the crown upon his head, Edward immediately removed it, declaring before the assembled great and good of the kingdom that he would only replace it once the lands lost to the crown by his father had been recovered – this new king it seemed was bent upon restoring the kingly authority he perceived had been lost in his father's time. Perhaps Edward had in mind a generality of lands, recalling the carefully worded homage he had recently made before the King of France, but very more likely he had in mind lands lost during the civil war to men like Llywelyn ap Gruffydd, who now rejoiced in the name Prince of Wales. Edward's appanage included the four cantrefs: Rhuddlan was mentioned by name, as was Builth, all these lands now in the possession of Llywelyn.[39] And worse, a notable absentee at his coronation that August day in Westminster Abbey was the aforesaid Llywelyn ap Gruffydd, Prince of Wales – it was an absence that had not gone unnoticed by the new king.[40]

Edward got on with setting the government of his new kingdom as he would wish it; on 21 September he replaced Walter de Merton as Lord Chancellor with loyalist Robert Burnell.[41] Robert Burnell, like Othon de Grandson, was of the same age as Edward, and like the Savoyard a long and loyal servant, companion and friend.[42] Burnell remained loyal to Edward throughout the Montfortian rebellion and was rewarded with being made Archdeacon of York in December 1270. He had remained in England while Edward was away on crusade – like Grandson, Robert Burnell was a man Edward could trust. The first witnesses to a charter of Edward's patronage were Thomas de Clare, Jean de Vesci, Othon de Grandson and Robert de Tibetot[43] – all these men had been on crusade with Edward. If Pierre de Savoie had been a veritable witnesser of over forty charters of the English crown in Henry's day, then the thirty-two out of thirty-seven charters that would be issued by Edward up to 1290 and witnessed by Grandson mark him as a close second in terms of Savoyard influence in England.[44] It was not their rank that marked them out, but their loyalty, it would be a distinction that Edward had learned from the reign of his father, and it would mark the way in which he would rule.

As we saw Grandson had remained in Savoy before returning to England in November 1274 only to be sent back to Savoy on a visit to Count Philippe at Saint-Georges-d'Esperanche where they shared Christmas. Once the Christmas festivities were done in the Viennois, Othon de Grandson then spent the following two years engaged upon much diplomatic work for Edward relating to Gascony and its neighbouring territories. In January 1275 he was in Paris with Antony Bek negotiating loans with the merchants of Piacenza that Edward might satisfy his Gascon creditors – that Edward might employ his former Keeper of the Wardrobe in this matter is understandable, but Othon's involvement again speaks to his trusted intimacy with Edward.[45]

It had been while Edward and Othon had been in Acre that the idea for a means to raise consistent revenue that might be used fighting wars or building castles had first germinated. Edward had begun to make recourse to a new way of funding royal expenses: the Riccardi and other merchants of Lucca in Italy. In the coming twenty years they would be crucial in providing the liquidity to fund his conflicts in Wales and Gascony, not to mention the capital outlay for an unprecedented royal castle-building programme. Before 1272, English kings had made some use of Italian bankers, particularly in papal relations, but Edward was about to take that to another level, and to begin with to fund his expenses on crusade and on his way home. Loans would be granted against customs revenue, providing a ready and continuous availability of liquidity.[46] As we saw earlier, Othon de Grandson, accompanying Antony Bek, had been key to Edward's finances from the beginning. In January 1275 they had been in Paris negotiating loans with the Italian merchants of Piacenza that he might satisfy his Gascon creditors.[47]

In April 1275, the newly crowned Edward called a parliament at Westminster. There too was Othon de Grandson returning from Paris with the loan from the merchants of Piacenza. Edward had called to parliament, in addition to the usual great and good nobles of the land, four knights from each shire and six or four men, burgesses, from each city, borough or market town. For what Edward had in mind was a far-reaching settlement to the financial issues only very partly solved by Othon's agreement with the Italians in Paris. Before we go on to explore the relationship with the Riccardi di Lucca we should pause to reflect that attending this first parliament of Edward's reign, was one Othon de Grandson[48] – some twenty years before the semi-mythical birth of democracy in what is now his native Switzerland, the son of Lac de Neuchâtel was attending the first English parliament to admit burgesses and the one responsible for suggesting that '*pur ceo q elections deivent estre fraunches, le Rey defent sour sa greve forfeture, a nul haut home, ne autre, par poer des armes, ne per manaces, ne desturbe de fere fraunche election*'. That is 'and because elections ought to be free, the King commands upon great forfeiture that no man by force of arms, nor by malice nor by menacing shall disturb any to make free election'.[49] His kinsman Pierre de Savoie had exported some elements of the Magna Carta to Savoy, now Othon de Grandson was at the parliament which issued the 1275 Statute of Westminster.

But the Statute of Westminster was not the main business of the spring parliament of 1275: that would be a new tariff on wool exports – England's greatest export. The record of Othon's attendance at parliament points directly to the new tariff: '[Grandson] Consents that the same customs shall be payable upon wool, &c. shipped from the ports of his liberties in Ireland as had been granted in England upon wool, &c, exported therefrom.'[50]

The proposal for this came from Edward's treasurer, Joseph de Chauncy, a Hospitaller Edward had met in Acre, who took up an idea of the Italian merchant Poncius de Ponto.[51] By agreement, the customs were collected directly from Italian merchants in the ports. The income from customs, which until 1279 amounted to about £10,000 annually, was directly offset against the debts the crown had owed to the Italian merchants. This in effect gave Edward what might now be described as a current account with an overdraft facility with his Italian bankers. Edward could call upon immediate loans irrespective of whether the accumulated income from customs could at that point bear the request; in the words of the English archives the Riccardi were called upon to provide liquid cash 'out of royal funds or their own'.[52] In fact, we know that for the crusading period and the coming First Welsh War, 1272 until 1279, their excess payments are listed as £23,000[53] and the period from 1290 until 1294 it's listed as £18,924[54] – like many of us since this was an overdraft facility much used by its holder. We do not know precisely when Edward came to a definite agreement with the Riccardi di Lucca, but it was most likely during his time in Acre and may have been consolidated during his journey through Italy.

The Riccardi di Lucca were among the new breed of Italian merchants who had evolved from so called 'caravan merchants', travelling to buy and sell in the markets north of the Alps, to 'sedentary merchants', who made use of a network of agents to carry on business on their behalf. These merchants had moved from buying and selling to finance, to support the increasing north–south payments in Europe generated by the wool trade, the crusades and papal relations – precisely the needs that drew them into Edward's orbit.[55]

The Riccardi family partnership was the foremost of the Luchesse merchant associations and founded as a simple partnership with joint and unlimited liability.[56] These partnerships were relatively new in their scope and breadth, growing out of father and son associations to take in many outside the immediate family, as is the case with the Riccardi. This ability to outgrow the family led to an increase in business acumen and capital and saw a significant rise to prominence from the 1250s onwards.[57] Perhaps the key individual on the Italian side of the relationship was the interestingly named Lucasio Natale, who appears in the English records as 'Luke de Luk' and his 'merchants of Lucca'. His partner at the London end was Orlandino da Pogio. Edward was not the first English king to make use of their services; his father Henry had bought fine cloths and ecclesiastical vestments from them in June 1245[58] – but the son would deal far more in raising finance for war than buying priestly robes. Richard Kaeuper notes well, that, 'if the label of capitalist is to be applied to any group of men in early European history, the Riccardi must be included'.[59] Prestwich estimated the bill for the ninth crusade as £100,000 – over £70 million in today's money.[60]

We can also add that it was not only to Edward and the crown that the Riccardi of Lucca would be bankers, but also to key members of his retinue who rode back with him through Italy that summer of 1273. Othon de Grandson also 'held an account' with the Riccardi. He was so well known to them that they familiarly referred to him as 'Messer Otto' in correspondence. He was not only a link to the English crown, but also to the *famille de Grandson* more widely.[61] We know that the crusade had been costly for Othon, he is mentioned alongside Jean de Vesci and Jean de Grailly incurring debts on crusade and borrowing 2,500 *Livres Tournois* from Acre merchants while in Outremer.[62] An example of both the influence of Othon de Grandson and the Riccardi at this point concerns the Italian involvement in the profitable wool trade. The Riccardi undertook to buy 120 sacks of wool from the abbot of the Cistercian house of Meaux in Holderness, Yorkshire, at the Boston fair. The abbot subsequently reneged on delivery of the wool; the Riccardi wrote seeking redress to, among others, their friend and customer, Grandson.

Another Riccardi customer travelling back with Edward would be Antony Bek, the future Bishop of Durham, and a key servant of Edward's. Indeed, we can say that both key negotiators of what will be the Treaty of Aberconwy of 1277 were Riccardi account holders, as was the crown, account holders of the bank that financed the coming Welsh Wars.[63] In the summer of 1279, the auditors of the annual accounts prepared by the Riccardi for Edward were listed as Robert Burnell, Joseph de Chauncy, Jean de Vesci, Othon de Grandson, Anthony and Thomas Bek[64] – the king's inner circle.[65] Jean de Vesci was a onetime ward of Pierre de Savoie and husband to the Savoyard Agnès de Saluzzo.[66] During the baronial war Vesci had been a Montfortian. The chronicler Thomas Wykes[67] describes the mercy shown to the onetime rebel who then became a lifelong servant to the king and lifelong friend and comrade of of Othon de Grandson.

The involvement of Othon de Grandson in the arrangement of the 1275 Paris loan from Piacenza, his attendance of the April 1275 parliament at which a tariff on wool exports and the Riccardi system was established when taken with his role as auditor of Riccardi accounts in England and his holding of an account with them point inexorably to the Savoyard having a leading part in the ordering of Edward's finances and setting them upon a footing that would bear the weight of the Welsh Wars and castle building that would inevitably come.

CHAPTER 4

But as Edward set about establishing his government and finances, and Othon seeing to the bishopric of Lausanne, trouble had been brewing. On 3 November 1274, that absentee from his coronation, Llywelyn ap Gruffydd, the Prince of Wales had been asked to come to the king at Shrewsbury to do the homage required of him by treaty.[1] Llywelyn ap Gruffydd was the son of Gruffydd ap Llywelyn Fawr, he that fell ignominiously while attempting escape from the Tower of London, and so the grandson of Llywelyn Fawr,[2] albeit an illegitimate grandson. Following his father's untimely end, he had defeated his brothers Dafydd and Owain at the Battle of Bryn Derwin in 1255 to claim ascendancy within the House of Gwynedd.[3] He had become a growing thorn in the side of the late Henry and now of Edward. We cannot be certain of when this Llywelyn was born, or indeed where; we cannot even be certain of who his mother was – but we can be certain that he had for all his life been trying to live up to the name of his grandfather Llywelyn Fawr.[4]

The Treaty of Montgomery seven years earlier in 1267 had not only granted Llywelyn title as Prince of Wales,[5] but also accorded him suzerainty over all other Welsh rulers, and had robbed Edward personally of his appanage land in Wales. What is more, it had created a dangerous source of conflict, for the native Welsh princes now owed allegiance to the Prince of Wales. But the native Welsh princes were not the only rulers of Wales – there were the marcher lords for all to contend with. The marcher lords occupied Welsh land outside the kingdom of England, and owed allegiance not to the Prince of Wales, but to the king of England. The marcher lords held lands along much of the Welsh border with England, but also most of South Wales, Glamorgan, and Pembroke. Llywelyn himself held Gwynedd, now extending from the Llyn peninsula all the way to Deeside and down the western coast, as far as the Dovey estuary. His vassals held Powys and Ceredigion, meaning that a cocktail of warring interests held Wales, with ultimately the Prince of Wales and the marcher lords subject to Edward. The Treaty of Montgomery would not provide the basis for a peaceful settlement of Wales. As the Lord Edward became King of England, trouble began to brew on his western border, and perhaps his coronation declaration showed and that he was determined to meet the threat. His father Henry had stayed his hand with the last Prince of Wales, Dafydd ap Llywelyn Fawr, when the Welshman reneged on earlier treaties. Henry had not invaded Gwynedd when he had had every right, showing leniency; however, his son had learned that to be a king you had to defend your *majesté*.[6] Not only Edward was resolved to claw back his lands lost to Llywelyn, so too were the marcher lords who would throw oil on to the fire – war threatened.

Contravening the express wishes of the government in London, Llywelyn had recently set about consolidating his hold over Powys with the construction of a castle in the Upper Severn valley at Dolforwyn, beginning in 1273, around the time Edward was visiting Count Philippe's castle under construction at Saint-Georges in the Viennois. But Dolforwyn was no palace; while it lacked entirely the military sophistication of the Savoyard castles, it was nonetheless a dagger held toward Edward's kingdom and the county of Shropshire in particular. The strategically important Montgomery and the nearby Ceri hills had been the flashpoint of an earlier confrontation between Llywelyn Fawr and a young Henry III in 1228.[7] Dolforwyn Castle was only 4 miles from, and obviously threatening, Montgomery Castle,[8] the very venue of the treaty of 1267. The regency government had attempted to prevent the castle's construction, across from the river Severn at Abermule. On 23 June 1273 they issued an 'inhibition of his [Llywelyn] erecting a castle at Abrunol, near the castle of Montgomery … so that the king may not be compelled to apply his hand otherwise to this'.[9]

Another castle as a source of conflict was that constructed by marcher lord Gilbert de Clare, Earl of Gloucester, at Caerffili, built from 1268 to consolidate his rule in Glamorgan. The Lordship of Glamorgan had been cut out of the Welsh Kingship of Morgannwg by the Normans, who had first extended their interests into the lands of welsh speakers after their conquests of the lands of the English. Robert Fitz[10] Hamo had established Norman rule, with his chief castle at Cardiff, from his lands in nearby Gloucestershire. After a period of royal custody, the lordship of Glamorgan passed into the hands of the Clare family[11] in 1217. But the Earls of Gloucester had only established their rule in lowland Morgannwg. They began to extend into the upland areas of the rivers Rhymney and Taff from 1246, bringing them closer toward Brecon and the southern extremities of Llywelyn ap Gruffydd's nascent principality of Wales. Clare rule had been extended to the commote of Glyn Rhondda and Meisgyn in 1246, Afan in 1247, and last Senghennydd in 1267.

Gwynedd had not extended its rule hitherto to south Wales, but Llywelyn was bent now upon this path, something Gilbert de Clare was equally bent upon resisting. The move into Senghennydd, nearly twenty years after the earlier extensions, was likely made following moves by Llywelyn into the area.[12] The Treaty of Montgomery had failed to define the relationship between Llywelyn and Gilbert; the latter would have felt a growing threat from the north. Caerffili, where the Rhymney begins a great bend in Senghennydd, was the response to the Welsh threat. On 13 October 1270, Llywelyn had burned the construction site to the ground, but on 1 June 1271 building was renewed,[13] and a castle so strong that the Marcher Lord's authority was firmly established over Glamorgan. 'Giant' Caerffili, as described by a Welsh chronicle,[14] was built as a magnificent concentric ring fortress, on a small island and surrounded by artificial lakes. Its scope and grandeur were no doubt not lost upon Edward, neither more importantly was its ability to successfully mark the authority of its builder upon the surrounding land.

North of Glamorgan lay Brecon, only recently, in 1263, brought into the lands of Llywelyn. When Humphrey de Bohun, who would succeed his elderly grandfather as Earl of Hereford in 1275, sought to restore his lands in Brecon, there would be more trouble. The Treaty of Montgomery had reserved Brecon for Llywelyn, and this encroachment, to the Welsh prince was a clear breech of the treaty. In the summer of 1273, it was a transgression formalised when the regency government – Henry having died, Edward not having returned – referred to Brecon as 'the land of Humphrey de Bohun'. Welsh historian R. R. Davies notes: 'These individual confrontations in the March need not have led to a more general breakdown of Anglo-Welsh relations … Yet their cumulative effect, especially as the years passed, was to create in Llywelyn's mind a suspicion that there was an orchestrated attempt to undermine his hard-won gains.'[15] If there had been an 'orchestrated attempt to undermine' Llywelyn, it seems that it had not lain with King Henry in his dying days, nor with his son Edward fighting

Mamluks at Acre, but perhaps with the regency government and one of mutual interest, between the Marchers Clare, Bohun and Mortimer. Mortimer was Roger Mortimer, 1st Baron Mortimer of Wigmore, whose wife Maude de Braose had been involved in the plot to free the Lord Edward prior to the Battle of Evesham that we explored more fully in my earlier book Peter of Savoy: The Little Charlemagne.

Llywelyn sat upon an uncertain perch in Gwynedd, and while there was a strong sense of Welsh identity, there was not yet a Welsh polity and so there were Welshmen who did not necessarily accept the overlordship of Gwynedd. Cracks, in terms of loyalty to Llywelyn, began to appear in Brecon and Deheubarth.[16] Both his brother Dafydd ap Gruffydd and Gruffydd ap Gwenwynwyn of Powys had been with Llywelyn when he had challenged Clare at Caerffili – both men may have begun to doubt the fight Llywelyn was picking. Llywelyn's retreat from Glamorgan in the face of the marcher lord was perhaps the beginning of the end for Llywelyn, not Edward's return from the Holy Land – Welsh historian J. Beverley Smith suggests wryly, that when he 'abandoned the siege of Caerffili and withdrew' that 'he was unable to arrest that withdrawal until he stood on the frontiers of Snowdon itself'.[17]

And so, we will soon have a new king who learned that perceived weakness in the face of opposition on behalf of his father led to civil war – a new king eager to assert his royal dignity. And we have a native Prince of Wales, becoming ever suspicious of this new English king and eager to assert this authority in the face of a perceived undermining of his position.

The Treaty of Montgomery was never meant to be a permanent solution to Anglo-Welsh relations. Historian of the Welsh Wars John. E. Morris described it as 'rather a truce than a peace'.[18] If a truce, it was ineffective: its less than precise definitions of what was owed by whom and for what meant that, in the climate of mutual suspicion prevalent in the early 1270s, the provisions of the treaty began to fall apart. In Llywelyn's troubled mind, he began to think of a way in which he could leverage the support of Edward in his disputes with Mortimer, Clare, and Bohun. That leverage appeared to be withholding the tribute owed by him to the crown. But in doing so, he was breaching a treaty with the crown. And remember this was a crown not yet placed upon Edward's head, when Llywelyn began to withhold the payments, even prior to Edward's return in February 1274.[19]

The regency government, as recorded in the Closed Rolls for Edward's reign, began at once, in December 1272, to display anxiety that Llywelyn was withholding treaty commitment payments.[20] Despite their 1272 request, no payment was forthcoming, Llywelyn was linking the lack of tribute payments with the failure of the crown to contain the Marcher Lords. But how able could the ailing Henry, a regency government and the absent Edward have been able to contain Clare, Bohun, and Mortimer? With the failure to maintain payments, the Treaty of Montgomery was in trouble, and Edward and Llywelyn set upon a collision course. By attempting to use the withdrawal of these payments to influence the actions of an uncrowned king, Llywelyn was catastrophically misjudging Edward. Importantly, we can see that the quarrel that ended with the First Welsh War in 1277 was not of Edward's making, he being at the time being most decidedly out of the country. In summary, Beverley Smith agrees that it was the confluence of a worsening position in the marches, alongside an absence of influence from Westminster that saw the deterioration of Anglo-Welsh relations between 1267 and 1276, saying that it was not 'something that dated from Edward's accession'.[21]

Llywelyn's paranoia would not have been helped, nor his position strengthened by a plot to assassinate him in early 1274. It had been arranged that Owain ap Gruffydd ap Gwenwynwyn would come with armed men on 2 February to carry out the assassination but were to be thwarted by a snowstorm. Llywelyn did not discover the full details of the plot until Owain confessed to the Bishop of Bangor. The plot implicated Llywelyn's brother Dafydd ap Gruffydd, who upon its discovery, in November 1274, fled to England and a sanctuary provided by Edward. The plotters also included the leading family of Powys Wenwynwyn: Gruffydd ap Gwenwynwyn, his wife Hawise and aforesaid son Owain. The plot laid bare the weakness of Llywelyn's position among Welshmen, particularly the rift within his own family and between Gwynedd and Powys. Llywelyn's expanded influence in Wales had always been built upon less than secure ground, evidenced by the necessity of taking hostages to guarantee agreements with lesser Welsh princes. Maerdudd ap Rhys back in 1261, many in Mid Wales in 1271 and Gruffydd ap Gwenwynwyn now in 1274 had been coerced in this way.[22] So, the plotters added further poison to the deteriorating relationship between the Prince of Wales and the king of England by increasing Llywelyn's internal paranoia. The harbouring of Dafydd ap Gruffydd and Gruffydd ap Gwenwynwyn by Edward has been offered by some as an excuse for Llywelyn not to pay homage to Edward. This might be true of 1275–76, but it cannot be said to apply to the first requests, and particularly that of the regency government for him to come to Rhyd Chwima in 1272. His continuing refusals to take an oath of fealty and pay homage due to his liege lord, Edward, began a downward spiral in Anglo-Welsh relations, that would march irrevocably to war.

Rhyd Chwima, in 1272, is a watershed moment in the build-up to the First Welsh War. Barely eleven days after Henry had passed away, and long before any internal Welsh conspiracy, the regency government issued, in Edward's absence, an order for Llywelyn to come to Rhyd Chwima. This was the ford of the river Severn near Montgomery, where traditional Anglo-Welsh meetings were held. Here Llywelyn was asked to pay due homage to Edward.[23] It is remarkable that this order appears on page two of Edward's Calendar of Close Rolls; it is only the third order of his government, and one issued in his absence. Llywelyn had not been summoned to leave Wales, but to come to the traditional meeting place of Rhyd Chwima. Those appointed to receive the homage on Edward's behalf, the abbots of Dore and Haughmond,[24] waited all day by the banks of the Severn. No one came; they waited and eventually left.

When Edward returned and was crowned in August 1274, the lack of Llywelyn's presence and homage would have been keenly felt by a new king who had seen the dignity of this father's reign compromised so often. But the failure, from the aforesaid order onward, to obey no less than five summons to attend Edward to do homage and give fealty was foolhardy and disastrous for Gwynedd – the leopard would exact revenge upon this slight against his honour. If fealty was 'the glue that held feudal society together'[25] then Edward had no choice but to defend his position. Edward had noted to the pope, regarding Llywelyn, 'in order to receive his homage and fealty' in August 1276, writing: 'we had so demeaned our royal dignity (*regiam dignitatem*) as to go to the confines of his land.' Edward was referring to a visit to Chester in 1275; an attempt had been made to get Llywelyn to come to pay the due homage in June 1275.[26] If ever there was a king conscious, because of the many challenges to his father's dignity, of his own '*regiam dignitatem*' then it was this king. At Chester, the chronicler of the monastery there, noted with dismay Llywelyn's 'contempt' for Edward by not coming to pay homage.[27] Edward had been in Cheshire awaiting his Prince of Wales since late August, his presence at Macclesfield noted on 24 August. He was at Chester to take Llywelyn's homage on 3 and 4 September, where he paced up and down awaiting the Welshman. However, he waited in vain – no Llywelyn. Edward went up to Birkenhead, on the nearby Wirral peninsula for a few days, on his return on 10 September – no sign of Llywelyn.[28]

Yet another mandate this time to Westminster, followed on 10 September; [29] however, Llywelyn again failed to show. Oddly, he still proclaimed a peace had been made to his people in Wales and levied a new tax to renew payments of monies owed to Edward. Since this is entirely at odds with his known failure to attend at Chester, and the above renewed summons to Westminster, we can only assume this was a pretext on Llywelyn's part and that he was, in fact, now preparing for war.[30]

Perhaps worse still for Edward, following the death, in the spring of 1275 of his Aunt Eleanor, wife of his slain uncle and onetime enemy, Simon de Montfort, their daughter, his cousin Eleanor, was married to none other than Llywelyn ap Gruffydd. The Prince of Wales and Eleanor de Montfort were married by proxy: he was in Wales, she in France.[31] So, here now for Edward was Llywelyn marrying the daughter of onetime rebel and man he had fought at Lewes and had brutally cut down at Evesham. Edward had last visited his aunt and the young Eleanor in an act of reconciliation, just two years earlier – so much for family reconciliations. The Plantagenet family was not famed for its even temper and patience, that by ignoring an order to refrain from castle building, with a breach of the Treaty of Montgomery, by refusal to pay him homage and give due fealty[32] and lastly marriage to the daughter of he and his late father's greatest enemy, then we can imagine that Llywelyn was trying that temper and patience beyond breaking point. The very last thing the new king wanted, especially after the peaceful uncontested succession, was a resurrection of a Montfortian faction. This raised the spectre of another civil war.

The two ships carrying Eleanor, her brother Amaury and their entourage, sailing off the south coast of England, were captured by sailors from the port of Bristol, just off the Scilly islands. Buried beneath the boards of the ship was found the banner of the *famille de Montfort*. The chronicler of Guisborough, writing later, would attribute the breakdown as having been brought to a head by 'Llywelyn, Prince of Wales' that he 'had taken himself a wife, daughter of Lord Simon de Montfort'.[33] In a marriage union between the Montfort family and the House of Gwynedd, the relationship betwixt king and prince had reached breaking point. And yet there had been another futile attempt to bring Llywelyn to the king.[34]

The business of the kingdom continued however, even as war clouds gathered. The position of Othon de Grandson at court was now so significant that his friend Edward would reward him with, in November 1275, the title 'Keeper of the Isles of Gernesye [Guernsey] and Gereseye [Jersey]',[35] something that would be extended to Lordship for life in 1277. The Channel Islands of Jersey and Guernsey were the remnants of the Duchy of Normandy that had once belonged to Edward's grandfather John, and like Ireland had been passed to Edward by the late King Henry as a part of his appanage in 1254. As in Ireland, the Vaudois knight would be an absentee landlord; nevertheless as his tenure continued into his very long life the harsh rule of his bailiffs would bring much criticism and establish a black mark against the name of Grandson, much as had been the case with a similarly absent Pierre de Savoie on the mainland decades earlier. How much of this bad reputation is justified is hard to tell at this distance, but both Savoyards were evidently keen to extract as much in the way of revenue as they could from their English landholdings. We will return to Othon's unhappy custody of the Channel Islands later.[36]

In October 1275 Othon was sent across the Channel once more, this time to Paris, and to make apologies to Philippe III that his Lord, Edward, was unable to attend the Martinmas French Parliament as he had pressing matters within his own kingdom. On this occasion Grandson was accompanied by Roger de Clifford and Maurice de Craon, and no doubt they both took the chance once more to press the claim of 1259 Treaty of Paris to the Saintonge and the Agenais – after all it was a product of this treaty by which Edward had been summoned to parliament in Paris as Philippe's vassal for Gascony.[37] Accordingly, from Paris Othon was to journey to Gascony, there along with its seneschal Luke de Tany to relieve the French king's seneschal of Périgord, Eudes de Fazel of his charge. Périgord would not receive an English seneschal until 1280, and then it would be Othon's fellow Savoyard, Jean de Grailly.[38] After a brief return to England, July 1276 saw Othon sail once more for Gascony, this time with Stephen de Pencestre to attend to a dispute with Philippe III over food and shipping subsidies required and to resolve a dispute with the Bishop of Bordeaux, Simon de Rochechouuart, over his revenues.[39]

Crossing the Channel with Grandson following the former mission would also be his brother Henri de Grandson, to whom Edward granted two years' protection on 26 May 1276. Henri travelled to the far north of Edward's realm to take up a position as parson of the church in Greystoke in the county of Cumberland.[40] The church at Greystoke had been recently built in 1255, some features from Henri's time remaining still. The rood beam bridging the chancel arch is the oldest item in the church and is blessed with floral emblems representing the wounds of Christ. The ancient choir stalls in the chancel have some well-preserved misericords (carved shelf underneath the seat). The movement of Henri to England must have been connected with the July 1275 instruction to sheriffs by Edward 'to collect the tenth of ecclesiastical revenue assigned in the general council [of Lyons A.D. 1274] for the aid of the Holy Land for six years, and the arrears thereof, whenever required to do so by G. bishop of Verdun or his collectors',[41] the 'G' as bishop of Verdun referring to Othon's and Henri's brother Gérard de Grandson, who had accompanied Edward and Othon on crusade. In return Edward had used his influence to obtain for him the see of Verdun. In 1278 Henri moved south once more to take up the see of Verdun, from his recently deceased brother Gérard,[42] Verdun then not yet in France but a prestigious Prince Bishopric within the Holy Roman Empire. Thus, the Plantagenet king was to have a hand in successive bishops of Verdun, chiefly to the benefit of the *famille de Grandson.*

Such cross-Channel journeys would, no doubt, have been unpleasant, uncomfortable and not a little dangerous to undertake. Othon's voyages would make him familiar with the dangers and pleasures of the open road. Indeed, his cross-Channel sojourns became so frequent he evidently became so well known by the men of Dover that when Thomas Salekyn, a boatman there, 'feared that he would lose the house which he was alleged to have built on the common soil' it was to his 'very dear lord, and it please him friend, Sir Otho de Granson [*sic*] that he appealed for protection.'[43]

1276 was the year of four popes. First, Edward's and Othon's crusading comrade Theobaldo Visconti, reigning as Gregory X, had died on 10 January. He had been followed by the Savoyard Pierre de Tarentaise reigning as Innocent V, but his brief reign had ended on 22 June with his premature death. Last, the former papal legate Ottobuono dei Fieschi, who had done so much to write the Treaty of Montgomery in 1267 and had come to the papacy as Adrian V, died after an even briefer reign on 18 August as he had fled the heat of Rome to Viterbo. None of these three dying popes would be able to intercede in Britain, and the fourth, John XXI, would only barely live out the year, passing in May 1277.[44]

The 'arduous affairs of my kingdom' of which Edward spoke in the autumn of 1275 to Philippe III were of course Llywelyn ap Gruffydd. The latest attempt at bringing Llywelyn to pay due homage looks to have been the straw that broke the camel's back, for the order now went out to Edward's Gascon *ingeniator*, Bertram, to travel to the forests of Kingsclere and Burghfield, on the Hampshire–Berkshire borders, to choose and fell timber appropriate for the construction of siege engines.[45] The timber was to be hauled to Caversham where the Sheriff of Berkshire and Oxfordshire was to arrange for it to be shipped down the Thames to the Tower of London.[46] The order to ship the timber was just twenty-four hours on from Llywelyn's latest failure to show, 26 April 1276. The drums of war were beginning to beat.[47]

However, Parliament had sat between 6 May and 3 June at Westminster, with no action yet taken. But, when Parliament sat once more at Westminster from 29 September, Edward arriving on 19 October, this time, there would be a response to Llywelyn's provocations. The king's patience finally snapped: Edward declared Llywelyn ap Gruffydd, the Prince of Wales, to be a 'rebel' and 'disturber of his peace' on 12 November 1276. The English Closed Rolls listed, impatiently, Llywelyn's failures to pay the due homage before Edward that he would 'go against Llywelyn as his rebel and disturber of his peace.'.[48]

One can hear the impatience of the Plantagenet king rising with every line. Despite last-minute protestations from Llywelyn, the Church declared he and his supporters to be excommunicate, and the principality placed under interdict.

So had war been inevitable? Well, perhaps Edward's coronation declaration suggests so, but equally there is a weight of evidence that Edward tried to avoid war. The failure to consolidate the Treaty (truce) of Montgomery into a lasting peace settlement, upon which the future of Anglo-Welsh relations could be built, was perhaps the starting point. The personalities of both Llywelyn, paranoid and wanting to hold what he had gained, and Edward, proud and wanting to regain what he felt the crown had lost – these personalities suggest an inevitable outcome. Llywelyn must have known the consequences of his failures to pay homage. He himself had acted against Maredudd ap Rhys Gryg of Deheubarth for such a breach, imprisoning him at Criccieth Castle.[49] That the Treaty of Montgomery built into the peace a tribute due to the crown that the Prince of Wales would find difficult to meet and made no account of marcher lords seeking redress – meant the treaty set up the pathway to conflict.

From the standpoint of the twenty-first century, it seems obvious that England and Gwynedd were set from an early point after Montgomery for war, but it did not seem like that at the time. Given Edward's leisurely return from his crusade, it seems that Wales was a long way from his thoughts. But when he did arrive back in England, Llywelyn would soon push his way up the young king's consciousness until the point he was left with little option but to declare him a rebel beyond the king's peace, a dangerous place to be in the thirteenth century. Prestwich is in no doubt 'it was Llywelyn's attitude, not Edward's, that explains why war broke out in 1276.'[50]

So, some 200 years since Duke William set foot among the English, a reckoning had long been brewing between the Anglo-Norman state, born in 1066, and the descendants of the Britons who had long resisted English incursions into their mountainous lands, such a reckoning now beckoning. Edward gathered to himself an army to invade Wales, an army larger than any seen in the British islands since the time of his ancestor, Duke William. Anglo-Norman kings, Edward's ancestors, had made incursions into Wales, they had made punitive raids, they had encouraged their nobles to establish semi-independent fiefs in the Marches, but now Edward prepared with all the thoroughness of a man about a business he knew well. His crusade to the Holy Land had been still born for lack of resources and planning, his father's incursions into Wales had also been found wanting – he was not to make that mistake this time, this time the remaining Britons would be brought to heel.

CHAPTER 5

Instructions for the invasion of Wales were issued from Westminster on 13 November 1276. There would be three armies invading Wales. First, William de Beauchamp, 9th Earl of Warwick, was despatched to garrison Chester in the north. Marcher Lord, Roger de Mortimer, 1st Baron Mortimer of Wigmore, a man with land to reclaim, was sent to his base at Montgomery on the Severn to secure the counties of Shropshire, Staffordshire, and Herefordshire adjacent to Mid Wales. Last, Payn de Chaworth, Lord of Kidwelly, a crusading companion of Edward's, was sent to south and west Wales.[1] His loyal Savoyard friend Othon de Grandson having been recalled from sunnier climes, went to Montgomery to join the push into central Wales. As the winter let hold of its chilly grasp the opening moves were made, the first target being Llywelyn's new castle at Dolforwyn. Shortly before 8 March of 1277, Master Bertram headed from London for the six-day journey to Montgomery, along with crossbowmen and miners, to prepare a siege, there to rendezvous with Grandson.[2] Master Bertram was an *ingeniator* of Gascon origin, who, as we saw, had been long in the service of the crown, working with Jean de Mézos before his move to Savoy.

Othon de Grandson joined the banner of Henri de Lacy, Earl of Lincoln, and a great-grandson of Amédée IV de Savoie, and the central army in Shropshire, commanding a troop of knights in January 1277. Edward had, late in 1276, sent to France for war horses, seventy-five being noted as passing through the French port of Wissant.[3] Morris suggested the final number received was more than a hundred in total.[4] Grandson himself caused two destriers[5] and thirty mounted crossbowmen to be brought from Gascony, where he had spent much recent time, also by way of Wissant in France.[6] When a medieval army mustered, it involved a lot of work over many days, lists to be made of the men, pay agreed, arms to be procured. Some 200,000 crossbow bolts were ordered from the Forest of Dean. Edward meant business; he had learned in the failed crusade and before that preparation was everything. Roger de Mortimer was accompanied by Henri de Lacy, who had twenty-five knights under his command, divided among eight bannerets.[7] Lacy himself had six knights and twenty-three troopers, Jean de Vesci had four knights and ten troopers, Othon de Grandson, a banneret, had also four knights and ten troopers; smaller numbers were divided among Guillaume de Leyburn, Robert FitzRoger, Jean de Vaux, Geoffrey de Lucy and lastly Jean de Bohun. Grandson had been assigned to Lacy's command; the other knights owed him feudal obligation – Grandson did not.

Henri de Lacy, 3rd Earl of Lincoln, was himself, as mentioned, descended from a Count of Savoy, and so related to his king by common Savoyard ancestry. His mother was Alésia de Saluce or Saluzzo, the daughter of Béatrice de Savoie, who in turn was the daughter of Count Amédée IV de Savoie – thus making Henri a great-grandson of the Savoyard. Edward, meanwhile, was the son of Alianor de Provence, herself a daughter of another Béatrice de Savoie who was a sister of the same Count Amédée IV de Savoie – such were the intricate ways in which the ruling families of Savoy and England were interrelated in the thirteenth century.

This force pushed up the Upper Severn to the castle at Dolforwyn – recently and provocatively constructed by Llywelyn and menacing the border – and laid siege to the castle. Othon de Grandson was not the only Savoyard invading Llywelyn's lands in the spring of 1277; indeed, the invasion of Wales might be said to have more than just a hint of Savoy. While Othon was among those laying siege to Dolforwyn, a messenger came to him on 3 April 1277: Jean de Bonvillars.[8] Jean was Othon's brother-in-law, married to Othon's sister Agnès.[9] Bonvillars was (and still is) a small village just over 5 kilometres north of Grandson by the Lac de Neuchâtel. Bonvillars's father Henri had been chatelain at Rue for Pierre de Savoie until 1266. His brother Henri de Bonvillars, a Cluniac dean responsible for the convent at the beautiful Romanesque monastery of Payerne, across the Lac de Neuchâtel, was later to come to England to be prior of Bermondsey, and later, its mother priory at Wenlock, in Shropshire,[10] just across the border from Dolforwyn.[11] Nonetheless, on that April morning at Dolforwyn, it was Jean de Bonvillars who was galloping up to the knights laying siege to the castle.

Earlier, another messenger between Edward and Othon had been yet another Savoyard, Guillaume de Cicon.[12] We first hear of Guillaume de Cicon in an archival reference dated 13 November 1276, the very day following Edward's declaration of Llywelyn as an outlaw.[13] This would have been the time Othon was away on Edward's business in Gascony and shows Guillaume de Cicon as a messenger from Othon to Edward. He was a knight from Cicon in the Franche-Comté de Bourgogne, then attached to Savoy by marriage of Alix, Countess of Burgundy, to Philippe, Count of Savoy. Cicon lies around 30 kilometres to the north of Pontarlier, by the village of Vanclans. Today, extraordinarily little remains of the castle, just several stone steps, but the House of Cicon had been long in Burgundian history and linked to the *famille de Grandson*. The arms of the family that Cicon would have borne into Wales was a black horizontal band across a field of yellow. Pontarlier would be one of the towns, along with the nearby Château de Joux, that Count Othon IV would pay homage for to Edward, in 1281,[14] in the same way that Philippe had paid homage for Savoyard castles in 1273. Such were the interests of both Savoy and Franche-Comté, bound up with the Plantagenet monarchy of England. A recent ancestor, Othon de Cicon, had been with the fourth crusade that had sacked Constantinople in 1204 and founded a fiefdom on the island of Euboea at Karystos. The Latin–Greek origins of Cicon will become fundamental to the castles in Wales, particularly at Caernarfon.

Along with Grandson, Bonvillars and Cicon was Gérard de Saint-Laurent, a knight who had also served with Edward on crusade in the Holy Land, in 1271–72. Gérard received arrears of wages, including a payment for a horse during his time at Acre, and expenses totalling 72 marks.[15] Arnold Taylor thought that his name might relate to Saint-Laurent-en-Grandvaux, in the Jura.[16] However, Chapuisat records a family of this name in Lausanne earlier in the century, these St. Laurents providing officers for the bishops of Lausanne and taking their name from a quarter of the city. Today the baroque Eglise Saint-Laurent lies at the heart of the Saint-Laurent quarter of Lausanne.[17] These four knights, as we shall see later, go on to fulfil key positions for Edward in Wales: Grandson as Justiciar of North Wales, Bonvillars, Cicon and Saint-Laurent as constables of Harlech, Rhuddlan, Conwy and Flint.

However, that is yet for the future. In the meantime, we have Othon de Grandson at the siege of Dolforwyn, a siege that ended with its surrender on 8 April 1277. The builders had not yet fully completed the castle; it lacked something vital for its defence: a water supply. The Welsh had neglected to dig a well, and so very quickly ran out of water. The fallen stronghold was left in the possession of Edward's Welsh ally Gruffydd ap Gwenwynwyn of

Powys, allowing him to fully regain control of Powys Wenwynwyn.[18] Indeed, Gruffydd ap Gwenwynwyn had been instrumental in bringing many Welshmen over to Edward's cause. Prestwich describes the First Welsh War as, in part 'a civil war in Wales',[19] given the many Welshmen who fought on Edward's side, Gruffydd ap Gwenwynwyn and Llywelyn's own brother Dafydd ap Gruffydd being perhaps the most notable. The extent to which we should not treat Wales and Gwynedd as synonyms is evidenced by the number of Welshmen serving with the royal armies of the First Welsh War: some 9,000 of 15,000 men. As Adam Chapman also said: the war 'was as much a conflict between Welshmen, as much as it was a conflict between Welsh and English'.[20]

With the fall of Dolforwyn, Llywelyn's position in mid Wales proved untenable, and by May he had vacated Brecon. Also, by 3 May, Henri de Lacy and Roger de Mortimer had moved the 40 miles on to Builth, where Mortimer had once been constable.[21] Builth had been specifically a part of his appanage, so Edward immediately instructed them to begin reconstruction of his castle destroyed by the Welsh prince seventeen years earlier in 1260. In the south Payn de Chaworth had been making good progress, bringing Deheubarth back to the king's allegiance, helped by local lords like Gruffydd ap Maredudd of Ceredigion and Rhys ap Maredudd (son of the imprisoned Maredudd ap Rhys Gryg) of Ystrad Tywi and thus gaining, much without a fight. By 16 May 1277 Chaworth was able to list those who would come to Edward at Worcester to pay due homage: the aforementioned, plus Rhys Wyndod, also from Ystrad Tywi, Rhys Fychan ap Rhys Maelgwn and Cynan ap Maredudd, also from Ceredigion. This swift collapse of Llywelyn's authority over and control of Welsh lordships, as established by the Treaty of Montgomery, is a marker of the First Welsh War.

Henri de Lacy's attackers had caused some damage at Dolforwyn; it seems likely that siege engines such as trebuchets had been employed, since stone balls have been subsequently discovered in and around the castle. The castle was, by Savoyard and recent English standards, a rather basic affair. There was no powerful gatehouse or flanking mural towers, so the attacking force was able to sack the nearby village and set up those siege engines to good effect. The latest castle-building developments of the thirteenth century had not yet reached Welshmen.[22] A Cadw artist's impression of 2002 by Ivan Lapper shows the small town alight, a trebuchet knocking lumps out of the curtain wall and the castle itself on fire.[23] The square donjon bears the scars of Master Bertram's siege engines to this day. As had fallen Benauges in 1253, so had fallen Dolforwyn in 1277 to Master Bertram's artillery. The primitive nature, by thirteenth century standards of the castle built by Llywelyn at Dolforwyn is further evidence that the repairs carried out following the siege have outlasted the original work.[24] Jean de Bonvillars arrived at Dolforwyn on 3 April 1277 with a message for Othon de Grandson and gave likely rise to a reply.[25]

The Calendar of Ancient Correspondence Concerning Wales collected by Sir John Goronwy Edwards, published in 1935, Edwards interprets in abstract not transcription the letter to Edward:[26]

> The sender reports that they laid siege to the castle of Dolvoreyn [*sic*] on the Wednesday in Easter Week [Mar. 31, 1277] … Informs the king that when the castle comes into his hands – il auera mester de grant amendement – it will need much repair. Wherefore there will be need of some man who will take these matters in hand and will loyally employ the king's money. For if the sender employs Master Bertram for the work, he fears that Master Bertram

> will devise too many things, and perhaps the king's money will not be so well employed as it needs to be. Asks the king's will in this matter. Thanks the king for the letter sent by the hand of John de Bevilar, which was of great assistance, for the sender's force looks like the force of a great lord and this cannot be done without money.[27]

Edwards suggests that the Earl of Lincoln might be the letters's author, but his index also lists Grandson as a potential source[28]. In addition to Edward's, perhaps ambiguous, attribution of either, Henri de Lacy or Othon de Grandson, several writers have variously suggested a number of potential authors.[29] Discounting Tanquerey as he misidentifies the date and recipient, what reasons do we have to suppose it was Grandson rather than Lacy?

First, the extreme familiarity of the greeting '*A sun tres cher seignur saluz*', which translates as 'To my very dear Lord Salut!' or Warmest greetings'. Both Othon and Henri were members of Edward's household – Othon having been brought to England as a boy by Pierre de Savoie, and Henri educated at court. Both men went on to serve Edward for many years, but Edward and Othon, as contemporaries, had in effect been raised together since boyhood, whereas Henri was over ten years their junior. Second, the original letter carried by Bonvillars from Edward to Dolforwyn was to Othon, and the reply is immediate, which implies a receipt and return. Third, all the men with the Earl of Lincoln were the 'king's men' – they were his vassals, except Othon[30] who was very much Edward's special friend. It may seem natural for Edward to write to Othon. Othon, as Edward's lifelong friend and confidant, would appear to have a greater interest in the protection of the king's purse than the young Earl of Lincoln, and greater access to a solution, namely the hiring of a better mason. Certainly, we can know in what esteem Grandson was held by Edward at this point: in March 1278 he had described him as someone who could 'do his will … better and more advantageously' than 'others about him', as well as 'if he himself were to attend to the matters in person'.[31] Othon de Grandson, along with Robert Burnell, was, perhaps, the man Edward trusted above all others to act on his behalf. Taylor points out that other letters from the Earl of Lincoln are formally dated with the regnal year – this one is not.[32] Then also, we have the certification of the wages for Master Bertram at Dolforwyn being '*par la veue sire Otes de Grauntson*' – 'by the wish of Sir Othon de Grandson'.[33] But perhaps the best evidence is from the archive records in August that it was again Othon showing a particular interest in castle building – this time, as we will see, at Flint. Prestwich agreed, writing: 'Taylor plausibly argued [the letter] was from Othon de Grandson' before confirming, 'Othon's influence was important in the choice that Edward made of the Savoyard Maître Jacques de Saint-Georges.'[34]

Given all this, it is most likely that Grandson was the author of the letter. It is this letter that is the 'smoking gun' which gives rise to what happens next. King Edward I summons the Master Mason he had been introduced to in Saint-Georges, in June 1273, Maître Jacques. Dolforwyn Castle has been described as the 'last Welsh castle', given its native Welsh construction. The coming Welsh castles would all be Savoyard.

But, in the Welsh Wars, the siege of Dolforwyn was a border preliminary: the real task of subduing Llywelyn and Gwynedd would now begin. Edward's initial feudal muster required a rendezvous at Worcester in July 1277,[35] followed by a division of his forces for a twin pronged assault on Gwynedd. A smaller force, perhaps 200 men, was to come from the south starting in Carmarthen. The main force would travel west from the old Roman city of Chester, along the coast and the four cantrefi, to the Conwy and Gwynedd. Payn de Chaworth would command the southern army, the Earl of Warwick the northern. With Payn would be the king's brother Edmund, Earl of Lancaster, and with Warwick would be the king himself. Edward had prepared well: he had arranged for the ships of the Cinque Ports to sail and meet him at Chester, a circuitous voyage indeed from the Channel.

That summer, as the ships docked, and horseman rode into the city from the southeast, Chester thronged with voices and the sound of military preparation not seen since the legions had departed. One can only imagine the cries of the knights, their squires, the foot soldiers, the sailors amid the usual panoply of merchants, innkeepers and citizens of Chester. The twice weekly markets at St. Peter's church and the abbey would have been overwhelmed by the travelling host. 300 sailors would have joined an army of nearly 3,000, English voices mixing with Savoyard and Gascon. Chester's normal trade with Wales would have been interrupted by the newcomers, but more than made up for by the assembling's army demands for corn at Eastgate, fish from the Dee estuary and meat from the cattle grazed on Saltney marsh. The smell of woodsmoke, the sound of clanging from blacksmiths re-shoeing warhorses, fixing coats of mail, fashioning crossbow bolts and arrows and tellingly sharpening swords – the sounds of an army preparing to invade would have carried across the Dee floating on the wind to the Welsh. Edward arrived at Chester from Worcester, by way of Shrewsbury, on 15 July 1277, aware that his army would soon exhaust the supplies available, and that the feudal obligation to serve owed to him by much of his army was time-limited. Just one week after his arrival by the Dee, on or about 21 July 1277, Edward and his army moved west.

Some 2,576 men, including 120 from Lancashire, 100 archers from Macclesfield, Cheshire, 640 men from Staffordshire and Shropshire and 1,000 foot spearmen and archers from Cheshire gathered their arms and began the invasion of Llywelyn's lands. Along with them went Dafydd ap Gruffydd and the 220 men of his bodyguard – Welshmen. So, along with the English infantry were Welshmen, Savoyard knights, Gascon crossbowmen – this was very much a multinational force of many tongues, the infantry largely speaking English and Welsh, the cavalry largely Norman French, Arpitan and Occitan. The army marched beneath no English flag, since no English flag was yet in use – the army marched behind the king's banner, three golden lions passant guardant (three golden lions on a red field); the banner had been brought into use by Edward's great-uncle Richard Cœur de Lion and represented the Kingdom of England, the Duchies of Normandy and Aquitaine. The lion had long been an emblem of the Anglo-Norman kings, and the lions were now marching across the Dee toward Wales. Behind the three lions came the yellow band and six yellow crosslets on a red field of the Earl of Warwick, the three red chevrons on a yellow field of Red Gilbert, Earl of Gloucester, the blue and yellow chequerboard of Jean de Warenne, Earl of Surrey, the three coquille St. Jacques on a red bend (band), crossed diagonally across a field of blue white paly (perpendicular stripes) of Othon de Grandson (Fig 1.3), the white coquille St. Jacques atop a black cross on yellow background of Jean de Grailly,[36] the three golden caveçons beneath a red lion of Geoffrey de Joinville,[37] the black cross on a yellow field of Jean de Vesci – the full colourful panoply of Anglo-Norman, Savoyard and even French heraldry glinting in the summer sun as they progressed across the Dee and followed the three lions into Wales. In 1300, the 'Song of Caerlaverock' gave us a description of a later campaign, but its imagery of 'many a beautiful pennon fixed to a lance', the sound of 'neighing horses' and of wagons loaded with 'provisions, and sacks of tents and pavilions' paints the picture we need.[38]

Davies writes of the army: 'It was a remarkable display of the capacity of the nascent nation-state to mobilise its resources for a co-ordinated and centralised war-effort.'[39] Finance for the expedition came, of course, from the Riccardi of Lucca. Thomas Bek's Wardrobe accounts for the year 20 November 1276 to 20 November 1277 show a receipt of £22,476 (equivalent today circa £16.5 million), against a war commitment of £20,220. The following year, 20 November 1277 to 20 November 1278 shows a receipt of a further £18,233 (today over £13 million).[40] Morris calculated the cost of the war to be £23,149, the total Riccardi receipts for these years amounting to £40,709. We can be clear: without the Riccardi Di Lucca this 'co-ordinated and centralised war-effort' would have been very difficult to achieve. Edward's army would be something relatively new in Britain as it was formed of many paid professionals rather than just the customary feudal host, and for this he had the liquid resources of the Riccardi. Sure, there would be the feudal host, but now the king needed a more competent group of men at arms who might be able to provide extended service with greater technical expertise, such as the crossbowmen – what we would call a professional army.[41]

Edward had seen his father's expeditions into Wales founder upon the rock of Welsh resistance but also a lack of preparation upon the part of the English. Faced with the sheer power of the Anglo-Norman war machine, the Welsh had fallen back upon the natural defences offered by their mountainous lands, fallen back upon hit-and-run guerrilla warfare. They had descended upon English columns advancing into Wales with cries and missiles emerging from the mists of the mountains only to disappear once more when a few of the attacking knights and soldiers lay dead and wounded. The Welsh had perfected the weapon of being the wasp that continually stings the dog until, maddened, it runs for cover.

But this time it would be different: marching into Wales, Edward would have passed the site of the Battle of Ewloe, where his grandfather Henry had come to grief at the hands of another Welsh prince, Owain Gwynedd, in 1157.[42] Henry had been defeated by ambush in a densely wooded valley, which no doubt influenced Edward's cutting his forest road deep into Wales. The Welsh had built a castle at Ewloe, commanding the road from England, but apparently and perhaps sensibly, given what had happened at Dolforwyn, had abandoned it prior to the invasion.

For with Edward's army that summer of 1277 marched new warriors – armies of woodcutters, carpenters, diggers, and masons. Edward had learned the lessons of previous campaigns, and indeed of his ill-fated crusade. As early as June, Lucasio and the Riccardi were ordered to pay 40 marks to Robert de Belvero and William de Perton, that Edward might collect masons and carpenters 'as many as he can get and in whatsoever works or service they may be, and to conduct them whither'.[43] First, the army made for Flint, on the Welsh side of the Dee, where Edward decided it would be useful to build a first stronghold from which to proceed along the coast. The chronicler Thomas Wykes described the land between Chester and the lands of Llywelyn as '*silva tantæ densitatis et amplitudinis*', that is a 'dense forest of great size.'[44] Just over a thousand years earlier the Romans had similarly advanced into the Teutoburg Forest of Germany and been annihilated by Germanic tribes in tactics similar to those now employed by the Welsh. But 1277 was not AD 9, Edward was no Publius Quinctilius Varus: he had brought with him those 1,800 axemen and proceeded to build himself a clear road along the coast as he went. So, the army moved slowly into Wales to the sound of axes ripping into wood and trees falling. To any Welshmen within hearing, this must have sounded like a monster was coming to devour Wales.

By 25 July, the army had hacked its way through to Flint, where it paused to build the planned advance headquarters, from which to move farther along the coast.[45] Edward chose the Flint site rather than occupying native Ewloe Castle, since Flint could be resupplied by sea, whereas Ewloe could not – an example of the king's intention to make recovery of the four cantrefi permanent. Following the war, Edward was described as granting land to Llywelyn's brothers Dafydd and Owain, as being 'in the camp of the Flint near Basingwerk'.[46] Basingwerk was the site of a Cistercian abbey just under 5 miles farther down the coast. According to legend, the name Flint came as an English corruption of the Latin word *fluentum*, meaning stream. But this legend takes no note of the archival records, where two later entries in the Calendar of Welsh Rolls[47] point elsewhere: on 3 December 1277, Flint is referred to as '*Le Chaylou*',[48] and on 18 January 1278 it is referred to as '*Le Cayllou*'.[49] The modern French word for a small pebble or stone is *caillou*, therefore, we can see that the scribes in Shrewsbury and Westminster translated the word 'flint' into French, and that 'flint' referred to 'stone' or 'rock' and not a corruption of 'stream'. While the area around the Flint site is marshy and wet, the castle itself would be built upon a small stone platform – a flint – hence the name.

Construction soon began on the small stone platform, or more accurately perhaps, the land surrounding it. We have reference to a payment made, upon the recommendation of none other than Othon de Grandson on 10 August, to build a palisade around the works there, to better defend the builders from Welsh attacks.[50] As we noted earlier that it is Othon de Grandson ordering construction work at Flint adds further credence to the belief that he is the author of the letter to Edward written at Dolforwyn. Morris describes the building works at Flint that summer: 'A strong post was thus made, though the works were but yet temporary and of wood, for there was no time to prepare stone.'[51] Others have, to a greater or lesser degree, made claims for something more solid begun in the four months that remained of the 1277 building season.[52] By analysis of the building records, Edwards pointed to three stages of construction, a first stage in 1277, a second from 1278 to 1280 and then a third to completion in 1286. For 1277 a determined start does seem to have been made, albeit one where payments for carpenters and diggers far outweighs that for stonemasons.[53] Morris set the scene of the defence at Flint that summer: 'Imbert, with his crossbows, and the Macclesfield archers, had the post of honour in defending the works.'[54] What we are seeing here at Flint in July and August 1277 is analogous to a movie portrayal of the US Cavalry constructing a fort deep in hostile 'Indian territory'. Morris added: 'the purchase of great numbers of quarrels means that there was plenty to do in the way of beating off the Welsh.'[55] The army was much in need of a palisade, as prescribed by Grandson, and arrows for the archers. Flint was, that summer, the front line of the invasion of Wales. Taylor confirms that the workers and works at Flint were 'treated as a military unit and placed under a knight'.[56] The Welsh chroniclers are also clear in their description of the works at Flint, recording that Edward 'fortified a court in Flint, with huge ditches around it'.[57]

So, who were the Welsh the army encountered in Wales that summer? First, we need to say that the Welsh fought on both sides, that the English army had many Welsh voices within it. Adding to its substantial Savoyard contingent, this English army, in addition to speaking many dialects of French, spoke an awful lot of Welsh. Edward had recruited many Welsh soldiers from the marches, men from Gwerthrynion, Maelienydd, Elfael, Builth, Radnor and Brecon.[58] Beverley Smith goes on to give us their names, these Welsh captains of the English army: Meurig ap Llewelyn of Brecon, Ifor ap Gruffydd of Elfael, Einion ap Madog of Builth, all led by Hywel ap Meurig of Radnor.[59] This Welsh army under Hywel ap Meurig amounted to some 2,700 footmen raised in Brecon and Radnor, Hywel ap Meurig had been passing intelligence of Llywelyn's castle at Dolforwyn to Edward since before the war.[60] But what did these Welsh soldiers look like? Christopher Rothero paints a vivid picture of 'migrant tribesmen, half warriors, half farmers'.[61] A Welsh chieftain would not have differed much from his ancestors who fought the Roman legions, equipped perhaps with a round wooden shield in the like of a Saxon or a Viking, rudimentary segmented armour around his upper body and armed with sword and spear. His ancestors had succumbed to the Roman, but not the Saxon and not entirely to the Norman. Gerald of Wales, writing a century earlier, gives us a description of 'mobile and lightly armed' men, who wore 'no armour at all' and 'who always prefer to do battle on rough terrain'. He went on to describe soldiers who would, not take prisoners, but 'cut off their heads' and rather than taking captives for ransom 'massacre them'.[62] Around 1300 a Flemish observer spoke of soldiers whose 'weapons were bows, arrows and swords' and 'javelins' but who 'never saw them wearing armour.'[63] They were, as Churchill admiringly described them, 'hardy and unsubdued'[64] and 'valiant Ancient Britons'.[65] They belonged to what R. R. Davies called a 'heroic society'.[66]

While Othon progressed along the north coast, in the south, Edward's younger brother Edmund Crouchback, Earl of Lancaster, had joined Payn de Chaworth and taken command of the southern army. They faced much less in the way of obstacles than the northern army and by 25 July had reached Aberystwyth from Carmarthen. On 1 August, within a week of arrival, on the Mid Welsh coast they began to build a castle.[67] The castle was begun by the mouth of the Rheidol and originally named in contemporary records as Lampader or Lampadarn.[68] Edward had given prior approval for a quick beginning of work to Master Henry of Hereford.[69] The wider West Country this time provided the source for the labour: 120 masons and 120 carpenters from Somerset, Dorset, and Wiltshire, soon followed by a barrel of some 6,000 nails, indicating that, like at Flint, the early works were of wood. They came by way of Bristol, thence by boat to Carmarthen, then on into Mid Wales.

What was created at Aberystwyth was a concentric castle of a very flattened lozenge shape, with the main entrance being a great twin-towered gatehouse on the eastern side. Work was concentrated into the first three years of the build, the 1277, 1278 and 1279 building seasons. The great gatehouse will be of interest as we go on, possibly being the means of a transmission of its type from Caerffili to Harlech, as Malcom Hislop has plausibly suggested.[70]

Meanwhile in the north Edward, on 16 August, renewed his drive into Wales from Flint. He left behind him there a garrison under the command of Reginald de Grey, with orders to protect and defend both Flint and the forest road. Edward was carefully attending to his lines of communication. The works underway, from 25 July, at Flint, were left with Ingeniator Master Richard of Chester[71] along with some 720 fossatores or diggers, 330 carpenters, 320 woodsmen, 200 masons, 12 smiths and lastly 10 charcoal burners.[72] The stonemasons from Lincolnshire, Nottinghamshire and Leicestershire[73] appear to have been under Master Thomas of Grantham, but with Master Richard in overall charge. Reginald de Grey was protecting this work along with Robert de Tatesdale, Aymer de St. Amand, Alex de Balliol, John d'Eyvil, Roger de la Zouche and no less than sixty-seven accompanying troopers. Master Richard appears for the first time in the archive that summer of 1277 at Flint and has been the subject of an excellent re-examination of his contribution by historian Rick Turner.[74] He is almost certainly the effective Master of Works at Flint for 1277 and into 1278, but this does not mean he was the designer of the castle, as we shall see.[75]

So, with work at Flint begun and the forest road protected, the axemen began again the work of clearing a road to the west, a road wide enough apparently for a man to loose an arrow from one side to the other. The road now gorging itself upon the Welsh forest has been described, perhaps with little exaggeration, as being wide enough to accommodate four modern three-lane motorways.[76] Within a week, by around 19 August, the army had progressed forward to Rhuddlan, onetime Saxon and then Norman township on the River Clwyd and only a few miles downstream from the cathedral town of St. Asaph. Henry III had preferred the nearby hilltop position of Dyserth for his castle, but as with Flint, Edward considered resupply by sea a key requirement. The king had learned from Llywelyn's destruction of his father's castles in Wales that in time of revolt the ability to quickly resupply a garrison was vital in their defence.

Rhuddlan first appears in history, in 796 when King Offa of Mercia won a battle by the Clwyd and later it's thought that Edward the Elder had founded a Saxon burh at Rhuddlan back in 921, although the precise location is unknown. The conquest and reconquest of the region is shown again as by 1063 it had once more become a part of the lands of Llywelyn ap Gruffydd, Prince of Gwynedd, only for him to lose it and his palace there burned by Earl Harold – the same Harold who would soon lose his life and England to the Normans. Literally Rhuddlan, named Roelent in the 1086 Domesday Book, means 'red bank', which described the colour of the soil making up the banks of the river Clwyd. What was then at Rhuddlan was a small Norman settlement protected by a motte and bailey castle, built by Robert de Rhuddlan in 1073.[77] Later, in 1258, a Dominican friary was founded.[78] Edward lodged, during his time at Rhuddlan, with the Dominicans, a record of payment which survives, along with a donation towards the glazing of their church – always an expensive thing in the Middle Ages.[79] The next year, Edward ordered that the prior and his friars at Rhuddlan should have wood from the forest and fish from the river and be able to 'grind freely at the king's mill there at the king's will'.[80] Rhuddlan commanded a bridging point of the Clwyd, but in addition to the coastal route east-west from the Dee to the Conwy, it sat at the head of Clwyd valley and its route inland to Denbigh and Ruthin. The Normans had thought this a good place for a castle, and likewise Edward, although he would build a little way from the original fortress.

The evolution of castle design, between the eleventh and thirteenth century, can be easily seen from the story of the castles in and around Rhuddlan: the Norman motte and bailey, Henry III's at Dyserth and then Edward's again at Rhuddlan. Originally, it was thought enough to place a castle high atop an artificial hill or mound: the motte. Then, as these castles fell, grew the need to build on higher ground to take advantage of nature's rocky outcrops as at Dyserth. But, as these higher-placed castles proved vulnerable to a sustained siege, then a coastal location seemed to offer the chance of resupply. Though Rhuddlan was not by the sea, Edward and Jacques would bring the sea to Rhuddlan. There is no record of work commencing in 1277 at Rhuddlan beyond the planning stage, and what Taylor called a 'veritable army of diggers'.[81] That Edward should want to build a castle at Rhuddlan is unsurprising: not only was it a key point on the road from Chester to the Conwy, but 'Rothelan' was specifically named way back in 1254, when Edward was a boy, as being his own, in his appanage.

Another week of westward cutting and hacking through the forest finally found Edward and his army, of now 15,000 men, by the wide expanse of the Conwy estuary. He had recovered the four cantrefi lost to Llywelyn, but the Prince of Wales retreated to the mountain vastness of Snowdonia and a position by Penmaenmawr. Henry III had constructed a castle at Deganwy in 1245, as the front line of the realm, but this had been destroyed by Llywelyn in 1263. Edward had no intention of playing into the prince's hands attempting a river crossing and frontal assault on the Welsh mountain strongholds. He had something considerably more effective in mind: he meant to starve Llywelyn into submission.

The four cantrefi recovered, work was underway at Flint and planned for Rhuddlan, the forest road from the Dee to the Conwy secure. Now Edward gathered a force, under Othon de Grandson and Jean de Vesci, of 2,000 foot and horse, collected by the Cinque Ports fleet at the Great Orme. Some 360 harvesters were also taken to the island, along with the army.[82] Anglesey was the Welsh breadbasket, where Llywelyn grew the wheat that would feed his people for the long winter ahead.[83] The force landed with the fields still full of unharvested cereal – Llywelyn had lost his winter grain supply. The corn was harvested, but to English, not Welsh granaries; for Llywelyn it was a grievous blow. Welsh cattle were gathered from upland areas above Flint and Rhuddlan to feed Edward's army;[84] there would be no repetition of previous English armies in Wales failing for lack of supplies.

By the late summer of 1277 Llywelyn had Edward to his front, across the Conwy, with a large army that had confiscated the four *cantrefi* from him. To his right and rear was Edmund Crouchback and his southern army at Aberystwyth, to his left he had another English army under Vesci and Grandson – and worst of all he had lost his grain supply. There was much of Caesar's conquest of Gaul and Alesia about the campaign. With Llywelyn playing the unfortunate role of Vercingetorix to Edward's Caesar – it was the methodical subjugation of an enemy by resource denial. Clausewitz many centuries later spoke of the need 'to take possession of his [the enemy's] material and other sources of strength, and to direct our operations against the places where most of these resources are concentrated'. Edward was following Caesar and foreshadowing Clausewitz.[85] He had invaded the principality and, unlike those that had come before, he had taken careful, methodical steps to slowly pin Llywelyn against his mountain home and encircle him in a chain-mailed vice without the resources to resist – it was as they say game, set and match.

Llywelyn made it known that he was prepared to submit to Edward – he had little choice. Edward could have pressed on and destroyed the Welsh prince, but he chose quite deliberately not to. The bad weather of autumn was coming, a frontal assault on Llywelyn would be costly and time consuming, and most tellingly he had the Welsh prince where he wanted him. Peace made sense for Edward too. Accordingly, the banner of the Three Lions retired from the Conwy to the Dominican friary at Rhuddlan on 12 September 1277, to await formal negotiations of a peace.

The English commissioners who negotiated what became known as the Treaty of Aberconwy were Antony Bek, Robert de Tibetot and none other than Othon de Grandson – the Savoyard had been at the siege of Dolforwyn, instrumental at Flint, helped seize the Welsh harvest, and now he was a key negotiator of the peace. Antony Bek, like Grandson, was a veteran of Edward's crusade and would later be rewarded with the Bishopric of Durham. Likewise, Tibetot had accompanied Edward on crusade and would be rewarded with being appointed Justiciar of South Wales. The commissioners were authorised to negotiate on behalf of the king on 2 November and crossed the Conwy to Aberconwy Abbey. The quiet of the Cistercian abbey provided a backdrop for the weeklong negotiations, Bishop Anian of St. Asaph acting as mediator, with the abbot acting, as in the past, for Llywelyn, along with his emissaries Tudur ap Ednyfed and Goronwy ap Heilin.[86]

An unusual transaction occurred at this time. Financiers of the war, the Riccardi, had followed Edward's army into North Wales. Orlandino da Pogio was one of their number. During or immediately after negotiations at the abbey of Aberconwy the Riccardi undertook to buy fleeces from the abbot and got a safe conduct to transport twenty sacks of wool back to Chester. The Riccardi were clearly not ones to let a war get in the way of a good business opportunity.[87] Nor had Edward's commanders been neglected, Othon de Grandson and Jean de Vesci, rewarded for their efforts in the war with twenty and twenty-six casks of wine, respectively.[88] The Treaty of Aberconwy was agreed on 9 November 1277, sealed by Llywelyn on this day, and ratified by Edward on 10 November at Rhuddlan. That day Llywelyn had crossed the Conwy to make his way to Rhuddlan to finally pay a homage to the king, homage asked of the Welsh prince by the Severn in 1272. He would have knelt before Edward, kissed his hand and given the oath of fealty. The terms of the peace were indeed Carthaginian: the four cantrefi would once more belong to the king of England. Thus, the continual passing of the Perfeddwlad between the Plantagenets and Gwynedd in then thirteenth century ended with Edward in possession of what had been his appanage. In a little over sixty years, it had been taken by his grandfather John in 1211, lost again to Llywelyn Fawr in 1216, retaken from Dafydd by Henry in 1247, granted to Edward in 1254, retaken by Llywelyn ap Gruffydd in 1264 and now lastly retaken by Edward – truly the middle country. Two of the cantrefi would be temporarily leased to Llywelyn's wayward and unreliable brother Dafydd – these being Rhufoniog (centred on Denbigh) and Dyffryn Clwyd (centred on Ruthin). The coastal and strategically vital cantrefi of Rhos and Tegeingl Edward retained for himself. Llywelyn would have to travel to England, to London, to swear fealty to Edward after first having done so at Rhuddlan. Although Llywelyn could still style himself Prince of Wales, the majority of the Welsh nobility would now be Edward's vassals, not Llywelyn's. Last and by no means least, Llywelyn was required to pay the sum of £50,000[89] as a fine for his disobedience – although this was soon remitted.[90] Dafydd was given the two cantrefi, and recognition would be given also to the rights of Owain Goch and Rhodri – Edward was imposing his peace between the brothers ap Gruffydd. Llywelyn was made to release Owain Goch from imprisonment. He would live out his life the next five years probably on the Llyn peninsula. The vanquished of Bryn Derwin in 1255 had finally achieved a restitution of sorts, courtesy of Edward. As a footnote Llywelyn was after all allowed to marry the daughter of Simon de Montfort, the ceremony taking place at Worcester in 1278, indeed Edward paid for the wedding of his cousin to the formerly outlawed Prince of Wales. In the end, Llywelyn paid homage to Edward and swore an oath of fealty. One is bound to ask at this point what he had gained from not doing so at Rhyd Chwima five years earlier. His subsequent actions had lost him the four cantrefi, his suzerainty of all but Gwynedd and a good deal of blood and treasure. Llywelyn ap Gruffydd was again what he had originally been, and in Edward's mind, what he should always remain – Edward's man. Perhaps a sign that, for Edward, the Welsh matter was now considered concluded was his despatch in the early months of 1278 of Othon de Grandson once more to Gascony.[91] Having ended Llywelyn's disobedience, Edward paid renewed attention to something he might have considered more important than Gwynedd: the stability of Gascony and the return to him of lost adjacent ancestral lands.

CHAPTER 6

With the situation in Wales now thought to be stabilised, Edward turned to concern for his more distant lands as Duke of Aquitaine, that is Gascony. To this end he despatched his most loyal servants, Robert Burnell and Othon de Grandson to Bordeaux. This reminds us that Llywelyn ap Gruffydd was for the moment an interruption to more pressing concerns in France. It is easy to take an Anglocentric view that the chief project of Edward's early reign was the suppression of the troublesome House of Gwynedd, but that would be to elevate the rain-sodden mountains of north Wales to an importance over the vineyards of Gascony that they do not perhaps deserve. So, for Othon de Grandson the voyage to Gascony was very much the resumption of work interrupted.

Robert Burnell, his companion on this venture, had been born in 1239 at the village which carried his family name, Acton Burnell in Shropshire. He had worked as a clerk in Henry's royal chancery, the office that wrote all the royal documents before, by 1257, moving into Edward's personal household. He had remained in England during the crusade to keep a watch on Edward's affairs at home and became regent following the death of the late King Henry. Upon his return to England Edward had appointed him Lord Chancellor in 1274 and a year later he had gained the bishopric of Bath and Wells – in short Burnell was leading player at court. Burnell and Othon were despatched to Gascony with the instructions to all there that they had 'full and free power to do all and everything that we would and would do there, if we were present'.[1] Edward wrote to them both warning of the Gascons' famed infidelity and unreliable nature, keen as they were ever to play the Plantagenets off against the Capetians to their own ends.

The appointment had been in January 1278, but Othon and Burnell made their ways separately to Bordeaux, Burnell by way of Paris where he reminded Philippe III that by the 1259 Treaty of Paris the Saintonge, Agenais and Quercy ought to be returned to Edward, and Othon by way of Compiègne where, along with his former Welsh War comrades Jean de Vesci and Henri de Lacy, they treated with the Jean I, Duke of Brabant regarding a marriage of Jean to Edward's daughter Margaret. Jean and Margaret were but each 2 years of age, but they would indeed be married in 1290. Brabant, today much of the southern Netherlands and central Belgium, then a part of the Holy Roman Empire, would be a useful continental ally. While at Compiègne Othon, along with Vesci and Lacy, took part in a grand tournament.[2] The event was highly attended by knights from both France and the empire and allowed Othon not only to indulge in that favourite activity of the medieval knight, fighting, but also a good deal of fruitful networking.

Geoffrey Chaucer writing a century later would give us the colour of a tournament: we should imagine the knight from Vaud upon his horse, proudly bearing the arms of the *famille de Grandson* among the great and good of the medieval world, with a reputation to win. Chaucer wrote:

> Then the gates were shut, and cried was aloud: 'Do now your duty, proud young knights!' The heralds left their spurring up and down; Now trumpets and bugles ring loud. There is no more to say, but from west and east. In go the spears very firmly in the lance-rests; In goes the sharp spur into the flank. There people see who can joust and who can ride; There splinter spears upon thick shields; He feels the stabbing through the breast-bone. Up spring spears twenty foot on height; Out go the swords bright as silver; The helms they hew to pieces and cut into shreds. Out burst the blood in strong red streams; With mighty maces they break the bones to pieces. He did thrust through the thickest of the throng; There strong steeds stumble, and down goes all, He rolls under foot as does a ball; On his feet he stabs with the broken shaft of his spear, and he hurtles him down with his horse; He is hurt through the body and then taken.[3]

The Rôles Gascons give us the nature of Burnell's and Grandson's business in Gascony, that is restitution of debts, the turning over of forest land to agriculture following bad harvest and the taking back into Edward's good graces that habitual problem, Gaston de Béarn.[4] Béarn lay in the south in the Pyrenees, its Viscount, Gaston VII de Béarn had long been troublesome to the Plantagenets. In 1252 he had been allied to the Castilians, something Henry III had remedied by marrying Edward to Leonor de Castille. On 2 April 1273 Gaston had been remarried to the daughter of Pierre de Savoie, Béatrice, Dame de Faucigny – a marriage that should have brought the Béarnais into the Plantagenet Savoyard sphere of influence.[5] Edward had lately imprisoned Gaston in Winchester, his release being on the promise of good behaviour, something Othon was to encourage. They would be working alongside Edward's seneschal and Othon's countryman, Jean de Grailly, former crusading comrade in Acre. Grailly from the Pays de Gex was now Lord of Benauges, a castle taken by Henry III in the Gascon rebellion of 1253–54. It had been at Benauges that Henry's engineer Jean de Mésot had come into the employ of Pierre de Savoie, returning to Savoy to mentor Edward's future castle builder Maître Jacques de Saint-Georges. Grandson as a Gascon specialist would have been well aware of the triangular nature of the relationship between England, Savoy, and Gascony.

Once matters were resolved in Gascony, Othon returned in the autumn of 1278 to Savoy by way of St. Denis. His reason for a visit home brings us to the matter of Othon's personal life, which has been the subject of some interest in the twenty-first century since he remained single throughout his life. The winter of 1278–79 was to bring a brush with a married life which reveals something of Othon's relationship, at this stage, with Edward. On 8 March 1279, Alix de Bourgogne died at Évian. As the co-ruler of the Free County of Burgundy she was also the wife of Count Philippe I de Savoie. It was during their marriage that Burgundy had been joined with Savoy, but for the time of their marriage only. Upon her death she was succeeded not by her still-living husband, but by her son as Count Othon IV de Bourgogne. Othon IV was the product of Alix's first marriage to Hugues de Chalon. Othon IV was married to Philippa de Bar, their daughter was another Alix de Bourgogne. Nothing came of the idea of Alix the younger being married to Othon de Grandson. In September 1279 Alix was betrothed instead to Jean de Bourgogne, son of Robert, Duke of Burgundy. With all these Burgundies we should perhaps recall at this point that the Duchy centred on Dijon was a duchy within the Kingdom of France and that the county centred in Besançon remained within the Holy Roman Empire. The marriage would begin a move by Count Othon to move his Burgundy into the French sphere of influence, something that would later lead Grandson to build a pro-Plantagenet alliance against him. But all of this lay in the future in 1279.

A letter from Edward to Grandson has survived, dated 11 March 1279, which while approving a match appears to do so in such lukewarm terms that it appears that Edward would prefer his friend and envoy remain single. Edward wrote:

> Edward, by the Grace of God King of England, Lord of Ireland and Duke of Aquitaine greetings to our beloved and faithful Othon de Grandson. The noble and distinguished man, our dearest friend, the count of Burgundy, has written us that there has lately been some talk and conversation between you both as to your marrying one of his daughters. Let it be that because we are as anxious for your well-being and honour as for our own, we hope with all our heart that you will marry neither there nor anywhere else, except in our presence, or at least, not until we have discussed this and other matters with you, so that the business may be carried out with the honour that we wish for you and that is fitting for your station, and be the more solemnly expedited in our presence. However, seeing that the wishes of the contracting parties usually win over the wills of others in these matters, we agree that if you have this really to your heart, and if our noble and beloved Othon of Burgundy, your relatives, and any others zealous for your profit and renown, advise you to accomplish it, then may the foregoing arrangements which you have discussed with the aforesaid count be brought to a fitting end, according to your desires and their advice and that everything be done as you see fit. We are writing the same to the count.[6]

Quite an extraordinary letter, reading much as a reluctant father would today send to a beloved daughter intent upon a less-than-favourable match. Perhaps given future events Edward ought to have acceded to the marriage, but in the short term the Franche Comté's move toward the Capetians appeared unlikely. In January 1281 Othon IV was in Lyon to enfeoff the strategically vital town of Pontarlier and Château de Joux, both on the Via Francigena to King Edward I of England, with Alix the elder's widower Philippe standing in for Edward.[7] So, in 1279–81 both Edward and Grandson would have felt the Free County of Burgundy remained safely in the Empire.

In early 1279, perhaps even to obtain a home sufficient to endow a lady, Grandson was confirmed in an earlier gift of 1275 by his travelling companion and colleague in Gascony, Robert Burnell, the manor of Shene in Surrey, today's Sheen.[8] The manor house was on the riverside and had a moat. The manor came with hunting rights and would be the base for Othon whenever he was at court in Westminster or Windsor, not quite the Savoy Palace of his kinsman Pierre de Savoie, but nonetheless a fine reward. Shene is recorded as having the benefit of garden, a dovecote and park, arable land, meadow, pasture, a rabbit warren and a fishery. The manor no longer survives; it was developed into a royal palace by Edward's grandson Edward III.[9]

Even as Edward wrote to Othon concerning marriage he travelled to France to resolve the question of the Agenais, to which Grandson had devoted much time. In May 1279 Edward voyaged to France, a journey which culminated in the Peace of Amiens in 1279, aided by Savoyards Othon de Grandson and Jean de Grailly. The Agenais lay to the immediate east of Gascony, south of Périgord and west of Quercy, and was in effect one of the doors to Gascony. The Agenais ought to have been returned to the Plantagenet dukes of Aquitaine by the 1259 Treaty of Paris, negotiated in part by Othon's fellow countryman Pierre de Savoie. However, in 1271, Philippe III had taken the Agenais for himself; now, along with the southern Saintonge they were by the 23 May 1279 Treaty of Amiens to be finally returned, Edward's father Henry would no doubt have been very happy.[10] That other matter of dispute, Quercy, remained to be resolved. In faraway Agen the Lords of the Agenais accordingly swore their allegiance to the Duke of Aquitaine, Edward.

From the absence of primary source evidence to the contrary it would seem that Edward, returning to England in July 1279, left Grandson in France to see to his affairs.[11] Primary sources do however, in connection with this considerable diplomatic activity, point toward the relationship between Edward and Othon at this point. The Calendar of Patent Rolls of 1280 attaches a word to Grandson when he once more enters the record a year later. On 26 July 1280, at Northampton, is issued a mandate to the usual source of finance, the Riccardi di Lucca, of a loan to Grandson. He is described as a member of the 'King's Household' but also the King's '*Secretarius*', which the translators of the CPR have helpfully rendered as 'king's secretary'.[12] But what did the word mean in the thirteenth century, and in an English context? Certainly not one, as in the modern sense, to undertake correspondence and administrative tasks, but rather, as the *OED* explains for the Middle Ages, a 'person entrusted with a secret' and more directly 'a confidential officer' of the king – in short what we might now call an envoy, and a senior one at that.[13]

In the summer of 1280 Othon, Gascon matters having been settled and Wales once more apparently pacified, was despatched to Rome on likely crusade-related business for his first visit to the Papal Curia,[14] but it would be into somewhat of a maelstrom he would arrive. Popes he'd known, such as Teobaldo Visconti, had passed as Gregory X in January 1276, and Ottobuono Fieschi as Adrian V that same summer of 1276. Othon's task was likely the substitution of Edward for Edmund in terms of crusading vows; Edward said that Othon was 'in those parts [Rome] on our brothers' business'.[15] – something in which Grandson would not succeed. When he had set out for Rome, Nicholas III of the Orsini clan, had sat on Peter's throne, but on 22 August he had succumbed to an apoplectic fit in Viterbo, some say poisoned. So Othon arrived for his first official visit to the Curia amid the fifth conclave to be held in five years.[16] The Annibaldi faction, backed by Capetian king of Sicily, Charles d'Anjou, had chased the Orsini from Rome amid much rioting. There was deadlock within the conclave between the rival factions, only to be followed by the kidnap of cardinals and a final vote to install the French Simon de Brion as Martin IV in February 1281. Martin was enthroned in Orvieto as Rome itself remained off limits. All of this being a first-hand lesson for Grandson in papal politics and the reality of the Curia.

During Othon's winter in Rome, as we saw earlier, another piece of the Anglo-Savoyard jigsaw was falling into place. In January 1281 Count Othon of the Free County of Burgundy travelled to Lyon, there to swear homage for the town of Pontarlier and nearby Château de Joux in the presence of Philippe de Savoie standing in for Edward, his nephew.[17] Both landmarks were along the *Via Francigena*, only lately travelled by Grandson en route to Rome. That his journey would have taken him by way of Pontarlier, the Château de Joux, Saint-Maurice and the Château de Bard, the latter two enfeoffed in 1246 to Henry, only emphasises the advantage of good Anglo-Savoyard relations sought by both Henry and now Edward. Savoy lay at the heart of Europe directly upon the main road to Rome.

But in Britain, was Wales pacified? This attention once more to Gascony, to Burgundy, to crusade, to the Papal Curia is a reminder that in 1281 Edward likely considered the question of North Wales settled, at least for now.

The royal castles at Flint and Rhuddlan were not the only castles being built in North Wales at the close of the decade. Llywelyn's brother Dafydd had rebelled against his brother's rule, then sought refuge in England and in the First Welsh War had sided with Edward against his brother. So, when the Treaty of Aberconwy was drawn up in the autumn of 1277, it sought not only to return the relationship between crown and Llywelyn to that prior to the Treaty of Montgomery, it also sought to compensate Dafydd ap Gruffydd for his support of Edward. When the four *cantrefi* had been taken into royal hands, two of them, Rhufoniog and Dyffryn Clwyd, along with the Lordship of Hope, had been granted to Dafydd. The two cantrefi granted were not the reward Dafydd had anticipated, as they were of less importance and certainly not what Dafydd felt was his due for supporting Edward. Rhos and Tegeingl had been retained by the crown and had become the site for the royal castles under construction at Flint (Tegeingl) and Rhuddlan (Rhos). In Edward's mind these new castles simply reinstated the control lost when Llywelyn had destroyed those at Dyserth and Deganwy, and of course, we should remember that Rhuddlan had been specified in his appanage.

The Lordship of Hope carried permission for a castle with it. Mentioned in the Domesday Book, the area was then the property of Gilbert de Venables. The castle would sit on a sandstone hill by the river Alyn, in the hills above the all-important coastal route into North Wales and with a good vantage of England. That building was underway at Hope, of Caergwrle Castle, can be seen from a gift of money made by Edward dated 12 November 1278: 'Dafydd ap Gruffydd, for the construction of his castle at Caergwrle. Sixty-six pounds. Thirteen shillings. Four pence [100 marks]'.[18] Taylor suggests that the payment may imply that the granted castle might have been previously damaged by Llywelyn, but also that the payment was retrospective and therefore covered the 1278 building season – that Dafydd put the works in place immediately he took possession. There is some debate whether Dafydd's castle was a new construction or merely a repaired earlier work. John Manley found 'no hint from the excavation results [1988–90] of an earlier thirteenth century castle',[19] so the castle is more likely to have been built as new by Dafydd. Taylor, goes on to suggest that, given the geographic proximity to Rhuddlan and Flint and Maître Jacques' role for Edward, that the mason may have undertaken some work at Caergwrle, but there is no evidence to support or deny this idea.[20] If the building date is accepted, then work at Caergwrle was underway simultaneously with those for the king at Flint and Rhuddlan. What the payment does suggest is that Dafydd was still the king's man in 1278, that any dissatisfaction he had with his allotment of 1277 did not extend to him not accepting the king's gift for the build or rehabilitation of his allotted castle.

Elsewhere, however, the façade of peace and harmony that had surrounded the relationship between Llywelyn and Edward at Worcester cathedral in 1278 began to fray at the edges. Perhaps the first fly in the ointment was the Welsh cantref of Arwystli, which lay on the southeastern border of Gwynedd, in Mid Wales, and had long been a disputed territory with Powys. Back in 1263, Llywelyn had ceded the cantref to rival Gruffydd ap Gwenwynwyn of Powys, before reversing his decision and reclaiming it in 1274. Following the Treaty of Aberconwy in 1277, the dispute arose again and was referred to Edward for conciliation. Llywelyn maintained that, as Arwystli was Welsh territory, then the Welsh law ought to apply, whereas Gruffydd ap Gwenwynwyn argued that as he was a Marcher Lord, the law of the

March, which was English common law, ought to apply. Edward decided not to decide and procrastinated upon resolving the matter. It has been suggested that Edward deliberately provoked Llywelyn in not deciding in his favour and not immediately treating his renewed vassal by Welsh law. Certainly, the matter belittled the Welsh prince, but I'm not so sure it was by design. The English naturally preferred their own law to what they saw as barbaric Welsh law, and this naturally equally alienated the Welsh.[21]

Morris suggests, something which I think governed Edward's motivations in pretty much everything he did, that his main concern was not to repeat the mistakes of his father's reign. Edward had learned the very hard way, at an early age, where perceived weakness got you as a thirteenth-century monarch. There was also a casual racism in terms of the English treatment of the Welsh in the immediate years following the First Welsh War: the English viewed the Welsh as being fierce in battle, but fickle and not to be trusted in their bargains and relationships, casual sexually, less than civilised and generally of a lower order – in short barbaric. The Welsh had begun to be poorly treated by the English newcomers, but it was an ill treatment born more of attitude than by design. One who was also to lay his claim to English justice was a certain Madog ap Llywelyn,[22] who had been exiled in England, received royal financial reward, and now claimed what he saw as his right to Meirionnydd. His reward later of land in Anglesey would not be seen by Madog as fair recompense and be the kernel of a grievance that would return to haunt Edward.

In addition, Archbishop John Peckham records a list of several other Welsh legal complaints of English rule.[23] Dafydd would later summarise this Welsh feeling of being ill used by the English and their laws: 'though it was provided in the peace agreement that the Welsh should be tried in their causes according to Welsh laws, this was not observed with respect to Dafydd and his men.'[24]

However, perhaps the poor state of the new defences at Aberystwyth suggests a general feeling of relaxed overlordship of a defeated enemy who would accept subjugation and being put firmly in their place. That the crown had not the least idea of what was to come is perhaps suggested by its willingness to allow key knights to leave the country, as evidenced by Pierre de Champvent being allowed leave to 'travel beyond seas' in the summer of 1281.[25] He would not return, most likely from Savoy, until September 1282, coming back to a very different country. This was of course the complacency of occupiers of foreign lands, in ignoring building resentment, which would come firmly back to bite them, the cause of surprise at many an uprising. As the new decade of the 1280s opened, unbeknown to the English for a long while, tensions began to rise again.

CHAPTER 7

Having returned to England in the summer of 1281, Othon was soon despatched once more by Edward, but this time it was more in support of Edward's maternal Savoyard family than English concerns. Pierre de Savoie had been at war with Rudolf von Habsburg until a truce had been made until the Savoyard's death in 1268. Thereafter Pierre's brother Philippe had come to the comital throne. As we have seen. Edward and Philippe had enjoyed good relations. In 1273 Philippe had formerly become Edward's vassal for real estate in the Alps, and only very recently Philippe had taken Count Othon of Burgundy's homage in the stead of Edward for other property along the *Via Francigena* in Burgundy. For decades earlier Philippe's brother Pierre had made war upon his kinsmen, the Counts of Geneva. Now in the winter of 1281–82 came news to England that the Habsburgs and Genevois were making common cause against Philippe. Edward would in February 1282 dispatch Othon, accompanied by John Derby, Dean of Lichfield, to Savoy to see if a renewed peace could be negotiated.[1]

But even as the Helvetian fire caught light once more, the Welsh fire only lately suppressed would also relight. During the night of 21 March 1282, a group of soldiers climbed the steep Norman motte of Hawarden Castle, close to the border with England. The castle was new: Llywelyn had destroyed the original Norman motte and bailey castle back in 1265, but this was border country, and it had been rapidly reconstructed. The men moved quietly into position – it was Saturday, but not just any Saturday, this was the eve of Palm Sunday. There had been peace in Wales and the Marches since the autumn of 1277. That peace was about to be broken by the determined Welshmen that fell into the quiet of an English Easter. The small garrison at Hawarden slept, no doubt, after an evening eating and drinking. Inside the castle it was warm, and the men rested by the glow of comforting fires. Outside the castle it was cold and dark, the ground most likely wet. The invaders steeled themselves for the attack. As the men climbed the castle walls and reached the battlements, the alarm would have been given, an alarm that sounded the beginning of the Second Welsh War.

The defenders were not expecting to be attacked as they slumbered that Easter, and the garrison was put to the sword. The holder of the castle, Marcher Lord Roger de Clifford, was very badly wounded in the assault but survived to be taken prisoner by Dafydd ap Gruffydd – he was a valuable prize. Clifford had fought with Edward at Evesham and accompanied him on crusade, being with him at Acre. On his return, as part of Edward's retinue that had traversed Italy and the Alps to Savoy in 1273, he had married while in Saint-Georges-d'Espéranche. Clifford had been rebuilding the castle at Hawarden, just 6 short miles from Dafydd's Caergwrle Castle.

The chronicler of Lanercost was one that wrote with monkish outrage that Dafydd, once allied to the King, had chosen Easter as a time to rebel.[2] It had long been the perceived custom among the men of Christendom that Easter was a time set aside from their bouts of periodic violence. This was a time of religious certainty; we should not overlook the sense of genuine horror that an attack at this time might provoke. If ever there was something that would reinforce among the English and French a sense of Welsh barbarism and somehow being on the extremity of Christendom, this was it. The capture of Hawarden that eve of Palm Sunday in March 1282 appeared to be the signal for a wider revolt; almost at once the Welsh flew into rebellion, launching themselves upon the English.

The causes of one war, especially those described as the 'Second' are often to be found in an earlier 'First' war. Most recently, in the last century, the seeds of the Second World War are to be found decisively in the First World War, the peace made at the end of the first war being in some way unsatisfactory to one party or incomplete. And so it was with the Second Welsh War: if we are to consider the reasons for the renewed conflagration, we must see the First Welsh War as the principal cause. Definitive historian of the Welsh Wars Morris wrote: 'No special cause for the rising need be sought beyond the natural wish for liberty and revenge.'[3] Quite so, the Welsh had been humiliated by the conclusion of the first war: Llywelyn ap Gruffydd had been once more reduced to being ruler of Snowdonia alone, and his brother Dafydd who had expected much reward for his assistance of Edward had felt ill used in receiving just the two cantrefi. Wales had once more been subjugated by the English, as they had been prior to the ascendancy of Llywelyn.

But still it was a tremendously risky and daring undertaking. The Gruffydd brothers had come to feel the full strength of Edward's determination in 1277–78 and must have known that his response would again be overwhelming. From the distance of many centuries, the rising looks to have had extraordinarily little chance of success and to have been the last throw of a dice by the princes of Wales, one that would ultimately lead not to their subjugation but to their destruction. But perhaps it did not seem that way to the rebels who took so quickly to arms in 1282, perhaps they did indeed think there was some chance of success. In revolt the Welsh nurtured an outrage at English occupation and interference in their affairs, an outrage that had repelled lesser kings than Edward. But the 'Leopard'[4] was cut of a different cloth than his father, and with hindsight we can see clearly that his response would be total.

The rebellion appears to have been coordinated[5] and premeditated, as the very next day the Marcher town of Oswestry was savagely attacked from Powys Fadog and elsewhere. Two days after Hawarden, the Welsh gained the castle at Aberystwyth by subterfuge, though at least the doors and gates had been locked this time. Gruffydd ap Maredudd and Rhys Fychan ap Rhys ap Maelgwn invited the castle's constable to dinner no less, and there took him captive, while his men took the castle.[6] Initially no damage was done, however within a day or two 'they burned the town and the castle and destroyed the rampart that was around the castle and the town'.[7] The castle at Aberystwyth had proven unequal to the task of restraining a Welsh rebellion. For the Welsh it was a hit-and-run attack since they did not hold Aberystwyth.

Meanwhile, the castles at Flint and Rhuddlan apparently fared better than Aberystwyth. They were attacked on Palm Sunday, 22 March,[8] the day after the night attack on Hawarden. There are some accounts of them having fallen, but it is almost certain they withheld the onslaught and that reports of destruction refer to the associated towns growing around them rather than to the castles themselves. That neither castle appears to have fallen is perhaps fortunate, since neither had been completed at this point. Morris writes that both castles were 'in connection with Chester by water' which, if accurate, bears out Edward's wisdom in siting the castles as he had.[9] Siege engines were put to use in the assault on Rhuddlan, as evidenced by the Welsh use of stolen lead from Northop that had been intended for construction at Flint.[10] At Flint the first constable, Gérard de Saint Laurent, appears to have fallen at this point, as he no longer appears in the records following 1282. We have no account of his death. On 25 March, writing to Roger de Mortimer, Edward, noting casualties at Flint, observed that certain of his men had been slain.[11] There is perhaps another allusion to his death in that his *valettus*,[12] or manservant, Sengin, was taken into the king's pay at this time. His replacement at Flint would be William de Perton, the clerk who had worked alongside Maître Jacques at Rhuddlan. St. Laurent was one of the first Savoyard casualties of the Welsh Wars – he would not be the last.

The extent of Llywelyn's prior knowledge of the rebellion is the subject of much debate; he himself later denied any prior involvement. Either way, his brothers's attack on Hawarden and the subsequent widespread revolt left him with no option other than to join a full and irrevocable rebellion against Edward. Welsh historian Davies recalls: 'he had little option but to join the revolt and to assume its leadership, indeed he had probably every inclination to do so.'[13] Prestwich is condemnatory of Edward in driving Dafydd into common cause with his brother Llywelyn, calling his policy toward them following the First Welsh War 'remarkably inept'.[14] Some have seen Llywelyn's remaining in north Wales, while Dafydd immediately went south to encourage rebellion there, as evidence of the former's reluctance to join the revolt, I think is unlikely. Having condemned Edward, Prestwich had earlier found it 'hard to imagine' that Llywelyn had been drawn into rebellion at the last moment.[15] The Chronicler of Guisborough was in no doubt, waxing lyrically, likening Llywelyn and Dafydd to Herod and Pilate who had been similarly agreed in insurrection.[16] The chronicler of Chester was also in no doubt that the brothers had been acting in concert.[17] Perhaps these English monks are partial witnesses, but they should not be disregarded lightly.

Dafydd would later assign much of the blame for his insurrection to Reginald de Grey.[18] On 14 November 1281 Grey had been appointed Justiciar of Chester; he was granted the county of Cheshire, the king's demesne lands in North Wales, described as 'Engelfield [Tegeingl] and Ros', together with the 'castles of Chester and Flint' but not 'the castle of Rothelan'. There was also a mandate to the Savoyard constable of Flint 'Gérard de Sancto Laurencio to deliver to him the castle of Flint'.[19] Gérard de Saint-Laurent was to give up the castle by Michaelmas of 1281, the extent to which this happened on the ground is uncertain – as mentioned earlier the Savoyard perished in the rebellion of 1282 and possibly never left the castle.

It would be the arrival of Grey, to which Dafydd later pointed to as the beginning of the downward spiral in relations between him and the crown. Beverley Smith calls Grey's rule 'harsh and capricious';[20] if this is so, then it took little time to incite Dafydd to armed revolt, November 1281 to March 1282 being little time to reign as a tyrant. Nonetheless, despite Grey's testimony not having survived, an impartial reading of Dafydd's later complaints would conclude that he most likely had a case to answer. We will never know for certain if Dafydd's complaints of Grey were of an overly sensitive Welshman or an overly insensitive Englishman, but we can be certain of the subsequent rebellion. The Hagnaby chronicler tells us that a meeting had been arranged to reconcile Dafydd with Grey and Clifford, but that Dafydd intended to kidnap both Grey and Clifford. Clifford on getting wind of the plot retired to the supposed sanctuary of Hawarden Castle which was then subsequently attacked by Dafydd.[21] Whether the infringements of Dafydd's dignity which he reported, warranted armed rebellion remains open to question, or whether the Hagnaby chronicler's tale holds water, we cannot tell – what is beyond doubt is the attack lit the fire of rebellion.

Edward had heard of the rebellion almost immediately, on 25 March 1282 he issued writs carried by Bogo de Knovill for three commanders of English forces to suppress the rebellion: Roger de Mortimer in the marches, Reginald de Grey at Chester and Robert Tibetot, another who had accompanied Edward and Othon on crusade, in west Wales. If Edward had thought ill of Llywelyn as a vassal who had refused to pay him due homage and had threatened his royal majesté, then one can only imagine how he might have responded to outright armed rebellion – and worse, outright armed rebellion of a man who had treated with him at Aberconwy. That the attack initially came from his one-time ally Dafydd ap Gruffydd would have filled him with feelings of betrayal and treachery. Had not his father been betrayed and deceived many times, but not responded ruthlessly? News of Hawarden would have played into every prejudice the king held of the faithless and devious Welsh. In making his proclamation he declared that he would 'repress the rebellion and malice of the Welsh'. A little of the sense of English outrage at perceived Welsh duplicity is conveyed by the Chester chronicler, writing of Llywelyn, as being of a '*Stirps mendax, causa malorum*', a 'lying race, the cause of evil'.[22] The use of the word '*mendax*' is striking, it can be literally translated as 'lying' but also as 'deceptive', it is the root of 'mendacious' and 'mendacity' in modern English. If Edward had learned one thing from his father's reign, it was that rebellion, betrayal and treachery had to be met with the full force a king's might.

A council was summoned to meet; it did so at Devizes on 5 April, where Tibetot was replaced as the southern army commander by the Earl of Gloucester, Red Gilbert. A general recall to arms brought Othon de Grandson back to England from Savoy, from where he had only been despatched in February, three weeks by horse in each direction brought him hot foot back to Britain. The fire in Savoy would at least be doused by another Savoyard Habsburg truce and finally the Treaty of Payerne in December 1283. Back in Britain, by 7 May Othon was commanding seventeen lances[23] at Montgomery in the Welsh marches.[24] Roger de Mortimer had a further eighteen and the Earl of Lincoln '100 horse and 600 foot' and that 'within a month of David's capture of Hawarden over 200, within two months over 300 lances of the household and paid squadrons were in arms'.[25]

Household knights, fifteen to be exact, along with nearly a hundred troopers, proceeded north to Chester under the command of Amédée de Savoie. The Savoyard was the second son of the late Thomas de Savoie, Count of Flanders, elder brother to Pierre and Philippe, and the man whose request for payment from Henry III had done so much to damage the king's relationship with Simon de Montfort. Amédée had been born in 1249 and, along with his younger brother Louis, both were long in Edward's service. Along with his brother Louis, Amédée had been left the lands in southern England of Pierre de Savoie.[26] However, this 1268 will had been overturned in England. Nonetheless Amédée had been compensated and Pierre de Savoie's will served its true purpose,[27] to provide an entrée into the English court.[28] Amédée was another that had been at Saint-Georges-d'Espéranche that summer of 1273 and had served in the First Welsh War in 1277 with the king – the King's Wardrobe expenses for 1278 note some £230 paid to Amédée in wages and expenses.[29] Following the Second war, as we shall see, Amédée would accompany Grandson on many diplomatic embassies on Edward's behalf.

Meanwhile, once at Chester, a relief expedition was mounted to come to the assistance of the beleaguered defenders of Flint and Rhuddlan. The Chester annalist suggests the castles had come under siege, '*eodem die*',[30] on the same day, as the attack on Hawarden, 21/22 March, and as mentioned earlier there is talk of lead for siege engines at Rhuddlan. Prestwich suggests that 'Llywelyn ap Gruffydd himself… took part in attacks on Flint and Rhuddlan.'[31] We may never know for sure, but nevertheless, after a siege of a month, on or about 21 April

1282, we know that Amédée de Savoie led his column along the road to Flint and Rhuddlan, a Savoyard-led English invasion of Wales. The evidence for the king having entrusted the relief of his castles to the future Count of Savoy comes from a letter dated 9 May: '*fu ozd nos a lever le sieche du Rodelan*', that is 'for our lift of the siege of Rhuddlan'.[32] The Welsh sieges of Flint and Rhuddlan now lifted, attention turned to the castles which had been damaged, as evidenced by the work in subsequent years to make good the attempts of the Welsh insurgents to bring them down. The relief operation was relatively short, Amédée being able to return to Chester within four days – on or about 25 April. The future Count of Savoy is recorded as '*domino ... Capitaneo*' of the English relief army.[33]

Once back in Chester, news reached him of the death of his elder brother and heir apparent as Count of Savoy, Thomas III de Piedmont.[34] Amédée would be needed to help maintain order in Savoy, particularly in view of the tense relations with the Habsburgs and Genevois.[35] As Othon had himself discovered fires could simultaneously catch light in Britain and Savoy, a perilous condition known to Anglo-Savoyards since the time of Pierre de Savoie. Within three years Philippe himself would be dead without an heir, leaving Edward a role in the Savoyard succession. Philippe's will arranged for his niece Queen Alianor de Provence and her son King Edward I of England the solemn duty of awarding the Savoyard inheritance. So, it was in 1285 that Edward decided between two knights formerly in his service, Amédée and Louis. Edward's judgement was to make Amédée the Count of Savoy, while creating a new Barony of Vaud for his younger brother Louis. Amédée went on to be a successful Count of Savoy, gaining the epithet grand – becoming Amédée le Grand de Savoie. That the king of England should decide the Savoyard succession and indeed that the future Count of Savoy should lead the relief of Flint and Rhuddlan castles in 1282 speaks volumes of the intimacy of the relationship between the Kingdom of England and the County of Savoy in the late thirteenth century – despite Matthew Paris's protestations, the seeds sewn by Henry and Alianor were continuing to bear fruit. David Carpenter in the second volume of his biography of Henry III noted, as we saw, that Pierre de Savoie had been thwarted in his attempt to have Amédée succeed him in his southern English lands. Time was however to show that Pierre's main goal of a position at the English court for Amédée while he came of age and succeeded both him and his brother Philippe was to come to pass. Pierre de Savoie had been right after all, even from the grave.

If Llywelyn had had any doubts as to the wisdom of joining Dafydd's rebellion, those doubts must have surely ended in June. His wife Eleanor de Montfort had been with child when the revolt erupted, and in June she gave birth to a daughter for Llywelyn, who would be christened Gwenllian. However, childbirth in the thirteenth century was not an easy passage, and Eleanor died on 19 June at Abergwyngregyn, and with her passed any hope Llywelyn had of a male heir. The body of this niece of Henry III, the daughter of Simon de Montfort, this cousin of Edward I and lately Princess of Wales was taken to the Monastery of Fagan the Little or Llanfaes. On 12 July, members of Eleanor's personal household were given safe conduct while travelling back into England, leaving Llywelyn to face his moment of destiny alone.[36] It has been speculated that in despair and losing all hope he joined his brother's fight.[37] We will never know for certain if this romantic lost cause led Llywelyn into battle, or if, as the Chester chronicler relates, that he was with Dafydd in rebellion from the beginning.[38] Following the war, little Gwenllian would be taken by Edward into the custody of a nunnery at Sempringham in Lincolnshire, there to live out her days in lonely contemplation of a life denied her, the last Princess of Wales.[39]

War was then, as now, an expensive business. Shortly after the attack on Hawarden the king was already resorting to the money houses of Italy to finance a campaign that he knew would be decisive in the struggle between king and prince. The Calendar of Welsh Rolls records, on 14 April, 1,000 marks were immediately made available in London 'by the Riccardi'[40] and further multiple supplies of 1,000 marks from Siena, Piacenza, Florence, and others to total 11,300 marks,[41] and further advances of thousand-mark portions for a similar sum from the same Italian wells on 10 June.[42] An order was sent to the Savoyard seneschal of Gascony, Jean de Grailly, for 'forty good crossbowmen on foot and twelve crossbowmen on horseback'.[43] At least half the cost of these Gascon crossbowmen would be met from Riccardi money.[44] The Gascons, along with their 70,000 bolts, including baneret Guillaume de Monte Ravelli, 'fought and swaggered, as befitted the forebears of d'Artagnan'. But the enormous financial demands of the Second Welsh War began to show the first cracks in the 'Riccardi system' as the merchants added the following ominous warning in a letter to Edward, 'thanks to God [the orders] have been paid up to the present and will continue to be paid if in our power'.[45] Requests were despatched to all corners of the king's realm, both in England and overseas for the resources, food and materials of war that would furnish one of the greatest armies ever to be put into the field by a medieval king of England.

By 16 June Edward was in Chester once more, 'pitching his tent at Newton', today a suburb northeast of the city.[46] By 31 July, his brother Edmund, along with his wife Blanche d'Artois had arrived in Chester.[47] There were to be two thrusts into North Wales this time. In addition to the coastal march from Chester to the Conwy by way of the forest road and Flint and Rhuddlan castles, there was to be a left flank to the English assault. Dafydd ap Gruffydd had been granted the two inland of the four cantrefi and his fiefdom would imperil the king's flank if not taken care of. Dafydd's territory encompassed Dyffryn Clwyd and Rhufoniog along with the castle at Caergwrle, but also Denbigh and Hawarden. Reginald de Grey was assigned the role of clearing the king's left flank, along with the traitorous Dafydd, from his lands. Edward moved along the coast road to Flint, where he had arrived and encamped by 6 July,[48] and by the next Thursday he was once more at his castle of Rhuddlan. It's possible to assume the formerly besieged castle had not fallen or was defensible, as he had taken Leonor with him[49] – quite something for a queen to travel into what was still to all intents and purposes a war zone.

Meanwhile, the English had also moved up the river Dee, Dafydd conceding Caergwrle without a fight, but not before slighting the castle he had so recently reconstructed at the King's expense. Reginald de Grey appointed Hugh de Pulford as constable of the castle and gave him a force of thirty crossbows and no less than 2,600 archers as protection for Maître Jacques, Master Richard and the men repairing the slighted castle.[50] Clearly, the English were expecting to be challenged, but Dafydd had withdrawn, not wishing to be caught in a besieged castle, fluidity of movement being the Welsh modus operandi. Grey took the castle of Ewloe overlooking the Dee estuary, uncontested as it had been back in 1277. As the English were protecting their flank for further progress, another castle was yielded without a fight by Dafydd, the seizure of which, earlier that year, had precipitated the whole revolt and subsequent war – Dafydd abandoned Hawarden Castle. Grey moved next into the two cantrefi granted to Dafydd for life by Edward, back in 1277, at the Treaty of Aberconwy: first, Dyffryn Clwyd and Ruthin, where a new castle had been begun in 1277, contemporaneously with those at Flint and Rhuddlan.

By August 1282, the English had once more taken possession of whatever there was in terms of a castle at Ruthin. An English army came inland from Rhuddlan, following the river

Clwyd by way of Llandyrnog to meet up with Grey at Ruthin by 28 August. We know that Edward himself was present at Ruthin between 31 August and 8 September and this visit is most likely in connection with a decision to resume work on the castle. That autumn the king dismembered the lands of Dafydd ap Gruffydd, Rhufoniog and Dyffryn Clwyd, and of Powys Fadog, among his loyal lieutenants.

The grants of land give us some idea of the king's movements, but also that of his household knights, including Othon de Grandson who bore witness to each of the three charters. Firstly, on 7 October at Rhuddlan, Edward granted Castell Dinas Brân, which occupied a prominent hilltop site above the river Dee in Powys Fadog, to Jean de Warenne, Earl of Surrey.[51] The castle had probably been built in the 1260s, before his death in 1269, by the Lord of Dinas Brân, Gruffydd ap Madog, Prince of Powys Fadog, on the site of several earlier structures. Then on 16 October again at Rhuddlan Henri de Lacy was granted Denbigh itself and the *cantrefi* of Ros ans Rhufoniog.[52] Lastly on 23 October at Denbigh, the Justiciar, Reginald de Grey, was granted the castle at Ruthin and *cantref* of Dyffryn Clwyd for himself.[53] Othon literally gave witness to Dafydd's former overlordship coming to an end, Edward installing men he could trust in Dyffryn Clwyd. The king had made the grant of Ruthin from Denbigh, the centre of the second *cantref* he had granted to Dafydd in 1277 – Rhufoniog. We are uncertain as to whether a castle had been begun at Denbigh by Dafydd; perhaps there is evidence of works in that Denbigh only fell to the English following a month-long siege that autumn of 1282.[54] The dismemberment of Dafydd's onetime land as spoils of war to men who could be trusted by Edward was now complete.

The king's left flank had now been secured, the two cantrefi granted to the treacherous Dafydd retaken and placed in loyal hands; order was being restored to the lands east of the Conwy. Ahead of Edward, Othon and the English army now lay the forbidding mountain fastness of Snowdonia, the very heart of Gwynedd. When he had had just cause to take Gwynedd, Edward's father Henry III had twice sheathed his sword in the 1240s. Edward too had foregone an invasion across the Conwy, deciding to leave Gwynedd in the hands of Llywelyn in 1277, despite having taken the breadbasket of Anglesey. But now there would have to be a final reckoning with the House of Gwynedd: this was not 1241, nor 1247 or even 1277, it was 1282, and Edward would now make an end of the perennial Gwynedd problem.

But also, that summer Edward had learned of a disaster that had befallen an English army in South Wales, which had given him reason to pause. Edward's plan had been to strike into Wales with three armies: himself in the north, marcher lord Mortimer in Mid Wales and Red Gilbert, the Earl of Gloucester, in the south. Edward had initially decided that his trusty fellow crusader Robert de Tibetot ought to lead the southern army but the Earl of Gloucester, perhaps living up to his fiery name, had insisted on control. Gloucester was to lead his army from Carmarthen and Dinefwr in the south toward Aberystwyth in Mid Wales, thus cutting Llywelyn off any hope of retreat southward from Gwynedd and restoring order to the south which had joined the rebellion.

On 17 June 1282, the army had sacked the Welsh castle of Carreg Cennen, whence they returned to Dinefwr Castle with the spoils. Traditionally English columns travelling in Wales had been beset by hit-and-run guerrilla tactics, the Welsh taking advantage of their intimate knowledge of the land. Edward had been meticulously circumspect in his progress in North Wales, both in 1277, by use of the forest road and castles at Flint and Rhuddlan, but also in 1282, by his careful protection of his left flank in taking Caergwrle, Ruthin and Denbigh before progressing to the Conwy. But the impetuous Red Gilbert was not Edward, and he had been travelling through South Wales with all the lack of care taken by earlier defeated English armies. As historian Morris confirms: 'carelessly without scouts'[55] they wandered into an ambush. Sure enough, at Llandeilo Fawr the Welsh descended like furies upon Gloucester's one hundred knights and some thousand foot soldiers and destroyed them almost to a man. The result was a temporary stalling of Edward's three-pronged assault on Llywelyn. Edward replaced Gilbert de Clare with his own half-uncle Guillaume de Valence. A salutary reminder to Edward and Grandson that the Welsh could be formidable opponents, something that would soon be brought especially home to Othon in a life-threatening way.

In the middle march, the King's commander and loyal servant Roger de Mortimer, 1st Baron Mortimer of Wigmore, the victor of Evesham, died on 26 October 1282, being replaced by Roger l'Estrange. What happened next would be pivotal in Anglo-Welsh history. No doubt Llywelyn felt the weakness of the English in the south, the potential weakness in Mid Wales following the death of Mortimer, the strong English army led by the king across the Conwy to his immediate front – all of these things pulled Llywelyn south from Gwynedd toward a date with destiny.

But before Llywelyn moved south, and as Edward paused at the Conwy, the Archbishop of Canterbury John Peckham[56] intervened to prevent further bloodshed. Perhaps also on the mind of the archbishop was the damage the war was doing to his church: the recent burning of the cathedral at Saint Asaph in the Perfeddwlad would have displeased him greatly. Ecclesiastical concern was not overly welcomed by the king, who felt he had the troublesome Prince of Wales cornered. Edward's terms for Llywelyn had hardened since those offered and accepted at Aberconwy in 1277, the latest revolt angering him to the point of losing all patience with the Welsh prince. Exile and land in England to the value of £1,000 for Llywelyn and banishment on crusade for Dafydd were the best and only terms Edward would offer. They were perhaps not meant to be accepted and accepted they were not. The intercession by the archbishop gives us an opportunity, not only to see the specific reasons the Welsh gave at the time for rebellion, but also the sentiment behind it, a sentiment that would echo down the centuries, as perhaps it was meant to.

Archbishop Peckham was an unlikely peacemaker between England and Wales, holding a traditional conservative worldview that saw the people of Wales as decidedly barbarian in their ways. Long before the war and his intercession, he had described Wales to Edward as '*vostre terre sauvage de Gale*'.[57] Nonetheless intervene he did, and his exchanges with both Llywelyn and Dafydd survive in Peckham's Registrum epistolarum. Dated, 11 November 1282, at Garthcelyn, we have recorded Llywelyn's response.[58] With a simultaneous appeal to myth and legend, in the Welsh prince's descent from the original founders of Britain, the descendants of the Trojan Brutus,[59] but also the status agreed by the Treaty of Montgomery, signed by the king and his father, as agreed by Ottobuono, and sealed at Rhyd Chwima, we see Llywelyn holding firm. But one has the distinct feeling that the Welsh prince was writing for posterity rather than as part of any ongoing negotiation likely to bear fruit. The correspondence with Peckham clearly coveys that any negotiation the archbishop might have thought possible was clearly futile, the Gruffydd brothers and King Edward bent upon a path that would decide the fate of Wales for generations to come.

Dated as they were, 11 November, we can see that the communication with Peckham was undertaken from a position where events had already taken England and Gwynedd beyond the point of no return: further hostilities had already recommenced. These events perhaps explain more than any other the hardening of the line taken by Llywelyn and Dafydd between 31 October and 11 November. Edward had a plan to complete the conquest and whereas in

1277 he had been content to merely punish the Welsh prince, now he intended to destroy him, and that required an assault on Snowdonia itself. His mood that November is expressed in a letter that survives in the Calendar of Welsh Rolls, in which he describes 'putting down the malice of the Welsh'.[60]

It seems it had been his plan all along; he had intended to occupy Anglesey, as in 1277, thus depriving Llywelyn of his larder. Edward had brought up the Cinque Ports fleet to Chester once more, first to assist in the supply of his army relieving Flint and Rhuddlan. But then the king had a new and remarkably audacious plan: he would build a bridge across the Menai straits from Anglesey to the mainland, a bridge of pontoon boats. The Menai Straits are some 16 miles (25 kilometres) in length, but only 1,300 feet (4,000 metres) wide at their narrowest point, the flow of water is tidal. On 24 May, he ordered Stephen de Pencester, the warden of the Cinque Ports, to choose up to twelve carpenters who might build boats and barges for the purpose, and they should be ready for work not later than 23 June. So, some 200 men from the Cinque Ports assembled on the Wirral shore of the river Dee. Sandwich, in the county of Kent, supplied twenty carpenters, following abortive attempts to build in Kent, and they found themselves journeying to the Wirral.

That summer, between 30 July and 9 August, the King's Wardrobe records payments made to Robert FitzJohn for poles from Chester to make punts and pontoons for the bridge. Master Richard began with a small construction camp near Llanfaes. The incredible structure soon took shape once the army under Luke de Tany, seneschal of Gascony before Savoyard Jean de Grailly, had occupied Anglesey. Striding across the Menai, floated a bridge of interlinked boats bearing upon them a flat section of sufficient width to allow the army to make a crossing. Final construction had seen sixty carpenters cross to the island under Master Richard and a further hundred under Master Henry of Oxford. It was a colossal undertaking, most likely from a work camp near the site of the future castle at Beaumaris.[61] Master Bertram appears to have supervised the undertaking, with Master Richard being his deputy on this occasion.[62] Their reward was a tun of wine each, along with wine for the workforce.[63] Guisborough suggests the bridge was wide enough for sixty men to proceed abreast, which is most unlikely, the Hagnaby chronicler has a more plausible fifteen. The perils of reading medieval sources are evident when we consider that the 'lx' in the Guisborough chronicle may well be a scribal copy error from an original 'ix' – nine men being a whole lot more plausible than sixty.[64]

Five days prior to the intervention of Archbishop Peckham, some of the English took events into their own hands in search of glory. On 6 November 1282 Luke de Tany led several knights, including Othon de Grandson who had earlier been at Montgomery and Rhuddlan, and around 300 men-at-arms across the bridge. They passed beneath the lower slopes of the mountains opposite Anglesey; behind them the tide reached its full height and cut off any route back – they were dangerously exposed to the classic Welsh tactic of ambush. The chronicler Walter of Guisborough, although he was not there and wrote from some years distance, gave a full account of what would become known as the Battle of Moel-y-Don,[65]

> *ut laudem acquirerent et nomen curiosum, necdum ponte plene firmato et perfecto, incautius transierunt et hoc in descensu aquæ et aquæ retracta cumque lustrassent pedes montium et essent a ponte aliquautisper remoti, superque venissent fluctus marisque inundantia ita quod ad pontem redire non posent præ aqua nimia, egressi sunt Wallenses a montibus excelsis dirigentes ad eos iter et gressus suos. At nostri attonti et multitudinem timentes magnam,*

> *se potius aquæ quam hosti credere volucrunt; ingressique sunt aquam ita ut erant onusti et armati, et quasi in puncto submersi sunt.*[66]

As originally translated by Morris: 'the Welsh came down upon them from the mountains. Our men, panic stricken at the sight of their numbers, preferred to face the water rather than the enemy. They plunged into the sea, burdened as they were with their armour, and were all drowned in a moment.'[67] An alternative translation of Walter of Guisborough reads

> When they had reached the foot of the mountain and, after a time, came to a place at some distance from the bridge, the tide came in with a great flow, so that they were unable to get back to the bridge for the debt of water. The Welsh came from the high mountains and attacked them, and in fear and trepidation, for the great number of the enemy, our men preferred to face the sea than the enemy. They went into the sea but, heavily laden with arms, they were instantly drowned.[68]

A Welsh chronicler wrote: 'And they desired to gain possession of Arfon. And then was made a bridge over the Menai; but the bridge broke under an excessive load, and countless numbers of the English were drowned, and others were slain.'[69]

Their leader Luke de Tany paid for his impetuosity and lust for glory with his life, others including the son of Llywelyn's prisoner Roger de Clifford and Lord Chancellor Robert Burnell's sons Philip and William – in total sixteen knights perished.[70] The Hagnaby chronicler, alone, suggests that Roger de Clifford not Luke de Tany, led the charge, anxious to avenge his father's capture at Hawarden, which does as Prestwich says, have a ring of 'plausibility' about it.[71] Remarkably, Othon de Grandson survived the battle, and his horse carried him to the safety of Anglesey – this would not be the first remarkable brush with death the Savoyard would have in his long ninety-year life. The chronicler wrote: 'With much difficulty Lord Othon de Grandson escaped.'[72]

The chronicler of Lanercost, who gives us very little detail of the Welsh wars, save for: 'During that war in Wales a bridge of boats was made in the place called Menai, that is, between Snowdon and Anglesey, where Sir William de Audley, Lucas Tanay and Roger de Clifford and many others, old and young were drowned.'[73]

Very likely the chronicle monk heard the tale from the survivor Othon de Grandson while the Savoyard was with the king's army later in the Scottish borderlands.

Morris criticises factual errors in the chronicler's story: the size of the army, the nature of the bridge, suggesting that our chronicler emphasised the catastrophic and shameful defeat as an admonishment of rash actions. Certainly, the effect of the disaster was to strengthen the king's resolve; one can only imagine Edward's response on first hearing of Luke de Tany's pre-emptive assault on Snowdonia. The chronicler Thomas Wykes saw in the attack an attempt to pre-empt peace negotiations, but although negotiations continued no peace or truce was in effect.[74] The defeat risked Edward's carefully laid plans and meticulous preparation, as had the earlier events at Llandeilo Fawr. It seemed that the king's servants were doing their best, in eagerness to please the king, to handicap his subjugation of Wales. Taylor suggests that the Welsh did not destroy the bridge following their 'hit and run' victory, recording new materials being sent to Anglesey for bridgework between 23 November and 28 December.

Archbishop Peckham fired one last salvo at Llywelyn: 'In what way did Brutus, after Dianæ's foretelling, and not without the tricks of the devil by the idolatrous sacrifice of a hunted doe, obtain entry to the British island, by the famous stories you proclaimed.'[75] The archbishop was, like Pontius Pilate, washing his hands of the Welsh, whom he said claimed descent from Brutus, then these men of Troy came by the island of Britain not without the tricks of the devil and idolatry. In short there was an adherence to prophecy and pagan ways that only the cleansing purification of Edward's army could give remedy.

With that, his patience exhausted, Archbishop John left Wales for Herefordshire and Snowdonia to the cleansing he was sure would come. Although we have no surviving record, many scholars believe that the archbishop now pronounced a sentence of excommunication on Llywelyn.[76] In one last intervention, after the war, in June 1284, the archbishop reminded Edward (as indeed he'd promised in 1282 in writing to the Princes of Gwynedd)[77] of the suffering of religious houses during the conflict. Peckham was as good as his word, and Edward duly compensated 107 religious houses, including those at Valle Crucis and Bangor. Edward, meanwhile, stood by the Conwy and would soon resume his assault, summoning more footmen to his ranks.[78] Edward's father had held back from a conquest of Gwynedd in 1247; When Edward would have been more than within his rights to go ahead, he himself had held back in 1277 when he left Llywelyn Uwch Gwynedd, but this time there would be no leniency toward what Edward's saw as the 'malice' that he thought continued to emanate from the wilds of Snowdonia; this time would be the reckoning for the House of Gwynedd. Despite the disaster on the Menai, he would go on, and news from Mid Wales would soon bring the king better news. On 11th December at Orewin Bridge near Builth Wells Llywelyn ap Grufydd met his end. Reports of his death are confusing, but he appears to have been ambushed. His head was severed from his body and sent to Edward. However, the fallen mantle carried by Llywelyn would be immediately raised once more by his brother Dafydd.

The war was not however, as we have said, over with the passing of Llywelyn, his brother Dafydd remaining at large. Edward sat that December by the Clwyd at Rhuddlan, his army weakened in Anglesey by the disaster of the Moel-y-Don; he needed reinforcement to pursue his cause to ultimate victory. He had not long after the beginning of the Welsh rising, in April sent to Jean de Grailly in Gascony for military assistance. There had been difficulty in responding to this request, since the king of France, as Overlord of Gascony forbad any participation of Gascon forces in his vassal (so far as Gascony was conferenced) Edward's Welsh war.

Nonetheless, eventually the Gascons began to appear, as Christmas 1282 passed in January of 1283 the great families of Edward's French lands arrived in Wales, as Morris lists: 'There came in person the Counts of Armagnac and of Bigorre, the lord of Bergerac, Roger de Mauleon, Arnald de Gaveston, Pierre de Greilly, Pierre Amanieu, Captal de Buch, the Viconte de Tarcazin and Guichard de Bourg, ex-mayor of Bordeaux.'[79] The nobles brought with them over 200 mounted crossbowmen and over 1,300 regular crossbowmen. Jean de Vesci had been to Gascony on Edward's behalf, with the Gascons he had returned; he was sent to join Othon de Grandson who'd narrowly survived Moel-y-Don to join the Anglesey army. The loyal Savoyard would now lead the newly rebuilt army in Anglesey, first making good the bridge of boats to the mainland. If the army did not have a French tinge to it before, it certainly did now – packed full and led by men from Savoy and Gascony.

Following the death of his brother, and having begun the revolt, Dafydd chose to fight on what became known from this point as 'Dafydd's War'. With 1283 but three weeks old

Edward was ready to make his next move: the army moved out from Rhuddlan and crossed the Clwyd, bound for the Conwy. But it was not to be the wide estuary by his father's old castle at Deganwy that would be his goal – Edward had other ideas, and ever the master strategist he moved inland and eschewed a direct assault upon the Welsh. They moved upstream along the Conwy to Betws-y-Coed, before arriving at the tower castle of Dolywyddelan. The castle, built on a rocky outcrop on the slopes of Moel Siabod overlooking the Lledr valley, was the gateway to passage across north Wales, situated at the head of waters that ran northward to Conwy and southwestward toward Harlech and Criccieth. The medieval road that passed from the Conwy valley into Meirionnydd passed close by the western side of the castle, not down in the valley as does the modern road.[80] The lonely castle had been built earlier in the century by Llywelyn Fawr or Llywelyn the Great, the late departed Llywelyn ap Gruffydd's grandfather. Although once reputed to be the birthplace of Llywelyn Fawr, it is now thought that he was born at Tomen Castell, a small tower that had previously stood on a nearby hill.

The castle comprised a small two-storeyed keep enclosed by a curtain wall. The enclosure was protected by rock-cut ditches and natural cliff edges. In besieging this outpost Edward fully knew that he was no longer containing the House of Gwynedd: he was now making a direct assault upon not only its actuality but its mythology. After a short siege, on '*die Lune*' Monday, 18 January 1283[81], Dolywyddelan Castle fell to Edward and his army; two days earlier the keeper of the wardrobe had already called for eleven masons to be sent there.[82] There in mid-winter the king now rested his army once more. He could strike the mountain fastness of Snowdonia now from the south, from the east and Othon de Grandson could strike from the north, and he controlled the sea to the west – Dafydd and Gwynedd were now caught in a suffocatingly deadly closing embrace.

Meanwhile, time, back in February had passed for Edward with the consolidation of his armies at Dolywyddelan and at Bangor by the Menai Strait, his quarry Dafydd it seems holed up at Castell y Bere to the south not far from Tywyn and the Dovey estuary. Simultaneously or closely thereafter four English armies moved in for the kill. The first headed by Edward himself moved northward along the western bank of the Conwy toward the abbey at Aberconwy – where it arrived in the second week of March. The second army headed by Othon de Grandson and Jean de Vesci moved in a southwestern direction from Bangor first by way of Caernarfon, then Criccieth on the Llyn peninsula. By 14 March, the native Welsh castle of Criccieth was also in English hands. One by one the strongholds of Gwynedd were falling. Two other English armies, that of the king's uncle Guillaume de Valence from Aberystwyth and Llywelyn's nemesis Roger L'Estrange from Montgomery came up from Mid Wales to threaten Castell y Bere, and with the army was Bogo de Knovill who had been earlier at Aberystwyth.

Castell y Bere was another constructed by Llywelyn Fawr or Llywelyn the Great and sat atop a rocky outcrop on the eastern side of the Dysynni valley protecting an old route from Tywyn to Dolgellau the southerly approaches to Gwynedd. The route then, as now to Meirionnydd by way of the coast, was difficult and presented you with the wide estuary of the Afon Mawddach before reaching deeper into Meirionnydd – far better to take the valley of the Afon Dysynni and the bridging point at Llaneltyd near Dolgellau and maybe the hospitality of nearby Cymer Abbey. Taylor, probably very rightly, suggests that Bere was the castle that Llywelyn Fawr had 'began to build for himself' in 1221, as recorded in the Red Book Version of the Brut Tywysogion.[83] On its northern and western approaches, the castle was protected by mother nature's precipitate faces, on the southern and eastern sides rock-cut ditches served as a moat defensive. The castle itself was a long slender affair, following the contours of the land; at its northern and southern extremity it featured D-shaped apsidal towers that were a feature of many native Welsh castles, the slender rear tail of the tower providing additional castle accommodation. The south tower was built apart from the curtain wall in isolation, the southernmost part of the curtain being protected by the square middle tower and the round tower. All the towers ran to two storeys, the middle square tower originally forming the function of central keep. Castell y Bere was much the largest of the castles built by Llywelyn Fawr and a worthy prize.[84]

At Castell y Bere, on his last assignment for Edward, was that master siege engine builder of Benauges and Dolforwyn, Master Bertram the Engineer. The archive records among the last entries we have for him: 'In the same place, at Castell y Bere, for engines made by Master Bertram.'[85]

It would seem Dafydd fled Castell y Bere shortly before or more improbably during the ensuing siege, heading north to Dolbadarn Castle in Snowdonia. The noose was tightening. The custodian of Castell y Bere, Cynfrig ap Madog, surrendered the stronghold to English forces, amounting to 3,000 men, on 25 April[86]. Immediately, as at Dolywyddelan, steps were taken for repairs in the allotment to Master Bertram, and his assistant Simon Le Counte, of five masons and five carpenters for new works.[87]

Within a few short months, Dafydd had lost Dolywyddelan, Criccieth and Castell y Bere along with the abbey at Aberconwy where Edward had subsequently set up his headquarters. The Abbot of Vale Royal was at the abbey by the Conwy from 6 April, perhaps to begin negotiations for the movement of the abbey to make way for what Edward saw as an ideal site to replace the former castle across the Conwy at Deganwy latterly destroyed by Llywelyn. Indeed, the movement of the abbey at Aberconwy and its replacement by a castle became another consciously vindictive act upon Edward's part to rid himself forever of the House of Gwynedd since the abbey had been the burial ground of the princes.

At some point between 22 and 25 April Othon de Grandson was detached, along with 560 men, from the forces surrounding Castell y Bere and sent north the 35 miles (56 kilometres) toward Harlech. The English archives record that the future site of Harlech castle was in English hands by late April, the archive saying: 'Given for pacifying, to Lord Othon de Grandson, for the support of five hundred and sixty of men going with him from Castel-y-Bere to Harlech, Twenty pounds by tally.'[88]

The record is the earliest mention of Hardelach or Harlech we have. By April of 1283 the future sites of Conwy, Caernarfon and Harlech castles were in Edward's hands – and it does not seem to have taken the king long to decide these three would be the home of the castles that would complete and hold his conquest of Gwynedd. Othon de Grandson and Jean de Vesci would join the king among his newly erected tents by the Cistercian monastery at Aberconwy as spring moved toward summer.

We are only certain of several of the elements of the movements across North Wales of Othon and the English army once at Anglesey. A bridgehead from the island to the mainland, most likely involving a rebuilding of the bridge of boats, is suggested for Bangor in late December 1282. Supplies for the army despatched from Chester and Rhuddlan to Bangor are dated to the period 28 December to 3 January 1283[89] and more thereafter. From Bangor we know it had passed Caernarfon, where once the Roman fort of Segontium had stood. Caernarfon took its very name from the Roman settlement there, Y gaer yn Afon, meaning 'the stronghold in the land over against Mon', Mon being the Welsh word for Anglesey.

Whatever remained of Roman Caernarfon it is most likely that there still stood there the Norman motte and perhaps the bailey too, erected by Hugh d'Avranches in the late eleventh century. The fall of Criccieth is recorded but not to which army. Criccieth was in English hands by 14 March since Henry of Greenford received pay from this date as its Constable – there is no record of a siege or battle. However, the archive is then precise in saying that Othon de Grandson, who commanded the Anglesey army, was at the siege of Castel-y-Bere. This would infer a movement of that army from Criccieth to Castel-y-Bere before returning north to Harlech, Othon then returning to the king at Conwy. The movement of this army would most likely have been over land, but they did have naval support also, which may have been used to ferry some of the army to besieged Castel-y-Bere, or at any rate three English commanders.

If we are to consider a birthplace for the iron ring of castles then it is most likely to have been at Aberconwy that spring – we can be almost certain that Othon de Grandson and Jean de Vesci had been at the future sites of Caernarfon and Harlech, Edward had yet to do so, therefore his loyal lieutenants had been his eyes as to the castle sites.[90] Although Prestwich cautions us against suggesting Grandson had too important a role in planning these castles, his role as a man with first sight of these sites and who could be trusted by Edward to see them, as if with his own eyes, should not be lightly discounted.[91] Perhaps in a tent in May 1283 we have the king's most trusted knights together with the king and the man he had sent to ordain the king's work in Wales, for given his presence at Dolywyddelan its very likely that Master James had been with the king's army. I do not believe it takes a large leap of the imagination to conclude that such a meeting was a possibility – we will never know for sure – but it remains a distinct possibility. If it happened, no records have been passed down to us, but then in the thirteenth century no records were ever kept of the process by which kings reached their decisions, or the counsel they sought and were given. It does seem that the parentage of Caernarfon and Harlech lay with those old friends of the king's who had accompanied him on crusade, dined with him in Savoy and recently returned from Gascon service to command his Anglesey army. (Fig 1.5)

That May the last stronghold of Gwynedd fell to the English, Dolbadarn Castle, located at the base of the Llanberis Pass deep in Snowdonia. There Dafydd despatched messages as a Prince of Wales to Ceredigion, but it was to a land now in English hands. Dolbadarn was unusual among the castles of its builder, Llywelyn Fawr, in boasting a round tower keep of two floors above a basement, that evoked English tower at Pembroke. Again, like Dolywyddelan, the keep had been surrounded by a curtain wall, of unmortared grit and slate stone. Within the courtyard, at the opposite end from the tower, sat the hall from which Dafydd gave his last orders as Prince of Wales. Some 3,000–4,000 English troops were still on the payroll and began searching the mountain passes for Dafydd. Morris writes that 'The Welsh evidently offered to surrender of their own accord … That the surrenders were made in abandonment of David.'[92] Welshmen in pursuit of royal pardon joined the hunt for their erstwhile prince. There was nowhere left for Dafydd to take refuge; he fled into the mountains there to await his fate like a wounded animal, his final realm being the Bera mountain above the home of the princes of Gwynedd at Abergwyngregyn. In June 1283 he attempted to evade capture in the mists of Snowdonia, just over a year since he had begun the rebellion at Easter 1282 by descending upon the castle at Hawarden.

It would be said that Enian (or Anion), Bishop of Bangor, betrayed his last hiding place of Nanhysglain to the English. He was there with his wife Elizabeth Ferrers, his two sons

Owain and Llywelyn hiding in a small dwelling in the desolate Carneddau wilderness – the last native Prince of Wales. On the night of 21/22 June men-at-arms climbed into the Welsh night to track down the fugitive. Medieval sources do not record the operation or the precise location of Nanhysglain, but we can imagine the commotion of their capture, and we do know a struggle ensued since Dafydd was apparently wounded in capture (*graviter vulneratus*). The last stand of the House of Gwynedd. That same night he was escorted to Rhuddlan by sixty archers to meet, no doubt, a jubilant Edward. From there he was taken to Chester, not far from the castle at Hawarden he had attacked the previous Easter, thence to Shrewsbury.

As Edward wrote, on 28 June 1283, to Gilbert de Clare from Rhuddlan:

> The tongue of man can scarcely recount the evil deeds committed by the Welsh upon the King's progenitors and him by invasions of the realm from time within memory … but God, wishing as it seems, to put an end to these evil proceedings has, after the prince had been slain, destined David, as the last survivor of the family of traitors aforesaid, to the king's prison after he had been captured by men of his own race.[93]

Dafydd himself was nursed back to health. Edward was determined that the Welsh prince whom he had sheltered from his brother, whom he had fought alongside in 1277 and 1278, whom he had rewarded with lands in the four *cantrefi*, was determined that an example be made of him. He called a parliament to be held in the border county of Shropshire, and notably omitted to call the clergy, who would have no blood on their hands.

Walter of Guisborough later recorded:

> Dafydd however, as he fled to the slaughter, from the aforesaid, hid in the marshes for almost a year, was taken prisoner at last on the eve of Saint Maurice, and in the Shropshire Parliament, which the King held after the feast of Saint Michael, like a deceiver and traitor and the killer is sentenced and hanged drawn and quartered and its four members sent into four parts of England, to be always remembered that way.[94]

And so it was that Dafydd ap Gruffydd met his end in Shrewsbury. The trial result was a foregone conclusion, the punishment meted out to the unfortunate Welshman was not new, but its use for a nobleman was. To be hung, drawn and quartered was a particularly barbaric medieval means of execution, and reserved for those that kings saw as traitors – which though he be Welsh, the English king as his suzerain saw him to be. To be hung, drawn and quartered meant being dragged through the town by horses along the ground to the place of execution, there to be hung until nearly dead, then to be cut down and literally cut into pieces while still alive. The chronicler of Lanercost wrote this verse:

> David of Wales, a thief and traitor,
> Slayer of men, of Church a hater,
> A fourfold criminal in life,
> Now dies by horse, fire, rope and knife.
> The ruffian thus deprived of breath.
> Most meetly dies by fourfold death.[95]

The fourfold punishment in the medieval mind reflected the multiplicity of Dafydd's crimes: he was to be drawn behind a horse since he was a traitor, he was to be hung since he had committed homicide, and lastly, the most gruesome of all, he was to be quartered since he had plotted the death of the king. For Dafydd one more torture was added: his bowels were to be removed at the point of his quartering and burned in front of him – this as punishment for having carried out his original attack on Hawarden during the Easter festivities, or as the Dunstable annalist wrote, '*Quia illud fecit tempore Dominicæ Passionis*'[96] or 'because it was done at the time of the Lord's Passion' – in an age of religious certainty such a despicable act met with particular approbation. It is recorded that his executioner, Geoffrey of Shrewsbury, was paid the grand sum of £1 for carrying out the sentence of death.

Dafydd was the first of Edward's enemies from the Celtic fringe to be executed, but he would not be the last. Some have seen this as a cruel retribution meted upon his enemies, but this would be to take the executions out of context and to misunderstand the king's motives, in short to be guilty of presentism. Katherine Royer in her paper on medieval justice says that 'Edward I inscribed on the scaffold his feudal fury rather than a strategy to bring Wales and Scotland to heel with displays of ceremonialised justice.'[97] Dafydd, like William Wallace to come, met his end because he was seen by Edward as a vassal who had rebelled against his suzerain. This 'feudal fury' explains entirely Edward's actions toward the slain Llywelyn ap Gruffydd in fighting the Welsh wars and his subsequent execution of Dafydd. We should remember that Dafydd was one who'd fought alongside Edward in the First Welsh War, that following that war, he had left his brother Llywelyn in possession of both his title and Gwynedd, and that previously he'd shown clemency to the rebel Jean de Vesci, now a key commander in the Welsh wars – Edward was more than capable of clemency but woe betide a man who might spurn this clemency. To be hung, drawn and quartered was a dishonourable death, an announced death, not the honourable death of an enemy in war – Dafydd was shown and seen to be as a man without honour in an age when this was fundamental to how the nobility self-identified.

The chronicler of Lanercost had it that his body parts were displayed:

> the right arm with a ring on the finger in York; the left arm in Bristol; the right and hip in Northampton; the left [leg] at Hereford. But the villain's head was bound in iron, lest it should fall to pieces from putrefaction and set conspicuously upon a long spear shaft for the mockery of London.[98]

Or as the Dunstable annalist put it, '*Caput autem ejus in Turri Londoniæ super palum altissimam est affixum*'[99] or 'his head is extremely high on a stake over the Tower of London.' Prestwich writes that there was some unseemly quarrelling of the prince's dead body, or more accurately body parts: 'the Londoners carried off the head in triumph, but the citizens of York and Manchester disputed possession of the right shoulder. The men of Lincoln refused to accept any part, and as a result incurred royal displeasure, only remitted once a substantial fine had been paid'.[100]

That trans-Pennine rivalry predated the Wars of the Roses in the form of Dafydd's right shoulders and that Lincoln was fined for not joyfully receiving their body part is the tragicomic conclusion to a macabre execution and to the Second Welsh War. From the distance of over 700 years, it seems perhaps inevitable that it should end this way: both brothers' heads would be displayed together in London on pikes at the Tower.

The ap Gruffydd brothers had attempted rebellion against Edward and a reversal of the results of the First Welsh War, these hopes would in the end prove futile. But the Welsh had always been able to hold the English at arm's length militarily and then politically in the past, letting the mountains and mists of Wales swallow invading armies before reducing them with hit-and-run tactics – what Clausewitz would later call the strategy of 'wearing out of the enemy'.[101]

English kings had always made efforts to subdue the Welsh before but had become dismayed and moved on to other things. For Llywelyn and Dafydd, they had no reason to believe the late thirteenth century would be any different – but they had not bargained with their nemesis Edward Plantagenet nor with his relentless lieutenants like Othon de Grandson. It is a truism that wars are often caused by one side of a political quarrel misunderstanding the other, or a mutual misunderstanding, and in the case of Llywelyn and Edward it was what Prestwich called 'any sympathy for, or understanding of, each other's position'.[102]

In the end the attempt to extend the polity of Gwynedd to encompass a nation of Welsh speakers failed, and failed because of the competing interests of Welsh princes, marcher lords that made it almost impossible to form a united polity – and a neighbouring kingdom in England keen to assert its own hegemony over the island of Britain. While attempting to create a greater extended polity of Gwynedd to more closely match the realm of Welsh speakers, Llywelyn had never attempted to overturn the king of England's overlordship of Wales; his citing descent from the Camber of legend implied the acceptance of the overlordship of a claimed descendants of the Locrinus of legend – but he had consistently failed to reach an accommodation with an English king, his acknowledged overlord – something for which, in the end, he paid for with his life.

March 1284 brought Othon a new title: Justiciar of North Wales,[103] to be based in the new town and castle Edward began to build at Caernarfon. (Fig 1.5) By the 1284 Statute of Rhuddlan Edward divided Llywelyn ap Grufydd's Gwynedd into three counties: Anglesey, Caernarfonshire, and Merionethshire.[104] Unlike his father Henry with his Savoyard counsellor and envoy Pierre de Savoie whom he rewarded by patronage with enormous English estates, Edward rewarded Grandson with position not land. Edward had learned how to place the most able man into positions of authority without upsetting his barony. In medieval England, a justiciar was analogous to what we might term a prime minister.[105] The English title Justiciar originated with the Latin *justiciarius* or *justitiarius* meaning 'man of justice' or simply 'judge'. Davies uses the appellation of 'king's governor general' in *The Age of Conquest*,[106] being given 'wide ranging military, governmental, and judicial powers.[107] The Lord of Grandson had in the words of the Statue of Rhuddlan responsibility for 'Custody and Government of the Peace of Us the King in Snowdon'. Davies goes on to conclude that 'much of his [Othon de Grandson's] attention … in these early years was devoted to … supervising the building of castles'.[108] Grandson was paid handsomely for 'keeping Wales', £1,000 per annum as justiciar and a further £100 for the castle at Caernarfon – in sum £1,100 which translates today to over £750,000![109] But, as we shall soon see, Othon, as he was in the Channel Islands, was mostly an absentee, delegating his role to deputy justiciars including variously his relative Jean de Bonvillars, his brother Guillaume, and John of Havering. During his time as Justiciar, there are some records of his hearing pleas in North Wales, including one judgement where he investigated a Welshman's right to some lands, and handed them over to him.[110] Events would soon bring Othon away from North Wales but still the appointment of Othon, as in effect, the king's viceroy in newly conquered Gwynedd, marked a notable moment in the career of the knight from Lac de Neuchâtel. During the First Welsh War Grandson had been rewarded with twenty casks of wine, for the Second War he had received another twenty tuns of wine, life was being very good to Othon de Grandson.[111]

CHAPTER 8

While Edward and Othon were occupied with the problem of the Welsh, word reached them of what became known as the Sicilian Vespers. At the end of May 1282 Edward received a letter from Ferrante of Aragon which suggested that 'five Sicilian cities have risen against King Charles and killed all the French living in them'.[1] Othon de Grandson's brother Henri (himself once a priest in England, now the Bishop of Verdun) soon wrote to Edward from Orvieto in more detail, including the danger of Aragon and France becoming embroiled:

> The news at the Curia is that the whole of Sicily is in open rebellion against the king, and it is feared that the king of Aragon, who has made the greatest preparations at sea, should enter that kingdom. The king of Sicily gathers a large army at Naples, intending to direct his steps against the Sicilians.[2]

Sicily was a part of the Kingdom of Naples and encompassed the island and much of southern Italy up to the Papal States. It had been born of the Norman conquest of Muslim Sicily by 1091 and the crowning at the behest of Pope Innocent II of King Roger II of Sicily, Roger I having been merely a count. This Hauteville dynasty had fallen in 1194 to be replaced by the Hohenstaufens in the form of King Henry I, crowned at Palermo in 1194. Henry was however better known as Holy Roman Emperor, having been crowned thus in Rome in 1191. Henry therefore ruled Italy to the north and south of the Papal States, something that made the papacy jolly uncomfortable in the context of the ongoing general dispute between the empire and the popes that was the Investiture Crisis from 1130 – essentially who had the power to appoint bishops, emperor or pope. By the mid thirteenth century, the conflict had been renewed between the much-excommunicated Frederick II and a succession of popes. Upon Frederick's death in 1250, having been declared *Antichristi* by Pope Innocent IV, the papacy sought to detach the kingdom from the empire by installing their own king. They ultimately brought an end to Hohenstaufen rule by introducing the brother of the sainted Louis of France, Charles d'Anjou as king. Charles was king of Sicily at the invitation of Pope Urban IV, the vacant kingdom having been previously offered to Edward's brother Edmund. This so called 'Sicilian affair' had been partly the cause of the recent baronial war in England. In short, not only did the expansionist Capetians now hold Sicily, but they did so at the behest of the papacy. Rebellion in Sicily would be then against both Paris and Rome.

The *Vespiri siciliani* broke out as a local response to the king of Sicily's eastward expansionist policies. Charles d'Anjou was not content with being king of Sicily: he sought far greater realms but expected the poor Sicilians to fund his empire building, something they were less than keen to do. Charles had already made himself king of Albania in 1272, which together with his Italian lands began to encompass an eastern Mediterranean empire for the

French king. Charles had designs upon the Kingdom of Jerusalem[3] and the Byzantine Empire when the rebellion erupted on Sicily.

The revolt takes its name from the uprising, which began at the start of Vespers, the sunset prayer marking the beginning of the night vigil on Easter Monday, 30 March 1282, at the Chiesa dello Spirito Santo (Church of the Holy Spirit) just outside Palermo. Runciman describes the events that Easter:

> To the sound of the bells messengers ran through the city calling on the men of Palermo to rise against the oppressor. At once the streets were filled with angry armed men, crying 'Death to the French' ('moranu li Francisi' in Sicilian language). Every Frenchman they met was struck down. They poured into the inns frequented by the French and the houses where they dwelt, sparing neither man, woman nor child. Sicilian girls who had married Frenchmen perished with their husbands. The rioters broke into the Dominican and Franciscan convents; and all the foreign friars were dragged out and told to pronounce the word 'ciciri', whose sound the French tongue could never accurately reproduce. Anyone who failed the test was slain … By the next morning some two thousand French men and women lay dead; and the rebels were in complete control of the city.[4]

Sicily had been ripe for rebellion, Charles had set foot their but once in all the years of his rule; he had made French not Italian the official language, and since he did not recognise his predecessors as legitimate kings, he had confiscated much land.[5] King Peter III of Aragon was married to Constance, daughter of the last Hohenstaufen to rule Sicily, Manfred, and Béatrice de Savoie, the daughter of the late Amédée IV de Savoie – Peter thought he had claim to the island on behalf of his wife. King Peter III of Aragon arrived on Sicily on 30 August, landing at Trapani, before moving on to be installed as the island's new king three days later in Palermo. Beleaguered Charles vacated the island but retained the kingdom's lands on the mainland, the two daggers now drawn across the straits of Messina.[6]

Receiving this news, Edward realised he had a problem developing. He understood from Henri de Grandson, the Bishop of Verdun, who had previously been in England with his brother serving as a priest in Greystoke, near Penrith in Cumberland, that an alliance of pope and king of France would soon be formed against the King Peter III of Aragon with Sicily as the prize. Worse perhaps for Edward was that Peter of Aragon's wife Constance, in addition to being the daughter of Manfred of the Hohenstaufen line, as we saw, was a daughter of Béatrice de Savoie, making her a granddaughter of Amédeé IV de Savoie. Worse still that Edward's daughter Eleanor was betrothed to be married to Peter's son Alfonso. This Sicilian broth threatened a mix of Aragonese, Hohenstaufen, Capetian, and Savoyard interests becoming enmeshed with Edward. The rebellion and potential conflict threatened to reopen the once-closed contest between Hohenstaufen and papacy – the ghost of Frederick II had come back to haunt the popes and the Capetians. As in later centuries a local conflict had the distinct potential for developing into a wider European conflagration, the distinct possibility that it might suck in England. After all Edward, in addition to being king of England held Gascony as a fief of the king of France and as such might be obliged to offer him military support in that capacity in any war with Aragon. On the other hand, Edward, on behalf of Gascony, had through years of diplomacy sought good relations with his neighbours across the Pyrenees, something his marriage to Leonor of Castile had successfully achieved. So, the Sicilian Vespers threatened to put Edward at odds with his Aragonese neighbours and Savoyard family on one side and his Capetian suzerain for Gascony on the other. It would pit his suzerain against his potential father-in-law. Indeed in 1282 and again in 1283, the French king did summon his Gascon vassal, the king of England, to provide forces for an upcoming French assault on Aragon.[7] Edward, a monarch reputed as a warrior king, had much to gain from keeping the warring kingdoms apart. Indeed, before even the Vespers had erupted, on 19 February 1282, Edward had had to send Jean de Grailly and Maurice de Craon to Philippe to excuse him from providing assistance due as Duc d'Aquitaine in an ongoing Capetian dispute with Castile.[8]

Events took on a farcical nature when Charles and Peter agreed to fight it out in a duel, backed by some one hundred knights. The Aragonese and Capetians chose Plantagenet Bordeaux as the venue for their duel placing Edward as Duke of Aquitaine right and centre. He appointed his seneschal Jean de Grailly to make arrangements. The appointed day of 1 June 1283 arrived; however, Charles and Peter arrived at different times for the event, saw the other was not present and left claiming victory. The real victor appeared to be Peter having been proclaimed king in Palermo and despite him and Sicily having been placed under interdict by pro-Capetian Pope Martin, went on to defeat Charles in battle, a real battle this time. What is more, Martin's preference for king, Charles's son (another Charles) was taken prisoner by Peter. We should remember at this point that the young, imprisoned Charles was Edward's cousin. Worse for Edward, his putative father-in-law was now under papal interdict, putting a hold over a marriage between Eleanor and Alfonso.

However, events subsequently concluded in a less than usual way, that is all combatants dying of natural causes. First, on his way to campaign in Sicily, Charles d'Anjou, King Charles I of Sicily (aka King of Naples and of Albania and of Jerusalem) passed away on 7 January 1285 at Foggia within his Kingdom of Naples. Then the pope, the French Martin IV departed this life on 2 April 1285. Then King Philippe III of France died at Perpignan on 5 October 1285 while trying to bring the Aragonese to battle – making him the second French king in succession, after his father Louis IX, to die of illness amid a failing army. Last King Peter III of Aragon was to die on 11 November 1285 at Vilafranca del Penedès.

The death of Charles d'Anjou would also mark the passing of the last of the four kings married by the famous four daughters of Provence – Louis, Charles, Henry, and Richard were now all gone, leaving behind just Alianor in England and Marguerite in France to grieve their husbands.

Edward would have to ensure that their successors, Pope Honorius IV, King Philippe IV of France, and King Alfonso III of Aragon also wanted peace. King Alfonso III of Aragon was crowned at Zaragoza on 9 April 1286, his brother King James II was crowned in Palermo, Sicily, while King Philippe IV of France had been crowned at Reims Cathedral on 6 January 1286. (Fig 1.7) This new king of France would eventually come to blows with Edward and the papacy, American historian Elizabeth A. R. Brown would describe him well as 'humourless, stubborn, aggressive and vindictive'.[9] The necessity of Edward paying him homage for Gascony presented the opportunity for a trip to France as peacemaker. But not before Edward had sent Othon ahead as his proctor and thence to Rome to press the new pope, who had come to Peter's throne on 2 April 1285, toward the peace table. This new pope, chosen after a short conclave, was an Italian, of an influential Roman family, Giacomo Savelli he would reign as the aforementioned Honorius IV. Although an Italian and not a Frenchman he responded to James's coronation in Palermo and entreaties of homage by excommunicating the Aragonese. Things were not going to be easy in Rome, Othon left England in December 1285 accompanied by Henry Cobham and a good deal of funds provide by the Riccardi di Lucca.[10] It would seem they were joined by Othon's oft-noted companion Jean de Vesci, as Honorius is recorded as making provision for them both to have a portable altar while at the Curia; the sensitive nature of Othon's diplomacy is further noted as requiring a 'discreet' 'confessor' – such were the trappings of medieval diplomacy.[11]

There is also a record of Othon's embassy to Rome at this point that touches upon the character of the knight from Savoy. The chronicler of Vale Royal Abbey wrote:

> Now there was at that time with the King a good and holy man, and a most strenuous knight in arms, named Otto de Grandison, whose memory be blessed for ever. Once he was sent as ambassador to the Apostolic see touching the business of the kingdom. And when he arrived there, led, I believe, by the inspiration of the Holy Ghost, he obtained from Pope Honorius IV the appropriation of the church of Kyrkham to the monastery of Vale Royal for ever. And when he returned to England, after having favourably accomplished all the King's business, he most devoutly gave to the abbot of Vale Royal the bull of the said church of Kyrkham. And the abbot, on his side, mindful of such great benefits, and considering that he held no knights in his own pay, offered a not inconsiderable quantity of gold and silver to the aforenamed knight. But he, preferring to be rewarded by God rather than by man, utterly refused to accept these things as vanities. Wherefore the abbot, with the unanimous consent of his convent, determined and decreed that the memory of the said knight should be specially preserved and cared for in the said monastery for ever. And for that reason, the deeds of that knight are recorded here, that thereby those who shall come in the monastery may be induced to pray without ceasing that he may receive an eternal reward in heaven for all his labour here on earth.[12]

Meanwhile, on 13 May 1286, Edward sailed from Dover to Wissant and thence, with no small baggage train, travelled first to Amiens where he duly paid homage to Philippe le Bel (the name he would be best known by in France) with the wording, 'I become your man for the lands which I hold overseas, according to the terms of the peace made between our ancestors' – that peace of course being the Treaty of Paris in 1259 and the ancestors being Henry III and Louis IX.[13]

An interesting name fleetingly appears once more at this point, Aigueblanche, in the form of a Jean d'Aigueblanche who accompanies Edward. The passing of Pierre d'Aigueblanche, Bishop of Hereford, in 1268 had not seen the end of Savoyard influence in Hereford, for from 1278 Jean had been the Dean of the Chapter of Hereford Cathedral. Interestingly, the accounts for Philippe de Savoie for 1272 describe him as '*archidiaconi*' and note a payment of eighteen *sol* and six *den* paid from Savoyard coffers – we are not told for what service.[14] Perhaps it related to Edward's crusade or his visit in 1273 to Savoy; in any case Mathew Paris would not have approved.[15] From Amiens the two kings, one also as Duc d'Aquitaine, travelled on to Paris. Edward was successful in negotiating a truce between France and Aragon, the ceasefire so to speak to last until March 1287, thus providing a breathing space to negotiate a more lasting peace. Philippe agreed to Edward playing mediator between himself and Aragon.[16]

Edward and Leonor stayed for two months in Paris, hospitality being provided by the *Abbaye Saint-Germain-des-Prés* on the left bank, less than a mile from Philippe's *Palais de la Cité*. After five months of negotiation in Rome, Othon and Jean de Vesci returned to Edward at Saint-Germain. On arrival in Paris, they would learn of the truce having been achieved. Edward despatched envoys back to Rome to ask Honorius to confirm the truce, this time not Othon; after all he had only just returned from Italy, and this time his fellow countryman, and former clerk to his brother Henri de Grandson would go, the Vaudois Raoul d'Allaman.[17]

A potential sticking point in any longer-term peace going forward, was Charles of Salerno the son of Charles d'Anjou, and as such Edward's cousin, who was being held by the Aragonese. To negotiate a permanent end to the Sicilian problem Edward and entourage journeyed south from Paris to Gascony in July 1286. En route we should add that he visited the abbey at Fontevraud in his ancestral lands of Anjou to visit the tombs of his great-uncle Richard and great-great-grandparents Henry and Eleanor. Gascony, the home of Master Bertram and Jean de Mésoz, was the rump of the Angevin empire in France encompassing the lands south and west of the Garonne and Dordogne rivers. It was a relatively underdeveloped region by medieval standards, being mountainous in many parts, but it did lend itself, as now, to the cultivation of the grape and so the production of wine – some 80,000 tuns of wine being exported annually through Bordeaux. The land of the English crown had been twice extended in Edward's reign as he sought to restore at least some of his great-grandfather's lands. In 1279 he had negotiated the addition of the Agenais, a large region to the east of Gascony centred upon Agen. The visit to Paris had yielded yet more territory in return for paying homage, this time the Saintonge, lands to the north of the Garonne up to the Charente. Edward was to spend the next three years in Gascony – his longest visit. Indeed, Edward and Leonor would, venturing south from Fontevraud, spend time in the Saintonge, where they spent all of September and October before following the Dordogne to the newly built (1270) bastide of Libourne,[18] near Saint-Émilion and Pomerol, where the wine remains among the finest to be had to this day. By 15 November they had reached the newly reacquired Agen before finally reaching Gascony itself.

Jean de Vesci was sent as an ambassador to Aragon to see Alfonso which resulted in a meeting between Edward and Alfonso in July 1287 at Oloron-Sainte-Marie. The ensuing festivities in the Gascon sun included Edward, Alfonso, but also Edward's familiar entourage: Guillaume de Valence, Henri de Lacy, Jean de Vesci, and the Savoyards Jean de Grailly and Othon de Grandson. It would be with Othon's advice of a treaty that might meet with approval in Rome that the Treaty of Oloron was agreed. Events turned a little surreal once more when the two met – Edward had brought along a lion as a gift, which promptly escaped and ate a horse. Alfonso had brought along two Saracens, who used the summit meeting as a means of escape. Alfonso made a harsh peace, which promised the release of Charles of Salerno for a significant sum of money (50,000 marks).[19] What is more, in return for his freedom Charles was to send three of his sons and sixty noblemen of Provence as hostages to his good behaviour. Failure to complete a lasting peace within three years would result in the forfeiture of Provence to which Aragon also had claim.[20] Perhaps surprisingly Edward acceded to Alfonso's demands but the want of papal blessing delayed peace – Honorius IV died on 3 April 1287 having occupied Peter's throne for only two years.[21] The Aragonese were in a strong position as not only had the pope died, but a papal invasion of Sicily that spring of 1287 had ended in disaster.[22] Also employed by Edward as an envoy between France, Aragon and Honorius had been a Savoyard knight latterly having the charge of the Château de Marmande in the Agenais – Aymon de Joulens. The little village of Joulens near Morges by

Lac Léman no longer exists, long ago swallowed by the commune of Marcelin, itself a suburb now of Morges. Aymon de Joulens would later be used by Edward as liaison with Amédée V de Savoie, lately of the English army in Wales.[23]

A witness to the war had been an envoy from the Mongol ilkhanate, Rabban Bar Sauma, who finding no pope in Rome, travelled to meet Philippe le Bel in Paris and Edward and Othon in Gascony where he arrived in the autumn of 1287. He would meet there an Edward who would have recently taken the cross once more and so receptive to ideas of crusade.

We will return to crusading plans later but meanwhile to continue with the Sicilian matter ar hand which was proving an impediment to them. A new pope, another Italian, Jerome of Ascoli reigning as Nicholas IV, came to the throne of Saint Peter in February 1288 and immediately condemned the treaty. Philippe IV also resisted the Treaty of Oloron; after all, the Capetians had spent so long acquiring Provence they were not prepared to put it back into the melting pot.[24] Charles of Salerno meanwhile languished in prison.

Nonetheless Nicholas, apparently alarmed that the struggle destabilised Western Europe at a time of renewed danger to the Holy Land, asked Edward to once more mediate.[25] So, in October 1288, a new treaty was agreed at Canfranc, but with no less Carthaginian terms. But this time, to ensure the release of Charles of Salerno and a prospect of ending the whole affair, the English crown agreed to pay 30,000 marks as a contribution to the total required for ransom of Charles and agreed to hand over some seventy-six English and Gascon hostages in place of the Provençals as a pledge of his subsequent good behaviour. As before the freed Charles was asked to prevail upon Philippe in Paris to extend the truce to a three-year armistice pending a long-term solution. Pledging himself for Edward was Othon's cousin Pierre de Champvent. Among the knights going over to the Aragonese as hostages was Jean de Vesci and the Justiciar of North Wales, Othon de Grandson.[26] Jean and Othon were old comrades from their days fighting their way from Anglesey to Caernarfon and Harlech back in the recent Welsh war. Most of the hostages were kept at Jaca in the foothills of the Pyrenees; however, Clifford was confident that 'Othon, because of his importance, was one of those who was sent down to the capital' of Zaragoza.[27] Given the lack of primary sources in Aragon we have no way to be certain, but Clifford's suggestion appears more likely than unlikely. Othon eventually spent his time as hostage without his long-time companion Jean de Vesci, as the latter was allowed to travel with Edward. As a valuable hostage Grandson is likely to have been held at Zaragoza, another former Roman city to add to his travels. Almoravid Zaragoza had only been conquered by Aragon and made the capital in the previous century, 1118, and so remained very much a Moorish city. It had become once more a place of pilgrimage: *Santa Maria del Pilar*, or Our Lady of Pilar, had attracted pilgrims taken with the notion that the yet living Mary had miraculously appeared to James the Greater in AD 40 whilst he was in Spain, and to that end a Romanesque cathedral was growing where the later cathedral now stands. Having visited Nazareth and Canterbury, the pious Othon was continuing his tour of places of thirteenth-century devotion. Indeed, Othon, with his experience of the Holy Land would not have felt quite so out of place in Moorish Spain than he had done in North Wales. Being a hostage of Alfonso was not apparently a troubling experience; he was allotted two guards who travelled with him, but although he had to return to lodgings on a nightly basis, he was free to hunt.[28] Charles of Salerno was duly freed and by Easter of 1289 Grandson was once more in Gascony.[29]

Othon was reunited with his cousin Pierre de Champvent, but Edward and Pierre would have given Othon unwelcome news: the passing of Edward's faithful servant and Othon de Grandson's comrade in arms Jean de Vesci. Although not a Savoyard himself, he had married into the family so to speak through his first wife Agnès de Saluzzo, a relative of both Alianor de Provence and Pierre de Savoie. He passed away at Montpellier in February 1289. Leonor de Castille travelled to Oloron-Saint-Marie to collect his body. She arranged for it to be sent taken back to England with great care, and he was buried at Alnwick Abbey in Northumberland.[30] So passed a man, who along with Grandson, commanded the army that had crossed the Menai Straits from Anglesey and been the first to see the site of the future castles at Caernarfon and then Harlech. The once-rebellious Vesci had fought alongside Montfort at Evesham and rebelled once more soon afterward, and yet Edward had offered clemency, which Vesci had rewarded with a life of service. Edward, Leonor, Vesci, and Grandson had been close friends, and had had many adventures together, but these were now beginning to draw to a close. His old friend and comrade of many battles, Grandson was an executor of his will.[31]

Also absent was Jean de Grailly, who had been removed from his position as seneschal sometime between the king's arrival and the spring of 1287. The trial had included Jean de Vesci, Henri de Lacy and Othon de Grandson, before his sojourn in Spain. An inquiry by the queen had found financial irregularities; Guillaume de Middleton, before the court of Gascogne, declared that the seneschal Jean de Grailly had misappropriated royal rights of justice in Saint-Emillion and its environs. Consequently, Jean de Grailly was condemned to restore what he had attributed to himself without rights and to the confiscation of all his lands and possessions in Guyenne. In fact, the limits of the jurisdiction of Castillon were blurred and Jean de Grailly had abused these imprecisions. Grailly returned first to Savoy before going on to find employment with the new French king, Philippe IV. Edward left John de Havering as the new seneschal of Gascony, but his tenure there would not be a happy one, resulting in yet another Gascon crisis and yet another crisis in Anglo-French relations.

Meanwhile joining Jean de Grailly in the service of the king of France leads us to bad news that year coming from Outremer. Edward's crusading adversary Baibars had died in 1277, the summer that Edward was himself engaged in his first Welsh war. Baibars had firstly been succeeded by his son Al-said Barakah, but he had soon been replaced by al-Mansūr Qālawūn, whom we shall henceforth know as Qālawūn.[32] The period of dynastic struggle in Egypt that followed the passing of Baibars might have brought Outremer respite and afforded the West a chance to strengthen their hand in the Levant – if such an opportunity existed it was one they did not take. Following the fall of the Principality of Antioch and earlier the County of Edessa, Outremer consisted of the County of Tripoli and the rump of the Kingdom of Jerusalem at Acre. When Qālawūn took the reins in Cairo, he kept treaties with what remained of Outremer, albeit heavily on his terms, but Outremer was living on borrowed time. The catalyst for the end came from an external source, a threat to both the crusader states and Muslims from the east – from Mongolia.

Back in 1255 Hülagü, a grandson of Genghis Khan, had sought to further expand the Mongol Empire into the Middle East under orders from his older brother, the Great Khan Möngke. Hülagü's forces subjugated many peoples along the way, most notably the centre of the Islamic Empire, Baghdad, which was completely sacked in 1258. But the threat to Muslim lands had ended for the moment with their defeat of Hülagü's commander Kitbuga at Ayn Jālūt on 3 September 1260. Arghūn, the new Ilkhan now tried once more to complete the conquest of the Middle East, and by some form of alliance with the West and crusader states. To this end, back in 1287 he had sent the aforementioned Rabban Bar Sauma on an embassy to Western Europe, meeting with Rome,[33] the Byzantine Emperor Andronikos II Palaiologos, the King Philippe IV of France and King Edward I of England (while Edward was in Gascony) along the way.[34] Sauma was an exotic fellow to meet Edward and Othon in Gascony, a Uyghur or Ongud monk of the Nestorian church of China, he had begun his journey west from what is now Beijing and the court of Kublai Khan before becoming an ambassador for Arghūn. As we saw and shall see again it is quite likely that Othon met Marco Polo, but to that we can add Rabban Bar Sauma to his list of meetings – that Othon de Grandson of thirteenth century Vaud might meet a traveller from Beijing is in and of itself remarkable. The flavour of the meeting between Sauma has survived in translation from Syriac by Wallia Budge

> And they went forth from that place, that is to say, from Paris, to go to the king of England, to Kasonia [Gascony]. And having arrived in twenty days at their city, the inhabitants of the city [Bordeaux] went forth to meet them, and they asked them, 'Who are ye? And Rabban Sauma and his companions replied, 'We are ambassadors, and we have come from beyond the eastern seas, and we are envoys of the King, and of the Patriarch, and the Kings of the Mongols.' And the people made haste and went to the king and informed him [of their arrival], and the king welcomed them gladly, and the people introduced them into his presence. And those who were with Rabban Sauma straightway gave to the king the *Pukdana* [i.e. letter of authorisation] of King Arghūn, and the gifts which he had sent to him, and the Letter of Mar Catholicus. And [King Edward] rejoiced greatly, and he was especially glad when Rabban Sauma talked about the matter of Jerusalem. And he said, 'We the kings of these cities bear upon our bodies the sign of the Cross, and we have no subject of thought except this matter. And my mind is relieved on the subject about which I have been thinking, when I hear that King Arghūn thinketh as I think.' And the king commanded Rabban Sauma to celebrate the Eucharist, and he performed the Glorious Mysteries; and the king and his officers of state stood up, and the king partook of the Sacrament, and made a great feast that day. Then Rabban Sauma said unto the king, 'We beseech thee, O king, to give [thy servants] in order to show us whatever churches and shrines there are in this country, so that when we go back to the Children of the East, we may give them descriptions of them.' And the king replied, ìThus shall ye say to King Arghūn and unto all the Orientals: We have seen a thing than which there is nothing more wonderful, that is to say, that in the countries of the Franks there are not two Confessions of Faith, but only one Confession of Faith, namely, that which confesseth Jesus Christ; and all the Christians confess it.' And King Edward gave us many gifts and money for the expenses of the road.[35]

After meeting Sauma at Saint-Sever, Edward, amid the Sicilian business which might threaten Gascony, and with news of the Rhys ap Maredudd rebellion in Wales could only show enthusiasm but make no immediate commitment to go east, only give him gifts and send Sauma back to Rome to meet with the then new Pope Nicholas IV. News of the Rhys ap Maredudd rebellion may well have also brought news of the death of Grandson's kinsman, Jean de Bonvillars,

Constable of Harlech Castle, believed perished under a collapsed mine during the siege of Dryslwyn castle in 1287.[36]

A letter following this embassy from Arghūn to Philippe IV survives and illustrates the attempted alliance, in translation it reading: 'If you send your warriors as promised and conquer Egypt, worshipping the sky, then I shall give you Jerusalem. If any of our warriors arrive later than arranged, all will be futile, and no one will benefit.'[37]

The enemy of my enemy is my friend as the old adage goes, and it is this reaching out once more between Mongol and Christian that sent Jean de Grailly to Outremer on behalf of the king of France, and that made Qālawūn wish to finally eliminate any residual threat from the crusader states by extinguishing them completely. As Runciman wrote, 'Had the Mongol alliance been achieved and honestly implemented by the West, the existence of Outremer would almost certainly have been prolonged.'[38] – but it was not to be so.

In April 1285 Qālawūn had marched against the formidable castle of the Knights Hospitaller at Margat, within the lands of the County of Tripoli, to punish the knights for their earlier support for the Mongols. After a thirty-eight-day siege, during which sappers and miners managed to dig several tunnels underneath the castle walls, a mine destroyed a salient of the southernmost wall. The defenders panicked and on discovering the numerous tunnels around the fortress, surrendered to the Mamluk commander Fakhr al-Din Mukri on 23 May, with Qālawūn entered Margat two days later. Margat like the Krak des Chevalliers before, it been a pillar upon which Tripoli stood. Margat also guarded the road from Tripoli north to Latakia, and so accordingly in 1287 Latakia also fell to Qālawūn – the noose around Tripoli was tightening – hence the despatch of Jean de Grailly to Acre. The West was beginning to finally fear for Outremer.

Qālawūn was at this time still bound by treaty with Tripoli, but a succession in 1288 following the death of Bohemond VII gave him the pretext he needed for decisive action. Elements within Tripoli sought Genoese help in the succession, some in Acre feared Genoese encroachment and warned Qālawūn that a firm, stronger Genoese base in the Levant might be a threat to him too. We cannot be sure that such a warning was sent from Acre to Cairo, but it does seem to fit well with the context of events. So, in March 1289, a large Mamluk army arrived at the gates of Tripoli along with attendant supply of trebuchets. Jean de Grailly marched north from Acre with the French knights under his command, Jean de Saint Oyend a fellow Vaudois was his lieutenant;[39] along with them were the Knights Templar under Geoffrey de Vendac, to attempt to forestall the onslaught.

The Mamluks fired their trebuchets and mangonels; two towers crumbled under the bombardment, and the terrified defenders hastily prepared to flee. The Mamluks soon overran the crumbling walls and captured the city on 26 April, marking the end of an uninterrupted Christian rule of 180 years, the longest of any of the major Frankish conquests in the Levant. The commander of the Temple Peter of Moncada was killed, the poor inhabitants of the city was massacred to a man, although a lucky few many managed to escape by ship. Those who had taken refuge on the nearby island of Saint-Thomas were captured by the Mamluks on 29 April. Days later the stench of the massacre at Saint-Thomas filled the air. Women and children were taken as slaves, and 1,200 pitiful prisoners were sent to Egypt and Alexandria to work in the Sultan's new arsenal.

Jean de Grailly, Edward's erstwhile seneschal of Gascony, escaped with his life to Acre. The County of Tripoli and Tripoli itself were no more – Acre rightly feared it would be next. Jean de Grailly would return to Europe, to Rome, Paris, and London to lobby for help in preventing the inevitable, imminent collapse of the last crusader foothold in the Levant – Acre. So, even as Othon was returning to Gascony that spring of 1289, there would be troubling news from the Holy Land. As news reached Edward there was only one thing to do:

he must consult with the pope, which meant having traversed the Pyrenees, Othon would be returning to Rome.

On 10 May 1289, Othon once more made for Rome, accompanied by the cleric William Hotham.[40] The journey was the one that the Savoyard knight was most familiar with: the road through the plains of France until the distant familiar outlines of the Jura came into view, on into the empire before threading his way through the mountains to his home at the Château de Grandson by Lac de Neuchâtel.

Remarkably Othon was able to spend time taking care of Vaudois business, attending to the future succession of the Bishop of Lausanne – the mitre, in 1289, was still in the hands of his cousin Guillaume de Champvent. Succession was arranged for his nephew Gérard de Vuippens, who in turn would be followed by another nephew Othon de Champvent and another Pierre d'Oron. This meant that from 1273 until 1323, the fifty years of his absence from the Pays de Vaud, the See of Lausanne was in family hands, thus in this way did Othon de Grandson take care of his lands during his time working for the English crown.[41] It is worth noting at this point, that Greystoke in the County of Cumberland, which had had the benefit of Othon's brother Henri de Grandson, now the Bishop of Verdun, would now have as parson none other than Gérard de Vuippens, who will as we just noted become the Bishop of Lausanne. So, Savoyard links with England at this time meant that a church in faraway Cumberland could, within a decade, be home to not one, but two Savoyards, both of whom would move on to important bishoprics within the empire – the thirteenth century was a most connected place. We know of Vuippens time at Greystoke, from a gift by Edward of ten oak trees for timber recorded in the Calendar of Close Rolls.[42] Gérard de Vuippens was the son of Ulrich de Vuippens and Othon de Grandson's sister Agnès; he had been born at some point between 1262 and 1267. Like many Savoyards he had moved to England, but for Vuippens it was to further a career in the Church, his first recorded position as a sub-deacon at the Benedictine Priory of Saint Leonard in Stamford before taking over as pastor at Greystoke.

Meanwhile on with the embassy to Rome. Horses rested, they made their way onward by way of Lausanne and the upper Rhône Valley to the Grand Saint-Bernard Pass, Turin, and the Papal Curia by way of the Via Emilia and Parma. We know the ambassadors took the usual route of the *Via Francigena* from the currencies that sustained them en route including *Livres Lausanneois*.[43] The journey in the summer heat took something of two months to complete. Arriving in July, one must pause at this point to reflect that Othon had lately arrived back in England from Spain and Gascony before making this new trek across the mountains and would be soon called upon to return to the Holy Land – for a knight now in his middle years this was some feat of endurance beyond most of us in the twenty-first century. A full account of the embassy has survived and was transcribed in the nineteenth century and is the source of all subsequent accounts.[44] The account relates the sheer complexity of organising an embassy of two individuals to travel in the thirteenth century from Edward's court to the Papal Curia. Some sixty or more horses are required to convey all those concerned on their thousand miles of journey. The alpine crossing needs special horses suited to the task and accompanying guides. These strings of horses winding their way up the mountain pass from the Rhône Valley needed shoes, fodder, saddle cloths, medication, harnesses. The men needed their own sustenance, and we know that disease struck en route: Aymon de Bonvillars and three servants died. What relation Edmund was to the late Jean and Henri in England we are not told. Another of the party, Raoul d'Allaman suffered a bout of gastroenteritis and broke an arm.

Financing of the embassy was again entrusted to the Riccardi di Lucca, the instructions sent to Labro Volpelli and his partners in Rome surviving:

> The king to his dear Labro Volpelli and his partners, citizens, and merchants of the Company of Riccardi of Lucca dwelling at the Roman Curia, greetings, and sincere affection. Since we have sent our dear secretary and faithful man, the noble Othon de Grandson, knight, to the said court, in order to expedite certain of our affairs there, we ask you that the loan which said Othon has sought be freely and securely advanced to him. And we will hold to repay fully the sum which Othon receives from you as witnessed by his letters.[45]

They arrived by mid-July only to find that a duplicitous Nicholas IV, having asked Edward to mediate at Canfranc, had on 19 June 1289 crowned the now-freed Charles of Salerno as king of Sicily and taken his homage. What is more he had granted him church tax revenues to pay for war on the Aragonese. Bartolomeo di Neocastro in his contemporary *Historio Sicula*, or *History of Sicily*, reports his version of Othon's protestations to Nicholas as:

> My lord the king of England, censures the kings who, wrangling over the realm of Sicily, are waging war, although which of them has taken up arms with greater justice, he cannot rightly determine. But in all friendliness, he is amazed that Your Paternity, by which the whole circle of the world is governed, should have suffered these kings to become embroiled in such a wicked struggle. For since the Sicilians, whether Italian or French or a mixture of the two, are all Christians, is not the Roman See to be censured? Or would you consider it wrong to put an end to as many of these disasters to your sons as possible? On the contrary, it would be acceptable to God and seem good to men if, turning the eyes of Your Holiness on the quarrelling kings, you would interpose the grace of your clemency between them, so that those whom you suffer to rage you might persuade to peace or at least admit them to a semblance of peace. For if you command, they will not disobey. And therefore, considering what perils the whole world undergoes from the dissensions of these kings and with what good reason men hold you to blame, my lord humbly prays that, so much as in you lies, you should put an end to their raging and establish a truce for two years between them and their allies, during which time my said lord together with you and the kings of France and of Castile should come to a final decision as to making a firm peace between them … For otherwise, it will not be pleasing to you, Holy Father, if the princes of the earth and indeed all Christian men, hearing of your wanton provocation of those whom, however unwillingly, you allow to fight when you might benignly make peace between them, treat you as an enemy of our universal Mother and of the Christian faith, even though they still pay all due regard to the honour of Mother Church. And you can be sure that when all the others are fighting you, my Lord will not be the last to take up arms against such perfidy, lest he too shall be undone.[46]

Neocastro misattributed this admonishment of the papacy to a 'Hugo' but it is indubitably Othon, although the actual words may well have been given a literate flow by the Sicilian chronicler of verse. Nonetheless, Nicholas agreed and appointed Othon to accompany a papal legate to travel to Gaeta in Lazio which King James of Sicily was besieging. Othon's negotiations proved successful and a truce between the competing kings of Sicily, Charles, and James, was renewed.[47] By November Grandson was back in Rome, but while the Western Europeans squabbled over Sicily the last foothold in the Levant, Acre, was now in mortal danger.

Pope Nicholas and the Curia received news of the fall of Tripoli. In September 1289 Henry II, King of Jerusalem at Acre, of the Lusignan clan, had despatched Jean de Grailly, who as we saw had fled Tripoli, to Europe to plea for help. Henry had succeeded in negotiating a further truce with Mamluk Qālawūn but following the massacre at Tripoli he no longer trusted the sultan. On 1 September 1289 he had reached Rome where Nicholas charged him to take twenty galleys with him to aid the defence of Acre. In Rome too was Buscarello de Ghizolfi, another envoy of the Mongol Arghūn, seeking alliance against the Mamluks, his mission proceeding to Paris in November. Buscarello then travelled to England to bring Arghūn's message to Edward, arriving in London on 5 January 1290 and remaining thirteen days at court.[48] This would be Edward's second meeting with a Mongol envoy. Edward answered enthusiastically to the project but deferred the decision about the date to the pope. The pope's Jean de Grailly-inspired expedition, meanwhile, was already in Outremer the summer of 1290, probably landing under the command of Nicholas Tiepolo, the son of the former Doge of Venice, Lorenzo Tiepolo, on 2 April 1290.[49]

Othon, meanwhile, was back in England from Rome by 8 March 1290. There was news of Outremer, the truce agreed for Sicily, but also no progress on the marriage of his daughter to Alfonso of Aragon due to the ongoing interdict, but he did have news of permission for Edward's son to marry the new queen of Scotland, the young Maid of Norway, for that's where she was living. The latter papal grant would begin a chain of events as momentous in Britain as the news from the Middle East. But, in Spring 1290 both Edward and Othon turned their thoughts once more to crusade,

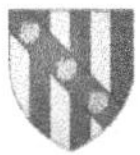

CHAPTER 9

Despite renewed clouds of war swirling around Sicily, Edward renewed plans for a possible crusade.

Edward had not forgotten Acre and the Holy Land. His time as king had been taken up with attending to domestic issues in north Wales and the outfall from the Sicilian Vespers but the 1287 visit of Bar Sauma to Gascony had brought crusade more firmly back on to the agenda. Edward had been in discussion Pope Martin IV in 1284 in terms of taking up the cross once more, but Sicily had intervened.[1] Edward had taken up the cross again in 1287, although the place and date are lost.[2]

As we saw Edward's crusade plans continued to involve Grandson as they were high on the agenda of the Grandson Hotham mission to Rome of 1289–90. Pope Nicholas IV had accordingly set the date for Edward's crusade ar June 1292, subsequently altered by Edward until June 1293.[3]

One of the lessons that Edward had learned in his time in Acre was the futility of making grand plans in London, Paris, or Rome for operations in Outremer without first having an accurate picture of the local political and military situation on the ground – in other words without a thorough reconnaissance. To this end it appears that he had decided first to send a small force commanded by a trusty lieutenant to carry out said reconnaissance – that trusty lieutenant would be of course Othon de Grandson. Whenever Edward needed representation as if he himself were there, then he always trusted his loyal friend and envoy.

That Othon was carrying out a crusade reconnaissance for his master has lately been called into question by the esteemed crusade historian Forey.[4] Historians since Kingsford, who wrote that Othon with overtones of John the Baptist was 'to prepare the way for the kings own coming'[5] have taken the crusade reconnaissance view. Esteemed crusade historian Christopher Tyerman has supported, though with more caveats Kingsford's theme, writing: 'the despatch of agents to reconnoitre both friend and foe in the east was a regular feature of western crusade operations.'[6]

Tyerman went on to add 'The expedition of Otho of Grandson to the east was the most tangible assistance that Edward gave to the Holy Land after his second assumption of the cross'.[7] Forey's questioning of this orthodoxy rests firstly upon it largely being based upon narrative sources rather than royal sources. Among these narrative sources is the writer of the *Excidium Acconis* who spoke of '*Oto de Grandisono miles, ex parte regis Anglie cum quibusdam aliis in subsidium terre sancte destinatus*', that is, 'Othon de Grandson, a knight, on the part of the King of England with some others destined for the support of the holy land'.[8] Back in England the London chronicler of the *Annales Londonienses* also wrote, '*Otho de Grandissono adivit Jerosolimam ad providentiam domini Edwardi regis Angliæ faciendam,*' that is, 'Othon de Grandson went to Jerusalem to make provision for Lord Edward, King of England.'[9] The chronicler of Guisborough added, '*Othone de Grandisono, qui cum thesauris*

Regis Angliæ ibidem missus ut viam pararet' or 'Othon de Grandson, who was sent thither with the treasures of the King of England to prepare the way'.[10] So, we have three chroniclers, two in England, one overseas, suggesting clearly this was king's errand, albeit Guisborough's is attached to his discredited accusation of Grandson's conduct at Acre and should be thus treated with caution. Forey suggests they may have been misled by the obvious impression that the king's closest envoy was working for the king, an impression given to historians ever since.

Forey suggests the royal sources point toward a private venture rather than some form of preparation for Edward. In a letter related to Othon's custody of the Channel Islands, recorded in the Gascon Rolls, Edward speaks of Othon staying '*in Dei obsequio in Terra sancta de nostra licencia et vo luntate*', that is, staying 'in the obedience of God in the Holy Land by our leave and free will'.[11] That reference to '*licencia*' or 'by our leave' is taken to point away from a similar role given to William de Henleye who, travelling with Grandson, is specifically referred to as an envoy.[12] These are good points – royal accountants and scribes could be as imprecise as chroniclers in their wording. I have in previous books, including *Welsh Castle Builders: The Savoyard Style*, insisted upon the exactitude of English scribes, referring to the builders of castles in north Wales; however, the writer of *Excidium* can only have got the impression of Othon's acting on behalf of Edward from the way Othon acted while in Acre, and the London and Guisborough chroniclers from the impression left at court in England. What is more, Forey in suggesting that when the Calendar of Documents Related to Scotland, mentions 'Otto de Grandison, who is in the K.'s service in the Holy Land' is in error, one is given to suppose that we may be looking at records to fit a thesis selectively.[13]

Forey does, however, accept that it was more likely Othon travelled east to fight rather than to pray. But to his central idea of a private errand, we must consider this, that it would represent the first time in his long service to the crown that he had acted on his own behalf rather than his master's – in short, out of character. The notion that Othon was acting at the behest of Edward is not only founded on what we know of Othon's character but also of Edward's, that is that he often learned well the lessons of life. After his failure at Lewes, he was sure to fight his Welsh wars in a sure and methodical way; after seeing how his uncle's castle at Pevensey withstood a year-long siege by being sited by the sea, he was sure to build his Welsh castles by the sea. The crusade of the Lord Edward must surely have taught him that it was foolish to arrive in the Holy Land unprepared, as he had done and indeed his uncle Louis had done. Far better, surely, to send your most trusted servant to report back on the strengths and weaknesses of the crusader position, the politics, the possible alliances to be made. We may never know for certain. Forey's suggestion is ultimately based on absence of evidence, that is Edward not spelling out his mission in the royal records, but we should not treat absence of evidence as evidence of absence. Forey's challenge to the traditional narrative is interesting but ultimately unprovable. In summary Forey may be right, but I find the absence of evidence not persuasive and the orthodox idea of a reconnaissance mission more in line with what we know of Edward's employment, before and after 1290, of Grandson.

So, Othon de Grandson prepared for the journey to Acre even as the bells of Westminster Abbey peeled for the weddings of Edward's daughters, Joan and Margaret. Archbishop Peckham preached and Grandson '*recuperunt crucem*' took up the cross once more.[14] On 10 June 1290 he granted the power of attorney to his brother Guillaume and to Henri de Bonvillars, brother of Jean de Bonvillars and the Prior of Wenlock.[15] Henri de Bonvillars 'going overseas for a year' nominated Brother James de Cosseneye as his attorney, the toponym being with reasonable certainty Cossonay in the *Pays de Vaud.*[16] Also dated 10 June 1290 a writ of 'Protection with cause *Volumus'* was issued at Westminster for three years to Othon.[17] In effect this meant that the crown would give protection to Othon's lands and people while he was away from England, and of course a breach of the king's protection was not to be undertaken lightly. We know of the names of at least some of his English companions, Hugh de Brok and William le Lange, who were given similar kingly protection.[18] A further fellow traveller and described as the 'king's envoy' was William de Henleye, Prior of the Hospital of Saint John of Jerusalem.[19] Another with the party was William de Cestria, one of Edward's chaplains and a trained lawyer involved in the new valuation of all benefices; others mentioned include Alexander de Esselington, Robert de Nevil, Gérard de Freyneyr and Simon le Taillur (both described as king's yeomen), Robert de Cadbury (Canon of St. Andrews in Wells), Hugh Fitz John, Edmund de Trop and Ralph de Waddon.[20] We can deduce that Grandson led the party, since the others were described as 'going with' him.[21] Also going with the English party were his Savoyard nephews Pierre de Vuippens and Pierre d'Estavayer.[22] Given there was a very real chance they might not return, and being young men without heirs, Grandson was careful to provide that lands he had just passed to them might go to other nephews upon their death – something that would sadly come to pass.[23] His cousin, the recently out-of-favour Pierre de Champvent, the boy who had long ago travelled with the young Othon for the first time to England and served Henry as a steward, remained with Edward's household also as a steward.[24]

Setting his affairs in order, after all a journey to Outremer was more than hazardous, Grandson disposed of some of his responsibilities in the British Isles. Dated 17 May 1290 we see the last reference to his being Justiciar of North Wales, a position he had in any case been largely absent from whilst lately in Gascony and Spain.[25] On 14 June at Westminster, he reached an agreement with Richard de Burgh, Earl of Ulster, for the leasing of Irish lands in Estremoy and Otheney.[26] Further, an *inspeximus* or confirmation of an earlier charter was issued 3 July relating to Othon, conferring lands he held in Ireland on his nephews Pierre de Vupplens and Pierre d'Estavayer.[27] Estavayer had been a household knight of Edward's, his home being on the eastern shore of Lac de Neuchâtel not quite across from Grandson itself. The brother of Pierre d'Estavayer, the cleric Guiilame, was at this time elevated by Pope Nicholas IV to the position of archdeacon in the great cathedral at Lincoln after having previously held a prebend in the county.[28] These lands held in Ireland, granted to Pierre d'Estavayer, of the king's grant by service of two knights' fees, included the castle, centred and land of Hokonagh, the town of Tipperary, the castle and town of Kilfecle [Kilfeacle], the land of Muskery [Muskerry], the manor of Kilsylam, the town of Clonmel, and the land of Estremoye – Othon was said to be Sheriff of Tipperary and the Lord of the Manor of Clonmel. Passing on such land in his absence is suggestive of a man setting his affairs in order – sad to consider then that his nephew Pierre de Vuippens would not return. Finance for the expedition was 3,000 marks, courtesy of a loan taken by the king from Lapus Bouchi, Gradus Pini and other merchants of the society of Amanati in Pistoia, Tuscany, Italy – an acknowledgement of the debt to the Italians is dated 13 July 1290: 'received by the hands of Othon de Grandson, to whom the King has given it in aid of his journey to Jerusalem'.[29] To set this in context 3,000 marks or £2,000 equates to almost £1.5 million in today's money – quite a sum to be 'received by the hands'.[30]

Also financially forthcoming was a grant by Archbishop of York, John le Romeyn, of 'the first fruits of the archdeaconry of Richmond'. Othon's cousin, Gérard de Vuippens, had lately been a canon at York, having been pastor at Greystoke in Cumberland; he would go on, like his uncle, to be a diplomat in Edward's service and Bishop of Lausanne then Basle. The grant to Grandson coincides with his becoming an archdeacon of Richmond. An Archdeacon of Richmond was a de facto bishop, having the privileges and prerogatives of a bishop save the right to confirm and ordain. Vuippens's elevation at Richmond would not be the first Savoyard power and influence in Richmondshire, Pierre de Savoie having held the Honour of Richmond until his death in 1268 and his steward Guichard de Charron having held the castle there successfully against the Montfortians in the second baronial war. Sadly, the value of the aforementioned 'first fruits' is unknown.[31]

The crusading party included some sixty knights, Edward's likely intention being that this advance reconnaissance guard would join and take command of the English knights of Saint Thomas in Acre.[32] We also know of the route taken, firstly to Paris, where they were noted by 18 July.[33] Then on to Vaud where Othon donated, from his revenues at Salins-les-Bains in the Franche Comté, to the priory church of Saint-Jean de Baptiste at Grandson, something that illustrates the perilous nature of his journey and task, the donation bears the surviving seal of Othon de Grandson and rests within the Vaudoise Cantonal Archive in Lausanne.[34] (Fig 1.9) Further prayers for a safe return will almost certainly have been offered to Notre-Dame de Lausanne in Jean Cotereel's cathedral before going forward to Rome and the Holy Land. It would not be the last times that the pious knight knelt in prayer to the Virgin Mary in the coming months. Othon was a Christian in an age of religious certainty, but also a man who viewed Mary as the Queen of Heaven, and just as his friend Leonor de Castile might intercede with Edward, he believed that Mary might intercede with God.

The donation to St. Jean read:

> for I hope, and trust to God, that through their prayers and suffrages, Blessed Mary and Saint John will see to it that my soul, after it has left my body, is presented to God, and received into Abraham's bosom. For I trust that through these prayers and because of what I hope to achieve, I shall, God willing, once I have put off this garment of flesh, deserve to gain a heavenly prize.[35]

The journey on from Vaud would have taken the group past Chillon and beneath the towering mountains into the Upper Rhône valley, a route Othon de Grandson knew well. No doubt a stop would have been made at the monastery of Saint Maurice before swinging right at La Batiâz up the Grand Saint-Bernard Pass and into Italy. Given the danger of what lay ahead perhaps each of the Savoyard took in their passing lands in the late summer sunshine, wondering if they would ever see them again. Down into the Val d'Aosta and Lombardy before the well-known route to Orvieto and the Papal Curia, arriving there by September. Their time in Rome was marked and recorded by Grandson obtaining an indulgence for the chancellor's nephew William Burnell from Nicholas IV.[36] But by mid-October they had left Rome and would take ship for Acre, but it would be a very different Acre than he had seen twenty years earlier.

The city had been a Christian city since the First Crusade, albeit with a brief interlude courtesy of Salah ad-Din between 1187 and 1191 and was home to a population of 40,000 people. Acre lay 15 miles (24 kilometres) across the bay from the city the crusaders new as Caiphas that we now call Haifa. Acre – Saint-Jean-d'Acre, the current francophone name, is perhaps a recent appellation – was a hook of land protruding from the Levantine coast into the

Mediterranean, providing a small and often choppy harbour. We have a map made between 1320 and 1325 by Italian Pietro Vesconte that allows us to reasonably describe the city.[37] The harbour itself, protected by the Tower of Flies, was divided into two, the inner harbour also benefitting from the protection of a chain. The approach to the harbour was a difficult one, passing the aptly named Cape of Storms (the southwesterly tip of Acre); a sharp turn was required to pass beneath the Tower of Flies, sandbanks awaiting the unwary seafarer. The city was surrounded on two of its three sides by water, and water controlled by the Franks – therein partly lay its longevity. To the landward side lay formidable defences, two city walls running together from the south until they parted at the Saint Anthony Gate to become three to encompass the Montsumart district. The Montsumart district had been an addition to the Old City following the recapture of Acre by Richard Cœur de Lion nearly a century earlier. Once past the L-shaped sea wall, at the very tip of the hook off to the arrivals' left as they made harbour would be the temple of The Poor Fellow-Soldiers of Christ and of the Temple of Solomon[38] – or the Knights Templar. Templar knights would have been immediately identifiable by their distinctive white mantles with a red cross. The Grand Master of the Templars that autumn was Guillaume de Beaujeu, whom Othon de Grandson would have known from his previous days in Acre. The Military Orders provided most of the manpower for the crusader states armies and were key players in politics and commerce. Tunnels ran some 430 yards (400 metres) from beneath the Templar palace under the Pisan quarter to the customs house in the harbour; such was the intimacy of the Templars' interest in the trade of the city. Of the others The Order of Knights of the Hospital of Saint John of Jerusalem[39] or Knights Hospitaller were based at their Palais des Malades or Hospital to the north of the Templars, in the Hospitaller quarter, and a hospice in the Montsumart district. The Hospitaller quarter itself encompassed the orders headquarters, their infirmary and the Church of Saint-John. The Hospitallers, whose origins were earlier than the Templars, of the Benedictine order, were identifiable by their white crosses on a scarlet[40] background. Jean de Villiers, their Grand Master since 1285, was also among the defenders of Acre.

The diverse nature of Acre would be at once obvious to the newcomers; by the inner harbour immediately adjacent to the Templars were the quarters of first the Pisans then the Genoese and the Venetians. But a sign of how that diversity might work against the city was that the Pisans and Venetians had walled off their quarters, and the Genoese had fortified the gates to theirs. Politically the city fell within the Kingdom of Jerusalem, whose name pointed toward the hope for recon quest of its former lands, but the aforesaid quarters and military orders had autonomy within their precincts. A further military order was ensconced to their right toward a turn in the city wall, The Order of Brothers of the German House of Saint Mary in Jerusalem[41] – or Teutonic Knights. The Teutonic Knights had been founded in Acre back in 1192 and were identifiable by their black crosses. Their Grand Master, Burchard von Schwanden, who was a Bernese neighbour of the Savoyards, had reluctantly joined the defenders in Acre, a city that held their headquarters. Unaccountably, Burchard von Schwanden would soon resign his position and leave the defenders – not a good sign.

Last would be the order with which Othon de Grandson was to liaise, an order which restricted its recruitment to Englishmen, The Hospitallers of St. Thomas of Canterbury at Acre – the Knights of Saint Thomas. The hospital and church of St. Thomas were to be found in the Montmusart district. On his visit to Acre, Edward had endowed the order with money to build a new church.[42] The order had, however, written to Edward in 1279 complaining of a lack of resources and apparently moves had been afoot before the new arrivals at Acre in 1290 to merge the order with the Templars. The English knights were identifiable by the emblem of the order, which was a red cross with a white scallop in the centre and the wearing of a white habit. Upon arrival, taking charge of the knights of Saint Thomas as Edward had asked, Grandson and his Anglo-Savoyard party would find just nine such knights of which to take charge.[43]

As they came ashore, perhaps the first thing to assail them would be the competing aromas of the royal slaughterhouse and fish market, the leftovers from which they would have seen floating in the harbour. Indeed, the French-speaking inhabitants of Acre called the harbour *lordemer* or filthy sea; worse for the arrivals from England the smell would have been worsened by the seasonal easterly wind then blowing combined with the still-hot weather.

Looking up from the harbour they would have seen tightly packed rooftops rising toward the city walls; the churches, including the beautiful new Gothic church of St. Andrew; houses and workshops built in the French style were the last busy crusader foothold in the Holy Land. Spanish Muslim traveller Ibn Jubayr had written of Acre a century earlier (1184) a description that would still hold good for 1290:

> A note on the city of Acre
> May God exterminate [the Christians in] it and restore it [to the Muslims]
>
> Acre is the capital of the Frankish cities in Syria, the unloading place of 'ships reared aloft in the seas like mountains' [Koran, LV, 24], and a port of call for all ships. In its greatness it resembles Constantinople. It is the focus of ships and caravans, and the meeting-place of Muslim and Christian merchants from all regions. Its roads and streets are choked by the press of men, so that it is hard to put foot to ground. Unbelief and unpiousness there burn fiercely, and pigs [Christians] and crosses abound. It stinks and is filthy, being full of refuse and excrement.[44]

The languages heard by Othon on his arrival would have been familiar Old French, Occitan and Arpitan but also German and Italian among those from the Latin west mixed with Arabic, Coptic, Hebrew, and Greek from the east: Acre was a veritable melting pot. The clean-shaven arrivals from England and Savoy would have noticed something else that marked them from the non-Latin occidentals they met: the Orthodox Christians, Muslims, and Jews proudly sported beards. The Templar knights they encountered too would have worn beards, something that may have marked them as oriental to occidental eyes.[45] Noticeable too would have been the dress of the locals, adorned in cotton, linen, muslin,[46] damask, and silk, even Latins adopting much occidental dress styles such as long robes and turbans, including so called 'tartar cloths' – even upturned shoes. The marketplace would have thronged with merchants buying and selling grain, cheese, poultry, fruit and vegetables from Acre's rural hinterland but also flax, wool, hides, straw for baskets, feathers for bedding and the more exotic precious stones from Damascus, silks and ceramics from Antioch, spices from Egypt, wine from Antioch and Laodicea, wine also from around Nazareth in Lower Galilee, dates from around Tiberias and the Jordan valley, and sugar from cane plantations in widely scattered regions. The food they saw would have seemed exotic, they would have seen locals sitting on divans and carpets eating food laced with lemon, sugar, rice and melons. The women would have used cosmetics and glass mirrors unknown at home. Should any of the travellers have lost horses on the long sea voyage from Italy, then fine destriers or war horses bred in the Levant were available for purchase on arrival. As today, an arrival from the west would be met with money changers and bankers awaiting their exit from the maritime customs to supply local currency and loans, and middlemen to arrange accommodation in public buildings – of course, Othon de Grandson had the 3,000 marks from the Italian money lenders with him and so the party would most likely have brushed these hawkers away.[47] The coins they would have seen bore the imprint of Arabic inscriptions, for all Outremer being Europe's first colony it was still the European tip of an Asian continent.

The city bore all the hallmarks of feverish anxiety that we recently saw in Saigon in the early 1970s, a combustible mix of ethnicities living on borrowed time. Before the English party had crossed the Channel, the pope's expedition under Jean de Grailly and Nicholas Tiepolo had docked in the harbour at Acre. The largely Viennese soldiers, some 3,000 or so, had then hit the fleshpots of Acre as an army with no fighting to do often does, whoring and drinking – they were the spark that lit the bone-dry tinder. One hallmark of Outremer, mostly unknown to the soldiering classes of Europe, was the extent to which oriental cities such as Acre traded with their Muslim neighbours. Acre was that summer, as it always was, filled with Muslim traders selling their exotic wares, the mix of occidental and oriental that was a heady mix. The exact circumstances of what followed in August 1290 have not been fully explained, but it seems that offence was taken at the action of a Muslim trader, perhaps involving a woman. The offence caused the Italians to rampage through Acre killing Muslims to the horror of the local population and even the military orders. Qālawūn had been waiting for a pretext to move on Acre, the Viennese had handed it to him gift-wrapped on a plate.

Back in London, Edward had belatedly written to Arghūn in September:

> To Arghūn, king of the Tartars …
>
> that he [Arghūn] will delight to rise against the perfidy of the sultan of Babylon and his people, in aid of the Holy Land and of the Christian faith … For the horses and other necessaries for the king's army, which Arghūn has liberally caused to be offered to the king by his said envoy when the king shall arrive in the Holy Land, the king tenders him renewed thanks. The king wishes him to know that the king, so soon as he can obtain the pope's consent for the passage of him and his army over the sea, will certify Arghūn thereof, and will direct his steps to the aforesaid land with the aid of Christ, to do which as speedily as possible the king has a great wish.[48]

But it was too late. While Othon de Grandson and the English were still in Rome, that October of 1290, Qālawūn had dissolved the truce with the Kingdom of Jerusalem at Acre and mobilised his Mamluk army – the situation in the east was unravelling before even the English had arrived.

To the sound of trumpets and with banners flying proclaiming jihad the mamluk war machine left Cairo by way of the fortified rectangular towered Gate of Victory – then seemingly for Acre a miracle. On 10 November 1290 Sultan Qālawūn, the vanquisher of Tripoli, died, almost certainly of that great medieval malady dysentery. The people of Acre 'rejoiced greatly and believed themselves saved' according to the Templar of Tyre – it was a forlorn hope. Qālawūn was replaced immediately by his son, Al-Ashraf Salāh ad-Dīn Khalil ibn Qālawūn or Khalil.

A new sultan did mean a delay, but it was not to be a stay of execution; that winter the sound of outraged religious fervour was heard throughout the Muslim world along with the ominous chopping of wood to construct great war engines: trebuchets, mangonels and other catapults on a scale the like of which the world had yet seen. Khalil used religious fervour as a weapon against Acre much in the same way Pope Urban II had once done to fan the flames of the First Crusade. Historian of the Fall of Acre, Roger Crowley citing one Muslim source speaks of the prevailing mood in Cairo and Damascus:

> O you, sons of the blood one [Christ], soon will God's vengeance rain down on you, of whom nothing will remain! Already al-Malik al-Ashraf is descending on your shores. Prepare to receive at his hands unbearable blows.[49]

> and:

> and when the order for this invasion reached me, and the decrees of the Sultan to prepare the arsenals and the machines arrived, my soul longed for jihad, yearning for it, like the craving of the thirsty earth for its rightful duty … I went to meet the Sultan and came to him while he had reached Gaza. I met with hospitality and joy and a smile from him, and I travelled with his horsemen to Akka [Acre].[50]

The rulers of Acre were in denial that autumn, winter, and spring even as the chopping of wood was carried out beneath their walls. They sent an embassy to Cairo to treat with the sultan; its envoys were simply locked up; war was coming to Acre.

As we saw for the Lord Edward's crusade, for the last twenty years of Outremer, we are primarily thankful to a man known as the Templar of Tyre for his eyewitness chronicle contained in *Les Gestes des Chiprois*.[51] He was almost certainly not a Templar, but probably one Gérard de Montréal, a Levantine nobleman of Cypriot origin and the secretary to Templar Master Guillaume de Beaujeu. The Templar is the only eyewitness account we have of the forthcoming events, a witness that shows little favour or bias, and is therefore the primary source we shall use. Of the embassy to Cairo the chronicle said:

> 485. And were the messengers Sir Philippe Mainebeuf, knight of Acre, who knew very well the Saracen language, and one brother knight of the Temple, by the name brother Berthelomé the Pizan, who was born in Cyprus, and one brother of the Hospital, and one scribe that was named Jorge; and were they before the sultan, who refused the letters and the present, and held back the messengers in prison.[52]

The Templar gives us the beginning of a letter from this time from the sultan to the Master of the Temple, which gives us both an idea of how Khalil styled himself and that the Templar was close to and privy to history. The Templar says that Khalil's letter announced himself as:

> 487. The Sultan of Sultans, the King of Kings, the Lord of Lords, al-Malik al-Ashraf, the Powerful, the Dreadful, the Chaser of Rebels, Chaser of Francs, and Tartars, and Armenians, Snatcher of Castles from the Hands of Miscreants, Lord of the Two Seas, Guardian of the Two Pilgrim Sites, Khalil al-Salih.[53]

Khalil was not one then for false modesty and understatement, and the 'Chaffeours des Frans' would soon let loose his dogs of war and indeed be true to his word chasing Franks.

On 6 March 1291[54] a great Mamluk army began the march across Sinai toward Acre, estimated to comprise over 160,000 infantry flanked by some 60,000 cavalry. But the most fearsome threat would be the Mamluk artillery, with no fewer than a hundred mangonels, known as the sultan's 'black bulls' trundling towards the city. These mangonels, catapults, would also be able to throw what the Arabs called *naft*, known to us as Greek Fire, at the defenders, likely a mixture of sulphur and other assorted ingredients that would bathe any defenders on the walls and behind with liquid fire that would cling to anyone unfortunate enough to be in the way,[55] a bit like napalm. The great trebuchets al-Mansour 'the Victorious' and Ghadaban 'The Furious'[56] travelled in carted parts to be assembled before the gates of Acre, Trebuchets were the heavy artillery of the medieval army; al-Mansour was among the deadliest being able to hurl stone weighing over 100 lb (50 kg) continually at a crumbling wall. One thing that marked the Mamluk war machine was its ability to assemble trebuchets and sufficient ammunition to hit a target with precise accuracy time and time again so that eventually the percussive impact would bring down even the strongest walls.

The troops of the sultan's vassals and of his provincial governors were also marching; they came from Aleppo in the north, from Homs and Damascus in the east and from Kerak in the southeast, and from all points of the compass they marched to converge upon Acre. Amid the camels, horses and carts, amid the infantry and the cavalry the sultan brought all sorts of specialists along with him, stonemasons, miners, and logistics experts. Musicians too as spectacle played a large part in providing the 'shock and awe' that was the Mamluk army on the march, with banners of all colours flying in the desert wind, accompanied by trumpets and enormous kettledrums beating out the march. With the sun glinting from the weapons, the flying banners and rhythmic beating of the drums, the trumpets heralding their arrival, the poor defenders of Acre would have been well aware of the arrival of their nemesis.

By early March advanced guards of the army had arrived in the vicinity of Acre, burning villages, establishing Mamluk control of the hinterland in preparation for the arrival of the main army. A steady stream of fleeing civilians began arriving at the city gates bringing tales of the approaching storm.

Bringing all this together, Crowley cites a Christian source describing the marching army; though the numbers are almost certainly exaggerated, they convey the scene:

> The sultan advanced towards Acre with the greatest multitude of unfaithful people, that no one could count, of all races, peoples, and languages, gathered from the east and the west. And the earth trembled at their sight, with the sound of a great number of trumpets, cymbals, and drums before them. The sun shone on their shields like gold as they passed and reflected on the mountains, and the tips of their polished spears shone against the sun like stars shining in the skies in a serene night sky. When the army marched, we could see a forest moving on the ground because of the multitude of spears. They numbered 400,000 soldiers and it was impossible not to admire the sight of so many infidels, since they covered all the land, the plains and the hills.[57]

The Mamluk *askari*, the name coming from the Arabic for solider, was quite different from the Frankish knights with which he was about to do battle. Iron was a much rarer commodity in the

Middle East than it was in Europe, so the mamluks blended the iron they had with softer metals such as bronze, but also, they made far more widespread use of leather in their armour. Helmets and body armour would be of laminated leather rather than iron, altogether lighter, the body armour being segmented and so allowing for great flexibility of movement. Unlike western kite-shaped shields, their shields were round, therefore lighter, and easier to wield. The Mamluk would also be a blaze of colour, flowing silks and cottons of all colours attached to horse and rider. Khalil introduced the wearing of the turban, and his horsemen may well have begun to wrap a brief turban around the bottom of their helmets in a style Westerners would become to associate with Islamic armies. The ruling Mamluks were of Turkish[58] rather than Arabic origin, and like the Turks they heavily favoured the use of cavalry archers shooting their arrows from composite bows in a hit-and-run manner to wear down their opponents.[59]

Khalil reached Acre on 5 April 1291[60] and formally laid siege to the city, as recounted later by the Templar of Tyre:

> The sultan had closed [pitched] his tents and his pavilions very close to one another, from holding the Touron, going until close to as-Sumairiya, in such a way that the whole plain was covered with tents; and the tent of the sultan himself is called the dehlis,[61] was a little high on the toron, where there was a beautiful tower and gardens and vineyards of the Temple, and the dehlis was all vermillion, and an open door faced toward the city of Acre, and such is the custom of the sultans that toward where the door of dehlis is opened, everybody knows that the sultan must go by this way.[62]

For those watching from the battlements of Acre, the pitching of the sultan's tent on Le Tournon,[63] with its entrance open and pointing to the city meant only one thing: there would be no negotiations, there would be only one way for the sultan and his army and in that way stood the defenders of Acre. Looking out then from his tent toward Acre, who would Khalil have seen atop the battlements of Acre?

Farthest to the sultan's right the Montsumart district section of the wall was guarded by the Templar knights under their Grand Master Guillaume de Beaujeu and Marshal Pierre de Sevrey, aided by the leper knights of Saint Lazarus. Moving to the left and the Gate of Saint Anthony were the Hospitaller knights under their Grand Master Jean de Villiers and Marshal Matthieu de Clermont. Then to the left came the English knights of Saint Thomas, and farther left the German Teutonic knights led by Hugo von Boland. The Tour Maudite or Accursed Tower, next, the keystone of the defence, and its associated barbican were guarded by the Lusignan Kingdom of Cyprus and Jerusalem, under Almaric, Lord of Tyre. Almaric was the eldest of the younger brothers of King Henry II who had successfully contested the kingdom with Charles d'Anjou. Lastly the sultan would have seen farthest left from his viewpoint, the wall running down to the harbour, the French knights of Jean de Grailly and the Anglo-Savoyard knights of Othon de Grandson.[64] The aforesaid knights specifically mentioned – Beaujeu, Villiers, Boland, Grailly, Grandson along with Almaric and the Patriarch, Nicholas de Hanapes – made up the 'council of war' of the beleaguered defenders, among whom might be the assistance of Italians, the Genoese, the Venetians, and the Pisans, though only the Pisans provided sustained support. In total, against the 150,000–200,000-strong army besieging Acre, the defenders could muster perhaps 1,000 knights and 14,000 infantry.[65] When Henry later joined his brother Almaric he brought along perhaps a further 700 defenders.

It took just over a week for the Mamluks to unpack their siege equipment, but the Templar of Tyre, on the receiving end, helpfully gives us their disposition:

> 490. One of his engines who had the name Ghadban, which is to say Furious, it was close to the guard of the Temple, and the other engine, which throws against the guard of the Pisans, had the name al-Mansouri,[66] this is to say The Victory, and the other large [engine], whose name I do not know, threw against the guard of the Hospital, and the fourth engine threw against a great tower, which has the name the Accursed Tower, which is at the second wall and was in the guard of the king.[67]

Nonetheless, with all this firepower at his disposal it was not a foregone conclusion that Acre would be taken by the sultan. We have already seen with the year-long siege of Pevensey Castle in England that a garrison resupplied by sea might be able to hold out, and the crusaders had command of the sea. In the Middle Ages there were but four ways to break into a heavily defended city: over the wall, through the wall, under the wall and by starvation. The latter method had allowed the royal faction to bring the Montfortian rebels to heel at Kenilworth but as we have suggested this option was not open to the sultan as he could not control access to Acre's harbour.

Going over the wall, escalade in the language of the day, involved scaling the walls using ladders, all the while taking fire from the defenders. Those attempting to climb the walls might be subjected to not only arrows and crossbow bolts but also rocks, scalding water, hot sand, and fire pots. A siege tower or *beffroi* (literally belfry) would require a flat-ground approach. Bringing down the walls by undermining them was time consuming, and as we have seen at Dryslwyn often dangerous, risking a collapsed mine, but could be highly effective. Siege engines to batter down the walls might also be effective, *artillerie* in Anglo-French, meant warlike munitions, especially ballistic weapons. Such engines could be employed to hurl rocks repeatedly against defences.

So, the sultan would have to bring down the walls by undermining them or simply beating them to a pulp – or as he chose to do a combination of both – and such a combination had proven successful for his predecessors Baibars at Krak-des-Chevaliers and Qālawūn at Tripoli. Chroniclers, such as the Templar of Tyre and artists were often imprecise in their descriptions of *artillerie* in use at Acre, using the generic *engin* or engine to mean all forms of ballistic device. But we can say that two forms of engine in particular were constructed: the mangonel[68] and the trebuchet.[69] Originally the mangonel was simply a form of catapult, using torsion to throw its missiles; however, by the medieval period the mangonel had evolved to be in effect a traction trebuchet. We can therefore divide mangonels from trebuchets by the use in the latter of a counterweight or counterpoise.[70] We should, for the medieval period, for mangonel read 'traction trebuchet' and for trebuchet read 'counterweight trebuchet'. To the Mamluks the mangonel was *al-manjanīq* in Arabic and the trebuchet the *huíhuípào*. The counterpoise trebuchet uses a counterweight to swing the arm; it was the only artillery on either side that had not originated with the Romans, making its way west from China borne by the Mongol invasions and taken up first in the Middle East then only recently in Europe. The trebuchet was a compound machine that made use of the mechanical advantage of a lever to throw a missile. They were invariably large constructions, from 30 feet (10 meters) in height to as much as three times that, built mostly of wood, but reinforced with metal, leather, rope, and other materials. Counterweight trebuchets used gravity, potential energy stored by slowly raising an extremely heavy box (typically filled with stones, sand, or lead) attached to the shorter end of the beam (typically on a hinged connection) and then released on command.

Khalil protected his bombardment artillery with lines of ditches, palisades and movable wooden shelters and the assault began. The Templar of Tyre again: 'They set up great barricades and wicker screens, the first night ranged them against our walls. The second night they advanced further; the third night, as well, they advanced. And so, they advanced so much that they came to the edge of the fosse [ditch].'[71]

Under the cover of darkness this assaulting ring would advance a little way, the defenders helpless to prevent the tightening noose around the beleaguered city. The Templar of Tyre bemoaned, 'and if anyone should ask why they let them so close, it was because they could not help it.'[72] Because the Mamluks had been able to advance as far as the fosse meant they were now just over 100 feet (30 metres) from the city walls – this meant that the heaviest defending trebuchets could not hit them because of the trajectory required.

And so, by day, the repeated assault would come, the continuously accurate thud of 50-kg boulders against the wall, like a giant hammering on a door. The defenders had to keep a careful lookout on the battlements since a rain of arrows and crossbow bolts, some of them flaming, would make a sustained occupation of the battlements impossible. The chronicler of Lanercost later wrote, almost certainly the voice of Othon de Grandson,[73] in these terms: 'shooting so hotly against it, as one who was there informed me, you might see the little arrows which they called 'locusts' flying in the air thicker than snowflakes'.[74]

The Templar of Tyre again, recounted the difficulty of those assailed defenders: 'And after this the enemy drew up their carabouhas, small Turkish catapults operated by hand, which can fire very fast and these did more damage to our men than the larger engines, since where the carabouhas fired, no one dared to appear in the open.'[75]

The word *carabouha* was Old French rendering of the Turkish *qarabugha* or 'black bull', a light slingshot trebuchet that was doing more damage, according to our witness, than the great trebuchets of the sultan. The 'black bull' was a traction catapult that could fire all manner of things at the defenders, including containers filled with excrement or burning fire.[76] All the time these trebuchets and catapults rained destruction down upon the crusader. The Mamluks were mostly impervious to counter-fire given the protection afforded to them by their barricades and wicker screens. So, although Acre could be resupplied by sea, the siege was tightening its hold on the city. Something would have to be done if there was to be any hope.

One of the avenues open to the defenders of a city beset by a siege would be to venture from behind their walls from time to time to disrupt the besieging army, in the terminology of the day to undertake a sortie.[77] The target for such a temporary armed breakout might be the great siege engines arrayed against them, the trebuchets or the tents of the opposing commanders.

The first such sortie was a clever attempt to outflank the Mamluks, taking advantage of the westerners' command of the sea. On the night of 13/14 April a small flotilla of vessels set sail from the harbour and headed north along the coast, positioning itself adjacent to the Mamluks outside the walls of the district of Montsumart. The Pisans had artfully crafted a barge that carried a mangonel, which was to be escorted by ships bearing crossbowmen. The little armada positioned itself by the outermost flank of the besieging army and opened fire, simultaneously landing a small force to harass the surprised Mamluks. The tables were now turned, rocks, arrows and crossbow bolts now raining down upon the sultan's army, the trebuchets they had built being of no use since they could not be turned toward the sea. Sadly, for the crusaders a storm blew and wrecked their little squadron of ships, breaking the arm of the mangonel beyond repair. The first attempt to break the siege ended in failure, but the imperative remained: something must be done.

And so, it was a second sortie was made from the city, following a council of war, on the night of 15/16 April. The Templar of Tyre again relates:

> 491. So it came that my Lord the Master of the Temple and his men and Sir Othon de Grandson and other knights [came] by night and went towards the Temple, who then went out of the Gate of Saint Lazarus, and the master ordered a Provençal, who is Viscount of the Burg of Acre, to set fire to the buches [frame] of the great engine of the Sultan, and they went out that night, and were until the said buches, and the one who must throw the fire, and throws the fire in fear in such a way it came short, and landed on the ground, and burned out on the ground. All the Saracens, which they found there, were all killed, men on horse and on foot, and of our, brothers and secular knights entering the pavilions, there horses legs stick together with the ropes of the tents and trebuchets, so the Saracens kill them, and in such a way we lost that night eighteen men on horse, brothers of the Temple and secular knights, but we took a number of Saracen shields and bucklers and trumpets and drums; and my lord and his men returned to Acre.[78]

The Templar refers to a Johan de Granfon which is almost certainly an error of recollection on his part, there being no other Granfon besieged in Acre other than Othon de Grandson – so we must read his name into the account.[79] Among the other knights the Templar does mention were likely to be the English knights of Saint Thomas. Sadly, the *chevaus s'encomberent* included one poor knight falling from his horse into a latrine where he met his end. The trophies the Templar mentions were duly hung from the battlements of Acre to taunt the besieging army, who in turn cut the heads from fallen knights and displayed them on the ends of pikes – but though the encounter might be seen as a draw, the sortie had failed in its attempt to break the siege. A further attempt was made on the night of 18/19 April, but the defenders were becoming increasingly desperate.

Easter came, and it seems that the following account given by the chronicler of Lanercost came directly from Othon de Grandson[80] and is related solely in his account:

> Those, then, who were in command upon the walls, perceiving that they could not hold the town for so long against so many foes, determined by common counsel to make confession and receive the communion, penitently imploring help for their arms from the Lord, and that all should sally forth on the day of our common redemption, with ranks arrayed and the prisoners set in the van, and adventure their lives for the Author of life. And when they had so resolved with undaunted hearts and kindled faith, they sent to the Patriarch, who was in the place, that they might accomplish under his authority and with blessing the purpose which they had begun. He broken in spirit and depending on the advice of perfidious persons, replied that none should attempt this, nor any of the city gates under pain of excommunication.[81]

The plan for this sortie was stillborn, but it illustrates the desperate minds of the defenders that they might seriously consider a venture beyond the city walls, perhaps some 10,000–15,000 against over 150,000, and to be protected by a human shield of prisoners. The desperate plan did not come to pass, but the relation to the chronicler at Lanercost gives us an insight into the blame game beginning in the face of impending disaster. There would be no more ventures from Acre to break the siege – the noose was now tied fast, and it remained only for the Sultan to pull the lever of execution; to this end he now asked his army to intensify their efforts.

The defenders' mood darkened; they looked in hope toward the sea and their king in Cyprus for deliverance, as the Templar of Tyre remembered: 'there was said news that the King Henry must come from Cyprus, bringing great help and they expected him day by day.'[82]

And so we come once more to the famed Lusignan clan from Poitou, a family married into by the widow of King John of England, Isabelle d'Angoulême, who found, as we saw in earlier chapters, much notoriety in England, a family whose Guillaume de Valence,[83] the great-grandson of Hugh VIII de Lusignan, was still the Earl of Pembroke, half-brother to the late King Henry III of England, marcher lord of King Edward I of England, and lord of Pembroke and Goodrich Castles. King Henry II of Cyprus and Jerusalem, of whom the defenders of Acre were so eagerly waiting, was another of the Lusignan clan, a great-great-great-grandson of the same Hugh VIII de Lusignan.[84] The reach of the francophone nobility in the thirteenth century can be easily expressed in that a king of Cyprus and Jerusalem might be related to a king of England by way of a family from Poitou, France.

Richard Cœur de Lion, who had taken Cyprus from a Byzantine rebel during his time on crusade in the Middle East, found it irksome to control and sold it to the Knights Templar, who in turn it passed to the Lusignan clan. Charles d'Anjou had for a time contested the Kingdom of Cyprus and Jerusalem but following the Capetian's death, Henry had become sole heir. Henry was crowned at Santa Sophia, Nicosia, 24 June 1285 as king of Cyprus and at Tyre in August 1286 the king of Jerusalem, followed by lavish festivities in the Hospitaller grand hall at Acre thereafter. So, it was natural that the citizens might look *jour en jour* for their king in their hour of need. But Henry was just 16 when the Sultan appeared to eradicate his kingdom.

Early on Friday, 4 May, ships appeared on the horizon; the people of Acre began to make out the flags, and they were the unmistakeable crosses of the Kingdom of Cyprus and Jerusalem: it was Henry. The ships docked in the harbour to a great fanfare, as some 700 knights and men-at-arms[85] stepped from the boats to reinforce the defence of the city. The citizens of Acre rejoiced, church bells rang out, but 700 was a paltry number. Once the cries at Henry's arrival had quietened, they soon gave way to the continual thud, thud, thud of the sultan's trebuchets.

Three days on from Henry's arrival, as hope began to fade, on 7 May, a ceasefire, and negotiations were attempted; perhaps Khalil might spare the people of Acre should the city be surrendered peacefully. The peace negotiations, if that is what they were, faltered when a rogue shot from a Christian siege engine landed close to the sultan's tent while they were still talking – thus ended the last hope for peace.

During the next week, the work of the great trebuchets and the patient undermining of the Mamluk engineers bore fruit. Eventually the incessant pounding, and the lack of solid ground beneath caused the English Tower, the Tower of the Countess of Blois, Saint Anthony's Gate, and the walls there and near the Tower of Saint Nicholas to crumble. The outer wall of the King's Tower succumbed on 15 May. The Templar again describes for us: 'The new tower, which they called the Tower of the King, was so badly undermined that the front face fell in a heap into the fosse.'[86, 87]

Friday, 18 May 1291 dawned with grey clouds and overcast conditions, but with the rhythmic boom, boom, boom, 'terrible and mighty'[88] of over 300 camel-mounted kettledrums, the clash of cymbals, the hurrahs of over a 100,000 Mamluks – the day of nemesis for the crusader states had dawned. Othon, commanding the English knights alongside Grailly and his French knights were responsible for the Tower of the Legate, having the Accursed Tower to their immediate left and the towers of the Germans and Patriarch to their right and the sea.[89] But the key Accursed Tower would fall, its loss critical, making Grandson's and Grailly's position to its right untenable.

For the coming end at Acre the chroniclers now disagree on the detail of events, which can undoubtedly be explained by the need of the various factions from the west seeking to explain the forthcoming disaster to their shocked populations at home. We can therefore not be sure of the actuality of events and the roles played by the key defenders, including Othon de Grandson, Jean de Grailly and the Anglo-Savoyard contingent. However, perhaps the most learned of later years, Runciman, distilled all the chroniclers' accounts into his own composite collation, so we shall begin with his account:

> During the next day, the Moslems strengthened their hold on the outer enceinte; and the sultan ordered the general assault for the morning of Friday 18th May. The attack was launched on the whole length of the walls from Saint Anthony's Gate to the Patriarch's Tower by the bay, but the main effort of the Moslems was against the Accursed Tower at the angle of the salient. The sultan threw all his resources into the battle. His mangonels kept up an unceasing bombardment. The arrows of his archers fell almost in a solid mass into the city; and regiment after regiment rushed at the defences, led by white turbaned emirs. The noise was appalling. The assailants shouted their battle cries, and trumpets and cymbals and the drums of three hundred drummers on camel back urged them on.
>
> It was not long before the Mamluks forced their way into the Accursed Tower. The Syrian and Cypriot knights that were in its garrison were pushed back westwards towards Saint Anthony's Gate. The Templars and Hospitallers came to their assistance, fighting together as if there had never been two centuries of rivalry between them. Matthieu de Clermont desperately tried to lead a counterattack to recover the tower, but though the two Grand Masters followed him, they could make no impression. Along the eastern wall of the city Jean de Grailly and Othon de Grandson held their own for some hours, but after the fall of the Accused Tower the enemy was able to pass along the crumbling walls and take possession of the Gate of Saint Nicholas. The whole salient was lost, and the Moslems were well established inside the city.
>
> There was fierce fighting in the streets, but nothing now could be done to save Acre. Guillaume de Beaujeu, Grand Master of the Temple, was mortally wounded in the fruitless counterattack against the Accursed Tower. His followers carried him to the Temple building where he died. Matthieu de Clermont was with him but returned to the battle and his death. The Grand Master of the Hospital, Jean de Villiers, was wounded, but his men brought him down to the

> harbour and put him protesting on board a ship. The young king and his brother Amalric had already embarked. King Henry was later accused of cowardice in deserting the city, but there was nothing that he could have done, and it was his duty to his kingdom to avoid capture. On the eastern sector Jean de Grailly was wounded, but Othon de Grandson took control. He commandeered as many Venetian ships as he could find and placed Jean de Grailly and all soldiers he could rescue on board, and himself was the last to join them.[90]

Stirring stuff of epoch-defining moments, Runciman took a lot of his account from the Templar of Tyre, particularly that relating to Guillaume de Beaujeu, Jean de Grailly and Othon de Grandson, all of whom the Templar sought to single out for honour in his account:

> 498. a javelin came at the Master of the Temple, just as he raised his left hand. He had no shield save his spear in his right hand. The javelin struck him under the armpit, and the shaft sank into the body a palms-length; it came in through the gap where the plates of armour were not joined. This was not his proper armour, but rather light armour for putting on hastily at an alarm.
>
> When he felt himself mortally wounded, he turned to go. Some of the defenders thought that he was retiring because he wanted to save himself. The standard bearer saw him go, and fell in behind him, and then all his household followed as well. After he had gone some way, twenty crusaders from the Vallo Di Spoletto saw him withdrawing and they called to him, 'Oh for God's sake, Sir, don't leave, or the city will fall at once!' And he cried out to them in a loud voice, so that everyone could hear him 'My Lords, I can do no more, for I am dead; see the javelin wound here!'
>
> And then we saw the javelin stuck in his body, as he spoke, he dropped the spear on the ground, and his head slumped on one side …
>
> Then entered a great number of Saracen men on horseback, so much that Sir Jean de Grailly, and Sir Othon de Grandson, and the men of the King of France made great[91] defence, so that there are assessed many wounded and dead; and Sir Jean de Grailly and Sir Othon de Grandson could no longer suffer the charge of the Saracens, and they departed from there and fled, and Sir Jean de Grailly was wounded.[92]

The Templar gives us the heart of Runciman's account, suggesting that Jean de Grailly and Othon de Grandson 'made great defence' causing many Saracens to be 'wounded and dead' and confirming that Jean de Grailly was indeed 'wounded'.[93] But in truth, as the Templar explained, 'there were too many Saracens'.[94] The Templar's account is clearly made up of events he has himself seen, other chroniclers recorded or imagined the horrors of those last hours at Acre, of women being torn apart by competing assailants, of babies crushed under the hooves of fleeing horses so much that even the invading Mamluks wept. We have in our time witnessed scenes of the fall of Saigon as an example of those last hours; whatever the details it must have been horrendous to witness and terrifying to undergo.

Thaddens or Thadeus of Naples, also used by Runciman, in his chronicle makes no mention of Othon, but is severe in his criticism of Jean de Grailly, heading his account of the aforementioned flight: '*De improbitate et reprehensione domini Johannis de Greliaco, capitaneo gentis regis Francie*' or 'The lack of integrity and the fault and Jean de Grailly, the captain of the nation of France', going on to add, '*laudabilem vel memoria dignum quoquo modo se ipsum exhibuit nec ostendit*', that is, he didn't 'in any way he present himself or showed himself to be praiseworthy or worthy of remembrance'. Thadeus finished with the most damning admonishment of Grailly he could summon up, writing, '*elegit pocius more femineo aufugere seu pugnandi*', that is, 'he chose to flee rather than fight, in a womanly fashion'.[95] Ouch, goodness the knives were out for Edward's former seneschal of Gascony.

It is the anonymous writer, not in Acre, but taking his account from disaffected eyewitnesses, of *Excidio Acconis* who claimed that not only Jean de Grailly behaved in a blameworthy fashion, but Othon de Grandson too, writing of '*actus militares turpiter*'[96] or 'shameful military actions', fleeing to their ships before the final assault, '*Vere non fugerunt a conflictu, quia nunquam in conflictum intrave runt*' or 'They did not really run away from the conflict, because they never ran into the conflict.'[97] Runciman used *Excidio* in his account but gave no credence to accusations of cowardice, in fact treating reports of the opposite, from the *Les Gestes des Chiprois* and *Chronicon Sythiense Sancti Bertini*[98] with greater credibility. So, who to believe? The anonymous writer of the *Excidio* or the Templar of Tyre? The account of the fate of a poor English squire, immolated, that we shall come to,[99] suggests perhaps that the Templar was close to the English and therefore Othon as the city fell, and so his account carries the weight of an eyewitness in assessing Grandson's conduct that day. Thus, Runciman gave greater weight to his testimony than others, and perhaps rightly so. Clifford in her epilogue used the words of 'a chronicler's voice', without taking the time to say whom: 'He [Othon] is a coward who tried to buy off the enemy, and when that failed, he deserted his men and fled from the battle'[100] But perhaps Swiss historian Jean-Daniel Morerod missed Clifford's use of the quote as a rhetorical tool, Morerod writing, '*Couard, je ne sais pa*' or 'Coward, I do not know', having earlier noted that his paper might lead to suggestions of having '*dés-héroisés*' or 'de-heroising' Othon.[101] Morerod cited Clifford in order to draw attention to Grandson's dubious financial affairs, but Clifford's rhetoric is an unsound basis for this critique, a better one as we shall see would be Grandson's financial links with the Templars and survival of those financial links at the orders suppression. Clifford's rhetorical use of an uncited chronicler, a non eyewitness source, reminds us of the perils of uncritically using medieval chronicles. Anglophone historians know only too well the peril of placing too much reliance upon medieval chroniclers, Matthew Paris being a notable example. So, who was Clifford's chronicler?

Blame for the fall of Acre was certainly flying in all directions; criticism of Othon's actions came from chroniclers who (unlike the Templar of Tyre) were not there. Clifford's words sound like one whom Runciman chose not to cite, the *Chronicon Domini Walteri de Hemingburgh*. The chronicler tells his readers that Othon having been '*qui cum thesauris regis Angliæ*', that is, 'with the treasure or treasury of the King of England' had attempted to 'pay off the enemy' but had fled with the '*thesauris*' or treasure or treasury to Cyprus before jibing '*mutato cognomine, in congressu militari parvum sonum fecit*',[102] that is, he 'changed his name and made a little noise in the military'. The jibe was a less than subtle play on the motto of the *famille de Grandson*, which was *Petit Cloche, Grand Son* or 'Small Bell, Big Sound.'[103] – a sneer that Prestwich describes as 'certainly not justified'.[104] Clifford's words, as they are not primary sourced sound like a mélange of the *Excidio Acconis* and *Hemingburgh*, otherwise known as Walter of Guisborough. But both these writers, though contemporary, were not at Acre, and so must surely be viewed with more suspicion than the writer of the *Les*

Gestes des Chiprois. Indeed, as we saw that the writer of the *Gestes* referenced the horrific demise of an English squire, and we know Grandson was commanding the English knights and squires, it could be reasonably suggested that the writer was an eyewitness to events directly of the part of Acre where Grandson fought. While this in no way proves his account is accurate, it does, I would venture, give it more credence in terms of a witness to Grandson's conduct at Acre than either Guisborough or the *Excidio*. In the end as Morerod wrote, we cannot know, but the Lord of Grandson deserves a more critical reading and assessment of the chronicler, that maybe even '*re-heroises*' him.

The 'treasure' that Hemingburgh refers to would be the 3,000 marks (£1.5 million) entrusted to him by Edward to prepare for a crusade, something that would now be next to impossible to arrange. There have been those that have suggested the 'treasure' was the fabled Templar treasure of fanciful legend since future Grand Master of the Templars Jacques de Molay (Fig 2.0) accompanied Othon on the flight from Acre – that such treasure made its way back to Savoy and that such treasure remained there in the safe keeping of the nascent Confederation of Switzerland born that same year in Grütli meadow by Lake Lucerne not that far from Château de Grandson. The conspiracy theory goes that said treasure in the hands of alpine peasants explains the rags to riches story of Switzerland. Such a notion ignores the fact that for most of its history Switzerland was in fact a relatively poor corner of the Holy Roman Empire, and that Château de Grandson lay in what is now the *Suisse Romande* or French-speaking Switzerland and only passed into the territory of the *Suisse Allemande* or German-speaking Switzerland by the Bernese conquest in the sixteenth century, over 200 years on from the fall of Acre – no, we can reasonably assume any 'treasure' was the money entrusted to Othon by Edward, since *Hemingburgh* clearly describes the treasure as '*thesauris regis Angliæ*'. But as we shall see any suggestion of arrival in Europe, with either Templar or Edward's 'treasure', is unlikely and not supported by evidence.

The Templars had in fact taken refuge in their citadel as the city fell, Grand Master Guillaume de Beaujeu had died there even as the others made for the boats. The garrison under their Marshal, Pierre de Sevrey held out behind their walls; they hastily elected a successor to de Beaujeu, Thibaud Gaudin. Attempts at an amnesty allowing withdrawal failed on 20 May with renewed death and slaughter. It was then that Thibaud Gaudin slipped away in a small boat for Sidon with the Templar treasure. This was witnessed by the Templar of Tyre[105] and concluded his eyewitness relation of the Fall of Acre, meaning that almost certainly he accompanied Gaudin.[106] As the chronicler had left Acre, accounts of the final denouement are varied; the remaining tower of the citadel withstood until at least 28 May, before Pierre de Sevrey and the last defenders were slain in battle and if captured, they were executed.

The precise manner, then, and the date upon which Othon de Grandson left Acre is the subject of some debate. The Templar of Tyre mentions him last there on 18 May as the city is overrun, and he appears to be a reliable eyewitness account. Others have suggested he left with Gaudin and the Templar treasure, but this appears to be a misreading of *Hemingburgh*, who was in any case neither reliable nor an eyewitness account. The most likely account is that of the Templar of Tyre recorded in the *Les Gestes des Chiprois* and relied upon by most historians since.[107] Pierre d'Estavayer was aboard the ships making for Cyprus, along with his uncle Othon, but Pierre de Vuippens was not among their number, having fallen with the defenders of Acre. They would have learned perhaps of the brave way the knights of the Temple had met their end in a desperate last stand, of the end of all the leper knights of the Order of Saint Lazarus defending Montsumart to the last man, save their leader Thomas de Sainville who had survived. Perhaps they learned of the fate of the Patriarch Nicholas de Hanapes who had drowned in the harbour, some said fallen into the water, some said perishing in a sinking overloaded boat. Some treasure of lost overboard in the desperate flight was found in the harbour in 1993 and 1994 in the form of gold florins.[108] It is very possible those fleeing had seen the patriarch perish themselves, since the chronicler of Lanercost, from whom we think owed his account to Grandson, wrote, 'the Patriarch, that vain image, was the first to flee, whom followed other rich folk.'[109] The historian Kingsford, writing over a century ago, perhaps more charitably, suggested that the Patriarch acted more heroically, his galley overloaded in his efforts to save as much of his flock as he could.[110] They would have had their ears still deafened by the terrified cries of the men, women and children screaming, caught between the onslaught of the rampaging Mamluks and the sea. Their nostrils would be still full of the stench of death. Perhaps too, it was only then they recalled the horror that they had seen, of their comrade, an English squire caught by Greek Fire and becoming a human fireball, as the Templar later described what he had personally witnessed:

> 498. one poor English *valé* [squire] was so badly hit by Greek Fire which the Saracens were hurling that his surcoat burst into flames. There was no one to help him. And so his face was burned, then his whole body. He burned as if he had been a cauldron of pitch, and he died there. He was on foot when this happened, because his mount had been slain under him.[111]

The people of Cyprus greeted a pitiable flotilla, carrying King Henry, the gravely wounded Master of the Hospitallers Jean de Villiers, the soon-to-be Master of the Templars, Jacques de Molay, (Fig 2.0) and the Savoyard knights. Wretched and or wounded, Othon de Grandson, Jean de Grailly and Pierre d'Estavayer were a long way from the serene *Pays de Vaud* – but they had survived. They wearily stepped ashore with little of their personal belongings, all that had been left behind them in their desperate flight from Acre. The Templar of Acre recalled that those who came ashore in Cyprus did so in '*grant povreté*' or 'great poverty'.[112] Othon's lack of his possessions is alluded to in the English Archive for 3 January 1292 at Westminster: 'Safe conduct until Michaelmas, for Peter de Weston, yeoman of Othon de Grandisono, whom some friends of Othon are sending to the land of Cyprus to him, with a horse laden with cloths and other things.'[113]

The poverty of his arrival was also later confirmed by Pope Boniface VIII, who in 1295 stated that he had lost almost all his possessions in 1291 and would run up large debts in Cyprus.[114] On arrival it seems he'd exchanged correspondence with his liege lord, Edward, on the disaster at Acre, and no doubt sought new instructions on how they might proceed. His personal poverty however would have been as nothing to the awful news he received from London: his friend Queen Leonor de Castile had died in his time in the Holy Land.

CHAPTER 10

The Savoyards had left England in July of 1290; now in Cyprus nearly a year later they learned that much had changed in England. Edward and Leonor had resolved to marry the heir to the English throne, young Edward of Caernarfon to the young heir to the vacant crown of Scotland, the so-called Maid of Norway. So, after the Savoyards had left England for Paris and Rome, the 7-year-old Margaret was sent for and began her own voyage. When she had joined her ship in Bergen, she was evidently in good health, but upon arrival in the Orkney Islands (then also a part of the Kingdom of Norway), she had been taken ill. Sometime between 26 and 29 September 1290, the young Margaret passed from this life, possibly of food poisoning.[1] The sad news reached both Edinburgh and London, the throne of Scotland vacant, her father King Alexander III having died in 1286, with no immediate heir, and the heir to the throne of England no longer with a marriage suitor. Not just the Guardians of Scotland[2] now responsible for their kingdom but also Edward and Leonor, responsible for their eldest son and heir, faced a problem. An empty throne in Scotland had no less than thirteen potential claimants. Political instability or civil war in a neighbouring kingdom was not good news for Edward. A letter from the Bishop of Saint Andrews at this point expresses the fears of civil war; in translation he wrote to Edward: 'let your excellency, deign, please, to approach he border to the consolation of the Scottish people and to staunch effusion of blood.'[3] What is more Edward and Leonor now needed another suitor for young Edward of Caernarfon – problems came in pairs that autumn for Edward.

En route to Scotland, Edward and Leonor had reached Clipstone in Sherwood Forest to greet the Maid had learned of her demise; when news broke a parliament was summoned – what to do. We are not certain of the exact dates of this Michaelmas Parliament, but Scotland does not yet appear as a named issue at hand, so perhaps Edward was still considering his options Scotland notwithstanding, of continuing consideration was the then still-live issue of crusade; with his advance retinue then arriving in Acre, on 25 October, the king agreed (presumably after consultation with his council) to the plans of Pope Nicholas IV for him to set out on crusade. Edward would receive the £130,000 already collected for the adventure plus monies collected from a new six-year tax for the purpose – departure day was set for June 1293 as previously negotiated by Othon de Grandson.

Clipstone was chosen as venue, despite its limited accommodation. The parliament itself was even by legend undertaken beneath an oak tree, in some measure due to the ailing health of the queen. Leonor's children were summoned to visit her in Clipstone - clearly a sign that Edward and Leonor feared the end may be near. Following the conclusion of the parliament Leonor and Edward set out the short distance from Clipstone to Lincoln. By this stage, the royal party was travelling barely 8 miles a day, and on 20 November, finally stopped at the village of Harby, Nottinghamshire, less than 7 miles (11 kilometres) from Lincoln. Poor Leonor, a lady who had survived sixteen pregnancies, was nearing the end of her long road from Burgos with her beloved Edward. Perhaps in the coming days, when Edward was continually at Leonor's bedside, the couple thought of that beautifully sunny day at the monastery of Las Huelgas, Burgos, in November 1254, where their journey together had begun. From Burgos to England to Sicily to the Holy Land to Italy to Savoy to France to Gascony to their coronation in London to Wales to Glastonbury, she had been as Guinevere to him. This would be a loss from which he would never fully recover.

The end came on Saint Andrew's Eve, 28 November 1290, in the evening, the archives recording her passing '*Decessus Regine*'.[4] They had been married for thirty-six years; we can begin to gauge Edward's grief, in that no government business (writs) were issued for three days – Edward's world as he had known it was gone. Leonor's embalmed body was borne in great state from Harby to Westminster Abbey; its resting places en route would later be marked by beautiful memorial crosses, perhaps the most famous being that in London at Charing or now Charing Cross. The 'Eleanor crosses' stood at Lincoln, Grantham, Stamford, Geddington, Hardingstone near Northampton, Stony Stratford, Woburn, Dunstable, St. Albans, Waltham, Westcheap, as well as at Charing – only three survive today.[5] The crosses were without precedent in England, finding only an echo in the montjoies erected for his lately sainted uncle Louis, on his last journey from Aigues-Mortes to Saint-Denis in France. We are not certain of the cause of death, perhaps it was a body weakened by malarial fever in Gascony, perhaps it was an inherited heart condition. The English didn't quite share Edward's grief and shed few tears it seems for Leonor; she had not acquired the language in her three decades in England, but her passing was also deeply mourned by her 'devoted' friend Othon de Grandson.[6]

Henry de Burg eulogised as recounted by the chronicler of Lanercost, 'How brief's the human span this Queen bears witness.'[7] Leonor's funeral took place in Westminster Abbey on 17 December 1290; she was interred in a temporary tomb. Eventually a magnificent tomb was fashioned for her, also in Westminster Abbey, a tomb that comprises a marble chest with carved mouldings and shields (originally painted) of the arms of England, Castile and Ponthieu but also the image of her good friend and champion, Othon de Grandson.[8] The knight was praying to the Virgin and Child, although the image is now decayed, the surcoat heraldry of the Grandson family clearly visible.

The fresco in Westminster was painted by Walter of Durham in early 1293[9] and raises interesting questions relating to Othon's time in Cyprus, as the image in London is replicated on an *antependium* or altar frontal created at Othon's behest, traditionally thought to have been created in Cyprus. The richly embroidered cloth is now held in the Bern Historical Museum, but originally rested on the main altar table at the Notre-Dame de Lausanne Cathedral – the very cathedral completed by Jean Cotereel. It was removed to Bern during the conquest of Savoyard Vaud by the Bernese in the sixteenth century but had come to the cathedral at the hands of a grateful Othon de Grandson as thanks to the lady for safe deliverance from Acre – he having prayed there for safe deliverance en route from England to Acre in 1290. The image was painted onto Leonor's tomb before Grandson set foot once more in England. So, how do we explain two images of Grandson kneeling in prayer before the Virgin and Child now being in London and Bern without apparently the painter and the embroiderers having met or the two objects, tomb and altar frontal, ever having been together?

We owe the idea that the *antependium* was of Cypriot origin and embroidered in the period immediately after the Fall of Acre to Michael Stettler, the onetime Director of the Bern Historical Museum and to Clifford, author of *A Knight of Great Renown*.[10] But Stettler was working entirely from 'artistic grounds' and Clifford from 'a half-formed theory' – a theory, subsequently oft repeated, that involved a visit by Othon de Grandson to Jerusalem in the aftermath of the flight to Cyprus.[11] The theory goes that Edward asked Othon to travel to the church of the Holy Sepulchre in Jerusalem to pray for Leonor and the fallen English knights of Acre. It is a compelling and romantic notion, and one that certainly provides a motive for the creation of both tomb and *antependium.* It is, then, in keeping with what we know of the character of both Edward and Othon, their friendship and the piety of the age. Certainly, the event was considered by Edward, in authorising the tomb, and Othon in, we assume, authorising the *antependium*, to be of some significance. Affection on Leonor's behalf for the good friend of her husband is attested to be the gift recorded in the Calendar of Patent Rolls: 'Confirmation of the legacy of Eleanor, late queen consort, granting to Othon de Grandisono, for life, her manors of Ditton,[12] co Cambridge, and Thurueston[13], co Buckingham, with reversion to the king.'[14] These English manors added to those he had acquired previously at Shene, Chelsfield, Easthall, Kemsing with Seal, Knole and Bradbourne , all in Kent, variously from Roger Burnell and Roger IV Bigod, Earl of Norfolk.[15]

Clifford's 'half-formed theory' is as good as any explanation as to the similarity of the images in London and Bern. It is possible that Khalil, conqueror of Acre, may have allowed pilgrimage to Jerusalem, but there is not a single shred of historical evidence for such an undertaking. We can neither prove nor disprove Clifford's theory; nonetheless, Sara Cockerill accepted the idea[16] as did Allison Weir who wrote: 'He [Edward] sent Sir Otto de Grandison to the Holy Land to offer prayers for Eleanor.'[17] Most plausibly crusade historian Tyerman suggested that Othon visited Jerusalem in lieu of his friend Leonor who may well have taken up the cross along with Edward back in 1287, we should remember she had accompanied Edward on his first crusade. He also added fuel to the suggestion that Othon's task in the east was crusade reconnaissance by reminding readers that Egyptian sultans were often wary of pilgrims, that 'a walking staff might actually be supporting a staff.'[18] Such an undocumented pilgrimage to Jerusalem would also fit in with Othon's timeline on Cyprus which, visit to Armenia notwithstanding, is hardly overburdened with activity.

The Bern Historical Museum where the *antependium* resides is reasonably certain of the centre piece being of Cypriot origin.[19] Susan Marti, of the museum, appears to be critical of '*auteurs anglophones*' adopting '*sans justification supplémentaire la thèse de Rowland Clifford*'. But Marti offers no alternative explanation as to why the *antependium* image so closely reassembles that in Westminster Abbey other than they share a common artistic mode. Frustratingly her focus on the *antependium* as an artwork, beautiful though it is, does seem to dismiss the rich wider historical context.[20] What we know of Othon's relationship with Edward and Leonor makes the idea of an association difficult to ignore. Surely an explanation would be in accordance with Clifford, Cockerill, Weir, and Tyerman that Edward asked Othon to offer prayers, perhaps in Jerusalem, to the Virgin and Child on behalf of his queen and Othon's dear friend Leonor. We must remember that neither fresco nor *antependium* could be or should be regarded solely as works of art – images on the tombs of queens of England are rarely without significance.

While Edward was away by the banks of the river Tweed attending to the ongoing Scottish succession, came more sad news. In November 1290 he had been at the bedside of his beloved[21] Queen Leonor de Castile as she passed away at Harby. Now came news, just six months later, that Queen Alianor de Provence, his formidable mother, had died on 24 June 1291. As Edward was calculating the great affairs of state, of the settlement of the relationship between England and Scotland, as he was making his procession around Scotland, how much one wonders did the thoughts of the king go back to his mother. Edward had visited his mother as lately as February before his journey to the north.

Her funeral would be delayed for the return of her son, but it had been a remarkable journey for the beautiful young girl from Provence. The woman whose marriage to King Henry III of England had begun the deepening of the Anglo-Savoyard relationship for a century to come, perhaps in those final days in the nunnery at Amesbury her mind returned to the journey she had undertaken north along the Rhône with her uncle Guillaume. She was the third of the four sisters of Count Ramon Berenguer V of Provence and Béatrice de Savoie to pass away, the four sisters who had all become queens of Europe. Sadly, her queenship and marriage to Henry had always been eclipsed by her sister Marguerite's to Louis, the soon-to-be-sainted Louis. She had tried to have her late husband, the irredeemably pious Henry elevated to sainthood, but in this she failed. She had never quite been accepted by the English - Matthew Paris's contemporaries always distrustful of foreigners - this she shared with her daughter-in-law. Both ladies from the sunny, fragrant Mediterranean had made their homes in cold, damp, gloomy old England. A more recent reappraisal of Alianor and her daughter-in-law Leonor comes from Hilton: 'Eleanor of Castille is the better remembered of the two. Yet it is the first of the southern princesses [Alianor] who was the greater English Queen.'[22]

Perhaps in her last moments her mind returned, as perhaps Leonor's may have, to her coronation in Westminster Abbey. That was over half a century ago now; she was now almost the only one alive who had been there. She had been a Queen of England and Duchess of Aquitaine. It had been a long journey from the Provence of her childhood. She had known Bordeaux and Gascony, the Paris of her elder sister Marguerite too, Fontevraud, Portigny, Chartres, Saint-Omer, Bourgogne, and Amiens and of course England. Her son had become a great king of England, her daughter Margaret a queen of Scotland, and her sisters had been queens of France, of the Germans and of Naples. Much if not most of this achieved through the family of her mother Béatrice and her uncles Guillaume, Pierre, Philippe, Thomas, Amédée and Boniface. She had led a long and fruitful life; with her at the end would have been her granddaughter Mary of Woodstock, Edward and Leonor's seventh daughter and now a nun at Amesbury. She had developed a love for the songs of the troubadours as a child – perhaps they played once more in her mind, perhaps she heard once more the choir singing at her coronation '*Christus vincit, Christus regnat, Christus, Christus imperat*'.

Alianor de Provence, perhaps the central character in forming the life of Othon de Grandson by forging the bridge to England, was laid to rest at Amesbury, not Westminster, on 8 September 1291. It was a quiet affair, not a state funeral. Professed nuns, for that she now was, were normally buried in their convents, dressed in the habit of their order, and so it was with Alianor. Edward asked the abbot of nearby Glastonbury to lay to rest his mother. She was placed in a tomb fit for a queen under the high altar; sadly, it has not survived, Amesbury Abbey being a casualty of the Reformation. So, the last resting place of Alianor de Provence is unknown; what is more she is the only queen of England with an unmarked grave; she may lie beneath a beautiful cypress tree within the grounds, and if this be so then it is a fitting memorial of a girl from Provence.

Edward had brought the heart of his beloved Leonor to Amesbury; he continued his mournful journey to London also with his mother's heart, '*duarum reginarum*', the two queens, wrote the Osney chronicler.[23] On Sunday, 6 December Leonor's heart was laid to rest next to that of her son Alphonso, in the Dominican Priory of the Blackfriars and on the same day Alianor's heart found its resting place in the Franciscan friary of Greyfriars by Newgate. Neither survive to this day, having both being consumed by the flames of the Great Fire of London in 1666. Alianor herself chose Amesbury and as Powicke noted, that she had 'made

England her home';[24] thus in the end, the girl from Provence, who had been much abused by Londoners, chose England as her place of eternal rest, which speaks volumes of her nature – she wanted to be close to her family.

The year 1291 ended with news both good and bad for this realm in the making. From Wales came news of the final capture of Rhys ap Maredudd, the Welsh noble from Deheubarth, who had been unhappy with his reward from Edward for service in the Welsh wars and rebelled in 1287. A rebellion made worse in Edward's mind, since it broke out in his absence while away in Gascony seeing to what he would have seen as far more important matters than the wounded pride of Rhys ap Maredudd. His rebellion which had brought the death of, among others, Othon's kinsman Jean de Bonvillars, constable of Harlech and Deputy Justiciar of North Wales would now be punished: he was executed.

Far worse the bad news came at last from Cyprus, the last stronghold of Outremer, the city of Acre, had fallen to the Mamluk sultan. News of the loss had taken from May until late August to reach Rome,[25] England a further number of weeks later, possibly not until late September or even early October. The Greek monk Arsenius reproached the papacy of the Fall of Acre: if only they had been so keen to defend Outremer as they had been to defend their rights in Sicily, declaring to Nicholas IV: 'Holy Father! If thou hast not heard of our sorrow, out of the bitterness of my heart will I reveal it. Would to God that thou hadst not been so intent on the recovery of Sicily.'[26]

Now the news from an impoverished Grandson from Cyprus was of the terrible events of the Fall of Acre. It cannot be stressed how much this calamitous news would have shocked Edward's court, and indeed all of Christendom. As the year closed correspondence, now lost to us, passed between London and Cyprus as to what on earth to do next. Edward had committed himself to setting forth for Outremer once more on 24 June 1293.

We do not know the contents of the letter from Cyprus that prompted Edward in January 1292 to allow aid to be sent to Othon de Grandson,[27] but it certainly carried news of the death of Leonor de Castile, but perhaps also instructions for Grandson to continue his envoy by going on to the Cilician Kingdom of Armenia, now the only entry point for a potential crusade. Nor do we know how Grandson had described the consequences of the Fall of Acre, its destruction, its death toll, for Christendom its affront to God.

Edward's intention to pursue his crusade and rectify this affront may be evidenced by the beginning, in 1292, of works to reconstruct Saint Stephen's Chapel within the Palace of Westminster. An 'English Saint Chapelle' had been his father's wish since he had seen the beautiful original in Paris. It would be innovative and influential in its design; built in the English perpendicular Gothic style, it sat at right angles to Westminster Hall. It was not the first chapel on the site, Edward's grandfather John's reign saw its first mention, but Edward's rebuilding was a statement of intent. It would be rebuilt in fits and starts, as funds allowed, for the remainder of Edward's reign. Louis had built Saint Chapelle in preparation for crusade, and it is very possible that the work at Saint Stephen's Chapel, and work on the king's chamber were similarly motivated. Further evidence that his thoughts in 1292 were of crusade, rather than matters closer to home, is evidenced by a letter received from the sultan, gloating of his victory at Acre and the massacre of Christians, being distributed widely to parishes, clearly an attempt to stoke righteous indignation on behalf of his subjects that might be used to fuel a crusade.[28]

However, Edward had received only half of the £130,000 funds earmarked for the crusade when news arrived from Rome that Girolamo Masci, Pope Nicholas IV, had gone to meet his maker on 4 April 1292. The ensuing two-year deadlock as the cardinals could not agree a new pope did little to further the cause of crusade.

But, if the contents of Edward's correspondence with Othon are lost, we do know how Grandson's erstwhile comrade at Acre has passed the Fall down to us in the *Les Gestes des Chiprois*:

> 513. *Enſi con vos poés entendre, fu toute la Surie perdue, & la prirent & deſtrurent Sarazins, ja ſoit ſe que devant furent prizes pluzors leus que je vos ay devizés. Ceſte fois fu tout perdu, que treſtous creſtiens ne tindrent.j. paume de terre en Surie.*[29]

> 513. Thus, as you have been able to learn, was all of Syria lost, taken and destroyed by the Saracens, although there were many places taken earlier that I have described for you. This time everything was lost, so that all together the Christians held not so much as a palm's breadth of land in Syria.[30]

Tout perdu, this time, everything was lost … as the Templar had written 'there were too many Saracens.'[31] Tyerman writes that for Edward crusade was 'always the next task but one, pushed into the future by domestic crises'[32] and if the domestic crisis in Wales was now done, that to the north, in Scotland, had not gone away. But not everything was *tout perdu* in the Christian east; the Kingdom of Cyprus remained, where Othon and the refugees had fled from Acre, but Cyprus was an island, not of the mainland.

Yet, a Christian kingdom had remained on the Asiatic mainland, a vassal for protection, of the Mongols, the Cilician Kingdom of Armenia. The Armenian presence in Cilicia had dated back to the first century BC, but the present kingdom to 1080, when Seljuk Turk incursions farther north had brought an exodus of Armenians south. It had become a kingdom with the crowning of King Leo I in 1198, the ruling Hethumid dynasty coming to the throne in 1226. Reigning monarch at the time of the Fall of Acre was King Hethum II.

Cilicia lay in Anatolia, to the north of Syria, along today's southern coast of Turkey, protected from the ravages of the Turks to the north by the Taurus mountains, pierced only by the Cilician Gates, and the Mamluks to the south by the lesser Amonos mountains. Its capital lay at Sis, today's Kozan, but its chief strategic asset was the port of Lajazzo, also known as Ayas, today's Yumurtalik, at the head of the Armenian Bay, today's Gulf of Alexandretta.

Othon de Grandson remained in the Middle East for around three years after the Fall of Acre, carrying out diplomatic work on Cyprus and in Cilicia. His regard for the Cypriots had not been great since the hesitant support for Acre he had witnessed for himself twenty years earlier. Nonetheless, it was a safe haven. Given that Edward had probably sent Grandson east to reconnaissance a future crusade, it is likely his thoughts turned to how his lord might fulfil his wish, and so his thoughts turned to Cilicia. Clifford expanded the view of Charles Köhler that Othon returned with a plan for a new crusade, the reconnaissance that Edward had required, that it involved using Ayas or Lajazzo as the base, a well-protected harbour, a hinterland not in hostile Muslim hands, a hinterland rich in provisions and horses, a base sitting within an orthodox Christian ally who was the vassal of Arghūn with whom an alliance was needed to ensure success.[33] The famous traveller Marco Polo, who first visited Ayas in 1271, reportedly described it as a 'city good for good trade', adding that 'all spices, silk, gold and wool from inland were carried to this town'. So, Grandson sailed from Cyprus to Cilicia, as he put ashore at Ayaş he would have disembarked by the recently built castle, a nod to the earlier predations of Baibars. We know of Othon's travels to Cilician Armenia from the contemporary Armenian historian and acquaintance of Grandson's, Hethum of Corycus, and his *Flos historiarum terre Orientis* or *Flower of the Histories of the East* which has survived to our own age.

The ruling King Hethum II abdicated his throne in 1293 to become a monk of the Franciscan order, in favour of his brother Thoros III. It seems from Hethum of Corycus that Grandson and that other refugee from Acre, the Templar Jacques de Molay, (Fig 2.0) had had a hand in affairs and the better reordering of the kingdom to meet the Mamluk threat and preserve it as a base for ongoing crusading ventures. However, in 1295 Hethum II was restored to his throne, Hethum of Corycus writing:

> When this was discovered, his second brother, lord Theodore, being summoned by lord Othon de Grandson, and several other nobles from the Kingdom of Cyprus, who had come to Armenia and other nobles and vassals of the Kingdom of Armenia, restored the dominion and kingdom to his eldest brother, lord Hethum … And upon these things I call to my witness the God of heaven, and the noble and wise man that Lord Othon de Grandson, and the masters of the house of the Temple and Hospital, and the brethren of their congregation, who were at that time in those parts, and in general all the nobles and men and people of the kingdom Armenia and Cyprus.[34]

Hayton makes two references to Othon, before and after the ellipses, which appear to be firstly 1293 and secondly 1295; however, since, as we will see, we know he was back in the west by 1295, the second dating must surely be in error. It has been suggested that the error may point to a second visit to Armenia, later in 1299,[35] but this too cannot be squared with his known whereabouts in the west.[36] The only known gap in Grandson's movements for this period are between June 1298 and February 1299, leaving no time for a 1299 journey east. Kingsford puts the visit to Armenia in 1294.[37] Therefore, we must conclude that Hayton, writing later, is separating one account of the same intervention into two, or that the second reference refers to the earlier. Forey notes that the second part of the text (after the ellipses) only appears in 'a few late manuscripts of the chronicle'.[38]

The reference to the Master of the Temple is to Jacques de Molay, (Fig 2.0) who would be its last Master, and as we saw earlier was known to Othon from his time as Visitor of the Order in England and would be referenced years later in payments from the order to Grandson. Molay was made Grand Master on Cyprus, no later than 20 April 1292,[39] when he his recorded acting as such; Forey sees Othon as having been 'involved'.[40] But as Alain Demurger has well suggested 'involved' cannot have meant direct participation in Molay's election since such a meeting would have been closed to Templars only.[41] The idea of being 'involved' came from a declaration given later during the suppression of the order; a Templar, Hugh de Fauro, gave testimony that Jacques de Molay had sworn before the Master of the Hospital and '*coram domino Odone de Grandisono milite*', that is 'before the knight Sir Othon de Grandson' but this must mean indirect not direct involvement.[42] Some have seen Grandson acting on behalf of the French king Philippe in the election, as evidenced by the 1308 pension payments from the French treasury upon suppression of the Templars discussed earlier; however, since this was entirely in fulfilment of an ongoing Templar obligation this can be safely discounted.

Grandson's closer relationship with Molay and the Templars seems to stem from his time at Acre, on Cyprus and in Cilicia between 1291 and 1294. Evidence of this comes not only from the aforesaid payments from the Templars to Grandson but also grants in the other direction. When both Molay and Grandson were back in the west, on 14 July 1296, Othon would grant the Templars 200 *Livres* from his revenues at Salins-les-Bains in the Franche Comté, a source of revenue he had used to similarly grant the monks of Saint-Jean Baptiste in Grandson before he had left for the Holy Land. (Fig 1.9) The first grant was in essence for prayers of safe return; the second grant looks like thanks for a safe return. The great salt works of Salins belonged to the Count of Burgundy; they were also known as the Seigneurs de Salins, and the works and its grander enlightenment era equivalent today enjoy UNESCO-listed status. The grant to the Templars was in consideration of the great help Othon had received from '*mes chiers amis en dieu freres Jaques de Molai*', that is, 'my dear friend in God brother Jacques de Molay' and he referred to the help which '*li freres du celle meismes Relegion ont fait a mes accessors, e a moi deca mer et de la mer en la sainte terre e ne cesse encore de faire*' or 'the brethren of that same order have given to my ancestors and to myself in the West and in the East in the Holy Land, and still continue to give'.[43] His reference to his *anccessurs* is likely to mean Barthélémy de Grandson who had died in 1158 in Jerusalem.

The Templar financial commitment to Othon is given to us in a papal confirmation of 17 August 1308 by Pope Clement V.[44] Upon suppression of the order Grandson was keen, obviously, that payments continue, since they were the enormous sum of 2,000 *Livres Tournois*, equating to £500 at the time, and over £350,000 in today's money. The pension arrangement was made by the Grand Master, named as Jacques de Molay, and variously dated to 1277, 1287 or 1296–97. Demurger wrote: 'Fault lay with the editor of Clement V's records … The editor put the date 1277, while M. L. Bulst-Thiele transcribed it as 1297, whereas the original, very clearly and without abbreviations or deletions says 1287.'[45] In his notes to this assertion, he cites the Vatican Archives date as '*Anno millesimo duecentesimo octuagesimo septimo*' or 'In the year one thousand two hundred and eighty-seven.'[46] Now of course, as we have seen Molay did not succeed Beaujeu until 1292, which renders the dating of the award problematic. Demurger then suggested that it was not Molay who made the award despite specific reference to him '*Jacobus de Mollay*', but his predecessor Beaujeu – in short, that the date was correct but the master's name incorrect. Forey argued the contrary, writing that it was: 'more likely that the grant was made by Jacques de Molay and that the date was wrongly copied'.[47] Given, Molay's 1292 election as Grand Master this would suggest 1296–97 – in short, the date was incorrect, but the master's name correct. Demurger acknowledged in his notes that 'a new problem arose … Grandson and the Temple were already connected in 1287: where, how and for what reason?' Indeed, Demurger's dating would create such questions, while Forey's dating would place them squarely in the context of the Fall of Acre and his time in the east with Molay. This '*compensare*' was given by the The Poor Fellow-Soldiers of Christ and of the Temple of Solomon for '*operibus virtuosis*' or 'virtuous actions' rendered by Othon in support of the order, but surely more likely post-Fall of Acre than before.

In confirmation of the pension, Clement V granted Othon three former Templar houses in France as a part of the continuing settlement, those at Thors, Épailly and Coulours,[48] an act unlikely to have been undertaken at the time in favour of a knight of the order. (Fig 2.2) And so, the 'virtuous works' referred to by Clement would appear to date from his time in Acre in 1291.(Fig 2.2) So, the date of 1277 attached to the payments by the transcription of them is certainly mistaken, and for the 1287 of the original 1308 manuscript we should read 1296–97.[49] Demurger gives 1296 clearly as the date for Molay meeting with Grandson and the Salins grant.[50] Othon de Grandson's intimate links with the Templars continue to intrigue, but in Cyprus and Armenia 1292–94, as at Acre 1291, and here with his pension payments they point to a significant and close ally in matters Outremer rather than a member of the order itself, of which there is no mention.[51]

The restoration of the Armenian monarch appears to have been in view of Hethum II's good relations with the Mongols, hence defence of the realm. It seemed then in the winter of 1294–95 that Othon's business in the east was done. He had learned of the assassination in December 1293 of the conqueror of Acre, Al-Ashraf Salāh ad-Dīn Khalil ibn Qalawūn. So, as Othon left the Middle East, although Acre had fallen, its assailant was himself no more, and there was at least some hope that Armenia might yet provide a foothold for another crusade. It is also likely that Grandson was hearing from England of renewed war clouds threatening, this time with Philippe IV's France. In December 1294 he was travelling home, as we have safe passage for him being arranged for him in southern Italy by Charles II of Naples dated 18 December.[52] As he did so, Pope Celestine V resigned on 13 December, something that would not happen again until 2013 with the resignation of Benedict XVI, so this meant a new pope. Pietro da Morrone reigning as Celestine V had been pope for just six months ending a two-year interregnum. The hermit Pietro gave way to a new pope, who would later have Pietro imprisoned, where he would die, something that would store up much trouble to come. Nonetheless, after a short conclave, on 24 December, a new pope, Benedetto Caetani, was elected, reigning as Boniface VIII – Grandson hastened to Rome as Edward's envoy. (Fig 2.1)

Caetani had been a member of the papal legation to England in the time of Simon de Montfort and had found himself once besieged in the Tower of London, only to be rescued by the then Lord Edward. Boniface had played a part in the resignation of Celestine and had him held safely or imprisoned in Fumone until his death a year later. He would reign as a pope ever conscious of papal authority and one who sought to defend the rights of the Church, and assert spiritual authority over temporal authority, something that would bring him increasingly into conflict with both Philippe and Edward. He would codify canon law, found Rome University, re-establish the Vatican archive, but it is collision path with the kings of Europe for which he will be mostly remembered. Many will see in his reign the final showdown between the idea of a United Christendom and the growing idea of nation states. It was said that Celestine had thrown these words at his successor, Boniface, 'you have entered like a fox, you will reign like a lion, but you will die like a dog.'[53] (Fig 2.1)

In October 1294, Othon's nephew Gérard de Vuippens had left England, on Edward's behalf, en route to the Papal Curia, and he would bring much news with him.[54] Given his grant of safe passage of December 1294 through Italy, Grandson likely arrived at the Papal Curia in the months shortly afterward, allowing time for Vuippens to bring him up to date with English affairs. His time at the Curia is likely to have ended in the early autumn as shown by the generous grant of 4,000 pieces of silver from the German crusade tenth (tax revenues) to Grandson as recompense for his losses in the Holy Land.[55] A further grant of 3,000 pieces of silver from the English crusade tenth (tax revenues) is later referenced in 1302 as being unpaid.[56]

It is at this point that some have seen his involvement in the struggle between the brothers Amédée and Louis for elbowroom in Vaud, and encroachment of the latter on *famille de Grandson* interests in Vaud, particularly Cossonay. This is perhaps overdramatised, though certainly Louis was ambitious in establishing himself as the Baron de Vaud. Nonetheless Grandson is likely to have asserted his family's rights and begun liaison with Louis' brother and Edward's ally Amédée in the obviously more important matters of Anglo-French relations.

In February 1295 Pope Boniface sent peace envoys to London and Paris, the nuncios being Cardinal Bertrand de Got, titular Bishop of Albano and future pope, and Cardinal Simon de Beaulieu, titular Bishop of Palestrina. (Fig 2.4) After a visit to Paris they arrived in London, even as in August Edward arrived from the now-subdued Wales. The disaffected Welsh noble Madog ap Llywelyn had taken advantage of Edward's occupation with his dispute with Philippe le Bel and flown into rebellion in 1294, a rebellion now suppressed. Edward told the bishops that he would indeed agree to an Anglo-French truce, should Philippe do the same of course, but that he could not do so without the agreement of his ally, Adolf of Nassau in Germany. Edward asked, since Edward wanted Othon and his onetime captain of an army invading Wales, Count Amédée V de Savoie, to represent him in peace negotiations which would attempt to calm the dire relations now with France.[57] Amédée and Othon were to travel to Cambrai, but Philippe delayed, awaiting Adolf's intentions. Accordingly, Grandson and the Count of Savoy travelled to Germany as an embassy to Adolf. Clifford with some irony writes that: 'it was the Germans who mistakenly believed the French when the latter swore that each territorial aggression would be the last.'[58] Then came news that on 23 October 1295 Philippe IV had outmanoeuvred Edward, signing the Treaty of Paris with King John Balliol of Scotland.[59] In trying to assemble an Anglo-German alliance, Edward had first been delayed by Welsh rebellion; now he faced an enemy to his rear – Scotland. (Fig 1.7) As Othon returned west hearing news of Welsh rebellion, war with France over Gascony, Scotland allying herself with France he may well have felt that he had left the eastern frying pan only to talk back into the western frying pan – *plus ça change, plus c'est la même chose* he may well have thought to himself.

CHAPTER 11

As Othon had returned to the west with thoughts on how a crusade might be attempted in the future, he would no doubt have been dismayed that the princes of Western Europe, divided over Sicily as he left, had now descended into many wars. The Sicilian War continued, although Alfonso of Aragon had died in the summer of 1291, thus rendering marriage to Edward's daughter Eleanor moot. His brothers James, who had now left Sicily and become king of Aragon and Frederick who had taken over in Sicily, continued the struggle. But war as we have seen had now also descended over Gascony, over Scotland, rebellion had broken out in north Wales, the very seat of his titular justiciarship at Caernarfon had been ransacked and burned – everywhere chaos seemed to reign. His master's kingship was foundering on the thorns of his problematic relations with Philippe IV of France and the Celtic fringe. He would have needed quite the catch-up; he had left Rome in 1290 with permission for Edward's son to marry the new queen of Scotland, the Maid of Norway. So, how had war after a peaceful century of relations with Scotland come to such a pass?

English kings had long claimed suzerainty over the neighbouring Scottish realm, and Scottish kings had claimed for an equally long time that no such relationship existed. Both monarchies reached back into the mythology masquerading as history of Geoffrey of Monmouth and his *History of the Kings of Britain* to support their claim. The status of the king of Scotland as a king was also called into question by the matter of unction, that is the action of anointing someone with oil or ointment as a religious rite or as a symbol of investiture as a monarch. The Treaty of York, of 1237, made between Alexander II of Scotland and Henry III of England, had regularised the border and the relationship between the two kingdoms. Alexander had quitclaimed his rights to the counties of Northumberland, Cumberland, and Westmorland in return for being granted some estate lands within these counties and becoming Henry's vassal '*de praedictis terris*' for these lands, not for the Kingdom of Scotland – there was no mention of any other feudal relationship.[1] However, the chronicler of Lanercost, writing a little later, was himself in no doubt: 'The kings of Scotland are bound to make submission to their overlord, the King of England and his heirs, as is proved from the time of King Edward named the Elder.'[2] Such a view might be firmly held but our chronicler is only expressing his belief not legal or historical fact, but it does allude to the fact that the English felt this to be true. Edward asked the monasteries and record keepers of England to find a precedent for his overlordship of Scotland, but what they found was such thin gruel. Nevertheless, Scotland had, this far, managed to maintain considerably more independence than had Wales, and developed into somewhat of a kingdom in its own right.

We can say that Scotland in 1291 was a quite different animal than Wales had been in 1276. Whereas Wales, outside of the marches, was ethnically and linguistically homogenous but politically divided then Scotland was ethnically and linguistically mixed but – and this is key– politically it was a united realm. Ethnically Scotland was made up of the descendants of that part of Northumbria that had found itself a part of Scotland and not England, these Anglo-Saxons in the southeastern part of the country were centred around Edwin's town or Edinburgh, in the southwest their descendants of Britons who hadn't fled to Wales and in the Highlands and islands of the north there were the Celtic descendants of the Irish Scotti tribe who'd lent their name to the kingdom. As recently as 2 July 1266 King Alexander III had acquired the Hebrides and the Isle of Man from Magnus VI of Norway, bringing reluctantly (as in the 1275 Manx rebellion) into Scotland a population of Norse descent. Ruling over these people was an increasingly francophone nobility of Anglo-Norman descent.

Included among the latter was John Balliol, who was the son of another John Balliol I, himself the son of Cecily de Fontaines and Hugh de Balliol of the *famille de Balliol* originating from the village of Bailleul in Picardy. Jean de Balliol was Lord of Barnard Castle and founder of Balliol College, Oxford. Another, Robert de Brus, 5th Lord of Annandale of the *famille de Brus* or *de Bruis*, derived from the lands now called Brix, close to the head of the Carentan Peninsula in Normandy. The *famille de Brus* held extensive lands in England as well as Annandale in southwestern Scotland, and his paternal ancestors were mostly buried at Guisborough Priory in North Yorkshire. Both John Balliol's father (Jean de Balliol I) and Robert de Brus V had been constables of Carlisle Castle and Sheriff of Cumberland, the former in 1244, the latter in 1255 and again in 1267. Indeed, the elder Jean de Balliol had been one of Henry III's leading counsellors between 1258 and 1265 and held the post Sheriff of Nottinghamshire and Derbyshire. The Battle of Lewes in 1264 had seen Jean de Balliol I, Robert de Brus V and Jean Comyn I all fighting on the royalist side alongside Henry III and the Lord Edward.[3] As mentioned earlier, Roberts V and VI de Brus accompanied Edward on crusade in 1270; Richard de Brus (brother of Robert V) was actually a household knight of Edward's. It's recorded that as he held both lands in England and Scotland and that Robert V de Brus attended both the English and Scottish courts when required.[4] His son Robert VI de Brus had in fact received pay for services in the Second Welsh War, infantry under his command fighting on Edward's behalf in Wales.[5] The *famille Comyn* is of Norman or perhaps Flemish origin. The surname is either a place name, possibly derived from Bosc-Bénard-Commin, near Rouen in the Duchy of Normandy, or from Comines, near Lille, in France. The Lady Isabelle, wife of Robert de Brus V was of the *famille de Clare*, and was the brother of Richard de Clare, father of the aforementioned Red Gilbert de Clare.

We can therefore say that not only were the nobility and monarchies of England, Scotland and France caught in a complex web of feudal relationships, but that they also intermarried to such a degree that they were also caught in a complex web of familial relationships. It is little wonder the kingdoms of England, Scotland and France would find themselves soon at war.

Following the death of the previously mentioned Maid of Norway the serious claimants to Scotland's throne were John Balliol and Robert de Brus.[6] Since other royal lines had died out, the claimants had to go back to asserting descent from King David I of Scotland, who had ruled as long ago as 1153, a century and a half earlier. He had been succeeded by his two eldest grandsons, whose lines had now perished, leaving the line of his third grandson, David the Earl of Huntingdon in England who'd died as long ago as 1216 in the reign of King John. This David, Earl of Huntingdon, had had daughters, the eldest of whom was Margaret, John Balliol's grandmother. David's second eldest daughter Isabel was mother to Robert de Brus V, David's third daughter Ada was mother to Jean de Hastings. Unhelpfully the *famille de Brus* kept calling their sons Robert and married Isabels.

Oh, but this was a complicated business, but in a nutshell, John Balliol claimed the best line by strict primogeniture: he was descended from the eldest ancestor and Robert de Brus V claimed closest blood line descent, as he was a generation closer to the last king.

In February 1291, when Edward was looking around for evidence to support his overlordship of Scotland, he was supported by an at first seemingly unlikely source – Robert V de Brus. The grandfather of the Bruce, and then rival for the Scottish monarchy, wrote to Edward in terms of English overlordship arising from the Treaty of Falaise. He recounted that 'in a war between the English and Scottish kings, Northumberland was lost'; this is an allusion to the war between King William I of Scotland and King Henry II of England of 1174 – William had been defeated at Alnwick during an invasion of Northumbria.[7] Robert V de Brus went on to say that in the resulting peace (Treaty of Falaise 1174) the English king's suzerainty over the Scottish king was established, writing, 'should the Scottish King make any *desobeisaunce* against England, then the Seven Earls were sworn to support the English king and his crown' – the Seven Earls being the original seven earldoms of Scotland. Robert acknowledged that this had subsequently been annulled (Quitclaim of Canterbury 1189), but that he thought this was 'invalid' because it would be 'unwise' to 'dismember the crown of such a limb' and 'that one must keep the crown whole'. This must have been music to Edward's ears, vindicating as it did the entire historic English claim to overlordship of the entire island of Britain, with a description that Scotland, was in effect, a limb of the British body and that Edward's crown represented the entire whole crown. Robert V de Brus ended this extraordinary letter by suggesting that should Edward make his '*demaunde droitureaument*' or 'request righteously' then he, Robert V de Brus, Lord of Annandale, and prospective king of Scotland would 'obey him' and 'will help him'. In the light of what we know to have followed in the coming decades this is an extraordinary document.[8]

So, to the succession crisis by where there were several claimants, Roman law favoured proximity of blood; feudal primogeniture as practised in England, Scotland favoured the strongest claim by seniority of birth. Interestingly Brus, arguing for proximity of blood in succession, cited Savoy as an example to follow, a succession crisis of 1285 which was also settled by Edward.[9] It was argued that primogeniture did not apply, since the descent had been through women, Margaret and Isabel, and that in such cases the estate ought to be divided between the claimants – that the kingdom was partible. Now the division (and weakening) of the kingdom of Scotland might have appeared tempting to an English king like Edward, but it appears to have not been considered. So Roman law or English and Scottish custom? If we lack detail of the discussions, then we are clear about the outcome: renewed deadlock. Edward appears to have lost patience (Duncan suggests this was 'fully justified')[10] with deliberations and prioritised the claims of Balliol and Brus over the remaining original claimants (now nine) on 16 June.[11] Edward seems to have acted scrupulously in this consideration, which for all concerned meant a further adjournment for international legal opinion (the University of Paris[12]) to be gathered on 3 July 1292,[13] but this time, thankfully, for only a further three months. As Duncan writes, 'he [Edward – and we might add Amédeé] must have been glad to leave Berwick and its intransigent and disputatious Scots.'[14]

Edward's position in terms of the Great Cause was neatly summed up in the question put to legal opinion in Paris, the English justification for considering Scotland a lesser kingdom is clearly described by its want of unction.[15] While it reiterated the English view of the kingdom of Scotland as dependent upon England, putting the case for both Balliol and Bruce, albeit by alias, the question as asked does refute the suggestion that Edward may have been angling for the throne of Scotland for lack of a viable heir, that is by escheat.

A royal council was held that summer, July 1292, in London while the king was away at the Scottish border, and Othon de Grandson was yet away in Cyprus, which tells us that the distant Grandson was now calling Westminster home as well as Queenhithe and the manor at Sheen. The record says that the council was held in '*domo Ottonis de Grandison extra palacium domini regis apud Westmonasterium*' or 'at the House of Othon de Grandson outside the King's Palace of Westminster.' The meeting, so held, confirms the position Grandson now held in royal affairs if we did not already need it.[16]

By the Tweed, the final sessions of the settlement of the Scottish succession, the Great Cause, began once more on 14 October 1292. But no sooner had they begun, when they had to be adjourned for several days; on 25 October, the Bishop of Bath and Wells, Lord Chancellor and perhaps one of Edward's most loyal servants, Robert Burnell, died. His body was taken for burial at Wells Cathedral, his heart at Bath Abbey. It is impossible to underestimate the influence Burnell had on Edward. Burnell had been a dominant figure during the first part of Edward's reign and had controlled many aspects of royal administration. For two decades he had worked alongside Othon de Grandson (in 1292 still absent in Cyprus) as being the cornerstone upon which Edward's foreign policy had been built. His dear wish had been to go on crusade, but unlike Edward and Othon, this wish would not be granted. His death at this juncture did not impact too much on the Scottish succession; what was to follow was likely a foregone conclusion, but his wise counsel and guiding hand in the storms that would soon come would be sorely missed. A letter survives in the UK National Archive written by Othon to Burnell's successor as Lord Chancellor, John Langton. The letter concerning the death of his friend Robert Burnell was written presumably from Cyprus and thus confirms ongoing correspondence between Grandson and England – it also confirms the status of the *famille de Bonvillars* as brothers-in-law, the late Constable at Harlech Jean de Bonvillars and the reference in the letter, Henri de Bonvillars, Prior of Wenlock noted by Othon as '*mon frere le prior de Wenloc*'.[17]

Also departing this life at Mortlake by the Thames on 8 December 1292 was Archbishop John Peckham of Canterbury, who would be interred in a tomb that survives to this day in the north transept of Canterbury Cathedral. Of late Edward had lost his mother, Alianor, his wife Leonor, his Archbishop of Canterbury, and his Lord Chancellor.

Nevertheless, following a short recess, things at Berwick moved quickly; on 6 November[18] the case of John Balliol was found to be stronger than Robert de Brus's; primogeniture had trumped proximity of blood, and Scottish custom had found favour over any recourse to imperial law. Subsequently, Balliol's case was then tested against the other claimants, until 15 November[19] when Edward and his council retired to reach a verdict. The Paris consultation had rendered opinion that supported the use of Scottish custom, failing that, English custom and not recourse to roman law, it favoured Balliol.[20]

On 17 November 1292, that verdict would finally be delivered: the next king of Scotland would be John Balliol. The announcement was made in the Great Hall of the castle at Berwick-upon-Tweed. On 19 November Edward duly issued instructions for the seisin of Scotland to be transferred to Balliol, castles handed over to him in his new realm. There was just enough time for him to be crowned on Saint Andrew's Day, Scotland's patron saint.[21] At the monastery of Scone, just north of Perth, on 30 November 1292 the Scottish crown was placed on John's head by Antony Bek, Bishop of Durham, officiating along with one of Edward's knights, John de St. John.[22] John was crowned in full ceremony, seated upon the ancient Stone of Scone, a hollowed-out stone in the form of a seat, but that Antony and John carried out the coronation gave the event a very English tone – Edward was now well and truly overlord of Scotland, the long dispute over the status of English kings vis-à-vis Scottish kings had been finally settled. On 26 December 1292 King John I of Scotland travelled south to Newcastle upon Tyne to pay homage to his liege lord, King Edward I of England – and everyone thought that was that.[23] So unlike John's predecessors, the words were not ambiguous: 'O Lord, My Lord Edward, King of England, the superior lord of the realm of Scotland, I, John de Balliol, king of Scotland, become your liegeman for the whole realm of Scotland with its appurtenances.'[24]

Many centuries later the unpredictability of the world would be summed up by British Prime Minister Harold Macmillan as 'events, dear boy, events' and events would soon blow Edward off course once more in his cherished wish to restore Christendom in Outremer. Earlier during the Lent of 1292, with Edward preparing to successfully conclude his Scottish business, unbeknown to him, his Gascon subjects, sailors from Bayonne were ashore fighting with the locals. The Île de Quémènès off the westernmost extremity of Brittany seems to have been the point of Norman Bayonnais conflict.[25] As the fists flew, insults exchanged in Occitan and Norman French, the tiny tremors that would lead to war began.

What Edward had established, or thought he had, was the feudal relationship between a king of Scotland and a king of England, but it would soon be the relationship of a king of England with the king of France that would, once more, throw the three kingdoms of England, Scotland, and France into turmoil. If John Balliol was now the vassal of Edward, then Edward remained a vassal of Philippe IV of France for the Duchy of Aquitaine. Edward, so jealous to protect his position in Britain, remained vulnerable in protecting his position in France. If Edward now regarded a Scottish king as a vassal, then, was it not right that a French king regard him similarly? This contradiction at the heart of Edward's realm would not be resolved, Edward could not have 'his cake and eat it' so to speak, and it would prove impossible to simultaneously assert his overlordship of Scotland and his independence in Gascony. The tripartite relationship would work if Edward respected John Balliol's kingship and Philippe IV respected Edward's dukedom – this was asking a lot of the individuals concerned. The hard-won retrieval of Saintonge, the Agenais and indeed the Treaty of Paris in 1259 would unravel as Philippe IV of France would attempt to do to Edward precisely what Edward had just done to John. As 1293 dawned this patiently erected status quo, much of it by Othon de Grandson, of Edward now having overlordship of the island of Great Britain while retaining Plantagenet lands in France was an edifice that would soon begin to be challenged. (Fig 1.8)

Trouble continued in French waters, the Normans retaliating for what they saw as Gascon aggression at Quémènès by attacking a boat from Bayonne, sinking it along with all her crew. During the summer of 1292 Norman ships continued to prey upon ships carrying out the wine trade between Gascony and England and Ireland, both off Normandy and in Norman ports.[26] On one occasion English pilgrims had, apparently, had their heads, feet and hands removed in Dieppe, an atrocity that saw Philippe IV finally act, calling for peace. But the attacks continued: seventy ships returning to England with wine from Gascony were attacked again off the coast of Brittany, worse perhaps, in Saint-Malo the Normans attacked seventy Gascon sailors from two Bayonnais ships and they were 'flayed or hanged in their skins with dogs.'.[27] The chronicler of Guisborough writes of '*suspendentes homines cum canibus*' or 'hanged men with dogs'.[28]

By now ships were sent to Gascony in convoy; one such assembled at Portsmouth on 24 April, was met and attacked on the outward voyage, by a Norman fleet off Cap Saint-Mathieu on 15 May.[29] But this time the English had armed themselves and expected attack, the location (close to the Île de Quéménès) looks deliberate, revenge was on their minds – a sea battle ensued and this time it was the Normans who were beaten.[30] The English then sailed for La Rochelle in the sensitive County of Poitou and proceeded to sack the town; this would now be a deliberate provocation for Philippe.[31] Now with the conflict threatening to get out of control, Edward too issued instructions for peace to be maintained between his Gascon subjects and Philippe's Normans; on 22 May 1293 he asked the sailors of the Cinque Ports and Bayonne 'to observe the recent peace with the King of France' despite what Edward called 'the malice' of their enemies.[32]

If La Rochelle was a sensitive provocation, then the reported raid of the Normans up the river Charente struck directly at the most sensitive point of all, the Saintonge, the carefully negotiated division between Edward's lands as Duc d'Aquitaine and Philippe's as king of France. Edward's sous seneschal Rostand de Soler wrote a report of the Norman raiding which survives. Rostand de Soler. the son of another Rostand de Soler (who had been seneschal of Gascony under Henry III from 1241 until 1242) and grandson of another, the youngest de Soler had been a mayor of Bordeaux, and now guarded Saintes from incursion from the north. Saintes was the scene of Henry's humiliation at the hands of his brother-in-law Louis back in 1243 and had only recently returned to Plantagenet hands thanks to the Treaty of Amiens of 1279. The peace of Amiens had divided the County of Saintonge along the river Charente, a Plantagenet bank from a Capetian bank with a bridge at Saintes. It is difficult to imagine a more sensitive spot for the Normans to choose in echoing their Scandinavian ancestors and going Viking. Sailing up the river the Normans used the French bank to raid the Gascon bank, the French side providing a haven for ongoing operations. Armed with crossbows and swords, wearing haketons[33] and bascinets[34] they descended upon Saint-Agnant, Saint-Nazareth-sur-Charente and Soubise, raping and pillaging like Vikings of old. They eventually sailed away following numerous raids with, among other things, money, jewellery, cheese, grain, bread, capons, chickens, cattle, weapons, ploughs, utensils, shirts, boots and perhaps most shocking altar cloths, candles and church ornaments.[35]

Blame for the breakdown in Anglo-French relations has, predictably, been apportioned differently on either side of the Channel, even in recent times.[36] At this distance it is difficult to know the truth: who threw the first blow, and are the atrocities recorded in English sources accurate or embellishment? In May 1293 Edward sent his brother Edmund Crouchback and one of his trusted lieutenants, Henri de Lacy, Earl of Lincoln, to Paris, on 10 May letters of credence to 'consult' with Philippe on 'the discord between the seafaring men of Normandy and England'. They were further empowered to 'make a truce between the said disputants until 15 August so that quarrels between them may cease and peace be reestablished.'.[37] An undated report from Edmund makes reference to a meeting on 11 July with the French queen, Jeanne de Navarre, who was of course the daughter of his wife Blanche d'Artois by her first marriage to Henry of Navarre – as always this would be family business.[38]

That summer Edward also had family matters on his mind in addition to the succession crisis in Scotland and war clouds over the Channel with France. His eldest daughter Eleanor was now to be wed to Henri III, Count of Bar. The County of Bar lay to the east of Champagne adjoining Henri de Grandson's Prince Bishopric of Verdun; at this point in history both Bar and Verdun were a part of the empire and not the Kingdom of France. On

20 September 1293 Henri was married to Eleanor at St. Augustine's Abbey which would, upon the Reformation, later become Bristol Cathedral.[39]

Meanwhile, on 24 July, Edmund was, once more, granted safe conduct while 'going beyond the seas'.[40] This time with Richard Gravesend, Bishop of London, and William Greenfield, future Archbishop of York and Lord Chancellor, for ecclesiastical company, they made three proposals to calm tensions with the French; first (and most unlikely to be accepted) that the grievances of French subjects be heard in English courts, or by four commissioners (two English, two French) to judge according to the rule of the sea, the *Loi d'Oleron*, or that failing these remedies papal arbitration might be invoked.[41] Philippe rejected these proposals and demanded that the mayor and leading citizens of Bayonne be brought and imprisoned at Perigueux in Périgord. On 16 October 1293 Philippe summoned Edward, his vassal as Duc d'Aquitaine, to present himself before the French *parlement*, at Christmastide, to answer for the actions of his Gascon subjects.[42] Philippe was going to treat with Edward exactly as Edward had been treating with John Balliol – Edward was to appear before parlement in January 1294. Edward once more despatched his brother Edmund to negotiate, who took with him his wife Blanche d'Artois, who was again of course the mother of Philippe's queen, Jeanne de Navarre – making Edmund not only Philippe's second cousin but also his stepfather-in-law. One might imagine that Edward imagined this could all be worked out, as it had before, by the intervention of the good offices of the related ladies, as it had been by Alianor and Marguerite de Provence. Edmund was authorised to bend to Philippe's requests and affirm Edward's position as Philippe's vassal provided that a prompt resolution was agreed, but Philippe IV was not his grandfather, or indeed his father, but the king who would find fame viciously suppressing the Knights Templar, and there was no Robert Burnell or Pierre de Savoie or Othon de Grandson present with diplomatic oil to pour on troubled Gallic waters.

When agreement had proven difficult, it had been Blanche and Jeanne that brokered a deal, as had Alianor and Marguerite before them. What they proposed and Edmund had readily and trustingly agreed was that various fortresses in Gascony would be given up and twenty Gascon hostages offered, if Philippe would cancel the order to appear before parlement, that a more longstanding solution would be agreed at a meeting of the two kings in Amiens and the bargain settled by the marriage of Philippe's sister Marguerite to Edward to put the relationship on a steadier footing. Sure, the agreement would have to be private, for now. French injured feelings had to be assuaged, but an agreement is what Edmund thought he had got. Morris suggests that Philippe went so far as to personally reassure Edmund, Blanche, and Jeanne that he was genuine and honest in his assurances that he would hand back the Gascon fortresses.[43] Prestwich goes as far as to declare that this was akin to the appeasement of the 1930s, that what Edmund had achieved was 'peace in our time'.[44] In agreeing to this bargain Edmund has been criticised, perhaps rightly, by Prestwich as being 'duped' by Philippe and marking a failure of English foreign policy. But Edmund, and Edward, were proceeding in the way that Plantagenet Capetian relations had proceeded since the partly Savoyard-facilitated rapprochement leading to and following the Treaty of Paris in 1259. Americans tend to speak more directly than English academics, and perhaps Philippe's duplicity is best summed up by Othon de Grandson's biographer, Clifford, suggesting that Edmund was 'generous, loyal, honourable and magnanimous' and that he had been deceived by 'a massive piece of double-crossing'.[45] Some have perhaps rightly argued that aforesaid treaty and rapprochement were flawed in leaving Aquitaine as the fief of a French king, and that it laid the ground for the future Hundred Years' War, but those taking part in negotiations in the 1250s or the 1290s were operating in an environment where it was thought peaceful coexistence was possible. The agreement was made before witnesses on 3 February 1294. The order was given to hand over the castles, and Jean de Lacy was despatched to Gascony to facilitate, along with seneschal Jean de St. Jean, the handover of Bordeaux and Gascony to French officials,[46] which happened in March 1294. As late as 19 April Jean de Bretagne was suggesting that he had seen a French safe conduct for Edward to come to France to fulfil the secret treaty.[47]

In the event the calculating Philippe reneged on his private agreement with Edmund and refused to give up his ill-gotten gains in Gascony. War was coming and Prestwich is in no doubt that it was 'of Philip's choice, not Edward's';[48] despite French academic protestations it is difficult to view Philippe's actions in any other way than a duplicitous means of depriving the great-grandson of Alianor d'Aquitaine his rightful patrimony. In the spring of 1294 Edward moved to Kent to bid Eleanor farewell on her journey to her new home in the County of Bar, and in expectation of a safe conduct to travel to Amiens to meet with Philippe to amicably resolve differences, man to man, anointed king to anointed king.

Edward, by accounts, turned red, purple, and perhaps a whole host of other colours when he heard that Philippe had deceived him, being met with a further summons to attend the French parlement to account for his Gascon vassals with Philippe in possession now of Gascony's fortifications. The poetic words of chronicler Pierre de Langtoft give us a flavour of the encounter. Langtoft asks, 'What does King Edward when he becomes aware of the fraud?'[49] – what indeed. The answer was the counsel of Bishop of Durham Antony Bek, who was, if these are close to the actual words he used, treading on dangerous ground: 'My Lord King thou art not a child.'[50]

The words may have been said of a friend to another, hence the '*tu*', but were clearly designed, if uttered, to break Edward from ideas of marriage to Marguerite and an ongoing warm relationship with Philippe to war. Bek, according to Langtoft, went on:

> If thou wilt recover thy land of Gascony,
> And take good care that Philip dissimulates with thee no longer,
> Arise, and bestir yourself,
> sleep not like a monk;
> Put on the hauberks,
> trample down the carrion,
> Mount the steeds,
> and take spear in fist.[51]

In this way, a king of England, was stirred to war with the king of France in the spring of 1294. But war with France was not going to be like anything undertaken by Edward so far. France was most definitely not Gwynedd, and he had the memory of his father's vain attempts to recover lost ancestral lands in France. But for Edward, like the recovery of the four cantrefs in North Wales, this was personal, and once more someone was attempting to take from him his appanage, something he had held for forty years now. Bek went on to point the way to the need to call in alliances now, the empire, Burgundy and of course Savoy. On 13 August, while at Portsmouth, in furtherance of this alliance, Edward mandated his son-in-law Duke John II of Brabant, Lothier and Limburg to deliver £22,000 to Count Amédée V de Savoie, himself only recently returned from England, 'for the payment of the people of Sauvoye [*sic*] and Burgoyne and those parts for their aid in the king's war against the king of France'.[52]

What Bek did not apparently say, is that Edward was going to need all his resources, which would mean his new lands in Wales and his now acknowledged vassal, John Balliol in Scotland.

Edward rejected Philippe's further summons to parlement of 19 May[53] and sent four friars across the Channel to formally renounce his homage to Philippe for the Duchy of Aquitaine. The friars' letters of credence are dated 20 June, but that may not have been the actual date of their departure for Paris. The breakdown of Anglo-French relations is perhaps best shown by Edward sending men of the church as envoys, likely thinking safe passage not possible for others, and in any case apparently the poor clerics were arrested upon arrival and spent days of incarceration before finally being allowed to make the formal withdrawal of homage – such were the feelings either side of the Channel. The rhyming verse of Langtoft gives us two of their names: William Gainsborough, a Franciscan, and Hugh of Manchester and gives Calais as the location of their prison for one week. He goes on to relate the indignation of the English king and his withdrawal of homage, in the medieval world a serious business. While we may not vouch for its accuracy we can hear the flavour of contemporary affront:

> Wherefore we are come here by command.
> Of our king sir Edward, whom God defend from evil !
> He signifies to thee by us openly,
> That he has strictly performed homage to thee
> For all Aquitaine, to hold freely,
> According to the peace arranged at the agreement
> Between your two ancestors by common assent,
> When their great strife was finally appeased.
> Thou hast not held it but broken it maliciously.
> And at his last repair to his people in Gascony,
> A covenant was made very solemnly
> To be held between you for ever.
> Thou hast not held it quite a year.
> Upon that I remind thee of the last dealing,
> Between, you and him it was made privately,
> Whereby he made thee a feoffment of Aquitaine,
> To refeoff him of the same tenement …
>
> Holdest him not thy man, nor does he mean to be so,
> Nor will he henceforward be to thee obedient.
> But when he shall have recovered his land to himself
> He will claim to hold it of God Almighty.[54]

All this, of course, meant that crusade was impossible, Edward's avowed intention to restore Outremer – the whole point of Othon de Grandson's reconnaissance of Acre where he and his nephews Pierre d'Estavayer and Pierre de Vuippens had sailed into the Fall of Acre – all this had been rendered null and void by the duplicity of Philippe. In June of 1294 Edward wrote to a potential eastern ally, Florent de Hainault, Prince of Achaea in Greece, of his changed circumstances; he wrote in anger, as the fate of Outremer had once more been decided by a divided Christendom.[55]

Meanwhile, writs had been issued for a feudal muster at Portsmouth for 1 September. The plan was to send a force to Gascony to try to recover at least some lost ground, while in the north Edward would amass an alliance as suggested by Bek, strong enough to directly challenge Philippe. Edward summoned not only the English nobles to come to his side, along with their knights and peasantry, but also the Scottish nobility led by John Balliol, and the Welsh peasantry. On 30 August, Reginald de Grey, from the castle at Ruthin he had been granted at the end of the Second Welsh War, was asked to raise men from the four cantrefs. Robert de Staundon, the Sheriff of Merioneth, was to supply men from the new counties that had once made up Gwynedd. Staundon had only lately taken custody of the castle at Harlech from Maître Jacques de Saint George, the order coming 28 December 1293 while Edward was at Canterbury.[56] James, and his wife Ambrosia, had held the castle since July 1290; it had been quite unusual for a master mason to hold the position of constable rather than a knight. Robert de Tibetot, Justiciar of South Wales, along with his deputy, Geoffrey Clement, were called upon on the same date to supply men from the marches and the south.[57] The army was to be led to Gascony by Tibbetot, along with Jean de Bretagne and Jean de St. Jean, the latter being the seneschal of Gascony on his way to recover the lands under his care given away in February. The Welsh contingent was summoned to be at Shrewsbury on 30 September.

When, years earlier, upon his return from Gascony, Edward had expelled the Jews from his kingdom, his grateful subjects had consented to a novel lay subsidy or tax of a fifteenth on movable goods (6.66 per cent). Having exhausted one source of money, Edward was now about to inexplicably exhaust another – he cut his links with his Italian bankers, the Riccardi Di Lucca, who had contributed so much to the success of his reign thus far by financing his Welsh wars and the castles that followed. The seals by which the Italians collected the customs revenues were broken on 29 July 1294.[58] Why he did this is, in the words of his biographer Prestwich, 'not easy to explain'.[59] After all, his brother Edmund had only recently been advanced just over 25,000 marks by the Riccardi in France for expenses incurred during his recent diplomatic mission to negotiate the ill-fated private treaty with Philippe.[60]

Edward moved to seize the assets of the Riccardi in England and imposed his own customs duty on wool exports of 3 marks (40 shillings) on a sack of wool – up until its repeal in 1297 it would render some £110,000 to the crown. So why at this critical juncture did Edward break with the Riccardi? Reasons put forward have included impending bankruptcy on the part of the Italian merchants brought about by their being hit by earlier demands from Philippe IV in France and others, resulting in the impending insolvency of the Riccardi. For Edward this was made clear by an inability to provide the crusade monies due – the money gathered by the Riccardi for his crusade amounted to a handy sum now that war with France was imminent, some 100,000 marks. But now when in urgent need of it, despite what his conscience and the pope might think of using money set aside for crusade, he was informed by the Italians it was not there. What Edward was suddenly faced with was a thirteenth-century credit crunch. If the Riccardi had been innovative in their novel money-raising and -lending activities, then they were novel now in experiencing a credit crunch.

The reason for abandoning a tried and trusted system lay in Edward's frustration and sense of inexplicable betrayal, at the loss of the money he was literally banking on. He had just learned that a treaty he had taken as negotiated, with Philippe, was now being reneged upon, and now too his Italian bankers were unable to provide their customary support. Kaeuper writes:

> We can picture Edward's going into a purple rage upon learning that not only were his bankers unable to finance the coming war with France, but also that the papal tenth, secured after years of negotiation, could not be fully recovered. In one of their letters the Riccardi quoted Edward's declaration that 'what he had taken as ours he had taken as from men who had deceived him.' A passage in what seems to be the earliest of the extant letters refers to 'the great indignation of the king.'[61]

Taken together, Philippe's 'double cross' of and what he saw as being 'deceived' by the Riccardi, then Edward's actions look understandable if not advisable.

Edward looked for allies that might help him to recover Gascony. As we saw earlier, in September 1293, his daughter Eleanor, whom Edward had tried to marry to the now-deceased Alfonso of Aragon, a match which had caused him great difficulty with Philippe, had now been married to Henry III, Count of Bar. The County of Bar lay on the eastern border of the County of Champagne and France, either side of the Prince Bishopric of Verdun, the recent see of Henri de Grandson, Othon's brother. Therefore, unsurprisingly, a treaty was drawn up in November 1294 whereby Henry would provide Edward with 1,000 horsemen for six months in return for 30,000 marks. Of course, Amédée V, Count of Savoy, who in effect owed his position to Edward, could be relied upon as an ally.[62] A further ally would be the suzerain of both Henry and Amédée, Adolf of Nassau, the king of the Germans, uncrowned Holy Roman Emperor. To that end, on the same day he despatched his refutation of homage to Philippe, Edward sent envoys to Germany to treat for an alliance with Adolf.[63] Capetian France had long adopted a policy of aggressive expansion into the lands it thought its own, of 'Gaul', that is uniting all francophones under their monarchy. This hostility to the princes and kings on its periphery had been successfully pursued by picking fights with each of them independently; in this way it had long been Philippe's aim to strip Edward of Gascony as Philippe Auguste had stripped John of Normandy, Maine, Anjou, and Poitou. Eventually Philippe's descendants would succeed in stripping the Counties of Burgundy, Bar, Savoy, and Prince Bishopric of Verdun among others from the empire too. However, at least in 1294, the Duke of Aquitaine in the form of Edward saw that the only way to meet this aggression from Paris was for the princes and kings to unite in common cause against Paris.[64]

If Philippe and the Riccardi had given Edward to a 'purple rage' then worse was soon to follow. In January 1291, the fifteenth tax imposed on an England which willingly accepted it, but a Wales which did not. Taxation was not new to Gwynedd; reference is made to Llywelyn causing a 'tribute to be assessed on all his lands' in 1273 before Edward had yet been crowned.[65] In 1275 as war clouds had gathered Llywelyn had imposed a tax of three pennies on every head of cattle within his lands, but the novelty of this tax is apparent from the astonishment registered by the Bishop of St. Asaph.[66] Wales was simply not used to the financial burdens that a medieval state like England might impose. Gwynedd had not minted its own coin; taxation, such as it was, had more usually been taken by the ruling house as payments 'in kind'. The medieval lay subsidy was according to economic historian J. F. Hadwin, 'the first national direct tax voted by English Parliaments to the crown'.[67] It was therefore novel in England, but the population there had been released from any debts owed to the expelled Jewry; in Wales, its novelty was sorely profound. The imposition of a centralised state's taxation hit the native population hard, having often little recourse but to sell livestock to raise coin money to pay the tax. Because of these problems it was not until the winter of 1292–93 that an assessment of taxation had even been possible.[68] What's more the financial burden appears to have fallen more heavily upon the Welsh than the English. Analysis of the surviving records for Merioneth and Flint for 1292–93 show the 2,669 inhabitants of Merioneth were obliged to pay a total of over £566 or over £400,000 in today's money, equivalent then to well over a thousand cows – and this for Merioneth alone. The final instalment of this tax was due on 30 September 1294.[69]

Also due by the same date was the order for able men, from Wales, to muster at Shrewsbury for military service in the king's war in France. There is evidence from Cambridgeshire that the general call to arms across England itself was not going well. The obligation of feudal military service was forty days, and this, because of travel times implied a geographical limit. The abbot of Ramsey had to resort to seizing cattle and horses from reluctant farmers and showing them from past records that their forebears had indeed fought for the king overseas, in order to raise men to arms.[70] Edward had apparently been forced to pardon criminals and outlaws in return for military service.[71] The departure for Gascony had been delayed from 1 September until 30 September by troubled recruitment, the difficulty raising quick finance and lastly and tellingly by that old opponent – the weather, and in particular the contrary weather of the English Channel in autumn.

Wales was a tinderbox waiting to catch fire once more. An unguarded tinderbox too, that was also seeing its royal garrisons being denuded of men for the war effort – newly built Harlech being reduced to just nineteen men.[72]

CHAPTER 12

With Othon still in the east there was rebellion now in Wales where he was still Justiciar – the Madog rebellion. We covered the rebellion more fully in my book *Welsh Castle Builders,* but Othon's Caernarfon was overrun by Madog ap Llywelyn, and the unfinished castle occupied, as were the castle at Castell y Bere which was then burned to the ground. Elsewhere in the four cantrefs Hawarden, Ruthin and Denbigh were attacked. Criccieth was besieged by Madog's forces for several months, and Morlais castle was captured by Morgan ap Maredudd in the south.

Harlech was besieged for the winter of 1294–95; among those sheltering in the castle would be the Savoyard Adam Boynard. The men of Harlech, and the women and children too, were Savoyard, English and Welsh.[1] The Savoyards were now on the edge of the world and menaced by something a good deal more threatening than the Bishop of Sion. Edward, meanwhile, found himself besieged that winter at Conwy Castle, (Fig 1.6) along with the Savoyards Guillaume de Cicon, Pierre de Champvent, and likely Maître Jacques de Saint George too. Champvent, we know then, spent some time within the walls of Conwy castle that winter. Which most likely explains why, when he later returned to the Pays de Vaud and undertook with his brother Guillaume de Champvent extensive works at the Château de Champvent that the Vaudois castle overlooking Grandson itself bears the hallmarks of Conwy. The architectural cross-fertilisation betwixt Savoy and the British Isles began to flow in both directions.[2]

However, once the winter had passed, the decisive engagement came in Mid Wales. The chroniclers Trevet and Guisborough mislead us, and countless historians including the otherwise excellent Morris, by next telling us that once the waters subside, Edward is relieved at Conwy by the Earl of Warwick, but without giving us many details. Morris took this to mean that the decisive engagement of the Welsh wars, the final battle, took place in the Conwy valley. Has the Earl of Warwick ridden all the way up from Mid Wales to relieve Conwy? – No. Thankfully for historians the chronicler at Worcester gives us the name of the battlefield – Meismeidoc. Edwards writing in 1924 was able to pinpoint the correct location, Maes Madog, now identified more accurately as Maes Moydog. He pointed to Meis as a rendering of the Welsh word for field, *maes*, and Moydog as the parish of Moydog, still today the site of farms Moydog Fawr, Moydog Fach and Moydog Uchaf. The name stretches back to the thirteenth century in the form of M'dok, Moydok and Moydauk.[3] If Trevet helped misguide us to the location, his description of the battlefield as '*in quondam planate inter duo nemora*', that is, on a 'plain between two woods' that does seem to fit with Maes Moydog even today. The Worcester annalist wrote:

> 5th March, Guillaume de Beauchamp, Earl of Warwick fought a war with the Welshmen in the place which is called in their tongue Meismeidoc; and they were laid low, of seven hundred noble men, in addition to the men who were

> drowned and fatally wounded. However, their Prince,[4] Madog ap Llywelyn, dishonourably, barely escaped.[5]

Morris also misidentified the date of the battle as 'a day or two before 24th January',[6] but the Worcester chronicler clearly sets the date of the last battle of the Welsh wars as 5 March 1295.

Madog, like Llywelyn before him, had been drawn to Mid Wales, and like the former prince, it would be his downfall. The Earl of Warwick had been at Montgomery since December, and got wind of Madog's move southwestward from Gwynedd in February, so accordingly he moved his army to Oswestry. On 4 March Warwick received very specific intelligence of Madog's movements and moved back to Montgomery and thence to Maes Moydog to meet the Welsh advance. Warwick's army had dwindled in size since December, and now counted 119 mounted bannerets, knights and cavalry, some 26 constables and just 2,689 foot soldiers plus a small number of crossbowmen and archers – Madog's number is unknown but thought to be smaller. Among the number of Warwick's army was Robert FitzWalter. Now was the time for him to take his revenge for the fall of Castell y Bere. Richard FitzAlan, Earl of Arundel, husband to the Savoyard Alésia di Saluzzo, was another at Maes Moydog seeking retribution for Bere. Also with Warwick was William de Pole, son of Gruffydd ap Gwenwynwyn, Powys as ever ranged against Gwynedd. The Mortimers were represented by William de Mortimer, the brother of Edmund, 2nd Baron Mortimer.[7] The foot soldiers were mostly men of Shropshire defending what they would have seen as an impending invasion of their county by men bent on pillage.

Madog was on the receiving end of a crushing defeat; if we take the Worcester chronicler at his word and compare with the known reductions in Warwick's payroll after the battle, we can see that the Welsh dead outnumbered the English by between seven and ten to one. That many of Madog's men were drowned, according to the Worcester chronicler, suggests that the battle ended in a rout and chaotic flight pursued by Warwick's forces. The river Vyrnwy and its tributary the Banwy to the north of the battle site, swollen by the known weather of that winter is where many found their end. The Hagnaby chronicler, likely drawing from an eyewitness wrote 'the Welshmen held their ground well, and they were the best and bravest Welsh that anyone has seen.'[8] Warwick's tactics were crucial in the overwhelming nature of the defeat, most likely by the encirclement of his enemy coupled with use of elite crossbowmen and some archery. Edward's mind now turned to increasing his hold on Gwynedd – he had another castle in mind, and this would be the crowning glory of his reign, and indeed the apogee of medieval castle design: it would be called Beaumaris.

So, the Scottish succession crisis, the Madog rebellion in Wales but most importantly the loss of Gascony and renewed war with France, this was the England to which Othon returned to from the East. As we said earlier out of the oriental frying pan into the occidental fryer. While the Welsh rebellion was concluding, the papal legates Bertrand de Got and Simon de Beaulieu had managed to bring the warring parties, the Anglo-Imperial alliance and France to the negotiating table at Cambrai in northern France in January 1296. The papal legates had asked Edward that the English church make prayers for peace, and accordingly on New Year's Day 1296 a request went out to Canterbury, York, and abbots of monasteries nationwide to pray for peace.[9] Thus Othon, with the dust of Cyprus and Armenia not yet off his surcoat, along with Earl of Pembroke, Guillaume de Valence, Walter Langton, Bishop of Lichfield, Jean de Pontoise, Bishop of Winchester, William of Louth, Bishop of Ely, and Hugh Despenser the Elder attended for Edward. The crusader Othon de Grandson would quickly become the diplomat and envoy Othon de Grandson. England's allies would number the Duke of Brabant, the Counts of Bar, Holland, and Count Amédée from Savoy.[10] Among the many clerks who might accompany such an embassy we have Master Albert de Bononia in the train of Jean de Pontoise and Henry of Newark, who would soon be Archbishop of York. This was some heavyweight embassy! However, it was all to come to nought, and Othon who had arrived at Cambrai with Amédée, accompanied him to England in late February to report on the collapse of peace talks.[11] Along with them journeyed a despairing Cardinal Béraud of Albano whose shuttle diplomacy was failing. So, it was to an England having only just suppressed a Welsh revolt, at war on two fronts with Scotland and France that Othon de Grandson returned to Britain. As the rhyming chronicler Langtoft wrote:

> The cardinal returns from Cambray with answer; And from the king of France, as you will hear afterwards, Sir Amery de Savoy, an earl of great renown, Came in his company, and Otho de Grauntsoun. The latter came out of Cyprus with his companions, Who, when Acre was taken, the neighbouring sea, Escaped in crossing without other accidents.[12]

On 1 March 1296 Edward moved to Newcastle; joining him there was Robert VI de Brus, now the 6th Lord of Annandale – his father the man passed over in favour of John Balliol, Robert V de Brus had died on 31 March 1295.[13] While the army waited, the Scots attacked and unsuccessfully besieged Carlisle castle where Brus had once been the constable. They had been emboldened by the February confirmation of their alliance with France, and with it offers of French support which never came.[14] But it was the date of the attack that would again, as it had earlier with Dafydd ap Gruffydd at Hawarden, shock contemporaries – the attack was made on Easter Sunday 1296. Edward moved his army to Berwick-upon-Tweed, the first of the towns he had demanded the previous October and offered terms to the burgesses of the town and the Scottish garrison at the castle, to both surrender[15] – they did not, and what is more offered the king the disrespect of offering them their naked backsides. There was now going to be only one outcome, and the rules of medieval warfare offered no hope of clemency for defenders of a town who refused to open their gates in times of siege and subsequently lost – the town was taken by Edward amid great bloodshed. To modern eyes what happened at Berwick sealed Edward's reputation as a 'tyrant', but this is to engage in presentism and to wilfully ignore the rules of medieval warfare. What is more, Edward offered terms to the garrison of the castle, who had seen what had happened to the town and surrendered, the 'tyrant' allowing those inside the castle to go about their business provided they promised not to make war upon him again. John Balliol now formally renounced his fealty and homage to Edward,[16] as Edward had indeed done himself when threatened by Philippe IV. Balliol's claim that the original fealty had been 'extorted by force' has been subsequently refuted by Scottish historian Duncan as 'manifestly false'.[17]

But, meanwhile, the Anglo-Imperial alliance was threatening to unravel, even as Edward moved against Philippe's new ally, the unfaithful John Balliol. Philippe managed to buy off Flanders in 1295 and on 6 January 1296 the onetime claimant to the Scottish throne, Count Floris V of Holland, switched sides in favour of Philippe. A furious Edward placed Holland under embargo and switched his wool trade to Mechelen in Brabant from Dordrecht in Holland. But worse, he may also have been implicated in the kidnap of the ill-fated Floris which led to his murder by Gérard de Van Velzen. Following the murder Holland changed sides once more as Floris's son John married Edward's daughter Elizabeth. Edward also had success in winning back Count Guy of Flanders, a wool embargo and Guy's resentment of Philippe's attention on Hainault doing the trick. Alliance building was a tricky and shifting process; in the matters of Holland and Flanders, it had been won, lost and won again. Edward and Philippe were sparring for position.

Meanwhile, earlier in Scotland, it was only after receipt of this revocation on 5 April that Jean de Warenne moved up the coast to Dunbar Castle, and an invasion of the Scottish kingdom began.[18] An attempt by the Scottish army to break the siege there resulted on 27 April 1296 in the Battle of Dunbar, and a wholesale and total defeat for the Scots.[19] The chronicler Bartholomew Cotton confirms that the knights who had fought together at Acre just five years earlier were once more with the English army – Othon de Grandson and Jean de Grailly feasting with Edward at Roxburgh that Pentecost.[20]

A short siege and capture by Edward of Edinburgh followed, then the capture of Stirling Castle before John Balliol sought terms. On 7 July, the Scottish-French treaty was revoked, and on 8 July at Montrose Balliol made his submission.[21] Edward, as overlord, revoked the four-year-old kingship of John Balliol, who by now must have been wishing he'd remained an English noble and the throne of Scotland was now vacant, and would remain so for some time as Edward had no plans to reopen the Great Cause, to the disappointment of Robert VI de Brus.[22] The Welsh rebellion had been suppressed, and war with Scotland won; now surely Edward could turn his reins once more toward France and attempt the recovery of his appanage in France, his ancestral lands of Gascony from the duplicitous scheming Philippe IV.

On 12 May 1296, Othon, having only briefly been with the king in Scotland was back on the diplomatic road. Along, once more with Amédée de Savoie, Hugh Despenser, Walter Langton, Bishop of Lichfield, and the clerk John of Berwick, Edward asked them to arrange a truce with Philippe. The Count of Bar and Duke of Brabant would again be present. Grandson was now putting in a lot of horse miles to find peace between England and France, a conflict that also threatened to engulf Savoy. It is while in Paris that Demurger places, rightly, the meeting of Othon and Templar Grand Master Jacques de Molay, (Fig 2.0) relating to Othon's Templar financial arrangements we discussed at length earlier.[23] But as negotiations with Philippe dragged on there would be more bad news for Edward.

After an illness in the previous autumn of 1295, Edward's brother Edmund, Earl of Lancaster, had finally been able to sail for Gascony accompanied by Henri de Lacy, Earl of Lincoln. Just before Edmund had left for Gascony, they had received news of the passing of another tower of the age, Gilbert de Clare, 7th Earl of Gloucester. Red Gilbert had passed away at Gloucester on 7 December 1295.[24] He had been married to Edward's daughter Joan for just five years, and though a Montfortian at Lewes, he had played a role in Edward's escape from captivity and joined him at Montfort's denouement at Evesham.

The force sent to Gascony was a much-reduced force than had been planned before the Welsh and Scottish rebellions: the treasury was now bare. The idea was for Edmund and Edward to catch Philippe IV in a twin attack, Edmund in Gascony, Edward, and his Flemish and Savoyard allies from Flanders. But first Edmund had to retake Gascony, and that was not going to be easy, as by now Philippe had been in possession of Edward's lands for two years and was well entrenched. Upon arrival they tried and failed to retake Bordeaux, then fell back upon Bayonne, where the expedition foundered upon the rock of poverty, the army dispersed for want of funds. It was a disaster. There on 5 June 1296 Edmund Crouchback, younger son of Henry III of England and Alianor de Provence, nephew of the House of Savoy, crusader knight, onetime king of Sicily, 1st Earl of Lancaster, Earl of Leicester since the demise of Simon de Montfort, departed this life of, so it was said, a broken heart. His body was firstly taken to Bordeaux, thence to England for burial; for Edward, it was another body blow – within a few short years he had lost his mother, his wife and now his loyal brother.[25]

It would be with Edmund in mind that Edward called a parliament in the autumn of 1296 at the town which bore the name of the saint for whom Edmund had been named, Bury St. Edmunds, and at a time to coincide with his feast day. Edward had been continuously in need of access to cash since his break with the Riccardi du Lucca – he would in the end come to terms with another Italian house, the Frescobaldi, but in the meantime, enemies pressed, and cash was short. In November 1296, the laity granted him a tax, but the clergy refused, or at least stalled. Pope Boniface, in February 1296, to bring the warring kings of England and France to their senses and the peace table, had issued a bull, the *Clericis Laicos*, which forbad the church from paying taxes to a lay authority, that is the king. Beneath the burden of taxation and now demands renewed for military service overseas, the bond between monarch and his barony, and indeed people, would now stretch almost to breaking point in the crisis of 1297. The fundamental weakness of the Plantagenets vis-à-vis the Capetians had always been their relative poverty and difficulty in persuading Englishmen to fight in France for the king's lands there.

Clericis Laicos made another enemy for Pope Boniface; however, Edward's opponent, Philippe IV of France, responded to the bull by forbidding the export of currency and valuables and the entry to France of papal tax collectors. Given that France was fairly high if not highest on the list of sources of papal revenue Boniface had to climb down, going so far as, on 11 August 1297, to make Philippe's grandfather Louis IX a saint. However, as we shall see Boniface had made an enemy that in the end would be his undoing.[26] (Fig 2.1)

Meanwhile, that summer of 1296, Othon, Amédée, Despenser and Langton laboured to bring about a truce between Edward, Adolf and Philippe. Langton's accounts for the embassy to France have survived and record payments to Grandson for July to October 1296 of some 725 *Livres Tournois* showing the embassy at Paris in July.[27] While Edward hoped to peacefully restore Gascony, Othon was simultaneously authorised to seek further alliances, this time with the Frederick III, Duke of Lorraine, and the nobility of imperial Burgundy, Philippe having temporarily paid off Count Othon, Edward's vassal – this was a time of manoeuvring for alliances on the part of both London and Paris. Indeed, while Langton returned to England in the autumn for the aforementioned parliament at Bury, Othon's movements that summer and autumn of 1296 seem to indicate he was more interested in alliance building for Edward than peacemaking, travelling to Burgundy and Savoy but also the Auvergne. His precise movements that summer and winter come from Bishop Langton. He was of course at Paris in July, travelling down to Moulins in the Auvergne by September, back to Cambrai in December before wintering almost certainly at his castle in Grandson with the clerk John of Berwick. It would be here that he was well placed to serve Edward by fomenting discord in nearby Burgundy where he had many ties of kin and interest. Edward knew well that Othon was 'our man in Burgundy' to borrow a more recent phrase – nobody knew better the Burgundians.[28]

In Burgundy Count Othon IV had lately become Edward's vassal for Pontarlier and the Château de Joux along the Via Francigena. But Othon of Burgundy's first marriage to Philippa of Bar, Edward's ally, ended with her death and he had remarried within the French sphere by marriage to Mahaut d'Artois. Indeed, the union provided two queens of France: Joan married Philippe V and Blanche married Charles IV. These marriage alliances would bring imperial

Burgundy toward France. What is more, Othon of Burgundy had in 1295 ceded his county to Philippe and France by way of appointing the French king administrator of her dowry. Together with Philippe allying himself with the County of Albon, also known as the Dauphiné to the south of Savoy, no doubt alarmed Amédée de Savoie and Othon de Grandson that Savoy might become the meat in a French sandwich. Grandson's and Amédée's machinations in the Free County led to an alliance of Comtois nobility who swore they would never become vassals of France and indeed joined the Anglo-Imperial alliance against Philippe.[29] Chief among this league of Comtois barony was Jean I de Chalon-Arlay, a not inconsiderable ally with many castles in and around the Jura. In the way that medieval families made war within themselves – Jean was the uncle of Count Othon IV. As the son of a Seigneur de Salins, from which seigneurs Grandson held the valuable salt revenues he'd just that summer awarded the Templars, Jean was a man with whom Grandson was well placed to foment discord. Other names among these rebel barons include families that had supported the Plantagenets before at the behest of Pierre de Savoie in Gascony and elsewhere; they included Gautier de Montfaucon, Jean de Montbéliard, the lords of Montrond, Joux (enfeoffed to Edward), Mornay, Concordray, Maugerex and Chessaigne. But also, notably, the Grandsons immediate neighbours to the north, the Lords of Neuchâtel. In such a way Grandson was able to remind the Savoyards and the Burgundians, both his kinsmen, that their interests better lay in an alliance with Plantagenet England than Capetian France.[30] So, we must imagine from what we know the nobles of the Franche Comté riding the short distance to the Château de Grandson that Christmas to plot their alliance, indeed for Thibaut de Neuchâtel and Jean de Montbélliard, the Seigneur d'Orbe, it would be a very short ride.

An alliance between the nobles of the Franche Comté and Edward was consummated in Brussels in the spring of 1297; it was agreed that the Comtois send 500 cavalrymen to support the English in return for 60,000 *livres* in the first year of the war and 30,000 *livres* thereafter.[31] Fighting alongside Edward for the Free County to remain within the empire, in effect their own independence, were Jean de Chalon-Arlay, Jean and Renaud de Bourgogne, (Fig 2.3) Gautier de Montfaucon, Simon and Jean de Montbélliard, Thibaut de Neuchâtel, Aymon de Faucogney, Etienne and Jean d'Oiselay, Gautier de Châteauvillain, Humbert de Clairvaux, Eudes de Montferrand, Guillaume de Corcondray, Jean de Joux, Guillaume and Gérard d'Arguel and Pierre de Joinville.[32] This latter seigneur was the son of Simon de Joinville, the close ally and kinsman of Pierre de Savoie. Simon had been younger brother to Jean de Joinville, the celebrated biographer of the sainted Louis, and Gefferoi now Edward's Baron Geneville – Pierre thus being a nephew of both. In the *famille de Joinville* we can again see how the Plantagenet–Capetian struggle might divide families. If Philippe was going to fish aggressively in the Scottish pond, then Edward could use his Savoyards to fish aggressively in the Burgundian pond.

The winter of 1296-97 is marked by a little uncertainty around Othon's activities brought about by a divergence of story between the English archive and chroniclers and a much later chronicle of Savoy which is generally found to be less than reliable. The uncertainty drew Belgian historian of medieval finance to question Grandson's loyalty to Edward. The whole affair concerns the marital status surrounding Othon's suzerains, namely King Edward I of England's daughter and Count Amédée V de Savoie himself. Count Amédée V de Savoie had been without a wife since the passing of Sybille de Bâgé in 1294. Meanwhile, Edward's daughter Joan of Acre, a young lady born when Edward, Othon, along with Leonor, had been in Acre some twenty-five years earlier, needed a husband. Joan had been married to Gilbert de Clare, Red Gilbert, the 7th Earl of Gloucester and had had four children by him in their five years of marriage, but Clare had died in 1295, thus leaving a perhaps exhausted Joan on the international marriage market once more, and in the context of 1296–97 a useful pawn to play in securing alliances. Edward asked Othon to secure a marriage with Amédée de Savoie; however, the Lady Joan had fallen for a squire in the service of the departed Clare, by the name of Ralph. The couple were secretly married in January 1297, a union that did not become known until April. Worse, it came to her father with news that the productive Joan was with child once more by the young squire. Edward was not best pleased as one can imagine, and had Ralph locked up in Bristol, eventually relenting and Ralph became Ralph Monthemer, 1st Baron Monthemer no less.[33] It is not difficult to have a little sympathy for Edward. Philippe had deceived him over Gascony, the Welsh had chosen that moment for rebellion, John Balliol in Scotland had allied himself with Philippe and now his own daughter had married and become pregnant by her former husband's squire!

But, citing the dubious *Chronique de Savoie de Cabaret* Kusman suggested that whilst with Edward's son-in-law Duke John II of Brabant in Louvain a secret marriage (yes, another one) was contracted clandestinely behind Edward's back with Othon's connivance matching Amédée with Maria of Brabant, the duke's sister.[34]What is certain is that Joan did not marry Amédée and that Maria of Brabant did, becoming Countess of Savoy. But is there any credence in Kusman's suggestion that whilst acting for Edward in matching Joan with Amédée, Grandson connived in matching Amédée with Maria? Firstly, such conduct would seem to be contradicted by all we know so far of the relationship between Edward and Othon, and indeed that between Edward and Amédée. Secondly Kusman bases the suggestion entirely upon a less than reliable chronicle written in 1419 in Savoy not England or Brabant. Thirdly Kusman neglects entirely to mention the affair, pregnancy and marriage to the charming squire of the lady Joan. The English archives, mostly through the *Fœdera* are quite clear that both Othon and Amédée are acting throughout this period as Edward's allies and indeed specifically as envoys.[35] Given that Amédée's marriage would actually strengthen Edward's alliance against Philippe le Bel by matching Savoy with Brabant I think it extraordinarily unlikely that either Othon or Amédée acted in the fashion suggested by the later chronicler highlighted by Kusman.

Meanwhile, Othon had been certainly in the Low Countries by at least 7 January 1297 when the alliance with Guy de Flandres was finally confirmed, and empowered along with Amédée, Langton and Berwick to make common cause with the Duke of Lorraine, the counts of Hainault and Guelders and the prince bishops of Liege and Utrecht. This was to be a rainbow alliance across the lands to the north and east of Philippe. On 10 May 1297 four of the Comtois nobility: Jean de Chalon-Arlay, its undoubted leader, Jean de Boulogne, Count Othon's brother, Gautier de Montfaucon and Simon de Montbéliard joined Langton, Grandson and Berwick in Brussels and made their pact. The Burgundians promised to wage war upon Philippe, which we must imagine meant opening another front for Edward by striking from the southeast, with although it's not mentioned Savoy, against Philippe's Duchy of Burgundy.[36]

As Edward was allying himself with Philippe's neighbours, as we saw the French king had made an ally of the king of Scotland who had been placed on that throne by Edward's own arbitration. As we saw, this alliance had prompted Edward to march north and defeat the Scottish king, John Balliol. Philippe now, in February 1297, sought to ask Edward to free his ally, but we know little of this communication back and forth, other than the English envoy responsible in this matter was, unsurprisingly the ever-faithful Othon de Grandson. Balliol was not released.[37]

In June 1297 Othon returned to England to make full reports to Edward, and to present his bill for service rendered to the Wardrobe. Othon's bill was for a salary payment covering some 393 days of service to the crown at 40 shillings a day, totalling £784. There was also a payment of £1,000 to keep his men and horses on the continent awaiting Edward's move against Philippe.[38] So, perhaps we should contextualise; according to the UK National Archive calculator £784 would represent £576,598 in today's money or 78,400 days wages for a skilled tradesman, and Othon had been salaried for 393 days. Othon de Grandson was an enormously well-paid servant of the crown!

CHAPTER 13

But when Edward finally sailed for Flanders on 24 August 1297 it would not be a leopard that landed on its shores but a declawed cat. Edward sailed to finally take on Philippe in support of Flanders with but 895 cavalry and less than 8,000 infantry.[1] It was a cavalry contingent little better than that promised by the Franche Comté and infantry support less than a third than had been in Scotland at Dunbar. Edward quickly found himself becalmed in a Flanders under very real threat from Philippe. So, after all the patient ally building and negotiation, not least all the horse miles put in by Othon de Grandson, how had this happened?

As we saw earlier the Riccardi system, from which Edward had financed his Welsh wars and castles, had collapsed amid a thirteenth-century credit crunch brought about by an unprecedented load upon the system. Edward had simultaneously been at war in Wales, France, and Scotland. Turning to his own people and church, Edward had been partially thwarted by Pope Boniface and his aforementioned *Clericis Laicos* which put church funds beyond his reach. Worse still, even as he planned to take on Philippe to restore Gascony, of which he was of course Duke, Edward had seen the 1294–95 Madog rebellion in Wales and 1296 Scottish alliance with France and ensuing military campaign to nullify same; all these distractions had been costly and drained his coffers. Robert Winchelsey, the successor to John Peckham as Archbishop of Canterbury, had returned from Rome determined to uphold *Clericis Laicos* and the independence as he saw it of his church. As we shall see this independence of the church would lead Philippe le Bel into conflict with Pope Boniface, but it would also lead Edward into conflict with Winchelsey.

If church opposition was bad enough, lay opposition to not only Edward's raising finance for the war, but opposition to the war itself also coalesced around the earls of Hereford and Norfolk, that is Roger Bigod and Humphrey de Bohun.

On 24 February 1297, while Othon was dealing with Philippe's attempt to free the Scottish king, Edward summoned a parliament at Salisbury to finalise plans to take on Philippe in Flanders. Edward asked those present for their support in providing the necessary military muscle. Bigod and Bohun flatly refused. In reply to Edward's furious 'By God, Earl, you shall either go or hang,' Bigod replied, 'By the same oath, O king, I will neither go nor hang.' Perhaps surprisingly Edward backed down and did not at that point issue a military call to arms. But on 15 April he did summons 130 magnates to muster at London on 7 July. This backfired as many of the magnates met beforehand at Montgomery in the Welsh marches. Bigod and Bohun were there of course, but also the Earl of Arundel, Richard FitzAlan newly returned from Gascony, Earl of Warwick William de Beauchamp, lately the victor at Maes Madog, John Hastings and Edmund Mortimer.

So, it was then that the English army's long planned incursion into the Low Countries arrived with more of a whimper than a growl. Philippe had in any case pre-empted Edward by marching against Lille, Robert d'Artois defeating Edward's German and Low Country allies on 20 August before taking Lille the day following Edward's arrival on the continent. As Prestwich put it, Edward had arrived 'to find the war already half lost'. Edward moved cautiously inland, first to Bruges and then by early September to Ghent. As the autumnal leaves began to fall, Edward's precarious position was rendered critical by calamitous news from Scotland. On 11 September, Jean de Warenne, 6th Earl of Surrey and onetime ward of Pierre de Savoie, had moved to Stirling in response to a renewed Scottish threat, this time not led by its imprisoned king, but by Andrew de Moray and a hitherto unknown William Wallace. By a narrow wooden bridge over the Forth of Firth, the Scots had enticed Warenne single file across the river only to crush them before they could gather sufficient strength to give battle – it was a ghastly error and a ruinous defeat. The road to England through Edward's back door now lay open even as Edward with a woefully inadequate army was trying after three years to do battle with Philippe.

Edward once more chose the pragmatic option: there was no way to prosecute a war with Philippe while the Scots threatened from the north' a truce had to be agreed. But would Philippe, whose fomenting of trouble on England's border had thus far proven more successful than Edward's on France's? The cleric William Hotham, who had accompanied Grandson to Rome previously, obtained an audience with the French king. Hotham was esteemed in France since his days studying theology at the University of Paris and so was a good choice as envoy on Edward's part. Edward was in effect at Philippe's mercy. Would the Capetian crush his Plantagenet opponent? Surprisingly perhaps is that the two cousins agreed the 9 October truce of Vive-Saint-Bavon which bought Edward time until 7 December to decide what to do next. What to do next was to despatch Othon de Grandson along with Hotham, Amédée de Savoie, Antony Bek and Aymer de Valence to the Cistercian abbey of Groeninge at Courtai to parley for a longer extension of the truce. Aymer was now 2nd Earl of Pembroke, having succeeded to his father Guillaume's extensive marcher lands. Surprisingly perhaps, again Philippe was magnanimous, agreeing on 23 November to an extension until Lent 1298. The English delegate authorised to oversee the truce was Gefferoi de Joinville, kinsman of the Savoyard comital family, and Pierre de Joinville, one of Edward's Comtois allies. A truce was one thing, a peace would be something else. Since Pierre de Savoie had so carefully helped to construct the 1259 Treaty of Paris and so reset Capetian–Plantagenet relations, a lot of water had flowed down *La Manche*. Not only were the two kingdoms once more at loggerheads over Plantagenet lands in France, but the matter had now expanded to include Scotland, Flanders, and a whole host of imperial fiefdoms to the east and southeast of France. On 27 December 1297 Pope Boniface intervened once more, the papal legates suggesting the whole matter be referred to him in Rome, but as the French insisted, acting in a personal capacity. On 24 January 1298 Othon and his fellow English negotiators at Courtai agreed to papal arbitration, a further extension of the truce for two years while the matter was referred to Rome. The peace of Tournai a week later formalised the papal arbitration.

This was going to take some sorting out. Philippe had renounced his vassal Edward's lordship of Gascony, while Edward, having then renounced him as suzerain had asserted suzerainty over John Balliol, who after renouncing this relationship had become a prisoner. This was indeed a tangled web of feudal obligations. On 18 February 1298 Grandson would once more be going across the Alps to the Papal Curia as envoy for Edward to untangle this mess, along with his Courtai colleagues, Hotham, Valence and Bek but with the addition of the Bishop of Winchester, John de Pontoise, and Hugh de Vere, 1st Baron Vere. Hotham was now Archbishop elect of Dublin, a promotion sought from Boniface by Edward, Hotham being consecrated at Ghent by Bek. Also, with the English and Savoyards in Rome was Robert de Bethune, the eldest son of Guy de Flandres. His letters which survive give us some of the flavour of the negotiations which followed.

So, Othon, accompanied on his journey by Hotham, left Flanders for Rome, perhaps taking the Mont Cenis route rather than Grand Saint-Bernard as the party called at Rivoli at the head of the Susa valley, guests of Count Philippe of Savoy Piedmont.[2] Philippe was the son of Thomas III of Savoy, whose death had prompted the Count of Savoy to appoint Alianor of Provence and Edward as arbitrator for the succession as count. It is often forgotten in Britain, especially in its northern regions, that Edward's arbitration of the Scottish succession was not his first; indeed, to evidence his abilities in this way Amédée de Savoie had made the long journey from Savoy to Scotland in 1292 to so witness. Othon had been at Rivoli, with its beautiful grandstand views across nearby Turin, over twenty years earlier on his first return from the Holy Land with Edward.

The case made by Grandson and the English to Boniface survives and appears as a response to Philippe's claim that Edward had forfeited Gascony as he had treasonably made war upon his suzerain these past four years. That Philippe had seized Gascony before the war and that Edward had subsequently revoked his homage appears not to have troubled the French. Edward's case was made in the hand of one Philippe Mantel, a Canon of Chichester, and Doctor of Civil Law. Edward's case was made to rest on three pillars: first, that Gascony had always been held by the *famille Plantagenet* and their ancestors by allodial right and not as a fief; second, that this had been superseded by the 1259 Treaty of Paris which as a contract required both suzerain and vassal to maintain each side of the bargain – and as the French king had not kept his side of the agreement the English king could not be held responsible for his – and third, thereby that the king of France had duly forfeited his own right of suzerainty.[3] This defence of Plantagenet rights would be used once more as the Capetian–Plantagenet relationship descended decades later into the Hundred Years' War. We can say with certainty that if the Treaty of Paris had attempted to build a bridge of trust between the two families, as Louis IX had said in 1259, 'if we are family how can we be enemies?'; then the 1294 confiscation by his grandson Philippe IV had begun the rupture that would lead to over a century of war – Philippe le Bel had surely poisoned the well. Indeed, Dante Alighieri would attribute these words to Philippe's ancestor Hugh Capet in purgatory, 'I was the root of the obnoxious plant that overshadows all the Christian lands, so that fine fruit can rarely rise from them.'[4]

The Flemings feared, rightly, that they were to be abandoned by their ally Edward. Bethune and his colleagues Jean de Namur and Philippe de Thiette appealed to Amédée and Othon, but were met with medieval realpolitik, what the Savoyards suggested could Edward do. The Flemings met a last time with Boniface, but they were indeed to cast adrift, poisoning Anglo–Flemish relations for some time.[5] It was pointed out that Philippe had stood by Balliol in a firmer fashion than Edward had Guy – John Balliol was duly released by Edward to the papal envoy, Raynald, Bishop of Vicenza, in the summer of 1299.

Pope Boniface delivered his arbitration in June 1298, proposing to restore the position to the status quo ante, that is to restore Gascony to Edward, but once more as Philippe's vassal per the Treaty of Paris. Until such time as this could be achieved Boniface ordered that Gascony be delivered into his hands by the good offices of the Archbishop of Toulouse. Boniface also proposed that the traditional tool of marriage ought to be tried again; after all, had not familial ties helped to bring about the 1259 rapprochement. Boniface suggested a marriage between Edward's heir Edward of Caernarfon, the future Edward II, and Philippe's daughter Isabelle. Given that the two shared the sisters Marguerite and Alianor de Provence as great-grandmother and grandmother, he granted dispensation of such a closely related marriage.[6] Meanwhile, the widower King Edward was to marry the Philippe's 20-year-old half-sister Marguerite – a double match had been proposed. Marguerite was the product of Philippe III's second marriage to Maria of Brabant whereas Philippe himself was the son of his father's first marriage to Isabella of Aragon. Marguerite was described contemporaneously as '*Francorum florem*' or 'Flower of France' and that she would offer '*concordia*' and '*amorem*' or 'peace' and 'love'.[7]

Nevertheless, this was an adjudication that would find little favour at the French court, one noble tearing it up and trampling upon it.[8] What is more, the arbitration, as the Flemings feared, effectively sold both Scotland and Flanders down the river by making no mention of either. Boniface was in effect in June 1298 giving Edward free reign to deal with Philippe's allies in Scotland and Philippe to deal with Edward's allies in Flanders. Edward's allies Guy de Flandres and the nobility of the Franche Comté were left to fight Philippe alone – the French tactic of expansion by isolating opponents working perfectly.

Even as Boniface issued his arbitration at the Papal Curia of Philippe's seizure of Gascony from his vassal Edward, Edward himself had returned to England from Flanders and was moving against his recalcitrant vassal, Scotland, with Othon's brother Guillaume de Grandson and cousin Pierre de Champvent close to the king. Again, we must say that the contradiction in his complaint as a mistreated vassal in France and as a misused suzerain in Britain did not seem to trouble Edward. On 22 July 1298 Edward defeated a Scottish army led by William Wallace at Falkirk. In September Wallace resigned as Guardian of Scotland in favour of Robert de Brus, the son of the Robert de Brus who had been a compatriot of Edward's and Othon's on the ninth crusade some twenty-odd years earlier. The son of their comrade-in-arms would not be so friendly to Edward and Othon as had his father.

French intransigence, meanwhile, continued, chiefly led by the French chancellor, keeper of Philippe's seals, the one-eyed nationalist zealot Pierre Flotte. French aims appear maximalist: they had uncoupled Flanders and the Franche Comté from England and would now try to swallow these whole but were reluctant to pay the price of Gascony. The French embassy with which Grandson and the English had to contend also included Duke Hugues V of Burgundy, Gilles I Aycelin de Montaigu of Narbonne (a later chancellor of France) and Count Guy IV de Saint Pol, the son-in-law of Edward's sister Beatrice. Pope Boniface in his arbitration had upheld the feudal bargain, which was in essence Edward's case; however, in the nascent nationalism of Pierre Flotte he had met an adversary he may well have struggled to comprehend. The whole dispute between Edward and Philippe – as indeed it had decades earlier between Simon de Montfort and Pierre de Savoie – was between the new forces of nationalism abroad in England and France and the old certainties of feudalism. Othon de Grandson saw no contradiction in paying homage to Edward for his English and Irish lands while simultaneously paying homage to Amédée de Savoie for his lands in Vaud. Likewise, he would have seen no difficulty in Edward being at once a king of England while holding an important duchy in France. This was not a view shared by Flotte who regarded with hostility the retention by a king of England of Aquitaine, even though he might hold it by ancestral right. In taking this view Flotte was undoubtedly following the wishes of his master Philippe. To quote his English language biographer, Joseph Strayer, 'no one has ever been able to blame the war of 1294–97 on anyone but Philippe' and that it was an 'unnecessary war' driven by his need to assert his suzerainty over the whole of France.[9] More recently Justine Firnhaber-Baker in her history of the Capetians attributed the war to Philippe being 'driven by his insecurities, his stubbornness, and his grandiose idea of royal majesty'.[10] When Boniface asked Flotte if he intended to drive the Plantagenets from France, Flotte let the cat out of the bag by answering simply '*Vous dites vrai.*' Thus, the French position since the time of Philippe Auguste and ongoing into the coming Hundred Years' War was made plain – France could not and would not tolerate a Plantagenet king of England retaining his ancestral lands in what they took to be their inheritance of the conquests of Clovis.

With that, Amédée and Othon returned to Savoy, the former to Chambéry, the latter to Grandson. In particular, what Othon's feelings as he arrived back at Grandson as his liege lord had been forced by circumstance to abandon his Burgundian neighbours to the French are lost to us. Assuredly, as an experienced diplomat Othon would have been used to the shifting sands of international relations: Edward in hopefully regaining Gascony and dealing with the Scottish rebellion was not in any position to aid the Flemings and Burgundians. Nonetheless, these were Othon's neighbours, and as he returned home the dispute with Amédée's brother Louis de Vaud simmered on – the macro and the micro of the medieval world. For William Hotham his service for Edward would be his last: on his way home, he departed this life at Dijon on 28 August; such were the perils of the medieval road that Othon de Grandson knew only too well.

Christmas 1298 passed but Edward was soon calling once more, in February 1299, sending one of his Gascon clerks, Arnaud de la Rame, to bring both Savoyards up to Paris for the next round in negotiations.[11] By April Grandson was in Paris, and May even saw a short visit across the Channel to England, no doubt to take personal instructions from Edward. A remarkable survivor in the English archives is a letter patent issued by Edward on 26 May while at Canterbury. Othon would be staying at his manor at Sheen, and may well have heard of its misuse by all and sundry staying there, Edward ordered:

> Mandate that no person, whether belonging to the king or any other person of whatsoever state, the king's son only excepted, shall enter, stay or lodge in Otto de Grandisono's manor of Shene, or put their baggage or other goods there, against his will or the will of the keeper of the said manor, as it appears that great damage has been done by people lodging in the houses there.[12]

Seemingly the issue of persons unnamed 'crashing out' at your London apartment is not entirely a twenty-first-century phenomenon.

Othon returned to France to join the embassy at Montreuil that was to negotiate the terms of the marriages suggested in Pope Boniface's arbitration the year before. Othon's kinsman Gérard de Vuippens was appointed to represent the English in handing their small portion of Gascony to the papal representatives, but both met with French reluctance to go along with their side of the adjudication. The embassy at Montreuil consisted of Grandson, but also Amédée recalled from Savoy as we saw earlier. The Savoyards were alongside John de Pontoise, Bishop of Winchester, Simon de Ghent, Bishop of Salisbury, Henri de Lacy, Earl of Lincoln, Guy de Beauchamp, Earl of Warwick, Aymer de Valence, Earl of Pembroke and lastly the Savoyard kinsman of Amédée, Gefferoi de Joinville, Baron de Geneville. This collection of Anglo-Normans, Savoyards and Poitevins provoked the French scribes at Montreuil to mock their accents, as their predecessors had earlier mocked Henry III. Othon,

Amédée and Gefferoi may well have hailed from Vaud, Burgundy, and Savoy but for the French they had spent too long in England; they were infected it seems by the peculiar way, they thought, that *les Anglais* spoke French. The scribes rewrote a poem mocking the visitors whereby Edward and Philippe replaced Henry and Louis.[13]

Perhaps one of the reasons Philippe acquiesced to the treaty is that a successful marriage between the young Edward and Isabelle would result no doubt he hoped in a grandson of his attaining the title Duke of Aquitaine, and it must be said the kingdom of England.[14] This suggestion by Elizabeth Brown is repeated by Seymour Phillips writing: 'Had it not been for the marriage [Edward and Isabelle] and the French king's [Philippe's] hopes to see a grandchild hold the lands [Aquitaine], he would never have considered relinquishing them.'[15] If this be so, given that the fruit of the marriage would come back to haunt the Capetian House of Valois in centuries to come; never can a dynasty have been so hoisted by its own petard.

The resulting Treaty of Montreuil of June 1299 made little mention of Gascony, kicking the can down the road, while prolonging the truce between Edward and Philippe. What it did do among great ceremony was the betrothal of Edward to Philippe's sister Marguerite and Edward's son to Philippe's daughter Isabelle. Edward senior's proxy at the ceremonies was none other than Count Amédée V de Savoie and Edward junior's proxy was Henri de Lacy, Earl of Lincoln.[16] Montreuil did not achieve peace, merely the promise of peace.

Following Montreuil, Grandson returned to England by August, given the task of investigating irregularities in the coinage of the Frescobaldi merchants who had succeeded the Riccardi di Lucca as a source of revenue for Edward.[17] English coin had been taken overseas and its silver had been used by continental mints for the production of sterling imitations of inferior weight. These low-grade 'pollards and crockards'[18] were finding their way into the English money by way of the Frescobaldi, something that appears to have been inadvertent on their part, as they were pardoned by Edward. The collapsed relationship with the Riccardi di Lucca had hamstrung Edward's finances at a critical moment; they would be replaced by the Frescobaldi in the coming years, but the coinage affair and its pardon speak to the uncertain beginnings of the relationship, and one in which Grandson, having been deeply involved with the Luccese, played his part.

In return for his services to the king Othon received further favours; first, six bucks from the forest of Ashendon in Buckinghamshire, a buck being an antlered male fallow deer.[19] Second, and much more remuneratively, he was given permission to hold a weekly Wednesday market at his manor of Acconagh in Tipperary, and furthermore, a yearly fair there on the vigil and feast of Saint Margaret and the thirteen days thereafter, the significance of the feast of this particular sainted lady being no doubt that she bore the same name as Edward's new wife. Third, Othon was granted free warren in his extensive lands in Ireland, that is in counties Tipperary, Waterford, Limerick, and Kerry.[20] Free warren was the grant of game and to hunt game within his lands, which, like all game, belonged to Edward as king. Grandson had also, a month earlier in June, acquired further lands in Vaud, this from Jean II de Cossonay and his wife Marguerite de La Tour du Pin, namely Suchy, between Savoyard Yverdon and Montfaucon Orbe.[21] The *famille de Grandson* had since 1292 been allied with the *famille de Cossonay* against the expansionist Louis de Vaud. In a few short months, thus Othon acquired gifts in England, rights in Ireland and land in Vaud. Grandson's arrangement for Edward of the Burgundian allies mentioned earlier touched also upon their mutual interest in the disputes with Louis de Vaud. On 28 September 1298 Jean de Chalon-Arlay and Gérard d'Arguel are involved in peace negotiations along with Guillaume de Champvent, Bishop of Lausanne, and Jean de Cossonay with Louis de Vaud.[22] In such a way could Grandson's efforts on behalf of Edward also touch upon his familial interests in Vaud.

In the month following this royal largesse Marguerite ventured across the Channel and the 20-year-old half-sister of Philippe was married to the 60-year-old Edward on 10 September 1299 at Canterbury. On 18 October Grandson was summoned to parliament held at the home of Knights Templar in England, the New Temple in London.[23] It was this summons to parliament that created the English barony Grandison that would later form the English cadet branch of the *famille de Grandson,* passing from the line of Othon's brother Guillaume – the Grandsons were now English nobility.[24] Events were once more unravelling the position in Scotland gained at Falkirk in 1298. Robert VII de Brus, known to history by his anglicised Robert the Bruce had renewed the struggle, and besieged Stirling Castle which duly fell. Matters had been complicated by Boniface in Rome, who had been petitioned by the Scots to make their country a papal realm. In response the pope issued, on 27 June 1299, *Scimus fili* or 'We know, my son', that asserted that Scotland belonged rightfully to the church and was not subject to English lordship. Pope Boniface ordered Edward to end his war with Scotland.

However, Edward planned a winter Scottish campaign immediately but was met with a lukewarm response to summons at Berwick; the matter would have to wait until the new century, the summer of 1300. This allowed Grandson to return to Vaud for the winter of 1299–1300, a journey of some three weeks by horse for a knight now in his sixties. He is noted in Vaud in January of 1300 putting his seal to agreements in connection with the ongoing dispute between his cousin Bishop Guillaume de Champvent of Lausanne and Amédée de Savoie's brother Louis de Vaud.[25] Clifford has his stay in Vaud until 29 February, but this is unlikely given that in London, Othon de Grandson was summoned to attend the parliament of 6 March 1300 at which Scotland was no doubt top of the agenda, along with Gascony and Flanders.[26] The ability of Othon to micromanage his affairs in Vaud while playing his part in the European struggle between Edward and Philippe that reached from the Scottish Borders to the Pyrenees is quite remarkable. Especially considering such a seemingly faraway dispute in Vaud, of little interest to the English, might include once more a Burgundian ally of Edward's, this time Gautier de Montfaucon, and his Chamberlain Pierre de Champvent. So, we see in October of 1299 and March 1300 Othon attending parliament in London, while finding time between to spend six weeks on horseback to journey to and from Vaud to attend to matters there – such was the life of Sir Othon de Grandson.

As the new century dawned the truce with Philippe expired, doing so with Scotland once more threatening from the north, Gascony nowhere nearer recovered and sad news coming from Flanders. The French had invaded Flanders knowing that Edward could offer his ally little support. In April Damme, the port once the home of Pierre de Savoie's invasion force of 1264, fell to the French. Ghent and Ypres followed suit in May, with Edward's ally Guy de Flanders and his son Robert who had been with Grandson in Rome taken captive. Flanders belonged to Philippe. Jacques de Châtillon, uncle to Philippe's queen was installed as military governor. If Flanders belonged to Philippe, then so too must Scotland belong to him, reasoned Edward, despite what Pope Boniface might say.

On 24 June Othon de Grandson was summoned by Edward to military service at Carlisle, but he would not be there.[27] During the month of June 1300, Othon was with Edward whose itinerant court was in Yorkshire, firstly at Pontefract then York. He was witnessing royal charters at Pontefract on 6, 7, 12 and 13 June before moving on with Edward to York.

There the prior of the Carmelites at York were granted oaks through the offices of Othon de Grandson. But then, on 15 June, and before the official summons to go north with Edward to Scotland as part of the general mobilisation, there is Edward deciding he needs to send Othon hastily to Rome. Edward had far better things for him to do than besiege Scottish castles: news had come of a Scottish embassy to Rome, and Edward had urgent need of him to go to Rome once more to argue the Plantagenet case regarding both Scotland and France. Furthermore, Edward was in receipt of a bull from Boniface that the English king either go on crusade or produce the tenth (tax revenues) he had collected for his crusade. Clearly Edward was not able to help Boniface financially or militarily given his differences with the French and the Scots. As always Edward needed Othon in Rome. In April John of Pontoise, Geoffroi de Joinville, William of Gainsborough, Gérard de Vuippens, Geoffrey Russell, and Raymond Arnaldi de Rama had been despatched to Rome to take care of bringing an end to the Gascon problem.[28] On 15 June Edward sent to Bishop Langton his treasurer and John Langton his chancellor:

> To send hastily to the king the letter which he formerly devised to send to the pope in answer to the news of the Holy Land which the pope sent by bull, so that the king can have the letter or the transcript at Durham on Friday next, or very early on Saturday, so that he may have advice on it before Sir Ottes de Granzon leaves him.[29]

Boniface's bull had clearly thrown a fly into the ointment. However, in July, as Othon made for Rome, Edward crossed the border and moved against Caerlaverock Castle in Galloway 8 miles (12 kilometres) south of Dumfries, only lately retaken by the Scots. The near-contemporary 'Song of Caerlaverock' gives us details of Edward's army of which was made up of at least one Grandson, Othon's brother Guillaume: 'William Grandison bore paly silver and azure surcharged with a red bend, and thereon three beautiful eaglets of fine gold.'[30] As the castle fell to Edward, and as Othon was on his way to Rome, Robert Winchelsey, Archbishop of Canterbury, delivered Boniface's June 1299 bull *Scimus Fili* to the king in Galloway.[31] Boniface wrote:

> The fact will doubtless have reached your highness' ears, and is, we doubt not, enshrined in your memory, how that from ancient times the Kingdom of Scotland has in full right belonged, and is still judged to belong, to the Church above named; and that that same kingdom, as we have heard, has never owed nor can ever owe feudal rights either to yourself, or to your predecessors on the throne of the kingdom of England.[32]

We should see in Boniface's bull the hand of Philippe as much as if not more than that of the Scots. The papal arbitration had supposedly placed Gascony in the hands of the pope pending a final settlement, but it had, as we saw earlier, made no mention of either Philippe's ally Scotland or Edward's allies the Flemish and the Burgundians. Accordingly, Philippe had, as we saw, moved against and taken captive Guy de Flandres. Now Philippe had pressured Boniface[33] to treat Scotland not like Flanders but like Gascony and bring the Scots under the papal cloak – Philippe had outmanoeuvred Edward. But as Boniface himself had observed regarding the French, 'he who deals with the French deals with the devil'.[34]

Edward wrote to the papal negotiator Raynald, Bishop of Vicenza that he 'had already sent Sir Otes de Grantzon and other messengers to the parts where the bishop is'.[35] This letter confirmed that Othon was on his way to Rome in August 1300. This was followed on 26 September 1300 by a further beefing up of Othon's mission to Rome, the appointment of Amédée V de Savoie and Henri de Lacy once more and the Gascon noble Amanieu d'Albret, who had been at Caerlaverock.[36] Edward's embassy to Boniface would now contain not just Englishmen but a Gascon, a Savoyard with close links to the Burgundians, and the Count of Savoy himself. The mission had begun as a general embassy to bring peace negotiations with Philippe to a conclusion but had now widened to include Boniface's attempts to collect the crusade tenth (tax revenues) and his attempt to take Scotland under his protection.

On the same day, 26 September, as the strengthened embassy to Rome was appointed, Edward issued a summons for a parliament to be held at Lincoln.[37] The barons there assembled from 20 January 1301 issued a letter refuting *Scimus Fili*; the arguments as to whether the Scots came within Edward's overall suzerainty, we discussed earlier in regard to his arbitration of the Scottish succession that delivered the Scottish crown to the lately rebellious John Balliol, but the baronial letter of 1301, in the event not sent,[38] was succinct:

> For we know, most Holy Father, and it is notorious in our country and not unknown to many, that from the first foundation of the Kingdom of England, the kings of that kingdom, as well in the times of the Britons as of the Angles, had in their possession superiority and direct dominion over the Kingdom of Scotland, or were captains of the sovereignty and rightful lordship of the same at successive periods, nor at any time did the same kingdom in temporalities belong, nor does it now belong in any way, to the aforesaid Church.[39]

But there were to be two letters, the other from Edward himself, drafted by the scholars of England's universities who had been sent away to give Edward the historical and legal ammunition to fire at the pope. In the words used by Edward:

> Thus, in the days of Eli and of Samuel the prophet, after the destruction of the city of Troy, a certain valiant and illustrious man of the Trojan race called Brutus, landed with many noble Trojans, upon a certain island called, at that time, Albion. It was then inhabited by giants, and after he had defeated and slain them, by his might and that of his followers, he called it, after his own name, Britain, and his people Britons … Arthur, king of the Britons, a prince most renowned, subjected to himself a rebellious Scotland, destroyed almost the whole nation, and afterwards installed as king of Scotland one Angusel by name. Afterwards, when King Arthur held a most famous feast at Caerleon, there were present there all the kings subject to him, and among them Angusel, king of Scotland, who manifested the service due for the realm of Scotland by bearing the sword of King Arthur before him; and in succession all the kings of Scotland have been subject to all the kings of the Britons … Æthelstan, king of England, established Constantine, king of Scots, to rule under him, saying 'it is a greater cause for pride to make a king than to be one.[40]

As was normal for the thirteenth century there was the resort to the myth and legend of Brutus and Arthur but also the historical Æthelstan. In AD 934 Constantine had indeed witnessed a charter at Buckingham in England as '*Constantinus subregulus*'[41] or 'Constantine under the rule', and described Æthelstan as '*Ethelstanus rex Anglorum per omnipotentis dexteram totius Britanniae regni solio sublimatus*'[42] or 'Æthelstan, king of the English, exalted by the right hand of the Almighty to the throne of the whole Kingdom of Britain'.

Edward was also advised that Pope Boniface had no right to Scotland, over interpreting as he was a claim that the Scottish church was a special daughter of Rome to mean that the entire realm of Scotland could thus be described.[43] Such was the mix of myth and history with which Othon was going to be armed to do intellectual battle with Boniface. Indeed, Boniface represents an intriguing figure, as he seemed to bend toward Edward and then toward Philippe, and no doubt Edward flew into a rage when he heard *Scimus Fili* read to him by Winchelsey, as Boniface had previously been seen to give him a free hand in Scotland and at least hold out the hope of regaining Gascony. But Boniface could blow both ways. The Flemish who had no love for him after he had abandoned them to the French, said of him '*à la fie dures, à la fie mols*' or that he was by turn 'hard and soft'.[44] He would, as we shall see, ultimately manage to infuriate both Edward and Philippe.

The Rome to which the English, Savoyards and Gascons were travelling to in 1300 was thronged with pilgrims as Boniface had decreed that the year be a jubilee year, the first of many in Rome. The city was heaving with apparently 30,000 pilgrims on one particular day, said to number 200,000 for the year. Boniface had offered the irresistible lure of 'full and copious pardon' to all who visited St. Peter's.[45] So many pilgrims visited that traffic regulations had to be instituted on the Ponte del Castel Sant'Angelo, one for pilgrims arriving, one for those leaving. Indeed, one pilgrim Dante Alighieri later likened the ordered queues to the regimentation in hell. The visitors would have been glad to find food plentiful after the long road and at reasonable prices, which would no doubt have pleased Edward as he was financing them. Expenses for the earlier (1300–1) embassy had come from the tenth (tax revenues) for the crusade, Gérard de Vuippens granted £309. 3s. 4d. and Othon de Grandson £332. This would equate to a figure approaching £250,000 in today's money, that is £235,000 for Grandson.[46] Clearly these were well paid envoys, but it also illustrates that their accommodation and expenses in easing the 'special affairs at the court in Rome' might be considerable. Negotiations began in the autumn of 1300 and dragged on for some time, but at least in the end Othon and his colleagues managed to persuade Boniface to back down from his claim to the tenth (tax revenues) for crusade that had been collected in England – and this at least was at least one of the primary goals of the embassy. However, Boniface would not back down from *Scimus Fili*, and there was no wider settlement of the now six-year-long dispute between Edward and Philippe over Gascony. The best that could be obtained was a further extension of the truce, this time until Epiphany 1302.

In March 1301 news came to Rome from Lausanne that Othon's cousin Bishop Guillaume de Champvent had departed this life. His successor in the see would be none other than Gérard de Vuippens, one of the party of negotiators with Grandson. Vuippens we should remember was not only a relative of Othon's, his nephew, but owed his clerical positions in England to Grandson and no doubt his role as envoy for Edward since coming to England. Vuippens had variously been a pastor at Greystoke in Cumbria, a position previously held by Othon's brother Henri, sub-deacon at Richmond and a canon at York. It is not reaching too far to imagine that his elevation to Bishop of Lausanne similarly owed a good deal to Othon de

Grandson. Vuippens's occupation of the see would be followed by another of the *famille de Grandson*, Othon de Champvent – thus representing a hold of the bishops's mitre at Lausanne by the family for nearly forty years. We should also remember that it would suit Edward in having a close ally sitting in such an influential bishopric on the pilgrims' route from England to Rome. Indeed, as the embassy concluded in the spring of 1301, it would be Vuippens who returned to England with news of the pope's relinquishment of the tenth (tax revenues); for that spring Othon returned not to England but to Vaud to attend to his affairs in light of the peace treaty now signed with Louis de Vaud. The summer of 1301 was, from 31 May, spent with the minutiae of the relationship between the castle of Grandson and the Savoyard castle at Yverdon, the castle built by Edward's Master of Works, Maître Jacques de Saint George. Apparently, some fields in the short distance between the two had lately been damaged – once more the micromanagement in Vaud after the macromanagement in Rome.

By November 1301 Othon had made the journey once more back to England and no doubt glad that he'd not been the bearer of tidings from Boniface that in effect chided Edward for the war as the elder king of '*maturitas*' or maturity who should know better while Philippe was still inexperienced and '*fervore juventutis impulsus*' or 'driven by the fervour of youth' – a view that would have pleased neither adversary. Nor would Edward have taken too kindly the description by this Roman pope of his appanage of Gascony, given to him by his father, the land of his great-grandmother Alianore being described as '*tam modica terra*' that is 'so little land'.[47] Grandson found upon arrival that he was going straight back to Rome, a meeting at Canterbury with French envoys having proven fruitless earlier in the year.[48] He had been appointed once more as envoy to the pope on 24 August. This time his colleagues would be Bishop Walter Langton and the Savoyards Amédée de Savoie and Gérard de Vuippens, granted letters of protection for the journey in September[49] once more. Grandson had in effect already been granted the necessary protection for the journey in advance from February 1301.[50] Langton had recently himself been the target of a baronial move to oust him on charges of murder, adultery and simony and was travelling with the Savoyards to Rome to be tried by Boniface, who promptly referred the matter back to Winchelsey, Archbishop of Canterbury. Langton aside, the negotiations of Edward's dispute with Philippe over Gascony, Flanders and Scotland were now taking on a distinctly Savoyard hue. It is quite remarkable that Edward should entrust the foreign relations of his realm to his foreign relations, a mark that whatever Matthew Paris might decades earlier have thought of the Savoyards in England, this king of England was more than happy to place his trust in his maternal family and their countrymen.

In December 1301, ratified by Edward at Linlithgow on 25 December, the truce of Asnières agreed a truce with the Scots until November 1302, a summer's campaigning.[51] The truce had been the work of Langton, Vuippens and accompanied by the clerk John of Berwick once more. For the French, the leading light was again Pierre Flotte who would not be long for this world. In view of this truce, which was pursuant to a wider agreement between Edward and Philippe, it appears that Othon and Amédée may well have pressed upon Edward the futility of ongoing negotiations with Boniface. Perhaps it might be more productive to follow up Asnières and negotiate directly with Philippe? So, despite all the arrangements made for Othon upon his arrival in the winter of 1301, Langton and Vuippens would be sole envoys to Boniface.[52]

Why was Edward's 'loyal Ottonis' excusing himself from Edward's service at this vital juncture? Edward's letter to Boniface explaining their absence cites '*quamplures causas notabiles & evidentes rationes*' or 'a number of notable and evident reasons.'[53] Clifford attributes the absence, rightly, to Grandson convincing Edward that further negotiation with Boniface was 'hopeless' and that 'their time would be better spent in negotiating directly with the French'.[54] Meanwhile, on 5 December 1301, the same month as Asnières, relations between Philippe and the hot and cold Boniface had deteriorated with the papal bull *Ausculta Fili* or 'Give ear my son', which invited Philippe in papal paternal fashion to mend his ways. Philippe responded with a public letter which described Boniface's intervention as '*tua maxima fatuitas*', that is to say, 'your greatest folly'.[55] Insults were flying between Rome and Paris, but in the very best Medieval Latin. Worse perhaps, the nobles of France, egged on by Flotte, wrote an angry letter to Boniface saying that such things as he was doing were '*ne sont choses qui plaisient à Dieu*' and that men would not expect such things except '*avecques Antechrist*', that is that Boniface's interventions were not pleasing to God and men could only expect such things with the Antichrist – nothing so much as the Antichrist could inflame the medieval mind.[56]

Boniface had created the see of Pamiers in the County of Foix in southern France, appointing the Occitan Bernard Saisset as its first bishop. Now Bernard was no lover of the Franks, suggesting that the people hated the Parisian bishop of nearby Toulouse 'because of that language', that language being *Langue d'Oil*. Saisset had been sent by Boniface as a papal legate to Philippe in order that the king should end his anticlerical ways. But on his return to Pamiers, Philippe charged Saisset of planning an Occitan rebellion against the crown. Saisset was arrested in his own bishop's palace and Pierre Flotte charged him with high treason, heresy, and blasphemy. Boniface of course looked upon Saisset's arrest in less than a kindly fashion and fired off *Ausculta Fili*. This Franco–Papal rupture cannot be overstated since it led to Philippe calling the very first Estates General in France, the assembly of nobles, clergy, and commoners, which can be very loosely seen to be analogous to the nascent parliaments in England. So, Philippe may now also have had reason to want to sideline Boniface and negotiate directly with Edward, king to king, an assertion of temporal authority.

Therefore, Othon and Amédée would not be going to Rome; they would be going to Paris. On 26 April both Othon de Grandson and Count Amédée V de Savoie, along with Henri de Lacy, Aymer de Valence, Hugh Despenser and again Amanieu d'Albret were appointed as the 'king's envoys to treat touching the reestablishment of peace with the King of France'.[57] In effect this was the Roman embassy of 1300 now going to Paris in 1302.

But even as the embassy arrived in France, the scales of power between Edward and Philippe – the former having had to agree a truce with the Scots at Philippe's levering was about to swing once more in Edward's favour. In the Flemish city of Bruges rebellion against French occupation was fanned by one named as Pierre le Roi or Peter the King. Italian chronicler Giovanni Villani describes him as a 'poor man, a weaver of cloth, and was small in person and gaunt, and blind in one eye, and over sixty years old: he did not know the French or Latin languages' but Villani added 'in his Flemish language he spoke better, more bold and distinguished than anything in Flanders and by his speech he moved the whole country to the great things that then followed'.[58] Sure enough, on 18 May, the people of Flanders, fed up with two years of French military occupation, rose up. If Scotland was proving a thorn in Edward's side, then Flanders was again to show that what was good for the goose was good for the gander. The Flemish militia of Bruges followed the lead of the Sicilians decades earlier, murdering as many Frenchmen as they could find. As the Sicilians had identified the French by their inability to pronounce Italian words, so the Flemish similarly found their victims by their inability to pronounce the Flemish word 'shield' without an accent.[59]

Echoing the Sicilian Vespers this rebellion would be known as the 'Matins of Bruges'. Military governor Jacques de Châtillon and Pierre Flotte no less were said to have fled Bruges 'in greatest terror'.[60]

In response Philippe sent a large army under Count Robert II d'Artois to suppress the rebellion, among them that thorn in Othon's side, Pierre Flotte. On 11 July at Courtrai the French army, mostly knights, met the Flemish militia. As Warenne had been found wanting at Stirling Bridge, with knights defeated by a determined pike-equipped militia, so Artois was found wanting at Courtrai. The French were heavily defeated, with around 1,000 knights and foot soldiers being killed. Among the French dead were Count Robert II d'Artois, Raoul de Clermont-Nesle, the Constable of France, Guy de Clermont, Marshal of France, Jean I de Ponthieu, Count of Aumale, Jean II de Trie, Count of Dammartin, Jean II de Brienne, Count of Eu, and Pierre Flotte. The very man who had used nascent French nationalism in his arguments in Rome with the decidedly feudal-minded Othon de Grandson had been killed by a Flemish nationalism that his French nationalism had brought to life – live by the sword, die by the sword indeed. Philippe's troubles in Flanders now quickly rendered his need for an accord with Edward more urgent. The war, begun by the fervour of youth in 1294 by the seizure of Gascony, finally after all the years of negotiation, the search for allies on both sides, all the journeys to Rome, seemed to have the prospect of an end in sight.

Worse was to follow for Philippe as Boniface issued in September 1302 his bull *Unam Sanctam* or 'One Holy'. In simple terms Boniface asserted, as he had with *Scimus Fili*, that temporal power must submit to spiritual power, that as pope he reigned supreme. Anglocentric historiography, especially that in Scotland, saw in *Scimus Fili* a repudiation of English claims over Scotland, overlooking its genuine wider context, a papal assertion of power over nations by claiming Scotland as belonging to the church. The New Testament had suggested that there were two swords, taken as a metaphor for the temporal and the spiritual. Thus, the bull concluded, the temporal authorities must submit to the spiritual authorities, not merely on matters concerning doctrine and morality, 'For with truth as our witness, it belongs to spiritual power to establish the terrestrial power and to pass judgment if it has not been good.' The bull ended, 'Furthermore, we declare, we proclaim, we define that it is absolutely necessary for salvation that every human creature be subject to the Roman Pontiff.' This was not something that Philippe could or would tolerate and launched him on a direct collision course with Rome.

So, it is against this background that we must see the peace negotiations of 1302 conducted in large part by the Savoyards Othon de Grandson and Amédée V de Savoie, in which Edward wanted the return of Gascony and a free hand in Scotland, while Philippe wanted a free hand in Flanders while dealing with his growing papal confrontation of the very nature of his realm. The age-old problem, as faced decades earlier in the 1259 Treaty of Paris, and one which would continue to plague Anglo-French relations for centuries to come – how to reconcile Plantagenet feudal claims to Gascony with Capetian claims to national sovereignty. The summer of 1302 and the following winter of 1302–3 would see Othon engaged in several diplomatic missions to France from England which would ultimately become the final peace treaty of 1303. Following the aforementioned 25 April appointment which retroactively applied to a 5 March embassy, there would be a 15 August appointment as envoy along with the usual suspects by now,[61] 10 January 1303,[62] before the final 20 May 1303 signing of the Treaty of Paris.[63] That these embassies were interrupted by journeys back to London is perhaps suggested by the 15 August 1302 appointment appearing in the Calendar of

Patent Rolls having the same date as actions taken at Westminster following the death of Archbishop Stephen O'Brogan of Cashel in Ireland by Edward on 'the information of Otto de Grandisono'.[64] There is also a letter to Othon and his fellow negotiators at Amiens of 21 November 1302.[65]

Before the formal treaty ending the nine-year war between Edward and Philippe, remarkably Othon was able to bring another difficulty to a conclusion. He arranged in Paris on 27 April 1303 for the marriage of the heir to the Grandson lands, Pierre de Grandson, the eldest son of Othon's brother Jacques, to be married to Blanche de Savoie-Vaud, daughter of Louis de Vaud. With this marriage of Grandson into the Barony of Vaud it was hoped, as it was for the marriages of Edward to Marguerite and Edward's son to Philippe's daughter Isabelle, to bring peace where there had once been discord.[66] The Grandson marriage to the daughter of Louis de Vaud had been facilitated by Louis' death in January 1302 and the presence of his heir Louis II de Vaud, Blanche's sister in Paris during Othon's time there. Two birds with one stone one might say, and again the affairs of Europe and Vaud happily coincided. It's also at this point, with this marriage that Othon makes his provision for the future of the family castle at Grandson and its lands and his lands in England, and having had no children himself, he named the married Pierre de Grandson as his heir.[67]

With the formal homage due by treaty, Henri de Lacy made the act of homage, or more accurately renewed the act of homage for Edward to Philippe for Gascony and it was all over. By 4 June Othon and Amédée were being sent to Gascony to take possession of the cities, towns, and castles of the duchy.[68] In anticipation Edward had written to them on 2 March establishing their credentials with the various communities of Gascony.[69] It had been a long road for Edward since Philippe had deceived his late brother Edmund and occupied Gascony, for occupation it was, and indeed Othon had only returned to England to find the struggle ongoing. There had been the Madog rebellion in Wales, the turning of John Balliol and Scotland, and the attempts to find allies in Flanders, Burgundy, and the empire. There had been the ill-fated campaign in Flanders, the disaster at Stirling Bridge, the victory at Falkirk. There had been the endless negotiations with Pope Boniface in Rome, the machinations of Pierre Flotte who had openly admitted the goal all along had been to rid France of the *famille Plantagenet*. But, in the end, Edward, Duke of Aquitaine, had regained what his father had given him all those years ago, his appanage, Gascony. It had been his kinsman Amédée and his old friend and envoy Othon de Grandson who had been there to retake possession upon his behalf.

CHAPTER 14

Wars are expensive businesses, true of today as it was true of the thirteenth century. Not only the payment of soldiers and the making of weapons of war, but also the restitution of affairs at war's end. So, it would be in the early fourteenth century, as Othon and Amédée, joined by Henri de Lacy, who'd lately paid homage on behalf of Edward for Gascony, returned to the war-weary duchy to retake possession for its duke. As Edward marched into Scotland once more in 1303 for yet another campaign there, it was Grandson the diplomat and administrator that would be found in Gascony, for Othon had now seen his sixtieth year and was rapidly advancing upon his seventieth. He was now less and less the soldier.

There had been the loans extended by communities and individuals to the crown to fight the war, there had been the castles which had changed hands leading to claim and counterclaim, and of course there had been the damages caused by soldiers trampling the wine crop and much else as they fought one another. It was into this sorry scene that the Savoyards and Earl of Lincoln rode in the spring of 1303.

All this, of course, was made ever more acute by the gap left in royal fund raising brought about by the absence of the Riccardi di Lucca. However, some respite was to be had by Grandson when Vuippens brought him news that Pope Boniface had granted the triennial tenth (tax revenues) which enabled him to take out loans against it. Into the vacuum left by the Riccardi were beginning to step another family of Italian bankers, the wealthy Frescobaldi of Florence. In the coming decade the Frescobaldi would loan £150,000 to Edwards I and II. In return they would be given virtual control of the revenues of England, including the mint and the customs, and were granted lands, honours, and privileges. Giovanni Frescobaldi of their number would write advice for his fellow Italians in England:

> Counsel for him who is passing into England. Clothe yourself in dingy colours, be humble, stupid in appearance, subtle in act. May evil come upon the Englishman if he molests you! Avoid cares and the man who injures you. Spend with a good heart and do not show yourself mean. Pay day by day. Be courteous in collecting debts, pointing out that necessity compels you. Do not ask awkward questions. Buy betimes if you see it is profitable. Do not have any dealings with men of the Court. Observe the commands of the powerful. It is to your interest to unite yourself with your fellow-countrymen, and have your door well bolted early.[1]

Also active in filling the financial void left by the Riccardi was another family of merchants from Lucca, the Ballardi, or more accurately perhaps the Bellardi. It would be from Giovanni Bellardi, rendered in English as John Ballard, that the Savoyards in Gascony depended upon for their wages.[2]

In terms the important task of setting up a Plantagenet administration for Gascony once more, a new controller was appointed for Bordeaux, Jean Gytardi or John Guitard.[3] There would also be a new lieutenant for the seneschal of the Agenais[4] and new governors of castles,[5] bailiffs,[6] king's clerks[7] and a new keeper of the royal forests.[8] There were also many claims and counterclaims arising from the disruption of war, an example being a complaint made by Guillaume de Cortosia that Pierre de Bordeaux and Raymond Gaufridi had maliciously stolen one hundred tons of wine from him, a rather serious crime in Gascony.[9] Bertrand de Ravignon, seigneur de Buzet, wanted letters patent that crimes committed during the war should be pardoned – fear of punishment for crimes of war being not a modern concern it seems.[10] Ravignan was something of a thirteenth-century ne'er do well as he had previously been pardoned for breaking into and robbing his own parish church.[11] French writer Pierre Courroux was less than complimentary suggesting that the Seigneur de Buzet had 'plundered both English and French' and that he inflicted '*nombreuses injures, dommages, violences et vexations*' on the people of the Agenais.[12] But Edward and Othon needed him in the castle of Buzet as it helped control access to Agen itself.

The 1303 treaty had created other local difficulties, not least of which was the town of Castillonès which found itself half in the now Plantagenet Agenais and half in Capetian Périgord, and as the townsfolk said, no man can serve two masters. Grandson and Lacy ordered John Hastings the seneschal to go to Castillonès to investigate. As said investigation could find no solution the matter was referred upward to Edward, who unsurprisingly decided Castillonès belonged in the Agenais.[13] Grandson and Lacy also inherited the ducal relationship with the ever-troublesome *famille de Béarn*. Gaston VII de Béarn had died in 1290, leaving the Béarnais to his four daughters: Marguerite, Constance, Mathe and Guillelme. The daughters did not get along, mostly because the ever-troublesome Gaston had seen fit to pass Béarn on to Marguerite, overlooking the eldest daughter, Constance. Grandson and Lacy would become referees. The sisters' relative husbands had made war one upon the other for the Béarn inheritance, going so far as to challenge one another to a duel. The matter was referred up the line past Edward as duke to Philippe le Bel as king. In January 1304 Philippe held a parliament at Toulouse, attended by Othon, Amédée and Henri de Lacy, where an adjudication was made. Philippe's arbitration simply said that the family ought to be at peace and forbad private wars. Marguerite, Viscountess of Béarn, decided that she might be better served by Edward and so paid homage to Othon and his colleagues.[14] Having failed to gain sufficient satisfaction from Philippe, she now sought the same from Edward – in such a way did the Gascons always play off the Plantagenets and Capetians against one another to their own ends. As Clifford put it succinctly, 'she could now devote herself to plaguing the English officials instead of the French.'[15] To complicate matters somewhat we should remember that the widow of the departed Gaston VII de Béarn was none other than Béatrice de Faucigny, the sole living offspring of Pierre II de Savoie, hence the involvement once more of her kinsman and count, Amédée de Savoie. We cannot pass once more without remarking upon the tangled web of familial relationships in the thirteenth and now fourteenth centuries.

In the autumn of 1303 as Othon was enmeshed in the minutiae of Gascon affairs, and Edward campaigned in Scotland, news came that the simmering antagonism between Philippe le Bel and Pope Boniface VIII had come to a head. On 3 April Boniface had issued an excommunication of anyone stopping French clerics coming to Rome, meaning Philippe or his officers. If we are in any doubt that Boniface intended this to extend to Philippe, the excommunication included even 'those that shine with imperial or royal dignity'.[16] This was an open challenge to the aforesaid 'royal dignity' that Philippe could not let pass. On 7 September, a small army of some 300 men under the fleur-de-lys banner, led by Philippe's new chief counsellor following Flotte's untimely demise, Guillaume de Nogaret, appeared outside of Boniface's palace at Anagni, 40 miles (64 kilometres) from Rome. Nogaret who had already been in Italy had allied himself with the Roman Colonna clan, enemies of Boniface's Caetani family.

The following day, 8 September, Boniface hurled a specific excommunication at Nogaret and Philippe le Bel. The French, however, fired back with a demand that Boniface abdicate the papacy. Boniface insisted he would rather die than abdicate. During a meeting between Nogaret, Sciarra Colonna and Boniface it is likely that the pope was beaten up. The citizens of Anagni revolted against Nogaret and the Colonna, allowing Boniface to free himself. However, Boniface was so shocked by this assault on the papacy he died on 11 October 1303 having fled Anagni to hold a council in Rome. Nicola Boccasini who had been with Boniface at Anagni succeeded him as Pope Benedict XI. His occupation of the Holy See would be a very short one. On 7 June 1304 Benedict released Philippe le Bel from his excommunication, but not Nogaret. Shortly after, on 7 July 1304, Benedict too expired in Perugia. He would be the last pope to reside in Italy during Othon's lifetime, until 1376 when Gregory XI returned to Rome. Benedict would be succeeded by the Gascon former Archbishop of Bordeaux and onetime papal envoy to Edward, Bertrand de Got, reigning as Clement V. (Fig 2.4) Clement would move the court of the papacy from Rome to Avignon. Clement was elected on 5 June 1305; he heard of his coming to the Holy See while in Lusignan, on his return to Bordeaux on 23 July 1305.[17] The seneschal John de Havering showered him with gifts and led him through the city[18] – the gifts Edward as duke had showered upon his Archbishop of Bordeaux included twenty barrels of wine, twenty oxen, twenty pigs, twenty rams, twelve bulls, twelve herons, two sturgeons and a golden cross with precious stones.[19] On 24 July at the Cathédrale Saint-André in Bordeaux Clement announced his intention to be crowned, not in Rome, but in Vienne on All Saints Day, 1 November, Vienne currently being a part of the empire and not France. On 22 August Philippe's brother Charles de Valois arrived in Bordeaux to represent the views of the French king. Philippe le Bel objected to Vienne and a compromise of Lyon was agreed, also not yet French but more agreeable for Philippe being in closer proximity.

That year, 1305, Bertrand de Got (Fig 2.4) began a castle at Villandraut, near his birthplace. British observers would note a remarkable similarity with Edward I's castle at Harlech. The castle would be quickly finished, completed by 1312, much of the work to allow the new pope to visit in 1307. Building records for the castle are not extant, but the new papal castle sat within Edward's Aquitaine, and was begun while Othon de Grandson was in Gascony; a knight with a long background and history in North Wales castle building cannot be entirely a coincidence. It seems likely Grandson arranged for castle builders he knew from Wales to come to Gascony in the service of Clement – who, when and how is lost to history. Some have seen the hand of Maître Jacques de Saint George at Villandraut; as yet there is no firm evidence to support the suspicions of his involvement, but in some form, in person or from a distance by influence such a link would not be surprising. If so, this would represent the completion of a circle that began at Benauges in Gascony in 1253 with Master Bertram and Jean de Mésot who began the castle-building triangle that linked Gascony, Savoy, and England. (Fig 2.5)

Othon had stayed on in Gascony even as his colleague Henri de Lacy had returned to England. Edward had reappointed John de Havering as seneschal in 1305. Accordingly,

Othon was able to partake of the festivities of Clement's return to Bordeaux. The yet-to-be-crowned pope's return to Bordeaux proved opportune since on 16 August news came that the Béarn matter had turned to warfare once more. Marguerite de Béarn's son Gaston I, Count of Foix, had invaded the territory of Count Bernard VI d'Armagnac. Young Gaston was also the Viscount of Béarn under his mother's regency. Armagnac lay between Foix and Béarn, these two having been joined by the marriage of Marguerite de Béarn into the comital family of Foix. This invasion was expressly violated the declaration against private wars made at Toulouse by Philippe. Given that Béarn lay within Edward's Duchy of Gascony and Foix within Philippe's realm had at least the potential to reopen conflict with Philippe. It would fall to Othon de Grandson with Clement's help to attempt to make the peace between Foix, Béarn, and Armagnac, between Marguerite and her son Gaston and the overlooked Constance. We see once more how a succession dispute in a far-off corner of Edward's duchy might entangle him with the French king even as he was trying to bring the troublesome Scots to heel. Once more the ever-loyal Grandson would be the fireman on the spot ensuring that this particular brush fire did not catch hold.[20] Unbeknown to Othon would be the capture on 3 August and execution on 23 August of that thorn in Edward's side, William Wallace.

But Grandson had neither news nor thoughts of the lands to the north of Edward's realm, merely his duchy of Aquitaine and as ever the crown's relationship with the papacy. He almost certainly accompanied the new pope at least as far as Nimes as Clement journeyed to Lyon for his coronation, having left Bordeaux on 4 September.[21] Othon was included among the list of participants in a 15 October English embassy to the new Papal Curia. Did he return to England before joining the embassy or join the embassy in Lyon? Given the entries in the Regestum Clementis papae V dated 19 October 1305 at Lunel and 22 October 1305 at Nîmes that reference Grandson, we can be reasonably certain that he journeyed that autumn of 1305 directly from Gascony to Lyon.[22] Joining Othon in Lyon to form the English party at the papal coronation were, among others, the familiar faces of Edward's treasurer, Bishop Walter Langton of Lichfield, Henri de Lacy, Earl of Lincoln, John de Benstede, Chancellor of Edward's Exchequer, Hugh Despenser and Amanieu d'Albret for Gascony. The newly enthroned Bishop Henry Woodlock of Winchester would be a late addition.

Amid great ceremony and splendour, the coronation of Bertrand de Got as Pope Clement V was witnessed by Othon de Grandson at the Church of Saint-Just in Lyon on 14 November 1305. (Fig 2.4) Also at the ceremony were the great and good of the medieval world, much like the recent coronation of King Charles in England. Present were Philippe le Bel who was now reconciled to the papacy, his brother Charles de Valois who had been lately in Gascony, Louis d'Évreux, later king of Navarre, Jean II de Bretagne and Henry of Luxembourg, future Holy Roman Emperor. Indeed, Charles de Valois, given the ill fate of Phillipe le Bel's line, would become the ancestor of the House of Valois on the French throne, something that would be contested by the Plantagenets for over a hundred years. So, much as today, a coronation was the excuse for a good deal of diplomatic networking, something at which Othon on Edward's behalf, excelled. However, all would not be well that day: as the newly crowned Clement processed through Lyon a wall collapsed, resulting in the death of Duke Jean II de Bretagne – an ill omen, but for whom?[23]

Clement moved on to the Dominican monastery at Avignon, where he would stay, choosing not to go to Rome, therefore beginning the era of the popes of Avignon. The English embassy, including Othon, went with them, spending the Christmas and New Year festivities of 1305–6 by the sunny banks of the Rhône. The embassy successfully persuaded Clement to annul certain reforms lately imposed upon Edward relating to the royal forest, although Prestwich casts doubt upon exactly what was meant. Another matter for the embassy was the position of Robert Winchelsey, Archbishop of Canterbury. If the late Boniface had been a thorn in Philippe's side, then Winchelsey had been a thorn in both Edward's and Langton's side. On 2 February Langton, Othon and company were able to persuade Clement to suspend Archbishop Robert from his duties at Canterbury. On18 May the bull was given to Winchelsey, and the next day he sailed from Dover never to return. In March 1306, the English had left Avignon, but Othon remained, likely said Clifford, as an early example of a permanent ambassador to the Papal Curia.[24] Othon was taking care of the detail, both in regard to Edward's realm and in regard to his own. Relations with the Frescobaldi of Florence, hoping to fill the void left by the Riccardi di Lucca, were attended to, Othon seeing to it that Clement restored a benefice in the diocese of Salisbury to Giovanni Frescobaldi.[25] His own familial concerns included obtaining a grant from Clement to the Promonasterian house of the Abbaye de Joux wherein his ancestors had lain since its foundation by Ebal de Grandson.[26] In February 1306, given his brother having the ear of the new pope, and access to the Curia without a trek across the Alps, Othon's younger brother Guillaume came to Lyon to obtain benefits for his sons John and Thomas.[27] Guillaume had had the benefit of an extensive career in England through Othon, Deputy Justiciar of North Wales included. Guillaume would be the Grandson that would in the end make his home in England, of which more later, and from whom no lesser lights than David Cameron and Diana Spencer, Princess of Wales, and indeed the English monarchy itself, are descended.

Also passing through Avignon it seems in 1306 was Héthoum de Koricos or Hayton of Corycus, to plead for claims to the throne of Cyprus of Amalric of Tyre, but also to plead the case for a new crusade in alliance with the Mongols. Amalric of the Lusignan clan had usurped royal authority from his brother Henry II. In the following year he would write *La flor des Estoires de la Terre d'Orient*, his account of the history of Cillician Armenia from which we get details of Othon's time in Armenia a decade earlier, as we discussed earlier. Hayton had joined the Premonstratensian order in Cyprus in 1305, the same order coincidentally as the aforementioned Abbaye de Joux, and would in 1307 be made prior of its house at Poitiers where he would commit his history to parchment. No doubt Othon and Hayton would be in much conversation with the crusade-minded Pope Clement.[28] Indeed, Clement issued a request for crusade proposals among his first encyclicals and would in 1308 issue a request for fresh proposals for the Council of Vienne which convened in 1311.[29]

Hayton has been attributed as the writer of *La Flor des estoires de la terre d'Orient* or *Flower of the Histories of the East*, a four-volume work, the first three volumes of which represent a geographical and historical survey of the east, while the fourth volume, which interests us, is a crusade proposal. These volumes dictated in French in Poitiers the next year, 1307, are taken to be Hayton's response to his meetings with Clement and the pope's request for crusading proposals. So what role, if any, did Grandson have in this? Which brings us to the authorship once more of the French text *Via Ad Terram Sanctam* and Latin text *Memoria Terre Sancte*, that is to say, works on how a future crusade might be undertaken. We mentioned earlier that in 1904 Charles Köhler had suggested the author was Othon de Grandson;[30] Paulin Paris had in 1869 and later J. Delaville le Roulx both suggested its author was Hayton of Corycus.[31] Here we have then in Avignon in early 1306 two of the suggested authors on crusading treatises at the court of a pope seeking crusade proposals.

The two texts have a common element which proposes that a crusading army lands in Armenia after the author rejects Egyptian and Levantine sites. The author also suggests an arrival season of summer, followed by a wintering to gather resources and strength in Armenia before attempting an invasion of the Levant the following spring. Köhler was able to show that the Latin text is in fact a translation of an original French text. The common text appears to have been written before 1289 since it refers to Tripoli still being in the hands of crusaders. Köhler held the opinion that the French text had been written by a westerner but while in the east – this being the use of the expressions '*nos gens*' and '*ceaus d'outre mer*'. Köhler went on to identify that the preamble to the French text appears to be a later addition in that unlike the pre-1289 dating earlier it gives evidence of being written later, that is after the Fall of Acre in 1291 and the death of sultan Khalil in 1293. Thus, he concluded the French text had been the combination of two writings, but that while it might be possible to have a common author it was more likely to have been written by two hands. After further confirming that the Latin text was much later Köhler summarised as follows: first, that a westerner had written a crusade proposal before 1289 in French, in draft, of which no copy has survived. Second, that the draft proposal was taken up between 1291 and 1293 by an author living in the east who added the preamble and a few passages, and that at the beginning of the fourteenth century a further revision was made and translated for the first time into Latin, thus creating the second Latin text. This later Latin text has a much fuller preamble and treatise on crusade finance. Köhler then suggested that the first revision between 1291 and 1293 and the later Latin text translation and revision were not made by the same hand.

Both Paulin Paris and J. Delaville Le Roulx attributed the later Latin translation and revision to Hayton, but Köhler was less certain. Although there are indeed close similarities between the *Memoria* and the fourth book of Hayton's *La flor des Estoires de la Terre d'Orient*, Köhler noted the differing advice in the *Memoria* and *Estoires* on using Cyprus as a landing point. Köhler firmly suggested Grandson as the author of the French text, and went on to say that the later revisions, the *Memoria*, were by an unknown hand, but that Hayton had used the *Memoria* in writing the fourth book of *Estoires* but was not the author of *Memoria*. Forey cast further doubt on the later Latin *Memoria* being the work of Grandson, since the Latin text suggests that crusading western kings might make peace to go on crusade, while an experienced diplomat like Othon would have known peace was a prerequisite for even contemplating crusade. *Memoria* also suggests that a western king gaining Jerusalem would cede the city to the church, something again Othon would have known to be impossible. Forey concluded by finding, like Köhler, that *Memoria* had an unknown revising author but also unlike Köhler that there was 'little justification for attributing any part of the two treatises to Otto'.[32] While Forey is convincing enough with *Memoria*, I do not believe he has yet provided a reliable enough critique of Köhler's attribution of the French text to Grandson.

However, we are dealing here with learned opinion, not verifiable fact. The reality is that while we may never know the author of these anonymous texts, the likely meeting of at least two of the potential authors in Avignon with Clement raises the intriguing possibility that were either of these candidates to be the author, he might have had considerable input from the other. Indeed, Köhler had left open the idea that there may well have been two authors to these texts.[33] The meeting between Grandson and Hayton certainly adds to Köhler's suggestion that *Estoires* may have been based upon the French text if Grandson was the author. Debate will no doubt continue, but it, remains a distinct possibility that in *Via Ad Terram Sanctam* held in the Ashmolean Museum in Oxford, we are reading the words of Othon de Grandson.

News would reach Othon in Avignon that as the late King Henry had granted Gascony to Edward as his appanage, now on 6 April 1306 he in turn had passed on the Duchy of Aquitaine, including the island of Oléron and the Agenais, to Edward the Prince of Wales as his appanage.[34] On 22 May, at Westminster, Edward knighted his son, along with many others, including one Piers Gaveston and one Hugh Despenser the younger, both of whom far more later.[35] The torch was being passed to a new generation, but was it to be a secure generation?

Grandson was to return to England in the late summer of 1306; once more dynastic marriage was on the agenda, Edward having married Marguerite, Philippe le Bel's half-sister in 1299 as a part of the peace had had a fruitful union. Two boys had been born to the couple: Thomas in 1300 and Edmund in 1301, but news reached Avignon of a daughter Eleanor, born in 1306. In the recent war Grandson had recruited the nobility of the Free County of Burgundy as allies for Edward and against their count, Othon IV who was moving the county into the French sphere of influence. Othon IV's death in March 1303 had seen him succeeded by his eldest daughter Joan, who was soon to marry, in January 1307, Philippe, the second son of Philippe le Bel. A marriage betrothal for the infant Eleanor to a son of the late Othon IV might protect English interest in the Free County, and the interests of its nobility and lastly their neighbours, the *famille de Grandson*. Accordingly, Othon IV's only son Robert, himself a young boy, was betrothed to Eleanor on 8 May 1306. On 4 October Pope Clement granted the necessary dispensation for the marriage.

Grandson then travelled back to England in this matter, but it was not Westminster but to the Scottish border at Lanercost Priory that Othon journeyed, as Scotland had once more caught fire. The knighting ceremony in London had in effect been a call to arms to take on Robert de Brus, who they thought had sacrilegiously taken up the throne of Scotland. Aymer de Valence had beaten Brus at Methven near Perth on 19 June. Kildrummy Castle, northwest of Aberdeen, was taken after a siege by 13 September, things appeared to be going well.[36] Othon had not seen his liege lord and lifelong friend Edward for some four years now and they were both long gained the grey hairs of old age. When Othon arrived at Lanercost he would find Edward not only plagued once more by the Scots but now dangerously ill too.

The Château de Grandson on the southern shores of the Lac du Neuchâtel in what's now Switzerland. The eleventh-century castle was much rebuilt in stages during the thirteenth and fourteenth centuries by Othon de Grandson, almost certainly financed by his account held with the Riccardi di Lucca and later his Templar stipend upheld by Pope Clement V on the suppression of the order. *John Marshall*

Above: The statue of King Edward I, by the grace of God, King of England, Duke of Aquitaine and Lord of Ireland. Othon de Grandson was brought to England, almost certainly by Henry III's counsellor and envoy, Pierre de Savoie. Grandson would be to Edward what Pierre was to Edward's father Henry. Grandson served Edward loyally throughout the king's life, from even before it began whilst on crusade in the Holy Land through two Welsh Wars, the Sicilian Vespers, the Fall of Acre and an Anglo-French war. *Wikimedia Commons*

Opposite above: A bridge at Lod in Israel bears the 1273 emblem of Al-Malik al-Zahir Rukn al-Din Baybars al-Bunduqdari, commonly known as Baibars or Baybars. The lion or panther is terrorising a mouse. In 1271–72 that mouse included the Lord Edward and Othon de Grandson. *Wikimedia Commons*

Right: The heraldry of the *famille de Grandson*, and Sir Othon de Grandson as Seigneur de Grandson featured a paly (a field divided by perpendicular lines into even parts) of argent (silver) and azure (blue) on a bend (band or strap running top left to bottom right) of gules (red). Displaying three coquille St. Jacques or escalopes. For the English cadet branch of the Grandison family, beginning with Othon's brother Guillaume, eagles replaced the coquille St. Jacques. *John Marshall, the family seal by kind permission of the ACV*

Edward I, then the Lord Edward, kills his attempted assassin in an 1850 engraving by Gustave Doré. *Wikimedia Commons*

The fabled Eagle Tower of Caernarfon Castle, deliberately styled by Edward I to allude to both Imperial and Arthurian connections. The site for Caernarfon Castle was first seen by Othon de Grandson as he and Jean de Vesci passed this way on their way from Anglesey to Criccieth, Castell y Bere and Harlech. The tower was to be the home of the Justiciar of North Wales but was not complete during Grandson's time in Gwynedd. *John Marshall*

Above: Conwy Castle, built by King Edward I at the end of the Second Welsh War directly upon the site of the Cistercian monastery of Aberconwy. The monastery was the scene of Othon de Grandson's negotiations to bring an end to the First Welsh War. *John Marshall*

Left: The tomb of King Philippe IV of France in the Cathédrale de Saint-Denis, France. Commonly known as Philippe le Bel or Philip the Fair, he was perhaps a statue both in life and in death. Philippe's counsellors Pierre Flotte and Guillaume de Nogaret were very much Othon de Grandson's diplomatic adversaries during the prolonged attempts to bring a conclusion to the Anglo-French War of 1294–1303. *Wikimedia Commons*

Right: Drawings of King Edward I of England and Philippe le Bel of France, from the Exchequer Memoranda Roll of the Lord Treasurer's Remembrancer for the twenty-fifth and twenty-sixth years of the reign of Edward I. 6 *L.T.R. Memoranda Roll, 69: mm. 54, 54d*

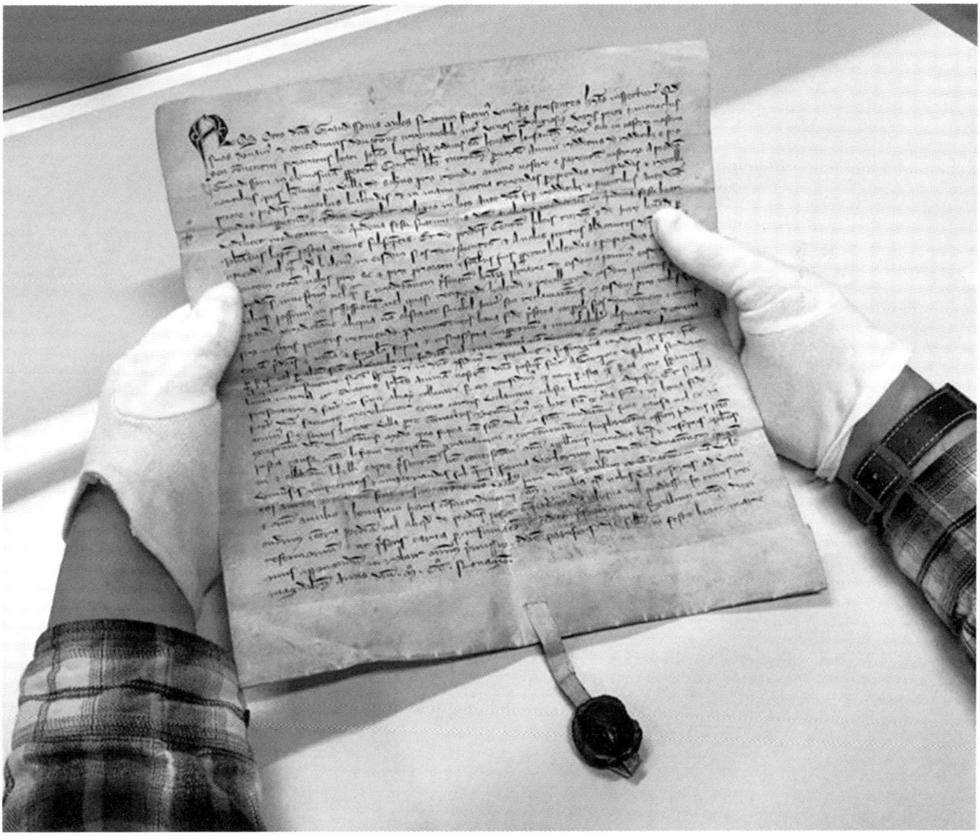

Below: The 1290 donation of 200 *livres* from his salt revenues to the house of Saint-Jean-de-Baptiste at Grandson bears the original seal of Othon de Grandson, and today resides in the cantonal archives of Vaud in Lausanne, Switzerland. The donation was made as Grandson was en route from England to the Holy Land and what would be his participation in 1291 of the last crusader defence of Acre. *ACV IB R 3/1–3. John Marshall*

Jacques de Molay, the last Grand Master of The Poor Fellow-Soldiers of Christ and of the Temple of Solomon, mainly known as the Knights Templar. His origin of Molay in Burgundy was near the Grandson lands, and indeed Othon de Grandson was 'involved' in Molay's election in 1292 following the Fall of Acre in 1291. Molay is named as responsible for the later stipend to Grandson, later upheld on the suppression of the order in 1307. Jacques de Molay was notoriously executed by Philippe le Bel in 1314, giving rise to the so-called *Rois Maudits* or Accursed Kings superstition that explained the end of the French Capetian dynasty. *Wikimedia Commons*

Benedetto Caetani reigning as Pope Boniface VIII whose clash with Philippe le Bel dominated Othon de Grandson's diplomatic work until Boniface's death in 1303 brought on by the attack of Guillaume de Nogaret on Rome in support of Philippe le Bel. *Wikimedia Commons*

The Templar Commandery of Epailly in Burgundy. Othon de Grandson was granted the Commandery in 1307, along with those at nearby Thors and Coulours, following the suppression of the Templars by Philippe le Bel and Pope Clement V in continuance of the pension he had enjoyed thereto from the Order. Upon Othon's death in 1327, the commandery reverted to the Hospitallers. Epailly itself had an income greater than the 2,000 *livres Tournois* needed to compensate Othon for his loss, therefore Coulours and Thors made no contribution. Grandson received the considerable sum, which equates to £350,000 per annum in today's money until the end of his life – so some £7 million in today's money. *John Marshall*

Renaud de Bourgogne, Comte de Montbéliard (1260–1321) the brother of Count Othon IV de Bourgogne yet sided with Comtois alliance against Philippe le Bel on the side of Edward I recruited by Othon de Grandson during the Anglo-French War (1294–1303) in 1296. Renaud's allies were his brother Jean along with Jean de Chalon-Arlay, Gautier de Montfaucon, Simon and Jean de Montbéliard, Thibaut de Neuchâtel, Aymon de Faucogney, Etienne and Jean d'Oiselay, Gautier de Châteauvillain, Humbert de Clairvaulx, Eudes de Montferrand, Guillaume de Corcondray, Jean de Joux, Guillaume, and Gérard d'Arguel and last Pierre de Joinville. His partly defaced tomb lies within the Abbaye Saint-Pierre de Baume-les-Messieurs in the Franche Comté. Renaud was related to Othon de Grandson by way of his wife Guillemette de Neuchâtel who was the daughter of Jordane, Dame de Belmont, herself the daughter of his cousin Aymon de la Sarraz. Pierre de Joinville, Seigneur de Marnay et Gex was the son of the Simon de Joinville who had been Pierre de Savoie's trusted assistant in Burgundy and had taken part in English affairs in the 1250s and 1260s. *John Marshall, access by kind permission of the Abbaye*

Bertrand de Got reigning as Pope Clement V, the Gascon pope and friend of Othon de Grandson's who became the first pope to base himself in Avignon and not Rome. Clement was involved in the suppression of the Templars at Philippe le Bel's insistence but managed to divert the resulting resources to the Hospitallers and protect Othon de Grandson's Templar stipend. His death in 1314 only added to the *Rois Maudits* Templar curse myth. *Wikimedia Commons*

Above: Château de Villandraut in Gascony, begun in 1304 by Othon de Grandson's friend Bertrand de Got, reigning as Pope Clement V. Its layout and plan are very suggestive of the Edwardian castles of North Wales and is another pointer to the involvement of Othon de Grandson in their construction, if not by design, then by common knowledge of builders. *Wikimedia Commons*

Left: The Priory of Lanercost in Cumbria, home of the Lanercost Chronicle. Founded between 1169 and 1174 to house Augustinian canons. Othon de Grandson spent the winter of 1306/7 there in the company of Edward I, likely being responsible for the chronicler's account drawn from an eyewitness of the Fall of Acre in 1291. *Wikimedia Commons*

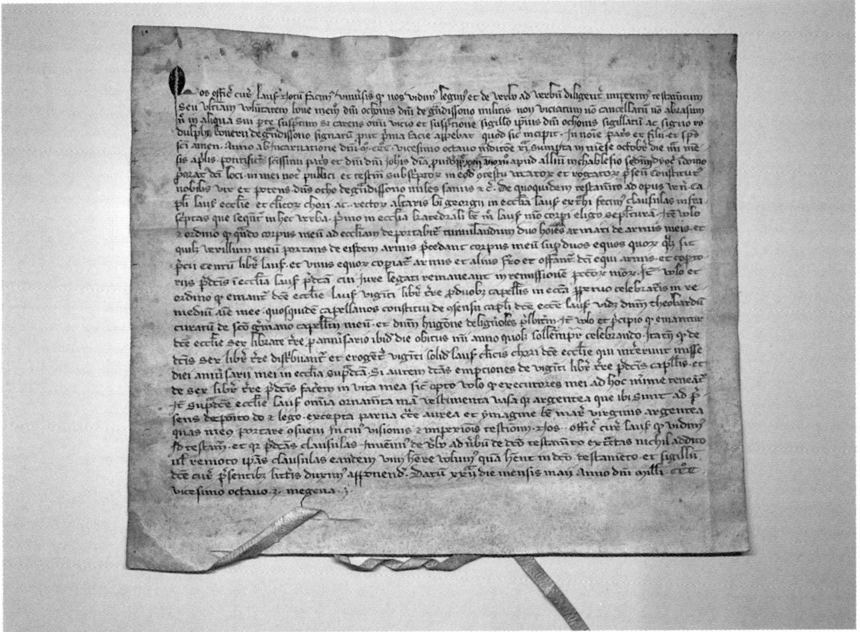

In his final years, in 1317, Othon de Grandson founded the small Carthusian monastery of La Lance just six miles (ten kilometres) north of the Château de Grandson. What survives in the Cantonal Archives of Vaud, Switzerland is the Charter of foundation and endowment of the Chartreuse de la Lance by Othon, lord of Grandson, knight, and his nephew and successor, Pierre de Grandson, Lord of Belmont, knight. ACV C X b 6. *John Marshall*

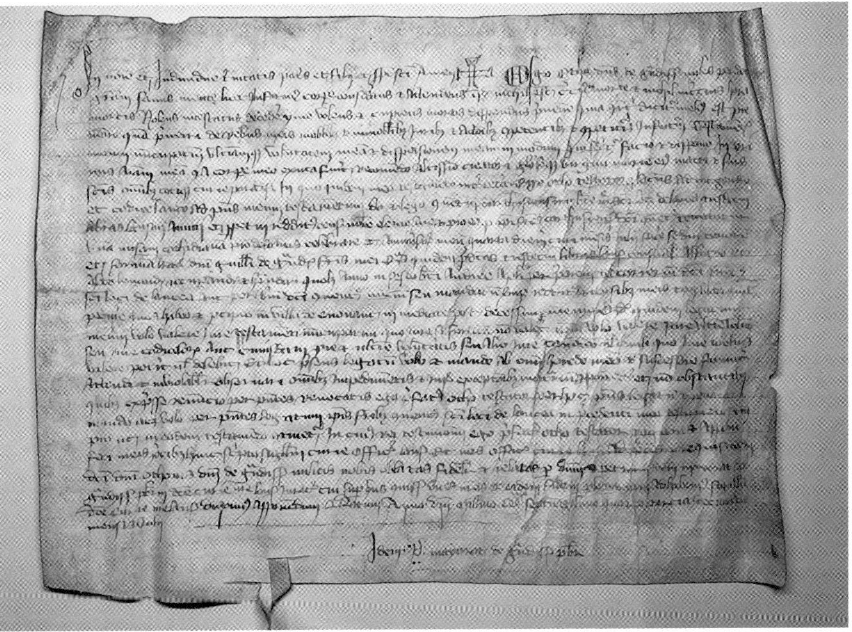

In 1317 Othon de Grandson founded a chapel in the Cathédrale de Lausanne in the name of Saint-Georges to be served by two chaplains. ACV C V b 37 & 38. *John Marshall*

Above: The last will and testament of Othon de Grandson no longer survives; what does survive is the *vidimus* of a clause from the will of Othon, lord of Grandson, knight, written in Aigle, in the prior's house, at the work of the chapter, the clergy, the choir and the rector of the Saint-Georges altar, which orders that his body be buried in Lausanne Cathedral: 'For the funeral service it is ordered that the coffin is preceded by 2 men carrying the arms of the testator, each holding a banner of arms and mounted on 2 horses worth 100 pounds each, one equipped with a raise to the said arms, and the other harnessed with iron, which horses with their crew will be given as an offering to the said church; he bequeathed to the said church 20 pounds of land for the foundation of 2 chaplains (Thibaud, priest of Saint-Germain, and Hugues de Lignerolles) and 6 pounds of land for the foundation of his anniversary. The *vidimus* is dated 22nd May 1328'. ACV C V b 53. *John Marshall*

Opposite: The tomb of Sir Othon de Grandson, Cathédrale de Lausanne, Switzerland. The tomb carries no identification and was mistakenly thought by locals for centuries to be that of Othon III de Grandson. The base and table are of black marble, the recumbent knight is of white marble, the decorative canopy is of a soft sandstone. The knight is clad in a coat of mail, worn together with a mail coif. His tabard and shield proudly display the unmistakable colours and heraldry of the *famille de Grandson.* His hands now missing once held a sword. Between 1725 and 1731 the tomb was opened to reveal the skeleton of a knight, clad in full armour, together with lance and shield. The opening also revealed his knightly golden spurs, likely those presented at his ennobling by Edward I. *John Marshall*

The John Grandisson Triptych was carved from ivory in England around 1330 AD. Since 1861, it has been part of the British Museum collection. John Grandisson, bishop of Exeter from 1327–69, was a man of education, culture and capital. This example of medieval English ivory carving is unusual because it is carved with the bishop's emblems. These two escutcheons bear the unmistakable heraldry of the *famille de Grandson. Wikimedia Commons*

CHAPTER 15

Robert VII de Brus, 7th Lord of Annandale, had on 10 February in Greyfriars, a Franciscan house in Dumfries, murdered the leading Scottish baron, John Comyn III of Badenoch.[1] Edward learned of the murder on 23 February. Brus had sided with Edward since 1302 but now the murder appeared to be a play for the crown of deposed John Balliol to whom Comyn was closely related. Like Rhys ap Maerdudd and Dafydd ap Gruffydd before him, Brus, apparently, felt not sufficiently rewarded for his efforts on behalf of Edward. In March Brus held the royal castle at Dumfries, but worse, on 25 March at Scone Brus the son and grandson of Edward's erstwhile crusading companions had himself crowned King Robert I of Scotland. One can only imagine how the news was received in London; Scotland had caught fire once more. Edward prepared a renewed military campaign and demanded that Clement excommunicate Brus.

Edward had been ill during the summer of 1306, but had recovered sufficiently to make the journey north, albeit by horse litter, to deal with the Scots only as the chill winds of autumn began to blow. But for Edward's life, now the king was 67 years of age, autumn would soon turn to winter. Along with Queen Marguerite, he arrived at Lanercost Priory on 29 September, a few short miles to the east of Carlisle. They did not, as can be imagined, arrive alone, the royal entourage numbering 200 people including the leading lights of government to the lowly keeper of the royal cows. This was more than could be accommodated by the canons and a tented city grew around the priory. New chambers were hastily added, both in wood and for Queen Marguerite in stone, all surrounded by an enclosing ditch. All were well furnished with fireplaces, as the legionaries of nearby Birdoswald could testify, the winters by the Solway could be more than a little cold.[2]

At Lanercost Edward's illness, despite the fresh milk from the cows, returned, and it was there Othon found him in the tranquil surroundings of the priory by the river Irthing. It is very possible that Othon stayed over at Greystoke in Cumberland, a day's ride, 25 miles (40 kilometres) from Lanercost. Othon's brother Henri and nephew Gérard de Vuippens had been pastors there and the *famille de Grandson* would be well known. As he made his way the short distance from Carlisle, he may have been accompanied by the many paupers who came to Lanercost in the hope of receiving alms from the king, of agents who had bought provisions for the king, of doctors from York bearing medicines of all kinds.[3] The accounts for the winter of 1306–7 do not tell us the malady from which Edward was suffering, but the list of medicines and potions ordered hint at afflictions of the legs and neck. The monastery's chambers were also to be fitted with glass windows against the chill winds that could blow across from the Solway Firth. Although they were most likely of almost the same years, old age had caught up with Edward earlier than it had Othon who had just made the 1,000-mile (1,650-kilometre) journey from Avignon to Lanercost.

During the Christmas festivities and into the New Year Othon spent time with Edward at Lanercost, (Fig 2.6) but also it seems the chronicler of the priory. Lanercost was home to a chronicler of some note. Lanercost had been founded between 1165 and 1174 by Robert de Vaux as the home of Augustinian canons or Black canons as they were known. 1306–7 was not Edward's first visit to the priory; he had been there before with Leonor in 1280 and before the siege of Caerlaverock in 1300. Indeed, its proximity to Scotland, just a mile south of Hadrian's Wall, had seen it suffer the cruel depredations of Scottish raiders, including William Wallace in April 1296. As such it was perhaps the natural home for chroniclers of the Scottish wars. However, the chronicler also gives us an account of the Fall of Acre in 1291. We can by no means be certain, but it seems very likely that the canons obtained their account of the disaster from one who was there, and that that someone was Othon de Grandson. The chronicle has this telling passage:

> The enemy, therefore, having had a taste of this bravery, increased their army so that it amounted to 300,000 light troops, investing the city once more and shooting so hotly against it that, as one who was there informed me, you might see the little arrows which they call 'locusts' flying in the air thicker than snowflakes. Those, then, who were in command upon the walls, perceiving that they could not hold the town for long against so many foes, determined by common counsel to make confession and receive the communion.[4]

That 'one who was there' might liken arrows falling 'thicker than snowflakes' does seem to point to the knight from Vaud who was more than familiar with the winters of the Jura. It would be normal for chroniclers to take advantage of travellers and visitors in their midst who had witnessed the great events of their time to enliven their histories.

From 20 January 1307 a parliament met at Carlisle. Edward, it seems was well enough to journey the 12 short miles (19 kilometres). Grandson also attended the parliament – it would be the last for both. The parliament mostly consisted of ecclesiastical rather than Scottish matters, cantering around the exactions of the papacy upon the English purse.[5] Clement had sent his fellow Gascon, Guillaume Testa to collect overdue papal revenues in support of his crusading ideals, and the English objected. Testa was called before an assembly to explain himself, the assembly being among the usual suspects' Langton, Despenser, Albret and of course Othon. The legate was advised to stay within the bounds of earlier legates and that representations would be made to the Papal Curia.[6] Cardinal Pedro Rodriguez, Bishop of Burgos, and Sabina arrived and was prevailed upon to excommunicate the murderers of John Comyn, that is Robert de Brus and company.[7] There was also the matter of Prince Edward's marriage to the young Isabelle de France. Edward was apparently unhappy that the key castle at Mauléon in the Pyrenees was yet to be handed back by the castellan who could hand it to the French. But Cardinal Pedro who must have known the castle well reassured Edward in this matter and an embassy was ordered to be ready to cross to France to finalise the marriage, Othon de Grandson of course being one of its members. The embassy was to be ready by 22 May but letters of protection for Othon dated 21 June, issued by Edward from Carlisle, show that there had been a delay in departure.[8] Remarkably Philippe had been claiming expenses due for the occupation of Aquitaine, only writing a letter cancelling fines incurred by Edward in the spring of 1307, this granted as a favour to Pope Clement who was anxious to secure the peace to further his crusading ambitions and no doubt peace in his homeland.[9]

Chapter 15

A portent of trouble to come that spring of 1307 was the young Prince Edward's Gascon friend and favourite, Piers Gaveston. He had lately been in trouble with the king for deserting the Scottish campaign for a tournament only to be pardoned in January at the insistence of the queen. But Edward reacted badly to the request made through the Bishop of Chester Walter Langton by the prince that Gaveston be granted the County of Ponthieu, lately granted to the younger Edward having earlier come into the family's possessions through the late Queen Leonor. The father went so far as to call the son 'son of a whore', seizing him by the hair. Now Edward I had by the end of his days somewhat of a temper, and the scene has been badly portrayed in the awful Mel Gibson film in the presence of Isabelle who of course was not there and amplified with the nonsense of throwing Gaveston out of the window, but as Seymour Philips has observed, the Guisborough-sourced account is 'suspect' let alone the filmic nonsense. Nonetheless, on 26 February, the king banished Gaveston from his realm (not his window), but he would soon be back and the source of much trouble.[10]

During the parliament came news from Scotland that would soon have grisly consequences. The Robert de Brus's brothers Thomas and Alexander had invaded nearby Galloway just to the northwest, aiming at the recovery of their ancestral lands. They sailed into Loch Ryan near Stranraer but were beaten by the local forces of Dungal MacDouall, who had remained loyal to the crown as he had been a supporter of the slain Comyn. An Irish sub-king and the Lord of Kintyre had accompanied them, both of whom Dungal had had beheaded on the spot. The heads, together with the Brus brothers, were sent to Edward at Lanercost. At Carlisle the Brus brothers met the same fate as had befallen William Wallace and Dafydd ap Gruffydd: they were hung, drawn and quartered, their heads displayed on the city gates and the keep at Carlisle Castle,[11] being the very castle their father Robert VI de Brus who had been on crusade with Edward and Othon and had held as Constable for Edward until his recent death in 1304. The executed brothers were also the grandsons of the Robert V de Brus who had fought alongside Edward at Lewes and Evesham all those years ago. As with Dafydd, Edward, rightly or wrongly, held the Plantagenet rage at being betrayed by a family he had thought his brothers-in-arms. Dungal for his part was knighted by Edward on Easter Day.[12]

It was however at some point that late spring, as Edward took out his vengeance on those he saw as traitors, that Othon left Carlisle for London. Neither would know, but it would be the last time they would see one another. It had been a long road together. Othon had come to the court in London likely as a small boy brought by Pierre de Savoie. They had experienced all the adventures of the medieval world together: the turmoil of the Second Baronial War, the crusade, its sortie to Nazareth, the attempted murder of Edward by the assassin, the news that Henry had died and that Edward was now king, the First Welsh War, the siege of Dolforwyn, the treaty negotiations at Aberconwy, the negotiations with the French over the Saintonge and the Agenais, the Second Welsh War, the disaster at Moel-y-Don, the march to Caernarfon, Castell y Bere and Harlech, being appointed Justiciar of North Wales, the crisis over the Sicilian Vespers and his time as a hostage in Zaragoza, the crusade reconnaissance that led to the Fall of Acre, then lately all the diplomatic work during the recent war with France to recover Gascony, something he had lately accomplished for Edward. It had been a long, long road and he had travelled many miles for Edward; as he took his leave of the king, he would not know that he was on the last of those miles.

Edward set out in early July for Scotland, by 6 July he had only got as far as Burgh-upon-Sands. The king, gravely ill, retired for the night. The next morning his attendants came to raise him but found him dying in their arms.[13] The chronicler of Lanercost, who had no doubt seen him a few days before and was close at hand, wrote:

> But alas! on the feast of the translation of S. Thomas, Archbishop of Canterbury and Martyr, in the year of our Lord aforesaid, this illustrious and excellent King, my lord Edward, son of King Henry, died at Burgh-upon-Sands, which is distant about three miles to the north from Carlisle, in the thirty-sixth year of his reign and the sixty-seventh of his age. Throughout his time, he had been fearless and warlike, in all things strenuous and illustrious; he left not his like among Christian princes for sagacity and courage. He is reported to have said to the Lord before his death 'Have mercy upon me, Almighty God! *Ita veraciter sicut nunquam aliquem nisi tantum te, Dominum Deum meum.*[14]

*Le roi est mort, vive le r*oi ![15] The death was not announced until the new king, Edward the second of that name could reach Carlisle and so 'messengers were sent in haste to give the bad tidings'.[16] Othon and the others perhaps received the news in London likely on or shortly after 11 July; a messenger announcing his father's death is known to have reached Prince Edward in London. We might assume the messenger also advised the king's council, and therefore Othon, of Edward's death.[17] Whether the messenger who visited the young Edward also alerted the council is a matter of doubt, which may explain the retention of the seal.[18] The very notification of Edward's death in the *Fœdera* mentions *Ottonis de Grandisono* by name, offering *consilium.* Othon and Edward are together side by side in the English record to the very end, the journey of the two little boys, one from Windsor the other the Lac du Neuchâtel had run its course from England to Italy, Outremer, Savoy, and Gascony and ended by the Scottish border. Othon remained Edward's counsellor even beyond the grave.[19]

King Edward the second of that name was proclaimed at Carlisle Castle on 20 July 1307.[20] Informed or not, on the old king's council's advice, including Othon, Ralph Baldock, Bishop of London retained the king's seal until 25 July whence it could be sent to the former Prince of Wales, now in Carlisle, on 2 August.[21] One of the young king's first acts, on 6 August, was the recall of Piers Gaveston whom he made Earl of Cornwall, his grand-uncle Richard's earldom.[22] Eyebrows were more than raised. Shortly after, on 7 August, Edward moved against his late father's treasurer, Othon's former colleague Bishop Langton, who was arrested. Edward scapegoated Langton somewhat for his father's debts but mostly for his attitude to Gaveston.[23] For Othon perhaps this new regime might be unwelcome.

When news reached Clement V in Poitiers where he had moved from Avignon, Clement had exequies held at the Papal Curia for Edward, the first time this had been done, and one that would serve as a model for future occasions. Clement praised Edward's 'justice and clemency, his crusading fervour and his many successes against all enemies.'[24] Clement had learned of his former duke's passing by the week ending 21 July, the exequies taking place the next week in the cathedral church at Poitiers, once within Edward's great-grandfather's duchy of Aquitaine.[25] Edward had asked that his body be carried into battle in Scotland, but understandably this wish was not fulfilled. The funeral cortège made its way from Cumberland to London. From August his body lay in state at Waltham Abbey in Essex until 18 October, Edward dressed in a royal mantle of crimson satin. His body moved on to the monastery of Holy Trinity and then St. Paul's Cathedral in London, thence to the churches of the Franciscan and Dominican friars before burial on 27 October at Westminster Abbey where he remains to this day.[26] The day before the funeral, on 26 October Othon would be granted protection for two years, going overseas on the new king's service.[27] It seems that the very last service that Othon performed for his great friend was attending his funeral. The service, given the absence of an Archbishop of Canterbury, was carried out by Antony Bek, Bishop of Durham. John of London gave the funeral oration:

> His stature was tall and fitting for each of his members … His eyes were round while he was placated and he was simple and dove-like in spirit, but in the anger and confusion of the heart of a lion, like sparking fire and thundering attack … A fierce lover of forests and beasts, while he ceased from battles, he sometimes entertained his mind with dogs and hawks, with these who play in the birds of the sky … Edward the great king … was beneficial to the peace of the kingdom, indeed, in building castles, in strengthening towers, in walls, in bastions, in fortifications, in moats … none is more refined, none more magnificent. And King Edward was an excellent warrior from his youth, most valiant in the games, in which his lance never failed or turned back, most daring in the tournaments … The most aggressive in war, the most shrewd in preparation … And the Lord was with him, through whom he was a man who prospered in all things. But to whom shall we compare and liken thee, most glorious among the kings of the earth? … O great King Edward, you are our leader in the war, you are the leader in the camp and our brave marches … By force and arms we recovered Gascony, which had been possessed by treachery; we prepared Wales for the slaughter of the enemy; first, he delivered the Kingdom of England from the mouth of the lion, when he delivered Daniel, king Henry the third, from the hand of the beast, Simon de Montfort, in the battle of Evesham. And so, we exalted the great Edward to the royal throne, both by virtue of war and by hereditary succession … Noble Arthur, king of Orkney, Norway, Aquitaine, Scotland, and Ireland, made them semi-full of people under tribute. Furthermore, he was unable to completely destroy the Saxon tribe which had entered Britain, from whom he finally escaped through his kinsman Modred in peace with the Britons. Not thus did our king Edward succumb … King Edward, who, when he was pleading the cause of the cross in the Holy Land, was mortally stabbed five times by a certain assassin, and did not perish; shot by many arrows, as at Strivelyn, he is unarmed and unharmed in the flesh. This king Edward raised above all kings a military glory, by a wide edict in France, in Flanders, in Aquitaine, in England, in Scotland, in Ireland, and in Wales … As much, then, as the English world remembers that great things were born under his leadership, the more abundantly it laments that it has lost so much in his absence. Yea, good comrades, look at what has happened to us, pay attention and see our disgrace. Our swords shall be beaten into plowshares, and our lances shall be reduced to sickles; for the worldly flower of the soldier, under whom he was to reign, to march, to advance, and finally to engage and triumph, has withered … O happy England and truly blessed country whose king is ours. Which certainly, during the reign of the magnificent Edward, shook all the kingdoms of the world with terror.[28]

As Othon sailed from Dover that November, he would not perhaps of known, but he would not see England again. There has been a lot of ink spilled in assessing the character of England's first Plantagenet king, Edward, but it is beyond doubt that the service of the Vaudois knight Othon de Grandson shows that Edward could inspire loyalty, lifelong loyalty. Edward and Othon were men of the thirteenth century. When thinking of the impact of their lives upon the nations of the British islands today, and indeed their legacy in France, and the Middle East as crusaders we should be careful not to project ideas of our own time. This loyalty attracted comment from Edward's latter day biographer Marc Morris, writing:

> The fundamental measure of Edward's wisdom, however, is that he was a good judge of other people. He could spot frauds (such as the knight who claimed to have been cured of blindness at the tomb of Henry III), and he had a talent for selecting men of outstanding ability to serve him. As one of the preachers in Poitiers put it: 'He did not rule in a frivolous state of mind, nor under the influence of flatterers … but with the prudent counsel of good and wise men.' Certain names spring immediately to mind. Robert Burnell, the longest serving chancellor until the eighteenth century; Otto de Grandson, a brave soldier and a brilliant statesman.[29]

Edward's father Henry had similarly made effective use of Savoyard counsel, Pierre de Savoie being his Othon de Grandson, but Edward had learned well the lessons of Henry's reign in the way this counsel ought to be employed. Edward made arguably better use of his mother's kinsmen and their followers, and we should add this to his obvious martial qualities.

That Savoy and Vaud supplied two of the greatest statesmen of the thirteenth century is something that seems to have passed the people of their homeland by. In my earlier work *Peter of Savoy: The Little Charlemagne* I discussed at length his contribution to the European stage, and to that contribution we must add Othon de Grandson in equal measure. Both Pierre and Othon for the seventy years from 1240 bestrode the world of European diplomacy on behalf of the English crown at a critical period in English history. It is a sad reflection on the prevalence of history as national myth making that dominated historiography in the nineteenth century that this has been largely ignored in Savoy, Vaud, and England. Pierre and Othon deserve a better memorial in their homeland than they have, especially Othon's tomb in Lausanne Cathedral that is unmarked. Even today the works of Swiss writers such as Bernard Andenmatten dwell upon their parochial achievements while paying less attention to their international accomplishments.[30] Until recently it was left to the American author Clifford to appreciate Othon de Grandson, the knight of great renown. English historians Prestwich and Marc Morris in their latter-day study of Edward are now correctly identifying Othon as both a brave solider and brilliant statesman.

Across the Channel, the France to which Othon and his embassy were shortly to travel was to be soon convulsed by much tribulation, one that touched Grandson closely. On Friday, 13 October 1307 Philippe le Bel's officers made dawn raids on all the hostels of the Templars within the Kingdom of France. In a raid planned and executed in secrecy they arrested all the brothers of the order they could lay their hands upon. The knights were dragged into Philippe's jails and subjected to torture, where they admitted to trumped-up charges of heresy. They had, apparently, denied Christ, spat upon the cross, peed on it, trampled it underfoot, worshipped idols including a cat and been guilty of sodomy.[31] These changes sprang from the ever-fertile imagination of Philippe le Bel, and most likely his twin ambitions of establishing his dominance over the church, to whom the Templars answered, not the king, and his constant need for money. In 1306 he had expelled the Jewry of France from the kingdom and netted himself 100,000 *Livres Tournois* in the process. The Genoese, Christian Spinola, wrote to King James II of Aragon: 'The pope and the king did this in order to have their money and because they wished to make one single house of the Hospital and the Temple and all the other brotherhoods, of which house the king intended and desired to make one of his sons the ruler.'[32]

Philippe had written to James, but also Edward in London, urging them to suppress the order in Aragon and England. Arrested that Friday 13th was the order's Grand Master Jacques de Molay. (Fig 2.0) He had been in France since the previous year, attending to Pope Clement's aforementioned request for crusade proposals.[33] Clement had received a visit from Philippe in Poitiers from 21 April until 15 May; mostly the aim was to blacken the name and reputation of his late enemy Pope Boniface, but the Templars had also been discussed.[34] Molay had then been in Paris in June to discuss rumours he had first heard in Marseille upon arrival in France, then spreading, of irregularities in the order's practices but seems to have thought the matter settled by a 24 August papal inquiry being ordered.[35] However, on 14 September secret orders had gone out from Philippe to his bailiffs and seneschals[36] and so on 13 October Molay found himself arrested with his brother knights.[37] Remarkably, the day before his arrest Molay had been among the ranks of honour, indeed pallbearer, at the funeral of Catherine de Valois, the newly deceased wife of Philippe's brother Charles.[38] Philippe's ability to be duplicitous would no doubt have been familiar to the late king of England and indeed Othon. Grandson, was, as we have seen, a close friend of the Templars, having fought alongside them at Acre in 1291, been there in Cyprus as a part of Molay's election as Grand Master, and in receipt of a handsome annual pension from the order. So Molay's arrest and the rumours swirling around France would have touched directly upon him, but at no point can we find him implicated in events, other than, as we saw earlier, petitioning Clement for the maintenance of his pension. But nowhere too can we find him leaping to the defence of Molay, his former friend and ally, at least not in a way that has left any trace. As Demurger said in conversation with the author of this book, Grandson did not try to defend Molay.[39] A character flaw? Demurger went to affirm that one cannot speculate about possible motives, Grandson was by now seventy years of age, had discretion become the greater part of valour?

On 22 November, to bring the Templar investigations under the spiritual and not temporal authority, Clement V issued the bull *Pastoralis praeeminentiae*. So, it was in a France convulsed by the arrest of the Templar knights that Othon de Grandson arrived on 25 November 1307. The embassy from the new king, Edward II, was to finalise arrangements for his marriage to Philippe's daughter Isabelle. Accompanying Othon this time was Antony Bek who had lately officiated at the late king's funeral, plus Othon's ofttimes colleagues of Anglo-French diplomacy, Aymer de Valence, Henri de Lacy, Amanieu d'Albret and John of Berwick. Matters were concluded quickly for once; on 30 December Edward II was writing to Philippe agreeing to arrangements and that he would be at Boulogne by 21 January 1308 in time to be married shortly after. Boulogne had been chosen for its proximity to the Plantagenet fief of Ponthieu. Edward raised concerns by appointing Piers Gaveston his regent during his trip to France.[40] On 25 January 1308 at the Notre-Dame de Boulogne the not 24-year-old uncrowned Edward II of England, great-great-grandson of Henri Plantagenet and Alianor d'Aquitaine, was married to the 12-year-old Isabelle de France, daughter of Philippe le Bel.

The Savoyards Pierre de Savoie and Othon de Grandson had laboured for some fifty years to bring about this rapprochement between the Capetians and Plantagenets, the descendants of Alianor and Marguerite de Provence. This was not just the royal marriage event of the year, but of the century, and would as we shall see have consequences reaching centuries into the future. Present along with the noble Lord of Grandson would be King Philippe le Bel of France, King Louis I of Navarre, later Louis X of France, Edward's stepmother Marguerite, Philippe's half-sister Marie of Brabant, Marguerite's mother and dowager queen of Philippe III, Albrecht I von Habsburg, King of Germany and King Charles II of Naples, Count Robert III of Flanders, his brother Guy de Namur, Duke Jean II de Brabant and his wife Edward's sister Margaret, Robert d'Artois, Count Louis II de Nevers, Count Guy IV de Saint Pol, Count Jean II de Dreux, Antony Bek, Bishop of Durham, Aymer de Valence, Earl of Pembroke, Henri de Lacy, Earl of Lincoln, Humphrey de Bohun, Earl of Hereford, Jean de Warenne, Earl of Surrey and of course Count Amédée V de Savoie – Othon's colleagues and adversaries of hours if not years of negotiations, some of whom he'd be seeing for the last time.[41] Isabelle wore a jewelled robe of blue and gold and a crimson mantle lined with yellow, Edward similarly well dressed – a golden couple, what could go wrong?

On 31 January, Edward, as the new Duke of Aquitaine paid homage but not fealty to his new father-in-law for Gascony,[42] Philippe having renewed his remission on Gascon penalties made to the late king the previous year.[43] The couple returned to England for their coronation, which was to be on 18 February but was delayed. The delay had been a baronial insistence, led by Henri de Lacy, backed up by Philippe's brothers and son who were to attend the coronation, that Gaveston be banished.[44] Eventually after an impasse Edward agreed to a formulation of coronation oath that led the barons to believe they would get what they wanted. The coronation proceeded therefore on 25 February 1308 at Westminster Abbey. However, even beforehand, Edward had sent Philippe's wedding presents to Piers Gaveston as a gift,[45] and during the coronation the newly ennobled Gaveston carried Edward the Confessor's crown ahead of the couple.[46] Othon did not attend the coronation, although Amédée de Savoie did, as did Othon's younger brother Guillaume.[47] At the coronation banquet in Westminster Hall, festooned with Gaveston's banners, Edward shunned his new queen to sit out the evening reclining on a couch with Gaveston.[48] The barons and the French royal party, including Philippe's brother Charles de Valois, were furious; civil war beckoned.[49] Edward's conduct has for centuries given rise to suggestions of homosexuality; however, lately this has been thought overplayed, his favour of Gaveston being most likely a deep brotherly affection rather than sexual; nonetheless, his actions in the Gaveston affair can be said to have threatened Anglo-French relations at an inopportune time.

Even before the coronation the English barons had, on 31 January, made a declaration at Boulogne that had some echoes of the declaration of 1258 that would ultimately lead to the Second Baronial War. The Boulogne declaration ambiguously sought to defend Edward II from what the signatories saw as his folly, but while not mentioning Gaveston by name it drew a distinction between the crown and the person of the king. But, unlike the 1258 oath which had Pierre de Savoie as a signatory, this time there was no Savoyard – Othon de Grandson had never been rewarded with English land in the way that Pierre had and so unlike his predecessor was not of the English baronage. What is more, despite its signatories numbering his familiar colleagues, Henri de Lacy, Aymer de Valence, Jean de Warenne and John of Berwick, Grandson does appear to be at over 70 passing on the chance to be as involved in the new king's reign as he was in the old. In short Othon's primary loyalty had always been to his friend Edward as much or more than it had been to the crown. This did not mean he would not continue to serve the crown in ways in which his diplomatic career would be obviously helpful, but 1308 does mark a stepping back. The Boulogne agreement foreshadowed a presentation to parliament in April 1308, but that would be for the English, not the Lord of Grandson.[50]

So, while Edward and Isabella set out on their unhappy marriage and the first rumblings of discontent with the new king may have been known to Othon, he left Boulogne not for London, but for the Papal Curia at Poitiers, where he is noted on 26 February 1308.[51] By May Philippe had arrived in Poitiers to press two points with Clement: first, he wanted a postmortem trial of Boniface, and second, he wanted to try the imprisoned Templars not Clement. Following *Pastoralis praeeminentiae* the Templars in England and elsewhere had been arrested but given Clement's bull Philippe had suspended his own investigations in favour of papal inquiry, after which Molay for one had recanted his confession. Things were getting messy. To pressure Clement, Philippe brought seventy-two Templars to Poitiers on 27 June, so that they might testify the guilt of the order.[52] Of lesser importance was the matter of claims arising from the recent war with England, and here we find Othon being employed on behalf of the English crown.[53] But Philippe also brought news from London of the king's coronation and subsequent events. Edward and Gaveston had made apparently for Windsor after the coronation. After an inconclusive parliament, the discontented barony had largely retired to Lacy's castle at Pontefract,[54] Philippe's brothers and son had returned to Paris with news of the affair. Lacy and the barons drew up 'three articles',[55] which in effect called for the exile of Gaveston. At parliament on 28 April these had been presented to the young Edward.[56] On 18 May Philippe had written to Edward calling for Gaveston's banishment – he was not about to see his daughter treated in this way. Philippe had sent the abbot of Saint Germain and three knights to England that '*pro statu de gaveston deteriorandu*' or that 'the state of Gaveston might deteriorate' and let it be well known that he thought of Gaveston and his supporters as his mortal enemies. It was even rumoured that Philippe sent money, £40,000, to Lacy and Valence to aid in their pursuit of Gaveston.[57]

News came also that Europe would be further destabilised. Albrecht von Habsburg, king of the Germans and only lately at the wedding in Boulogne, was murdered at Windisch, now in the Swiss canton of Aargau, in May. This would present an opportunity for the ever-acquisitive French king but also a threat to the Grandson lands from both Paris and an unstable German land to the immediate north. Written on 8 August and proclaimed on the 12th, Clement responded to Philippe's pressure with another bull, *Faciens misericordiam*, which established a church commission to investigate the Templars and called for a council to be held in 1310. All this meant of course, a new king in England mired in a potential civil war with Scotland still at odds with him, France convulsed by the Templar affair, the empire without a head, that any crusade plans drawn up for Clement, by Hayton, Molay or Othon were for the birds.

There was also the matter of Othon's Templar pension, and it is in August that Clement and Philippe made arrangements for its continuance and award of former Templar property in France to Grandson.[58] As we saw earlier when discussing Othon's Templar links the pension was the enormous sum of 2,000 *Livres Tournois*, equating to £500 at the time, and over £350,000 in today's money. In confirmation of the pension, Clement V, on 17 August, having left Poitiers on 13 August for nearby Ligugé, and no doubt with Philippe's acquiescence, granted Othon, by what he called 'opportune remedy', three former Templar houses in France as a part of the continuing settlement, those at Thors, Épailly and Coulours.[59] (Fig 2.2) Neither Philippe nor Clement appears at this distance in time to have associated Grandson with the Templars, other than as a recipient of payments from the order. Perhaps the Lord of Grandson was too associated with the English crown to be pursued by Philippe without diplomatic entanglement, but more likely, as we have said in matters Templar, Othon was a fellow traveller rather than member.

News reached the Curia that matters in England had, for now, resolved. By 18 May Edward had been forced to exile Gaveston[60] and on 24 May the recalled Archbishop of Canterbury Robert Winchelsey had pronounced excommunication on him should he return.[61] Edward made Gaveston Lieutenant of Ireland; on 25 June 1308 he took ship at Bristol for Dublin.[62] This followed letters of 16 June, from Edward to Philippe,[63] to Clement,[64] to Amanieu d'Albret[65] and to Othon de Grandson,[66] begging them to use their influence to enable papal nuncios to facilitate Gaveston's return and revocation of the excommunication. Clement replied that he would send the Bishop of Poitiers in mediation, but he appears to have been delayed by Philippe. The matter rumbled on into the autumn, by which time, on 5 October, Clement wrote again, this time to Philippe, that he was sending Othon de Grandson to make the peace in England, writing: 'And also, we charged and urged by our letters our beloved son, the noble Othon de Grandson, whom we consider most useful in making the aforesaid peace according to your and our desires.'[67]

By October Arnaud d'Aux, Bishop of Poitiers, for Clement and Count Louis d'Ëvreux for Philippe were in England to mediate, but despite Clements's letter to Philippe, no Othon de Grandson.[68] In order to placate Philippe Edward agreed to the suppression of the Templars in England, something he had been resisting since the previous December.[69] He also agreed to the release of Othon's erstwhile companion Bishop Walter Langton, on 9 November.[70]

That summer, between 28 June and 2 July, Clement at Poitiers heard at least fifty-four Templars 'confess' their sins. When they were asked if their statements were given freely many said that while they had been tortured and threatened, restricted to bread, and water and had undergone other forms of harsh treatment, their confessions were not, apparently, the results of this torture. As Othon was no doubt there or nearby, one wonders what the old knight, who knew so many Templars, and had been with them at the Fall of Acre, thought of the confessions and proceedings.[71] Grandson appears to have left on his mission by September of 1308, as there are numerous 8 September indulgences issued in his name to his family and clerks contained in the Registres de Clement V.[72] These dispensations included also benefits to the Franciscan church in Grandson and the *famille de Grandson* Premonstratensian Abbaye de Joux, the latter being granted permission to found a daughter abbey at St. Jean. However, Othon seems to have got only so far from Poitiers as Philippe's Fontainebleau.[73] Philippe had, it seemed, discussed the matter with Philippe during the king's visit to Poitiers a few months earlier; indeed, Clement's confirmation of 17 August 1308 from the Abbaye Saint-Martin at Ligugé near Poitiers (see appendix) follows a mandate from Philippe to the bailiff of Sens on the matter of 30 July 1308 (see appendix).[74] Philippe confirmed Grandson in the former Templar *commanderies* of Thors in the diocese of Troyes, Coulours-en-Onthe in the diocese of Sens (hence the mandate above) and lastly Épailly in the diocese of Langres.

So first we must consider what was a *Commanderie,* or in English a Commandery? The military orders had adopted since their beginning structures like the existing monastic orders, which made sense since they were in effect monks with swords. We saw earlier that Bernard de Clairvaux, a major figure in the early days of the Cistercians had been instrumental in giving the Templars their rule at Troyes at 1128 along with Barthélémy de Grandson, just fifty miles (eighty kilometres) from Épailly. The lowest subdivision of their order as the

Commanderie, a local recruiting centre and source of revenue from rent and donations under a commander. These *commanderies* had been in royal hands since the suppression the previous autumn. Épailly itself had an income greater than the 2,000 *Livres Tournois* needed to compensate Othon for his loss, therefore Coulours and Thors made little or no contribution. Templar historian Demurger published a fascinating window on to the *Commanderie* of Épailly at the time of its passing to Grandson. Firstly, we know that some 550 people in the locale were responsible for '*là ou l'on fait feu*' or 'where the fire is fired' that is the hearth, which is in effect a count of households, giving us an estimated population of 1,925 to 2,750 inhabitants who might contribute to coffers of the commander – much the same population as the villages surrounding Épailly to this day.[75] The Templars had owned the house of Épailly and its outbuildings, the wood of Épailly, the orchard of Fay and large quantities of meadows.[76] The inhabitants of the local villages; Courban, Bissey-la-Côte, Louesme and Layer-sur-Roche owed royalties and or service to the Commanderie – the Templars were in effect the local lords, thus Othon de Grandson might be described as the Lord of Épailly.[77] Demurger published for us a breakdown of Othon's newly found income:[78]

Income from houses and outbuildings	£100
Pasture and woodland	£30
Income from vineyards	£70
Income from meadows	£225
Income from arable land	£262. 10s.
Malmaison Farm	£25
La Réserve Total	£712. 10s.
Income from tenant royalties – wax	£9. 6s. 8d.
– Wheat	£220. 16s.
– Rye	£35
– Barley	£275
– Oats	£210. 8s 4d.
– Wine	£35
– Hens	£261. 13s. 4d.
Royalties Total	£812. 4s. 4d.
Income from labour – *Corvée*	£37 10s.
– Harvest	£27. 10s.
– Ploughing	£45
– Saint Rémi Rents	£55
– All Saints Day Rent or *Corvée*	£65
Income from labour total	£192. 10s
Total	**£1717. 4s. 4d.**

Grandson received the considerable sum of £2000 *Tournois*, which equates to £350,000 per annum in today's money until the end of his life – so some £7 million in today's money.[79] The grant was not considered hereditary, Othon's heir Pierre tried to claim the revenue of Épailly, but it remained with the Hospitallers after Othon's tenure.[80] (Fig 2.2) However, the *famille de Grandson* might well be said to have kept some interest in Épailly as the Hospitallers placed Épailly under the successive command of the brothers Jean and Gérard de Montagny. The brothers were sons of Aymon de Montagny and Agnès de Grandson – Agnès being a niece of Othon's.[81]

From Fontainebleau it was not to London as we saw, but to Vevey by Lac Léman, where he is noted six weeks later. John Maddicott suggests that Othon had once more taken up the cross in 1307,[82] and a line in a papal letter just before he set out for Vevey does allude to another journey to the Holy Land, Clement writing on 25 May 1308 '*ita tamen ut quam primum dictus Otto proficiscetur in Terrae sanctae subsidium*' or 'so, however, that as soon as the said Otto would set out for the relief of the Holy Land'.[83]

But it was not the Holy Land that called Grandson south instead of north in the autumn of 1308. The hostilities between Louis de Vaud, Amédée V de Savoie's late brother, and the see of Lausanne, the latter in the hands of the *famille de Grandson* in the person of Guillaume de Champvent, Pierre de Champvent's brother, had not died with the passing of the protagonists. A renewed conflict, this time between Louis II de Vaud and Bishop of Lausanne Gérard de Vuippens, lately in Edward's diplomatic service, had broken out. Against this we should also set renewed Capetian encroachment of the Grandson sphere of influence, recalling Othon's recruitment of the nobility of the County of Burgundy to alliance with England against Philippe le Bel in the recent war. This had been possible, in part, due to the nobility's dislike of the pro-French stance taken by the late Count Othon IV de Bourgogne. The count having died in 1303 had been succeeded by his daughter Jeanne II who had become a very eligible heiress. Philippe le Bel then took advantage of the weakness of the empire, of which the County of Burgundy was a part, by marrying his son Philippe to Jeanne in January 1307. Albrecht von Habsburg's murder in May 1308 had weakened the pro-imperial faction in the county in favour of the French, to the potential disadvantage of the Grandsons. With all England's problems, and imperial instability, the last thing either pope or Grandson might have needed was a renewed conflict between the Savoyard Barony of Vaud and its episcopal see of Lausanne. So, England would have to wait. Grandson made for Vaud at Christmas 1308–9 to intervene there. The 1311 prolongation of the truce made at Vevey early in 1309 survives, made '*par la main de noble baron monsire Othe segnor de Grancon*' or 'by the hand of the noble baron Othon Lord of Grandson'.[84] The Vaudois political problem would be resolved once Othon returned to the Papal Curia, as no doubt at Othon's bidding Gérard de Vuippens was moved from Lausanne north to the see of Basel and replaced immediately by his kinsman Othon de Champvent, brother of the late Bishop Guillaume, Othon having been a member of the Lausanne chapter and a safe pair of hands. Vuippens replaced at Basel the former Prince Bishop, one Othon de Grandson, son of Jacques de Grandson, our Othon's late brother – the bishoprics of Helvetia being something of a game of *famille de Grandson* musical chairs at this time. Othon de Champvent marked the third successive Bishop of Lausanne having been of the *famille de Grandson*, and Vuippens being the second successive Prince Bishop of Basel. Still living at this point and to at least 1313 was Othon's sister and Gérard's mother, Agnès, we don't know which year she would final pass away, but we do know she was taken on a 9th December.[85]

The treaty at Vevey is said to have been sealed on or by 2 January 1309, but by 16 January we have Othon visiting his newly benefitted former Templar *Commanderie* at Épailly, 180 miles (290 kilometres) distant. Now it is possible that in those two weeks he made that journey, but also that he returned north earlier and that the treaty, having been his doing, was simply sealed in January. Given that the Vevey treaty is not extant but referred back to in 1311, we cannot be certain, but the letter from Épailly to John Langton, Bishop of Chichester and Lord Chancellor, is marked '*Donees Espalli le xvj jour de jenuier*' and so we can at least know that he visited his newly acquired *commanderie* in mid-January 1309.[86] The subject of his letter was his clerk in England, Eudrich de Vuippens, a kinsman of both Othon's and Gérard's, lately Bishop of Lausanne. The letter gives us the name which Grandson would have used of himself. I have called him Othon in this book, which is the modern rendition in French of his name, but in the letter, he uses the name he would have himself used and known, Othes, this all being a cautionary example of writing the history of a life based upon such fragmentary evidence. But by March 1309 Othon had returned to the Papal Curia, once more to take up the cause of the young Edward, since the summer and autumn of 1308 had called him to Paris and Vevey matters had developed further in England that had rendered his papal peace mission redundant, overtaken by events.

As we saw in mid-January Othon was at Épailly; by March he was being granted protection to once more cross Philippe's territory to the Papal Curia on Edward's business.[87] He would be joined at Avignon by an embassy from England, despatched on 4 March, likely to seek the return of Gaveston, which included Aymer de Valence.[88]

In April 1309 at parliament Edward proposed the return of Gaveston, but this was rejected by the barony. However, the barony did suggest a return might be possible with a reform of the kingdom. Perhaps anticipating, Edward had written to Clement giving assurances that the matter had been resolved and peace returned to England. Accordingly, by 21 May 1309, in response to the embassy and letter, Clement issued a bull annulling the excommunication of Piers Gaveston,[89] meaning that after its arrival in England in June,[90] on 27 June Edward was able to recall him to England and on 5 August restore his former favourite to the Earldom of Cornwall. The English matter appeared to be resolved – only appeared resolved since the returned Gaveston also returned to his habits of getting under the skin of the barons and going so far as to establish nicknames for them: Warwick being the 'black dog of Arden', Lincoln the 'burst belly', Pembroke 'Joseph the Jew', Gloucester 'whoreson' and Lancaster the 'churl'.[91] How to win friends and influence people the Gaveston way. Becoming chief among the baronial opposition was a man of the royal blood himself, Thomas, Earl of Lancaster, the son of the late king's brother Edmund.[92] Edward and Gaveston were developing the bad habit of not just making enemies of the barony but also barons with a good claim themselves to the throne. Whether Othon in Avignon became aware that his good friends and colleagues Henri de Lacy and Aymer de Valence were 'burst belly' and 'Joseph the Jew' is unclear, but he would certainly have counselled a king not to make such enemies.

Othon was still in Avignon when the envoys of the newly crowned king of the Germans Henry of Luxembourg arrived there in June 1309. Following the murder of Albrecht von Habsburg, the election of a successor had been quick. He had been elected king in Frankfurt on 27 November 1308 and crowned in Aachen on 6 January 1309, this despite Philippe lavishly spending much treasure in the hope of placing his brother Charles de Valois on that throne, Charles being a head much in want of a crown. Philippe acquiesced in Henry's success mostly because Henry – although Luxembourg was supposed to be a part of the empire, like the County of Burgundy it was falling under the influence of Paris and Henry – was a vassal of Philippe's. Clement confirmed Henry's election but also considered that it might be a good idea to have Henry adopt the imperial throne in Rome as a way of checking Philippe's ambitions. Clement felt in need of imperial protection. Technically there had not been a Holy Roman Emperor since the days of the much-excommunicated Frederick II – his successors in Aachen had not been crowned emperor by the pope, something required to consider oneself emperor. The envoys chosen by Henry to the Papal Curia were Guy de Namur, the son of the late County Guy of Flanders, Amédée V de Savoie, Guillaume III de Genève, and Jean II de Vienne of the Dauphiné. For Othon their visit must have been something of a reunion. We should mention at this point that Jean, as Dauphin, that is Count of Albon, still ruled a county a part of the empire which had yet to become a part of France, which would not happen until his descendant Humbert III sold his land and titles to Philippe VI of France. These envoys to Clement had one thing in common: they were from French-speaking parts of the empire nervous or resisting Capetian advances – an interest Othon knew well from his alliance building a decade earlier. However, Othon's involvement now in imperial affairs also marks somewhat a disentanglement from English affairs. The stability of the western environs of the empire touched directly upon his own lands and their welfare following Edward's death was becoming ever more important.

In England, the Gaveston affair was again steering the kingdom toward conflict; given Gaveston's behaviour the barony refused on 18 October 1309 to attend the 'parliament' at York.[93] This was followed by a refusal to attend the parliament called in February 1310 – sure enough they had come to London but stayed away from Westminster.[94] Eventually parliament did sit from 27 February but then Edward was presented with proposals for reform once more. A commission would be begun, lasting eighteen months, to reform Edward's government. If he refused to accede, then the barons threatened deposition.[95] It was a return to the strife of his grandfather Henry's later reign, a curtailment of royal power. With little choice, on 16 March 1310 Edward agreed to the Lords Ordainers – seven bishops, eight earls, six barons – who would draw up reform plans. Pointedly, Gaveston would not be among the Lords Ordainers.[96] Grandson, meanwhile, at the Papal Curia was no longer playing any discernible role in English affairs.

In Avignon, Grandson appears now to have the interests of the empire, and so his own lands front and centre of his concerns. Following the counsel of Othon, and the imperial envoys, Clement sent word to Italy that they should receive Henry as the new emperor. Othon's counsel was referenced to the northern Italian towns as 'of our … beloved son, Othon de Grandson, the most zealous of your honour.'.[97] So, Henry made for Italy, swearing fealty to Clement in Lausanne on 11 October. Grandson was at this time rewarded by Henry with the fief of Laupen near Bern, a castle garrisoned nearly fifty years earlier by Pierre de Savoie against earlier Habsburg inroads.[98] Othon appears that autumn to have been making for Italy too, getting as far as Aiguebelle by the confluence of the Maurienne and Tarentaise by which way he could have made for either the Petit Saint-Bernard or Mont Cenis passes; however, it is there that a great illness befell him.[99]

The nature of Othon's great illness is unknown, but it is the first recorded instance of his old age catching up with him. It is likely that his being now over 70 with decades in the saddle were beginning to catch up with the old warhorse. All that we know is that he was laid up that winter of 1310–11 at Aiguebelle and that he was attended by a physician who became, not unsurprisingly, his friend.[100] Whatever the 'great illness' may have been, Clement was soon writing to Grandson, along with Amédée de Savoie, Guy de Namur and the Bishop of Trent, Henry of Metz the imperial chamberlain, with affairs relating to his crusading ambitions.[101] Clement was urging upon the imperial chamberlain, envoys and Othon de Grandson the need for an all-embracing peace between the empire and France which might bring Europe to stability and render a crusade possible. A covering letter to his nuncio in Italy reveals that Othon must have been in contact with Clement regarding his illness and situation in Aiguebelle as the legate is advised to go to Othon en route to Italy 'who is, as it were, on your journey' or as Clifford translated 'not much out of your way'.[102] Henry had crossed into Italy in the autumn of 1310, and on 6 January 1311 he was crowned king of Italy in Milan with the iron crown of Lombardy. But the Italian cities, divided between Guelph and Ghibellines held out variously against him and he would not be crowned Holy Roman Emperor in Rome until 29 June 1312. However, his reign would not last long, as he died of malaria in August 1313. His successor would be Louis IV, elected in 1314; however, the nature of the Italian divide would mean Othon de Grandson would not see another Holy Roman Emperor in his lifetime.

In England, 1311 would see the Lords Ordainers demand and eventually get the expulsion, again, of Piers Gaveston as the affair rumbled on. In May Edward caught sight of a draft of the proposed ordinances; he was less than happy.[103] By May, Othon had aborted any journey to Italy for Clement and Henry he may have intended and was back at the Papal Curia in Avignon in the service of the young king Edward. Othon would soon receive his appointment from Edward who was by the Scottish border at Berwick, to be a representative of the English crown at the coming great council to be held just to the north of Avignon in Vienne.[104] That Edward had lost touch with Grandson is indicated by the preserved chancery warrant, which read:

> also, as the king wills that Sir Othes de Grantson be named one of his said messengers, to request him by letters under the Great Seal to charge himself with the message, with the other messengers, and meet them a day or two on this side of the pope's court to inform himself from them on the points touching the message, and to deliver these letters to the treasurer to send to Sir Othes wherever he may be found, without delay; also to let the messengers have letters of credence to the pope and the cardinals.[105]

Sir Othon de Grandson, wherever he may be found indeed. Edward needed the old knight's counsel. Othon would be joined by Edward's other representatives, William Greenfield, Archbishop of York, John de Halghton, Bishop of Carlisle, Henry Woodlock, Bishop of Winchester, Ralph de Baldoc, Bishop of London, and his old colleague the Gascon Amanieu d'Albret. This time there would be no Henri de Lacy, as the Earl of Lincoln, a long-standing colleague of Grandson's had passed away in February 1311.[106] News would also be brought of the passing of the Bishop of Durham Antony Bek on 3 March.[107] This was the passing of Othon's generation and yet the old warhorse remained. The English brought with them a protestation to Clement from Edward that the proposed ordinances of the Lord Ordainers ought to be annulled if they found against the young king.[108] In England, on 27 September 1311, the ordinances were published: Edward's realm was to be reformed. Gaveston was required to leave the kingdom by 1 November and did so on 3 November.[109]

Clement had ordered the council to meet in his bull *Regnans in Coelis* of 1308; it was to have met earlier but had been delayed as evidence for the main business of the council had been slow in gathering – the council was to consider the fate of the Order of the Temple of Jerusalem. The gathering in Vienne the old Roman city by the Rhône brought together 20 cardinals, 4 patriarchs, 108 archbishops and bishops of the church, and 62 other clerics, all of which around a third were from France itself. Since some 240 clerics had been invited, we can imagine that a good many found convenient reasons to be elsewhere. The matter was largely a foregone conclusion – the order was to be suppressed, but Clement was fighting a rearguard action; he wanted to retain control of the orders assets and not cede them to Philippe. The French king duly arrived to fulfil his suppression of the order and promptly parked an army at nearby Lyon to concentrate the mind of the clerics. On 22 March 1312 Clement pronounced his bull *Vox in Excelso*:

> After long and mature deliberation, having in mind God alone and the good of the holy land, without turning aside to right or to left, we elected to proceed by of provision and ordinance, in this way scandal will be removed, perils avoided, and property saved for the help of the holy land … Therefore, with a sad heart, not by definitive sentence, but by apostolic provision or ordinance, we suppress, with the approval of the council the order of the Templars, and its rule, habit and name.

With that the Templars became history. Philippe had his way, but Clement had held on to the Templars' property and would in effect fold the order into the Hospitallers. Clement also managed to bring an end to proceedings against the late Pope Boniface, against Philippe's charges of sodomy among other things – Philippe does seem to have had a thing about sodomy, although Clement had been forced to rescind the excommunication of Nogaret a year earlier in April 1310. Once more we can only imagine the thoughts of the old knight from Vaud watching on who had fought so valiantly alongside the Templar knights at Acre some twenty years earlier.

Meanwhile, Othon's work for Edward apparently done, it seems his response to the fall of the Templars, if he had already done so, was to take up the cross himself once more and make for Outremer. From Avignon in the spring of 1312 Othon appears to have sent word to England for his affairs to be set in order,[110] and made a visit back to Vaud before returning to Avignon down the Rhône for a papal blessing of his endeavour. We know of Othon's taking up of the cross once more from a letter written by Clement. All did not go well with Othon's journey back to Avignon; he and his retinue were assailed at Pons Durino, todays Pont d'Ain, a bridging point of the Ain some 22 miles (35 kilometres) west of Nantua on the road from Geneva to Lyon. His assailants were led by Aymon de Palud, the seigneur de Varambon, a castle near Pont d'Ain. His uncle Guy de la Palud had been in the service of Alianor de Provence in England and more lately an archdeacon in Lyon.[111] But young Aymon was not quite so peaceable, taking Othon a prisoner and killing and wounding some of his entourage. His goal appears to have been largely robbery as he made off with some 20,500 gold florins, some 72 kilograms of gold, these being gold coins struck in Florence. Given that there were 3.54 grams of gold in a florin then Othon had at October 2024 gold prices been robbed of £4.8 million! The Florin was a gold coin minted in Florence since 1252, and indeed were the first gold coins minted in Europe since antiquity. They carried the fleur-de-lis (the symbol of Florence) on one side, Saint John the Baptist on the other. By the early fourteenth century, they had become the currency of the international nobility and the church, they have been found in the harbour waters of Acre witnessing their use by those in Outremer.[112] Othon de Grandson could have come by his 20,500 florins in the east but most likely the majority if not all were a part of the Templar dispensation, either before or after the suppression.

We know of the attack and robbery from Pope Clement who quickly wrote to the Archbishop of Lyon, Pierre de Savoie (not to be confused with his namesake the Count of Savoy of English fame) and the bishops of Mâcon and Chalon. Aymon was to be excommunicated, and his lands placed under interdict unless he made full satisfaction of the monetary loss and injuries. Clement wrote:

> To the venerable brothers, the archbishop Lyon, the bishops of Chalon and Mâcon. The enormity of the crime against the person of our beloved son, the noble man Otto de Grandisson, our knight and friend disturbed us the more deeply and still shocks us to the depths of our heart because of the great love that we deservedly bear to him for his devotion and probity. We have learned from the same knight, who complained gravely to us, and spread public fame rather than infamy that I hate, that when he himself, who was kindled by the zeal of faith and devotion, had already for long time, having assumed the life-giving sign of the cross, he [Othon] intended in the month of August next to come, as he still intends to cross the sea to the Holy Land, to come to our presence for a blessing. And with the permission obtained from us, he would come at our command, and then he would make his way down the Rhône in peace. Aymon de Palude, lord of Varambon spoke to some the sons of the noble men of Amédée, Count of Savoy, and subjects of the Dauphin of Vienne, who were associated with him as accomplices in this part. When the knight himself [Othon]had happened to pass through the place which is commonly called the pons Durino [Pont d'Ain], which was situated below the Dauphin's own land ... as we do not doubt that he [Aymon] arrived, armed with a hostile force, and the same knight [Othon], with twenty thousand five hundred florins of gold and his other possessions, was carried away by him [Aymon], violently plundering him and the same retinue, so that they could not approach the apostolic see, hindering them. He [Aymon] assumed by his own recklessness to capture and detain the captives for several days, some of the said retinue being fatally wounded in a capture of this kind, and one of Octo's [Othon's] own squires being cruelly killed, others being inflicted with the same grievous injuries. From which force the aforesaid knight afterwards escaped, as it pleased the Lord; because of this, there is no doubt that Aymon and his accomplices, through the various processes of the apostolic see, inflicted the decree of excommunication on all those who came to the aforesaid see and hindered or harassed the promulgation in any way.[113]

For someone who had travelled so many miles in his life, fought in countless battles from North Wales to the Holy Land it was ironic he should have faced such danger so late in life by the banks of the Ain so close to home. The reason for the attack appears to have been a family quarrel. Aymon de Palud was in dispute with the *Seigneurs de Cossonay*, over a dowry payment, Grandson was related to the *famille de Cossonay*. It seems therefore that Aymon had taken things rather into his own hands. Aymon had married Marguerite de Thoire-Villars, the lady having been previously married to the late Jean II de Cossonay and mother of his children including Louis now Seigneur de Cossonay. Aymon had a son by his first marriage, his heir Pierre II de la Palud who had married, yes you guessed it a Cossonay, Eléonore de Cossonay, the daughter of the aforesaid Jean and Marguerite. So, we have Aymon's son by his first marriage marrying his second wife's daughter and being in want of a dowry. One wonders why Clement did not grumble about the proximity by which this family conducted its intimate business! The matter appears to have been resolved on 5 April 1315 by a device by which the Cossonays gave castle revenues to Othon for nine years in exchange for a loan by which to pay Marguerite, Aymon's wife, for the dowry of her daughter Eléonore. So, it seems Othon got his money back by means of the castle revenues and repayment of the loan and Eléonore got her dowry.[114]

But all this meant that upon release it was not to the Holy Land, but back to Vaud for Othon de Grandson – the crusade as it had been for the late king of England would be delayed by mundane matters closer to home. His relative Othon de Champvent had, on 19 April 1312, departed this life, creating a new power vacuum adjacent to the family's lands and doubt over the latest 1311 truce between Baron Louis II de Vaud and the see of Lausanne.

The preferred candidate would be another kinsman, his nephew Pierre d'Oron, but the good bourgeoisie of Lausanne would not put up with this and flew into rebellion, a rebellion fanned by Louis. One of the ringleaders of the revolt was a Michel Guerri, a bourgeois of Lausanne. We know his name from some remarkable documents of June 1314 which both pardon a sentence of death given to him and in the same Lausanne chapter session authorise Bishop Pierre d'Oron in taking a loan from him, subsequently repaid.[115] They tell of a revolt of 10 August 1313 that involved more than fifty in number; details are few, but it does seem to have been sudden and related to the episcopal interregnum. The pardon given to Guerri is noted as having been '*ad requisitionem et de consilio et instancia domini Othonis de Grandissono*' that is, 'at the request and at the counsel and authority of Lord Othon de Grandson'.[116] The following year, on 19 April 1314, Othon would add his name as'*magnifico domino Othone, domino Grandissoni*' to the final arbitration.[117] Arbitration is what the 'Great Lord Othon, Lord of Grandson' did best.

It seems that the knight so often bringing peace between the Plantagenets and Capetians across the broad span of Western Europe was now called upon to bring peace to Lausanne. So, the Grandsons continued their hold over the see of Lausanne, strengthened in effect by Othon's kinsman and former crusading partner Pierre d'Estavayer taking up the position of bailli.

That summer of 1312 as Othon had returned to Vaud during a civil war between the see of Lausanne backed by the Grandsons on the one part and the bourgeoisie of Lausanne backed by Louis II de Vaud on the other, another conflict had reached its conclusion, that between Edward II and Piers Gaveston on one side and the barony of England on the other. In mid-January 1312 Piers Gaveston had returned from his latest exile and met up with the king in Yorkshire. The nobles in London were alarmed and the Archbishop of Canterbury excommunicated Gaveston. Edward and Gaveston while being pursued by the earls found themselves firstly at Newcastle and then by boat along the coast to Scarborough Castle, somewhere that Edward thought could be defensible. Edward left Gaveston at Scarborough and made for the northern stronghold of York while immediately Scarborough was besieged. On 19 May Gaveston surrendered the castle by an agreement whereby Aymer de Valence, Jean de Warenne and the others would take him safely to join Edward at York pending a fuller settlement. Aymer de Valence then took Gaveston south for apparent safekeeping as negotiations with Edward continued. On 9 June 1312, leaving Gaveston a while in Deddington, Oxfordshire, the Earl of Warwick, the black dog, seized his moment and took Gaveston for himself. What followed was in effect a lynching, Gaveston being run through with a sword and beheaded. Valence was embarrassed, Edward was furious, relations between the barons and Edward verged on civil war. Whether the relationship between Edward and Gaveston had been sexual has been the subject of much debate, but we should perhaps remember that Philippe le Bel had consented to the marriage of Edward to Isabelle which is unlikely of one given to see sodomites under every bed if his new son-in-law had indeed been a well-known homosexual. More likely perhaps, the barons simply resented the hold Gaveston had had over the king and patronage. Peace came to England in the autumn of 1312, and in November Edward and Isabelle were blessed with the arrival of a son. The boy, born at Windsor Castle on 13 November 1312, was given the name Edward after his father and late grandfather, he would become Edward the third of that name – boy with the blood of Edward I and Philippe IV in his veins. (Fig 1.8)

Meanwhile, having left Vaud for Avignon before the aforementioned revolt in Lausanne had broken out in August 1313, Othon was once more summoned by Edward into his service, this time for his experience of Gascon affairs. Grandson's onetime colleague Amanieu d'Albret was locked into disputes with Edward's seneschal. The ailing John Hastings had left the role in 1312 (he died in February 1313, another of Othon's contemporaries had gone) to be replaced firstly by John de Ferrers then by Estèbe Ferréol. It is rumoured that Ferrers had met an untimely end by poisoning. Gascony was as it often was in turmoil, the local nobility once more playing off the Plantagenets against the Capetians. Albret who held the important territory of Landes was increasingly using his elbows to assert himself over and above Edwards seneschals. With Scotland unresolved, civil war seemingly only always just around the corner, the last thing young Edward needed was trouble in Gascony. As the trouble was Othon's erstwhile colleague and as Grandson was an acknowledged Gascon expert, he was summoned to consult with the king at the next opportunity. That opportunity presented itself when Edward and Isabelle left England for France on 23 May 1313 for a visit to Philippe le Bel in Paris.

On 2 June, the citizens of Paris marched out from their walls to welcome Edward and Isabelle, and that evening Philippe provided a royal banquet. The occasion, apart from the diplomacy, was chiefly the knighting of Isabelle's brothers on 3 June in Paris, King Louis of Navarre, Count Philippe of Poitiers, and Count Charles of la Marche– all would be future kings of France. This was Isabelle's first return home since her marriage and would be something of a family get together, much in the way Edward's grandfather Henry had done with Philippe's grandfather Louis all those decades ago. After the war of 1294–1303 it was the chance for a Plantagenet–Capetian reset. As with Henry and Louis there were sumptuous banquets, Edward hosting his own at the Abbaye Saint-Germain-des-Prés, just outside the city walls, where the royal couple stayed.[118] The ceremonial dubbing and belting of the brothers as knights along with hundreds of their contemporaries was preceded by a night vigil at Notre-Dame Cathedral. The chronicler Godefroy de Paris gives us an extraordinary account of the festivities enjoyed by Grandson along with the two royal families and the denizens of fourteenth-century Paris. There is talk of thousands of candles burning even by day, a fountain of wine, the nobility changing costume three times a day, actors staging tableaux including a mini-heaven replete with nightly singing angels, the resurrection enacted, the apocalypse foretold, the artisans and city watchmen processing in their finery, trumpets, drums and bells – this was indeed *la grant feste*.[119] During Edward's and Isabelle's stay 189 pigs, 94 oxen, 380 rams 160 pike, 200 carp and no less than 80 barrels of wine were consumed. This was the seal for Othon on all those years of patient diplomacy on behalf of the late king. During a puppet show, Isabella gave embroidered purses to her brothers and sisters-in-law, gifts that would prove fateful. Othon the crusader would have approved the taking of the cross by the Capetian brothers, Edward, and Isabelle – though perhaps not Edward and Isabelle oversleeping as the chronicler thought they had been having too much fun in bed, something that does contradict later claims of homosexuality.

Following the Paris show, the parties, and given his calling to Paris, Othon, decamped to Pontoise 18 miles (30 kilometres) northwest of the city to undertake the diplomatic business. It was at Pontoise on 19 June that Othon witnessed a performance of *Bernard the Fool* and fifty-four naked dancers – what the old knight made of this we can only imagine.[120] It is common for one generation to take a dim view of the next and surely Othon must have wondered what his old crusade friends and compatriots Edward, Henri de Lacy, Jean de Vesci and Jean de Bonvillars would have made of all this. Perhaps Othon had lived too long. When he had arrived in Paris he would have found no scheming Guillaume Nogaret, as he had died in April 1313. Othon was outlasting them all.

When Edward and Isabelle returned to England in July, Othon took his leave and returned south; it would be in this summer of 1313 that he last met a king of England. It had been a long road for Othon de Grandson since first he had been taken to the English court by Pierre de Savoie. But in Paris with the immediate memory of fifty-four naked dancers, the road ended.[121]

CHAPTER 16

1314 would be a fateful year for all concerned as Othon returned to Vaud to lend his name *Magnifico domino Othone* to the peace between the see of Lausanne and the bourgeoisie of Lausanne; events elsewhere concluded; these were now events of which the knight of approaching 80 would learn not witness.

In March Philippe le Bel finally had his pound of flesh from the Templars, having held them prisoner for seven years and subjecting them to unimaginable tortures; having had Clement annul the order, he had its leaders executed. Historian Henry Charles Lea described the sad and terrible demise of Othon's comrade-in-arms Jacques de Molay (Fig 2.0):

> The cardinals dallied with their duty until 18th March 1314 [or 11 March],[1] when, on a scaffold in front of Notre Dame, Jacques de Molay, Templar Grand Master, Geoffroi de Charney, Master of Normandy, Hugues de Peraud, Visitor of France, and Godefroi de Gonneville, Master of Aquitaine, were brought forth from the jail in which for nearly seven years they had lain, to receive the sentence agreed upon by the cardinals, in conjunction with the Archbishop of Sens and some other prelates whom they had called in. Considering the offences which the culprits had confessed and confirmed, the penance imposed was in accordance with rule — that of perpetual imprisonment. The affair was supposed to be concluded when, to the dismay of the prelates and wonderment of the assembled crowd, Jacques de Molay and Geoffroi de Charney arose. They had been guilty, they said, not of the crimes imputed to them, but of basely betraying their Order to save their own lives. It was pure and holy; the charges were fictitious and the confessions false. Hastily the cardinals delivered them to the Prevot of Paris, and retired to deliberate on this unexpected contingency, but they were saved all trouble. When the news was carried to Philippe, he was furious. A short consultation with his council only was required. The canons pronounced that a relapsed heretic was to be burned without a hearing; the facts were notorious and no formal judgment by the papal commission need be waited for. That same day, by sunset, a pyre was erected on a small island in the Seine, the *Ile des Juifs*, near the palace garden. There de Molay, de Charney, de Gonneville, and de Peraud were slowly burned to death, refusing all offers of pardon for retraction, and bearing their torment with a composure which won for them the reputation of martyrs among the people, who reverently collected their ashes as relics.[2]

The Templar of Tyre in his account gleaned from an eyewitness in Paris confirmed that Molay and Gonneville had retracted their forced confessions, 'But merchants who happened to be there said that the master turned towards the people and said very loudly that all that was written was false, and that he had never said nor confessed such things, and moreover that the Templars were good Christians.' He continued:

> 698. Upon these words a sergeant struck him with his hand across the mouth, so that he might speak no further, and he was dragged by his hair into a chapel, and they kept him there until it was very late, and the crowd had thinned out and most people had left. And then the master and the commander of Gascony were placed in a small boat and taken onto an island in the river, and there a fire was burning. The master begged them to suffer him to say his prayers, which he did say to God; and then his body was bound over to the working of their will.
>
> So, they took him and cast him into the fire, and he was burned. And if Almighty God, who knows and understands hidden things, knows that he and the others who were burned were innocent of those deeds of which they were accused, then they are martyrs before God; and if they received what they had deserved, they have been punished – but I may truly say that, to all appearances, I knew them for good Christians and devout in their masses and in their lives.[3]

It was said that some heard Molay calling to God for judgement upon those that had so wickedly brought about his end. According to Godefroy de Paris, as the flames began their work, he cried out '*Diex set qu'à tort et à péchié, S'en vendra en brief temps meschié! Sus cels qui nous dampnent à tort: Diex en vengera nostre mort*',[4] that is, 'God knows who is in the wrong and has sinned. Soon misfortune will come to those who have wrongly condemned us: God will avenge our deaths.'[5]

Events would soon suggest to the fertile medieval mind that it was so. Sure enough, on 20 April, Pope Clement V followed Molay to the grave at Roquemaure near Avignon. Apparently dying of lupus, the not yet 50-year-old pope had evidenced God's wrath upon his acquiescence in the Templar affair by having the church where he lay in state be burned to the ground with his unburied body yet inside. The Italian chronicler Francesco Pipino wrote, 'It is also said that on the night in which he died, he was so deserted by everyone, that a part of his body was burned by the fire of the candles that fell upon him.'[6] Bertrand de Got was laid to rest in the church at Uzeste in Gascony by his castle at Villandraut. We mentioned earlier the Grandson–Grailly connection with Villandraut and Benauges, and the castle-building trail that led from Benauges to Villandraut by way of Savoy and North Wales. Satisfyingly, for lovers of historical symmetry, Clement was laid to rest at Uzeste alongside a member of the *famille de Grailly*. (Fig 2.4)

For Philippe, scandal and worse was to be his story of 1314. When two Norman knights, Gautier, and Philippe d'Aunay, travelled to England, Isabelle apparently noticed them in possession of the embroidered purses gifted to her sisters-in-law. Her recently knighted brothers Louis, Philippe and Charles had married into the Duchy of Burgundy and, as we saw Othon's neighbours the County of Burgundy then within the empire. We saw earlier how this French encroachment had been resisted, with Grandson's encouragement, by the Burgundian nobility. Louis had married Marguerite, the daughter of Duke Robert II of Burgundy, while Philippe and Charles had married the late Count Othon IV of Burgundy's daughters Jeanne and Blanche, respectively. Philippe had thus thought Burgundy to be on its way into his arms. However, these daughters-in-law were all apparently either in the arms of not his sons but the Norman lovers d'Aunay for some three years past,[7] Marguerite and Blanche certainly and both with Jeanne's knowledge – meeting, apparently, illicitly in the Tour de Nesle in Paris, after which the whole affair is known. It is possible that Isabelle herself alerted her father to the scandal, as she certainly had the means, the motive, and the opportunity, having just paid a visit to her father in March 1314. Writing years later the chronicler of the *Scalacronica* thought so.[8] Isabelle's accounts certainly evidence private nocturnal visits to her father.[9] Following surveillance Philippe had all of those involved arrested, including all his daughters-in-law who were sheltering at the nunnery of Maubuisson. The Aunay brothers of course met a grisly end; according to Godefroy of Paris they were '*Por leur traison et péchié, Qu'il furent vif escorchié*', that is, 'For their treachery and sin, that they were flayed alive.'[10] Given that the crime was *lèse majesté* their punishment did not end there. The writer of the *Chronique de Guillaume de Nangis* went further: 'they were in the sight of everyone flayed alive in the public square. Their virile and genital parts were cut off, and their heads were cut off, and they were dragged to the public gallows where, stripped of all their skin, they were hanged by the shoulders and the joints of the arms.'[11] Philippe was in no mood to have his majesty defamed, Burgundy or no Burgundy. The French writer Maurice Druon in his *Les Ross Maudis*, dramatised twice by French television, left out mercifully the gorier details of Philippe's vengeance including the removal of the private parts. Meanwhile back in the fourteenth century, Blanche and Marguerite were found guilty, of which there is little doubt, as Godefroy de Paris wrote '*n'est nul feu sans fumée*' or 'there is no fire without smoke.'[12] They had their heads shaven (this punishment not being new it seems in 1944) and imprisoned. The ladies were interred in Richard Cœur de Lion's Château Gaillard.[13] Godefroy of Paris used the word *garce* which we might translate as slut.[14]

Jeanne escaped permanent imprisonment, being later found innocent only after incarceration at Dourdan.[15] But the whole affair or we might say affairs rocked Philippe's court to its very foundations – quite the scandal. Some have seen Isabelle as the Machiavellian princess furthering the claims to the French throne of her infant Edward, but this seems a little too artful to be true. Nonetheless, its rumour and the misogyny it helped create in the French establishment may well have brought about their sudden fondness of the Salic Law in the years to come. For Othon de Grandson and his Burgundian allies the scandal arrested the French threat for now. The English author of *Scalacronica* attributed the misfortune coming to the House of Capet not to the fate of the Templars but to the three queens.[16]

Meanwhile in Britain, in the summer, young Edward, accompanied by Aymer de Valence, invaded Scotland to bring Robert VII de Brus, 7th Lord of Annandale, now King of the Scots to heel, at Bannockburn near Stirling where on 23–24 June the Scots soundly defeated their army. All his father's attempts to establish the Scottish monarchy as vassals of the English king came rapidly to nought. The Scottish kingdom would remain independent of the English kingdom for centuries more to come. Edward's military reputation, not the best, would never recover and his realm be once more unstable.

In early November Philippe was out hunting north of Paris and seems to have had a heart attack. He was only 46 years of age. He was taken from the hunting lodge to Poissy where he recovered somewhat. However, the king undertook, weeks later, a 37-mile (60-kilometre) horse ride to Essonne where his health gave way again. He was carried this time to nearby Fontainebleau where he departed this life on 27 November 1314 – he had survived his far older cousin and rival Edward I by barely seven years. The deaths of Philippe and Clement within the same year as Molay gave rise to the legend of the Capetian curse. Unsurprising perhaps since Philippe's successor Louis X would reign but a year before dying on 5 June 1316, his son John I dying on 19 November later that year aged just 4 days old. Father and son would be followed by Louis' brother Philippe, reigning as Philippe V. (Figs 1.7, 2.4 & 2.0)

For Othon de Grandson the departures from the stage of life of Philippe and Clement meant a return to the quieter pastures of Vaud and the Lac de Neuchâtel. With the Holy See vacant for the next two years and two months there was little else to do. By now the ageing Lord of Grandson was like many knights before him viewing his coming afterlife and seeking ways in which his departed soul might receive prayer in the long years after his passing. It had long been common practice for the kings and nobles of Europe to found monastic houses where monks might pray for the repose of their immortal soul, and Othon de Grandson would be no exception. Upon his return to Vaud his thoughts turned to the foundation of a religious order. The region had long been a centre for monasterial activity: the Cîteaux and Clairvaux of the Cistercians lay to the north in Burgundy, the enormous House of Cluny to the west and the Carthusians of Chartreux to the southwest. Indeed, as we saw earlier the abbey at Romainmôtier and later the Abbaye de Joux close by had long played a role in the Grandson family story. Indeed, Grandson itself was home to the monks of Saint-Jean Baptiste. Many of these houses had received direct financial support from Othon and the family. (Fig 1.9) But Othon's heir Pierre, through the support of Othon himself, would now go further and found their own monastic house for monks of the Carthusian Order.

At the end of the eleventh century Bruno of Cologne had founded a new order of monks in the middle of the Chartreuse massif in Savoy, indeed the name of the order itself coming from their beginning in the Chartreuse, the *Ordo Cartusiensis*. Following the Benedictine rule the central idea of these Carthusians was to be priests who lived singly in their own living spaces or cells rather than for example the dormitories of the Cistercians. The order declined the use of music in their services. One might say the order was one of shared solitude– they were to be eremitic, that is hermits. The statutes of the order had been written by Guigues du Pin by 1133, which would place a Grandson foundation under the authority of the mother house in the Chartreuse. In England, a good example of a Carthusian house would be Mount Grace Priory in North Yorkshire.[17]

On 17 October 1317 Pierre de Grandson granted land in the parish of Concise to the Carthusians on the northern borders of the family lands where they met those of the lords of Neuchâtel in the Val de Lancy[18] by the stream of the same name which emptied into the Lac du Neuchâtel.[19] The Carthusians were to found a monastery at La Lance for thirteen monks, although in reality the community never reached this number. In foundation the order received grazing, logging, and fishing rights from the Grandsons, Pierre's act being approved by Othon, still the Lord of Grandson. The cornerstone of *Bienheureuse Marie du Saint-Lieu de la Lancy* was duly laid in April 1318.[20] According to an anonymous chronicler of the order, two years later, in 1320, Othon visited the order's mother house in Chartreuse, his stay there causing something of a disaster. As his cell was warmed beforehand by the monks who didn't take care to watch the fire, a general conflagration followed.[21] Othon de Grandson donated some 6,000 florins to the order, that is £1.43 million in today's money, for the foundation of their house, and so can be considered its lay patron.[22] Andenmatten posits a number of reasons, beyond piety, why the Grandsons might found the monastery, either as a family necropolis or a way of marking the northern boundary of their lands.[23] In England Coppack and Douglas note that in every case 'the founder came from the literate upper levels of society', this being a result of the contemplative life of the Carthusians.[24] It is perhaps not then such a surprise that the most renowned noble in Vaudois society might found a Carthusian house. What is more, we can venture that the overriding motivation of Othon de Grandson, twice the crusading knight, benefactor of religious houses, having spent long hours with popes, weeks and months in the saddle and having reached advanced years, might place a value upon contemplative Christian piety. (Fig 2.7) Indeed, earlier on 10 October 1317 Grandson had donated 20 *livrées* to be paid annually to the Cathédrale de Lausanne for the support of a chapel there in honour of Saint George.[25] (Fig 2.8)

While Othon was setting his affairs in order with God, affairs of this life came back to haunt him once more, in particular his lordship, granted many, many years ago by his friend Edward, of the Channel Islands. There had been rumbling disputes going back to the beginning of his almost fifty years' lordship which we must now recount.

Othon de Grandson had been awarded custody of the Channel Islands by Edward in 1275 and outright title in 1278, but we must really begin its history centuries earlier to understand its relationship to the English crown and thus to Grandson. What we now call the Channel Islands is a more recent appellation of the principal islands of Jersey, Guernsey, Alderney, and Sark that lie off the western coast of the Contentin peninsula of Normandy. They had been granted, in 933, by Rodolphe, King of West Francia to Williame de lon Espee, that is William I Longsword. This Williame was the son of Rollo who had been similarly granted Normandy by Charles the Simple. Thus, the Channel Islands subsequently belonged to the dukes of Normandy, who in 1066 subsequently became also kings of England. From 1066 until 1204 the islands remained a part of the Duchy of Normandy. The Capetian Philippe II's conquest of Normandy from Plantagenet John in 1204, had, because John managed to retain the islands, the effect of detaching the islands from the mainland. Although in 1259 Henry III renounced his claim to Normandy by the Treaty of Paris, he did not renounce his lordship of the islands. Indeed, he had in 1254 passed them to his son Edward, along with much territory elsewhere, as Edward's appanage. Thus in 1278 it was the Lord Edward, now King Edward I, who passed them for safekeeping to his closest friend, Othon de Grandson. The islands would be held by Othon for fifty years.

The islanders had enjoyed from 933 until 1278 a direct feudal relationship with the dukes of Normandy and subsequently kings of England. Edward in passing responsibility to Othon was creating an intermediary and in so doing a constitutional novelty not welcomed by the islanders. This imposition of Grandson between the king and the islanders is the source of what proved to be Othon's unhappy tenure of the islands. Repeatedly over these fifty years we see the islanders claiming that their ancient rights and customs were being infringed, without ever being able to point, when challenged, to any firm source of these ancient rights and customs. Of necessity, as we have seen, Edward had far more important things for Grandson to be doing than sitting on Jersey actually running the islands, and so he was an absentee landlord with all the problems this always creates. As Othon's predecessor Pierre de Savoie had delegated the actual running of his English estates to his stewards, so Othon de Grandson delegated his running of the islands to bailiffs. As with Pierre de Savoie's stewards before them in Sussex, so Othon de Grandson's bailiffs would be accused of going too far in exacting revenue from tenants and riding roughshod over their rights. In this way Othon can be said not to have learned from Pierre's time in England. The locals did not take kindly to being told what to do by absent foreign landlords.

Writing in the nineteenth century historian Julian Havet said of Othon's government of the islands that '*Le gouvernement d'Othon de Granson fut une longue oppression*' and added the word '*tyrannie*'.[26] Let us turn to some of the specifics. As we saw earlier Othon had been first granted custody of the islands on 25 November 1275 '*Writ de intendendo* to the tenants of the islands of Gernese and Gereseye for Otto de Grandisono, appointed to the custody of those islands' at a *ferme* of 500 marks.[27] This *ferme* was acquitted on 25 January 1277 and Othon was to hold the islands even to five years after his death – this was the letter patent that, as we saw earlier, described the relationship between Edward and Othon:

> Acquittance to Otto de Grandisono of the farm by which he holds the islands of Guernsey and Jersey and the adjacent islands, and grant of the said islands and their issues for life, and grant, on account of his intimacy with the king, and his long and faithful service from an early age, and for the acquittance of debts incurred in the king's service in the aforesaid time, that his executors shall hold the said islands and their issues for five years after his decease for the acquittance of his debts, and the fulfilment of his will without rendering any account therefor.[28]

Grandson would be given, so the sources tell us, a number of titles over his fifty-plus years' tenure of the islands, notable among which would be in 1289 the title '*domini insularum*' or Lord of the Isles.[29] So then to the '*tyrannie*', one problem that Othon, or more accurately his representatives, had to deal – the entanglement of the islands with neighbouring Normandy. Although Philippe Auguste had in effect detached the islands from the reminder of the duchy in 1204, something underlined by the granting of Edward's appanage in 1254 and the Treaty of Paris in 1259. It was not a clean break, a rupture which readers familiar with Brexit might know well. Religious houses on the mainland still held rights on the islands. Philippe had broken temporal links but not spiritual links, as the islands had remained within the diocese of Coutances.[30] These priories still held rights, for example to levy dues on fishermen, the most important activity of the islands. What is more, successive kings, John, Henry then Edward, had decided not to unduly upset the islanders by interfering with long-held customs, rights, and relationships as they felt that enough Plantagenet land had been lost already and didn't want to lose any more.[31] The islands, in an age when you navigated at sea by staying within sight of land if you could, were an important link in the journey from England to Gascony, as was the island of Oleron – all these territories becoming a part of Edward's appanage. But Edward had given the islands to Othon in what historian of the islands Alexander Kelleher called 'effectively a sinecure', that is a position requiring little or no work but giving the holder financial reward.[32] Clifford agreed, writing 'that his [Edward] grant to Othon was in recognition and repayment of his services, and the latter had never for a moment looked on his wardenship as anything but a source of revenue'.[33]

As with Pierre de Savoie, Othon made much use of compatriots, indeed kinsmen, to look after his interests on the islands, including his brother Guillaume,[34] Henri de Bonvillars, Prior of Wenlock,[35] and Gérard d'Oron.[36] Even when Edward temporarily renewed his direct control of the islands during the French war, he took care to appoint Henry Cobham as sub-warden, a fellow ambassador along with Othon to the Roman Curia in 1285 – in simple terms, a trusted colleague.[37] Earlier Othon's representatives had begun to assert control in a way that these kings had not. When the king did appoint justices to investigate, these would include Othon's own clerks Jean de Ditton and William Russell.[38]

In terms of the complaints, on 10 June 1280 we hear of:

> Complaint by the men of Jersey and Guernsey that the bailiffs of Otto de Grandisono of those islands lately took into the king's hands, without reasonable cause, certain lands whereof the former were enfeoffed there long since by the bailiffs of Henry III, and still detain them, and immoderately amerced them for certain trespasses in the king's warrens in the said islands in taking rabbits unlawfully, of which trespasses they have never been convicted, nor have ever put themselves on the grace of the said Otto or his said bailiffs therefor, nor made any fine with them; and that the said bailiffs distrain them by their beasts and other goods for the said amercements, and refuse to permit them to salt, dry, and sell their fish, as they have always up to the present time been wont to do according to the grant of the king's predecessors, kings of England.[39]

These complaints continued on and off for the next forty years until such time as a knight of over eighty winters finally travelled to the islands in an attempt to resolve matters. The islanders had not been happy to return to the distant absentee lordship of the Lord of Grandson; during the recent war St. Peter Port had twice been raided and burned by the French and the trade and fishing by which they depended upon for a living had suffered. Unhappy despite Othon writing to the chancellor in England, William de Greenfield, likely in June 1303, at war's end, 'let my people of the Isles and their goods pass freely.'[40] In August 1308, while with Pope Clement, Othon had addressed the latent issue of French clerics holding authority in the islands by getting Clement to forbid the Bishop of Coutances from citing islanders to appear before him.[41] Credit does not seem to have been given by the 'people of the isles'.

What brought matters to a head, along with disputes with the Bishop of Coutances, was a dispute relating to the Abbaye of Mont Saint-Michel in Normandy and the Priory of St. Clement on Jersey.[42] As we saw earlier, Othon's latest sub-warden was Gérard d'Oron, a nephew, appointed to the islands in 1320. Arriving in Jersey likely only in 1321, he had quickly made himself less than popular, so much so that Jersey and Guernsey were unsafe, and he took refuge on Sark. In February 1323, the young Edward appointed new commissioners to investigate the islander's complaints, appointing sub-warden Gérard d'Oron as one of them. It was at this instance, possibly at Edward's request, that the commissioners were joined on Jersey by 6 June 1323 by Othon de Grandson.[43] Ensconced in the castle at Jersey it was his first and only visit to the Channel Islands of which he had been for fifty years lord. But Othon's famed powers of diplomacy failed him, and the islanders were not to be placated. By December when Edward despatched Gérard d'Oron on a diplomatic mission to the empire, Grandson left Guernsey with him, never to return.[44]

Back in 1318 a new pope had succeeded Clement, Jacques d'Euse; reigning as John XXII, he had been chosen at Lyon and would continue with Clement's residence at Avignon and indeed would be its longest resident. While Othon was experiencing the hostilities of the islanders of Jersey, his old friend, ally and liege lord Count Amédée V de Savoie was making for Avignon where he arrived on 4 February 1323. However, during his stay by the Rhône Amédée fell ill that summer and passed away on 16 October 1323. When the news reached Othon, likely on his return to Vaud, he would have mourned the loss of another long-time friend and colleague of not only diplomatic missions around Europe but also service in England. It was fitting that Amédée's successor as Count of

Savoy would be Edouard, named for their late good friend, the king of England. The late king has had many detractors over the centuries since, mostly in Wales and Scotland, but not in Savoy where he inspired such loyalty among so many, including Othon and the departed Amédée, known forever in Savoy as *le Grand.* After a journey of eleven days back from Avignon, Amédée was laid to rest among his illustrious ancestors at Hautecombe Abbey in Savoy on 27 October.[45]

The next year, 1324, Grandson travelled again, this time a shorter distance, to Bar-sur-Aube, 30 miles (50 kilometres) to the east of Troyes and similarly distant to the north of Othon's Épailly. The so-called Capetian curse had seen to it that Philippe le Bel's son Philippe V had not lasted long, dying on 3 January 1322. He had been succeeded by his brother Charles IV. Charles was the first Capetian king to carry the name of the illustrious Charlemagne; he would also be the last. Leopold I, Duke of Austria, a Habsburg, had recently suffered a setback in Helvetia still seen as one of the foundations of modern Switzerland. In 1315 he had been defeated by the nascent Swiss confederacy at the Battle of Mortgarten. As we saw earlier, like Courtrai in 1302 and Bannockburn in 1314, Mortgarten had seen a knightly chivalric army defeated by a seemingly lesser host of infantry – the age of the knight, of Othon de Grandson, was it seems drawing to a close even while he lived. As we saw earlier Holy Roman Emperor Henry VII had died in 1313, thus creating a vacancy for the elected throne. In 1314 Leopold had supported his brother Frederick but had been outvoted by Louis of Bavaria as King of the Germans, of Italy and emperor. Louis had subsequently supported Swiss independence of the Habsburgs but within the empire – the beginnings of Switzerland, the country that now encompasses the Grandson lands, but not in Othon's lifetime or for centuries yet to come. Louis' title had continued to be contested by Frederick, but on 18 September 1322 at Múhldorf he had been taken captive by Louis, leaving Leopold to uphold the family claims. Louis was the subject of Marsilius of Padua's 1324 tome *Defensor Pacis*, which asserted imperial secular authority over that of the papal interference, following much in the same way as Dante Alighieri's 1313 *De Monarchia.* Othon lived in a time when national rather than feudal authority began to hold sway and secular rather than spiritual power was becoming increasingly dominant. Eventually this would lead to the Reformation and the world of nation states. The mind of men was turning from Othon's world toward our own.

Charles IV of France had his own designs, in the meantime, on the francophone imperial lands, those of the counties of Burgundy, Savoy, Albon and Provence, the former Second Kingdom of Burgundy. He would meet Leopold at Bar-sur-Aube to garner his support in this endeavour in return for French support in gaining Basel, Constance, and Zurich for the Habsburgs. All this was of course a threat to Grandson, Vaud and Savoy and could not be allowed to come to pass. Othon, we will remember, in the context of supporting Edward's fight with Charles's father had long supported the nobility of Burgundy against Capetian expansion. Charles at this point had been freed from his marriage to the ill-fated Blanche, daughter of Count Othon IV de Bourgogne by the lady's death in the prison of the Château Gaillard in 1322. He had remarried quickly to Marie de Luxembourg, daughter of the late Henry VII, Holy Roman Emperor – accordingly Charles had designs on as much of the empire as he could lay his hands on,[46] if not all of it as emperor with his new wife. Had not Pierre Dubois written in 1306 that the French king should bribe the German electors to be emperor, seize Constantinople, reign over all European sovereigns, and reduce the papacy to a French royal chaplaincy.[47] Indeed, Dubois had specifically referenced potential French overlordship of Grandson's Savoy. After such hubris however often follows nemesis' disaster was to befall the House of Capet once more, Charles had taken the pregnant Marie with him to Avignon to meet and plot with Pope John, who had excommunicated the emperor Louis on 23 March and would pronounce him deposed in July. However, first the Capetian disaster: an accident overtook poor Marie who then miscarried a boy, Louis, who died hours later, followed to the grave by his mother on 26 March 1324 – it would be the only boy Charles would have; the Capetian line would end with him.

So, it was a bereaved Charles that met Leopold in July 1324 at Bar-sur-Aube to further his imperial claim.[48] The prevention of Capetian expansion and hegemony would, as it had been for all his life, be among Othon de Grandson's last concerns. We know nothing of his work there, but we do know Othon was also at Bar. An expense claim for messengers in the employ of Edouard de Savoie reads 'in going to Bar, to the Lord Othon de Grandson, sent there by the Lord [Edouard]'.[49] So, Grandson was at Bar in the service of Count Edouard de Savoie. Charles would not be emperor, Leopold would not reclaim Helvetia, Burgundy, and Savoy, despite the dreams of Pierre Dubois, and would not be French until many centuries later. So, whether it was the death of Marie and her links with the empire or that king and duke could not agree, Grandson's last mission, it seems, met with success. The struggle between pope and emperor would continue and soon there would be pope and anti-pope. Charles had more immediate fish to fry; in August 1324 he invaded Gascony to begin what became known as the War of Saint Sardos. He achieved little, but it would be the negotiations for peace with Edward that would have catastrophic consequences for the Plantagenet king. The struggle between pope and emperor would continue and soon there would be pope and anti-pope.

Edward and Isabelle had been growing increasingly estranged. In the years since Gaveston's death Edward had taken to another favourite, Hugh Despenser, the son of the chief adviser of the same name, Hugh Despenser the Elder– the Younger was the problem. In March 1325 Isabelle travelled to France to negotiate peace terms, something in earlier decades the province of Othon de Grandson. While in Paris she met up with Roger Mortimer, 1st Earl of the March and grandson of his namesake grandfather, the couple fell in love and would plot the downfall of both Despenser and Edward. Noticeable in 1324 is that Grandson is in the service of Edouard de Savoie regarding Capetian expansion into imperial lands and not Edward II of England regarding Capetian expansion into Plantagenet Gascony – despite Othon's long Gascon experience. As Grandson returned to Vaud, we might forgive him for thinking the world was turning upon its head, but it was a world he was not long for.

As he rode back through Burgundy, the Jura and finally into Vaud, perhaps his thoughts turned to his friends and comrades of these many years now departed, of Jean de Vesci, Jean de Grailly, Antony Bek, Robert Burnell, Jacques de Saint George, Henri de Lacy, Pierre de Savoie, Amédée de Savoie, Jean de Bonvillars, Pierre de Champvent, Bertrand de Got, Jacques de Molay, Hayton of Corycus and of course Edward – now all gone, with only Othon left. Perhaps he heard their voices once more, oh such adventures they'd had. Now the old knight returned to his castle and lit a fire. In the dancing flames perhaps he saw again the castles in North Wales, the Eagle Tower, the bridge of boats, the harbour at Acre, the sound of the Mamluk drums, the escape to Cyprus, the cypress trees of Rome, the Taurus mountains of Armenian Cilicia, the cathedral in Zaragoza, Westminster Abbey, the Sainte-Chapelle in Paris, the vineyards of Gascony, the blue waters of the Mediterranean, the Bay of Biscay, the Pyrenees, the Grand Saint-Bernard Pass, the Aosta valley, the Viennois, Avignon, Nazareth, his Channel Islands, Lanercost Priory, so many miles, so many, many memories. Wearied of the tedium of living he brought a log out of the wall and threw it on the fire.

> Our revels now are ended. These our actors,
> As I foretold you, were all spirits and
> Are melted into air, into thin air;
> And, like the baseless fabric of this vision,
> The cloud-capp'd towers, the gorgeous palaces,
> The solemn temples, the great globe itself,
> Yea, all which it inherit, shall dissolve,
> And, like this insubstantial pageant faded,
> Leave not a rack behind. We are such stuff
> As dreams are made on and our little life
> Is rounded with a sleep.

CHAPTER 17

Sir Othon de Grandson departed this life in April 1328, living a life of some ninety years. He died at Aigle, having given his last will and testament there on 4 April; he probably died the following day, 5 April 1328, according to the Carthusians at La Lance.[1] The cathedral at Lausanne dated his death to 12 April, although Clifford suggested the obit was the date of his funeral not his death.[2] His body was then transported back along the Rhône, by the beautiful Léman, past Villeneuve, Chillon, Montreux, Vevey and the aromatic vineyards of Lavaux to his last resting place of Lausanne.[3] His will requested burial at the Cathédrale de Lausanne, so much of which had been built by the likely father of Maître Jacques de Saint George, Jean Cotereel. The funeral probably took place on 12 April, as described in his last will (Fig 2.8):

> I choose burial in the cathedral church of B[lessed]. Mary [Lausanne]. Also I will and order that when my body shall be carried to the church to be laid thereupon, two men armed with my arms, and each carrying my banner with the same arms, shall precede my body on two horses, each of which shall be worth 100 *livres Lausanneois*, and let one of the horses be covered with my arms and the other with iron [carapace], and let the said horses be offered [with] the aforesaid arms and coverings to the aforesaid church of Lausanne, who as rightful ambassadors shall remain for the remission of my sins.[4]

He closed by bequeathing gifts to the cathedral, save for the 'small gold cross and a statue of the Virgin Mary, of silver,[5] which I usually carry with me.' These last words give us an insight into the man behind the legend, the pious crusader knight to the end.[6] The cathedral gratefully noted that he gave 'many good ornaments for his service in solemn festivals, namely, the best capes, three noble crosses and gold plates, ribbons, several cups and cloths of gold for the repair of the great altar'.[7] His tomb is there to this day, to the left of the chancel, paying silent witness to the seven centuries that have passed. It seems that his body was divided at his death, his body being buried as willed in Lausanne Cathedral, but his heart and entrails appear from later documents to have been entombed in the Franciscan house at Grandson and Carthusian foundation at La Lance, respectively.[8]

His brother, Guillaume de Grandson, former Deputy Justiciar of North Wales and lifelong knight and friend of Edmund Crouchback, stayed on in England. He was with Edmund when he died in Gascony, and it is said is commemorated on his tomb – if so then both the Grandson brothers are memorialised in Westminster Abbey. He went on to serve Edward in Scotland, notably at Falkirk in 1298, alongside his kinsman Pierre de Champvent. Becoming the first Baron de Grandison, he like his brother would live to old age, but unlike his brother he would found a dynasty in England, married to Sybil Tregoz – the Grandisons. Sybil was of the Anglo-Norman Tregoz family of Herefordshire, the see of late Savoyard bishop, Pierre d'Aigueblanche in Henry's time. Having lived at Ashperton,[9] to the west of Ledbury for many years, Guillaume died in 1335, and was buried along with Sybil, who had died the year before, at Dore Abbey in Herefordshire. Reputedly Guillaume had gifted the abbey a piece of the true cross which Othon de Grandson had acquired during the Fall of Acre in 1291. Their son John Grandison would become the Bishop of Exeter in 1327, the year before his Uncle Othon died, several works of art associated with him surviving in the British Library, the British Museum in London and the Louvre in Paris, his books in the Bibliothèque National in Paris.[10] Indeed, John kept up the family link with the papacy and diplomacy, becoming a friend and envoy of John XXII. John Grandison donated the tenor bell to his cathedral, which still sounds to this day adorned with the family name, Grandson, from the Lac de Neuchâtel.[11]

When founding a church at Ottery St. Mary in Devon, John Grandison perhaps spoke well of his father and uncle when he wrote that it was his desire:

> for insuring the never ending remembrance of the deeds of valour and charity wrought by his family and friends, noble and gentle, who together with their willing followers and loyal comrades, whether in England, in France, in Scotland or the Holy Land, helped to fashion the realm and win the nation's place in the world's history which we now gratefully inherit.[12]

Perhaps most idiosyncratically, the amateur football teams of Devon still compete to this day for the Grandisson Cup! Its latest winners are Sidmouth Town Reserves.[13]

Guillaume's daughter, Bishop John's sister Katherine de Grandison, would marry William Montacute, 1st Earl of Salisbury around 1320, during Othon's lifetime. In 1348 Jean Froissart linked Katherine as the lady at the origin of the Order of the Garter story. Katherine's son, another William, 2nd Earl, would go on to be a founding member of the order and a commander of Edward III's armies in France. In 1360 he helped negotiate the Treaty of Bretigny that returned Gascony and much more of Aquitaine to the Plantagenets – Othon would no doubt have been proud.

What is more Guillaume's daughter, Othon's niece Mabilia, anglicised as Mabel, married member of Parliament John de Pateshull. Mabel would therefore, through the Beauchamp and Beaufort families be an ancestor too of the Tudor kings of England - once more Othon would no doubt have been proud.[14]

Othon's niece Katherine in marrying William Montacute, 1st Earl of Salisbury, gives us perhaps the most interesting of the descendants of the *famille de Grandson* in England. The couple in addition to the aforementioned son William, 2nd Earl, had a daughter Philippa. Now Philippa was married to Roger Mortimer, 2nd Earl of the March. Philippa and Roger had a son Edmund, 3rd Earl of the March, who in turn was followed by Roger, 4th Earl, his daughter Ann Mortimer the origin of the Yorkist claim to the English throne. Edmund, 3rd Earl of the March, had married into royalty, Philippa of Clarence, daughter of the Duke of Clarence, second surviving son of Edward III. It was Ann Mortimer, the ancestor of Edward IV and by his daughter Elizabeth of York, that however distant, means that the blood of Othon's brother Guillaume de Grandson has flowed in the kings and queens of England even to our present day[15] – once more Othon would no doubt have been proud.

Othon de Grandson was a knight of his time, a knight of feudal loyalties to the counts of Savoy and kings of England, but more especially a king of England, his lifelong friend Edward.

We should remember that the contemporary caricature of Edward Longshanks is often the product of Welsh and Scottish writers of later times and indeed more recently an anglophobic Australian actor's film of William Wallace. Othon's lifelong loyalty to Edward born of lifelong friendship challenges that caricature, and at the very least nuances Edward's character.

Othon fulfilled much the same role for Edward as another Savoyard, Pierre de Savoie, had played for his father Henry. Othon was very much Edward's Pierre de Savoie. He was quite simply a man Edward could trust implicitly, a valuable asset for a medieval king. Grandson, remarkably, was of the line of Savoyard diplomats serving the Plantagenet crown of England from the 1240s through the 1320s. There had been Guillaume de Savoie, Pierre d'Aigueblanche, Pierre de Savoie, Gérard de Vuippens, Amédée de Savoie and of course Othon de Grandson. During Henry's reign there had been, thanks to the chronicler Matthew Paris, a good deal of criticism of the Savoyard role in English affairs. The successful continuation of this role in Edward's reign has often been overlooked by historians of Henry's reign. Of course, the second generation of Savoyards were not rewarded with land in the way of the first and there was no Monfortian-style challenge to Edward's reign. But we should see the continuation by Edward of Henry's use of Savoyard diplomacy as a vindication of Henry's policy of using these skilled, able, and well-connected diplomats. In *Peter of Savoy*,[16] I challenged the notion that a nation had by definition to employ as its servants native-born sons – the life and service of the Savoyard knight Othon de Grandson to the English crown only goes to underline my point. Nationalists and xenophobes ought to remember that nations are best served by the best talents irrespective of birth.

Not only was Othon de Grandson a skilled diplomat and envoy but he was a knight and soldier who had managed to survive numerous battles from the Menai Strait to the Holy Land. He led Edward's armies at the siege of Dolforwyn Castle, along the coast to Flint, the ill-starred Battle of Moel-y-Don and then from Anglesey by way of Caernarfon, Castell-y-Bere and Harlech to Conwy. As a crusading knight he twice ventured to the Holy Land, seeing off an assassin's attempt on Edward's life, and then decades later leading the English knights in the heroic but doomed defence of Acre. It may well even have been Othon that wrote that treatise on how to conduct future crusades that never came. In this long military career Othon de Grandson was a knight, and if we are to believe the Templar of Tyre a brave and courageous knight of great renown.[17] That Grandson lived some nine decades amid such danger is testimony to a knight skilled with the sword as well as diplomatic wits. To stand by the Accursed Tower at Acre surrounded by over a 100,000 Mamluks and deafening sound of drums took courage beyond most of us. But also, the Templar of Tyre speaks of a loyalty that is the hallmark of Othon de Grandson the man, saving the life of his Savoyard compatriot Jean de Grailly. We should remember that Grailly was a man tried and in effect fired by Grandson in Gascony when the former was seneschal, and yet here Othon was risking his life to save him.[18]

During Othon's long life, he had spent many years in the saddle. Grandson travelled the length and breadth of the roads of thirteenth- and fourteenth-century Europe. In our modern age its tiring enough to travel, but it takes a train less than twelve hours to journey from North Wales to Vaud – in Othon's time it took over three weeks. And yet Othon in his time knew Europe from Anglesey to Zaragoza, from Scotland to Sicily, from Gascony to Palestine, from Flanders to Cillician Armenia. Othon de Grandson amassed an incredible number of horse miles. He frequented the Channel crossing so often from Wissant to Dover, that when the ferryman Thomas Salekyn was in trouble and needed the help of someone important, it was to Othon he turned' Salekyn wrote to Othon as his '*amy*' or 'friend'.[19]

So, was Othon the 'little noise' of Guisborough?[20] Or perhaps the 'coward' pointed to by Morerod?[21] Or was he the Templar of Tyre's knight 'of great renown'?[22] Or the Vale Royal chronicler's 'good and holy man, a most strenuous knight in arms whose memory be blessed forever'?[23] Renowned English historian J. R. Maddicott in writing Othon's entry in the English Oxford National Biography summed Grandson up, writing: 'It is hard to think of any comparable figure in medieval English history who lived so long, travelled so widely, or had a career so diverse and adventurous.'[24] King Edward I's definitive biographer Prestwich described Othon as above all a knight who had rendered such 'loyal service to Edward I and Eleanor, his queen.'[25]

We shall give the last word to the chronicler Jean d'Ypres whom we began with as perhaps sums things up best

> I have heard the following story from the lips of certain honourable and trustworthy men of Savoy, who, however, told me not of what they had seen but of what they had heard. Now these men alleged that once upon a time there was in Savoy a certain lord of Grandson, whose wife bore him a son. When the astronomers were summoned to examine, calculate, and decide the child's nativity, they declared that if he grew to manhood, he would be great, powerful, and victorious. There was also present on this occasion a person full of superstition, or shall I rather say of divine inspiration, who taking a brand from the hearth declared that the boy would live only so long as the brand lasted, and that he might live the longer thereupon had the brand built up in a wall. The boy lived, grew to manhood, and to old age, with ever increasing honour; until at last, weary of life through the burden of his years, he ordered the brand to be taken out of the wall and cast into the fire. Hardly was the brand consumed, ere the good knight expired. My informants told me further that this fateful lord of Grandson was beyond sea in the company of the son of the King of England; and that when he heard how the prince had been poisoned, he alone, trusting, as I suppose, in the fate that had been foretold for him, dared to suck the venom from the wound; and thus through his aid was Edward healed. Afterwards this lord of Grandson and his kinsfolk rose to high honour with the Kings of England, and unto this day have they great repute in that country. But of this can I avouch no more than was told to me.[26]

He was great, powerful and victorious, of ever-increasing honour. Today he rests in the cathedral in Lausanne. Sadly, perhaps the cathedral does not mark his tomb with his illustrious name. English visitors, of whom there are not apparently many, would pass by unknowing that the crown of England had been so long and so well served by this knight in repose. Parochial history, in England and Switzerland, has not remembered his service well. But in Lausanne does indeed lie perhaps one of England's greatest and loyal servants.

SAVOYARD DIPLOMACY IN ANGLO-FRENCH RELATIONS 1272–1303

Date	**Envoys**	**Notes**
11 November 1275	Othon de Grandson	Return of the Agenais
23 July 1276	Othon de Grandson	Gascony
February 1278	Othon de Grandson	Gascony
23 November 1278	Jean de Grailly	Return of the Agenais
6 February 1279	Jean de Grailly	Return of the Agenais
23 May 1279		**Peace of Amiens**
13March 1280	Jean de Grailly Gefferoi de Joinville	Castille
21 June 1281	Jean de Grailly	Treaty obligations 1259 & 1279
17 October 1281	Jean de Grailly	Provence
19 February 1282	Jean de Grailly	Aragon
13 June 1282	Jean de Grailly	Treaty obligations
June 1286	Othon de Grandson	Crusade and Gascony
23 April 1292	Gefferoi de Joinville	Ponthieu
14 August 1295	Othon de Grandson Amédée V de Savoie	Anglo-French War – truce
12 May 1296	Othon de Grandson Amédée V de Savoie	Anglo-French War – truce
21 November 1296	Othon de Grandson Amédée V de Savoie	Anglo-French War – truce
23 November 1297, 24 January 1298 & 18 February 1298	Othon de Grandson Amédée v de Savoie	Anglo-French War – peace
22 April 1299	Gérard de Vuippens	Anglo-French War – Gascony
18 May 1299	Amédée V de Savoie	Anglo-French War – treaty

Date	Envoys	Notes
5 June 1299	Othon de Grandson Amédée V de Savoie Gérard de Vuippens	Anglo-French War – Gascony
19 June 1299		**Treaty of Montréal**
18 July 1299	Amédée V de Savoie Gérard de Vuippens	Anglo-French War – release of John Balliol
15 April 1300	Gefferoi de Joinville	Anglo-French War – treaty
24 August 1301	Othon de Grandson Amédée V de Savoie Gérard de Vuippens	Anglo-French War – peace
26 January 1302	Gérard de Vuippens	Anglo-French War – treaty
25 April 1302	Othon de Grandson Amédée V de Savoie	Anglo-French War – treaty
15 August 1302	Othon de Grandson Amédée V de Savoie	Anglo-French War – treaty
10 January 1303	Othon de Grandson Amédée V de Savoie	Anglo-French War – treaty
20 May 1303		**Treaty of Paris**

Source: Mary C. L. Salt. 1929. 'List of English Embassies to France, 1272–1307'. *The English Historical Review* 44: 263–78.

APPENDIX

Selected Primary Sources

1263. *Le Vendredi après la decolation de St. Jean Baptiste*

Echange entre Agnès Dame de Granson tutrice de Pierre Guillaume Gérard Jacques Henri et Othon ses enfans et le comte Pierre de Savoie du Péage de Granson en contréchange de six livres de rente annuelle sur les revenus de Cuarnie Pomers et Crotnai.

Source: House of Lords. Minutes of Evidence taken before the Committee of Privileges: Petition of Sir Henry Paston Bedingfeld of Oxborough, Baronet, in the Matter of the Abeyance of the Barony of Grandison. 7 April 1854–26 June 1858. London: HMSO. 169–70.

'*Nos Agnes domina de Grandisono tutrix legitima liberorum nostrorum Petri et Willelmi Girardus Jaquetus et Henricus pro se et fratre suo Otonino filii predicte domine ex una parte et nos frater Aymo de Crusillia ordinis predicatorum Willelmus prior Lustriaci magister Arnaudus canonicus Lugdunensis dominus Hugo de Palvesvel vice et nomine illustris viri domini Petri comitis Sabaudie ex altera notum facimus universis quod nos scientes prudentes et spontanei talem ad invicem permutationem contraximus videlicet quod nos Agnes et filii nostri predicti pro nobis et heredibus nostris permutamus et vice permutationis tradimus et assignamus totum pedagium nostrum de Grandisono quod habemus vel habere debemus in illis rebus que venient apud Yverdunum vel transitum facient per Yverdunum ita quod de illis rebus pedagium alibi quam apud Yverdunum levari non possit. Nos vero frater Ayno Willelmus prior magister Arnaudus et Hugo predicti vice et nomine domini comitis supradicti nomine permutationis assectamus eisdem apud Charnie Pomers Crocneri sex libras annui redditus promittentes nobis ad invicem res predictas ultro citroque nomine permutationis traditas et assignatas defendere et garentizare ad justiciam contra omnes. Nos eciam Agnes et filii nostri predicti ad instanciam et requisicionem predictorum de gratia speciali ex causa donacionis cedimus et concedimus predicto domino comiti quicquid juris et racionis habemus vel habere debemus in ortis sive curtilibus et claperiis factis datis et constructis per castellanum Yverduni sive de ejus auctoritate et mandato in pascuis comunibus inter telam et brianam die confectionis presentium litterarum adjecto quod a dicta die in antea ullum ibi denuo fiat curtile. Et quod contra caminum factum in mariscis non veniemus nec de ipso de cetero movebimus questionem promittimus eciam et ad hoc nos obligamus quod predicta omnia faciemus laudari et approbari ab Otone supradicto. In quorum omnium testimonium nos partes predicte fecimus fieri duo paria litterarum unius ejusdemque tenoris quibus apposuimus sigilla nostra. Ego vero Henricus cum sigillum non habeam sum contentus sigillis aliorum. Datas apud Yverdunum die Veneris post festum decollationis beati Johannis anno Domini millesimo ducentesimo sexagesimo tercio.*'

1263. The Friday after the decolation of St. John the Baptist

Exchange between Agnès Dame de Granson, guardian of Pierre Guillaume Gérard Jacques Henri and Othon her children and Count Pierre de Savoie du Péage de Granson in exchange for six pounds of annual income on the income of Cuarnie Pomers and Crotnai.

Source: House of Lords. Minutes of Evidence taken before the Committee of Privileges: Petition of Sir Henry Paston Bedingfeld of Oxborough, Baronet, in the Matter of the Abeyance of the Barony of Grandison. 7 April 1854–26 June 1858. London: HMSO. 169-70.

'We, Agnès, lady of Grandson, the legal guardian of our children, Pierre and Guillaume, Gérard, Jacques, and Henri, for himself and his brother Othon, the son of the aforesaid lord, on the one hand, and us, brother Aymo de Crusillia, of the order of preachers, William, prior of Lustria, master of Lustria, Arnaud, canon of Lyons, lord Hugo de Palvesvel, vice and name to the illustrious man Lord Pierre, Count of Savoy, on the other hand, we make it known to all that we, knowingly and prudently, have contracted such an exchange with each other, that is to say, that we Agnès and our children aforesaid exchange for us and our heirs, and in exchange for the exchange we deliver and assign all our toll of Grandson that we have or ought to have in those things which will come to Yverdon or pass through Yverdon, so that no toll can be levied on those things elsewhere than at Yverdon. But we brother Ayno Guillaume prior master Arnaud and Hugh of the aforesaid vice and in the name of the lord of the aforesaid count in the name of the aforesaid exchange obtain the same from Charnie Pomers Crocner six *livres* yearly rent promising us to each other the aforesaid things delivered and assigned to each other in the name of the exchange to defend and guarantee to justice against all. We, the aforesaid Agnès and our children, at the instance and request of the aforesaid, by special grace for the cause of the donation, yield and grant to the aforesaid lord the earl whatever right and reason we have or ought to have in the orchards or curtilages and clapperies made given and built by the castellan of Yverdon or by his authority and by commandment in the common pastures between Tela and Briana on the day of the making of the present letters, that from the said day onward any curtilage should be made there again. And we promise that we will not come against the stove made in the seas, nor will we raise any other question about it, and we bind ourselves to this that we will do all the aforesaid to be praised and approved by the aforesaid Othon. In witness of all of which we have made the parts aforesaid to be two pairs of letters of one and the same tenor, to which we have affixed our seals. As for me, Henri, since I have no seal, I am content with the seals of others.'

Dated at Yverdon on the Friday after the feast of the beheading of the blessed John in the year of the Lord one thousand two hundred and sixty-three.

25th January 1277

King Edward I Letter Patent

Source CPR Edward I vol 1 1272-1281

'Edwardus dei gratia. Rex Anglie, Dominus Hibernie et Dux Aquitanie, omnibus ad quos présentes littere pervenerint salutem. Cum nuper concessissemus dilecto et fideli ac familiari

nostro Otoni de Grandisono insulas nostras de Gernes. et Geres, cum insulis adjacentibus et omnibus aliis ad easdem insulas spectantibus habendas et tenendas de nobis et heredibus nostris ad totam vitam ejusdem Otonis per certam firmám nobis inde annuatim reddendam, Nos eidem Otoni gratiam facere volentes uberiorem, concedimus pro nobis et heredibus nostris quod idem Oto quietus sit de eadem firma in tota vita sua, et quod habeat et teneat insulas illas cum insulis adjacentibus et omnibus aliis ad easdem insulas qualitercumque spectantibus ad totam vitam suam, et percipiatet habeat omneš exitus et proventus eanmdem quocumque nomine censeantur et commodum suum inde faciat prout sibi magis viderit expedire. Ob familiaritatem etiam ipsiu Otonis et diutina ac laboriosa et fidelia obsequia sua nobis a primeva etate nostra et sua multipliciter impensa, et ut acquietet débita quibus indebitatus est in servicio nostro tempore predicto, et insuper propter specialitatem quam erga ipstim intime gerimus, sibi specialiter subvenire cupientes, volumus et concedimus, pro nobis et heredibus nostris, quod executores ipsius Otonis vel ejus assignati seu attornati quicumque habeant et teneant insulas predictas cum omnibus suis pertinenciis predictis, et percipiant et habeant omneš exitus earundem, per quinquennium post decessum ejusdem Otonis, ad acquietandwm indedébita sua, et ad completionem testamenti sui, sine occasione et impedimento nostri, heredum, ballivorum et ministrorum nostrorum quorwmcumque; volumus insuper et concedimus pro nobis et heredibus nostris, quod predictus Oto et heredes et executores sui quieti sint de omnimodis compotis, ratiociniis, arreragiis, receptis, demandis, et exactionibus quibus-cumque, que ab eo exigi possent de tempore quo eas tenebit in vita sua, vel sui executores, assignati seu attornati post ejus decessum easdem insulas tenebunt per quinquennium supradictum: ita quod nos vel heredes seu ballivi aut ministri nostri nichil in eisdem insulis aut exitibus earundem, quocumque nomine censeantur, interim clamare, vendicare seu exigere valeamus, complete autem termino predictorum quinque annorum, insuie predicte cum pertinenciis ad nos et heredes nostros intègre revertantur. In cujus rei testimonium presentibus sigillum nostrum fecimus apponi. T. me ipso, apud Wygorn., vicesimo quinto die januarii, anno regni nostri quinto.'

'Edward, by the grace of God. The King of England, the lord of Ireland, and the Duke of Aquitaine, Greetings to all those present and that receive this. Since we had recently granted to our beloved and faithful and familiar Othon de Grandson our islands of Guernsey and Jersey, together with the adjacent islands and all others pertaining to the same islands, to be held and held by us and our heirs for the whole life of the same Othon, to be rendered to us annually by a certain farm. Othon let him be quiet about the same farm during his whole life, and that he may have and hold those islands with the adjacent islands and all others in any way related to the same islands for the whole of his life, and let him perceive all the results of the same by whatever name they are considered and make his profit therefrom as he thinks best for himself. Because of your familiarity also with Otho himself, and your long laborious and faithful service to us from our early age and his own, which has cost him many times, and to settle the debts which he owed in our service at the aforesaid time, and moreover, because of the specialty which we intimately bear towards him, desiring to assist him in a special way, we will and grant, on behalf of ourselves and our heirs, that the executors of Othon, or his assigns or attorneys, whoever may have and hold the aforesaid islands with all their aforesaid appurtenances, and receive and have all the proceeds thereof, for five years after the decease of the same Othon, to settle the debts his own, and for the completion of his will, without the opportunity and hindrance of our heirs, bailiffs, and servants; We also will and grant for ourselves and our heirs, that the aforesaid

Othon and his heirs and executors be at rest from all manner of accounts, accounts, arrears, receipts, demands, and exactions of any kind, which may be exacted from him during the time that he shall hold them in his life. his own, or his executors, assigns or attorneys after his decease shall hold the same islands for the aforesaid five years: so that we or our heirs or bailiffs or our ministers shall have nothing in the same islands or issues of the same, by whatever name they may be considered, meanwhile we shall be able to cry, avenge or demand, complete but at the end of the aforesaid five years, they shall return to us and our heirs in their entirety, as aforesaid, together with their appurtenances. In witness whereof we have hereunto affixed our seal. By myself, at Worcester, on the twenty-fifth day of January, in the fifth year of our reign [1277].'

3rd April 1277

Letter from Dolforwyn to King Edward I variously attributed to Roger de Mortimer (incorrectly), Amédée V de Savoie (incorrectly), Henri de Lacy (possibly) and Othon de Grandson (plausibly). The letter is the nearest thing we have to a request to bring Maître Jacques de Saint George from Savoy to England to build castles.

Source : Frédéric Joseph Tanquerey. 1916. *Recueil de Lettres Anglo-Françaises, 1265–1399.* Paris : Librairie Ancienne Honoré Champion. 5–6.

'*Au Roy de Englterre. Al sun tres cher seignur saluz. Sachez sire ke nous asegames le Chastel de Doluereyn le mekreydy en la simeine de Paskes ... Sachez sire ke quant le chastel sera en vostre mein, il auera mester de grant amendement; por quoi nous auerrums mester de eukun homme ke de tels choses se feust entremettre e ke leument vosist empleer vos deners, kar nous y mettoms Mestre Bertram je dout ke il ne devisast trop de choses e par aventure vos deners ne serreint assez bien emplee com serreit, e por ce sire mandez nous de ceste chose vostre volonte. Sachez sire ke la lettre ke vus nous avez envoye par mon sire Joh de Bevilar nous vint a graund socour, kar sachez sire ke nostre ost semble bien ost de graunt seignur, e ce ne poet on mine fere sans deners. Sire a Deu ke vous gard, mandez nous votre estat e vostre volonte. Ceste lettre feu fete a Dolverein le Samedy apres Paskes.*'

'To my dear Lord Salut! Be aware that we besieged the castle at Dolforwyn on the Wednesday in Easter Week [31 March 1277] … Please know sir that when the castle will be in your hands it will be in need of great reworking; for what we have to tell you about a man, such things must be mediated, and that you save your money. Master Bertram, I doubt he does not estimate too much of things and by adventure your money. By this sir, tell of this your will. Know sir that the letter we have sent by my Lord Jean de Bonvillars has come to us in great earnestness. By the knowledge of our Lord that our host seems to be great and of a great Lord, and that this is not creation without money. Sir, God keep you, let us know how you are and what your will is. It is the letter at Dolforwyn, the Saturday after Easter [3 April 1277].'

As summarised by John Goronwy Edwards

'The sender reports that they laid siege to the castle of Dolvoreyn [*sic*] on the Wednesday in Easter Week [Mar. 31, 1277] … Informs the king that when the castle comes into his hands –

il auera mester de grant amendement – it will need much repair. Wherefore there will be need of some man who will take these matters in hand and will loyally employ the king's money. For if the sender employs Master Bertram for the work, he fears that Master Bertram will devise too many things, and perhaps the king's money will not be so well employed as it needs to be. Asks the king's will in this matter. Thanks the king for the letter sent by the hand of John de Bevilar, which was of great assistance, for the sender's force looks like the force of a great lord and this cannot be done without money.'

Source : John Goronwy Edwards, Ed. *Calendar of ancient correspondence concerning Wales.* Cardiff: Cardiff University Press Board, 1935. 30–31

June 1303

(Date suggested since it follows peace with France)

Othon de Grandson to the Chancellor of England (William de Greenfield)

Source : Ancient Correspondance, xxxvi. 133

'Sire, mandez moy se vous auez mande aus pors qui les chouses des ij Royames soient comunes, si come il a este ordene, et veullez mander aus gardeyns des pors & aus ballifs que eus leyssent passer ma gent des ysles et leur chouses franchement.'

Endorsed: Au Chancelier. O. de Granson.

30th July 1308

Philippe IV of France to the Bailiff of Sens.

Source : ANF Série JJ 40, No. 64 Robert Fawtier (dir.), *Registres du Trésor des Chartes*, Vol 1 *Règne de Philippe le Bel.* Analytical inventory by Inventaire J. Glénisson et J. Guérout, Paris, 1958, 64-65

'Philippus Dei gratia Francorum rex, ballivo Senonensi vel ejus locum tenenti salutem. Cum sicut accepimus, magister et fratres milicie templi retroattis temp(ori)bus ex certis dum fertur causis, dum adhuc sui status libertatem haberent, tenerentur obligati nobili viro Othoni de Grandi sono militi, in duobus milibus libris turonensium annui redditus solvendis Parisius vel Lugduni singulis annis quibus vitam duxerint in humanis, ac sanctissimus pater C. (Clemens) divina providentia summus pontifex pro illis duobus milibus libris eidem Ottoni reddendis assensu nostro super hoc requisito et ad hoc interveniente ordinaverit assignare domos de Turribus et de Espalliaco dyocesis Lingoniensis et de Coulors Senonensis et Trecensis dyocesis cum suis pertinenciis, redditibus et proventibus, exitus, obvenciones et jura eorumdem percipiendis et habendos ab ipso usque ad summam redditus supradicti residuo Templo, si quod fuerit remansuro quamdiu dictus miles vitam duxerit in humanis,

in solucionem et satisfactionem pro duobus milibus libris turonensium. Mandamus et committimus vobis, vocatis superintendentibus ad Templariorum negocium et aliis probis viris quos ad hoc videritis evocandos, assignetis dicto militi vel procuratori suo in domibus ipsis vel illis earum que ad hoc sufficere poterunt, aut si non sufficiant in ipsis et aliis magis propinquioribus et commodioribus dicto militi dictum redditum duarum millarum librarum turonensium ad vitam ipsius tenendum omnibus certa hoc legitime estimatis que in assignacionibus predictorum radentur, prout rationabiliter fuerit faciendum. Datum Pittavis XXX die julii anno Domini m° ccc octavo.'

'Philip, king of the Franks, by the grace of God, greet the bailiff of Sens or the holder of his place. When, as we have received, the master and the brothers of the militia of the temple having been withdrawn from the temp(ori)s for certain reasons, as it is said, while they still had the freedom of their state, they were bound to be bound to the noble man Othon de Grandson, a knight, paying an annual rent of two thousand *Livres Tournois* o each of Paris or Lyons in the years in which they led their lives in human life, and the most holy father C. (Clement) the divine providence of the supreme pontiff for those two thousand *Livres* to be returned to the same Othon, with our assent to this requirement and intervening for this purpose, ordered to assign the houses of the Towers and of Épailly to the diocese of Lingoniensis and the Coulors of Sens and the Diocese of Trece, with its appurtenances, rents, and revenues, receiving and holding the same issues, encumbrances, and rights, from him up to the sum of the remaining rents of the aforesaid temple, if any remain as long as the said knight leads his life in human life, in payment and satisfaction for two thousand *livres tournois* We command and entrust to you, having called the superintendents to the business of the Templars, and other honest men whom you see to be summoned for this purpose, you will assign the said soldier or his agent in the houses themselves or in those of theirs which may be sufficient for this purpose, or if they are not sufficient in themselves and in others more near and convenient to the said soldier, the rent of two thousand *Livres Tournois* to be held for his life, to be held by all those lawfully estimated, who shall be shaved in the aforesaid assignments, as was reasonably to be done. Given at Poitiers on the 30th day of July in the year of the Lord 1308.'

17th August 1308

From Pope Clement V

Source : Reg. Clement V, vol 2–3,137–38. no 2938.

Tue nobilitatis devota sinceritas, per quam te gratum nostris affectibus representas, digne nos excitat et inducit, ut personam tuam plenitudine favoris apostlici prosequentes indemnitatibus tuis paternis precaveamus affectibus teque condignis favoribus honoremus. Oblata siquidem nobis tua petitio continebat, quod ab olim magister domus militie Templi Ierosoimitani attente considerans profectus multiplices, qui ex tuis operibus virtuosis eidem ordini provenerant et sperabat imposterum provenire ac volens premissa digne retributionis premio compensare, tibi de consensu sui conventus duo milia librarum Turonen. parvorum certis locis et terminis quoad viveres per manus preceptoris Francie et thesaurarii domus Parisien. eiusdem ordinis qui essent pro tempore solvere et dare promisit, prout in patentibus litteris super hoc confectis predicti conventus sigillo plumbeo munitis plenius dicitur contineri. Nos *itaque tuis supplicationibus inclinati promissionem huiusmodi ratam et gratam habentes illam auctoritate apostolica ex certa scientia confirmamus etc. usque communimus.* Et quia *ex certis impedimentis provenientibus magistro et ordini supra- dictis eiusdem pecunie summam ab eodem magistro iuxta promissionem huiusmodi ha- bere non potes, nobis humiliter supplicasti, tibi super hoc per apostolice sedis providentiam de oportuno remedio provideri.* Nos *igitur volentes personam tuam huiusmodi devotionis obtentu dono specialis providentie prevenire tuisque providere indempnitatibus in hac parte tibi de Turribus, de Espaillierco et de Coulours domos eiusdem ordinis Lingonen., Senonen. et Trecen. diocesium cum omnibus iuribus et pertinentiis suis per te quo ad vixeris retinendas ac earum fructus, redditus et proventus usque ad summam dictorum duorum milium librarum in usus proprios convertendos tibi auctoritate apostolica duximus concedendum.* Volumus *autem, quod reliquum fructuum predictorum vel pecunie percipiendum ex ipsis alicui ex generalibus per nos vel specialibus per singulos prelatos regni Francie in singulis eorum diocesibus administratoribus et gubernatoribus bonorum ipsius ordinis in eodem regno seu diocesibus consistentium deputatis annis singulis facias exhiberi.* Non *obstantibus quibuscunque statutis et consuetudinibus ordinis supradicti iuramento, confirmatione apostolica seu quacunque firmitate alia roboratis, et quibuslibet privilegiis et indulgentiis et litteris apostolicis generalibus vel specialibus magistro et ordini supradictis vel quibusvis aliis comuniter vel divisim sub quacunque forma verborum concessis, de quibus oporteat in presentibus fieri mentionem et per que effectus presentium impediri valeat quomodolibet vel differri.* Tenorem *autem predictarum litterarum presentibus inseri facientes, qui talis est:*

> *Vniversis presentes litteras visuris et audituris frater lacobus de Mollay divina gratia magister humilis pauperis militie Templi salutem in Domino. Noverint omnes, quod nos inspicientes et considerantes et diligenter advertentes grandia bona et profectus, quos nobilis et potens vir carissimus et dilectus noster in Domino dominus Otho dominus de Grandissono fecit et facit mansioni sive domui nostre et faciet toto tempore vite sue, prout firmiter credimus et speramus, nos in recompensationem et remunerationem omnium predictorum de consilio nostro et conventus nostri donamus, concedimus et assignamus tenore presentium predicto domino Othoni duo milia librarum Turonen. parvorum solvenda et reddenda ipsi domino Othoni vel suo certo mandato quolibet anno sine aliqua dilatione toto tempore vite sue, scilicet mille libras die Purificationis Domine nostre et alias mille libras die Mercurii proxima post festum apostolorum Petri et Pauli mensis iunii et sic quolibet anno toto tempore vite sue et debemus eidem dictam monetam tradere quolibet anno apud mansionem nostram Parisien. vel Lugdunen. Supra Rodanum, ubi sibi melius placuerit, et nos districte precipimus in virtute sancte obedientie. preceptori Francie et thesaurario nostre domus de Parisius, qui pro tempore fuerint, quod dictam pecuniam tradant, solvant et benigne assignent omni dilatione remota domino Othoni prefato vel suo certo mandato secundum formam predictam, et pro maiori securitate et firmitate nos dedimus dicto domino Othoni presentes litteras sigillatas bulla nostri conventus factas in mansione nostra apud Parisius anno Domini millesimo ducentesimo septuagesimo septimo mense iulii die dominica post festum apostolorum Petri et Pauli.*

Nulli ergo etc. nostre confirmationis, concessionis et voluntatis etc. ... Dat. Lugusiaci, XVI kal. septembris, anno tertio. In eundem modum venerabilibus fratribus. archiepiscopo Senonen. et Lingonen. Ac. Trecen. Episcopis.

The devout sincerity of your nobility, by which you show yourself grateful to our affections, worthily arouses and induces us to pray for your person in the fullness of your apostolic favour, to pray for your paternal indemnities, and to honour you with favours worthy of you. Your petition, which was presented to us, contained the fact that, from the former Master of the Order of the knights of the Temple of Jerusalem, carefully considering the many occasions that had come from your virtuous actions for the same order, and hereafter and in future, and wishing to compensate the premises with a worthy retribution, he gave you, by the consent of his assembly, two thousand Livres Tournois in certain places and terms as to be given by the hands of the [Templar] preceptor of France and the treasurer of the order [of the Temple] of Paris. He promised to pay and give those who were of the same order for the time being, as it is said to be more fully contained in the open letters of the aforesaid meeting concluded upon this, sealed with a leaden seal. We, therefore, bowing to your supplications, having approved and accepted this kind of promise, confirm it by apostolic authority from certain knowledge, etc. we still share And since, due to certain impediments arising from the aforesaid master and order, you cannot have the sum of the same money from the same master according to this kind of promise, you have humbly begged us, that the providence of the apostolic see may be provided for you in this matter by means of an opportune remedy. We, therefore, wishing to obtain a gift of this kind of devotion from your person, will by special providence prevent and provide you with indemnities in this part of of Thors, of Épailly, and of Coulours, the temples of the same order in the dioceses of Langres., Senones and Troyes. the diocese with all its rights and appurtenances, which we have decided to grant you, by apostolic authority, to be retained by you for living and their profits, rents and proceeds up to the sum of the said two thousand pounds to be converted into your own use. We wish that the rest of the aforesaid fruits, or money received from them, should be presented to any one of the generals through us, or special through each of the prelates of the Kingdom of France, in each of their dioceses, the administrators and governors of the goods of that order existing in the same kingdom or dioceses, appointed for each year. Notwithstanding any statutes and customs of the aforesaid order strengthened by oath, apostolic confirmation or any other firmness, and any privileges and indulgences and general or special apostolic letters granted to the aforesaid master and order or to any others jointly or separately under any form of words, of which it may be necessary in the present to be mentioned, and by which the effect of the present might be hindered in any way, or postponed And making the tenor of the aforesaid letters to be inserted in the present, which is as follows:

> Every day you will see and hear the present letters, brother Jacques de Mollay, divine grace, teacher, humble, poor, knight of the Temple, peace in the Lord. Let them all know what, observing and considering us, and paying careful attention to the great goods and progress, which the noble and powerful man, dearest and our beloved in the Lord, Lord Othon de Grandson, has done and is doing for our Order and will do all the time of his life, as we firmly believe and we hope, that in recompense and

remuneration of all, the aforesaid of our council and of our assembly, we grant and assign to the aforesaid Lord Othon two thousand Livres Tournois, according to the tenor of the present. to be paid and returned to Lord Othon himself, or to his sure command, every year without any delay throughout his life, that is to say, one thousand livres on the day of the Purification of Our Lord, and another thousand livres on the Wednesday next after the feast of the apostles Peter and Paul, in the month of June, and so every year throughout his life sue and we must deliver to him the said money every year at our Temple in Paris. or Lyons, by the Rhône, where it pleased him better, and we command the district in virtue of holy obedience. to the preceptor of Francia and the treasurer of our Temple of Paris, who are for the time being, that they deliver the said money, pay it, and kindly assign it to the aforesaid lord Othon, after any delay removed, or by his sure command, according to the aforesaid form; The sealed meeting of our meeting held in our residence at Paris, in the year of the Lord one thousand two hundred and seventy-seven [although the transcript reads 1277 the manuscript reads 1287] of the month of July, on the Sunday after the feast of the apostles Peter and Paul.

Therefore, none etc. of our confirmation, concession and will, etc. Ligugé, 16th September, in the third year [of our reign – 1308] [17th August 1308]. In the same way to our venerable brothers. Archbishops of Sens and Auxerre [Guillaume de Paris], Langres [Guy de Genève] and Bishop of Troyes [Jean de Nanteuil].

16th January 1309

Othon de Grandson to John Langton, Bishop of Chichester, and Chancellor of England)

Source : Ancient Correspondance, xxxv. 59

'A reverent pere en dieu et son chier seignur et amy, mon seignur Jehan par la grace de Dieu, Evesque de Cycestre, Chancelier d'Angleterre, Othes de Gransson salut et li apparellie a son playsir et a sa volunte. Sire, pur ce que ie sui desirranz doir bones novelles de voustre estat, le quel Diousface touz iours bon, je vous pri sire que le plus sovant que vos porrez le me veullez mander. Endroit dou mien sire, sil vous plait a savoir, i'estoye seins et haitiez, le dieu merci, quant ceste lettre fu faite. Sire, cum aucunes genz facent grief a sire Wdry de Wyppeyns, mon clerc, et le quel est en mon servise en l'eglise de Wyrkinthone dont il est persone, je vous pri, sire, que vous ses procurours voullez avoir recommande aus besoignes qui le thocheront, et que vous, sire, pour ce qu'il est en mon service, li veuillez aydier, s'il vous plait, comant il ait la proteccion le Roy a toutes ses clauses tant que a iij anz. Et me veullez, sire, si vous plait, voustre volonte mander, la quel ie feroye a mon povoir. Sire, nostre seignur vous gard. Donees Espalli le xvj iour de Jenuier. [1309]

Endorsed: *A Reverent pere en dieu, mon seigneur Jehan, par la grace de Dieu Evesque de Cicestre, Chancelier d'Angleterre.*

Unknown date

VIA AD TERRAM SANCTAM

Source: Oxford, Bodleian Library., ms, Ashmole 342, fol. 1–6 v

'Por ce que le reaume de Jerusalem est apelés le reaume qui est [le rois des rois, ouquel roiaume il deigna et vost souffrir mort et passion et espandi son digne et precious sanc por nos raembre des poines d'enfer et geter dou poer del ennemi et rapeler a sainte gloire en sa sainte cité de la celestial Jerusalem, la ou est joie et beneurté sans fin par tous les siecles des siecles, devroilslt chascuns crestiens estre destrois, angoissous et ententis coment ce saint roiaume fu slt osté et netoié des mains et dou poer des mis de la sainte foi crestiene el fust franchi de tous servages. Et moult est grant honte et grant laid a tous crestiens, especiau ment as empereors, as rois, as princes et as autres grans sei gnors, quant il sueffrent a estre en servage et subiection le saint royaume ou nos avons esté racheté de si grant servage come dou deable et des dolouroses poines d'enfer, les queles sunt sans fin. Et moult covendra a rendre grant conte a Dieu a tous ceaus qui pooir en ont, quant il sueffrent que li mescreant et li ennemi de la sainte foi tienent son herilage, ou il vost el deigna espandre son saint et precious sanc. Dont nos prions Dieu le tot poissant, sans la cui grace nulle chose gui bone soil ne peut estre, gue il mete en cuer et en volenté as grans seignors d'outre m de metre cure et pooir et volenté de delivrer cest saint royaume des mains des mescreans, qui ont tantes habominacions faites en sains leus que ce seroit dolour a retraire. et que il vuillie ouvrer de să grace en eaus, [sans] laquel nul n'auroit pooir de riens faire. Et le conseill que l'en porroit metre, si est cestui., et faire se peut.

Et le conseill que l'en porroit metre, si est cestui, et faire se peut.

Se nostre Sires voloit metre sa grace au cuer d'aucun des rois dou Ponent, si come le roi de France, le roi d'Angleterre, le roi de Castele, le roi d'Allemaignie, ou le roi de Cezillie, que tous partie ou aucuns d'eaus emprist metant son pooir de venir con querre la sainte terre nostre Seignor, a nos semble que chascun dessus dis rois par soi mettant son poor acheviroit ce fait, au point et en l'estat que la painisme est dou Soudan qui a a nom Melec el Essraf gui fu filz del Melec el Mensor. Car son pere et lui ont ocis et bezillié tous les grans chevetaines et bons qui soloient estre dou tems del Melec el Vaher, que on apeloit Ben docdar. Et por ce aveuc trois mille chevaliers et n aubalestriers o l'autre gent a cheval, qui aveuc eaus seroient, les Sarrazins ne les porroient souffrir ni atendre en nul leu. Et. se il les atendoient en champ, noz gens, o l'aye de Dieu, les desconfiroient et gaaignieroient tout.

Or devons regarder de quel port il movroient, et laquel saison seroit plus profitable.

A ceaus de France et d'Angleterre, le meillior port seroit a Marseillie ou a Aigue Morte et a celle riviere de Provence. Au roi de Castele, sa riviere et ses pors sunt assés coneus. A celui d'Ale maignie, le [port de Venise et sa riviere. Au roi de Cesillie et a ceaus d'Itaillie, le port de Brandis et l'autre riviere de Puillie.

La meillior saison que il porroient avoir por passer, si est a la sainte Crois, en septembre, et por trop de raisons. La premiere raison si est que en celle saison l'on passe plus tost que n autre. L'autre si est que les gens et les chevaus si ont freschure et passent plus aiseement, et l'aigue meismes est plus froide, qui est grant aise et grant saveté sur mer. D'autre part, en celle saison le chaut et l'enfermeté de la mer est passé. Si est aussi grant avantage as chevaus qui vienent maigres et au desous de la mer, et se truevent plus près de l'erbage en celui passage que au pas sage de mai. D'autre part, la gent de la mer' ont adonc receu lur rentes, et le pays est plus planteif adonques que en nulle saison de l'an. Ceaus d'outre mer meismes sunt nez et norris en terre froide, et quant il vienent contre yver, il aprenent et usent la terre, si que, quant ce vient en esté, il sunt plus sains et la terre les comporte meaus.

Il ya vi places principaus la ou le passage peut et doit ariver de venue par raison. La premiere si est Alicandre. l'autre Damiate, l'autre Accre, l'autre Triple, l'autre Chipre, l'autre Ermenie.

La riviere d'Alizandre ne loeree je en nule maniere la venue, por ce que Alizandre est une fort ville; et d'autre part tout le pooir de la painisme si est ores ou reaume d'Egipte; et verteroit tout la. Encor, a la plage d'Alixandre n'a neent d'aigue douce, et qui beveroit de cele aigue gaires de tems il seroit trop euferme et se corromperoit tout. D'autre part, les chevaus seroient maigres et au desouz dou travaill de la mer, et ne trouveroient point d'erbage, quar erbage n'a neent la, se l'on ne le seme, et celui qui seroit semé, les Turs le gasteroient tost et legierement, et les chevaus demorreroient a grant meschief sans herbage, et pelit s'en porroit l'on aidier d'eaus au besoing. Et chascun peut savoir que des chevaus qui vienent d'outre mer l'on ne se peul gaires bien aider jusques a ce que il soient en erbes. De l'autre part, qui vodroit chevaucher par la terre, l'on ne le porroit faire, quar l'on n'auroit point de somage, ne la ne recoverroit l'on a nul somage ne acroistre sei de nulle chevau cheure. D'autre part, celle plage dou reaume d'Egipte est moult ennuiouse et mauvaise en celle saison, laquel chose seroit grant ennui et grant perill a la navie. D'autre part, se yver se meist, les viandes et les refreschemens ne porroient neent aler en l'ost, de laguel chose l'on auroit grant disete. Plusors autres raisons y a que l'on porroit dire sur la riviere d'Alixandre: mes nos empasserons ores. Bien est voir que, se a Nostre Seignor pleust que l'on peust prendre la cité en brief terme, l'on auroit achevé une grant partie dou fait, et se aiseroit l'on en la ville de bone aigue et de grant parlie d'autres bones choses. Mes ce est une chose que nul ne doit deviser ni aficher.

La riviere de Damiate ne seroit mie bone de venue; car la ville est abatue et gaste; et n'en y a mais nul repaire ni nul recet, si com nos gens orent autre fois, avant que la ville ne fust abatue. Et le chevaucher contremont, l'on ne le porroit faire por les bestes gui seroient foibles et debrisées de la mer, et de somage auroit l'on grant disete. D'autre part, erbage n'auroil on point, quar les Turs le gasteroient maintenant. Et de demorer la tot yver aler amont, seroit grant meschief, quar l'on se porroit amermer et non croistre. Et d'autre part a Damiate n'a nul port d'iver, ni por navie ne por grant vasseau. Et plusors autres raisons y a que l'on porroit dire sur cest fait, mes nos nos empassons.

A ariver a Acere ni a Triple ne seroit gaires profitable, quar a chevaucher de venue par la terre l'on ne porroit, car les bestes dou passage seroient lasces et travailliées. D'autre part, l'on ne porroit chevaucher par la terre sans grant somage por porter les viandes et les choses qui besoing seroient en l'ost. Et en ces 1 leus porroit l'on recovrer a poi de somage ni de bestes. D'autre part, en grant meschief seroient ceaus qui iroient en forage, por les chasteaus que les Sarrazins tienent près de ces deus leus, ne port n'en a a l'un ni en l'autre, la ou granment de naves peussent yverner. Or vos ai mostré por coi ne seroit pas bon que le passage arivast en nul de ces v leus devans dis A ariver en Chipre, si come le roi de Frauce fist, ne seroit pas bon aussi, quar il ne fist autre se non amermer, sans croistre: quar il s'amermeront moult en Chipre et de gens et de chevaus et de deniers; et quant il vostrent aler a Damiate, le passage lur costa près autant come celui d'Aigue Morte en Chipre. D'autre part, erbage a il poi en Chipre, et est cher; ni de chevaucheures l'on ne se peut de riens acroistre en Chipre, ne il n'a en Chipre nul port ou naves peussent yverner, se ce ne fust a grant meschief et a grant travaill. Et sachés que au roi de France et a tous les barons ennuia moult de ce qu'il ariverent en Chipre, quar il s'aparsurent bien qu'i lur avoit esté grant meschief.

Or mosterrons coment il seroit bon en totes manieres, por plusors raisons, que le passage arivast en Ermenie, c'est a savoir a la contrée de Laias, mais qu'il ne demorast que l'iver sans plus, car le pays d'Ermenie est moult sain en yver et moult enferme en esté. Le reaume d'Ermenie est moult fort et avironé de moult hautes montaignes, ne nus ne peut entrer en la terre que par certains pas, et les pas sunt tous garnis de bons chasteaus et de fors: et font a savoir maintenant as gens qui suut en Ermenie l'entrée des ennemis, si qu'il la sevent deux jors ou trois avant qu'il n'en trent et se peuent garnir a lur volonté. Le reaume d'Ermenie est garni de moult grans erbages et de moult bons et ne costeront neent. Si est aussi garni de moult grant bestiaill por charnage, c'est a savoir buès et vaches et bufles et pors et autre menu bestiaill, et planteif de blé et de chace et d'oiselis et de poisons de mer el d'aigue douce, car il y a trois grans rivieres de bone aigue. Port a il un des meilliors dou monde. la ou toules les naves dou monde porroient yverner, c'est a savoir le port de Paus, qui est a liues de Laias. En nul leu de la Surie l'on ne peut recovrer a somage ni a chevaucheures qu'en Ermenie, car il y a ou païs somage et bestes a grant planté. Et la Turquie est a meismes d'eaus, la ou il y a plus de somage et de bestes que en nul leuc dou monde, et de la recoverroit l'on a grant planté une grant partie de ceaus dou passage qui seroient a pié, se le passage arivoit autre part que en Ermenie, que la se monteroient tous a cheval; et d'autre part il recoverroient de la Turguie tentes et plusors autres choses qui sunt besoing a ostoier. Il s'acrestroient aussi dou roi d'Ermenie et de sa gent, qui est grant chose, ce qu'il ne feroient point se il estoient arivés autre part. Le roi de Chipre et sa gent vanroient trop legierement, car de l'un chief de Chipre jusques en Ermenie n'a que LX millies. Les vins et les viandes de Chipre yroient totes en l'ost et legierement; les gens de l'ost se porroient espandre par tot le reaume d'Ermenie et por forages et por totes autres choses que besoing lur seroit et sans perill, quar le reaume d'Ermenie est de tel condicion cum je ai dit devant. Toutes les fois que tout l'ost ou partie vodroit chevaucher ou corre en la painisme, il le porroient faire et sans nul perill. Quar en celle painisme qui est en la marche d'Ermenie demorrent poi de gens d'armes; et si tost cum vos estes hors dou reaume d'Ermenie, l'on trueve la terre moult garnie et planteive de menue gent et de bestiaill, et ce est la terre d'Antioche et de Tarpesac' et de Gaston et le plain de Harenc, la ou il y a moult de riches casaus et de bien garnis. Et qui vodroit passer outre vers la terre de Halape faire le peut aiseement, car la cité de Halape est a deus petites jornees de la marche d'Ermenie; et qui vodroit garnir Antioche, faire le porroit, quar les murs de la vile sunt tous enterins et empiés, et tous les casaus entor sunt garnis de Crestiens. Les chasteaus qui sunt entor Antioche auroit l'on legierement aussi, si comme Gaston et le Tarpesac et Harenc et Dargous et le Coursaut et aucuns autres chasteaus qui sunt la. Et, se les seignors de l'ost veissent ou coneussent que l'acorder et le complater [*sic*] *aveuc les Tatars lur fust profitable, laquel chose a moi semble que bone seroit, il porroient meaus traitier et porchacer cest fait d'Ermenie que de nul autre leu, car Ermenie si est veisine des Tatars. Le roi d'Ermenie porroit aussi moult aidier en ce fait, car il se tient por lur home et il les conut et eaus lui, et il a eu a faire a eaus sovent. Dedens cel yver gue le passage yverneroit e Ermenie, ceaus de lost se garniroient de soumage et de bestes che vaucheures et de toutes les autres choses que besoing lor seroit por chevaucher et ostoier. Et les chevaus qu'il auroient mené aveaus d'outre mer seroient en erbes et mis en bon point et seroient acreus dou roi d'Ermenie et de sa gent, dou roi de Chipre et de sa gent, dou covent dou Temple et de celui de l'Hospital;*

et en cel yver seroient refreschis et reposés, eaus et leur chevaus; et, vers le nouveau tems, porroient chevaucher. Et le chemin qu'il tearoient seroit tel:

Issir de la Portelle, et aler vers la terre d'Antioche par le Pont dou Fer, et chevaucher par la Murre, et par Sermin et par Meguaret Mesrin, et par tote celle terre jusques a Haman. Celle terre est trop bien garnie et planleive et riche, et plaine terre et large chemin, et n'a neent de gens d'armes. Haman si est grant ville et foible et pernable, et y a poi de gens d'armes. L'ost de Babiloine, se il issoit, je ne cuit neent qu'il iroit plus avant d'un leuc qui s'apele le Caneis. Le dit Caneis est a VI liues de Haman et a vi liues de la Chamele, quar tous jors ont il ce usé que, quant grant gent entrent au Ssem, l'ost de Babiloine. et de Domas les alendent au Casab, por ce que le leu est estroit; et a moi semble que ce seroit a souhaid de pooir combalre aveaus et speciaument en leu estroit. Et, se il avenoit en aucune maniere que l'ost de Babiloine n'en issist, l'ost de Doumas et dou Ssem est neent, et n'atendroit a nul leu. L'on chevaucheroit de Haman par la Chamelle et par Maubec droit a Domas et pren droit l'on tote la terre legierement et sans grant contrast. De Domas iroit l'on en Jerusalem et auroit l'on destruite tote la pai nisme dou Ssem et recoverroit quanque les Crestiens tindrent onques en la Surie. Et de la et avant et après feroit l'on ce qu'il plairoit a Nostre Seignor. Et, se il avenoit que l'on fust acordé o les Tatars, je loeroie que il chevauchassent le chemin de haut, c'est a savoir par Halape et par tote sa terre et par tous les autres leus qui sunt haus, la ou nos gens ne seroient point avenus; et seroit tous jors lor ost au mains a une jornée loins dou nostre. Quar le chevaucher ensemble aveuc eaus, ne l'estre de lur gens aveuc les nos, sovent ne seroit neent profitable chose, et por trop de raisons. Les naves et les vasseaus dou passage, qui yverneroient au port des Paus, porteroient le gros harnois de l'ost et le blé et les autres grosses viandes, et les dames et les femes et les anfans de l'ost et les autres pesantes choses, et iroient droit a Acre; et la porroient laisser ce que il lur plairoit et aler a Japhe, et porroit l'on recouvrer de lur navie as choses que il auroient besoing. Les pelerins sejorneroient en Jerusalem tant come il lor plairoit por aourer et visiter les saias leus. Après il porront chevaucher et aler a Gadres [3] tenir leur herberges la, car Gadres si est sain leu et planteive place de tot quanque besoing est a ost, et est près de la marine, qui est graut avantage et grant aise, et est la porte de l'entree en Egipte. Et, se nostre Seignor eust ordené que nos gens entrassent par la berrie conquerre Egipte, de Gadres se pren droit le chemin. Et sachés que il n'est mie si grevous, ne si hainos de sablon, ni de mauvaises aigues, com l'on dit; et por ce le vos deviserons tout ordeneement et a tire et herberges et aigues et quanque il y a de Gadres jusques au Caire.

Ce est le chemin de la berrie de Gadres jusques au Caire, et les herberges et les aigues.

De Gadres au Daron, trois liues; bon chemin el bones her berges et bones aigues.

Dou Daron a Rafah, II liues; bon chemin et bone aigue et assés.

Dou Rafah a la Zahque, IIII liues; bone herberge et bone aigue et assés; poi de sablon.

De la Zahque jusques a Heus, IIII liues tot sablonous; boné aigue et assés.

De Heus jusques a Larris, IIII liues tot sablon; bone aigue et assés; estassons de vendre et d'acheter.

De Larris jusques a Bir el Cani, III liues tot sablon; aigue assés et bone.

De Bir el Cani jusques à Bousser, III liues; et là se prenent I chemins; celui de haut est tot sablon et mauvaise aigue; celui de bas est le chemin usé et s'en vait par un leu ou le roi Baudoin morut, et celui leu s'apele Sabaquet Bardoill et vait a l'Aorade, et a sablon assés. La dite Aorade si est bone herberge et aigue assés et bone place de vendre et d'acheter; et si ne I a de Bousser jusques a la Aorade que II liues.

De la Aorade a la Saoede, a IIII liues; si a grant sablon et bone herberge et bone aigue et assés, et place de vendre et d'acheter.

De la Saoede au Meteileb, V liues, grant sablon; mauvaise herberge et mauvaise aigue, mes il y a assés.

Dou Meteileb a Nahlet Sabiha, m liues; bone aigue et assés, grant sablon

De Nahlet Sabiha a Catie, I liues, grant sablon. Catie est bone ville, aigue assés et bone, et si est a i liues de la baherie de Tennis

De Catie se prenent deus chemins [por] aler au Caire, l'un bas et l'autre haut; et les deus fierent a une bone ville qui a a nom la Habesce

Le chemin de bas, lequel est usé, si est de Catie au Horabi, et y a IIII liues, grant sablon, aigue assés, mais elle est poi salée. Dou Gourabi a Cousser, V liues, sablon assós et assés d'aigue, mes moult mauvaise. Dou Couseir a Birhysce, IIII liues; sablon poi, aigue assés, mes salée. De Birhysce a la Salehie, IIII liues; bone vile, aigue assés et très bone. De la Salehie a la Habesce VI liues, bon chemin, et la Habesce bone vile et grant, bone aigue dou Nil, terre tote habitée et garnie.

Le chemin de haut de Catie a Ahras, v liues, sablon assés, aigue assés et mauvaise. De Ahras a Bouhoroc IIII liues, sablon ', assés et mauvaise aigue, salée et amere. De Bouhouroc a Hocar IIII liues petites; sablon assés, mauvaise aigue, mais assés.

Et dou Houcar au Hascebi I liues; sablon assés, bone her berge et bone aigue et place de vendre et d'acheter. Dou Hassebi a Essiuont IIII liues; sablon assés, bone aigue et assés dou flum. De Essiuont a Masinat, III liues; sablon assés, bone aigue dou flum. De Masinat jusques a la Bebie, III liues; sablon assés, bone aigue dou flum. De la Bebie comence la terre de labor, et a jusques a la Vaherie III liues. La Vaherie est bone vile et grant, et aigue assés dou flum. De la Vaherie a la Habbesce, III liues; bon chemin et terre gaaignable. La Habesce est bone vile et grant, et aigues et totes choses a planté.

De la Habesce a Belbeis, III liues; terre gaaignable. Belbeis est bone ville et grant et riche et planteive de bones aigues et de totes bones choses.

De Belbeis à Bir Elbeina IIII liues, terre gaaignable, bone aigue et assés. De Bir Elbeina au Huss, IIII liues; terre gaaignable, bone aigue et assés.

De Huss a Quiryacos, IIII liues; terre gaaignable. Quiriacos est bone ville et grant et planteive de bores aigues et de plusors autres biens.

De Quiriacos au Caire, quatre liues de bon chemin.'

4th April 1328

Last Will and Testament of Othon de Grandson

Vidimus (Attested Copy) of a clause of the will of Othon, lord of Grandson, knight, written at Aigle, in the house of the prior

Source: ACV C V b 53

'Meum ecclesia cathedrali beatae Mariae Laus mo eligo sepultra Item volo et ordino quod, quando corpus meum ad ecclesiam deportabitur tumu landum, duo homines armati de armis meis et quilibet vexillum meum portans de eisdem armis precedant corpus meum super duos

equos, quorum quilibet sit precii centum libre lausannensium; et unus equorum coperiatur armis et alius ferreo et offerantur dicti equi [cum] armis et copertoriis predictis in ecclesia Lausannensi predicta, cui iure legati remaneant in remissionem peccatorum meorum.'

'I choose burial in the cathedral church of B[lessed]. Mary [Lausanne]. Also, I will and order that when my body shall be carried to the church to be laid thereupon, two men armed with my arms, and each carrying my banner with the same arms, shall precede my body on two horses, each of which shall be worth 100 *livres Lausanneois*, and let one of the horses be covered with my arms and the other with iron [carapace], and let the said horses be offered [with] the aforesaid arms and coverings to the aforesaid church of Lausanne, who as rightful ambassadors shall remain for the remission of my sins. I want and order that 20 liveries of land be purchased for the church of Lausanne, for two chaplains to celebrate in perpetuity for the rest of my soul; these chaplains, constituted with the consent of the chapter, are D. Thibaud, parish priest of Saint-Germain, my chaplain, and D. Hugues de Lignerolles, priest. I want and prescribe that one buys for. The said church 6 liveries of land for my birthday, and we will give 20 *sols* to the clerics of the choir who will have attended the service, on the anniversary day of my death. My executors will be able to buy back these 20 and 6 liveries of land. I give and bequeath to the church of Lausanne all my ornaments, clothing and silverware which are now deposited there, with the exception of a small gold cross and a statue of the B[lessed]. Mary.'

NOTES

Without Whose Help ...

1. Michael Ray. 2006. 'The Savoyard Cousins: A Comparison of the Careers and Relative Success of the Grandson (Grandison) and Champvent (Chavent) Families in England'. *The Antiquaries Journal* 86.

Prologue

1. Steven Runciman. 1954. *A History of the Crusades: Volume III The Kingdom of Acre and the later Crusades*. Eleventh ed. London: The Folio Society. 263.
2. Chron. Bertini. '*Et audivi qui scribo, narrantibus [michi] quibusdam Sabaudinis viris honestis et fide dignis, sed narrata non visa narrantibus; dicebant enim, quod in Sabaudia dudum erat quidam dominus de Gransone, cui natus est filius. Vocati astronomi ad pueri nativitatem inspiciendam, calculandam seu iudicandam; qui dixerunt, puer natus, si viveret, magnus esset, potens et victoriosus. Interfuit unus supersticiosus seu forte divinus, qui, sumpta ex igne facula, dixit, quod hic puer tantum durabit quantum facula presens'. Pater assumptam faculam clausit in parietes, ut diucius duraret. Vixit iste puer, crevit et ad etatem senectam et senium duravit, semper in honore accrescens, donec nimio senio et vivendi tedio pertesus, faculam predictam parieti inclusam extrahi fecit et in igne proici; qua' penitus in igne consumpta', miles cito post expiravit. Dixerunt ultra narrantes, quod iste fatalis dominus de Gransone tune cum aliis ultra mare existens', cum audiret filium regis Anglie, tam valentem virum, sic invenenatum, solus ausus fuit suggere[1] vulnera eius sic invenenata, forte confidens in fato suo predicto de facula; suxit igitur, et sic Edoardus sanatus est. Et exhine dominus iste de Gransone et sui penes reges Anglie elevati sunt et honorati, et adhuc hodie per Angliam magni reputantur et potentes*.' Frédéric Gingins in Chronique historique et généalogie du donjon de La Sarra (1818) had erroneously attributed this Lord of Grandson to Ebal III or IV de Grandson, however historians are now certain that given its clear description of the attack upon the named Lord Edward the attribution to Othon I de Grandson is certain.
3. Charles L. Kingsford. 1909. *Sir Otho de Grandison 1238? -1328*. Transactions of the Royal Historical Society 3. Appendix of Documents I, 188–89. Citing Ancient Correspondence VIII. 51. '*Edwardus, dei gratia Rex Anglie, dominus Hibernie, et dux Aquitannie, dilecto et fideli suo Otoni de Grandisono salutem*'
4. Othon III de Grandson was the grandson of Othon I's brother Jacques the Sire de Belmont, his grand nephew. Born between 1340 and 1350, he died in 1397. This younger Othon had fought on the Plantagenet side in the Hundred Years' War and met his end in a duel with kinsman

Gérard d'Estavayer. Othon III had a reputation for knightly valour, named thus by French chronicler Froissart, and gained a reputation as a poet writing some 80 of 6,000 verses. See Arthur Piaget. 1890. *Oton de Granson et ses poésies. Romania*, 19. 237–59, 403–48.
5. Marie-Louise Françoise de Pont-Wullyamoz. 1796. *Anecdotes Tirées de L'Histoire et des Chroniques Suisses. Lausanne: Chez Henri Vincent.* 375. n1.

Chapter 1

1. Sapaudia first appears in Ammianus Marcellinus, who described it as the southern district of Provincia Maxima Sequanorum, the land of the Sequani enlarged by the Diocletian Reforms. It originally covered the area around Lac Léman, the land of the ancient Allobroges. Its prefect appeared in the late Roman List of Offices. During the fifth century, the Burgundians settled in the area, forming the Kingdom of the Burgundians, the capital of which was Lugdunum Segusianorum (Lyon). For centuries thereafter, the names Burgundy and Sapaudia/Savoy became closely linked. In the mid-ninth century, Sapaudia was ruled by the Bosonid duke Humbert as part of the realm of Upper Burgundy. In 933, it was incorporated into Rudolph II's Kingdom of Arles, the Arelat or Second Kingdom of Burgundy.
2. Manfred W. Wenner. 1980. The Arab/Muslim Presence in Medieval Central Europe. International Journal of Middle East Studies 12: 61.
3. Bernard of Aosta also likely erroneously named Bernard of Menthon.
4. Canon Jean-Pierre Voutaz & Pierre Rouyer. 2013. *Discovering the Great Saint-Bernard.* Martigny: Les Editions du Grand-Saint-Bernard. 12–13.
5. The First Kingdom of Burgundy was a successor to the Western Roman Empire in what is now southeastern Gaul and western Helvetia. The Burgundian tribe had migrated, possibly from Scandinavia, to settle in western Helvetia in the dying years of Rome. Their first king was Gunther in 411 and last Gundomar until his defeat by the Merovingian Franks under Childerbert and Clothar in 534.
6. C. W. Previté-Orton. 1912. *The Early History of the House of Savoy (1000–1233).* Cambridge: Cambridge University Press. 2. Arpitan is what we used to call Franco-Provençal, but since it is neither French nor Provençal the name was changed. It is a Romance language which grew from Latin as did its neighbours. The names for the towns and cities of the region illustrate the differences with standard French; for example, Genève becomes Geneva, Lausanne becomes Losena, Aoste becomes Aousta, Grenoble becomes Grenoblo, Annecy becomes Enneci, Chambéry becomes Chamberi and Martigny becomes Martegne.
7. Peter H. Wilson. 2017. *The Holy Roman Empire*. Second Edition. London: Penguin 37.
8. Manfred W. Wenner. 1980. 'The Arab/Muslim Presence in Medieval Central Europe'. *International Journal of Middle East Studies* 12: 59–79.
9. René Poupardin. 1907. *Le Royaume de Bourgogne (888–1038)*. Paris: Librairie Honoré Champion. 144. C. W. Previté-Orton. 1912. *The Early History of the House of Savoy (1000–1233)*. Cambridge: Cambridge University Press. 30. King Rudolf III the last independent King of Burgundy died 6 September 1032 and was buried in Lausanne.
10. C. W. Previté-Orton. 1912. *The Early History of the House of Savoy (1000–1233).* Cambridge: Cambridge University Press. 6.
11. Ibid. 5.

12. Ibid. 6. Manfred W. Wenner. 1980. 'The Arab/Muslim Presence in Medieval Central Europe'. *International Journal of Middle East Studies* 12: 59–79.
13. Bernard Demotz. 2000. The county of Savoy from the 11th to the fifteenth century: Power, castle and State in the Middle Ages, Geneva: Slatkine. 51. Emperor Sigismond I of the Holy Empire elevated the county of Savoy into a duchy in 1416. The deed was signed in Montluel on February 3, 1416.
14. Of course, Voltaire was describing the Empire of his time saying, '*Ce corps qui s'appelait et qui s'appelle encore le saint empire romain n'était en aucune manière ni saint, ni romain, ni empire'* but the Empire of the thirteenth century could have merited the same epithet. Quoted from *Essai sur l'histoire générale et sur les mœurs et l'esprit des nations*, Chapter 70 (1756).
15. Peter H. Wilson. 2017. *The Holy Roman Empire*. Second Edition. London: Penguin.196–197.
16. Albert Naef. 1905. *Les mosaïques de Boscéaz près Orbe*. Imprimerie L. Vincent.
17. Recueil des chartes de l'abbaye de Cluny. Tome 3, 174–76. '*Rodulfus rex. Burchardus archiepiscopus. Hugo episcopus Genevensis. Aynricus episcopus Lausonensis. Hugo episcopus. Teuto abbas. Lambertus comes.*'
18. M.L. Charrière. 1866. *Les Dynastes de Grandson Jusqu'au XIII Siècle*. Lausanne: Georges Bridel. 91. n5. '*Reddimus Deo et sancto Petro ad Romanum monasterium in comitatu Vvaldense uillam Ferrieris cum omnibus appendiciis suis.*'
19. Ibid. 18. '*C'est la première fois que le nom de Grandson apparaît dans les documents.*' Or 'This is the first time Grandson's name appears in the documents.'
20. M.L. Charrière. 1866. *Les Dynastes de Grandson Jusqu'au XIII Siècle*. Lausanne: Georges Bridel. 16–17. '*Selon les religieux, Abalbert, sans concession de l'abbé ni des moines, avait violemment occupé un rocher entouré d'une épaisse forêt dépendante du village de Ferreyre qui appartenait au monastère romain, et y avait construit un château, d'où il pillait le village pré- cité, extorquant aux sujets du couvent de l'argent et d'autres choses; il avait commis des exactions à Agiez et envahi, à plusieurs reprises, les possessions du couvent à Champvent.*' Or 'According to the monks, Abalbert, without concession from the abbot or the monks, had violently occupied a rock surrounded by a thick forest dependent on the village of Ferreyre which belonged to the Romainmotier, and had built a castle there, from where he plundered the aforementioned village, extorting money and other things from the subjects of the monastery; he had committed abuses in Agiez and invaded, on several occasions, the possessions of the monastery in Champvent.'
21. M. L. Charrière. 1866. *Les Dynastes de Grandson Jusqu'au XIII Siècle*. Lausanne: Georges Bridel. 17. n2. '*Convenit etiam Adalbertus, princeps castri Grantionensis, cum suis militibus, contra quem sanctus papa valde comotus est pro loci depredationibus; nec non cleri vel populi maxima multitudo, quorum non potuit comprehendi numerus; ergo patre nostro beatissimo Hugone suggerente, sanctus apostolicus super altare beati Petri missam celebravit, in auribus confluentis populi pristinam loci auctoritatem confirmavit, invasores et vastatores ejus excommunicavit, et nisi resipiscerent ab universalis ecclesiæ catholicæ sancta communione, sub anathematis obligatione, sine fine segregavit.' Cartulaire de Romainmotier*. 418.
22. Herman of Laon, *De miraculis*, cols. 966–67; *Genealogiae Fusniacensis*, 255–56.
23. Frédéric Jean Charles de Gingins-La Sarraz. 1842. *Annales de l'abbaye du Lac-de-Joux depuis sa fondation jusqu'a sa suppression en 1536. Mémoires et documents publiés par la Société d'histoire de la Suisse romande, 1st ser.*, 1. Lausanne: Marc Ducloux.

7. '*Ainsi, la fondation de ce monastère remonte réellement à l'année 1126, et la charte de l'année 1140 qui consacre sa mémoire est postérieure de plusieurs années à cette fondation.*' Or 'Thus, the foundation of this monastery really dates back to the year 1126, and the charter of the year 1140 which consecrates its memory is several years later than this foundation.'

24. M. L. Charrière. 1866. *Les Dynastes de Grandson Jusqu'au XIII Siècle*. Lausanne: Georges Bridel. 120.
25. David Williams. 'Ebal III and Ebal IV de Grandson'. 2021. *Foundations* vol 13, 2–43.
26. Jean Gremaud, Ed. 1863. *Nécrologe de l'église cathédrale de Lausanne. Mélanges. Mémoires et documents publiés par la Société d'histoire de la Suisse romande*, 1st ser., XVIII. Lausanne: Georges Bridel, 104; Cart. Lausanne, 636, '*VII. Kal. Februarii. Pro dono yblone domino grandisono.*'
27. Cart. Lausanne, 523; *Fontes rerum Bernensium*, 2: 74–75 '*Testes ... Yeblo de Granzon et Girardus de Sarata.*'
28. David Williams. 2021. 'Ebal III and Ebal IV de Grandson'. *Foundations* vol 13, 34–35.
29. Maxime Reymond. 1920. '*Le Chevalier Othon I de Grandson*'. *Revue Historique Vaudoise* 28: 162. '*Dès 1234, Pierre de Grandson, fils de Ebal IV est l'ami de Pierre de Savoie le charge d'affaires et le porte-parole du Petit Charlemagne.*' Or 'From 1234, Pierre de Grandson, son of Ebal IV, was the friend of Pierre de Savoie, the chargé d'affaires and the spokes person of Little Charlemagne.'
30. Eugene L. Cox. 1974. *The Eagles of Savoy: The House of Savoy in Thirteenth Century Europe*. Princeton: Princeton University Press. 194.
31. AST, BV, 12.2: 300, Pailly 1. 28 November 1251, '*Ego Aymo dominus de Sarrata significo universis quod feudum illud quod ego tenebam a domino Petro de Sabaudia racione comitatus Gebennensis*'. And AST, BV, 12.1: 4, Index 3.15. 28 November 1251, '*Ego Aymo dominus de Sarrata significo universis quod ego accepi in feudum a nobili viro domino Petro de Sabaudia castrum de Bellomonte situm in diocesi Lausannensi quod castrum Richardus dominus de Bellomonte consanguineus meus habet in feudum a me et hoc factum et presente et consenciente predicto Richardo domino de Bellomonte.*"
32. David Williams. 'Pierre de Grandson Part One'. 2022. *Foundations* vol 14, 7.
33. Wurstemberger vol 1. 264. n22. '*Von Petern von Granson findet sich zwar keine Belehnungs urkunde aber er selbst kömmt so häufig im Gefolge Peters von Savoyen vor, dass sich an seinem Lehensverhältniss.*' Or 'but he himself appears so often in the entourage of Peter of Savoy that his feudal relationship is evident.'
34. Bernard Demotz. 2000. *Le Comté de Savoie du XIe au XVe siècle.* Genève: Editions Slatkine. 27. '*En revanche de nombreux vassaux ont sans doute prêté hommage sans que l'on ait trace écrite.*' Or 'On the other hand, many vassals have undoubtedly paid homage without a written record.'
35. CCR Henry III vol 9 1251–53, 109. '*Pro Petro Gransun et magistro Willelmo de Wytsand '.-Mandatum est J. Maunsell' quod una cum W. de Haverhull ', thesaurario regis, et camerariis suis provideant quod Petrus dominus Gransun sine dilacione habeat super annuum feodum suum xx. libras, qualitercumque perquirantur, mutuo aut alio modo; et quod similiter magister Willelmus de Wytsand' habeat x. libras, de dono regis. Et hoc nullatenus omittant. Teste ut supra. Per regem.*' Or 'For Peter [of] Grandson and William of Wytsand. Ordered by J[ohn] Maunsell that together with W[iliam]. of Haverhill let the king's treasurer and his chamberlains provide that Peter the lord of Grandson shall, without delay, have upon his annual fee 20 pounds. in whatever way they are sought,

mutual or otherwise; and that in like manner Master William of Wytsand has 10 pounds of the gift of the king. And they will by no means omit this. Witnessed as above. By the king.' That a Hanekin de Wissant is recorded as Constable of Pierre de Savoie's Pevensey Castle in 1264 and so was a close associate of the Savoyard may well point to Guillaume de Wissant mentioned along with Pierre de Grandson in 1252 being a family member and or another associate of the Savoyard. Such a link would reinforce the inference that the English archive is pointing strongly to a Pierre de Savoi–Pierre de Grandson link.

36. CLR Henry III vol 2 1240-1245, 309. 'June 13 [1245], Westminster. Liberate to Guinun messenger of Peter de Grauntzun 30 marks to Peter's use for this Easter term of his yearly fee of 30 marks.
37. David Williams. 'Pierre de Grandson Part One'. 2022. *Foundations* vol 14, 16. 'We do not know when Ulrich III of Neuchâtel married Jolante of Urach, when Agnès was born, her place in the order of her siblings, or when she married Pierre I de Grandson.'
38. Michael Prestwich 2020. *Othon de Grandson et la Cour d'Edouard I, Othon I de Grandson (vers 1240–1328)*. Lausanne: Cahiers Lausannois d'Histoire Médiévale. Published in French '*C'était donc assurément par la frère de Beatrice [de Savoie] Pierre, qui vint Angleterre en 1240, que les contacts d'Othon de Grandson avec l'Angleterre furent etablis.*' Or 'It was therefore assuredly through Béatrice [of Savoy] Pierre's brother, who came to England in 1240, that Otho de Grandson's contacts with England were established.'
39. Maxime Reymond. 1920. '*Le Chevalier Othon I de Grandson*'. *Revue Historique Vaudoise* 28: 162. '*est l'ami de Pierre de Savoie, le chargé d'affaires.*' Or 'is the friend of Pierre de Savoie, the chargé d'affaires.'
40. Aug. Burnand. 1911. *La date de la naissance d'Othon 1er, Sire de Grandson. Revue Historique Vaudoise* 19: 130. Writes '*Il faut fixer 1238 comme la date de la naissance d'Othon.*' We can translate to 'we must fix 1238 as the date of the birth of Othon.' Later Maxime Reymond. 1920. 'Le Chevalier Othon I de Grandson' in *Revue Historique Vaudoise* 28: 163. Suggested '*date de naissance d'Othon vers 1240*'.
41. More recently Swiss historiography has cautiously settled on '*vers 1240*' or 'around 1240'. See Bernard Andenmatten. 2020. *Othon I de Grandson (vers 1240–1328)*. Lausanne: Cahiers Lausannois d'Histoire Médiévale. v–vi.
42. House of Lords. 1858. Minutes of Evidence taken before the Committee of Privileges: Petition of Sir Henry Paston Bedingfeld of Oxborough, Baronet, in the Matter of the Abeyance of the Barony of Grandison. 7 April 1854–26 June 1858. London: HMSO. *'Nos Agnes domina de Grandisono tutrix legitima liberorum nostrorum Petri et Willelmi Girardus Jaquetus et Henricus pro se et fratre suo Otonino.'*
43. Charles L. Kingsford. 1909. *Sir Otho de Grandison 1238?–1328*. Transactions of the Royal Historical Society 3: 127. n3. 'The order is determined by a deed of August 31, 1263, under which Agnès and her sons sold the '*Peage de Grandson*' to Peter of Savoy for an annual rent charge on Cuarnie, Pomers and Crotnei. It begins: *'Nos Agnes, domina de Grandisono, tutrix legitima liberorum nostrorum Petri et Willelini, Girardus, Jaquetus et Henricus, pro se et fratre suo Otonino, filii predicte domine &c.*' Peter and William were clearly underage. Henry was probably just of age, for, having no seal of his own, he was '*contentus sigillis aliorum*'. 'Otho was plainly absent; for his brothers contracted in his behalf and promised to obtain his consent.' The full charter is reproduced in the Appendix.
44. David Williams. 2022. 'Pierre de Grandson Part One'. *Foundations* vol 14, 17.

45. Jean Gremaud. Ed. 1863. *Nécrologie de l'église cathédrale de Lausanne. Mélanges. Mémoires et documents publiés par la Société d'Histoire de la Suisse Romande*, 1st ser., XVIII: 89–246. Lausanne: Georges Bridel. 155.
46. Chron. Bertini. '*Et audivi qui scribo, narrantibus [michi] quibusdam Sabaudinis viris honestis et fide dignis, sed narrata non visa narrantibus; dicebant enim, quod in Sabaudia dudum erat quidam dominus de Gransone, cui natus est filius. Vocati astronomi ad pueri nativitatem inspiciendam, calculandam seu iudicandam; qui dixerunt, puer natus, si viveret, magnus esset, potens et victoriosus. Interfuit unus supersticiosus seu forte divinus, qui, sumpta ex igne facula, dixit, quod hic puer tantum durabit quantum facula presens'. Pater assumptam faculam clausit in parietes, ut diucius duraret. Vixit iste puer, crevit et ad etatem senectam et senium duravit, semper in honore accrescens, donec nimio senio et vivendi tedio pertesus, faculam predictam parieti inclusam extrahi fecit et in igne proici; qua' penitus in igne consumpta', miles cito post expiravit. Dixerunt ultra narrantes, quod iste fatalis dominus de Gransone tunc cum aliis ultra mare existens', cum audiret filium regis Anglie, tam valentem virum, sic invenenatum, solus ausus fuit suggere[1] vulnera eius sic invenenata, forte confidens in fato suo predicto de facula; suxit igitur, et sic Edoardus sanatus est. Et exhine dominus iste de Gransone et sui penes reges Anglie elevati sunt et honorati, et adhuc hodie per Angliam magni reputantur et potentes.*'
47. David Williams. 2022. 'Pierre de Grandson Part Two'. *Foundations* vol 15. David Williams's article forms the latest body of evidence and thinking that we have on the daughters of Pierre de Grandson.
48. CPR. Edward I vol 1 1272–1281, 188. 'January 25th [1277], Worcester, Acquittance to Otto de Grandisono of the farm by which he holds the islands of Guernsey and Jersey and the adjacent islands, and grant of the said islands and their issues for life, and grant, on account of his intimacy with the king, and his long and faithful service from an early age, and for the acquittance of debts incurred in the king's service in the aforesaid time, that his executors shall hold the said islands and their issues for five years after his decease for the acquittance of his debts, and the fulfilment of his will without rendering any account therefor.' We will discuss Othon's overlordship of the islands later.
49. Julian Havet. 1876. *Série chronologique des gardiens et seigneurs des îles normandes (1198–1461).* Seigneurs des *îles normandes (1198–1461).* Bibliothèque de l'école des chartes. Tome 37. 225. Has the Latin text in full. '*Edwardus dei gratia. Rex Anglie, Dominus Hibernie et Dux Aquitanie, omnibus ad quos présentes littere pervenerint salutem. Cum nuper concessissemus dilecto et fideli ac familiari nostro Otoni de Grandisono insulas nostras de Gernes. et Geres, cum insulis adjacentibus et omnibus aliis ad easdem insulas spectantibus habendas et tenendas de nobis et heredibus nostris ad totam vitam ejusdem Otonis per certam firmám nobis inde annuatim reddendam, Nos eidem Otoni gratiam facere volentes uberiorem, concedimus pro nobis et heredibus nostris quod idem Oto quietus sit de eadem firma in tota vita sua, et quod habeat et teneat insulas illas cum insulis adjacentibus et omnibus aliis ad easdem insulas qualitercumque spectantibus ad totam vitam suam, et percipiatet habeat omneš exitus et proventus eanmdem quocumque nomine censeantur et commodum suum inde faciat prout sibi magis viderit expedire. Ob familiaritatem etiam ipsiu Otonis et diutina ac laboriosa et fidelia obsequia sua nobis a primeva etate nostra et sua multipliciter impensa, et ut acquietet débita quibus indebitatus est in servicio nostro tempore predicto, et insuper propter specialitatem quam erga ipstim intime gerimus, sibi specialiter subvenire cupientes,*

volumus et concedimus, pro nobis et heredibus nostris, quod executores ipsius Otonis vel ejus assignati seu attornati quicumque habeant et teneant insulas predictas cum omnibus suis pertinenciis predictis, et percipiant et habeant omneš exitus earundem, per quinquennium post decessum ejusdem Otonis, ad acquietandwm indedébita sua, et ad completionem testamenti sui, sine occasione et impedimento nostri, heredum, ballivorum et ministrorum nostrorum quorwmcumque; volumus insuper et concedimus pro nobis et heredibus nostris, quod predictus Oto et heredes et executores sui quieti sint de omnimodis compotis, ratiociniis, arreragiis, receptis, demandis, et exactionibus quibus-cumque, que ab eo exigi possent de tempore quo eas tenebit in vita sua, vel sui executores, assignati seu attornati post ejus decessum easdem insulas tenebunt per quinquennium supradictum: ita quod nos vel heredes seu ballivi aut ministři nostri nichil in eisdem insulis aut exitibus earmzdem, quocumque nomine censeantur, interim clamare, vendicare seu exigere valeamus, complete autem termino predictorum quinque annorum, insuie predicte cum pertinenciis ad nos et heredes nostros intègre revertantur. In cujus rei testimonium presentibus sigillum nostrum fecimus apponi. T. me ipso, apud Wygorn., vicesimo quinto die januarii, anno regni nostri quinto.' The regularly cited CPR abbreviates the grant in English. CPR Edward I vol 1 1272–1281, 188. 'Jan 25 [1277], Worcester. Acquittance to Otto de Grandisono of the farm by which he holds the, islands of Guernsey and Jersey and the adjacent islands, and grant of the said islands and their issues for life, and grant, on account of his intimacy with the king, and his long and faithful service from an early age, and for the acquittance of debts incurred in the king's service in the aforesaid time, that his executors shall hold the said islands and their issues for five years after his decease for the acquittance of his debts, and the fulfilment of his will without rendering any account therefor.'

50. House of Lords. 1858. Minutes of Evidence taken before the Committee of Privileges: Petition of Sir Henry Paston Bedingfeld of Oxborough, Baronet, in the Matter of the Abeyance of the Barony of Grandison. 7 April 1854–26 June 1858. London: HMSO.
51. CChR Henry III Edward I vol 2 1257–1300, 254. 'July 26 [1281], Copford. Gift to Otho de Grandison, for his homage, and for the service rendered by him from his and the king's youth, of the castle and cantred and land of Hokonagh in Ireland, and of all the town of Tipperary, and the castle and town of Kilfecle, the land of Muskery, the manor of Kilsylan and the town of Clonmel, which the said Otho previously had for life of the king's gift and which he restored to the king; gift also of all the land of Estremoy, which the king had formerly given to John Ferre, and which the said John had restored to the king: to be held from the king by the said Otho, the hoirs of his body and his assigns, by the service of two knights' fees. Mandate to Robert de Ufford, justice of Ireland, to give seisin. Mandate to the same to accept Richard de Exonia as the attorney of the said Otho. Mandate to the knights, free-men and others of the said lands to be intendent to the said Otho.'
52. And David Williams. 2022. Foundations Vol 14, 19. 'Kingsford is almost certainly correct when he dates Othon's birth to c.1238, but less so when he dates Othon's arrival in England to 1258. . . A more realistic date would seem to be 1244–5.
53. Charles L. Kingsford. 1909. Sir Otho de Grandison 1238?-1328. Transactions of the Royal Historical Society 3: 127. 'No doubt Agnès was glad enough when on his fourth visit to England in 1258.'
54. Michael Prestwich. 1997. *Edward I.* Yale: Yale University Press. 127. 'Personal details about the king's [Edward] relationship with his sons are very scant, but it is tempting to

see his hand in the choice of toy castles … a miniature siege engine as well.' In the way that to this day men give their sons the toys familiar to them from their own childhood, it must also be tempting to see Edward and thus Othon playing with toy castle and miniature siege engines also.

Chapter 2

1. Emmanuel Davin. 1963. *Béatrice de Savoie, Comtesse de Provence, mère de quatre reines (1198-1267).* Bulletin de l'Association Guillaume Budé 2: 176-189.
2. P. Chaplais. 1952. The Making of the Treaty of Paris (1259) and the Royal Style. The English Historical Review 67: 235–53. André Perret. 1983. Le comte Pierre II de Savoie. L'expansion savoyarde et l'alliance anglaise au xiiie siècle. Revue Savoisienne 95-119.
3. Darren Baker. 2017. Henry III: The Great King England Never Knew It Had. Stroud: The History Press. David Carpenter. 2020. Henry III: The Rise to Power and Personal Rule 1207 - 1258. New Haven: Yale University Press. David Carpenter. 2023. Henry III: Reform, Rebellion, Civil War, Settlement 1259–1272. London: Yale Publishing Ltd. E. F. Jacob. 1924. What were the 'Provisions of Oxford'? History 9: 188-200. H. W. Ridgeway. 1989. Favourites and Henry III's Problems of Patronage, 1247-1258. The English Historical Review 104: 590–610. H. W. Ridgeway. 1983. The politics of the English royal court, 1247-65, with special reference to the role of aliens. University of Oxford.
4. Margaret Howell. 1998. Eleanor of Provence. Oxford: Blackwell Publishers Ltd. 226.
5. Charles L. Kingsford. 1909. *Sir Otho de Grandison 1238?–1328.* Transactions of the Royal Historical Society 3: 126. And Maxime Reymond. 1920. 'Le Chevalier Othon I de Grandson'. *Revue historique vaudoise* 28: 163. 'Sir Otho de Grandison (or Graunzun) appears as one of Edward's knights in 1268, and had no doubt fought under him at Lewes and Evesham.'
6. Michael Prestwich. 1997. *Edward I.* Yale: Yale University Press. 53.
7. CPR Henry III vol 5 1258-1266 464-5. Oct. 16 [1265]. The like to Peter de Chaumpvent of 5 marks of yearly rent in Westminster. Westchepe in the said city late of Thomas de Exeporte, sometime citizen of London, the king's enemy, which the said Thomas used to receive from the stalls of Robert de Muntpelers in Westchepe; to hold by the due and accustomed services.' And 465. 'Oct. 16. Westminster. Grant to Peter de Chauvent and his heirs of the houses in the city of London late of Robert de Montpelers, sometime citizen of London, the king's enemy.'
8. CPR Henry III vol 5 1258–1266, 465. 'The like to the following houses late of the king's enemies in the said city [London] . . .Otoninus de Graunzun, those late of Simon de Hadestok.' And Ibid. 467. 'The like to the following of like houses in London: Ottonin de Grauncun, those houses with their appurtenances and rents in the street of the Thames by Quenehithe late of Simon de Hadestok.'
9. CPR Henry III vol 5 1258–1266, 464–65. 'Oct. 16 [1265]. The like to Peter de Chaumpvent of 5 marks of yearly rent in Westminster. Westchepe in the said city late of Thomas de Exeporte, sometime citizen of London, the king's enemy, which the said Thomas used to receive from the stalls of Robert de Muntpelers in Westchepe; to hold by the due and accustomed services.' And 465. 'Oct. 16. Westminster. Grant to Peter de Chauvent and his heirs of the houses in the city of London late of Robert de Montpelers, sometime

citizen of London, the king's enemy.' And Ibid. 514. 'Grant to Peter de Chaumpvent, to whom with Ottonin de Graunzun the king granted all the lands late of William le Blund the king's enemy, of the goods of the said William, which belong to the king by reason of his forfeiture.'

10. CPR Henry III vol 6 1266–1272, 282–83. 'This is the agreement made between Peter de Chaumpvent and Otto de Granzun, of the one part, and William son of William de Criketot, one of the heirs of William le Blunt, of the other part, to wit, that the latter is bound to the former in 400 marks for his ransom whereby he made fine for the lands late of William le Blunt in Assefeld which the king gave to the said Peter and Otto by occasion of the trespasses charged against the said William de Criketot and William le Blunt in the disturbance had in the realm, of which sum the said William de Criketot will pay to Peter and Otto or their heirs or attorneys at the New Temple, London, before the preceptor or brethren of the Temple at the Nativity of the Blessed Mary, 52 Henry III, 200 marks, and at Hilary following 200 marks; and for greater security the said William grants for him and his heirs that the whole of the said land of Assefelt shall remain in the hands of Robert Burnel, clerk, until satisfaction have been made to the said Peter and Otto for the said sum. Further the said William has made a charter of feoffment of the same to Peter and Otto which is placed in the keeping of the treasurer of the Temple, London, so that if the said payments are made it shall be restored to him and be of none effect, and if not, it shall be delivered to the said Peter and Otto, and the said Sir Robert Burnel shall then give them seisin of the said manor. And if the said William wills that the wood of Assefeld or part thereof be sold to make the said payment at the said terms, the said Peter and Otto grant that the said William shall have someone appointed on his behalf together with the men of the said Robert to make faithfully the sale of the said wood, so that the money received therefrom be not put to other uses than the said payment. Witnesses, Sir Hugh son of Otto, Sir William Belet, Matthew de Teltenham, Robert de Bosço and John de Pelteham, knights, William de Neketon, John de Geddinges, Robert de Neketon, William de Midd', clerk, and others.'
11. What we now call 'Old St Paul's Cathedral', the one lost in the Great Fire of London (1666) had been consecrated as recently as 1240, just some twenty odd years before.
12. Leo T. Gourde, 'An Annotated Translation of the Life of St. Thomas Becket by William Fitzstephen' (1943). Master's Thesis. 622.
13. Ibid.
14. Ibid.
15. Charles L. Kingsford. 1909. *Sir Otho de Grandison 1238?–1328*. Transactions of the Royal Historical Society 3: 128. Kingsford suggested that Grandson had 'no doubt fought under him [Edward] at Lewes and Evesham'.
16. CPR Henry III vol 5 1258–1266, 467. 'Oct.17 [1265]. The like to the following of houses late of the king's enemies in the City of London. . . Geoffrey de Genvill, those houses late of William, son of Benedict.'
17. Michael Prestwich. 2005. Geneville [Joinville], Geoffrey de, first Lord Geneville. *Oxford Dictionary of National Biography.* For the escape of Edward see Margaret Howell. 1998. Eleanor of Provence. Oxford: Blackwell Publishers Ltd. 224.
18. RG i, no. 2870. '*et Willielmo de Pesmes et duobus militibus sociis suis robas, scilicet eidem Willielmo tres pecias. et Simoni de Greenvilla et duobus militibus sociis suis robas,*

scilicet eidem Simoni tres pecias. T. ut s' The *famille de Pesmes* would a century later find themselves linked to the *famille de Grandson*. CCR Henry III vol 10 1256–1259, 223–24. '*Pro militibus Burgundie.-Mandatum est Philippo Lovel, thesaurario, quod Henrico de Peiny, Willelmo de Pemes, Ricardo de Mumbiliard, Simoni de Genvyle, Johanni de Dornay, Guidoni de Rens', Baldewino de Villa, Johanni de Castellione, Petro de Chaunteny, Hugoni Espaulard et Willelmo de Puncayle, qui jam ad mandatum nostrum venerunt in Angliam pro expedicione nostra Wallie, sine dilacione habere faciat feodum suum quod eis debemus ad scaccarium nostrum, vel saltem medietatem ejusdem feodi, cuilibet eorum modis omnibus persolvi faciat ad expensas suas quibus se preparare possint ad veniendum ad regem ad instans parleamentum Oxonie, sicut rex eis mandavit, exinde cum rege in expedicionem regis Wallie progressuri: et, cum rex sciverit quantum eis liberaverit, faciet eis habere breve de Liberate ubi illud prius non habuerit. Teste rege apud Clarendon XXV. die Maii.* 'Or 'For the knights of Burgundy. It was ordered to Philip Lovel, the treasurer, that Henry de Peiny, Guillaume de Pesmes, Richard de Mumbiliard, Simon de Joinville, John de Dornay, Guidon de Rens', Baldewin de Villa, John de Castellion, Peter de Chaunteny, Hugh Espoulard and William de Puncayle, who have already come to England for our expedition in Wales, at our command, shall without delay have their fee which we owe them to our treasury, or at least the half of the same fee, to be paid to each of them by all means for their expenses which they that they may prepare to come to the king to the immediate parliament at Oxford, as the king commanded them, and thence to proceed with the king to the expedition of the king to Wales; Witness the king at Clarendon 25th day of May [1258].'

19. Wurstemberger. vol 4. No. 657. '*In dorso testamenti legitur: Nos Petrus Comes Sabaud. hanc nostram vltimam uoluntatem per manum Villi de Aug. capellani nostri subscribi fecimus et sigillari, ac propria manu signauimus Testes, signantes per monogrammata sua, et qui sub scripserunt per manum Will. de Augusta, capellani Comitis, qui solus manu propria subscripsit: Humbertus de Monteferrato, Girardus de Grancione prepositus S. Thomæ de fornerio lug dun. Camillus falasterius miles. Amadeus de Boczesello, petrus de amaysino. Johannes de gllr (?). Ebalus de Montibus, petrus capellanus. Will. de Augusta capellanus propria manu subscripsi.' For Chaplaincy see Charles L. Kingsford. 1909. Sir Otho de Grandison 1238?–1328. Transactions of the Royal Historical Society 3: 127.*
20. David Williams. 2022. 'Pierre de Grandson Part One'. *Foundations* vol 14, 14. 'His obit is recorded in the necrology of Lausanne cathedral on 2 July, '*Visitatio beate Marie virg. Obiit Petrus dns Grandissono*', which is confirmed by an entry for the same day in the Grandison Obits, '*Obit. dni Petri dns de Grandisone ii die July*', and also in the Beaufort–Beauchamp Book of Hours, '*6 Non. Jul. Obit. dni Petri dns de Gandesone*'. The year is almost certainly 1258; for on 15 July 1259 a letter of pope Alexander IV to the prior of Romainmôtier regarding the provision of his son Girard to a canonry of Metz cathedral mentions Pierre thus: *'Petitio dilecti filii Girardi subdiaconi nostri nati quondam P[ietri] domini de Grancano nobis exhibita continebat'*.
21. Charles L. Kingsford. 1909. *Sir Otho de Grandison 1238?–1328*. Transactions of the Royal Historical Society 3: 128.
22. Othon de Grandson and Jean de Grailly would be reunited some twenty-six years later on the walls of Acre in 1291.
23. CPR Henry III vol 5 1258–1266, 632. 'Aug 27 [1266], Kenilworth. Notification that Reynold de Grey, constable of the castle of Nottingham, delivered by order of the king

to Peter de Chaumpvent one balistam de trullio and four balistas ad duas pedes of the king's baliste in his keeping in that castle, by the hand of William de Grey, the receipt of which the said Peter has acknowledged before the king.'

24. Richard K. Morris. 2006. *Kenilworth Castle*. Third Edition. London: English Heritage. 40. The Dictum of Kenilworth was a peace treaty with the rebels following the death of Simon de Montfort. The document marks the end of the reform movement and the restoration of royal power.
25. St. Martin Le Grand was a college of secular canons of ancient origin, with a collegiate church to dedicated to St. Martin of Tours. The church was especially interesting since it was responsible for the sounding of the curfew bell in the evenings, which announced the closing of the city's gates. The college church of St. Martin Le Grand was not very far from the house granted to Othon de Grandson following the late baronial war. Following Savoyards Guillaume de Champvent and Louis de Vaud as Deacons of St. Martin would be William of Louth, Keeper of the Wardrobe.
26. CPR Henry III vol 5 1258–1266. 566–67. 'March 16th [1266], Westminster. Notification to Pope Clement of the appointment of William de Chavent dean of the church of St. Martin, London, and William Bonquer as the king's proctors and special envoys to lay before him the damages, injuries, oppressions and grievances inflicted upon the king by occasion of the late disturbance in the realm, to sue and obtain general and special things for the king and his right, and the advantage and honour of the king's dignity; and to ask and obtain specially graces and indulgences and a timely subsidy for the relief and amelioration of the estate of the king and the realm.'
27. Chron. Thomas Wykes, 197–98.
28. Accounts of the Great Roll of the Pipe of the Exchequer for the reign of Henry III. Thirty-fifth report of the Deputy Keeper of Public Records and Keeper of the State Papers of Ireland, 50.
29. Mark Hennessy. 1996. 'Manorial organisation in early thirteenth-century Tipperary'. *Irish Geography,* vol 29:2. 118.
30. Cal Docs Ireland 1293–1301, no. 511
31. CChR Henry III Edward I vol 2 1257–1300, 254. 'Gift to Otho de Grandison, for his homage, and for the service rendered by him from his and the king's youth, of the castle and cantred and land of Hokonagh [Coonagh] in Ireland, and of all the town of Tipperary, and the castle and town of Kilfecle [Kilfeacle], the land of Muskery, the manor of Kilsylan [Kilsheelan] and the town of Clonmel, which the said Otho previously had for life of the king's gift and which he restored to the king; gift also of all the land of Estremoy, which the king had formerly given to John Ferre, and which the said John had restored to the king; to be held from the king by the said Othon, the heirs of his body and his assigns, by the service of two knights' fees. Mandate to Robert de Ufford, justice of Ireland, to give seisin. Mandate to the same to accept Richard de Exonia as the attorney of the said Otho. Mandate to the knights, free-men and others of the said lands to be intendent to the said Ötho.'
32. CChR Henry III Edward I vol 2 1257–1300, 149 & 177. 'Aug 2 [1270], Winchester . . . *Inspeximus* and confirmation of a charter . . . witnesses. . . Sir Otho de Graunzon. . . dated at York, 18 September [1267] 52 Henry III.' And 'Nov 1 [1271], Westminster. . . *Inspeximus* and confirmation of a charter . . . witnesses. . . Sir John de Greylli. . . Sir Otho de Grandisono. . . given by the hand of the said Edward at Woodstock, 14 July [1267] 52 Henry III.'

33. Arnold Taylor. 1985. *Studies in Castles and Castle-Building*. London: The Hambledon Press. 61. n26.
34. Michael Prestwich. 2010. *Knight: The Medieval Warrior's (Unofficial) Guide*. London: Thames & Hudson. 45–6.
35. Marie-Louise Françoise de Pont-Wullyamoz. 1796. *Anecdotes Tirées de L'Histoire et des Chroniques Suisses. Lausanne: Chez Henri Vincent.* 375. n1. '*Les tombeaux de la cathédrale ayant été ouverts sous la préfecture de Monsieur de Gross, baillif de Lausanne, on trouva dans le cercueil de Grandson, le fquelette du bon chevalier, revêtu de son armure complette, casque en tête, éperons dores aux talons; et près de lui, sa lance et son ecu.*' Or 'The tombs of the cathedral having been opened under the prefecture of Monsieur de Gross, bailiff of Lausanne, we found in Grandson's coffin, the skeleton of the good knight, clad in his full armour, helmet on his head, golden spurs on his heels; and near him, his lance, and his shield.'
36. Reg. Clement IV, Numbers 1110 and 1146.
37. *Princeps Walliae*, Prince of Wales was a new term in 1245, one Dafydd ap Llywelyn Fawr had begun styling himself thus in 1244, before the Norman conquest Welsh leaders had sometimes styled themselves 'Reges or Kings of the Britons'.
38. The term crusade is ultimately derived from a Middle Latin *cruxata, cruciata*. The adjective *cruciatus* had been used in the sense of 'marked with a cross' from the twelfth century; *cruciatus* (also *cruxatus, croxatus, crucesignatus*) was used of crusaders by the mid-thirteenth century, from their practice of attaching a cloth cross symbol to their clothing. Use of *cruxata (cruciata)* for 'crusade, military expedition against enemies of the church' is in use by the 1280s. The Middle French croisade is recorded from at least the fifteenth century. The French spelling *croisade* is recorded in English still in the sixteenth century; the modern spelling crusade dates to c. 1760. See *OED*.
39. Christopher Tyerman. 2012. *Chronicles of the First Crusade*. London: Penguin Books. 20.
40. The Eighth and Ninth crusades are often considered to be one and the same crusade, the eighth being King Louis XIV's expedition to Tunisia, and the ninth Edward's expedition to Acre since they were originally planned to be one and the same.
41. One of those who died on the Seventh Crusade was the half-brother of Henry III, Hugh XI de Lusignan.
42. Steven Runciman. 1954. *A History of the Crusades: Volume III The Kingdom of Acre and the later Crusades*. Eleventh ed. London: The Folio Society. 263.
43. Ibid. 265–66.
44. Ibid. 266.
45. Ibid. 270.
46. Joseph Michaud, 1881. *History of the Crusades*. Wm. Robson, trans. 3 vols. London: Routledge. vol. 3. 17.
47. Geoffrey Hindley. 2003. *A Brief History of the Crusades*. London: Constable & Robinson Ltd.293
48. For the Lord Edward 'taking up the cross' see letter from Cardinal Ottoboni to Pope Clement IV reprinted in Rose Graham, 1900. Letters of Cardinal Ottoboni. *The English Historical Review*, Volume XV, Issue LVII, January 1900, 112. '*Adhec de viro egregio, regis filio, bone voluntatis, accionis pie, nobilitatis strenue fideique deuote, penes sancte paternitatis vestre animum non sine attestacione multorum testimonium in consciencie sinceritate deponens, eundem, qui signum crucis in terre sancte subsidium deuote*

suscipere intendit, precordiali affeccione in Domino recommendo, supplicans vt qui Deo et Christo eius vult humiliter abnegare seipsum sanctum dominum et vicarium Christi propicium et benignum inueniat adiutorem.' For Othon de Grandson see Esther Rowland Clifford. 1961. *A Knight of Great Renown: The Life and Times of Othon de Grandson*. Chicago: University of Chicago Press. 16.

49. James A. Brundage. 1966. "Cruce Signari': The Rite for Taking the Cross in England'. *Tradito* 22. 289–310.
50. Thomas Wright. 1839. The Political Songs of England from the Reign of John to that of Edward II. 130–1.
51. Joinville quoted in Nancy Goldstone. 2010. *Four Queens: The Provençal Sisters Who Ruled Europe*. London: The Orion Publishing Group. 320–21.
52. Simon Lloyd. 1988. *English society and the crusade, 1216–1307*. Oxford: Clarendon Press. Appendix 4 n33. 'CPR 1266–72, p. 480: Gessevill; but PRO, C 66/88, m. 15 d. reveals a misreading of 'Geneville'.
53. Ibid. 115.
54. Thomas Asbridge. 2010. *The Crusades*. London: Simon & Schuster UK Ltd. 888.
55. Steven Runciman. 1954. *A History of the Crusades: Volume III The Kingdom of Acre and the later Crusades*. Eleventh Edition. London: The Folio Society. 244.
56. Nancy Goldstone. 2010. *Four Queens: The Provençal Sisters Who Ruled Europe*. London: The Orion Publishing Group. 329.
57. Esther Rowland Clifford. 1961. *A Knight of Great Renown: The Life and Times of Othon de Grandson*. Chicago: University of Chicago Press. 17. Rowland Clifford described the crossing as from Portsmouth, but as the Winchester chronicler wrote, an account which Prestwich described as the route by which Edward 'probably crossed'. Michael Prestwich. 1997. Edward I. Yale: Yale University Press. 73. n21. Ann. Winchester. 109. '*Et sic iter suum versus Portesmue, ubi transfretare proposuerat, arripuit; et cum eo dominus Willelmus] de Valencia, dominus Thomas de Clare, dominus Rogerus de Clyfford, et multi alii, qui mutato proposito Cantuariam adiverunt, et apud Doveriam transfretaverunt xiii. kal. Septembris.*' Or 'and so he set out on his way towards Portsmouth, where he had proposed to cross; and with him lord William de Valencia, lord Thomas de Clare, lord Roger de Clyfford, and many others, who, with a changed purpose, went to Canterbury, and crossed over at Dover. 13th cal. September.' See also following note.
58. Ann. Winchester 109. '*Item dominus Edwardus in castello Wyntoniæ, petita licentia a domino rege transfretandi versus Terram Sanctam, venit in capitulo Wyntoniæ non. Augusti, et accepit licentiam a conventu, rogans humiliter ut pro se orarent, et sic iter suum versus Portesmue, ubi transfretare proposuerat, arripuit; et cum eo dominus W[illelmus] de Valencia, dominus Thomas de Clare, dominus Rogerus de Clyfford, et multi alii, qui mutato proposito Cantuariam adiverunt, et apud Doveriam transfretaverunt xiii. kal. Septembris. Item x. kal.*' Or 'Likewise, lord Edward in Winchester, having requested permission from the lord king to cross over towards the Holy Land, came in the chapter of Winchester. Augustus, and received leave from the convent, humbly begging them to pray for him, and thus took his way towards Portsmouth, where he had proposed to cross; and with him lord William de Valencia, lord Thomas de Clare, lord Roger de Clyfford, and many others, who with a changed purpose went to Canterbury, and crossed over at Dover. cal. September. Also x. cal.'

59. Chron. Wykes. 236. '*Obtenta quoque licentia, dominus E[dwardus] satagens dominum Robertum Burnel clericum suum, quem sincerissime diligebat, ad tantæ celsitudinis apicem promovere, relicta classe cum quanta poterat celeritate secessit Cantuariam, ut personæ suæ præsentia supradictos induceret electores, ut in dictum clericum suum vota sua dirigerent.*' Or 'having also obtained leave, the Lord Edward, endeavouring to promote Sir Robert Burnel, his clerk, whom he loved most sincerely, to the pinnacle of such highness, left the fleet and retired to Canterbury with all the speed he could, in order to bring in the aforesaid electors in his person, to give his wishes to the said clerk they would direct.' He then goes on to suggest that Edward returned to Portsmouth to continue with the plan to travel to Aigues Mortes by way of Bordeaux and Gascony, but the timeline is very tight and the Winchester chronicler, closer to Portsmouth, has a date for the Dover embarkation whereas Wykes merely recites the original plan. Ann. Winchester. 109. '*Et sic iter suum versus Portesmue, ubi transfretare proposuerat, arripuit; et cum eo dominus Willelmus] de Valencia, dominus Thomas de Clare, dominus Rogerus de Clyfford, et multi alii, qui mutato proposito Cantuariam adiverunt, et apud Doveriam transfretaverunt xiii. kal. Septembris.*' Or 'and so he set out on his way towards Portsmouth, where he had proposed to cross; and with him lord William de Valencia, lord Thomas de Clare, lord Roger de Clyfford, and many others, who, with a changed purpose, went to Canterbury, and crossed over at Dover. 13th cal. September.' King Henry writing to Llywelyn ap Gruffydd also describes a move of origin from Portsmouth to Dover see CCR King Henry III vol 14 1268–1272, 290. '*Edwardi primogeniti nostri versus Terram Sanctam, qui, illis qui sunt de consilio nostro et aliis regni nostri magnatibus et fidelibus nostris secum existentibus, cum crucesignatorum multitudine apud Portesmuth' auram expectando jam diu est perhendinavit et pretextu contrarietatis aure predicte ab inde usque Dovor.*'
60. Michael Prestwich. 1997. *Edward I*. Yale: Yale University Press. 71.
61. CPR Henry III vol 6 1266–1272, 588. 'Jan 30 [1271], Westminster. Special protection and protection *volumus* for four years. . . going beyond seas in aid of the Holy Land . . . Gérard de Grandisono.'
62. CPR Edward I vol 3 1292–1301, 58. '13th December 1293, Tower of London. Inspeximus of a charter sealed with the seal which the king used before he assumed the governance of the realm, dated Sicily, 15 January, 50 Henry III, whereby he granted to William son of Warin land to the yearly value of 301. in the County of Connaught in Ireland, as extended by Roger de Clifford, with all the rights thereto pertaining, to hold to him, his heirs and assigns by the service of half a knight's fee. Witnesses: Sir Henry de Almania, William de Valencia, Thomas de Clare, John de Verdone, Roger de Clifford, Robert Tibotot, John de Vescy, Otto de Grandisono, Richard de Rupella, Hugh son of Otto, and others. By K., on the information of G. de Roubury.' Chron. Bertini. '*Et audivi qui scribo, narrantibus [michi] quibusdam Sabaudinis viris honestis et fide dignis, sed narrata non visa narrantibus; dicebant enim, quod in Sabaudia dudum erat quidam dominus de Gransone, cui natus est filius. Vocati astronomi ad pueri nativitatem inspiciendam, calculandam seu iudicandam; qui dixerunt, puer natus, si viveret, magnus esset, potens et victoriosus. Interfuit unus supersticiosus seu forte divinus, qui, sumpta ex igne facula, dixit, quod hic puer tantum durabit quantum facula presens'. Pater assumptam faculam clausit in parietes, ut diucius duraret. Vixit iste puer, crevit et ad etatem senectam et senium duravit, semper in honore accrescens, donec nimio*

senio et vivendi tedio pertesus, faculam predictam parieti inclusam extrahi fecit et in igne proici; qua' penitus in igne consumpta', miles cito post expiravit. Dixerunt ultra narrantes, quod iste fatalis dominus de Gransone tune cum aliis ultra mare existens', cum audiret filium regis Anglie, tam valentem virum, sic invenenatum, solus ausus fuit suggere[1] vulnera eius sic invenenata, forte confidens in fato suo predicto de facula; suxit igitur, et sic Edoardus sanatus est. Et exhine dominus iste de Gransone et sui penes reges Anglie elevati sunt et honorati, et adhuc hodie per Angliam magni reputantur et potentes.'

63. Michael Prestwich. 1997. *Edward I*. Yale: Yale University Press, 83.
64. Ruth Margaret Blakely, 2005. *The Brus Family in England and Scotland, 1100–1295*. Boydell & Brewer. 81.
65. We have different reports from three chroniclers concerning Edward's journey from Aigues Mortes to Tunis. Chron. Wykes. 238. Makes no mention of Sardinia. Nor does Chron. Guisborough. Vol 1, 330. It is the continuation of Chron. Flores, vol 3. 20. '*Edwardus noster sulcavit maria versus Acon, et a longe aspiciens insulam Sardaniæ, ibidem applicuit, rumores certos de morte regis Francia Lodowici.*' Or 'Our Edward ploughed the seas towards Acre, and seeing from afar the island of Sardinia, he landed there and heard certain reports of the death of King Louis of France.'
66. Chron. Guisborough. Vol I, 331. '*Quid est, domini charissimi, nonne convenimus huc et caracterem Domini assumpsimus ut in inimicos crucis Christi procedere et non componere deberemus? absit a 'nobis hoc, nam modo patet introitus, et terra nobis est plana et dura, ut possimus procedere usque ad sanctam civitatem Jerusalem.*'
67. C. Köhler, 1903–4. '*Deux projets de croisade en terre-sainte composée à la fin du xiiie siècle et au debut du xive*', *Revue de l'Orient Latin*, 407–8, 427–28. For the view that Othon de Grandson was 'very possibly' the author see Michael Prestwich. 1997. *Edward I*. Yale: Yale University Press. For the contrary view see
68. Gestes des Chiprois. 199. English translation, Paul F. Crawford. 2003. *The Templar of Tyre: Part III of the deeds of the Cypriots*. Abingdon: Routledge. 86. '376. the ninth of May in the same year the Lord Edward, son of the king of England, arrived in Acre. He encountered a great storm at sea on the voyage out, so much so that a waterspout hit his ship, so that it nearly foundered.'
69. 'Sultan' is Arabic for 'power.'
70. Steven Runciman. 1954. *A History of the Crusades: Volume III The Kingdom of Acre and the later Crusades.* Eleventh Edition. London: The Folio Society. 278.
71. Krak de Chevaliers was militarily fallen upon hard times, down to 300 defenders from 2,000 in 1220.
72. Paul F. Crawford. 2003. *The Templar of Tyre: Part III of the deeds of the Cypriots*. Abingdon: Routledge. 86 '376 In the year 1271 of the Incarnation of Christ, on the eighteenth of February, Baibars, sultan of Babylon, besieged the castle of Krak des Chevaliers, which was held by the Hospital of St. John of Jerusalem. He took it on terms on the eighth of April, sparing their lives.'
73. Steven Runciman. 1954. *A History of the Crusades: Volume III The Kingdom of Acre and the later Crusades.* Eleventh Edition. London: The Folio Society. 279.
74. Paul F. Crawford. 2003. *The Templar of Tyre: Part III of the deeds of the Cypriots*. Abingdon: Routledge.87 '378 In this year the sultan besieged Montfort of the Germans, a castle very near Acre, and took it on the twelfth of June, on terms and sparing their

lives. On the sixteenth of July he conducted the men to Acre and let them go.8 On this day the men of Acre were all in arms, ready to defend their lands. Then the Lord Edward saw the sultan's host and his great power, and knew too well that he did not have the men to fight the sultan with. So, none of the Christians dared go out against him, and the next day the sultan left, and went back to Babylon.'

75. Gestes des Chiprois. 199. *'376 En l'an de M & CC & LXXI de l'incarnaſion de Criſt, à .xviij. jours de mois de fevrier, Bendocdar ſoudan de Babiloine, aſega la chaſteau dou Crac, quy fu de l'Oſpitau de Saint Johan de Jeruſalem, & le priſt à fiance à .viij. jors d'avril, ſauve lor vies. Et en ſel an meymes, à .ix. jours de may, ariva à Acre monſeignor Odoart, fis dou roy d'Engleterre, que en ſon veage ot mout de tempeſte de mer, que .j. ſIſon fery en ſa nave que poy ne la nea; & amena ſa feme o luy, & vint le conte de Bretaine, & au més de ſetembre, vint à Acre meſſire Arniot, frere de meſſire Odoart. Et en ſe dit an aſega Bendocdar, ſoudan de Babiloine, Gebelacar, quy eſtoit dou prince d'Antioche, & la priſt à fiance.'* English translation, Paul F. Crawford. 2003. *The Templar of Tyre: Part III of the deeds of the Cypriots*. Abingdon: Routledge. 86.

76. Gestes des Chiprois. 199–200. *'378 En cel ans, aſega le ſoudan Montfort des Alemans, .j. chaſtyau bien près d'Acre, & le priſt à .xij. jours dou mois de jun à fiance, ſauve lors vies & à .xvj. jours de gunet mena les gens devant Acre, & ſeluy jour la gent d'Acre ſI furent tous as armes pour defendre la terre, & adons meſſire Odoart vy l'oſt dou ſoudan & ſon grant poier, & conut bien que il n'en avoit pas gens de combatre au ſoudan, & por ce n'en oza nul des creſtiens yſſir à luy, & l'endemain ſe parti le ſoudan, & ala en Babiloine.'* English translation, Paul F. Crawford. 2003. *The Templar of Tyre: Part III of the deeds of the Cypriots*. Abingdon: Routledge. 86.

77. Gestes des Chiprois. 200. *'379 Et des puis meſſire Odoart fiſt une chevauchée, & ala briſer un riche cauzau quy a nom Saint Jorge, qui eſt près d'Acre à .iij. lines, & furent o luy Temple & Oſpitau, & l'autre gent d'Acre, & ce fu à lſſue de gunet quy faiſet mout grant chaut, & brizerent le dit cauzau & tuerent mout de Sarazins, & firent grant guain, mais de noſtre gent y morut acés par chaiſon dou miel d'abeille & d'autre choſes quy managerent, ſI con gens à pié ſont uſés de faire, ſI que il moreent par le chemin & pour le chaut & pour le travaill & pour les viandes chaudes qu'il aveent mangé.'* English translation, Paul F. Crawford. 2003. *The Templar of Tyre: Part III of the deeds of the Cypriots.* Abingdon: Routledge. 86.

78. Paul F. Crawford. 2003. *The Templar of Tyre: Part III of the deeds of the Cypriots.* Abingdon: Routledge. 86.n2.

79. Ibn al-Furat, 1971. *Ayyubids, Mamlukes and Crusaders*, vol 2: Translation, ed. Jonathan Riley-Smith, Malcolm Cameron Lyons, Ursula Lyons. Cambridge. W. Heffer & Sons Ltd. 157.

80. Paul F. Crawford. 2003. *The Templar of Tyre: Part III of the deeds of the Cypriots.* Abingdon: Routledge. 57 'In September Sir Edmund, brother of the Lord Edward, also came to Acre.'

81. *La Finanza Sabauda.* Vol 2, 124 *'dominum Eidmundum Anglie.'* And ibid. 125. '*Die dominice in crastino assumptionis beate Marie ibidem ... domino Eidmundo.*'

82. Peter W. Edbury. 1994. *The Kingdom of Cyprus and the Crusades, 1191–1374.* Cambridge: Cambridge University Press. 92.

83. Paul F. Crawford. 2003. *The Templar of Tyre: Part III of the deeds of the Cypriots.* Abingdon: Routledge. 57. 'The sultan of Babylon armed eleven Saracen galleys and

sent them out to do damage to Cyprus. When they reached the waters off Limassol, they all wrecked and broke up due to pilot error, by God's will and not for any other reason, for both the wind and the sea were perfectly calm. They were all taken as slaves, though two galleys escaped and went back to Alexandria. 5 If things had not turned out thus, they would have destroyed Limassol and other places in Cyprus.'

84. Ibn al-Furat, 1971. *Ayyubids, Mamlukes and Crusaders*, vol 2: Translation, ed. Jonathan Riley-Smith, Malcolm Cameron Lyons, Ursula Lyons. Cambridge. W. Heffer & Sons Ltd. 152. 'Sultan Baibars had written to Egypt directing that the galleys be sent out against Cyprus so as to distract the attention of its King [Hugh III] and force him to leave Acre.'
85. Simon Lloyd. 1988. *English society and the crusade, 1216–1307*. Oxford: Clarendon Press.
86. Steven Runciman. 1954. *A History of the Crusades: Volume III The Kingdom of Acre and the later Crusades*. Eleventh Edition. London: The Folio Society. 280.
87. Ibn al-Furat, 1971. *Ayyubids, Mamlukes and Crusaders*, vol 2: Translation, ed. Jonathan Riley-Smith, Malcolm Cameron Lyons, Ursula Lyons. Cambridge. W. Heffer & Sons Ltd. 150
88. Hugh Kennedy. 1994. *Crusader Castles*. Cambridge: Cambridge University Press. 37.
89. Caco or Qaqun is in fact around 50 miles, not 15 miles from Acre.
90. Chron. Guisborough, Vol 1, 333. '*Iterato, circa festum nativitatis sancti Johannis Baptistæ, cum audisset Edwardus convenisse Saracenos apud Kakehowe [Caco], quod distat ab Acra quasi 'xv milliaribus, exivit ibidem, et irruens in eos summo diluculo percussit ex eis quasi mille viros, cæteris in fugam velocem conversis, tuleruntque spolia multa.*'
91. Turcoman or Turkmen were and are semi-nomadic Turkic peoples who had come to the Levant with the Seljuk Turks in the eleventh century, today making up parts of the populations of Syria, Iraq, and Turkmenistan.
92. Gestes des Chiprois. 200–1. '*381 A .xxiiij. jours dou mois de novembre dou dit an, monſeignor Odoart et le roy Hugue & la chevalrie de Chipre & d'Acre, & le Temple & Oſpitau alerent brizer .j. cazau quy a non Cacon, quy eſt en la terre de Sezaire loins d'Acre .xij. liues & plus, & firent grant damage à Sarazins & gaignerent .ij. herberges de Turquemans, & tuerent Sarazins aſés & prirent beſtiail gros & menu .xijm., & aſegerent aucuns Sarazins dedens une tour quy eſt à Caco mout fort environée de focés plains d'aigue, & bien l'eüſſent priſe, mais nos gens douterent de trop demorer pour le cry quy eſtoit par la terre, & la Sarazins eſtoient ja aſemblés de toutes pars, dont noſtre gent ſe partirent & vindrent à Acre tout lor guain ſain & ſauf.*' English translation, Paul F. Crawford. 2003. *The Templar of Tyre: Part III of the deeds of the Cypriots*. Abingdon: Routledge. 86–87
93. Ibn al-Furat, 1971. *Ayyubids, Mamlukes and Crusaders*, vol 2: Translation, ed. Jonathan Riley-Smith, Malcolm Cameron Lyons, Ursula Lyons. Cambridge. W. Heffer & Sons Ltd. 157.
94. Chron. Flores, vol 3, 23. '*Edwardus, cum magna militia exivit Acon transiens per Nazareth.*'
95. Michael Prestwich. 1997. *Edward* I. Yale: Yale University Press. 75. '. . .had Edward not arrived when he did, Acre would have been surrendered to Baibars' Mamluk troops. Baibars had certainly been conducting a most successful campaign, taking Chastel Blanc, Gibelacar, and the greatest of all crusader fortresses, Crac des Chevaliers.'
96. Steven Runciman. 1954. *A History of the Crusades: Volume III The Kingdom of Acre and the later Crusades*. Eleventh Edition. London: The Folio Society. 281.

97. William of Tyre. 1943. *Deeds Done Beyond the Sea*, Volume II, Ed. Austin. P. Evans. Columbia University Press. New York. 391. Latin original see *HISTORIA RERUM IN PARTIBUS TRANSMARINIS GESTARUM LIBER VIGESIMUS, CAPUT XXXI. Describitur Assissinorum secta, et missio legati eorum ad dominum regem.* '*Senem vocant; cui tantae subjectionis et obedientiae vinculo solent obligari, ut nihil sit tam durum, tam difficile tamque periculosum, quod ad magistri imperium, animis ardentibus non aggrediantur implere. Nam inter caetera, si quos habent principes odiosos aut genti suae suspectos, data uni de suis, vel pluribus, sica, non considerato rei exitu, utrum evadere possit, illuc contendit, cui mandatum est; et tam diu pro complendo anxius imperio, circuit et laborat, quousque casu injunctum peragat officium, praeceptoris mandato satisfaciens. Hos tam nostri quam Sarraceni (nescimus unde deducto nomine) Assissinos vocant.*'
98. Larousse defines '*Braie*' as '*culotte, pantalon, dans les costumes traditionnels de la Gaule et pendant le haut Moyen Âge.*'
99. Gestes des Chiprois. 201. *'382 Or vos diray ſe quy avint à monſeignor Odoart: il avint que .j. Sarazin home d'arme ſe vint batier à Acre, & meſſire Odoart le fiſt faire creſtien & le tint de ſon hoſtel. Ceſtu ſI fiſt atendant à meſſire Odoart que il yroit eſpier les Sarazins là où l'on lor poroit mauſaire, & avoir ja fait ce ſervize aucune fés; & par luy alerent nos gens à Saint Jorge & a Caco, dont meſſire Odouart ſe fia tant en luy, que il comanda que il ne fuſt defendu de parler à ly ni de jour ni de nut. Se que il avint une nut que il vint à la chambre où monſeignor Odoart ce dormoir o la raine, & mena o luy le durgeman, & fiſt etendant que il venoit d'eſpier & voloit parler à monſeignor Odoart, ſi que monſeignor ly ovry ſa chambre il meiſmes, veſtu ſoulement en chemiſe & braie, & le Sarazin s'acoſta à luy & le fery d'un coutiau ſur la hanche, quy ly fiſt un parſonde plaie & perelyouſe, & meſſire Odoart ſe ſenty feru & le fery .j. cop dou poin, par mi le temple, quy l'abaty eſtordi à terre une pieſſe, & puis priſt .j. coutiau de table quy eſtoit en la chambre, & le fery en la teſte & l'ociſt. Le cri ſe leva entre la mahnée, & virent lor ſeignor feru & jeterent le cry par la ville d'Acre, dont les ſeignors s'aſemblement là & firent venir tous les mieges & eſclas quy li ſuſerent ſa plaie & en traïſtrent le venim, dont il fu bien guary, la mercy Dieu, & ſe party à xxij. jors de ſetembre, & ala Outremer en ſa terre.*' English translation, Paul F. Crawford. 2003. *The Templar of Tyre: Part III of the deeds of the Cypriots*. Abingdon: Routledge. 86–87
100. Ibn al-Furat was a fourteenth-century Egyptian historian whose noted for verbatim quoting of primary sources.
101. Ibn al-Furat, 1971. *Ayyubids, Mamlukes and Crusaders*, vol 2: Translation, ed. Jonathan Riley-Smith, Malcolm Cameron Lyons, Ursula Lyons. Cambridge. W. Heffer & Sons Ltd. 159.
102. Charles L. Kingsford. 1909. *Sir Otho de Grandison 1238?–1328*. Transactions of the Royal Historical Society 3: 125–95. Citing 1 Chron. Bertini. '*Et audivi qui scribo, narrantibus [michi] quibusdam Sabaudinis viris honestis et fide dignis, sed narrata non visa narrantibus; dicebant enim, quod in Sabaudia dudum erat quidam dominus de Gransone, cui natus est filius. Vocati astronomi ad pueri nativitatem inspiciendam, calculandam seu iudicandam; qui dixerunt, puer natus, si viveret, magnus esset, potens et victoriosus. Interfuit unus supersticiosus seu forte divinus, qui, sumpta ex igne facula, dixit, quod hic puer tantum durabit quantum facula presens'. Pater assumptam faculam clausit in parietes, ut diucius duraret. Vixit iste puer, crevit et ad etatem senectam*

et senium duravit, semper in honore accrescens, donec nimio senio et vivendi tedio pertesus, faculam predictam parieti inclusam extrahi fecit et in igne proici; qua' penitus in igne consumpta', miles cito post expiravit. Dixerunt ultra narrantes, quod iste fatalis dominus de Gransone tunc cum aliis ultra mare existens', cum audiret filium regis Anglie, tam valentem virum, sic invenenatum, solus ausus fuit suggere[1] vulnera eius sic invenenata, forte confidens in fato suo predicto de facula; suxit igitur, et sic Edoardus sanatus est. Et exhine dominus iste de Gransone et sui penes reges Anglie elevati sunt et honorati, et adhuc hodie per Angliam magni reputantur et potentes.' John of Ypres died in 1383, but he entered the monastery in 1339, and may have heard the story not many years after Othon's death.

103. Alan Forey. 2017. 'Otto of Grandson and the Holy Land, Cyprus and Armenia'. *Crusades* 16. Taylor & Francis. 80. Otto's action is not mentioned in any contemporary source. The first writer to relate the sucking of poison from the wound was Ptolemy of Lucca, writing some forty years after the crusade, and he attributed the deed to Edward's wife Eleanor. He reports the story as merely a rumour, and the St. Bertin chronicler himself similarly referred to Otto's supposed action as something said by Savoyards: he even expressed his own doubts, as he added: '*Hec non assero nisi, ut dictum est, ex relatu.*' It would therefore appear unlikely that there was any substance in the claim.
104. Chron. Guisborough, Vol 1, 334–37.
105. Chron. Bertini. '*Et audivi qui scribo, narrantibus [michi] quibusdam Sabaudinis viris honestis et fide dignis, sed narrata non visa narrantibus; dicebant enim, quod in Sabaudia dudum erat quidam dominus de Gransone, cui natus est filius. Vocati astronomi ad pueri nativitatem inspiciendam, calculandam seu iudicandam; qui dixerunt, puer natus, si viveret, magnus esset, potens et victoriosus. Interfuit unus supersticiosus seu forte divinus, qui, sumpta ex igne facula, dixit, quod hic puer tantum durabit quantum facula presens'. Pater assumptam faculam clausit in parietes, ut diucius duraret. Vixit iste puer, crevit et ad etatem senectam et senium duravit, semper in honore accrescens, donec nimio senio et vivendi tedio pertesus, faculam predictam parieti inclusam extrahi fecit et in igne proici; qua' penitus in igne consumpta', miles cito post expiravit. Dixerunt ultra narrantes, quod iste fatalis dominus de Gransone tunc cum aliis ultra mare existens', cum audiret filium regis Anglie, tam valentem virum, sic invenenatum, solus ausus fuit suggere[1] vulnera eius sic invenenata, forte confidens in fato suo predicto de facula; suxit igitur, et sic Edoardus sanatus est. Et exhine dominus iste de Gransone et sui penes reges Anglie elevati sunt et honorati, et adhuc hodie per Angliam magni reputantur et potentes.*'
106. Christopher Tyerman. 1996. *England and the Crusades, 1095–1588*. Chicago: University of Chicago Press. 125.
107. Fœdra, 495.
108. Alan Forey. 2017. 'Otto of Grandson and the Holy Land, Cyprus and Armenia'. *Crusades* 16. Taylor & Francis. 80.
109. Michael Prestwich. 2020. 'Othon I de Grandson (vers 1240–1328)'. Lausanne: Cahiers Lausannois d'Histoire Médiévale. 5. The article was published in French, but I am indebted to Michael Prestwich for supplying the original English text which has been cited here.
110. TNA E101/333/15.
111. Chron. Guisborough, Vol 1, 336. '*et ait duobus primo nominatis, domino scilicet Edmundo et domino Johanni de Vescy, 'Numquid et vos diligitis dominum vestrum?'*'

et dixerunt 'Utique:' et ait, 'Tollite ergo mulierem hanc et non videat eam dominus ejus quousque dixero vobis;' tulerunt ergo eam flentem et ejulantem; et dixerunt, 'Sine, domina, melius est quod tu effundas lachrymas quam quod lachrymetur tota terra Anglicana' Or 'and he said to the two first named, namely Sir Edmund and Sir Jean de Vescy, 'Do you also love your master?' and they said, 'Of course.' And he said, 'Take this woman away, and let her master not see her until I tell you.' therefore they took her away weeping and wailing; and they said, 'No, madam, it is better that you should shed tears than that all the land of England should weep.'

112. CChR Henry III Edward I vol 2 1257–1300, 149 & 177. 'Aug 2 [1270], Winchester . . . *Inspeximus* and confirmation of a charter . . . witnesses. . . Sir Otho de Graunzon. . . dated at York, 18 September [1267] 52 Henry III.' And 'Nov 1 [1271], Westminster. . . *Inspeximus* and confirmation of a charter . . . witnesses. . . Sir John de Greylli. . . Sir Otho de Grandisono. . .given by the hand of the said Edward at Woodstock, 14 July [1267] 52 Henry III.'
113. Steven Runciman. 1954. *A History of the Crusades: Volume III The Kingdom of Acre and the later Crusades*. Eleventh Edition. London: The Folio Society. 282.
114. Alain Demurger. 2018. '*Othon de Grandson et les templiers d'Épailly*' in *Communicating the Middle Ages: Essays in Honour of Sophia Menache*. London: Routledge. 39. '*Le prince Edouard rentra en Angleterre en novembre 1272, toujours accompagné d'Othon de Grandson. Il faut corriger l'erreur, encore souvent reproduite, qui veut qu'en quittant la Terre sainte, le prince ait laissé sur place un important corps de chevaliers avec Othon de Grandson comme capitaine En réalité c'est un autre familier du prince, un quasi compatriote d'Othon, le genevois Jean de Grilly, (Grilly, c. Gex, Ain, France) qui fut laissé sur place comme sénéchal du rovaume de Jérusalem.*' Or 'Prince Edward returned to England in November 1272, always accompanied by Othon de Grandson. We must correct the error, still often reproduced, which says that when leaving the Holy Land, the prince left behind a large body of knights with Othon de Grandson as captain. In reality it is another familiar of the prince, a quasi-compatriot of Otto, the Genevan Jean de Grilly, (Grilly, c. Gex, Ain, France) who was left behind as seneschal of the Kingdom of Jerusalem.' Henri Moranvillé. Ed. 1891. *Chronographia regum Francorum,* 2 vols. Paris. 2: 5 'In *Acon vero tunc erat Otho de Grandissone quem dudum, ut dictum est supra, custodem seu capitaneum reliquerat rex Anglorum Edowardus cum magna milicia*' or 'In Acre, then, was Othon de Grandson, whom Edward, king of the English, had left a long time ago, as has been said above, as guard or captain, with a large army.' Alain Demurger. 2018. '*Othon de Grandson et les templiers d'Épailly*' in *Communicating the Middle Ages: Essays in Honour of Sophia Menache*. London: Routledge. 47. n5. '*Chronographia regum Francorum, éd. Henri Moranvillé*, 2 vols., (Paris, 1891), 2: 5 '*est à l'origine de cette erreur: Edouard, alors qu'il quittait la Terre sainte, relinquit, loco sui, capitaneum Othonem de Grandisono, militem probum ac in armis strenuum, cui dimisit ad manutenendum guerram contra Saracenos.*' Or 'Chronography of the Kings of the Franks, Ed. Henri Moranvillé, 2 vols., (Paris, 1891), 2: 5 is at the origin of this error: Edward, while he was leaving the Holy Land, 'leaves, in his place, captain Othon de Grandisono, a good soldier and in the mighty men of arms, whom he sent to maintain the war against the Saracens.'
115. Baibars would die before the eventual fall of Acre, dying at Damascus on 1 July 1277, but his dynasty the Bahriyya Mamluks would last in Egypt and the Levant until 1517.

116. MS. Ashmole. 342.
117. C. Köhler, 1903–4. '*Deux projets de croisade en terre-sainte composée à la fin du xiiie siècle et au debut du xive*'. *Revue de l'Orient Latin*. 435–36. '*fecit sermonem proclamari in maiori ecclesia Anco[ni]- tana, scilicet Sancte Crucis, in quo nos, huius scripti compositores. presentes affuimus.*' Or 'he [Gregory X] caused the sermon to be proclaimed in the greater church of Ancon[ni]-tana [Acre] that is, of the Holy Cross, in which we, the composers of this writing, we were present.' For the view that Othon de Grandson was 'very possibly' the author see Michael Prestwich. 1997. *Edward I*. Yale: Yale University Press. 75. 'A treatise written within the next twenty years, very possibly by Otto de Grandson, implies that all was not well with the English forces when they disembarked. With the knowledge of hindsight, the treatise argued that it was best for crusaders to arrive in autumn, preferably in Armenia, so that the army and in particular its horses could be ready to march on Jerusalem in the following spring. To land at Acre in early summer had major disadvantages, as the horses would be in bad condition after the sea voyage, and fodder was hard to obtain.' And Esther Rowland Clifford. 1961. *A Knight of Great Renown: The Life and Times of Othon de Grandson*. Chicago: University of Chicago Press. 27. For the contrary view see Alan Forey. 2017. 'Otto of Grandson and the Holy Land, Cyprus and Armenia'. *Crusades*. 16.
118. Chron. Thomas Wykes, 247-8. '*Eodem anno quarto nonas Aprilis apud castrum de Berkamestede obiit Ricardus rex Alemanniae, et sepultus est in abbatia de Hailes, quam a fundamentis sumptibus suis construxerat.*' Or 'In the same year [1272], on the fourth of April, Richard, king of Germany, died at the castle of Berkhamstead, and was buried in the abbey of Hailes, which from the foundations he had built it at his own expense.'
119. Chron. Thomas Wykes, 252. '*Die Mercurii in festo Sancti Edmundi quondam Cantuariensis archiepiscopi, videlicet xvi. kal. Decembris piæ recordationis Henricus rex Anglorum serenissimus, carnis mole deposita, hominem terrenuin exuens, momentaneam mundi gloriam cellesti palatio commutavit, cum Rege regum perpetuo regnaturus in cœlis; Dominica proxima sequente, videlicet in festo beatissimi regis et martyris Edmundi, in nobilissima basilica Westmonasterii, quam opere sumptuoso et incomparabili a fundamentis extruxerat, regni magnatibus exequias debitas impendentibus, cum ea qua decuit honorificentia tumulatus: sane corpus ipsius pretiosissimis indumentis et diademate regio, prout decuit, adornatum, omni assistentium judicio, cum a nobilioribus regni ad hoc officium praeelectis in locello portatili deferretur ad tumulum, ampliori splendore decoris effulgebat mortuum, quam prius dum vixerat appareret.*' Or 'On Wednesday, on the feast of St. Edmund, once archbishop of Canterbury, viz. 16 cal. In December of pious remembrance, Henry, the most serene king of the English, laid aside the bulk of the flesh, put off the earthly man, exchanged the momentary glory of the world for the heavenly palace, and was to reign eternally in heaven as the King of kings; On the following Sunday, that is to say, on the feast of the blessed king and martyr Edmund, in the most noble basilica of Westminster, which he had built from the foundations with a sumptuous and incomparable work, the grandees of the kingdom were given the due funerals, and he was buried with the honour due to him: of course, his body was clad in the most precious clothes and the royal diadem, as it was due adorned, according to the judgment of all the attendants, when it was carried to the tomb in a portable casket by the nobles of the kingdom pre-selected for this office, with a greater splendour of beauty the dead king shone brighter than before when he had lived.'

120. Walter of Guisborough quoted in Darren Baker. 2017. *Henry III: The Great King England Never Knew It Had*. Stroud: The History Press. 803.
121. Ibid. 813.
122. James Birchall. 1873. *England under the Normans and Plantagenets: An Historical Manual*. London: Simplin, Marshall & Co. 108.
123. Robert Bartlett. 1993. *The Making of Europe: Conquest, Colonization and Cultural Change 950–1350*. London: Penguin Books Ltd. 404.

Chapter 3

1. Dante Alighieri. *Canto XII.* In translation 'A spirit by itself apart retir'd, Exclaim'd: 'He in God's bosom smote the heart, Which yet is honour'd on the bank of Thames'.' The spirit cast alone and by itself is taken to be Guy de Montfort as he is in the seventh circle reserved for men of violence having committed murder in 'God's bosom' that is to say a church of Henri d'Almayne, a man 'honour'd on the bank of the Thames.'
2. Chron. Flores. vol 3. 22. '*Unus de interfectoribus suis, Symon, filius Symonis de Monte Forti, in castro quodam juxta civitatem Senensem obiit in hoc anno, qui nuper, tanquam Chaim, maledictus a Domino, vagus fuit et profugus super terram.*' Or 'One of his slayers, Simon, the son of Simon of Montfort, died in this year in a certain castle near the city of Siena, who had lately, like Cain, cursed by the Lord, been a wanderer and a fugitive on earth.'
3. CPR Henry III vol 3 1232–1247, 469. 'Jan 16 [1246], Westminster. Grant to Amadeus, count of Savoy and marquess in Italy, for the homage which he has done to the king for the castle of Avyllan [Avigliana], the town of Susa, with the palace and castle of Bard and the town of St. Maurice in Chablais, to hold to him and his heirs of the king and his heirs in perpetual fee, of 1,000l. at London at the Exchequer, whereof the king has paid 500 marks in hand and will pay 500 marks at Easter next and the remaining 500 marks at Michaelmas following.' Latin text Wurstemberger, vol 4. No 191. '*Amedeus IV Comes recognoscit in feudum a rege Angliæ castra de Aviliana, de Bardo, et villas Secusiæ et S. Mauritii in Chablasio, pro qua recognitione accipit Comes a rege Mille libras Sterlingorum. 1246. Januarii 16. ap. Westmonasterium. Tria diplomata Heorici Regis, pro Amedeo, Comite Sabaudiæ et Marchione Italiæ. Rex concedit Amedeo, Com.Sab, et March, in Italia, pro homagio quod fecit pro Castro Auyllan et villa Secucie, cum Pallacio et castro de Bardo et villa S. Mauritii in Chablasio, tenendis de Rege et heredibus suis sibi et heredibus suis in feodo imperpetuum, M. libras bonorum Sterlingorum de thesauro suo, percipiendas London. ad Scaccarium Regis de dono suo. De quibus M. libris Rex solvit ei, pro manibus, D. marcas, et ei solvere tenetur D. marcas ad festum Pasche anno regni suo tricesimo; et residua D. marcarum ad festum S. Michaelis anno eodem, preter feodnm suum quod percipere debet ad eundem terminum.*'
4. Michael Prestwich. 1997. *Edward I.* Yale: Yale University Press. 84. 'The accounts of his officials show that much was made of Edward's arrival in Savoy. The castellan of Rivoli sent two messengers to meet him, and another to inform the count of his arrival. Edward was then presented with gifts of wine, beef and other foodstuffs. The bailiff of Montmelian bought ten oxen and fifty-nine lambs ready for a feast for Edward and

provided him with an escort.' Citing AST Inv. Sav. 51. Fo. 257. Mazzo I, no 8. Eugene L. Cox. 1974. *The Eagles of Savoy: The House of Savoy in Thirteenth Century Europe*. Princeton: Princeton University Press. 411.

5. At Conwy castle. See the authors earlier book. John Marshall. 2022. Welsh Castle Builders: The Savoyard Style. Pen & Sword Books: Barnsley, 23 & 123.
6. Those in Edward's party are detailed in Arnold Taylor. 1985. *Studies in Castles and Castle-Building*. London: The Hambledon Press. 29 and 35. See also Michael Prestwich. 1997. *Edward I*. Yale: Yale University Press. 84. 'Edward's most important companions at this stage of his journey were John de Vescy, Roger Clifford and Otto de Grandson.'
7. Chron. Thomas Wykes. 255. *'die Mercurii proxima post festum Sanctæ Trinitatis descendit de monte Cenisii, et in quindena Sanctæ Trinitatis venit apud Sanctum Georgium prope Lugdunum.'* Or 'from the Wednesday next after the feast of the Holy Trinity they descended from Mont Cenis and arrived at Saint-Georges near Lyon.'
8. Ibid. Dates added in the margin by the translator. See also Henry Gough. *Itinerary of King Edward the First throughout his reign, A.D. 1272–1307, exhibiting his movements so far as they are recorded.* vol 1. Paisley: Alexander Gardner, 1900. 24.
9. Eugene L. Cox. 1974. *The Eagles of Savoy: The House of Savoy in Thirteenth Century Europe*. Princeton: Princeton University Press. 411–12.
10. Writing in Arnold Taylor. 1985. *Studies in Castles and Castle-Building*. London: The Hambledon Press. 34 Taylor suggest that 'work on the castle probably began in about 1268 or 1269; that by the beginning of 1271 some part of it was already in use … building went on for a further three years or so'.
11. Chron. Thomas Wykes. 255. Dates added in the margin by the translator. See also Henry Gough. 1900. *Itinerary of King Edward the First throughout his reign, A.D. 1272–1307, exhibiting his movements so far as they are recorded.* vol 1. Paisley: Alexander Gardner. 24.
12. *La Finanza Sabauda*. vol. 1, xiv and xvi. '[For] 1270 à 1272 *Deux comptes de Thomas de Becunet châtelain de St. George de Livrées par lui faittes à divers ouvriers pour la fabrique et des livrées à l'occasion du reçu des droits de la Châtelainie de St. George.*'
13. Arnold Taylor. 1985. *Studies in Castles and Castle-Building*. London: The Hambledon Press. 33. '*Sentence prononcée par Edmond, fils du roi d'Angleterre ... Attum apud Sanctum Georgium de Speranchia.*' Citing *Rég. Dauph ii,* no. 10980. And *La Finanza Sabauda*. vol. 2, 123 *'Die June in festo beati Laurencii* [10 August 1271] *apud Sanctum Georgium de Sperenchi ... [Pro] Camera domini mundanda.'*
14. M. Chabord was Engineer of the Bridges and Roads of the Isère Department in 20th Fructidor of the Second Year of the French Republic one and indivisible – 11 September 1794.
15. The name *Carré Savoyard or Savoyard Square* is a non contemporary description of a castle building style common in thirteenth century Savoy. Typically, the curtain walls make a square with a round tower at each corner, often one of which is enlarged to form the *donjon* or keep. At Saint-Georges the standard was adapted by the use of polygonal towers.
16. Malcolm Hislop. 2020. *James of St. George and the Castles of North Wales*. Barnsley: Pen & Sword Books Ltd.
17. ADI Serie L, no. 198, pacquet 1. The letters in the following report by Chabord relate to the accompanying colour-wash plan '*Le cydevant Château d 'Espéranche est flanque de quatre tours A, octogones (voir le plan cyjoint figure), dont les murs ont cinq pieds d'épaisseur.*

Vers le sommet de ces tours, il existe quelques embrasures. Les murs extérieurs de cedit bâtiment, ainsi que le mur BC servant de clôture à la grande cour du côté du nord, ont aussi semblable épaisseur. Des fossés, comme le plan l'indique, regment tour au tour de ce vaste bâtiment, et ont de largeur depuis trente a cinquente pieds, sur dix a dix-huit pieds de hauteur.' Or 'The side of the Château d'Espéranche is flanked by four towers (A), octagons (see the plan attached figure), the walls of which are five feet thick. Towards the top of these towers there are a few embrasures. The exterior walls of this building, as well as the wall (B–C) serving as an enclosure for the great courtyard on the north side, are also of similar thickness. Ditches as the plan indicates, surround this vast building, and are thirty to fifty feet wide, and ten to eighteen feet high.' We thus have the best description we can now have of the Château d'Espéranche. The surviving elements of the castle in 1794 being the four towers (A), one face of the curtain wall (B–C) and the surrounding moat, which was then drained to a marsh on its northern face. But enough had survived until 1794 to identify a Carré Savoyard, but with octagonal not round towers.

18. *Fœdera*. 504. *'UNIVERSIS presentes literas inspecturis, Philippus comes Sabaudia, salutem in Domino. Noverit universitas vestra quod nos fatemur recepisse serenissimo principe, domino Edwardo, DEI gratiâ, ilustrissimo Rege Angliæ, in feodum, castrum Avillan', villam secus, cum palatio & castro de Bardo, & villam sancti Mauritii in Chablay, qua & quas sub eo modo retinemus & retinebimus, sicut ea tenuit à, recolende memorie, domino H, patre dicti domini Regis, quondam dominus Amedeus comes Sabaud• frater noster; Et, pro predicts feodo & terris, fatemur nos magium, in manibus predicti domini Regis. fecisse presentialiter ho- In cujus rei testimonium presentes literas fieri fecimus patentes, nostro sigillo munitas, apud Sanctum Georgium de Sperench', xxv. die Junii, anno Domini MCCLXXIII.'*
19. Arnold Taylor. 1985. *Studies in Castles and Castle-Building*. London: The Hambledon Press. 41.
20. Ibid. 42.
21. *Fœdera*. 504. *'en la presence le noble baron mon sire Phelip counte de Sauvoye e de Burgoyne. Mon sire Johan de Vescy. Mon sire Roger de Clyfford. Sire Simon de Genevile. Sire Otes de Grantson'*. See also Michael Prestwich. 1997. *Edward I*. Yale: Yale University Press. 84. 'The witness list to this deed reveals that Edward's most important companions at this stage of his journey were John de Vescy, Roger Clifford and Otto de Grandson.'
22. *Fœdera*. 504. *'quoddam castrum apud Abrunol prope castrum de Monte Gomery de novo engere ... Vobis mandamus districte inhibentes, ne castrum illud construere'*. Or 'a new castle at Abrunol near to the castle of Montgomery ... we order strictly prohibiting the construction of a castle'.
23. Jean-Pierre Chapuisat. 1964. *'Au service de deux rois d'Angleterre au XIIIe siècle: Pierre de Champvent,' Revue historique vaudoise* 72: 163. n.2.
24. Ibid. The charter bears the usual Savoyard witness list: Imbert Pugeys, Ebal II de Mont, Pierre de Champvent, Imbert de Montferrand and Guillaume de Champvent.
25. CPR Edward I vol 1 1272–1281, 49. 'April 24 [1274], Westminster. Grant to Lewis de Sabaudia of the deanery of the church of St. Martin-le-Grand, London, void by the promotion of William de Chaumpvent, late dean, to be bishop of Lausanne.'
26. CCR Edward I vol 1 1272–1279, 119. 'April 7 [1274]. Peter de Chaumpvent, who is going to parts beyond sea by the king's licence, has given power to William de Bonevill

to make attorneys for him until Michaelmas next, unless he return to England in the meantime.'

27. Jean-Daniel Morerod. 2012. *La Cathédrale Notre-Dame de Lausanne: Monument européen, temple vaudois.* Lausanne: La Bibliothèque des Arts. 22.
28. Esther Rowland Clifford. 1961. *A Knight of Great Renown: The Life and Times of Othon de Grandson.* Chicago: University of Chicago Press. 46.
29. Sara Cockerill. 2014. Eleanor of Castile: The Shadow Queen. Second Edition. Stroud: Amberley Publishing. 267.
30. Henry Gough. 1900. *Itinerary of King Edward the First throughout his reign, A.D. 1272–1307, exhibiting his movements so far as they are recorded vol. 1.* Paisley: Alexander Gardner. 25.
31. Edward interestingly uses the same words in paying homage to Philippe as his father Henry had earlier used with Louis following the Treaty of Paris in 1259. Edward swearing that he was Philippe's man for 'all the lands I ought to hold from you'. Opinion is divided as to whether we should read anything into the 'ought' in terms of lost Plantagenet lands in France, but since it would have been expressed in French as *devrait* which can be translated as either should or ought and thus implied criticism of Capetian holding of Plantagenet lands. Furthermore, the language can be read as confirming that Aquitaine had been an allodial fief before 1259 and had not subsequently lost that status by the terms of the treaty of Paris, because the homage depended, upon complete fulfilment of the terms of the 1259 treaty. Since the lost lands had not been restored as agreed, then Aquitaine, so the argument goes, reverted to being an allod, and was not the subject of French suzerainty. It was argued that the homage performed by Henry III applied only to those lands given him by Louis IX in exchange for Henry's renunciation of Normandy, Poitou, Maine, Touraine, and Anjou. Thus, when Edward performed his homage in 1273, he swore fealty for those lands which he 'ought to hold' from the king of France by implication, Edward neither recognised, nor owed, any feudal obligations for Aquitaine because the kings of France had failed to relinquish the lands promised in the treaty of Paris, and so were, essentially, in breach of contract. These legal niceties would become crucial twenty years later when Philippe IV attempted to seize Gascony from Edward.
32. Ann. Trevet. 281-3.
33. The name *Curtana* or *Curtein* (from the Latin *curtus*, meaning short).
34. Michael Prestwich. 1997. *Edward I.* Yale: Yale University Press. 90.
35. Edward would not be seated on the well-known 'King Edward's Chair' used most recently at Elizabeth II's coronation in 1953, since Edward had the chair made in 1296, some twenty-two years after his own coronation.
36. The *Laudes Regiæ* had its origins in ancient Rome, when emperors had entered the Eternal City after triumph in a great battle, they were met by the chants of the people.
37. CCR Edward I vol 1 1272–1279. 68. 'Feb 10 [1274], Westminster. To the Sheriff of Gloucester. Order to provide 60 oxen and cows, 60 swine, 2 fat boars, 60 live sheep, 3,000 capons and hens and 40 bacon-pigs against the king's coronation feast at the octaves of Easter … Like orders for various quantities of provisions to the sheriffs of the following counties: Buckingham and Before, Oxford, Kent, Surrey and Sussex, Warwick and Leicester, Somerset and Dorset and Essex.' There are further copious orders of food to be provided 'for the king's use' dated 28 February on the subsequent pages of the CCR.

38. Robert Kilwardby would be an archbishop with but a walk-on part in the life of Edward, he had been appointed by Pope Gregory X in 1272 while Edward was returning from the Holy Land and would leave Canterbury and England for an Italian cardinal's hat in 1278. He died in Italy in 1279 and was buried in the Dominican convent in Viterbo, Italy.
39. CPR Henry III vol 4 1247–1258, 270. 'Charter granting to Edward, eldest son and heir of the king ... all of the county of Chester with its castles and towns, with the conquest of Wales by the king within these limits, namely Rothelan, Dissard and Gannoc [Deganwy] and the other land of Pervethelat [Perfeddwlad]; ... the castle of Buelt [Builth] ... 14th February 1254, Bazas, Gascony, France.' We should note also that two of the witnesses of Edward's appanage were the Savoyards Pierre de Savoie and Pierre d'Aigueblanche.
40. *Fœdera.* 505. '*Litteræ L. principis Walliæ, de invitatione suâ ad festum coronationis Regis Angliæ.*' or 'Letter to Llywelyn, Prince of Wales, on his invitation to the feast of the coronation of the King of England.'
41. E. B. Fryde, D. E. Greenway, S. Porter & I. Roy. 1986. *Handbook of British Chronology*. Third Edition. London: Offices of the Royal Historical Society. 85.
42. Robert Burnell had been born in 1239 at the village which carried his family name, Acton Burnell in Shropshire. He had worked as a clerk in Henry's royal chancery, the office that wrote all the royal documents before, by 1257, moving into Edward's personal household.
43. CChR Henry III Edward I vol 2 1257–1300, 187. The Witness list to this charter is not recorded in the CChR but is listed in The Royal Charter Witness Lists of Edward I (1272–1307) from The Charter Rolls in the Public Record Office transcribed and edited with an introduction by Richard Huscroft, List and Index Society, no. 279 (1999), 2. (Then Huscroft, Witnesses)
44. Michael Prestwich. 2020. *Othon de Grandson et la Cour d'Edouard I' in Othon I de Grandson (vers 1240–1328)*. Lausanne: Cahiers Lausannois d'Histoire Médiévale. 14.
45. CPR Edward I vol 1 1272–1281: 77. 'Jan 18 [1275], Clarendon. Power to Otto de Grandisono and Antony Bek to contract a loan from merchants to the amount of 3^000 marks.' 85. 'April 29 [1275], Westminster. Acknowledgment of a loan of 391l. 13s. 4d. sterling, received from Perogius. Scoualaco, William Ganebieu, Reginald de Molin[is], and Reginald de Monachaco, and their fellows, of the society of Scotusof Piacenza, merchant of the pope, by Otto de Grandisono and Antony Bek, at Paris, for the expediting of the king's business, with promise to repay the same within the feast of All Saints next.' 98. 'June 24 [1275], Westminster. The like to the same to pay out of the said money at the said fair to Teglarius Amadoris, James Aymery, Hugelin de Vicchio, and their fellows, merchants of Florence, 500 pounds of Tours, which they advanced, as a loan to the king, to Otto de Grandissono and Antony Bek, for the latter to deliver to Enieric, vicomte de Rocheciiouard and Stephen de Monte Forti, knights, in payment of the king's debts, and which the said knights acknowledge they have received.'
46. The English archives give us some of the detail of his expenses at this time, all handled by the Wardrobe and the good offices of the Riccardi of Lucca: merchants at Acre some 880 *livres* and a further 1,333 *livres* 6 *sol* and 8 *den*.
47. CPR Edward I vol 1 1272 – 1281, 77, 85, 98. Text above.
48. Francis Palgrave. 1827. The Parliamentary Writs. London. Vol 1. 642. '1275. Grandisono, Otto de. Present in Parliament at Westminster, on Sunday the Feast of Saint Dunstan. 19 May.'

49. Danby Pickering. 1762. The Statutes at Large: From the Magna Charta to the End of the Eleventh Parliament of Great Britain, Anno 1761 [continued to 1806]. Vol. I. Cambridge: Joseph Bentham. 80. Cap V. And Tomlins, Thomas Edlyne; John Raithby. 1810. Statute of Westminster 1275 [3 Edw. I.–A.D. 1275 Statute I]. The Statutes of the Realm: Printed by Command of His Majesty King George the Third; in pursuance of an Address of the House of Commons of Great Britain. Vol. I. London, Great Britain: Dawson of Pall Mall. 28.
50. Francis Palgrave. 1827. The Parliamentary Writs. London. Vol 1. 642.
51. Prestwich suggests the Annalist of Dunstable, who is our source in this regard, may have meant Orlandino da Pogio who was a leading member of the Riccardi of Lucca. See Michael Prestwich. 1997. *Edward I.* Yale: Yale University Press. 100. n39.
52. Richard W. Kaeuper. 1973. *Bankers to the Crown: The Riccardi of Lucca and Edward I.* Princeton: Princeton University Press. 81.
53. TNA E101/261/1.
54. TNA E372/143 m 35d.
55. Richard W. Kaeuper. 1973. *Bankers to the Crown: The Riccardi of Lucca and Edward I.* Princeton: Princeton University Press. 2–4.
56. Thomas W. Blomquist, 1971. 'Commercial Association in Thirteenth-Century Lucca,' *The Business History Review* 45: 159.
57. Ibid. 160.
58. Richard W. Kaeuper. 1973. *Bankers to the Crown: The Riccardi of Lucca and Edward I.* Princeton: Princeton University Press. 5.
59. Ibid. 27.
60. Michael Prestwich. 1997. *Edward I.* Yale: Yale University Press. 81. Philip de Berizon of Genoa another 666 *livres* 13 *sol* and 4 *den*, to the Templars in Paris some 4,000 *livres*, the carriage of a chest with silks and carpets 18 *sol*, furs acquired in Bruges for the upcoming coronation another 100 *livres*, in total 7,687 *livres* paid to Robert Burnell in London on his behalf by the merchants of Lucca. Loans from the Riccardi, to cover the period from his arrival at Trapani until his arrival in England totalled another £22,364, being a king on crusade and his travels was proving a costly business, but one the merchants of Lucca were happy to finance. See CPR Edward I vol 1 1272–1281, 131–32. An example of both the influence of Othon de Grandson and the Riccardi at this point concerns the Italian involvement in the profitable wool trade. The Riccardi undertook to buy 120 sacks of wool from the abbot of the Cistercian house of Meaux in Holderness, Yorkshire at the Boston fair. The abbot subsequently reneged on delivery of the wool, the Riccardi wrote seeking redress to, among others, their friend and customer, Grandson. See Richard W. Kaeuper. *Bankers to the Crown: The Riccardi of Lucca and Edward I.* Princeton: Princeton University Press, 1973. 37.
61. TNA E159 / m 63 31d. His brother, Henri de Grandson, the Bishop of Verdun from 1278, is known to have received loans from the Riccardi in the 1290s, another who received loans was the Prior of Wenlock, Henri de Bonvillars, brother of Jean de Bonvillars, who would owe some one hundred marks in 1290.
62. Francis Palgrave, Ed. 1836. *The Ancient Kalendars and Inventories of the Treasury of his Majesty's Exchequer*, vol 1: London, 80. '*Consimilis obligacio Johis de Vescy [e]t Ottonis de Grandissono de. jiml. D. li. Turon, sub dat a°. Dñi mittmo. como. lxxiido.*'

63. Richard W. Kaeuper. 1973. *Bankers to the Crown: The Riccardi of Lucca and Edward I.* Princeton: Princeton University Press. 28–30.
64. E. B. Fryde, D. E. Greenway, S. Porter & I. Roy. 1986. *Handbook of British Chronology.* Third Edition. London: Offices of the Royal Historical Society. 35. Burnell had been one of the regents ruling England in Edward's absence on Crusade, along with Walter Giffard, Archbishop of York, and Roger de Mortimer. Antony Bek, Joseph de Chauncy, Othon de Grandson and Jean de Vesci had been with Edward in the Holy Land.
65. Richard W. Kaeuper. 1973. *Bankers to the Crown: The Riccardi of Lucca and Edward I.* Princeton: Princeton University Press. 85.
66. CPR Henry III vol 4 1247–1258, 237–8. 'July 25 [1253], Portsmouth, Notification that William de Vescy, in the king's presence at Portesmuth, on the day of St. Mary Magdalen, 37 Henry III, bound himself by oath to procure that his firstborn son and heir, or in case of his death his next heir, should marry one of the daughters of the lord of Chambre or one of the daughters of the vicomte of Aosta so that by the award of four good men selected by the said William, and four good men selected by the counsel of the queen and Peter de Sabaudia, or either of them, there shall be provision of a certain sum of money to be assigned to the said son for his marriage. For the observance of all these things faithfully and without fraud, the said William bound himself on his fealty in the king's hand (fide media in manu nostra) and Peter de Sabaudia in the same hand swore to procure performance thereof, and the said William laid himself under the royal and ecclesiastical jurisdiction that he and his heirs should be distrained by any compulsion of the king or the ecclesiastical court to fulfil this covenant under pain of 1,000 marks he laid himself also under the compulsion of the archbishop of Canter- bury by ecclesiastical censure. Witnesses: John de Plessetis, earl of Warwick, John son of Geoffrey, justiciary of Ireland, John de Grey, Robert Walerand, Master W. de Kilkenni, archdeacon of Coventry, Philip Luvel, treasurer of London, Henry de Wengham and others.'
67. Chron. Thomas Wykes, 197–8. '*Edward. cordia, gratiso se submisit, qui pius et misericors non solum distulit ultionem, sed et veniam tribuit transgressori.*' Or 'Edward of the heart willingly submitted himself, which is not only pious and merciful, but he not only deferred vengeance, but also pardoned the transgressor.'

Chapter 4

1. CCR Edward I vol 1 1272–1279, 136. '3 Nov [1274], Northampton. 'To Llywelyn, son of Griffin, Prince of Wales. Order to come to the king at Shrewsbury on Sunday after St. Andrew and the other things he ought to do to him.'
2. Llywelyn Fawr or Llywelyn the Great was Llywelyn ap Iorwerth. He succeeded as Prince of Gwynedd in 1200 and during the reign of King John sought to turn the English king's troubles to his advantage by growing Gwynedd into an overlordship of all Welsh rulers.
3. Dr. Adam Chapman. 'Bryn Derwin 1255' The Inventory of Historic Battlefields in Wales. Last modified Jan 2017. http://battlefields.rcahmw.gov.uk/wp-content/uploads/2017/02/Bryn-Derwin-1255-Chapman-2013.pdf.
4. J. Beverley Smith. 2014. *Llywellyn ap Gruffudd: Prince of Wales*. Ebook. ed. Cardiff: University of Wales Press. 82. Suggests his mother to have either been a Senana (more likely) or a Rhunalt (less likely.)

5. *Princeps Walliae*, Prince of Wales was a new term in 1245, one Dafydd ap Llywelyn Fawr had begun styling himself thus in 1244; before the Norman conquest Welsh leaders had sometimes styled themselves '*Reges* or Kings of the Britons'.
6. Dafydd ap Llywelyn had signed the Treaty of Gwerneigron in 1241. Clause 12 said, 'In these and all other matters Dafydd will be at the wish and command of the king and obey the law in all things in his court.' TNA C66/49. Following a rebellion and the death of Dafydd, Llywelyn ap Gruffydd, his nephew had signed the Treaty of Woodstock in 1247. Clause 1 said, 'Owain and Llywelyn will likewise give their homages to the king and his heirs.' And Clause 2, 'Owain and Llywelyn grant and quitclaim for ever the Four Cantrefi.' TNA E36 /274. Henceforth the four cantrefi were given to the then Lord Edward as his appanage. Subsequently Llywelyn ap Gruffydd had taken advantage of royal weakness in following the Second Baronial War to recover the cantrefi and the title Prince of Wales at the 1267 Treaty of Montgomery. TNA C5 3/56.
7. David Carpenter. 2020. *Henry III: The Rise to Power and Personal Rule 1207–1258*. New Haven: Yale University Press. 74–77.
8. Montgomery Castle had first been built from 1071 by Roger de Montgomery who had come to Britain with William the Conqueror, the family fief lying in Normandy, including Saint-Germain-de-Montgomery and Sainte-Foy-de-Montgomery.
9. CCR Edward I vol 1 1272–1279, 51. 'June 23 [1273], Westminster. To L[lewelyn] son of Griffin, prince of Wales. Inhibition of his erecting a castle at Abrunol near the castle of Montegomery, or a borough or town there, or a market there, ordering him t o supersede entirely the repair and construction of the same, so that the king may nut be compelled to apply his hand otherwise to this, as the king learns that he proposes to erect anew the said castle and to erect anew & borough or town and market'
10. Fitz being 'son' (of) from the Old French *filz*, the origin of the modern French *fils*.
11. The *famille de Clare* had its origins like most of the Anglo-Norman nobility, in Normandy itself. Gilbert was descended from Richard de Clare, the eldest son of Gilbert de Brionne, a fief midway between Lisieux and Evreux and south of Rouen. Richard (and his brother Baldwin) had crossed the Channel with William in 1066, and were rewarded with much land, including Tonbridge (of which more later) and the fief of Clare in Suffolk, hence the family name.
12. J. Beverley Smith. 2014. *Llywellyn ap Gruffudd: Prince of Wales*. Ebook. ed. Cardiff: University of Wales Press. Apple.
13. Derek Renn. 1989. *Caerffili Castle*. Revised ed. Cardiff: Cadw. 10.
14. Ibid. 3.
15. R.R. Davies. 1987. *The Age of Conquest: Wales 1063–1415*. Oxford: Oxford University Press. 322.
16. J. Beverley Smith. 2014. *Llywellyn ap Gruffudd: Prince of Wales*. Ebook. ed. Cardiff: University of Wales Press. Apple.
17. Ibid.
18. John E. Morris. 1901. *The Welsh Wars of Edward I*. Oxford: Clarendon Press. 111. 'It was rather a truce than a peace, for obviously there was not yet a final settlement.'
19. J. Beverley Smith calculates those payments were made in full and promptly between 1267 and 1269, that the 1270 payment was only partially made in part payments, thereafter payments continue in sporadic fashion until they dry up completely.
20. CCR Edward I vol 1 1272–1279, 2. 'Dec 2 [1272], Westminster. To Llywelyn, son of Griffin, Prince of Wales. Whereas according to the form of peace concluded between

the late king and Llewelyn, the latter is bound to the king in 3,000 marks to be paid at Christmas next ... This Llywelyn is to neglect in no wise, as he loves the king and his honour, and as the king specially trusts him.'

21. J. Beverley Smith. 2014. *Llywellyn ap Gruffudd*: Prince of Wales. Ebook. ed. Cardiff: University of Wales Press. Apple.
22. Michael Prestwich. 1997. *Edward I*. Yale: Yale University Press. 172. 'One means frequently employed by Llywelyn to retain allegiance of Welsh rulers is evidence of their reluctance to accept his lordship. In 1261 he demanded that Maredudd ap Rhys should hand over twenty-four hostages, and in 1274 Gruffydd ap Gwenwynwyn gave his son Owain to him as a hostage. The same technique was used on a wide scale in 1271, when Llywelyn was reinforcing his authority in Mid Wales.'
23. CCR Edward I vol 1 1272–1279, 2. '29 Nov [1272], The New Temple [London]. Order to L[lywelyn, son of Griffin, Prince of Wales. Order to come to the ford of Montgomery in person, so that he be there in the octaves of St. Hilary next, to make oath of fealty to the king before the kings envoys whom the king shall send there specially to receive the fealty, as they shall cause him to know on the king's behalf, as the government has come to the king by his father's death, and he has caused his peace to be proclaimed, and the prelates, earls, barons and other proceres of the realm have promptly and without omission made oath of fealty and have done the other things that they could do or make to the king in his absence by reason of his crown and royal dignity, and L [lywelyn] is bound, to do the like, as he knows.'
24. CCR Edward I vol 1 1272–1279, 2. '22 Nov [1272], The New Temple [London]. To the abbot of Hagheman. Order to go to the ford of Montgomery with the abbot of Dore, as the king has ordered L[lewelyn] son of Griffin to be there to make fealty before them as they shall enjoin him on the king's behalf. Given by the hand of W. de Merton, the chancellor. The like, '*de verbo ad verbum*,' to the abbot of Dore. To all, etc. Grant to the aforesaid abbots of power to receive the fealty of Llewelyn (Leulini), prince of Wales, so that if both of them cannot be present, the one who shall be present shall have full power to receive Llewelyn's fealty.
25. Derek Wilson. 2017. Medieval Kings and Queens. Bristol: Immediate Media Co. 43.
26. CCR Edward I vol 1 1272–1279, 241. '24 June [1275], Westminster. To Llywelyn, son of Griffin, Prince of Wales. Order to do before the king at Chester in the octaves of the Assumption next to do homage and take the oath of fealty and to do the other things that he, like other nobles and liegemen (*fideles*) of the king, is bound to do the king by reason of the crown and royal dignity.'
27. Ann. Cestrienses, 102–3. '*Idem Rex apud Cestriam venit ut tractaret cum principe Wallie Lewelino et cito pro contemptu dicti principis recessit.*' Or 'Also the king came to Chester, that he might treat with the prince of Wales, Llywelyn, and soon left in cause of the contempt from that prince. '
28. Henry Gough. Itinerary of King Edward the First throughout his reign, A.D. 1272–1307, exhibiting his movements so far as they are recorded vol 1. (Paisley: Alexander Gardner, 1900). 50–1.
29. CPR Edward I vol 1 1272–1281, 104. '10 September [1275], Chester. Mandate to Llewellin, son of Griffith, Prince of Wales. whom the king has several times commanded to be at Chester to do his homage and fealty to be at Westminster three weeks after Michaelmas [October] next to do so and the king summons him hereby, and moreover has ordered

him to be summoned by the bearers, the abbot of Deruhale, Thomas de Meynewarin and Adam de Button, or two of them.'

30. Michael Prestwich. 1997. Edward I. Yale: Yale University Press. 174. 'However, he [Llywelyn] claimed in proclamations to his own people that peace had been made, and raised tax, on the pretext that he needed the money to pay Edward what was due to him. This alarmed some of the Welsh, and it must be suspected that Llywelyn was in fact collecting funds with a view to war.'
31. Eleanor de Montfort and Llywelyn ap Gruffydd were married as originally her uncle Henry and aunt Alianor had once married, '*per nuncios per verba de presenti* '- canon law endorsed a marital bond that was made in this way, with the full consent of both individuals before witnesses.
32. *OED*, March 2019, Oxford University Press. Origin of fealty. Middle English: from Old French *feau(l)te,* fealte, from Latin *fidelitas* (see fidelity). Fidelity. Origin of fidelity. late Middle English: from Old French *fidelite* or Latin *fidelitas*, from fidelis 'faithful', from fides 'faith'. Compare with fealty. Therefore, in Old French, and so the word as understood by Edward and his contemporaries, Fealty had a common root in the Latin word for faithful.
33. Chron. Guisborough. Vol 2, 5. '*Leulinus, princeps Walliæ . . .sibi in uxorem quondam domini Symonis de Monteforti'*
34. CCR Edward I vol 1 1272–1279, 325. '23 January [1276], Winchester 'To Llywelyn, son of Griffin, Prince of Wales . . . the king again re-summons him to be before him fifteen days from Easter . . . '
35. CFR Edward I 1272–1307, 65.
36. Alexander Kelleher. 2022. 'The King's Other Islands of the Sea': The Channel Islands in the Plantagenet Realm, 1254–1341 History. vol 107. Issue 376. 22. 'The administration under Otto de Grandison's lordship substantiated this view. Otto was unsurprisingly an absentee lord. However, his officials were frequently accused of maladministration, namely the gross neglect of their administrative and judicial responsibilities and, worse, their aggressive efforts to extract as much revenue from the Islands as possible.'
37. *Fœdera*. 151. '*Verum quia, ob ardua Regni noftri negotia, que habemus trac tanda, ad illum diem vobis accedere non valemus, Dominationi veftre fupplicamus, quatinus abfentiam noftram in hac parte, fi placet, habere velitis favorabiliter cxcufatam. Dantes infuper dilectis & fidelibus noftris, Mauritio de Credo mo, Ottoni de Grandifono, & Rogero de Cliford, ad hujufmodi excufationem noftram plenius faciendam, cum noftro mandato fpe ciali, plenariam poteftatem.*'
38. CPR Edward I vol 1 1272–1281, 113. 'Nov 13 [1275], Westminster. Mandate to Otto de Grandisono and Luke deTany, seneschal of Gascony, Westminster, to absolve the above Eblo from the seneschalship of Perigord committed to him in the king's name by the king's uncle, on his prayer to be relieved from it by reason of certain affairs which have recently arisen, and to receive from him the castle of Bourdeilles (Bordelia). Writ de intendendo directed to all persons of the dioceses of Perigeux, Cahors, and Limoges, for the person whom the said Otto and Luke shall provide to be seneschal of Perigord in place of the said Eblo.'
39. CPR Edward I vol 1 1272–1281, 155. 'July 25 [1276], Westminster. Grant to Otto de Grandissono, Stephen de Penecestre, and Luke de Tany, seneschal of Gascony, of full powers to treat with Simon, archbishop of Bordeaux, as to the fruits received by or

on behalf of the king of the temporalities of the archbishopric of Bordeaux during the voidance of the see.'

40. CPR Edward I vol 1 1272–1281. 143. 'May 26 [1276], Westminster. Simple protection, for two years, for Henry de Grandisono, parson of the church of Creystok [Greystoke].'
41. CPR Edward I vol 1 1272–1281, 155. 'July 24 [1276], Westminster. Precept to all sheriffs to collect the tenth of ecclesiastical revenue assigned in the general council [of Lyons A.D. 1274] for the aid of the Holy Land for six years, and the arrears thereof, whenever required to do so by G. bishop of Verdun or his collectors, certain of the clergy having retained the same for two of the aforesaid years, and having been excommunicated by the executors appointed to collect the same.'
42. Charles L. Kingsford, 1909. 'Sir Otho de Grandison 1238? -1328,' Transactions of the Royal Historical Society 3: 128.
43. Ibid.
44. Gregory X died 10 January, Innocent V died 22 June, Adrian V died 18 August, the next Pope was John XXI who began his reign 8 September.
45. CCR Edward I vol 1 1272–1279, 278. 'April 17 [1276], Langley. To Ralph de Sandwyco, the king's steward, Order to cause Master Bertram, the king's engineer, to have six oaks in the park of Odyham or in the foreign wood there, to make therewith the king's engines, as Bertram shall cause him to know on the king's behalf.'
46. TNA C47/ 35/7. A no 24. 'To the Sheriff of Oxon' *Precipimus tibi quod meremium illud quod magister Bertramus Ingeniator noster, tibi liberabit sive fuerit infra ballivam tuam sive extra cariari usque London' ad ingenia nostra ibidem inde facienda prout idem Bertramus tibi dicet ex parte nostra. Teste me ipso apud Langele xxvij die Aprilis anno regni nostri quarto.'* And is endorsed '*Ad cariandam meremium domini regis de boscho qui vocatur Bocholte extra Kyngesclere in comitatu Suhamptes usque ad aquam apud Kaversham. Et ad cariandum meremium de boscho de Burhfildebur in comitatu Berks' ad eundem locum, xiiij.libr. xj.s.'*
47. Arnold Taylor. 1989. Master Bertram, Ingeniator Regis. Studies in Medieval History presented to R. Allen Brown. Woodbridge: The Boydell Press. 295.
48. CCR Edward I vol 1 1272–1279, 359–361. 'November 17 [1276], Westminster. The king after his coronation, in the second year of his reign, ordered Llywelyn (Lewelino) son of Griffin, prince of Wales, to come to do the homage and fealty due to him for the land of Wales; and Llywelyn did not come for this purpose within a year of the coronation, so the king caused him to be summoned at Chester in the quinzaine of the Assumption in the third year of his reign to do the said homage and fealty, and he offered him safe and secure conduct in coming, staying, returning etc, although the king was not bound to do so. And Llywelyn did not come at that day but sent certain frivolous excuses by his envoys and by letter to the king, so that it was decided he should be summoned again to be At Westminster for the aforesaid purposes in three weeks from the following Michaelmas. At which day he did not come, but sent unreasonable excuses as before, so that it was decided that he should be again summoned to come to Westminster in the octaves of St. Hillary following for the aforesaid purpose. And Llywelyn did not come at that day, but excused his absence by letters and envoys insufficiently, as above, so that the king, of his grace, caused him to be summoned a third time to come to Westminster in three weeks from the following Easter to do his homage and fealty. On which day Llywelyn did not come, but pretended insufficient excuses by his letter and envoys, as before so that R. Archbishop of Canterbury and certain bishops and other prelates, earls and barons strongly besought the king that

they by themselves and their envoys might ask inform and induce Llywelyn to do his homage and fealty, and that the king would supersede for the time further extension of the said matter. To which prayers the king acceded, so that they frequently sent the archdeacon of Canterbury as their envoy to Llywelyn to treat upon this matter, which could not be consummated, although the archdeacon laboured much to this end with due expedition. Afterwards, in fifteen days from Michaelmas, in the fourth year of the reign, at Westminster Llywelyn signified to the king by his letter that he would come to Montgomery or Oswestry (Album Monasterium Johannis filii Alani) to do his homage to the king . . . And hereupon . . . it is agreed by common council of all the aforesaid prelates, earls, barons and others that the king shall not hear the aforesaid petition of Llywelyn, and shall not admit his excuses noted above, but that he shall go against Llywelyn as his rebel and disturber of his peace.'

49. Maredudd ap Rhys Gryg (died 1271), was the son of Rhys Gryg, a Welsh prince of Deheubarth. he swore allegiance to Llywelyn in 1258, he later that year sided with the king. Consequently, on 28 May 1259, Maredydd was put on trial for treason, the first trial of its kind in Wales. He was found guilty by a council of native lords and imprisoned in Criccieth Castle. In 1261, Maredudd was granted reconciliation with Llywelyn under severe terms.
50. Michael Prestwich. 1997. Edward I. Yale: Yale University Press, 1997. 170. '. . . but it was Llywelyn's attitude, not Edward's, that explains why war broke out in 1276. The survival of Llywelyn's rule depended on his achieving notable success against the English: Edward, in contrast, did not need to bolster his prestige by means of a struggle with the Welsh.'

Chapter 5

1. CCR Edward I vol 1 1272–1279, 358. 'Nov 13 [1276], Westminster. The king has given power to William de Bello Campo, earl of Warwick, captain of his garrison (*municionis*) in co. Chester, to receive the attorneys of all those who are staying in garrison with the earl in all pleas within the realm until Midsummer next, so that when the earl shall have certified the king or his chancellor of the names of the attorneys, a writ of chancery shall be made to them as ought to be done and has been wont to be done. The king gave like power to Payn de Cadurc[is], captain of his garrison in West Wales. The king gave like power to Roger de Mortuo Mari, captain of his garrison in cos. Salop, Stafford and Hereford.'
2. TNA C47/2/2 no 5. *'E fet a sauer ke ceaus ke vent a Montgomery dirront ke mester Bertram, les charpentiers e les alebasters ke vindrint de Lundres, les mineors e le deaus monceors Henry de Greenford e Robert de Vilers receuerunt leur gages par les mains sire Richard de Boys et Lyone le fiuz Lyone, e par la vueue sire Otes de Grauntson, des deners le queues le Roy fitliuerer as auaundiz Richard d Leone pur fere une partie de ses besoines.*
3. CPR Edward I vol 1 1272–1281, 184. 'Dec 7 [1276], Windsor. Request to the keepers of the port of Whitsaund to permit the bearer of the.se presents, whom Otto de Grandisono has sent beyond seas to bring two destriers into England, to cross over.'
4. John E. Morris. 1901. The Welsh Wars of Edward I. Oxford: Clarendon Press. 12.
5. *OED*, March 2019, Oxford University Press. ORIGIN *Destrier.* Middle English: from Old French, based on Latin *dextera* 'the right hand', from *dexter* 'on the right' (because the squire led the knight's horse with his right hand).

6. CPR Edward I vol 1 1272–1281, 184.' Dec 8 [1276], Windsor. The like to the same [Keepers of Wissant], to permit 30 mounted crossbowmen, whom the king has commanded to come from Gascony, to cross over.'
7. A banneret was a knight who commanded his own troops in battle under his own banner. His banner was square or rectangular rather than a long pennon. The rank was entirely military rather than the socio military rank of knight.
8. Jean de Bonvillars is variously recorded in English archives; Bevillard, Beylard, Bevilar, Beuillar, Beuillard Byvelard, Beillar, Bomlard, Bonovillario, Byveillard and Bonouillar We will continue to use the form in use today – Bonvillars.
9. Aug. Burnand. 1911. '*Vaudois en Angleterre au XIIIe siècle, avec Othon Ier de Grandson: (d'après M.C.-L. Kingsford),* '*Revue historique vaudoise* 19 no 7: 212. We can discern his relationship from the description of his son, also Jean de Bonvillars as '*neveu d'Othon de Grandson'*.
10. Fellow Vaudois, Jacques de Cossonay would follow Henri de Bonvillars at Wenlock from 1291. CPR Edward I vol 2 1281–1292, 481. 'March 26 [1292], Westminster. Henry, prior of Wenlok, going beyond seas, nominating brothers Bartholomew de la Douse and James de Cossenay his fellow monks until All Saints ... March 29 [1292], Westminster, Henry, prior of Wenlok, going beyond seas, until All Ssints.' Bonvillars status as a brother-in-law of Grandson is suggested by a 1292 letter from Othon de Grandson to John Langton, TNA SC 1/26/34 in which Othon describes Henri de Bonvillars as '*mon frere le prior de Wenloc'*. A familial attribution concurred with by Arnold Taylor. 1963. *Some notes on the Savoyards in North Wales, 1277–1300. With special reference to the Savoyard element in the construction of Harlech Castle*. Genava 11: 290. n5. And more recently by David Williams. 2023. *A Letter of Henry de Bonvillars, Prior of Wenlock?* Foundations 16. no3. 29.' I follow Arnold Taylor in interpreting 'frere' as 'brother-in-law."
11. Jean Pierre Chapuisat. 1989. '*De Mont-sur-Rolle à Windsor, de la Dullive à Dumfries ... La Maison de Savoie et le Pays de Vaud,' Bibliothèque historique vaudoise* 97: 119.
12. Guillaume de Cicon appears in the English archives variously as; Cykun, Cycons, Chycun, Sicoms, Sicun, Sycun and even Dygoin.
13. Arnold Taylor. 1963. 'Some notes on the Savoyards in North Wales, 1277–1300. With special reference to the Savoyard element in the construction of Harlech Castle'. *Genava* XI: 290. A n6 citing TNA C 62/52. '*Willelmi Cykun nuper venientis ad nos in nuncium a portibus transmarinis ad partes Angl' ex parte Ottonis supradicti.'* Or 'Guillaume de Cicon recently came to us with news from overseas to parties English on the side of the above named Othon.'
14. *Fœdera.* 588. *'De homagio Othonis com 'Palatini Burgundia. A. D. 1281 . Nos Otho comes palatinus Burgondiæ, & dominus Salinen' notum facimus universis præsentas litteras inspecturis, quod nos tenemus, in feodo & in homagio, ab excellentissimo viro, domino Edwardo, divina gratia, Rege Angliæ, Duce Aquitaniæ, & principe Dirlande, pontarliam, & castellaniam, & pediagium ejusdem loci, & totum illud quod habemus en Veras, cum apenditiis eorumdem. Item Calamontem, & Joygne, & la Chandarlie, cum suis pertinentiis universis, prout tenet a nobis Johannes de Cabilone, avunculus noster. Item castrum de Jou, cum suis appenditiis, prout dictus Johannes de Cabilone, avunculus noster, tenet a nobilis ariere feodum. Et prædicta omnia confitemur, & recognoscimus nos tenere a dicto domino Rege in feodo & homagio, secundum quod est expressum;*

salva fidelitate nostrorum dominorum. In quorum testimonium damus & concedimus dicto domino Regi præsentes litteras, nostro sigillo sigillatas. Dat' Lugd' anno Domini MCCLXXXI. Mense Januarii.'

15. TNA C 62/69 m 5 bis.
16. Arnold Taylor. 1963. 'Some notes on the Savoyards in North Wales, 1277–1300. With special reference to the Savoyard element in the construction of Harlech Castle'. *Genava* XI.: 290–1.
17. Letter 29.9.99. CR 1251–53, 465. For the St Laurents in the mid-thirteenth century, C. Roth. Ed. 1948. *Cartulaire du Chapitre de Notre Dame de Lausanne, première partie*, Lausanne: n.339.
18. J. Beverley Smith. 2014. *Llywellyn ap Gruffudd: Prince of Wales*. Ebook. ed. Cardiff: University of Wales Press. Apple.
19. Michael Prestwich. 1997. *Edward I.* Yale: Yale University Press. 177. 'In what was in many ways a civil war in Wales, it must have been obvious to the English king that it was to his advantage to give full encouragement to Prince Dafydd, Gruffydd ap Gwenwynwyn and those Welsh rulers who were ready to throw off their allegiance to Llywelyn.'
20. Adam Chapman. 2010. 'Welshmen in the Armies of Edward I' in *The Impact of the Edwardian Castles in Wales*. Oxford: Oxbow Books. 175. 'The final conflict between Gwynedd and the English Crown was as much a conflict between Welshmen as it was between Welsh and English.'
21. C. J. Spurgeon, 1978. 'Builth Castle', *Brycheiniog* 18: 54.
22. Robert J. Dean. 2009. *Castles in Distant Lands: The Life and Times of Othon of Grandson.* Willingdon: Lawden Haynes Publishing. 19.
23. Ibid. iii.
24. Lawrence Butler & Jeremy K. Knight. 2004. *Dolforwyn Castle, Montgomery Castle.* Cardiff: Cadw. 27.
25. Arnold Taylor. 1963. 'Some notes on the Savoyards in North Wales, 1277–1300. With special reference to the Savoyard element in the construction of Harlech Castle,' *Genava* XI: 298. 'In a letter to King Edward, written at Dolforwyn during the siege, and dated 3 April 1277, Othon de Grandson said that when the castle surrendered it would need much repair, and expressed his fears that if he assigned the work to Master Bertram the latter would 'devise too many things and perhaps waste the king's money, and therefore some other man would be needed who would take the matter in hand' (Cal. Ancient Correspondence concerning Wales, p.31.)'
26. Frédéric Joseph Tanquerey. 1916. *Recueil de Lettres Anglo-Françaises, 1265–1399.* Paris: Librairie Ancienne Honoré Champion. 5–6. Incorrectly dated as '*Avant 1272*' or 'Before 1272' and misidentified as a letter from '*Roger de Mortimer à Henri III*' but reproduced otherwise correctly as '*Au Roy de Englterre. Al sun tres cher seignur saluz. Sachez sire ke nous asegames le Chastel de Doluereyn le mekreydy en la simeine de Paskes ... Sachez sire ke quant le chastel sera en vostre mein, il auera mester de grant amendement; por quoi nous auerrums mester de eukun homme ke de tels choses se feust entremettre e ke leument vosist empleer vos deners, kar nous y mettoms Mestre Bertram je dout ke il ne devisast trop de choses e par aventure vos deners ne serreint assez bien emplee com serreit, e por ce sire mandez nous de ceste chose vostre volonte. Sachez sire ke la lettre ke vus nous avez envoye par mon sire Joh de Bevilar nous vint a graund socour, kar sachez sire ke nostre ost semble bien ost de graunt seignur, e ce ne poet on mine fere sans deners. Sire a Deu ke vous gard,*

mandez nous votre estat e vostre volonte. Ceste lettre feu fete a Dolverein le Samedy apres Paskes.' Or 'To my dear Lord Salut! Be aware that we besieged the castle at Dolforwyn on the Wednesday in Easter Week [31 March 1277] … Please know sir that when the castle will be in your hands it will be in need of great reworking; for what we have to tell you about a man, such things must be mediated, and that you save your money. Master Bertram, I doubt he does not estimate too much of things and by adventure your money. By this sir, tell of this your will. Know sir that the letter we have sent by my Lord Jean de Bonvillars has come to us in great earnestness. By the knowledge of our Lord that our host seems to be great and of a great Lord, and that this is not creation without money. Sir, God keep you, let us know how you are and what your will is. It is the letter at Dolforwyn, the Saturday after Easter [3 April 1277].'

27. John Goronwy Edwards, Ed. 1935. *Calendar of ancient correspondence concerning Wales*. Cardiff: Cardiff University Press Board. 30–1. Edward spent the Easter of 1277, not with his army, but on pilgrimage to Walsingham. Henry Gough. 1900. *Itinerary of King Edward the First throughout his reign, A.D. 1272–1307, exhibiting his movements so far as they are recorded. vol. 1*. Paisley: Alexander Gardner. 69.
28. Ibid. index.
29. The historiography of this is long, in 1916, Frédéric Joseph Tanquerey. *Recueil de Lettres Anglo-Françaises*, 1265–1399. Paris: Librairie Ancienne Honoré Champion, 1916. 5–6. Misidentified the author as Roger de Mortimer. Then John Goronwy Edwards, Ed. *Calendar of ancient correspondence concerning Wales*. Cardiff: Cardiff University Press Board, 1935. 30–31. Identified as 'probable' that the author was Henri de Lacy, but ambiguously perhaps, qualified his identification by listing in his index 'Sir Otto de Grandison' as a potential author, marked with a '?' Taylor, writing in 1976 in his paper *'John Pennard, Leader of Gwynedd'* added to the debate 'the possibility must not be overlooked that the king's correspondent was de Grandson rather than de Lacy.' Taylor had then muddied the water by suggesting another author, Amédée de Savoie, Arnold Taylor. 1985. *Studies in Castles and Castle-Building*. London: The Hambledon Press. 5. n2. 'It is not unlikely that he [Amédée] was the writer of the letter' also collected in this publication was the earlier paper 'John Pennard, Leader of the Men of Gwynedd' 212. n1. Nicola Coldstream. 2003. 'Architects, Advisers and Design at Edward I's Castles in Wales,' *Architectural History: Journal of the Society of Architectural Historians of Great Britain* 46. 26. 'Was probably Amadeus of Savoy' but this was taken from Taylor's aforesaid 1985 note. However, Taylor, having identified two possible authors, finally in 1989 came down on the side of Grandson, not Amédée (or indeed Henri de Lacy), as the author. Arnold Taylor. 1989. *Master Bertram, Ingeniator Regis. Studies in Medieval History Presented to R. Allen Brown*. Woodbridge: The Boydell Press. 296. n41. 'For a number of reasons, however, the author of this present paper believes them [the Dolforwyn letters] to have been sent by Sir Otto de Grandison.' The Cadw guidebook of 2004, for Dolforwyn, written by Lawrence Butler and Jeremy K. Knight, says 'the Earl of Lincoln [Henri de Lacy] reported to the king' such are the perils of an unsigned letter.'
30. John E. Morris. 1901. *The Welsh Wars of Edward I*. Oxford: Clarendon Press. 121. 'Otto de Grandison had no feudal obligation, but the others were all tenants-in-chief and men of position.'
31. CCR Edward I vol 1 1272–1279. 493. 'March 21 [1278], Down Ampney. To R. [Robert Burnell] Bishop of Bath and Wells, the chancellor, and to Othon de Grandisono. The

king commends the care and solicitude exhibited by them in his affairs in the court of France … especially as the king has no one about him whom he believes could know the premises and do his will in the premises better and more advantageously than them, not even if he himself were to attend to the matters there in person.'

32. Arnold Taylor. 1989. *Studies in Medieval History Presented to R. Allen Brown*. Woodbridge: The Boydell Press. 296.
33. TNA C47/2/2 no 5.
34. Michael Prestwich. 2010. 'Edward I in Wales' in *The Impact of the Edwardian Castles in Wales*. Oxford: Oxbow Books. 4. 'A letter of April 1277, which Taylor plausibly argued was from Otto de Grandson … It is very likely that Otto's influence was important in the choice that Edward made of the Savoyard Master James of St. George to play a leading role in the castle-building programme in Wales.'
35. A Muster was the assembly of troops in preparation for battle. The word comes from the Old French '*moustrer*' which itself came from the Latin '*monstrare*', meaning 'to show'. Military service for most of the medieval period was based on land ownership. This feudal system determined that all holders of a certain amount of land were obliged to accept knighthood and do military service for their feudal overlord, either in person or by raising forces.
36. Jean de Grailly will appear often in this story, for a full biography see Henri Buathier. 1995. Jean Ier de Grailly un chevalier européen du XIIIe siècle.
37. Geoffroi de Joinville, commonly known in England as Geoffrey de Geneville, brother of French chronicler of Saint Louis, Jean de Joinville, had been Justiciar of Ireland from 1273 until 1276. The younger brother of Geoffroi and Jean being Simon de Joinville, Seigneur de Gex et Marnay in Savoy and Burgundy. Gefferoi, like Othon de Grandson had been brought to England by Pierre de Savoie. Like the famille de Grandson the famille de Joinville were related to the comital family of Savoy. Simon de Joinville had been Pierre de Savoie's vassal and ally in Savoy during his absences in England, likewise his son Pierre de Joinville will act similarly for Othon de Grandson.
38. *Song of Caerlaverock* from 1300 cited in Michael Prestwich. 2010. *Knight: The Medieval Warrior (Unofficial) Guide*. London: Thames & Hudson. 169. 'On the appointed day, the whole host was ready, and the good King with his household, then set forward against the Scots, not in coats and surcoats, but on powerful and costly chargers; and that they may not be taken by surprise, well and securely armed. There were many rich caparisons embroidered on silks and satins; many a beautiful pennon fixed to a lance, and many a banner displayed. And afar off was the noise heard of neighing horses: mountains and valleys were everywhere covered with sumpter horses and wagons with provisions, and sacks of tents and pavilions.'
39. R. R. Davies. 1987. *The Age of Conquest: Wales 1063–1415*. Oxford: Oxford University Press. 335.
40. Richard W. Kaeuper. 1973. *Bankers to the Crown: The Riccardi of Lucca and Edward I*. Princeton: Princeton University Press. 178.
41. Sir Maurice Powicke. 1953. *The Thirteenth Century 1216–1307*. Oxford: Oxford University Press. 543.
42. Gerald of Wales. *The Journey Through Wales and The Description of Wales*. London: Penguin Books Ltd, 1978. 209. 'It was there [the forest of Coleshill] in our own time that Henry II, King of the English, was badly mauled when he made his first assault

on Wales. In his youthful ardour and rash enthusiasm, he was unwise enough to push on through this densely wooded pass, to the great detriment of his men, quite a few of whom were killed.' The Battle of Coleshill also known as the Battle of Ewloe, was fought in July 1157. The description of Henry's struggles in the densely wooded pass no doubt influenced Edward in cutting his road through the forest.

43. CPR Edward I vol 1 1272–1281, 213–14. 'June 13 [1277], Brill. Writ of aid, until Michaelmas, for Barunsinus Walterii and his fellows. merchants of Lucca, king's merchants, appointed to do certain arduous business in the realm. The like for the following: Abbas de Brakalyen and his fellows, merchants of Lucca. Orlandinus de Podio and his fellows, merchants of Lucca. Frederic Ventur and Matthew Rogyumpel and their fellows, merchants- of Lucca. June 16 [1277], Brill The like for Master William de Perton, king's clerk, sent to the counties of Lincoln and Leicester to provide, with the counsel of the sheriffs, masons (*cementariis*), and carpenters, as many as he can get, and in whosoever works or service they may be, and to conduct them whither he has been enjoined. The like for Master Robert de Belvero, sent to divers parts of the realm for the same purpose.'
44. Chron. Thomas Wykes, 272. *'silva tantæ densitatis et amplitudinis'* or 'the dense forest of great size.'
45. John E. Morris. 1901. *The Welsh Wars of Edward I.* Oxford: Clarendon Press. 130.
46. *Fœdera*, 544. '*in castris apud le Flynt prope Basingwerk*'.
47. The Calendar of Welsh Rolls are 7 rolls held by the UK National Archive in Kew, Ref C77, calendared and published in 1912. They comprise enrolments of letters patent, letters close and charters issued under the Great Seal and other documents relating to Welsh affairs, Welsh rulers and to Edward I's conquest of Wales. They cover the period from 1276 until 1294 and are here abbreviated in reference as CWR.
48. CWR 1277–1326, 160. 'Jan 18 [1278], Westminster. To all to whom, etc. Notification that the king has granted to Nicholas Bonel, receiver of aU the money arising from the issues of the king's two cantreds and the parts adjoining and viewer of the king's works in those parts both at Le Chaylou and at Rothelan'.
49. Ibid.
50. TNA E101/3/15. *'Vincencio clerico pro duobus solidis quos dedit diversis hominibus precepto O. de Grandisono pro maremio leuando apud Flind, ijs.'* Or 'Vincent gave to the clerk for the two *sol* [shillings] that he gave to various men by order of Othon de Grandson for having carted timber in Flint, two shillings.' The horse drawn cart was the most common way of transporting material.
51. Ibid.
52. J. G. Edwards. 1944. 'Edward I's Castle-Building in Wales,' *The Proceedings of the British Academy* XXXII: 18–9. 'in the Middle Ages building operations in British were concentrated into what was called 'the season' – the period of the year extending from about April to about November … this fact is reflected very clearly in the accounts.' We need to remember that the 'building season' at Flint in 1277 did not being until the last week of July, with the arrival of the English army, at the earliest and was thus clearly not a full building season. Edward confirms the term 'season' as being contemporary to the thirteenth century in North Wales by citing '*seisonam*' and *'la seeson'* and *'ceste seeson'* in references in his footnote Ibid. 19. n1.
53. John E. Morris. 1901. *The Welsh Wars of Edward I.* Oxford: Clarendon Press. 130. 'A strong post was thus made, though the works were but temporary, and of wood, for there was no

time to prepare stone.' This was a view with which Edwards disagreed. J. G. Edwards. 1944. *Edward I's Castle-Building in Wales*. The Proceedings of the British Academy XXXII: 33. 'the mistaken idea that Flint castle was at first only a wooden structure … first propounded by the late Dr. J. E. Morris.' But this rather depends upon what we mean by 'at first'. Morris was clearly referring to the summer and autumn of 1277. In his paper J. G. Edwards. 1951. *The Building of Flint*. The Flintshire Historical Society XII: 14. Edwards modified his view somewhat, writing, 'At Flint during the first five weeks building in stone would be less important.' He evidenced this by a ratio of '3 masons to 1 carpenter' at Flint compared to '13 masons to 1 carpenter' later at Beaumaris. More recently Vicky Perfect. 2012. *Flint Castle: The story of Edward I's first Welsh castle*. Mold: Alyn Books Ltd. has suggested that as building work commenced in 1277, and Maître Jacques was not yet in Wales, then he was not involved in its planning or scope – that an entire summer building season had been undertaken before his arrival. Her argument rests and falls on the extent of the 1277 works in stone. Edwards had clearly set out that for the first five weeks this was negligible, so what of the period thereafter until the end of November? Well, Edwards again confirmed that for the period until 10 October, the ratio remained '1 mason to 3 carpenters'; only for the six weeks to 21 November does the ratio of masons improve, and then only to '33 masons to 57 carpenters to 100 diggers' – at no time, unlike later at Beaumaris, is the number of masons in relation to the number of carpenters even close to what we might expect for castle building to be underway in a substantial way. Edwards seems to have rested his suggestion of stone works at Flint in 1277 on a 1278 account, '*Et in stipendiis cuiusdam plumbarii cooperientis turres* [*sic* in full] *in castro predicto per predictum tempus*'. The lead roofing was attached to *turres* or towers at Flint in 1278. He surmised, correctly, that one would only add lead to the roof of a finished tower. This would suggest that at least two of the towers at Flint were extant in 1278, and given that work paused in 1278, were built largely in 1277. However, Arnold Taylor. *The Welsh Castles of King Edward I*. London: The Hambledon Press, 1986. 20 n1. observed, rightly, that we cannot be thinking of one of the completed towers as the *donjon* tower, since that was only completed in 1286, leaving three towers to consider. Furthermore, he noted, 'it should not be forgotten that there was a fifth – the outer gate tower shown in the plan of Flint inset in Speed's map of Flintshire (1610). When the Pipe Roll records the purchase of lead '*ad turres cooperiend' in eodem castro*' and the wages of a plumber … the reference might be this tower and only one of the others.' Going on to add that early completion of the Gate Tower is evidenced by the Grant of Burgages of 1281. In short that it may well have been only one of the four castle towers completed in 1277. This suggestion would, in effect, square with the thinking of Morris, Edwards and Taylor – and render Perfect's suggestion unlikely.

54. John E. Morris. 1901. *The Welsh Wars of Edward I*. Oxford: Clarendon Press. 130.
55. Ibid.
56. Arnold Taylor. 1986. *The Welsh Castles of King Edward I*. London: The Hambledon Press. 17. 'For the first few weeks each labour category was treated as a military unit and placed under a knight who shared with the clerk who had directed its recruitment responsibility for the issue of its wages.'
57. Brut, 267.
58. J. Beverley Smith. 2014. *Llywellyn ap Gruffudd: Prince of Wales*. Ebook. ed. Cardiff: University of Wales Press. Apple.
59. Ibid.

60. C. J. Spurgeon. 1978. 'Builth Castle', *Brycheiniog* 18: 54.
61. Christopher Rothero. 1984. *The Scottish and Welsh Wars 1250–1400*. Twentieth Edition. Botley: Osprey Publishing Ltd. 3. 'They were migrant tribesmen, half warriors, half farmers, often living out meagre lives (when they were not raiding and feuding) by keeping cattle and sheep, as they had done so for thousands of years. Not content with their own lands, the men of the tribe left the bards and concealed homes above the valleys each spring to raid and pillage in the lands around their principality. Such was their reputation that pious Englishmen regarded two pilgrimages to St. Davids as being equal to the hardship and dangers of one to Jerusalem.'
62. Gerald of Wales. 1978. *The Journey Through Wales and The Description of Wales*. London: Penguin Books Ltd. 297–98.
63. Lodowyk van Velthem, 1725. (Ed. Le Long). Spiegel Historiaal, Book IV, c. 5. 'Edward, King of England, came to Flanders. He brought with him many soldiers from the land of Wales. In the very depth of winter, they were running about bare-legged. They wore a red robe. They could not have been warm. The money they received from the King was spent in milk and butter. They would eat and drink anywhere. I never saw them wearing armour. I studied them very closely and walked among them to find out what defensive armour they carried when going into battle. Their weapons were bows, arrows and swords. They also had javelins.'
64. Winston S. Churchill. 2013. *A History of the English-Speaking Peoples*. New York: Rosetta Books. 240.
65. Ibid. 241.
66. R. R. Davies. 1987. *The Age of Conquest: Wales 1063–1415*. Oxford: Oxford University Press. 76.
67. Brut, 383. cited in J. Goronwy Edwards. 1944. 'Edward I's Castle-Building in Wales' The Proceedings of the British Academy XXXII: 30. 'on St. James's day [25 July] Edmund the King's brother, accompanied by an army, came to Llanbadarn, and began the building of Aberystwyth castle.'
68. Aberystwyth Castle is generally referred to in medieval records as Lampader or Lampadarn as noted, or Lampadervaur from the local Welsh place name Llanbadarn Fawr, and should not be confused with Lampeter or Llanbedr some 20 miles distant to the south.
69. J. Goronwy Edwards. 1944. 'Edward I's Castle-Building in Wales' The Proceedings of the British Academy XXXII: 30. '*Henrico de Hereford cementario eunti apud Kaermerdyn pro castro de Lampader firmando, ad suas expensas, Xs*.' Or 'Mason, Henry of Hereford, moving to Kaermerdyn [Carmarthen] for the strengthening of the castle of Lampader [Aberystwyth], at their own expense, 10 shillings.'
70. Malcolm Hislop. *James of St. George and the Castles of North Wales*. Barnsley: Pen &Sword Books Ltd, 2020. 70.
71. TNA SC 1/23/53 '*Richard le Enginour le Rey, un Burgeys de Cestr*.'
72. TNA E101/485/19.
73. Arnold Taylor. 1989. *Master Bertram, Ingeniator Regis. Studies in Medieval History presented to R. Allen Brown*. Woodbridge: The Boydell Press. 298. n49.
74. Rick Turner. 2010. 'The Life and Career of Richard the Engineer' in *The Impact of the Edwardian Castles in Wales*. Oxford: Oxbow Books. 46–58.
75. Ibid. 46. 'Richard was put in charge of 1,850 men mustered at Flint to begin work on the castle there and at Rhuddlan … but how much [design] was left to Master Richard

[at Flint] and Master Bertram [at Rhuddlan] is a matter of speculation. Once Master James took overall charge of work at Flint and Rhuddlan in April 1278, Richard may have moved on to other works for he disappears temporarily from the records.'

76. Marc Morris. *A Great and Terrible King*. London: Windmill Books, 2009. 154. This colourful picture comes from the Annals of Thomas Wykes. Chron. Wykes, 272–73. '*et quia inter Cestriam et terram Lewelini interjacet quaedam silva tantae densitatis et amplitudinis, quod exercitus regis eam nullatenus poterat sine discrimine pertransire; prostrata sen secata ipsius silvæ portione non modica, progrediendi in terram principis sibi et complicibus suis latissimum patfecit ingressum et terram ipsum violentis ausibus occupatam triumphaliter introivit.*' Or 'Between Chester and Llywelyn's country lay a forest of such denseness and extent that the royal army could by now means penetrate through without danger. A large part of this forest being cut down, the king opened out for himself a very broad road for an advance into the prince's land and having occupied it by strong attacks he entered through it in triumph.'
77. The motte of Robert of Rhuddlan's castle remains, the line of its Bailey traceable in nearby fields, a little downstream of the Edwardian castle at Twthill. It was reputedly built upon the site of Llywelyn ap Gruffydd's Hall.
78. Arnold Taylor. 2008. *Rhuddlan Castle*. Cardiff, Cadw. 1.
79. Arnold Taylor. 1986. *The Welsh Castles of King Edward I*. London: The Hambledon Press. 27. n6. 'Edward was at Rhuddlan intermittently from 19 August and continuously from 27 September to 18 or 19 November … For part if not all of his stay he was accommodated by the Rhuddlan Dominicans, who were paid for their hospitality and given a donation towards the glazing of their new church.' TNA E101/350/23.
80. CChW 1244–1326, 4. 'Oct 1 [1278], Macclesfield. To Master Thomas Bek and John de Kirkeby. Order to make letters to the prior and convent of the Friars Preachers of Rhuddlan that they shall have their estovers in the forest of Pervethald by Rhuddlan and free fishery in the river of Rhuddlan and that they may grind freely at the king's mills there at the king's will; also to let Juorius their prior have letters directed to Bogo de Knovill, sheriff of Salop, to put David de Rydemayn in any competent service in his bailiwick.'
81. Arnold Taylor. 1986. *The Welsh Castles of King Edward I*. London: The Hambledon Press. 27.
82. Michael Prestwich. 1997. *Edward I*. Yale: Yale University Press. 180. Gerald of Wales. 1978. *The Journey Through Wales and The Description of Wales*. London: Penguin Books Ltd. 199. 'This island produces far more grain than any other part of Wales. In the Welsh language it has always been called '*Mon mâm Cymru*' which means 'Mona the mother of Wales'.'
83. Gerald of Wales. 1978. *The Journey Through Wales and The Description of Wales*. London: Penguin Books Ltd. 199.
84. J. Beverley Smith. 2014. *Llywellyn ap Gruffudd: Prince of Wales*. Ebook. ed. Cardiff: University of Wales Press. Apple.
85. Carl von Clausewitz. 2003. *Principles of War*. Mineola: Dover Publications Inc. 50–1.
86. J. Beverley Smith. 2014. *Llywellyn ap Gruffudd: Prince of Wales*. Cardiff: University of Wales Press. Apple.
87. Richard W. Kaeuper. 1973. *Bankers to the Crown: The Riccardi of Lucca and Edward I*. Princeton: Princeton University Press. 179.

88. TNA E101/4/3.
89. The chronicler of Lanercost records '50,000 pounds of silver' Herbert Maxwell. 1913. The Chronicle of Lanercost, 1272–1346. 16.
90. The £50,000 fine was pardoned as early as 11 November 1277 and was most likely originally imposed to establish in the treaty Llwellyn's war guilt.
91. CPR Edward I vol 1 1272–1281, 253. 'Jan 18 [1278], Westminster. Protection with clause volumus, until Midsummer, for Philip Burnel, going beyond seas with Otto de Grandisono.'

Chapter 6

1. RG vol 2 1273–1290. 50. no 187. '187. *Rex archiepiscopis, episcopis, abbatibus, prioribus et ceteris prelatis, comitibus, vicecomitibus, baronibus, militibus, vassallis, majoribus, communitatibus civitatum et villarum, et omnibus fidelibus et subditis suis ad quos, etc., salutem. Sciatis quod transmittimus in Vasconia et in aliis terris quas habemus et habere debemus in duratu Aquitanie et comitatu Pictavie venerabilem patrem R. Batlioniensem et Wellensem episcopum, cancellariuum nostrum, et dilectum et fidelem nostrum Ottonem de Grandisono, loco nostri, dantes eisdem et alteri corumdem plenam et liberam potestatem faciendi omnia et singula que faceremus et facere possentus ibidem, si presentes essemus, et eciam si mandatun exigant speciale, mandantes tenore presencium quod ab omnibus pareatur eisdem; el quod per eos vel cum eis actum, quoquo modo literit, vel ordinatuma, ratum et gratum habebimus et habenus: et, cum de ipsis per litteras sigillis corum vel alterins, una cum sigillis ipsorum quos al hoe sibi associare dxuerint vel duxerit, signatas nobis constiterit, illa faciemus sigilli nostri munimine roborari. In cujus, etc. Datum apud Dovoram,. vij. die Ffebruarii, anno predicto.*'
2. P. Coss. 1993. *The Knight in Medieval England 1000–1400*. 85. 'Present at a tournament at Compiègne in 1278, for example, were the earls of Lincoln and Gloucester, Hugh de Courtenay, Roger de Clifford, Thomas de Molton, Hugh Despenser, Otto de Grandison, William de Say, John de Vesci and John Comyn.'
3. Geoffrey Chaucer, *The Knight's Tale*.
4. Ibid. nos 180, 187–88.
5. Eugene L. Cox. 1974. *The Eagles of Savoy: The House of Savoy in Thirteenth Century Europe*. Princeton: Princeton University Press. 378.
6. Charles L. Kingsford. 1909. *Sir Otho de Grandison 1238? -1328.* Transactions of the Royal Historical Society 3. Appendix of Documents I, 188–89. Citing Ancient Correspondence VIII. 51. '*Edwardus, dei gratia Rex Anglie, dominus Hibernie, et dux Aquitannie, dilecto et fideli suo Otoni de Grandisono salutem. Scripsit nobilis vir egregius et amicus noster karissimus, Comes Burgundie, quod inter ipsum et vos de filia sua vobis matrimonio copulanda habita sunt diebus istis colloquia et tractatus. Set quia vestrum sicut proprium commodum et honorem cupimus et optamus, nollemus, quantum in nobis est, quod ibi vel alibi nisi in nostra presencia, vel saltem quousque vobiscum super hiis et aliis loqueremur, aliquam duceretis in uxorem: ut negocium sub illa honorificencia, quam vellemus et que decet statum vestrum, per nostram presenciam honorabilius posset et sollempnius expediri; verumptamen considerantes quod voluntates contrahencium vincere solent in huiusmodi voluntates aliorum, volumus et assentimus, quod si*

contractus ille vobis cordi sit, et vir nobilis et dilectus noster Otto de Burgundia, et alii consanguinei ac ceteri zelatores honoris vestri id ad vestrum profectum et honoris titulum cedere videant et id vobis consulant cum effectu, tunc premissa, iuxta cor vestrum et ipsorum consilia et secundum ordinaciones et tractatus inter pre- dictum Comitem et vos inde habitos vel habendos, fini debito mancipentur, prout statui vestro congruit et fore videritis, facienda. Et hoc ipsum eidem Comiti per nostras litteras respondemus. Teste me ipso apud Wodestoke xj die Martii, anno regni nostri septimo.'

7. *Fœdera*. 188–89. '*De homagio Othonis com. Palatini Burgundia. A. D. 1281. 'Nos Otho comes palatinus Burgondiæ, & dominus Salinen' notum facimus universis præsentas litteras inspecturis, quod nos tenemus, in feodo & in homagio, ab excellentissimo viro, domino Edwardo, divina gratia, Rege Angliæ, Duce Aquitaniæ, & principe Dirlande, pontarliam, & castellaniam, & pediagium ejusdem loci, & totum illud quod habemus en Veras, cum apenditiis eorumdem. Item Calamontem, & Joygne, & la Chandarlie, cum suis pertinentiis universis, prout tenet a nobis Johannes de Cabilone, avunculus noster. Item castrum de Jou, cum suis appenditiis, prout dictus Johannes de Cabilone, avunculus noster, tenet a nobilis ariere feodum. Et prædicta omnia confitemur, & recognoscimus nos tenere a dicto domino Rege in feodo & homagio, secundum quod est expressum; salva fidelitate nostrorum dominorum. In quorum testimonium damus & concedimus dicto domino Regi præsentes litteras, nostro sigillo sigillatas. Dat' Lugd' anno Domini MCCLXXXI. Mense Januarii.'*
8. CCR Edward I vol 1 1272–1279, 520. '25th January [1279], Westminster. To the sheriff of Surrey. Order to deliver to Otto de Grandisono the manor of Shene, as Hugh de Wyndesor lately granted to R. bishop of Bath and Wells, the chancellor, then archdeacon of York, the manor of Shene, which grant the late king afterwards confirmed, and the bishop lately enfeoffed Otto of the manor aforesaid.'
9. J. Cloake. 1995. *Palaces and Parks of Richmond and Kew vol 1, The Palaces of Shene and Richmond.* 13–14, 219.
10. The 1229 Treaty of Paris put an end to the conflict between the King of France, Louis IX, and the Count of Toulouse, Raymond VII, and provided for the marriage of the latter's daughter, Joan of Toulouse, to King Louis' brother, Alphonse of Poitiers. If they did not have heirs, their estates were to revert to the Crown of France. Among these estates the Agenais and Quercy, were originally part of the dowry that Joan of England, sister of Richard I of England, brought when she married count Raymond VI of Toulouse in October 1196. The 1259 Treaty of Paris signed between King Louis IX and Henry III, King of England, had provided that, if Joan of Toulouse did not have an heir, the estates brought by her grandmother, Joan of England, would return to the Duchy of Aquitaine, the Duke of which held prior claim through Joan of England.
11. Esther Rowland Clifford. 1961. *A Knight of Great Renown: The Life and Times of Othon de Grandson.* Chicago: University of Chicago Press. 58.
12. CPR Edward I vol 1 1272–1281, 389. 'Mandate to John Simonetti, Bonroneinus and Richard Guidichun, and their fellows, merchants of Lucca, to advance by way of loan to Otto de Grandisono, one of the king's household and king's secretary, whom the king is sending to the court of Rome on special business, at the times and places the said Otto shall enjoin upon them to do so in the king's name.'
13. *OED*, March 2019, Oxford University Press. ORIGIN [Secretary] late Middle English (originally in the sense 'person entrusted with a secret'): from late Latin *secretarius* 'confidential officer', from Latin *secretum* 'secret', neuter of *secretus*

14. CPR Edward I vol 1 1272–1281, 389. 'king's secretary, whom the king is sending to the court of Rome on special business'.
15. *Fœdera*. 187.
16. Pope Gregory X died 10 January 1276, Innocent V 22 June 1276, Adrian V 18 August 1276, John XXI 20 May 1277 and Nicholas III 22 August 1280.
17. *Fœdera*. 188–89. '*De homagio Othonis com. Palatini Burgundia. A. D. 1281. Nos Otho comes palatinus Burgondiæ, & dominus Salinen' notum facimus universis præsentas litteras inspecturis, quod nos tenemus, in feodo & in homagio, ab excellentissimo viro, domino Edwardo, divina gratia, Rege Angliæ, Duce Aquitaniæ, & principe Dirlande, pontarliam, & castellaniam, & pediagium ejusdem loci, & totum illud quod habemus en Veras, cum apenditiis eorumdem. Item Calamontem, & Joygne, & la Chandarlie, cum suis pertinentiis universis, prout tenet a nobis Johannes de Cabilone, avunculus noster. Item castrum de Jou, cum suis appenditiis, prout dictus Johannes de Cabilone, avunculus noster, tenet a nobilis ariere feodum. Et prædicta omnia confitemur, & recognoscimus nos tenere a dicto domino Rege in feodo & homagio, secundum quod est expressum; salva fidelitate nostrorum dominorum. In quorum testimonium damus & concedimus dicto domino Regi præsentes litteras, nostro sigillo sigillatas. Dat' Lugd' anno Domini MCCLXXXI. Mense Januarii.*'
18. John Manley, 1994. 'Excavations at Caergwrle Castle, Clwyd, North Wales: 1988–1990,' *Medieval Archaeology* 38: 86. '*David fillio Griffini, ad construendum castrum suum de Kaierguill, de dono Regis. Lxvj. li. xiij.s.iiij.d.*'
19. Ibid.
20. Arnold Taylor. 1985. *Studies in Castles and Castle-Building*. London: The Hambledon Press. 177 8. 'It would not be surprising if those works [Caergwrle] were under James's overall direction also.'
21. Marc Morris. 2009. *A Great and Terrible King*. London: Windmill Books. 175.
22. Madog was the son of Llywelyn ap Maerdudd, the onetime Lord of Meirionnydd who'd fought against Llywelyn ap Gruffydd at the Battle of Bryn Derwin in 1256 and had been accordingly deprived of his patrimony.
23. Reg. John Peckham. Lists the following: Complaint of Lord David (445–47), Complaints of the Men of Ros (447–51), Complaint of Rys the Little of Estrad Tywy (451–52), Complaint of Llewellyn and Howel, Sons of Rys (452–53), Complaint of the Sons of Maredud son of Oweyn (453–44), Complaint of the Men of Ystradaluy (454–55), Complaint of the Men of Penliti (455–58), Complaint of Goronou Son of Heylyn (458–60), Complaint of the Men of Tregeayl (460–63)
24. Huw Pryce. 2005. *The Acts of Welsh Rulers: 1120 to 1283*. Cardiff: University of Wales Press. 652.
25. CPR Edward I vol 1 1272–1281, 454. 'Aug 15 [1281], Hurst. The like for Peter de Chauveut, going beyond seas, nominating Hugh de Kendale and Walter de Bocking until a year after Michaelmas. Protection with clause volumus for him.'

Chapter 7

1. *Fœdera*. 190. '*REX dilecto & fideli fuo Ottoni de Grandifono, falutem. Cum, inter Magnificum Principem, Dominum R Romanorum illuftrem, & dilectum confanguineum noftrum, Philippum Comitem Sabaudie, ficut noftis, contentio feu gucrra lit mota; Nos,*

qui partem utramque fpecialis dilectionis brachiis amplexa mur, dedimus vobis, & dilecto Clerico noftro Magiftro Johanni de Derby Decano Lychefeld, quem propter hoc ad vos tranimitti mus, fpecialem & plenam poteftatem, per noftras patentes litteras quas ei liberari fecimus, tractandi inter partes iplas.'

2. Chron. Lanercost, 33. 'the Welsh nation, unable to pass their lives in peace, broke over their borders on Palm Sunday, carrying fire and sword among the people engaged in procession, and even laid siege [to some places – probably referring to Flint and Rhuddlan] whose Prince Llywelyn, deceived [more's the pity] by the advice of his brother David, fiercely attacked his lord the King; as we read written about Christ, 'him whom I loved most hath set himself against me'.'
3. John E. Morris. 1901. *The Welsh Wars of Edward I.* Oxford: Clarendon Press. 149–50.
4. Edward had been compared to a Leopard in the 1264 Song of Lewes. 'Whereunto shall the noble Edward be compared? Perhaps he will be rightly called a leopard. If we divide the name, it becomes lion and pard … A lion by pride and fierceness, he is by inconstancy and changeableness a pard, changing his word and promise, cloaking himself by pleasant speech.'
5. J. Beverley Smith. 2014. *Llywellyn ap Gruffudd: Prince of Wales*. Ebook. ed. Cardiff: University of Wales Press. Chap. 9. Apple. 'It would seem … [there was] a single purpose and a co-ordinated plan.'
6. Ibid.
7. Brut, 383 cited in J. G. Edwards, 1944. 'Edward I's Castle-Building in Wales', *The Proceedings of the British Academy XXXII*: 30.
8. Ann. Cestrienses, 108–9. '*et castrum de Rothelan eodem die obsedit*'. Or 'and laid siege to the castle of Rhuddlan on the same day'.
9. John E. Morris. 1901. *The Welsh Wars of Edward I.* Oxford: Clarendon Press. 154. 'but the castles of Flint and Rhuddlan held out and were in connection with Chester by water'.
10. Ibid. 31
11. CWR 1277–1326, 212. 'March 25 [1282], Stanley. To Roger de Mortuo Mari. The king learns that certain Welsh malefactors went by night to the castle of Hawardyn, with horses and arms … and in addition their aiders went feloniously to the king's castle at Flynt and burned certain houses their as far as possible (*ut potuerant*) and slew certain of the king's men there.'
12. Would translate literally as Valet but perhaps manservant is better, from Old French *vaslet*, from *vassellittus*, diminutive of Late Latin *vassallus* ('manservant, domestic, retainer'), from *vassus* ('servant')
13. R. R. Davies. 1987. *The Age of Conquest: Wales 1063–1415*. Oxford: Oxford University Press. 348–349.
14. Michael Prestwich. 1997. *Edward I.* Yale: Yale University Press. 232. 'It was after the first Welsh war that he [Edward] made political errors. To have driven two men who had been such bitter rivals as Llywelyn and Dafydd into the same camp was remarkably inept.'
15. Ibid. 183. 'He [Llywelyn], more than anyone else, was capable of organising nationwide resistance to the English, and it is hard to imagine that he was merely drawn into the rebellion at the last minute.'
16. Chron. Guisborough. Vol 2, 9. '*et sic Herodis et Pilati inita concordia et facta conjuratione valida insurrexerunt*'.

17. Ann. Cestrienses, 108–9. '*de consilio fratris sui Lewelini*' *or* 'with the counsel of his brother Llywelyn'.
18. Reginald de Grey had long experience in English law, he had been Sheriff of Nottinghamshire, Derbyshire and the Royal Forests and a Constable of Chester Castle, a Constable of Nottingham Castle (1265–66) and Constable of Northampton Castle (1267–68). He was Justice of Chester in 1270 and Sheriff of Chester (1270–74).
19. CPR. Edward I vol 1 1272–1281, 464. 'Nov 14 [1281], Westminster. Mandate to Gerard de Sancto Laurencio to deliver to him the castle of Flint with its armour, with all the receipts thereof for the same period.'
20. J. Beverley Smith. 2014. *Llywellyn ap Gruffudd*: Prince of Wales. Ebook. ed. Cardiff: University of Wales Press. Chap. 9. Apple.
21. Michael Prestwich, 2002. 'Document: Edward I's Wars in the Hagnaby Chronicle', *Journal of Medieval Military History* X: 199. and for full Latin text 206–7.
22. Ann. Cestrienses, 110. '*Stirps mendax, causa malorum.*' Or 'From a lying race, a cause of all evils.'
23. John E. Morris. 1901. *The Welsh Wars of Edward I.* Oxford: Clarendon Press. 156.
24. Arnold Taylor. 1985. *Studies in Castles and Castle-Building.* London: The Hambledon Press. 49. n4. '*Die Iovis vij Maii, Waltero de Bello Campo, eunti In municionem Montis Gomerii cum domino Otone de Grandisono capitaneo eiusdem municionis.*' Or 'Thursday, the seventh of May, Walter de Beauchamp, going to the fortification of Montgomery and Lord Othon de Grandson as the captain of the same fortification.'
25. John E. Morris. 1901. *The Welsh Wars of Edward I.* Oxford: Clarendon Press. 156.
26. Wurstemberger, vol 4. No 750. *'1268. Maji 11. Petræcastelli. 'Legamus vltra legata per nos in primo testamento nepotibus nostris Thome, Amedeo et Ludovico, filiis fratris nostri quondam Thome de Sabaudia Comitis, facta quidquid habemus et tenemus vel habere etc. in Anglia in terra Sussessia cum toto honore Aquile.'* Or '1268 11th May, Pierre-Châtel. 'Let us read beyond the legacies by us in the first testament to our grandsons Thomas, Amédée and Louis, to the sons of our brother, formerly Thomas Earl of Savoy, whatever we have and hold or have etc. in England in the land of Sussex, with all the Honour of the Eagle.'
27. CPR Henry III vol 6 1266–1272, 487. 'Whereas Peter de Sabaudia bequeathed the honours of Laigle and Hastings to Thomas de Sabaudia and Amadeus and Lewis his brothers, and these by reason of the bequest sued the said honours before the king; and whereas Edward the king's son, holding the honour of Hastings, is in remote parts, so that the king cannot make any order in this matter; grant to the said Thomas, Amadeus and Lewis of 100 marks a year at the Exchequer until the return of Edward.' This settlement appears to be temporary not permanent as it was made during Edward's return. We know thereafter they are both found in the retinue of household knights upon his return. Quite correctly the payment refers to the Honour of Hastings.
28. Bernard Andenmatten. 2000. '*Contraintes lignagères et parcours individuel: Les testaments de Pierre II de Savoie*' in *Pierre II de Savoie 'Le Petit Charlemagne'* Ed. Bernard Andenmatten, Agostino Paravicini Bagliani and Eva Pibiri. (Lausanne: Université de Lausanne). 277. '*Le premier en faveur de ses trois neveux leur confirme les donations en Angleterre et les recommande aux souverains anglais. On peut y voir le souci de leur assurer un avenir à la cour d'Angleterre*' Or 'The first [codicil] in favour

of his three nephews confirms their donations to England and recommends them to English sovereigns. We can see the concern to ensure them a future at the English court.'

29. John E. Morris. 1901. *The Welsh Wars of Edward I.* Oxford: Clarendon Press. 45.
30. Ann. Cestrienses, 108. '*et castrum de Rothelan eodem die obsedit*'. Or 'and laid siege to the castle of Rhuddlan on the same day'.
31. Michael Prestwich. 1997. *Edward I.* Yale: Yale University Press. 182. 'Llywelyn ap Gruffydd himself was not slow to join in what was rapidly becoming a nationwide rebellion and took part in attacks on Flint and Rhuddlan.' Citing the Welsh Assize Roll, 1277–1284, Ed. J. Conway Davies. Cardiff, 1940, 352.
32. Arnold Taylor. 1986. *The Welsh Castles of King Edward I.* London: The Hambledon Press. 31. n1. Citing TNA SC1/24/94. The letter quoted is from John Wyall of 9 May testifying to have served under Amédée de Savoie.
33. Arnold Taylor. 1985. *Studies in Castles and Castle-Building.* London: The Hambledon Press. 49. n4. '*Die mercurii viiij April, domino Amadeo de Sabaudia Capitaneo municionis Cestrie cum viij equis coopertis percipienti per diet ix.s. pro vadiis suis per idem tempus, x. Li.vij.s*' Or 'On Wednesday 8th April, the Lord Captain Amédée de Savoie at Chester and eight horses covered securing by day nine shillings, for the wages of men by the same time, Ten livres, seven shillings.'
34. Thomas III de Piedmont had felt aggrieved at being previously passed over as count in favour of his uncles, Pierre and then Philippe. Jean I, the Dauphin had died falling from a horse and as Humbert I the new Dauphin coming to power by marriage of Jean's sister Anne to Humbert, Baron of La Tour de Pin, had brought more land to the Dauphine then Thomas III had seen an opportunity to settle old scores with the Dauphine. He had been making war on the Dauphin for land in the Manche de Coligny when he died near La Côte-Saint-André. Thomas and Amédée's younger brother, Louis, had written to King Edward from Savoy begging leave for his brother to return. Count Philippe had previously delegated Piedmont to Thomas.
35. CPR Edward I vol 2 1281–1292, 30. Amédée was granted two years protection to travel 'beyond seas' on the 14th.
36. CWR 1277–1326, 231.'July 12 [1282], Rhuddlan. Richard le Taillur, Hugh le Serjaunt and Jul[iana] Daunsele, who were of the household of Eleanor, late the wife of Llewelyn son of Griffin, the king's enemy, have letters of [safe] conduct in coming into England and staying there so long as they behave themselves, lasting until St. Peter ad Vincula.'
37. J. Beverley Smith. 2014. *Llywellyn ap Gruffudd: Prince of Wales.* Ebook. ed. Cardiff: University of Wales Press. Apple.
38. Ann. Cestrienses, 108. '*David filius Griffini pacis perturbator efectus est, de consilio fratris Lewlini principis Wallie.*'
39. Following the deaths of Llywelyn and Dafydd the fate of their children was firstly that little Gwenllian, daughter of Llywelyn and Eleanor de Montfort, was placed in the Priory at Sempringham in Lincolnshire, where she remained until her death in 1337. As for the children of Dafydd, his daughter, Gwladys was also sent to a religious house in Lincolnshire, the convent at Sixhills, where she also spent the remainder of her life. Of the sons of Dafydd ap Gruffydd, Llywelyn ap Dafydd was arrested and taken to Rhuddlan to be imprisoned alongside his brother, Owain ap Dafydd. A force of cavalry and infantry were deployed to escort Llywelyn and Owain out of Gwynedd to Bristol before the end of July 1283. Llywelyn ap Dafydd died at Bristol Castle in 1287

and was buried in the nearby Dominican church (now known as Quakers Friars). His burial was paid for by Edward. His brother Owain would remain a prisoner until the end of his life, he was reportedly still alive in 1325, the last male heir of the House of Gwynedd.

40. The thousand marks being made available by '*Bonruncinus Walterii* and his fellows, merchants of Lucca of the society of the Riccardi.' Prestwich writes that 'the Riccardi received little by way of financial reward' for their loans to Edward, given the church's prohibition on usury, which is in and of itself quite remarkable. The answer as to why, lays in the access crown patronage gave them to English markets. such as using the King's Exchequer Courts to pursue their debtors and special access to the English wool market. During the period where they were bankers to the English Crown, the Riccardi were involved in around half of all the forward contracts with English wool producers. See Michael Prestwich. 1997. *Edward* I. Yale: Yale University Press. 241.
41. CWR 1277–1326, 215–16. 'April 14 [1282], Devizes. To all to whom. Notification that the king is bound to Devizes. Bonrunoinus Walterii and his fellows, merchants of Lucca (*Luk'*) of the society of the Ricardi, in 1,000 marks, which he paid to the king at London on Thursday before St. George, in the 10th year of his reign, by the hands of Master William de Luda, keeper of the wardrobe, for the expedition of certain of the king's affairs, which sum the king will cause to be paid in full to him and his fellows within a year from Whitsunday next, which the king promises to do in good faith. . .'
42. CWR 1277–1326, 230–31. 'June 10 [1282], Rhuddlan. To all to whom, etc. Notification that the king is bound to Rhuddlan. Bonrunci[n]us Walter' and his fellows, merchants of Lucca of the society of the Ricardi, in 1,000 marks, which he paid to the king at London on Friday after the Translation of St. Thomas the Martyr by the hands of Master William de Luda, keeper of the king's wardrobe, for the expedition of certain of the king's affairs, which sum the king will cause to be paid to Bonruncinus and his fellows within a year of Michaelmas next. . .'
43. CWR 1277–1326, 217. 'April 17 [1282], Devizes. To John de Greilly, seneschal of Gascony, or to him who supplies his place. Order to provide without delay forty good crossbowmen on foot and twelve crossbowmen on horseback at suitable wages to be assigned to them by him, and to send them to England to the king with the victuals that Master Poncius Amati, Bernard Fraunconn, and Elias le Carpenter shall cause to be provided in Gascony for the king's us^, and to cause them to have their wages from the constable of Bordeaux in coming to the king, which the king will cause to be allowed to the constable in his account.'
44. Michael Prestwich. 1997. *Edward I*. Yale: Yale University Press. 240..
45. Richard W. Kaeuper. 1973. *Bankers to the Crown: The Riccardi of Lucca and Edward I*. Princeton: Princeton University Press. 185,187.
46. Ann. Cestrienses, 108. '*fixit tentoriam apud Neuton*' Or 'pitching his tent at Newton'.
47. Ibid. '*Vigilia Sancti Petri ad Vincula venit Eadmundus frater Regis cum uxore sua Regina Navere apud Cestriam versus regem.*'
48. Ibid. '*In octavis Apostolorum Petri et Pauli castra metatus est cum exercitu suo apud Flint et munivit Castellum.*'
49. Ibid. '*Die Jovis proxime post octavus apostolorum venerunt rex et regina cum exercitu suo apud Rothelan.*'
50. John E. Morris. 1901. *The Welsh Wars of Edward I*. Oxford: Clarendon Press. 161.

51. CWR 1277–1326, 240. 'Oct. 7 [1282], Denbigh. To the archbishops, etc. Notification that the king, for the greater tranquility and common benefit (*utilitatem)* of him and his heirs and of all his realm of England, has granted by this charter to John de Warenna, earl of Surrey, the castle of Dynasbran. . . Witnesses. . . Otto de Grandisono.'
52. CWR 1277–1326, 241. 'Oct. 16 [1282], Rhuddlan. To the archbishops, etc. Notification that the king has granted by this charter to Henry de Lacy, earl of Lincoln, the cantreds of Ros and Roewynnok and the commote of Dynmael. . . Witnesses. . . Otto de Grandisono'
53. CWR 1277–1326, 243. 'Oct. 23 [1282], Denbigh. To the archbishops, etc. Notification that the king has granted by this charter to Reginald de Grey the castle of Ruthin and the *cantref* of *Defferencloyt . . . Witnesses. . . Otto de Grandisono'*
54. L. A. S. Butler. 2007. *Denbigh Castle*. (Cardiff: Cadw). 6. 'Whatever the nature of the defences at Denbigh, they were strong enough to withstand a month's siege by the English in the autumn of 1282.'
55. John E. Morris. 1901. *The Welsh Wars of Edward I.* Oxford: Clarendon Press. 166.
56. Archbishop John Peckham had come the see of Canterbury on 25 January 1279. He was a native of Sussex who was educated at Lewes Priory; as a Franciscan he studied at the University of Paris under Bonaventure, where he would later teach theology. While in Paris his Franciscan theology came up against, among others, the great theologian Thomas Aquinas. In around 1270, Peckham returned to England, where he had taught at the University of Oxford.
57. J. Beverley Smith. 2014. *Llywellyn ap Gruffudd: Prince of Wales*. Ebook. ed. Cardiff: University of Wales Press. Chap. 10. Apple.
58. Reg. John Peckham.469. '*Responsiones Walensium. Primo, quod licet dominus rex de Quatuor Cantredis et aliis terris ab eo datis magnatibus suis ac de insula Engleseye, nullum voluerit habere tractatum, tamen consilium principis non permittit, si contingat aliquam pacem fieri quin tractetur de praemissis eo quod isti cantredi sunt de puro principis tenemento in quibus merum ius habuerunt principes et praedecessores sui a temporibus Kambri filii Bruti; tum quia sunt de principatu, cuius confirmationem princeps obtinet per bone memoriae Ottobonum sedis apostolice legatum in regno Anglie, consensu domini regis et sui patris ad hoc interveniente, sicut patet cartas eorum inspicienti; tum quia etiam equius est quod veri heredes teneant dictos cantredos de domino rege pro pecunia et servitiis consuetis, quam eos dari extraneis et advenis, qui etsi fuerunt regis aliquando, tamen per vim et potentiam.*' Or 'Welsh Responses. First, although the king has not wished to the four cantrefi and the other lands given by him to his magnates, and the island of Anglesey, the prince's council does not permit any discussion of these should peace be made, since those cantrefi belong solely to the prince, and the princes predecessors from the time of Cymryw Camber, the son of Brutus have had the sole right to them because they belong to the principality whose confirmation the prince obtained from the papal legate Ottobuono with the consent of the king and his father, as their charters show, and because it is fairer that the true heirs hold the said cantrefi from the king for the accustomed money and services than for them to be given to strangers and newcomers; true, the lands were held for a time by the king, but only by force.' And '*Item, idem princeps non tenetur dimittere hereditatem suam et progenitorum suorum in Wallia a tempore Bruti, et etiam sibi confirmatam per Romanae sedis legatum, ut dictum est, et terram in Anglia receptare, unde linguam, mores, leges ac consuetudines ignorat; ubi possent etiam sibi quaedam maliciouse imponi ex odio inveterato a vicinis Anglicis,*

quibus terra illa privaretur imperpetuum.' Or 'Also, the prince is not obliged to abandon his inheritance and that of his ancestors in Wales since the time of Brutus, and confirmed to him by the papal legate, and receive land in England, where he is ignorant of the language, manners and laws and customs and where certain things could be maliciously imposed upon him by the inveterate hatred of the neighbouring English who would be deprived of that land forever.' 'Item, populus Snaudon' dicit quod licet princeps vellet dare regi seysinam eorundem, ipsi tamen nollent homagium faceri alicui extraneo, cujus linguam, mores, legesque penitus ignorant. Quia sic posset contingere eos imperpetuum captivari, ac crudeliter tractari, sicut alii cantredi circumquaque per ballivos regis ac alios regales alias tractati fuerunt, crudelius quan Saraceni, pront patet in rotulis quos vobis miserunt, sancte pater.' Or 'Also, the people of Snowdonia say that, even if the prince wished to give possession of them to the King, they do not wish to do homage to a stranger, of whose language, manners and laws they are entirely ignorant, since they could be captured and treated cruelly, just as the other cantrefi everywhere were treated more cruelly than the Saracens by the king's bailiffs and other royal officers as it is clear from the rolls they have sent to the archbishop.'

59. Geoffrey of Monmouth. 1966. *The History of the Kings of Britain*. London: Penguin Books Ltd. 15 'from Brutus the first King of the Britons'. And 40 'Brutus had … three famous sons whose names were Locrin, Albanact and Kamber … Kamber had that part which now lies beyond the River Severn, now called Wales.'
60. CWR 1277–1326, 275. 'to put an end finally to the matter that he has now commenced of putting down the malice of the Welsh, as Llywelyn son of Griffith and other Welshmen, his accomplices, have so many times disturbed the peace of the realm in the king's time and in the time of his progenitors, and they persist in their resumed rebellion.'
61. CWR 1277–1326, 235. '18th August 1282, Rhuddlan. To the king's barons and the subjects of the Cinque Ports in his garrison in Anglesey. Writ of aid in favour of Luke de Tany whom the king is sending in garrison and defence of those parts and to provide and make a bridge there and order to cause him to have cords and anchors necessary for the construction of the bridge as he shall direct.'
62. Rick Turner. 'The Life and Career of Richard the Engineer' in *The Impact of the Edwardian Castles in Wales*. Oxford: Oxbow Books, 2010. 49. '*Master Bertram et R socio suo*' Or 'Master Bertram and Richard his companion'.
63. Ibid.
64. Michael Prestwich, 2002. 'Document: Edward I's Wars in the Hagnaby Chronicle,' *Journal of Medieval Military History* X: 200. n13.
65. The encounter has become known as the Battle of Moel-y-Don, suggesting a site opposite Moel-y-Don, Anglesey. However, this site does not fit the description very well and originated in a ferry crossing, recent examination has suggested a site farther north nearer to Llanfaes, Edward's Anglesey work camp. This would mean either a mainland site at Traeth Lafan or Abergwyngregyn.
66. Chron. Guisborough, Vol 2, 10–11.
67. John E. Morris. 1901. *The Welsh Wars of Edward I*. Oxford: Clarendon Press.179–80.
68. J. Beverley Smith. 2014. *Llywellyn ap Gruffudd: Prince of Wales*. Cardiff: University of Wales Press. 860.
69. Brut, Penarth MS. 20, Jones 120 & 228, cited The Inventory of Historic Battlefields in Wales at http://battlefields.rcahmw.gov.uk/collections/getrecord/404319 retrieved

6 November 2018. '*Ac a vanassant goresgin arvon ac ena y gwanaeth pwyd y bont ar venei ac y torres y bont o tra llwith ac y bodes aneirif or season ac ereill a las.*'

70. Ann. Cestrienses, 110–112. Has a full list of the knights who perished: Dominus Willelmus de Audethleye, Dominus Lucas de Taneiey, Dominus Ricardus de Wellis, Amari Burdet, Petrus de Lamare, Ph. Burnell, Willelmus Burnell, Henricus Tyeis, Howelus fil. Griffini, Roger de Clifford Junior, Willelmus de Lindeseye, Willelmus le Butiler, Thomas de Halton, Willelmus de Oudingishelys, Petrus de la Quarere and Walterus le Jaie.
71. Michael Prestwich. 2002. 'Document: Edward I's Wars in the Hagnaby Chronicle'. *Journal of Medieval Military History* X: 200.
72. Ann. Cestrienses, 112. '*Cum magna difficultate evasit dominus Otto de Graunson.*'
73. Chron. Lanercost, 38. 'During that war in Wales a bridge of boats was made in the place called Menai, that is, between Snowdon and Anglesey, where Sir William de Audley, Lucas Tanay, Roger de Clifford and many others, old and young, were drowned.'
74. Chron. Thomas Wykes, 290. '*Interim dum archiepiscopus in Snowdounia triduo moraretur, regii proceres clam sed tamen insipienter ingressi sunt Snowdouniam, sestimantes se posse in dolo ipsam suis viribus occupare.*' Or' 'Meanwhile, while the archbishop was in Snowdonia for three days the nobles of the king would stay secretly, but still unwisely they entered Snowdonia, thinking that they could take possession of her by means of their own strength.'
75. Reg. John Peckham. 474. '*Qualiter demum Brutus, Dianæ praesagiis, non sine diaboli praestigiis per idoloatriam immolate cervæ venatitiæ obtentis, insulam Brittanicam pervaserit, per famosas historias declarator.*'
76. J. Beverley Smith. 2014. *Llywellyn ap Gruffudd: Prince of Wales*. Cardiff: University of Wales Press. 876. n141.
77. 'In addition you strike against the king, saying that the royal churches and church people are cruelly ravaged and killed by tyranny, to which we reply that the lord king was attacked by evils not that he made then, certainly neither has he considered making them; conversely he has voluntarily offered to us, of which I will urge him on when opportune, he intends to repair the churches at his own cost, though he puts this off until he can forever calm this period of warfare, as if he did this earlier they might again be destroyed by brigands.'
78. CWR 1277–1326. 259. 'Dec. 6 [1282], Rhuddlan. To all the king's bailiffs and faithful subjects of the counties of Nottingham and Derby to whom, etc. Writ of aid lasting until the Epiphany in favour of William Wyther, whom the king is sending to those counties to choose 300 footmen and to bring them to the king, as the king has enjoined upon him. The like in co. Lancaster in favour of Geoffrey de Langel[ey] to choose 200 footmen. The like in co. Hereford and the adjoining parts of the Welsh marches, to last until the Purification, in favour of Hugh de Turbervill, whom the king is sending to those parts and to other parts of the marches of Wales to choose footmen, to wit from the lands of Edmund, the king's brother, 200 men, from the parts of Went 300 men, from the lands of Reginald son of Peter 200 men, from the parts of Ewyas 100 men, from the parts of the forest of Dene 100 men, from the parts of Urchenfeud 100 men, from the community of the county of Hereford 200 men, from the parts of Ardeleyes, Lenhales and Kynton 100 men, and from the lands of the prior of Leministre 100 men. The like in cos. Stafford and Salop in favour of Richard de Bosco, whom the king is sending to choose 1,000 footmen in those counties. To the sheriffs of those counties. Order to cause to come

before Richard at certain days and places to be made known to them by him all the strong and powerful men of both counties, and to cause the thousand men aforesaid to be chosen from them.'

79. John E. Morris. 1901. *The Welsh Wars of Edward I.* Oxford: Clarendon Press. 188.
80. Richard Avent. 2004. *Dolywyddelan Castle, Dolbadarn Castle, Castell y Bere.* 2010 Edition. Cardiff: Cadw.25.
81. TNA E101/351/9 para 38.
82. Arnold Taylor. 1986. *The Welsh Castles of King Edward I.* London: The Hambledon Press. 44. n2.
83. Ibid. 75.
84. Richard Avent. 2004. *Dolywyddelan Castle, Dolbadarn Castle, Castell y Bere.* 2010 Edition. Cardiff: Cadw. 37–40.
85. TNA E101/351/9 '*Magistro Bertramo Ingeniatore apud castrum de Bere pro ingeniis ibidem faciendis.*'
86. Guillaume de Valence and Roger L'Estrange offered terms on 22 April 1282. £80 to be given for its surrender, TNA C47/2/4 records a payment so made of £53, 6s and 8d.
87. John E. Morris. 1901. *The Welsh Wars of Edward I.* Oxford: Clarendon Press. 193.
88. TNA, C47/2/4 '*pacatum domino Othon de Grandisono ad sustentacionem D et lx peditum secum euncium de Castro de Bere usque Hardelach xx.li per talliam.*'
89. TNA E101/4/1.
90. The key role of Othon de Grandson in building the Welsh castles had been highlighted by: Maxime Reymond. 1920. *Le Chevalier Othon I de Grandson. Revue Historique Vaudoise* 28: 164. '*Le pays conquis, Othon fut chargé d'en administrer la partie nord et d'y construire deş forteresses sûres: il avait appris de Pierre de Savoie, comme aussi pendant son séjour en Terre Sainte, la manière de les édifier.*' 'The country conquered, Othon was responsible for administering the northern part of it and building there secure fortresses: he had learned from Peter of Savoy, as also during his stay in the Holy Land, how to build them.' Michael Prestwich. 1997. *Edward I.* Yale: Yale University Press. 209. 'Other Savoyards assisted Master James. John de Bonvillars, a knight, was paid late in 1283 to go to Wales 'to supervise the king's works there', and the accounts of building work at Conwy show that he was involved in the details of allocating work to teams of masons. William Cicon, a Savoyard household knight, constable at Rhuddlan and then at Conwy, was probably influential, and Otto de Grandson doubtless had a part to play.' J. R. Maddicott, 2005. 'Grandson (Grandison), Sir Otto de'. *Oxford Dictionary of National Biography.* 'Grandson was essentially viceroy of the newly conquered lands, a position suggestive of the confidence placed in him by Edward; and he may have had some influence, as his Savoyard friends and kinsmen certainly did, on the design of the castles by which Wales was to be held down.' And indeed, as we saw the very instigator of Edward hiring Maître Jacques de Saint George to build castles in Wales. See Arnold Taylor. 1963. Some notes on the Savoyards in North Wales, 1277-1300. With special reference to the Savoyard element in the construction of Harlech Castle. Genava 11. 298. n28. 'In a letter to King Edward, written at Dolforwyn during the siege and dated 3 April 1277, Otto de Grandson said that when the castle surrendered it would need much repair, and expressed his fears that if he assigned the work to Master Bertram the latter would 'devise too many things and perhaps waste the king's money, and therefore some other man would ne needed who would take the matter in hand' (Cal. Ancient

Correspondence concerning Wales. 31). This evidence of Otto de Grandson's lack of confidence in Master Bertram and his wish to employ someone else is of the greatest interest, seeing that it might point to one of the reasons that led to the bringing of Master James over from Savoy to take charge of the works in Wales.'

91. Michael Prestwich. 2020. *Othon de Grandson et la Cour d'Edouard I. Othon I de Grandson (vers 1240–1328)*. Lausanne: Cahiers Lausannois d'Histoire Médiévale. 12. 'In 1283 Othon was the first commander to reach the site where Harlech castle was built'
92. John E. Morris. 1901. *The Welsh Wars of Edward I.* Oxford: Clarendon Press.194–195.
93. CWR 1277–1326, 281.
94. Chron. Guisborough. Vol 2, 14. 'David *autem, a praedicta caede fugien, tandem vero et mariscis latitabat fere per annum, tandem vero captus in vigilia Sancti Maurine adductus est, et in parliamento de Solopeshire, quod tenuit rex post festum Sancti Michaelis, tanquam seductor et proditor et homicida judicatus tractus est et suspensus, et postes membratim divisus et quatuor ejus membra in quatuor partes Angliae missa sunt in memorium rei perpetue*.'
95. Chron. Lanercost, 35. '*David Walensis, epuos, ignis, funis, et ensis, Infelix, fatum tibi dant recis et cruciatum. Es nece – fur, proditor, ac homicida, Hostis et ecclesiae debes de jure perire.*'
96. Ann. Dunstable, 294. '*Quia illud fecit tempore Dominicæ Passionis*' or 'because it was done at the time of the Lord's Passion.'
97. Katherine Royer. 2003. 'The Body in Parts: Reading the Execution Ritual in Late Medieval England'. *Historical Reflections/Réflexions Historiques* 29: 327.
98. Chron. Lanercost, 35.
99. Ann. Dunstable, 294.
100. Michael Prestwich. 1997. *Edward I*. Yale: Yale University Press.203.
101. Carl von Clausewitz, 1968. *On War*. London: Penguin Books. 182.
102. Michael Prestwich. 1997. *Edward I*. Yale: Yale University Press. 359.
103. CCR Edward I vol 2 1279–1288, 273. 'Aug 22 [1284], Bangor. To the Justiciary of Ireland. Whereas the king has left Otto de Grandisono in Wales to keep that land, and to expedite certain other things in those parts, as the king has more fully enjoined upon him by word of mouth, he orders the justiciary to cause 500 quarters of wheat and as many quarters of oats and 200 quarters of malt and 50 tuns of wine to be bought and sent to Wales, as Otto's attorneys to be sent to him in this behalf shall explain to him on Otto's behalf.'
104. Ivor Bowen. Ed. 1908. The Statutes of Wales. London: T Fisher Unwin.2-3. No. 12 'The Statute of Wales. Edward, by the Grace of God King of England, Lord of Ireland, and Duke of Aquitaine, to all his Subjects of his Land of Snowdon, and of other his Lands in Wales, Greeting in the Lord. . . We have Provided and by our command ordained, That the Justices of Snowdon shall have the Custody and Government of the Peace of Us the King in Snowdon, and our Lands of Wales adjoining; and shall administer Justice to all Persons whatsoever, according to the original Writs of Us the King, and also the Laws and Customs underwritten. We likewise will and ordain that there be sheriffs, Coroners, and Bailiffs of Commotes in Snowdon and our Lands of those parts. A Sheriff of Anglesey, under whom shall be the whole Land of Anglesea, with its Cantreds, Metes, and Bounds. A Sheriff of Caernarvan, under whom shall be the Cantred of Arvan, the Cantred of Arthlencoyth, the Commote of Cruthin, the Cantred of Thleen, and the

Commote of Yvionith. A Sheriff of Meirioneth, under whom shall be t h e Cantred of Meirioneth, the Commote of Ardovey, and the Commote of Penthlin, and the Commote of Deyrinoin, with their Metes and Bounds.' CWR Edward I 1277-1294, 284. 'March 20 [1284], Rhuddlan. To the king's sheriffs, constables, bailiffs, ministers and all his men of his land of Snaudon and of his other lands in Wales to whom, etc. Notification that the king has appointed John de Havering during pleasure his justiciary under Otto de Grandisono, justiciary of Snaudon and of other lands of the king in Wales, and order to be intendent to him in that office.'

105. J. H. Baker. 2007. An Introduction to English Legal History (4th ed.). Oxford: OUP. 15.
106. R.R. Davies. 1987. *The Age of Conquest: Wales 1063–1415*. Oxford: Oxford University Press. 364.
107. Ibid.
108. Ibid. 365–66.
109. TNA 101/351/2.
110. TNA SC8/296/14779.
111. TNA E101/4/3 and TNA E101/4/6.

Chapter 8

1. *Fœdera*. 204. '*Qui etiam pro certo dixerunt mihi quod 5. Civitates Sicilie infurrexerunt contra Regem Caro um, & interfecerunt omnes Gallicos, habitantes in eis*.' Or 'who also told me with certainty that the 5 cities of Sicily were enraged against King Charles and killed all the French who lived in them.'
2. C.V. Langlois. 1905. '*Notes et documents relatifs à l'histoire du Xiii siècle*' *Revue Historique LXXXVII* Issue 1 . 67. '*Nova Curie sunt quod tota Sicilia in manifesta rebellione est contra regem, et timetur ne rex Aragonum qui maximum apparatum fecit in mari intrare debeat illud regnum. Rex Sicilie magnum exercitum Neapoli congregat, contra Siculos intendens dirigere gressus suos*.' Or 'The news at the Curia is that the whole of Sicily is in open rebellion against the king, and it is feared that the king of Aragon, who has made the greatest preparations at sea, should enter that kingdom. The king of Sicily gathers a large army at Naples, intending to direct his steps against the Sicilians.'
3. In 1277 Charles d'Anjou had purchased a claim to the disputed Kingdom of Jerusalem.
4. Steven Runciman. 1958. *The Sicilian Vespers: A History of the Mediterranean World in the Later Thirteenth Century*. Cambridge: Cambridge University Press. 115.
5. John Julius Norwich. 2016. *Sicily: A Short History from the Ancient Greeks to the Cosa Nostra*. London: John Murray. 110–11.
6. Ibid.
7. Michael Prestwich. 1997. *Edward I*. Yale: Yale University Press. 321.
8. Mary C. L. Salt. 1929. 'List of English Embassies to France, 1272–1307'. *The English Historical Review* 44: 269. '19 February 1282, John de Greilly was at Paris, sent with Maurice de Craon to excuse Edward from the auxilium owing to Philip against Spain.'
9. Elizabeth A. R. Brown, 1987. 'The Prince is Father of the King: The Character and Childhood of Philip the Fair of France', *Mediaeval Studies* 49, 315.
10. CPR Edward I vol 2 1281–129, 213. 'Mandate to Baruncinus Galteri, Rcyner de Luk', and Orlandinus de Podio and their fellows, merchants of Lucca, to pay to Otto de

Grandisono as much money as he may require of them for the king's affairs, and the king will reimburse them.' And Protection, with *clause volumus*, until St. Peter ad Vincula for Henry de Cobeham, going beyond seas with Otto de Grandisono on the king's affairs.'

11. Reg. Honorius IV. 371. Nos 534 and 535. 'Sainte-Sabine, 13 juin 1286. 534 *Johanni de Vescie, regis Anglie militi, habendi secum altare portatile in quo sibi et familie sue possit per capellanum pro prium divina officia facere celebrari, concedit facultatem. (n° 38, fol. 139 vo.) Nobili viro Johanni de Vescie, militi carissimiin Christo filii nostri. regis Anglie illustris. Apostolice Sedis beni gnitas-. Dat. Rome ut supra. In eundem modum pro nobili viro Octone de Grandisono, Lausanensis diocesis. Sainte-Sabine, 13 juin 1286. 535 Nobili viro Octoni de Grandisono concedit ut aliquem discretum presbiterum possit in confessorem suum eligere. (no 39, fol. 139 v°.) Nobili viro Octoni de Grandisono, Lausanensis diocesis. Personam tuam sincera -. Dat. ut supra.*'
12. John Brownbill. Ed. 1914. The History of the Abbey in Ledger of Vale Royal Abbey. Manchester: Manchester Record Society. 11. See also H. Fishwick. 1874. The History of the Parish of Kirkham in the County of Lancaster. Chetham Society. Vol 92. 30. 'In 1286 Otto de Grandison obtained a bull from pope Honorius IV., by which the advowson was conferred upon the abbey of Vale royal for ever, and on the 27th January 1287 the king confirmed his previous grant.'
13. Michael Prestwich. 1997. *Edward I.* Yale: Yale University Press. 323.
14. *La Finanza Sabauda.* vol 2, 291.
15. Jean-Pierre Chapuisat. 1964. 'Au service de deux rois d'Angleterre au XIIIe siècle: Pierre de Champvent'. *Revue Historique Vaudoise* 72: 170. n2.
16. *Fœdera.* 15.
17. Esther Rowland Clifford. 1961. *A Knight of Great Renown: The Life and Times of Othon de Grandson.* Chicago: University of Chicago Press. 91.
18. Libourne gets its name from the Lieutenant of Gascony who built the bastide there Roger de Leybourne.
19. Steven Runciman. 1960. *The Sicilian Vespers.* London: Penguin Books. 289.
20. Ibid.
21. Ibid. 288.
22. Ibid.
23. Jean Pierre Chapuisat. 1989. *De Mont-sur-Rolle à Windsor, de la Dullive à Dumfries ... La Maison de Savoie et le Pays de Vaud* 97: 120.
24. Steven Runciman. 1960. *The Sicilian Vespers.* London: Penguin Books. 289.
25. Ibid.
26. *Fœdera.* 30. '*Nomina vero Obsidum prædictorum sunt hæc ... Johannes de Vescy, Otto de Grandisono*' or 'These are the names of the aforesaid hostages … Jean de Vescy, Othon de Grandson.'
27. Esther Rowland Clifford. 1961. *A Knight of Great Renown: The Life and Times of Othon de Grandson.* Chicago: University of Chicago Press. 96. 'Some of the hostages were kept at Jaca, a frontier town whose protecting ring of walls with their twenty-eight towers and seven gates was guarded in turn by the surrounding white circle of the Pyrenees, but it is probable that Othon, because of his importance, was one of those who was sent down to the capital, Saragossa [sic].'
28. *Fœdera.* 34. '*ad venandum cum Canibus & Avibus*' or 'to hunt with dogs and bird'.

29. Jean Paul Trabut-Cussac. 1952. '*Itinéraire d'Édouard Ier en France 1286–1289*'. *Bulletin of Historical Research* XXV. Issue 72. 180. n63. RG ii. No. 1119. 'June 1289. . . *Dei permissione Bathoniensis et Wellensis episcopus, et Oto de Grandisono, miles, illustris domini nostri regis Anglie vices gerentes in Vasconia, dilecto suo magistro Ade de Norfouk, constabaulario Burdegale, et qui pro tempore fuerit, salutem in Domino sempiternam.*'
30. Alison Weir. 2020. *Queens of the Crusades: Eleanor of Aquitaine and her Successors*. London: Penguin Random House UK. 644.
31. CPR Edward I vol 2 1281–1292, 356. 'May 18 [1290], Westminster. *Inspeximus* and confirmation of a deed, dated at London, xv. Kalends Westminster. June 1290, whereby Anthony, bishop of Durham, and Otto de Grandisono, executors of the will of John de Vescy.'
32. Born Qālawūn as-Sālihī he would become known as al-Mansūr Qālawūn that is Qālawūn the Victorious
33. He arrived too late to meet Pope Honorius IV, who had recently died. So, Bar Sauma instead engaged in negotiations with the cardinals and visited St. Peter's Basilica.
34. Rabban or Rabbi Bar Sauma was born circa 1220 in or near modern day Beijing, China. His name Bar Sauma is Aramaic for 'son of fasting'. He became a Nestorian monk and then religious teacher. The emperor, Kublai Khan is thought to have sent Bar Sauma west to Jerusalem. En route he came into the employ of the Ilkhanate in Baghdad. Hence the embassy to Europe on behalf of Arghūn. Bar Sauma travelled with a large retinue of assistants, and 30 riding animals. Companions included the Church of the East Christian (archaon) Sabadinus; Thomas de Anfusis or Tommaso d'Anfossi, who helped as interpreter and was also a member of a famous Genoese banking company; and an Italian interpreter named Uguetus or Ugeto (Ughetto). Bar Sauma likely did not speak any European languages, though he was known to be fluent in Chinese, Turkish and Persian. Europeans communicated to him in Persian.
35. Sir E. A. Wallis Budge. 1928. Trans. *The Monks of Kublai Khan Emperor of China*. London: Harrison & Sons Ltd. 58.
36. Benjamin. F. Byerly and Catherine Ridder Byerly. Ed. 1986. Records of the Wardrobe and Household 1286-1289. London, No. 543 (to Peter Crerges, *valetto episcopi orientalis nuncii Argoni Tartarorum*, October) and No. 1082 (to Passarat, *menestrallo et vigilatori Mar de Barsauma, episcopi orientalis nuncii Argoni Can Tartarorum*, 2 November). 67, 117.
37. French royal archives, via https://web.archive.org/web/20080618170019/http://chass.colostate-pueblo.edu/history/seminar/sauma/saumaletter.htm accessed 21 February 2020.
38. Steven Runciman. 1954. *A History of the Crusades: Volume III The Kingdom of Acre and the later Crusades*. Eleventh Edition. London: The Folio Society. 336.
39. Maxime Reymond. 1920. '*Le Chevalier Othon I de Grandson*'. *Revue Historique Vaudoise* 28: 165. '*Il [Jean de Grailly] avait pris femme à la Côte, à Saint-Symphorien près Rolle, et son lieutenant à Saint-Jean d'Acre fut Jean de Saint-Oyend, localité voisine, alors qu'un autre de ses compagnons d'armes était Aymon de Sallenove, qui fut châtelain de Rolle? Ainsi Jean de Grailly groupait autour de lui à Acre une partie de la noblesse de la Côte [Vaud].*' Or 'He [Jean de Grailly] had taken a wife of *La Côte* [Vaud], at Saint-Symphorien near Rolle, and his lieutenant at Saint-Jean d'Acre was Jean de Saint-Oyend, a neighbouring town, while another of his companions in arms was Aymon de

Sallenove, who was castellan of Rolle 1. Thus, Jean de Grailly gathered around him at Acre a part of the nobility of *La Côte* [Vaud]. Saint Oyens remains a village of the heights above Rolle.

40. *Fœdera.* 47. *Litera de Credentia Nicholao Papa, Cardinalibus. Anctiffimo Patri in Chrifto, ac Domino reverendo, Domino Nicholao, Dci gratia facrofancte Romane & Univerfalis Ec clefice Summo Pontifici, Edwardus, &c. devota pedum ofcula beatorum cum omni reverentia & honore. Dilectos confiliarios & fideles noftros, Nobilem virum Otho nem de Grandifono militem, ac religiofum & difcretum Virum & Fratrem Guillielmum de Hothum, de ordine prædicatorum, pro quibufdum Negotiis noftris, ad Sanctitatis veftra præfentiam defti nantes: Paternitatem veftram humiliter inploramus, quatenus præfatos Nuncios noftros folita benignitate recipere, & eifdem, vel corum altcri, fuper omnibus & fingulis, que vobis, ex parte noftra viva vocis oraculo, duxerint, vel duxerit exponenda, indubitabilem fi dem & firmam credentiam adhibere velitis, veluti nobis, ipfis, ac ea, quæ vice noftra petierint, ad gratiam exauditionis admittere, & profequi gratiofe. Vitam profperam & longævam annuat vobis Deus, ad Regimen Ecclefia fue Sancte & Pacem totius populi Chriftiani.Dat. apud Lauerdake octavo die Maii, Anno Domini millefimo ducentefimo octogefimo nono.*
41. Ibid. 104.
42. CCR Edward I vol 2 1279–1288, 312. 'Jan 28 [1285], Canterbury. To Geoffrey de Nevill, justice of the Forest beyond Trent. Order to cause Gerard de Wypeyns, parson of the church of Creystok, to have in the forest of Inglewode ten oaks fit for timber, of the king's gift.'
43. Esther Rowland Clifford. 1961. *A Knight of Great Renown: The Life and Times of Othon de Grandson.* Chicago: University of Chicago Press. 97. n28. 'Othon was paid in the currencies of Lausanne, Turin, Parma, Bologna, and Florence, which is a good indication that he probably followed what is still the most usual route from the north to Rome.'
44. Joseph Stevenson. 1870. 'Documents Illustrative of the History of Scotland'. 134–38. Used in Esther Rowland Clifford. 1961. *A Knight of Great Renown: The Life and Times of Othon de Grandson.* Chicago: University of Chicago Press and Michael Prestwich. 1997. *Edward I.* Yale: Yale University Press.
45. Richard W. Kaeuper. 1973. *Bankers to the Crown: The Riccardi of Lucca and Edward I.* Princeton: Princeton University Press. 87.
46. Bartolomeo di Neocastro. 1900. *Historia Sicula 1250–1293.* Vol XIII. Part 3. Ed. Guiseppe Paladino. Bologna: Nicola Zanichelli. 110–1. '*Dominus meus rex Angliae reges arguit, quod altercantes de Regno Siciliae bella committunt, licet quis arma justius sumpserit, ille non recte decernat; sed ad amicam conscientiam rediens mira tur, quod tuae paternitatis conscientia, qua totius orbis circulus gubernatur, reges ipsos tam nefaria proelia patitur miscuisse. Nonne, cum christiani sint Siculi, si ab Italis aut Galliae populis, et e converso si ipsi a Siculis confundantur. Romana Sedes arguitur? Aut dicis nefas esse, si, quas potes, clades eruas filiorum ? Deo quidem foret acceptum et pium hominibus, si, erga reges discordes tuae sanctitatis aperiens oculos, inter ipsos interponeres tuae clementiae gratiam, ut quos saevire permittis, ad pacem utinam declinares, saltem 'pacis ad instar eos admitteres. Quod si jusseris, non negabunt. Et propterea dominus meus humiliter supplicat, ut considerans quanta ex seditione regum ipsorum discrimina aubeant partes orbis, et quantum, a singu'is creaturis proinde rationabiliter arguaris, eorum quod potes, furoribus impone silentium, statuens Fœdera treguarum annorum duorum inter*

ipsos et eorum valitores, infra quos dictus dominus meus una tecum et rege Franciae, ac 'rege Castellae finali decisione provideat de pace ipsorum firmiter obtinenda. Alioquin piacere tibi, Sancte Pater, non poterit, sì cum hos certare permiseris, quos recipere potes benignus ad pacem, ceteros principes orbis terrae, et cunctum populum christianum, ad quorum notitiam jam protervitas ista pervenit, honore matris Ecclesiae semper salvo, in te tamquam contra hostem Universalis Matris, et aemulum fidei Christianae, licet invitos, procul dubio provocabis; sciturus, quod dominus meus non erit e sociis ultimus, qui, furentibus 'aliis, ne simili forsan exemplo depereat, ille arma proposita contra tantam perfidiam sumera non tardabit.'

47. Ibid. 54. '*Litera a Carolo Rege Sicilie, ad Alfonfum Regem Aragonia ... mediante Domino Odone de Grandifono, pro parte illuftris Principis Domini Edwardi Anglorum Regis Magnifici.*'
48. T. Hudson Turner. 1851. 'Unpublished Notices of the Times of Edward I, and of his Relations with the Moghul Sovereigns of Persia'. *The Archaeological Journal* 8: 48. Jacques Paviot. 2000. England and the Mongols. *Journal of the Royal Asiatic Society 10.* no *3: 314.*
49. Roger Crowley. 2019. *Accursed Tower*. New Haven: Yale University Press. 129.

Chapter 9

1. Calendar of Papal Registers Relating to Great Britain and Ireland: Volume 1, 1198–1304, Ed. W. H. Bliss (London, 1893). 473–74, 477. British History Online www.british-history.ac.uk/cal-papal-registers/brit-ie/vol1/pp512–527 (accessed 18 September 2024).
2. Michael Prestwich. 1997. *Edward I.* Yale: Yale University Press.328. Christopher Tyerman. 1996. *England and the Crusades, 1095-1588.* Chicago: University of Chicago Press. 235.
3. Michael Prestwich. 1997. *Edward I.* Yale: Yale University Press. 329.
4. Alan Forey. 2017. 'Otto of Grandson and the Holy Land, Cyprus and Armenia'. *Crusades* 16. Taylor & Francis. 81.
5. Charles L. Kingsford. 1909. *Sir Otho de Grandison 1238?–1328.* Transactions of the Royal Historical Society 3: 138. 'In the meantime, Sir Otho de Grandison was to go to Acre and prepare the way for the King's own coming.'
6. Christopher Tyerman. 1996. *England and the Crusades, 1095–1588.* Chicago: University of Chicago Press. 238.
7. Ibid. 236.
8. *Excidium Acconis*, 57.
9. Ann. London. 99. '*et in crastino dominus Otho de Grandissono adivit Jerosolimam ad providentiam domini Edwardi regis Angliæ faciendam.*' Or 'and on the morrow Lord Otho de Grandisson went to Jerusalem to make provision for Lord Edward, King of England.'
10. Chron. Guisborough. Vol 2. 24. '*Othone de Grandisono qui cum thesauris regis Angliæ ibidem missus ut viam pararet ante faciem ejus, habuit enim in proposito rex in terram proficisci, durante din subsidione hostium cum eisdem thesauris in Cyprum fugiens, mutato cognomine, in congressu militari parvum fecit sonum.*' Or 'Otho de Grandison, who was sent thither with the treasures of the king of England to prepare the way before his face, for the king had purposed to march into the land, during the din with the aid

of the enemy, fleeing to Cyprus with the same treasures, having changed his surname, made little noise in the military meeting.'

11. RG iii. 21. No 1924. '1924. *Rex magistro Willelmo de Sancto Remi gio, ballivo insularum Gerneseye et Gereseye, salutem. Cum dilectus [et] fidelis noster Oto de Grandisono, cui insulas illas commisimms et conce simus, easdem insulas vobis commiserit sub ipso eustodiendas, sub confideneia speciali quam de vobis reportat, et idem Oto moram faciat in Dei obsequio in Terra sancta de nostra licencia et vo luntate, per quod denariis ad debitorum suorum exoneracionem plurimum indiget hiis diebus, vobis mandamus firmiter injungentes quod omnia arre ragia et debita et eciam firmas que sibi in insulis predictis debentur de tempore retroacte. et attornato mercatorum nostrorum Lucanensium de societate Rieardorum has litteras nostras defe renti, sine dilacione aliqua, nomine ipsins Ottonis liberetis per eyrograffum inter vos et ipsum lato rem hinc inde conficiendum. Et hoc, sicut hono vestrum diligitis, et dampnum et seandalum vitare volueritis, nullo modo omittatis; et quid in hae parte feceritis et statum insularum predicta rum venerabili patri R., Bathoniensi et Wellensi episcopo, generali attornato * prefati Otonis, distincte et aperte per vestras litteras remandetis.*'
12. CPR Edward I vol 2 1281–1292, 367. 'June 20 [1290], Westminster. Protection with clause volumus, for two years, for William de Henleye, prior of the Hospital of St. John of Jerusalem in England, going to the Holy Land as envoy of the king.' Christopher Tyerman. 1996. *England and the Crusades, 1095–1588*. Chicago: University of Chicago Press.237.
13. CRRS, 131.
14. Hist. Anglicana, 177. '*Et statim post, dominus Joannes de Peccham, archiepiscopus Cantuariae, prædicavit de cruce Christi, et plures magnates Angliae sumpserunt crucem, videlicet, dominus Thomas de Bek, episcopus de Sancto David, comes Gloverniæ et domina Johanna uxor sua, dominus Robertus de Thateshale, et dominus Robertus filius suus et haeres, et dominus Oto de Grantoun receperunt crucem sine spe remeandi; et statim festo prædicto, ut dictum est, cum omni sollemnitate finito iter suum arripuerunt in Terram Sanctam.*' Or 'And immediately after, lord John de Peccham, archbishop of Canterbury, preached about the cross of Christ, and several magnates of England took up the cross, namely, lord Thomas de Bek, bishop of St. David's, [the] earl of Gloucester [Gilbert de Clare] and lady Joan [of Acre] his wife, lord Robert de Tattershall, and Lord Robert, his son and heir, and Lord Othon de Grandson, received the cross without hope of recovery; and immediately after the foretold feast, as has been said, when all the solemnities were over, they took their journey to the Holy Land.'
15. CPR Edward I vol 2 1281–1292, 362. 'June 10 [1290], Westminster. Otto de Grandisono, going to the Holy Land, nominating [his attorneys] Henry, prior of Wenlok, and William de Grandisono for three years.'
16. Ibid. 367. 'June 20 [1290], Westminster. The prior of Wenlok, going beyond seas, nominating Brother James de Cosseneye and Thomas le Enfaunt for one year.'
17. Ibid. 363. 'June 10 [1290], Westminster. Protection with clause volumus, for three years, for Otto de Grandisono, Westminster. going to the Holy Land.'
18. Ibid. 366 and 372. 'June 20 [1290], Westminster. Protection with clause *volumus*, for three years, for Hugh de Brok, going to the Holy Land in the company of Otto de Grandisono.' And 'July 11 [1290], Westminster. Protection, with clause volumus, for: William le Lunge, going with Otto de Grandisono to Jerusalem, for three years.'

19. Ibid. 367. 'June 20 [1290], Westminster, Letters for William de Henleye, prior of the Hospital of St. John of Jerusalem, going to the Holy Land as the king's envoy.'
20. Charles L. Kingsford. 1909. *Sir Otho de Grandison 1238?–1328*. Transactions of the Royal Historical Society 3: 138. n6 and CPR Edward I vol 2 1281–1292, 356–76.
21. CPR Edward I vol 2 1281–1292. 372. 'July 11 [1290], Westminster. Protection, with clause volumus, for: William le Lunge, going with Otto de Grandisono to Jerusalem, for three years.'
22. Esther Rowland Clifford. 1961. *A Knight of Great Renown: The Life and Times of Othon de Grandson.* Chicago: University of Chicago Press. 111.
23. CPR Edward I vol 2 1281-1292, 372-3. 'July 3 [1290], Havering. Inspeximus and confirmation of a charter of Otto de Grandisono to Peter de Wypeyns [Vuippens] his nephew, whereby the said Otto-after reciting that Edward I. had granted to him in fce tail by the service of two knights' fees, the castle, cantred and land of Okonagh, the town of Tiperari, the castle and town of Kilfekle, the land of Muskerye, the manor of Kilsilam, the town of Clummele and the land of Estremoyc, and also Hynaon (which he formerly had of the gift of the king for life)-grants to the said Peter the whole land of Estremoye and Oenny for ever for the service to the king of half a knight's fee, with remainder to Gerard de Crous [Oron], nephew of the said Otto. Witnesses: -R. bishop of Bath and Wells, J. bishop of Winchester, P. bishop of Exeter, Edmund, earl of Lancaster, brother of the king, Edmund, earl of Cornwall, Gilbert de Clare, earl of Gloucester and Hertford, Robert Tibotot, John de Sancto Johanne, Walter de Bello Campo, Peter de Chaumpaigne, knights, and others. Inspeximus and confirmation of a charter of the said Otto granting in fee simple to Peter de Estanayaco (or Estanayco) [Estavayer], his nephew, out of the above lands, the castle and land of Okonagh and the town of Tiperari, for the service to the king of half a knight's fee, with remainder to John de Estratelinges [Estavayer], called 'Russelet,' another nephew of the said Otto; witnessed as above.' Thus, should Vuippens not return his lands pass to Gérard d'Oron, should Pierre d'Estavayer not return his lands pass to Jean d'Estavayer.
24. E. B. Fryde, D. E. Greenway, S. Porter & I. Roy. (Eds) 1986. *Handbook of British Chronology*. Third Edition. London: Offices of the Royal Historical Society. 76.
25. CCR Edward I vol 3 1288–1296, 80. 'May 17 [1290], Westminster. To the treasurer and barons of the exchequer. Order to cause Oto de Grandisono to be acquitted of 1321. 7s. 6d. exacted from him for the stores (warnestura) lately sent from Ireland to Wales for the munition of the king's castles and the maintenance of Oto's household there by Stephen, late bishop of Waterford, then justiciary of Ireland, wherewith the justiciary charged him in the exchequer of Ireland, as appears in the king's letters patent made to Otto concerning this, as the king has pardoned Oto by his letters patent.'
26. CCR Edward I vol 3 1288-1296, 137. 'Enrolment of agreement made, on Tuesday after St. Bartholomew, 18 Edward, between Sir Otto de Grandisono and Sir Richard de Burgo, earl of Ulster, whereby Otto demises to Richard all the lands that Otto had in Estermoye and Oheny, for the term of Otto's life; rendering therefor 721. yearly at Clomele. Richard grants to Otto power to distrain him for this sum if he fail in payment by his cattle, goods and chattels in Estermoye and Oheny, and in his manors of Lislathelach, Tristelanranth and Esclou, with power for the treasurer and barons of the exchequer of Dublin to distrain for the said sum if Otto be insufficient to distrain therefor, and granting that he will give the king 601. at the said exchequer as often as he shall fail in payment, and to

the treasurer and barons 201. for their labours in the like case. Witnesses: Sir Robert, bishop of Bath and Wells, Anthony, bishop of Durham, Sir William de Vescy, Sir John de Sancto Johanne, Sir Hugh de Brok, knights.'

27. CPR Edward I vol 2 1281–1292, 372. 'July 3 [1290], Havering. *Inspeximus* and confirmation of a charter of Otto de Grandisono to Peter de Wypeyns his nephew, whereby the said Otto-after reciting that Ed. ward I. had granted to him in fce tail by the service of two knights' fees, the castle, cantred and land of Okonagh, the town of Tiperari, the castle and town of Kilfekle, the land of Muskerye, the manor of Kilsilam, the town of Clummele and the land of Estremoyc, and also Hynaon (which he formerly had of the gift of the king for life)-grants to the said Peter the whole land of Estremoye and Oenny for ever for the service to the king of half a knight's fee, with remainder to Gerard de Crous, nephew of the said Otto. Witnesses: -R. bishop of Bath and Wells, J. bishop of Winchester, P. bishop of Exeter, Edmund, earl of Lancaster, brother of the king, Edmund, earl of Cornwall, Gilbert de Clare, earl of Gloucester and Hertford, Robert Tibotot, John de Sancto Johanne, Walter de Bello Campo, Peter de Chaumpaigne, knights, and others. Inspeximus and confirmation of a charter of the said Otto granting in fee simple to Peter de Estanayaco (or Estanayco), his nephew, out of the above lands, the castle and land of Okoragh and the town of Tiperari, for the service to the king of half a knight's fee, with remainder to John de Estratelinges, called 'Russelet,' another nephew of the said Otto; witnessed as above.'
28. Aug. Burnand. 1911. '*Vaudois en Angleterre au XIIIe siècle, avec Othon Ier de Grandson: (d'après* M.C.-L. Kingsford)'. *Revue Historique Vaudoise*, 214.
29. CPR Edward I vol 2 1282–129. 373. 'July 13 [1290] Westminster, Acknowledgment of the king's indebtedness to Lapus Bonchi, Gradus Westminster. Pini and their fellows, merchants of the society of the Amanati of Pistoia, in 3,000 marks, received by the hands of Otto de Grandisono, to whom the king has given it in aid of his journey to Jerusalem; with promise to repay the same at All Saints.'
30. TNA Currency Calculator.
31. William Henry Dixon. 1863. *Fasti Eboracenses:* Lives of the Archbishops of York. London: Longman, Green, Longman & Roberts. 337. '1290, May 15. The archbishop grants the first fruits of the archdeaconry of Richmond to Sir Otho de Grandison to enable him to go to the Holy Land.'
32. Roger Crowley. 2019. *Accursed Tower*. New Haven: Yale University Press.127.
33. Esther Rowland Clifford. 1961. *A Knight of Great Renown: The Life and Times of Othon de Grandson.* Chicago: University of Chicago Press. 113.
34. ACV IB R 3/1-3.
35. Ibid.
36. Reg. Nicholas IV, 521. No 3279. '3279 15 Septembre 1290, Orvieto. *Dispensatio super pluralitate beneficiorum. (REG. 45, c. 419, f. 83 vo.) Willelmo Brunell, preposito ecclesie Wellensis, quocum olim, ad supplicationem Octonis de Grandisono, dispensatum est ut praeposituram Wellensis ecclesiae, sine cura, ecclesiam de Vesterham (sic), Roffensis dioecesis, curam habentem, quas minor viginti quinque annos natus, rece pit et insimul, absque apostolica dispensatione, detinuit, una cum canonicatibus et praebendis in Lichefeldensi, Saresbiriensi, Landavensi, Menevensi et Sancti Adomari, Morinensis dioecesis, ecclesiis, retinere posset, rursus in dulgetut, ecclesia de Westerham (sic) dimissa, ecclesiam de Donton, Saresbiriensis dioecesis, curam animarum haben tem,*

accipere et cum aliis beneficiis suis retinere valeat. Exigunt tuarum virtutum ... Dat. apud Urbemve terem, xVI kalendas octobris, anno tertio.' For translation see Regesta 45: 1290–1291', in Calendar of Papal Registers Relating to Great Britain and Ireland: Volume 1, 1198–1304, Ed. W. H. Bliss (London, 1893). 512–27. British History Online www.british-history.ac.uk/cal-papal-registers/brit-ie/vol1/pp512–527 (accessed 2 December 2020). 'To William Brunell, who, being under age after the council of Lyons, accepted the provostship of Wells, and afterwards the church of Westerham, in the diocese of Rochester, and was not ordained priest within a year, and, at the request of Odo de Grandison, in his twenty-third year, obtained a papal dispensation enabling him to retain the same, together with canonries and prebends of Lichfield, Salisbury, Llandaff, St. Davids, and St. Omer. Indult to him to accept the church of Donton, in the diocese of Salisbury, on resigning that of Westerham, and to retain his other benefices with a canonry and prebend of York, which he has obtained since the above dispensation, the cure of souls not being neglected.'

37. British Library. Department of Manuscripts. The British Library, Guide to the Catalogues and Indexes of the Department of Manuscripts. London: British Library, Reference Division Publications, MS 27376, ff.189v–190.
38. In Latin, *Pauperes commilitones Christi Templique Salomonici.*
39. In Latin, *Ordo Fratrum Hospitalis Sancti Ioannis Hierosolymitani.*
40. David Nicolle. 2001. *Knight Hospitaller*. Twelfth Edition. Oxford: Osprey Publishing. 27.
41. In Latin, *Ordo domus Sanctæ Mariæ Theutonicorum Hierosolymitanorum* or in *German, Orden der Brüder vom Deutschen Haus der Heiligen Maria in Jerusalem.*
42. Desmond Seward. 2000. *The Monks of War: The Military Orders.* London: The Folio Society. 54.
43. Ibid. 57.
44. Ronald. J. C. Broadhurst, 1952. *The Travels of ibn Jubayr.* London: Jonathan Cape.
45. Helen Nicholson. 2004. *Knights Templar 1120–1312.* Eleventh Edition. Oxford: Osprey Publishing Ltd. 27.
46. Muslin, so called because the Europeans thought it originated in Mosul.
47. David Jacoby. 2005. 'Aspects of Everyday Life in Frankish Acre'. Taylor & Francis. 73–115.
48. CCR Edward I vol 3 1288–1296, 145.'Sept 12 [1290], Nottingham. To Arghūn, king of the Tartars . . . '
49. Roger Crowley. 2019. *Accursed Tower*. New Haven: Yale University Press. 145.
50. Ibid. 147.
51. *The Gestes des Chiprois* is in itself a remarkable survivor, the manuscript survived until at least 1343 in Kyrenia, Cyprus where it was copied by a prisoner, Jean le Miege as something to do to pass the time. The manuscript perished, most likely in the Ottoman invasion of Cyprus in 1571. The copy we have is that of Jean le Miege, thanks to two Italian amateur historians, Count Massimo Mola di Larissé and Carlo Perrin who found the Jean le Miege copy in an Italian castle in 1882. From this a copy was made that was transcribed for publication in 1887 – it is this transcription we have used for the Old French Templar of Tyre text as published.
52. Gestes des Chiprois. 241. '485. *Et furent les mefages meffire Phelippe Mainebeuf, chevalier d'Acre, quy favoir mout bien le lenguage farazin, & j. frere dou Temple chevalier, quy et nom frere Berthelomé Pizan, & eftoit nés de Chipre, & j. frere de l'Ofpitau, & j.*

escrivain quy et nom Jorge; & furent devant le soudan, quy refuza les letres & le presant, & retint les to mesages en prison.'

53. Gestes des Chiprois. 242. '487. *Le soudan des soudans, le roy des roys, le seignor des seignors, Melec el Esseraf, le puyssant, le redouté, le chasseours de rebels, le chasseours de Frans & des Tatars & des Ermins, aracheour des chaffiaus des mains des mescreans, seignor des .ij. mers, serveour des .ij. sains pelerinage Calohonel & Salahie.*'
54. Roger Crowley. 2019. *Accursed Tower*. New Haven: Yale University Press. 145.
55. Marcus Graecus, a writer of the tenth century, gives a rough recipe: 'Take pure sulphur, tartar, sarcocolla [Persian gum], pitch, dissolved nitre, petroleum [obtainable from surface deposits in Mesopotamia and the Caucasus] and pine resin; boil these together, then saturate tow with the result and set fire to it. The conflagration will spread, and can be extinguished only by urine, vinegar, or sand.' Footnote from John Julius Norwich's *Byzantium: The Early Centuries*. 342–43.
56. The Templar of Tyre calls these '*engins*' or trebuchets 'Haveben' and 'Menfour'. Gestes des Chiprois. 243.
57. Roger Crowley. 2019. *Accursed Tower*. New Haven: Yale University Press. 149.
58. The name Mamluk Sultanate is a modern appellation, al-Dawla al-Turkiyya or Dawlat al-Turk would have been their own description of their state. Literally State of Turkey or State of the Turks.
59. David Nicolle. 2014. *Mamluk 'Askari 1250–1517*. Oxford: Osprey Publishing Ltd.
60. Gestes des Chiprois. 243. 'a .v. jours d'avril'
61. *Dehlis* being a Frankish rendition of the Arabic *dihliz* meaning threshold or vestibule.
62. Gestes des Chiprois. 243. '*Le soudan si fist fermer ses tentes & ses pavellions mout pres l'un de l'autre, quy tenoient dou Touron, alant jusues vers le Semerrie, que tout le plain fu couvert de tentes; & La tente dou soudan, quy s'apele dehlis, estoit sur .j. toron hautet, la ou ele avoit une bele tour & jardins & vignes dou Temple, lequel dehlis estoit tout vermeill, & une porte overte vers la sité d'Acre, & est ensy huze des soudans que vers [la ou] la porte dou dehlis est overte, chascun seit que le soudan doit aler par sel chemin.*'
63. In pre–Latin Frankish *tournon* meant 'little hill'. The Arabic name was *Tal al-Fukhar*.
64. Roger Crowley. 2019. *Accursed Tower*. New Haven: Yale University Press. 161. David Nicolle. 2005. *Acre 1291*. Third Edition. Oxford: Osprey Publishing Ltd. 54–55.
65. David Nicolle. 2005. *Acre 1291*. Third Edition. Oxford: Osprey Publishing Ltd. 39.
66. The Templar of Tyre may be in error in his translation of al-Mansūri. It is translated as 'aided or assisted by God', see Paul F. Crawford. 2003. *The Templar of Tyre: Part III of the deeds of the Cypriots*. Abingdon: Routledge. 231. n6.
67. Gestes des Chiprois. 243. '490. *L'un de ses engins quy avoir nom Haveben, quy vient a dire yrious, si estoit devers la garde dou Temple, & l'autre engin, quy geter contre la garde des Pizans, avoit nom le Mensour, ce est a dire le victoire, & l'autre gran, que je ne vos le say nomer, getoit contre la garde de l'Ospitau, & le cart engin getoit contre une grant tour, quy a nom la Tour maudite, quy est a segons murs & est de la garde dou roy.*'
68. From the Old French *mangonel(le)*, French *mangoneau*, itself from Medieval Latin *manganellus*, *mangonellus* from Greek *manganon* meaning 'engine of war', *Oxford Dictionary of English*.
69. From the Old French *trebucher* meaning 'overthrow', *Oxford Dictionary of English*.
70. Christopher Gravett. 1990. *Medieval Siege Warfare*. Sixteenth Edition. Oxford: Osprey Publishing Ltd. 49.

71. Gestes des Chiprois. 243. '*Il mirent efcus grans & efcus fais de verges, la premiere nut renges contre nos murs, & la fegonde nut, les acofterent plus avant, & la tierce nut, auffi les acofterent, & tant les acofterent que il vindrent fur la doune dou foce.*'
72. Gestes des Chiprois as translated by Esther Rowland Clifford. 1961. *A Knight of Great Renown: The Life and Times of Othon de Grandson*. Chicago: University of Chicago Press. 119.
73. This attribution to Othon de Grandson seems almost certainly accurate, since the knight later visited Lanercost Priory on the border between England and Scotland with the Edward's army en route to Scotland, and we know of no other witness to the events of Acre in 1291 who later might have been with the chronicler at Lanercost. David Nicolle. 2005. *Acre 1291*. Third Edition. Oxford: Osprey Publishing Ltd. 65. And Roger Crowley. 2019. *Accursed Tower*. New Haven: Yale University Press.180. And Esther Rowland Clifford. 1961. *A Knight of Great Renown: The Life and Times of Othon de Grandson*. Chicago: University of Chicago Press. 120, all concur.
74. Chron. Lanercost, 79. 'The enemy, therefore, having had a taste of this bravery, increased their army so that it amounted to 300,000 light troops, investing the city once more and shooting so hotly against it that, as one who was there informed me, you might see the little arrows which they call { locusts 'flying in the air thicker than snowflakes. Those, then, who were in command upon the walls, perceiving that they could not hold the town for long against so many foes, determined by common counsel to make confession and receive the communion, penitently imploring help for their arms from the Lord'
75. Gestes des Chiprois. 244. '*& apres dreferent lor carabouhas, quy font engins peris turqueis, quy fe tirent as mains & geteent mout fouvent, faizoient plus de maus a la gent que les grans engins, que le leuc ou le carabouha lanfet, nul n'en ozer acofter*'.
76. Roger Crowley. 2019. *Accursed Tower*. New Haven: Yale University Press. 219.
77. Old French *sortie* meaning literally 'a going out', the past participle of *sortir*, 'go out'. The word remains in English to this day to denote an operational flight by a single military aircraft or a short trip or journey.
78. Gestes des Chiprois. 245. '491. *avint que mon feignor le maiftre dou Temple & fa gent & meffire Johan de Granfon & autre chevaliers [vinrent] une nuit devers la partie dou Temple, qui eftoit a l'utremer de la Porte de Saint Ladre, & ordena le maiftre .j. provenfau, qui eftoit vifconte dou Bort a Acre, de metre le feuc a buhcher dou grant engin dou foudan, & niffirent celle nuit, & furent jufues au dit buhcher, & feluy qui dut geter le feuc, & la geta fur paor en tel maniere quy vint court, & chay a terre, & alumet fur terre. Tous fiaus Sarazins, quy la fe troverent, furent tous mors, gens a chevau & a pie, & de noftre, freres & chevaliers dou fiecle alerent fy avant entre les paveillons, quy lor chevaus s'enconberent as jambes des cordes des tentes & trabucheent, adons les Sarazins les tueent, & en tel maniere perdimes fele nuit. xviij. homes a chevau, freres dou Temple & chevaliers dou fiecle, mais l'on prift pluzours efcus & targes farazinezes & trombes & nacares; & retorna mon feignor & fa gent a Acre.*'
79. Esther Rowland Clifford. 1961. *A Knight of Great Renown: The Life and Times of Othon de Grandson*. Chicago: University of Chicago Press. 120. n27. David Nicolle. 2005. *Acre 1291*. Third Edition. Oxford: Osprey Publishing Ltd. 61. Roger Crowley. 2019. *Accursed Tower*. New Haven: Yale University Press. 206. All concur.
80. His authorship is agreed upon by Roger Crowley. 2019. *Accursed Tower*. New Haven: Yale University Press. 212. & David Nicolle. 2005. *Acre 1291*. Third Edition. Oxford: Osprey

Publishing Ltd. 65. Whereas Esther Rowland Clifford. 1961. *A Knight of Great Renown: The Life and Times of Othon de Grandson*. Chicago: University of Chicago Press. 121, goes so far as to suggest the whole scheme may have been Othon de Grandson's idea.

81. Chron. Lanercost, 80.
82. Gestes des Chiprois. 246. '*ſe dilſoi[en]t noveles que le roy Henry devet venir de Chipre a bon ſecours qu'il amenoit, & l'on l'atendoit de jour en jour.*'
83. Guillaume took his name de Valence not from the more commonly known Valence by the Rhône south of Lyon but of Valence near the family fief of Lusignan in Poitou.
84. Guy de Lusignan, King of Jerusalem (1186–1192), defeated by Salah ad-Din at Hattin in 1187 and the king who lost Jerusalem was also a son of Hugh VIII de Lusignan.
85. Roger Crowley. 2019. *Accursed Tower*. New Haven: Yale University Press. 218–219. The number is estimated elsewhere to be '100 knights and 2,000 infantrymen'. David Nicolle. 2005. *Acre 1291*. Third Edition. Oxford: Osprey Publishing Ltd. 68.
86. Paul F. Crawford. 2003. *The Templar of Tyre: Part III of the deeds of the Cypriots*. Abingdon: Routledge. 130.
87. Gestes des Chiprois. 247. '*La tour neuve que l'on diſoir la Tour dou roy ſi fu ſi menée, que la frontiere devant chey en .j. mont par dedens le focé.*'
88. Ibid. 131.
89. Christopher Marshall. 1992. *Warfare in the Latin East 1192–1291*. Cambridge: Cambridge University Press. 82.
90. Steven Runciman. 1954. *A History of the Crusades: Volume III The Kingdom of Acre and the later Crusades*. Eleventh Edition. London: The Folio Society. 349–350. The account cites the following sources: Gestes des Chiprois, 43–54; Samudo, 230–31; Amadi. 220–25; *De Excidio*, Cols 760–82; Thaddens, 18–23; Ludolph of Suchem (P.P.T.S. 54–61); al-Jazari. 5; Maqrisi, Sultans II, i, 125–26; Abu'l Feda. 164–65. Abu'l Muhasin in Reinaud. op. cit. 589–92. There is a picaresque account (unfortunately without references) in Schlumberger. *Byzance et Croisades*. 207–79. Muntaner. Cronica (ed. Caroleu). 378, tells of Roger of Flor's conduct.
91. The translation by Paul Crawford uses the words 'fierce defence' Paul F. Crawford. 2003. *The Templar of Tyre: Part III of the deeds of the Cypriots*. Abingdon: Routledge. 134.
92. Gestes des Chiprois. 251–52. '498.*j. pilet vint vers le maitſtre dou Temple, & au lever que le maiſtre fiſt de ſa main feneſtre, n'en avoit point d'eſcu fors ſon dart á ſa mayn deſtre; aſel piler le fery ſous l'aſelle, & li entra une paume de canne dedens le cors, quant il vint au vent là où les plates ne joinent point, car ſes ne furent mye ſes curaſſes fiables, ains furent curaſſe legiere, d'armer ligierement à .j. cry. Et quant il ſe ſenty feru àu mort, ſi ſe miſt aler, & l'on cuyda que il s'en alaſt volentiers pour foy ſauver; & celuy dou confanon le vy aler, ſi ſe miſt aler devant luy, & adons toute ſa mehnée le ſeguyrent, & enſi come il s'en aloit bien, .xx. des cruſſés do Val d'Eſpolite li vindrent au devant, & ly diſtrent: 'A pour Dieu, ſire, ne vous partés car la ville ſera tant toſt perdue! 'Et il lor reſpondy hautement, que chaſcun l'oy: 'Seignors, je ne peus plus, car je ſuy mort; veés le cop.*'Et adons veyme nos le pilet clavé en ſon cors; & ſur cel parole, il jeta la dart en terre, & torſa le col... Adons entrerent grant gent a chevau Sarazins, ſe que meſſire Johan de Grely, & meſſire Ote de Gualanſon,& la gent dou roy de France firent grant defence, de quey il y ot aſes nafres & mors; & meſſire Johan de Grely & meſſire Ote de Gualanſon ne porent plus ſoufrir le charge des Sarazins, & ſe deſpartirent dou leuc & ſe ſauverent, et fu meſſire Johan de Grely nafré.'

93. David Nicolle. 2005. *Acre 1291*. Third Edition. Oxford: Osprey Publishing Ltd. 81 concurs with Runciman's account. 81, citing the Gestes des Chiprois.
94. Paul F. Crawford. 2003. *The Templar of Tyre: Part III of the deeds of the Cypriots*. Abingdon: Routledge. 131.
95. Magister Thadeus. 121. '*De improbitate et reprehensione domini Iohannis de Greliaco capitaneo gentis regis Francie. Dominus vero Iohannes de Greliaco, solo nomine miles et professione solummodo Christianus, qui tunc temporis pro parte Francorum regis illustris super ipsius gente, quam ob terre sancte reverenciam ac civitatis precipue Acconensis rex ipse christianissimus deputarat cotidiana presidia, generalis capitanie fungeretur officio multorumque militum esset ac peditum comitiva vallatus, in nullis omnino militarium exercitationum actionibus, prout ducem principis tam gloriosi decebat, laudabilem vel memoria dignum quoquo modo se ipsum exhibuit nec ostendit, quin pocius, velut sue fame prodigus, virtutis egenus, armorum inpaciens, deliciarum commestionumque usibus nimium resolutus et deditus ac proinde viribus enervatus, tam in Tripolitane olim desolationis quam in Acconensis denuo conculcationis casibus elegit pocius more femineo aufugere seu pugnandi onera quasi timidus declinare quam contra crucis hostes ut miles dimicare auderet strenuus vel saltem ut catholicus confligere Christianus*.'
96. *Excidium Acconis*. 90. '*Similiter Iohannes de Grilliaco capitaneus Aconis et Oto de Grandisono iam dictus, suas relinquentes custodias, cum quibusdam se gerentibus generosos, integris armaturis, in rei principio ad mare fu gientes, actus militares turpiter abnegantes caritatisque ter minos inhumaniter exeundo naviculam concenderunt. Heu, hii omnes in Galliis dum vigerent inter Gallos eque pares, ferrum simulantes fera cum dentibus audacia corrosuri, lin gue procacis iactitatione inaniter asserebant se potius mor tem pati quam fugere a conflictu quoquomodo. Vere non fugerunt a conflictu, quia nunquam in conflictum intrave runt, sed intacti recedentes, quos regebant relinquendo, effu gerunt pre timore, desperantes ex seipsis, sicut credo, nec querentes quo in deo firmarentur*.'
97. Ibid.
98. Charles L. Kingsford. 1909. *Sir Otho de Grandison 1238?–1328*. Transactions of the Royal Historical Society 3: 147. n4. Cites *Excidio Acconis* 12, *Gestes des Chiprois* 499 and Chron S. Bertini 770 in this regard.
99. Gestes des Chiprois. 249. '498. *fu pris dou feuc .j. povre valet engles ſi malement, que ſon ſuvreſegniau fu alume, qui n'ot nul quy le ſecouruſt, que il ot ars la chere, & puis tout ſon cors & alumet auſi con ſe fuſt .j. chauderon de puis, & la morut; & quant ſe le avint, il eſtoit a pie, que ſa beſte li fu tuee de ſous luy.' Or in* English translation, Paul F. Crawford. 2003. *The Templar of Tyre: Part III of the deeds of the Cypriots*. Abingdon: Routledge. 100. '498. one poor English *valé* [squire] was so badly hit by Greek Fire which the Saracens were hurling that his surcoat burst into flames. There was no one to help him. And so his face was burned, then his whole body. He burned as if he had been a cauldron of pitch, and he died there. He was on foot when this happened, because his mount had been slain under him.'
100. Esther Rowland Clifford. 1961. *A Knight of Great Renown: The Life and Times of Othon de Grandson*. Chicago: University of Chicago Press. 273.
101. Jean-Daniel Morerod. 2020. *Finances et Sentiments* in *Othon I de Grandson (vers 1240–1328)*. Lausanne: Cahiers Lausannois d'Histoire Médiévale. 125 and 131.

102. Chron. Guisborough, Vol 2, 24. '*Othone de Grandisono qui cum thesauris regis Angliæ ibidem missus ut viam pararet ante faciem ejus, habuit enim in proposito rex in terram proficisci, durante din subsidione hostium cum eisdem thesauris in Cyprum fugiens, mutato cognomine, in congressu militari parvum fecit sonum.*' Or 'Otho de Grandison, who was sent thither with the treasures of the king of England to prepare the way before his face, for the king had purposed to march into the land, during the din with the aid of the enemy, fleeing to Cyprus with the same treasures, having changed his surname, made little noise in the military meeting.'
103. *Histoire généalogique des sires de Salins au comté de Bourgogne*, Vol 1.
104. Michael Prestwich. 1997. *Edward I*. Yale: Yale University Press. 329.
105. Gestes des Chiprois. 257. '510. *Le maiſtre novyau ſi avoit nom frere Tibaut Gaudy; ſi ſe vy [aſſailly] & penſa que à ſon comenſement il ne abandoneroit mye le chaſtiau, & ei conſeil à ſes freres, & par lor volenté, proumetant leur quy lor manderoit ſecours, & s'en ala en Chipre.*' *Or in* English translation, Paul F. Crawford. 2003. *The Templar of Tyre: Part III of the deeds of the Cypriots.* Abingdon: Routledge. 105. '510. The new master was named Theobald Gaudin. He saw his position assaulted, and thought that he ought not to begin his term of office by abandoning the castle. He took counsel with his brethren, and with their consent he went off to Cyprus.'
106. Roger Crowley. 2019. *Accursed Tower*. New Haven: Yale University Press. 262–63.
107. Bartholomew Cotton. *Historia Anglicana*, 432, states that Othon was present after 18 May, also David Nicolle. 2005. *Acre 1291*. Third Edition. Oxford: Osprey Publishing Ltd. 84, writes that 'Othon de Grandson probably also left [with Gaudin] but that accusations of his appropriating the Templar treasure were later slander' and that 'Othon de Grandson arrived in Cyprus destitute.' Roger Crowley. 2019. *Accursed Tower*. New Haven: Yale University Press. 251, quotes the Templar of Tyre and makes no mention of Othon de Grandson having been at Acre after 18 May. Esther Rowland Clifford. 1961. *A Knight of Great Renown: The Life and Times of Othon de Grandson.* Chicago: University of Chicago Press. 122, bases her account also on the Templar of Tyre and implies an 18 May departure with the wounded Jean de Grailly. Steven Runciman. 1954. A *History of the Crusades: Volume III The Kingdom of Acre and the later Crusades.* Eleventh Edition. London: The Folio Society. 350, wrote as we saw that Othon de Grandson joined the departing boats of 18 May 'and himself, was the last to join them'. The account recorded in the Gestes des Chiprois is also that of Cronaca del Templare, cap. 224, ed. Minervini, 269.
108. Robert Kool. 2006. A Thirteenth Century Hoard of Gold Florins from the Medieval Harbour of Acre. The Numismatic Chronicle vol 166. 301-320.
109. Chron Lanercost, 139–40.
110. Charles L. Kingsford. 1909. *Sir Otho de Grandison 1238?–1328*. Transactions of the Royal Historical Society 3: 148.
111. Gestes des Chiprois. 249. '498. *fu pris dou feuc .j. povre valet engles ſi malement, que ſon ſuvreſegniau fu alume, qui n'ot nul quy le ſecouruſt, que il ot ars la chere, & puis tout ſon cors & alumet auſi con ſe fuſt .j. chauderon de puis, & la morut; & quant ſe le avint, il eſtoit a pie, que ſa beſte li fu tuee de ſous luy.*' English translation, Paul F. Crawford. 2003. *The Templar of Tyre: Part III of the deeds of the Cypriots.* Abingdon: Routledge. 100.
112. Gestes des Chiprois. 259. '516. *En ceſte ihle de Chipre ſe recuillirent la gent quy eſchaparent d'Acre & des autres leus de Surie, & là furent à grant povreté, & ſe aucun*

fu qui eiift peu traire dou fien & aporté o luy, fi valut mains la mité, por ce que les chofes de vitaille encherirent mout, & meifmes les maifons, qui fe leueent à .x. bezans l'un[e] le més, mon- terent à .c. bezans l'an, & tous lor amis de Chipre le[s] mefconurent ni fayzoient d'yaus menfion de mité & d'amifté aucune, mais le roy Henry confillia, & fe fift, metre à fodées les povres chevaliers & fergans, dont il fift grant amone & grant bien, & la rayne eftablirent & le roy amohnes ordenées à douner à povre gens.' Or in English translation, Paul F. Crawford. 2003. *The Templar of Tyre: Part III of the deeds of the Cypriots.* Abingdon: Routledge. 100. '516. Those who escaped from Acre and the other places of Syria retreated to this island, but they were in great poverty. Even if there was anyone there who had been able to bring away something of his own and carry it to Cyprus with him, it was worth less than half of what it had been, because foodstuffs were in great scarcity. Even houses which had been renting for ten bezants a year went up to a hundred bezants a year. All their friends in Cyprus forgot about them and made no kindly mention of them. But King Henry took counsel, and had the poor knights and sergeants put on a payroll, and he gave great alms and many good things to them, and the King and the Queen established relief specifically to be given to these poor people.'

113. CPR Edward I vol 2 1281–1292, 465. 'January 3 [1292], Westminster. Safe conduct, until Michaelmas, for Peter de Weston, yeoman of Otto de Grandisono, whom some friends of Otto are sending to the land of Cyprus (Cipre) to him, with a horse laden with cloths and other things.'
114. Reg. Boniface VIII 1: 277–80. docs 826, 830; 388–89, doc 4490.

Chapter 10

1. A.A.M. Duncan. 2002. *The Kingship of the Scots, 842–1292: Succession and Independence.* Edinburgh University Press. 221. 'How long she had lain ill on land is unknown, but it could have been for as much as a week, and certainly from about 23 September; the ship was her father's, whose suppliers may have poisoned her with decaying food.
2. Scottish nobles acting as collective Regents of Scotland.
3. A. M. Duncan. 2002. *The Kingship of the Scots, 842–1292: Succession and Independence.* Edinburgh University Press. 423–24. 'Finally Fraser looks at the 'worst case' scenario: 'if [the Maid of Norway] has in truth died – God forbid – let your excellency deign, please, to approach the Border to the consolation of the Scottish people and to staunch effusion of blood, so that the true men of the kingdom can maintain their oath unbroken and set up (*preficere*) as king him (*illum*) who by law should inherit, if so be that he (ille) is willing to abide by your advice'
4. Sara Cockerill. 2014. *Eleanor of Castile: The Shadow Queen.* Second Edition. Stroud: Amberley Publishing. 343.
5. The surviving crosses are at Geddington, Hardingstone and Waltham.
6. Sara Cockerill. 2014. *Eleanor of Castile: The Shadow Queen.* Second Edition. Stroud: Amberley Publishing. 260–61. 'A third member of Edward's male circle with whom a close friendship [with Leonor] can be inferred is his childhood friend Otho de Grandison, who not only appears often as a witness but was a recipient of gifts from Leonor ... Obviously Leonor had no interest in anyone except her husband, other than by way of friendship. However, there seems a possibility that Otho's feeling for her was more

tender ... There seems some reason to speculate that he [Othon] was devoted to her.' Ibid. 345. CPR Edward I vol 2 1281–1292, 417. 'Jan 18 [1291], Ashridge. Confirmation of the legacy of Eleanor, late queen consort, granting to Otto de Grandisono, for life, her manors of Ditton, co. Cambridge, and Thurueston, co. Buckingham, with reversion to the king.'

7. Chron. Lanercost, 77. 'O reader pause and pray: 'Dear Christ, allow No ill to vex her who is laid below ! How brief's the human span this Queen bears witness; Pray for her soul, and mend thine own unfitness. Nor birth nor worth nor wealth nor strength availeth To ward off death, which over all prevaileth. Mourn not too long: thou canst not by much weeping Bring back her soul who in this tomb lies sleeping; But pray that she abide with Christ in glory, While here below her virtues live in story. Long live the King, and prosper in achievement ! Would'st thou record the year of his bereavement ? Write once a thousand and a hundred thrice, Add them, and from the total take five twice. Also the month and day thou must remember, Queen Alianora died on fifth November.6'
8. Alison Weir. 2020. *Queens of the Crusades: Eleanor of Aquitaine and her Successors.* London: Penguin Random House UK. 661. Describes Othon Grandson as 'her champion'.
9. B. Botfield, Ed., 1841. *Manners and Household Expenses of England in the Thirteenth and Fifteenth Centuries.* London. 121.
10. Esther Rowland Clifford. 1961. *A Knight of Great Renown: The Life and Times of Othon de Grandson.* Chicago: University of Chicago Press.
11. Marc Morris. 2009. A Great and Terrible King. London: Windmill Books. 433, citing Christopher Tyerman. 1996. *England and the Crusades. 237–8,* who in turn is citing Esther Rowland Clifford. 1961. *A Knight of Great Renown: The Life and Times of Othon de Grandson.* Chicago: University of Chicago Press. 126.
12. The then manor of Ditton Camoys, today Woodditton in the District of East Cambridgeshire.
13. Today, Turweston, Buckinghamshire.
14. CPR Edward I vol 2 1281–1292, 417. 'Jan 18 [1291], Ashridge. Confirmation of the legacy of Eleanor, late queen consort, granting to Otto de Grandisono, for life, her manors of Ditton, co. Cambridge, and Thurueston, co. Buckingham, with reversion to the king.'
15. Michael Ray. 2006. The Savoyard Cousins: A Comparison of the Careers and Relative Success of the Grandson (Grandison) and Champvent (Chavent) Families in England. The Antiquaries Journal 86: 155.
16. Sara Cockerill. 2014. *Eleanor of Castile: The Shadow Queen. Second Edition.* Stroud: Amberley Publishing. 362. 'making a pilgrimage to Jerusalem'.
17. Alison Weir. 2020. *Queens of the Crusades: Eleanor of Aquitaine and her Successors.* London: Penguin Random House UK. 662.
18. Christopher Tyerman. 1996. England and the Crusades, 1095-1588. Chicago: University of Chicago Press.237-8.
19. Susan. Marti. 2020. '*L'Antependium d'Othon de Grandson*' in *Othon I de Grandson (vers 1240–1328).* Lausanne: Cahiers Lausannois d'Histoire Médiévale. 45. '*Dès les années 1960 ancien directeur du Musée d'Histoire de Berne. Michael Stettler estimait en se fondant sur des éléments artistiques que la par centrale était d'origine chypriote, La thèse d'une confection de la broderie à Chypre vers la fin du XIII siècle est depuis lors généralement admise par les chercheurs.*' Or 'From the 1960s former director of the Bern History Museum. Michael Stettler estimated, based on artistic elements, that

the central piece was of Cypriot origin. The thesis of a development of embroidery in Cyprus towards the end of the thirteenth century has since then been generally accepted by researchers.' The idea that the end pieces are *Opus Anglicanism* comes from William Richard Lethaby, Surveyor of the Fabric of Westminster Abbey, 1857–1931, cited in Esther Rowland Clifford. 1961. *A Knight of Great Renown: The Life and Times of Othon de Grandson.* Chicago: University of Chicago Press.

20. The author met up with Susan Marti in Bern before the *antependium* and was unable to interest her in the wider historical context,
21. Many authors have written of Edward and Eleanor being a true love match, including, for example, Lisa Hilton. 2008. *Queens Consorts: England's Medieval Queens.* London: Weidenfeld & Nicolson. 20.
22. Lisa Hilton. 2008. *Queens Consorts: England's Medieval Queens*. London: Weidenfeld & Nicolson. 246.
23. Chron. Osney, 330. '*Corda duarum reginarum in eorum præsentia, cum ea qua decuit honorificentia Dominica proxima et die Lunæ post festum Sancti Nicholai, sepeliri constituit.'* Or 'The hearts of the two queens, in their presence, were to be buried with the due honour on the next Sunday and on the Monday after the feast of St. Nicholas.'
24. Sir Maurice Powicke. 1953. *The Thirteenth Century 1216–1307*. Oxford: Oxford University Press. 73.
25. Michael Prestwich. 1997. *Edward I*. Yale: Yale University Press. 329.
26. Charles L. Kingsford. 1909. *Sir Otho de Grandison 1238?–1328*. Transactions of the Royal Historical Society 3: 150.
27. CPR Edward I vol 2 1281–1292, 465. 'January 3 [1292], Westminster. Safe conduct, until Michaelmas, for Peter de Weston, yeoman of Otto de Grandisono, whom some friends of Otto are sending to the land of Cyprus (Cipre) to him, with a horse laden with cloths and other things.'
28. Matthew M. Reeve. 2006. 'The Painted Chamber at Westminster, Edward I, and the Crusade'. Viator-medieval and Renaissance Studies 37: 189–221.
29. Gestes des Chiprois. 258. '513. Enſi con vos poés entendre, fu toute la Surie perdue, & la prirent & deſtrurent Sarazins, ja ſoit ſe que devant furent prizes pluzors leus que je vos ay devizés. Ceſte fois fu tout perdu, que treſtous creſtiens ne tindrent.j. paume de terre en Surie.'
30. Paul F. Crawford. 2003. T*he Templar of Tyre: Part III of the deeds of the Cypriots.* Abingdon: Routledge. 157. '513. Thus, as you have been able to learn, was all of Syria lost, taken and destroyed by the Saracens, although there were many places taken earlier that I have described for you. This time everything was lost, so that all together the Christians held not so much as a palm's breadth of land in Syria.'
31. Ibid.100.
32. Christopher Tyerman. 1996. *England and the Crusades, 1095–1588.* Chicago: University of Chicago Press. 231. 'As king he [Edward] never went to war except to defend his self-proclaimed and frequently challenged rights, in Wales, Gascony, or Scotland. Conversely Edward never gave up announcing publicly his intention to support the crusade in person or by proxy Throughout his reign, and in common with many contemporary rulers, he placed his actions in the context of the needs of the Holy Land. . . The crusade was always the next task but one, pushed into the future by domestic crises, but not forgotten.'

33. Esther Rowland Clifford. 1961. *A Knight of Great Renown: The Life and Times of Othon de Grandson.* Chicago: University of Chicago Press. 129–31, citing Charles Köhler in *Revue d'Orient Latin*, X, 406ff.
34. C. Köhler. Hayton, *La flor des Estoires de la Terre d'Orient.* 327. '*Quo comperto, frater ejus secundus, dominus Theodorus, convocatis domino Hotono' de Grandisono, et aliis pluribus nobilibus, de regno Cipri, qui venerant apud Armeniam et aliis regni Armenie nobilibus et vassallis, fratri suo primogenito, domino Haytono*' And, Ibid. 330. '*Et super hiis testem mihi invoco Deum celi, et virum nobilem et pruden tem dominum Odonem' de Grandisono, et magistros domus Templi et Hospitalis, et fratres eorum conventus, qui tunc temporis in partibus illis erant, ac generaliter omnes nobiles et homines ac populos regni Armenie atque Cipri.*'
35. Alain Demurger. 2002. *The Last Templar*. London: Profile Books Ltd. 78. 'Any intervention … still with Otton de Grandson, must be deferred to 1298 or 1299.'
36. Alan Forey. 1973. *The Templars in the Corona de Aragon.* Oxford: Oxford University Press. Doc XXXVI, citing Charles L. Kingsford. 1909. *Sir Otho de Grandison 1238?–1328.* Transactions of the Royal Historical Society 3: 151. n2. 'Otho cannot … have been in Armenia between 1299 and 1303.'
37. Charles L. Kingsford. 1909. *Sir Otho de Grandison 1238?–1328.* Transactions of the Royal Historical Society 3: 151. n1. 'Otho's visit to Thoros was clearly in 1294.'
38. Alan Forey. 1973. *The Templars in the Corona de Aragon.* Oxford: Oxford University Press. Doc XXXVI.
39. Alain Demurger. 2018. '*Othon de Grandson et les templiers d'Épailly*' in *Communicating the Middle Ages: Essays in Honour of Sophia Menache*. London: Routledge. 41.
40. Alan Forey. 1973. *The Templars in the Corona de Aragon.* Oxford: Oxford University Press. Doc XXXVI.
41. Alain Demurger. 2018. '*Othon de Grandson et les templiers d'Épailly*' in *Communicating the Middle Ages: Essays in Honour of Sophia Menache*. London: Routledge. 41. '*Il est totalement invraisemblable qu'il ait participé de manière directe à l'élection; ni lui, ni le maitre de l'Hôpital. La réunion du chapitre général (ou du couvent, c'est-à-dire un organe plus restreint) n'était ouverte qu'aux seuls templiers.*' Or 'It is totally implausible that he participated directly in the election; neither him nor the master of the Hospital. The meeting of the general chapter (or of the convent, that is to say a more restricted body) was open only to the Templars.'
42. Jules Michelet. Ed. 1841–51. *Procés des Templiers. Tome* 2. Paris. 224–25. '*Nunc grandia scandala, suspicio et infamia sunt exorta contra dictum ordinem, cujus fratres credit quod scirent abnegacionem predictam, et quod eam Magister et alii sint confessi; et dixit quod dictus Magister, cum esset discordia ultra mare in conventu eorum de creacione Magistri, et pro vinciales Lemovicinii et Alvergnie, qui faciebant majorem partem conventus, vellent habere in Magistrum fratrem Hugonem de. Penrando, et minor pars dictum Magistrum, prefatus Magister juravit, coram Magistro Hospitalis qui tunc erat, et coram domino Odone de Grandisono milite, et pluribus aliis, quod ipse consentiret in dictum fratrem Hugonem, et quod ipse nolebat esse Magister.*'
43. Anthony Luttrell. 2015. 'Observations on the Fall of the Temple' in *Élites et Ordres Militaires au Moyen Age*. Casa de Velasquez: Madrid. 365.
44. Reg. Clement V, *vol 2–3,137–38. no 2938. '2938. Lugudiaci, 17 aug. 1308. 'Confirmatur pensio facta Ottoni per magistrum militiae Templi. (cap. 581, f. 114a). Dilecto filio*

nobili viro Othoni de Grandissono. Tue nobilitatis devota sinceritas, per quam te gratum nostris affectibus representas, digne nos excitat et inducit, ut personam tuam plenitudine favoris apostlici prosequentes indemnitatibus tuis paternis precaveamus affectibus teque condignis favoribus honoremus. Oblata siquidem nobis tua petitio continebat, quod ab olim magister domus militie Templi Ierosoimitani attente considerans profectus multiplices, qui ex tuis operibus virtuosis eidem ordini provenerant et sperabat imposterum provenire ac volens premissa digne retributionis premio compensare, tibi de consensu sui conventus duo milia librarum Turonen. parvorum certis locis et terminis quoad viveres per manus preceptoris Francie et thesaurarii domus Parisien. eiusdem ordinis qui essent pro tempore solvere et dare promisit, prout in patentibus litteris super hoc confectis predicti conventus sigillo plumbeo munitis plenius dicitur contineri. Nos itaque tuis supplicationibus inclinati promissionem huiusmodi ratam et gratam habentes illam auctoritate apostolica ex certa scientia confirmamus etc. usque communimus. Et quia ex certis impedimentis provenientibus magistro et ordini supra- dictis eiusdem pecunie summam ab eodem magistro iuxta promissionem huiusmodi ha- bere non potes, nobis humiliter supplicasti, tibi super hoc per apostolice sedis providentiam de oportuno remedio provideri. Nos igitur volentes personam tuam huiusmodi devotionis obtentu dono specialis providentie prevenire tuisque providere indempnitatibus in hac parte tibi de Turribus, de Espaillierco et de Coulours domos eiusdem ordinis Lingonen., Senonen. et Trecen. diocesium cum omnibus iuribus et pertinentiis suis per te quo ad vixeris retinendas ac earum fructus, redditus et proventus usque ad summam dictorum duorum milium librarum in usus proprios convertendos tibi auctoritate apostolica duximus concedendum. Volumus autem, quod reliquum fructuum predictorum vel pecunie percipiendum ex ipsis alicui ex generalibus per nos vel specialibus per singulos prelatos regni Francie in singulis eorum diocesibus administratoribus et gubernatoribus bonorum ipsius ordinis in eodem regno seu diocesibus consistentium deputatis annis singulis facias exhiberi. Non obstantibus quibuscunque statutis et consuetudinibus ordinis supradicti iuramento, confirmatione apostolica seu quacunque firmitate alia roboratis, et quibuslibet privilegiis et indulgentiis et litteris apostolicis generalibus vel specialibus magistro et ordini supradictis vel quibusvis aliis comuniter vel divisim sub quacunque forma verborum concessis, de quibus oporteat in presentibus fieri mentionem et per que effectus presentium impediri valeat quomodolibet vel differri. Tenorem autem predictarum litterarum presentibus inseri facientes, qui talis est: Vniversis presentes litteras visuris et audituris frater Iacobus de Mollay divina gratia magister humilis pauperis militie Templi salutem in Domino. Noverint omnes, quod nos inspicientes et considerantes et diligenter advertentes grandia bona et profectus, quos nobilis et potens vir carissimus et dilectus noster in Domino dominus Otho dominus de Grandissono fecit et facit mansioni sive domui nostre et faciet toto tempore vite sue, prout firmiter credimus et speramus, nos in recompensationem et remunerationem omnium predictorum de consilio nostro et conventus nostri donamus, concedimus et assignamus tenore presentium predicto domino Othoni duo milia librarum Turonen. parvorum solvenda et reddenda ipsi domino Othoni vel suo certo mandato quolibet anno sine aliqua dilatione toto tempore vite sue, scilicet mille libras die Purificationis Domine nostre et alias mille libras die Mercurii proxima post festum apostolorum Petri et Pauli mensis iunii et sic quolibet anno toto tempore vite sue et debemus eidem dictam monetam tradere quolibet anno apud mansionem nostram Parisien. vel Lugdunen. supra Rodanum, ubi sibi melius placuerit, et nos districte precipimus in virtute sancte obedientie. preceptori Francie et thesaurario nostre domus de Parisius, qui pro tempore fuerint, quod dictam pecuniam tradant, solvant et benigne assignent omni dilatione remota domino Othoni prefato vel suo certo mandato secundum formam predictam, et pro maiori securitate et firmitate nos dedimus dicto domino Othoni presentes litteras sigillatas bulla nostri conventus factas in mansione nostra apud Parisius anno Domini millesimo ducentesimo septuagesimo septimo mense iulii die dominica post festum apostolorum Petri et Pauli. Nulli ergo etc. nostre confirmationis, concessionis et voluntatis etc ... Dat. Lugusiaci, XVI kal. septembris, anno tertio. In eundem modum venerabilibus fratribus. archiepiscopo Senonen. et Lingonen. Ac. Trecen. episcopis.'

45. Alain Demurger. 2002. *The Last Templar*. London: Profile Books Ltd. 81–82.
46. Ibid. n43.
47. Alan Forey. 2017. 'Otto of Grandson and the Holy Land, Cyprus and Armenia'. *Crusades 16.* Taylor & Francis.
48. Alain Demurger. 2019. La Prisée de la maison templière d'Épailly en 1308. In *Bulletin archéologique et historique du Châtillonnais* Ser. 7, vol. 1.35. Thors in the diocese of Troyes, Coulours-en-Onthe in the diocese of Sens and lastly Épailly in the diocese of Langres.
49. Anthony Luttrell. 2015. 'Observations on the Fall of the Temple' in *Élites et Ordres Militaires au Moyen Age*. Casa de Velasquez: Madrid. 365. 'In Paris, probably in 1296 or possibly in 1297, Molay and the Temple granted Granson an annual pension for life of 2,000 *livres*; apparently, Granson was securing a conspicuous income for his lifetime while the Temple acquired a revenue which was payable in perpetuity.' Alain Demurger, *Jacques de Molay*, 121–123 and 339, argued that the grant was made by Guillaume de Beaujeu in 1287.
50. Alain Demurger. 2018. '*Othon de Grandson et les templiers d'Épailly*' in *Communicating the Middle Ages: Essays in Honour of Sophia Menache*. London: Routledge. 42. '*Othon de Grandson n'est donc de passage en France et plus précisément à Paris qu'au début de l'été 1296. C'est à ce moment et en ce lieu que Jacques de Molay a pu le rencontrer*.' Or 'Othon de Grandson was therefore only passing through France and more precisely in Paris at the beginning of the summer of 1296. It was at this time and in this place that Jacques de Molay was able to meet him.'
51. Alain Demurger. 2002. *The Last Templar*. London: Profile Books Ltd. 26. 'It is nonetheless true that when Jacques de Molay became Grand Master, a number of Comtois orbited around him: Aymon d'Oiselay, Marshal of the Order, Jacques de la Rochelle, already mentioned, and Otton de Grandson, although he was not a Templar.'
52. George Digard. 1936. *Philippe Le Bel et le Saint-Siège*. 2 vols. Paris. 1: 206. n2.
53. John Julius Norwich. 2011. *The Popes*. London: Chatto & Windus. 335–36.
54. *Fœdera*. 142.
55. Reg. Boniface VIII. 1: 278–79. Nos 826 & 830. 826. '*Executoria donationis Oddoni de Grandisono facte. (fol. 198 verso. Venerabilibus fratribus ... archiepiscopo Treverensi et episcopo ac dilecto filio magistro Humberto de Bellavaile, canonico etensibus. Cum dilectus filius nobilis vir Oddo de Grandisono, fidei zelo succensus, dudum tempore in felicis exterminii civitatis Aconensis, pro defensione ipsius civitatis et eircumadjacentium partium in ipsa civitate personaliter commorans ac personam et bona periculis exponere non formidans, grandes expensas pro suis et comitive sue necessilatibus ac aliorum fidelium subventione subierit, majori parte rerum quas secum habebat ibidem amissa, ita quod propter ea, secundum ejus assertionem et aliorum*

fide dignorum testimonium, importabilibus debitis secundum suarum facultatum vi res ab eo urgente necessitate contractis, facultes ipsas alienieris opprimat gravis moles, nos eidem nobili quatuor milia marcarum argenti de pecunia decime Ala mannie pro Terre Sancte deputate subsidio, in diversis locis deposita, que nondum in ejusdem Romane ecclesie potestate pervenit – donavimus. – Quod dictam summam dicto nobili solvi faciant, et omnes alias pecunie quantitates de dicta decima provenientes penes mercatores camere apostolice deponi faciant infrascriptos, videlicet dilectos filios Thomam Spiliati, Jobannem Jacobi ac Rogerium Maunecti, Lupum Hugonis de sotietatibus Mozo rum et Spinorum de Florentia, et Clarentinum Anselmi et Marguliese Brachii, de sotictate Clarentum de Pistorio et ipso rum mereatorum sotios.' 830. Recompensatio expensarum pro defensione Aconis factarum. (fol. 199 vo.) *Dilecto filio nobili viro Oddoni de Grandisono. Dignus es et nota tue devotionis obscquia promerentur ut circums pecta benignitas matris Ecclesie te, qui fidei zelo succensus, olim in transmarinis partibus pro ipsius ecclesie honore, ipsarum partium subsidio propriaque salute indefessa sollicitudine laborasti, oculis respiciat gratiosis. Sane cum tu dudum, tempore infelicis exterminii civitatis Aconensis, pro defensione ipsius civitatis et dictarum partium in eadem civitate personaliter commorans ac personam et bona periculis exponere non formidans grandes expensas pro tuis et comitive tue necessitatibus ac aliorum subventione subieris, majori parte rerum quas tecum habebas ammissa ibidem, ita quod propter ea, secundum assertionem tuam et aliorum fide dignorum testimonium, importabilibus debitis secundum tua rum facultatum vires a te urgente necessitate contractis facultates ipsas alienieris opprimat gravis moles, nos super hiis – compatientes – tibi quatuor milia mar charum argenti de pecunia decime Alamanie Terre Sancte deputate subsidio in diversis locis deposita, que nondum in ejusdem ecclesie potestate pervenitlargi mur et de illis tenore presentium providemus, ita quod de prima que de cetero perveniet ad personas ad cam recipiendam seu colligendam deputatas vel deputandas per prefatam ecclesiam, ipsarum quatuor milium mar charum solutio tibi fiat. — DaL. Anagnic, id. septembris. anno primo.*'

56. Esther Rowland Clifford. 1961. *A Knight of Great Renown: The Life and Times of Othon de Grandson*. Chicago: University of Chicago Press. 139. n6. 'The grant from the German tenth was made on September 13, 1295. The date for the other, is uncertain, as the only reference to it is in a letter from Boniface to the collectors in England, written on 19 March 1302, complaining that it had not been paid. However, since the wording of the two letters is almost identical, they were probably both written at about the same time.'
57. Mary C. L. Salt. 1929. 'List of English Embassies to France, 1272–1307'. *The English Historical Review* 44: 271. '14 August 1295, Edward I informed Boniface VIII in response to his requests that, if Philip IV were willing, he would grant a truce until All Saints' Day (*Fœdera*, 149). Amadeus of Savoy and Otto de Grandison were requested to be present at the negotiation.'
58. Esther Rowland Clifford. 1961. *A Knight of Great Renown: The Life and Times of Othon de Grandson*. Chicago: University of Chicago Press. 142.
59. A. A. M. Duncan. 2002. *The Kingship of the Scots 842–1292*. Edinburgh: Edinburgh University Press. 651. 'There is absolutely no trace in these English records of any knowledge of the treaty which four ambassadors from the Scottish council had made with Philip IV at Paris on 23 October 1295, a treaty which we know was to infuriate Edward.'

Chapter 11

1. Michael Prestwich. 1990. 'Edward I and the Maid of Norway'. *The Scottish Historical Review* 69: 157–58.
2. Chron. Lanercost, 89. The kings of Scotland are bound to make submission to their overlord, the King of England and his heirs, as is proved from the time of King Edward named the Elder and can still be learnt from deeds and papal bulls.'
3. Ruth Margaret Blakely, 2005. *The Brus Family in England and Scotland, 1100–1295.* Boydell & Brewer. 80.
4. Ibid. 83.
5. Michael Prestwich. 1997. *Edward I.* Yale: Yale University Press. 196.
6. Other pretenders to the throne, by legitimate descent included Jean de Hastings, 1st Baron Hastings; Floris V, Count of Holland; Jean II Comyn, Lord of Badenoch (even though he was a guardian) and Eric II, King of Norway. Those claiming by illegitimate descent included Nicholas de Soules; Patrick Galithly; William de Ros, 1st Baron de Ros; William de Vesci, Baron de Vesci; Patrick Dunbar, 7th Earl of Dunbar; Roger de Mandeville and Robert de Pinkeney.
7. If English kings claimed overlordship of Scotland, then Scottish kings in the form of William claimed the English counties of Northumberland, Cumberland, and Westmorland as their own in counterclaim.
8. A. A. M. Duncan. 2002. *The Kingship of the Scots 842–1292.* Edinburgh: Edinburgh University Press. 431–32. 'Let him [King Edward] know by Elias de Hauville that 'whenever he wishes to make his *demaunde droitureaument*, I will obey him and will help him by myself and by all my friends, and by my lineage whatever my friends want to do.'
9. Ibid. 549. 'Custom of royal succession in Scotland is for Bruce, because it has happened that where a king had two sons, the younger reigned before the son of the older, by nearness of blood, as chronicles can show; Scottish examples and others from England, Castille and Savoy are cited in D.76(E).'
10. Ibid. 557. 'Edward, so far as we can tell, was fully justified in losing patience with the Scots and even with his own twenty-four and should be given credit for allowing the Scots every opportunity to act as judges in their own Cause in August 1291 and June 1292.'
11. Ibid. 546. 'Between 6 June and 2 August, the Great Roll has nothing about the Cause except an adjournment on 13 June to 2 August. But the last royal letters dated at Norham were of Sunday, 17 June,31, and the more likely date for adjournment is 15 or 16 June, forty days before convening at Berwick on 2 August.'
12. University of Paris, had emerged around 1150 as a corporation associated with the cathedral school of Notre, considered in 1292 as the premier university in Europe. It had been officially chartered in 1200 by King Philippe Auguste, it was later often nicknamed after its theological College de Sorbonne, in turn founded by Robert de Sorbon, itself chartered by Louis IX around 1257.
13. A. A. M. Duncan. 2002. *The Kingship of the Scots 842–1292.* Edinburgh: Edinburgh University Press. 558. The Cause was probably adjourned on 3 July, after which the council continued to sit in parliament in the first half of July to hear complaints by Macdougalls and Macdonalds on 7 July.'

14. Ibid. 'He must have been glad to leave Berwick and its intransigent and disputatious Scots.'
15. G. J. Hand. 1970. 'The Opinions of the Paris Lawyers upon the Scottish Succession c. 1292'. *Irish Jurist* 5: 144. 'The king of a certain kingdom was neither anointed nor crowned but placed in a customary royal seat by the earls, magnates and prelates of the kingdom. He held his kingdom by homage in fee from another king, as from the superior and direct lord of his kingdom. He died without any children or lineal heirs descendant. The king who is the superior and direct lord of that kingdom took it into his own hands, because many appeared, each asserting himself to be the heir, until it should be decided by process of law before him who was to be preferred in the succession. In particular two claimants came forward who were said to be descended from the brother of the grandfather of the dead king. One of them-let us call him Titius-was descended from the elder brother of that brother, as the great-grandson of that brother. The other-let us call him Seius-was descended from the second daughter of that brother, as the grandson of that brother. In this way the two were related to the deceased king in a collateral line. But Titius enjoys the right of primogeniture, Seius is by one degree the nearer in kin. Wherefore, granted that the kingdom is impartible, it is inquired which of these two should be preferred in the succession.'
16. Charles L. Kingsford. 1909. *Sir Otho de Grandison 1238?–1328.* Transactions of the Royal Historical Society 3: 130. n2.
17. TNA SC 1/26/34.
18. A. A. M. Duncan. 2002. *The Kingship of the Scots 842–1292.* Edinburgh: Edinburgh University Press. 597. 'Judgement against Bruce was given on Thursday, 6 November 1292.'
19. Ibid. 616. 'From 15 November King Edward and his council took two days to formulate their judgement.'
20. A good summary of the Paris consultation can be found in G. J. Hand. 1970. 'The Opinions of the Paris Lawyers upon the Scottish Succession c. 1292'. *Irish Jurist* 5: 141–55.
21. Chron. Guisborough, Vol 2, 38. '*Die vero Sancti Andreæ Apostoli idem Johannes de Balliolo effectus est rex Scotiæ more Scotorum, qui sequitur. Apud monasterium de Scone positus erat lapis pergrandis in ecclesia Dei juxta majus altare, concavus quidem et ad modum rotundæ cathedræ confectus, in quo futuri reges loco quasi coronationis ponebantur ex more.*' Or 'But on the day of St. Andrew the Apostle, the same John of Balliolo was made king of Scotland in the manner of the Scots, which follows. At the monastery of Scone there was a large stone placed in the church of God near the high altar, hollow indeed and made in the manner of a round chair, in which the future kings were placed in the place of coronation as was customary.'
22. Michael Prestwich. 1997. *Edward I.* Yale: Yale University Press. 562.
23. Ibid.
24. *Fœdera.* 782. '*Domine mi, domine Edwarde, Rex Angliæ, superior dominus regni Scotiæ, ego Johannis de Balliolo, Rex Scotia, devenio vester bomo ligius de toto regno Scotiæ, cum pertinentiis, & omni eo quod appendet.*'
25. Thomas K. Heeboll-Holm. 2013. *Ports, Piracy and Maritime War: Piracy in the English Channel and the Atlantic c. 1280–c. 1330.* Leiden: Brill. 86.
26. Ibid. 86.
27. Ibid. 87.

28. Chron. Guisborough, Vol 2. 41. '*Et cum die quadam sex Anglicanas naves obviam habuissent, easdem hostiliter aggressi duas ex ipsis continuo peremerunt suspendentes homines cum canibus ad trabes navium suarum, et sic per mare navigantes nullam faciebant differentiam inter canem et Anglicum.*' Or 'And when one day they met six English ships, they attacked them with hostility, immediately killed two of them, hanging men and dogs to the beams of their ships, and thus sailing through the sea they made no difference between a dog and an Englishman.'
29. Michael Prestwich. 1997. *Edward I.* Yale: Yale University Press. 576.
30. Thomas K. Heeboll-Holm. 2013. *Ports, Piracy and Maritime War: Piracy in the English Channel and the Atlantic c. 1280–c. 1330.* Leiden: Brill. 87.
31. Sir Maurice Powicke. 1953. *The Thirteenth Century 1216–1307.* Oxford: Oxford University Press. 644.
32. CPR Edward I vol 3 1292–1301, 16. 'May 22 [1293], Westminster. Mandate to the men of the commonalty of the whole fleet of England and Bayonne, on pain of their bodies and goods, to observe the recent peace with the king of France, and as God has given them victory over the malice of their enemies, to abstain from harming the Normans or others in the dominion of France.'
33. A haketon being a stuffed jacket usually worn beneath a coat of mail.
34. A bascinet in 1293 being a steel or iron open faced skull cap, unlikely at this time to have gained the pointed visor they would later sport.
35. Thomas K. Heeboll-Holm. 2013. *Ports, Piracy and Maritime War: Piracy in the English Channel and the Atlantic c. 1280–c. 1330.* Leiden: Brill. 113–15.
36. Michael Prestwich. 1997. *Edward I.* Yale: Yale University Press. 577. n5. Prestwich, disagreeing with, and citing French historian Favier (1978), as one who even now sought to blame Edward for events. If Edward was responsible, as Favier suggests, then it is difficult to reconcile that it was Edward who sent peace embassies to France to resolve the dispute.
37. CPR Edward I vol 3 1292–1301, 15. 'May 10 [1293], Westminster. Letters of credence to Philip, king of France, in favour of Edmund, the king's brother {*germano*\ and Henry de Lacy, earl of Lincoln, sent to consult with him touching the discord between the seafaring men of Normandy and of England. Notification that these are empowered to make a truce between the said disputants until August 15, so that the quarrels between them may cease and peace be re-established.'
38. Mary C. L. Salt. 1929. 'List of English Embassies to France, 1272–1307'. *The English Historical Review* 44: 270. '10 May 1293, Edmund of Lancaster and Henry Lacy were empowered to conclude a truce until 15 August to permit settlement of maritime disputes (CPR 1292-1301. 14), and received credences (ibid.15). Philip IV replied (*Lettres des Rois*, i. 424, a later copy), asking for speedy restitution. A report from Edmund (undated) at the French court mentions an interview with the queen of France on 11 July, and a council proposed for the octave of Michaelmas to discuss maritime disputes (C. M. 29/3/11). Complaints of piracy by the Normans were made by the seneschal of Saintonge and exist in C. M. 31/5.'
39. Kelcey Wilson-Lee. 2019. *Daughters of Chivalry: The Forgotten Children of Edward I.* London: Picador. 131.
40. CPR Edward I vol 3 1292–1301, 33. 'July 24 [1293], Canterbury. Protection with clause volumus, for one year, for Edmund, the king's brother, going beyond seas.'

41. Mary C. L. Salt. 1929. 'List of English Embassies to France, 1272–1307'. *The English Historical Review* 44: 270. '15 July 1293, Richard Gravesend, William Greenfield, and Roger Brabazon were empowered to act in the affair of the truce (*Lettres des Rois*, i. 404), and offered three alternative methods of procedure (ibid. i. 426-9). They returned unsuccessful (*Flores Historiarum*, ii. 86). 18 October, Edward was cited to appear in the Parlement at Christmastide (Boutaric, i. 282, no. 2858; *Fœdera*, 793; C. M. 27/'
42. *Fœdera*. 793.
43. Marc Morris. 2009. *A Great and Terrible King*. London: Windmill Books. 486.
44. Michael Prestwich. 1997. *Edward I*. Yale: Yale University Press. 578.
45. Esther Rowland Clifford. 1961. *A Knight of Great Renown: The Life and Times of Othon de Grandson*. Chicago: University of Chicago Press. 137.
46. Mary C. L. Salt. 1929. 'List of English Embassies to France, 1272–1307'. *The English Historical Review* 44: 270. '3 February [1294], John Lacy was sent to John of St. John with the instructions to fulfil the secret treaty which Edmund had made with Philip IV (*Lettres des Rois*, i. 406)'
47. Ibid. 270–71.
48. Michael Prestwich. 1997. *Edward I*. Yale: Yale University Press. 579.
49. Chron. Langtoft, 202–3. '*Ke fet li rays Eduuard quant seet la desccayvance*'.
50. Ibid. '*My sir rays, tu n'es pas enfaunce.*'
51. Ibid. '*Si tu veus recoverer la terre de Gascoyne, Et garder ben de Phelippe ke plus sur tay ne foyne, Levez, si te movez, ne dormez pas cum moyne, Endossez les haubers, defolfe la karoyne, Mountez le destreus, et pemez launce en poyne.*'
52. CPR Edward 1 vol 3 1292–1301, 83. 'Aug 13 [1294], Portsmouth. Mandate to John, duke of Lother', Breybant and Leynburg', to deliver to the person authorised by the count of Sauvoye, the king's cousin, the 22,000l. sterling, sent with the said John in the fleet to those parts for the payment of the people of Sauvoye and Burgoyne and those parts for their aid in the king's war against the king of France.'
53. Mary C. L. Salt. 1929. 'List of English Embassies to France, 1272–1307'. *The English Historical Review* 44: 271. '19 May, Edward was summoned to appear at Paris (*Fœdera*, 800). Edmund reported events and the deception practised on them (ibid. 794; A. C. xxx. 4.'
54. Chron. Langtoft, 205–6.
55. Christopher Tyerman. 1996. *England and the Crusades, 1095–1588*. Chicago: University of Chicago Press. 236.
56. CWR 1277–1326, 353.
57. John E. Morris. 1901. *The Welsh Wars of Edward I*. Oxford: Clarendon Press. 240–41.
58. TNA E159/68 m. 86d.
59. Michael Prestwich. 1997. *Edward I*. Yale: Yale University Press. 612.
60. Richard W. Kaeuper. 1973. *Bankers to the Crown: The Riccardi of Lucca and Edward I*. Princeton: Princeton University Press. 213.
61. Richard W. Kaeuper. 1973. *Bankers to the Crown: The Riccardi of Lucca and Edward I*. Princeton: Princeton University Press. 219.
62. Michael Prestwich. 1997. *Edward I*. Yale: Yale University Press. 379.
63. Ibid.
64. G. Barraclough. 1940. 'Edward I and Adolf of Nassau: A Chapter of Medieval Diplomacy'. *The Cambridge Historical Journal* VI: 225–7. 'French policy, based on Carolingian

tradition and directed to the 'reintegration' of Gaul … The ultimate aim of French policy during the reigns of Philip III and Philip IV seems to have been the creation, in place of the German, of a French Empire … And the technique of French aggression was the more insidious and the less easy to challenge and defeat, because it was simply the extension to non-French lands of the technique and policy applied within France against the feudal princes, and because each prince of Lorraine and Burgundy was dealt with individually. If this policy was only made possible by the weakness of the German monarchy, which meant that no prince on the western frontiers of the Empire could rely on the consistent support of the German king in resistance to French aggression, it was nevertheless pursued with consummate skill. So long as counties, bishoprics and principalities could be dealt with individually, French policy had no reason to fear effective opposition; and the only serious danger was the possibility of the alliance of all opponents in an overwhelming coalition … Philip the Fair's diplomatic agents and advisers skilfully used this shortsighted inability to combine against the common enemy as a means of furthering French policy. The only serious danger was the possibility that the princes on France's northern and eastern frontiers might be united in opposition by the joint action of the German and English kings; for French expansion was a direct threat not only to the territorial integrity of the English possessions in Gascony but also to English commercial interests in the Low Countries.'

65. CCR Edward I vol 1 1272–1279, 57. 'Oct 10 [1273], Westminster. To L[lewelyn] son of Griffin, prince of Wales. Order to deliver 2,000 marks to Poncius de Mora, the king's merchant, and 3,000 marks to Reginald de Grey, the king's justiciary, without delay. . . '
66. James Given. 1989. 'The Economic Consequences of the English Conquest of Gwynedd'. *Speculum* 64: 32.
67. J. F. Hadwin. 1983. 'The Medieval Lay Subsidies and Economic History'. *The Economic History Review New Series*, Vol. 36, No. 2, 200.
68. CWR 1277–1326, 353.
69. Michael Prestwich. 1997. *Edward I*. Yale: Yale University Press. 341.
70. Marc Morris. 2009. *A Great and Terrible King*. London: Windmill Books. 496.
71. John E. Morris. 1901. *The Welsh Wars of Edward I*. Oxford: Clarendon Press. 240.
72. R. R. Davies. 1987. *The Age of Conquest: Wales 1063–1415*. Oxford: Oxford University Press. 382.

Chapter 12

1. J. Griffiths. 1935–7. 'Documents Relating to the Rebellion of Madoc, 1294–5'. *Bulletin of the Board of Celtic Studies* VIII:
2. Jean-Pierre Chapuisat. 1964. '*Au service de deux rois d'Angleterre au XIIIe siècle: Pierre de Champvent*'. *Revue Historique Vaudoise* 72: 169. Chapuisat notes the arrow loops by example; we are frustrated from knowing more by the complete lack of building records for Champvent. Our understanding of post-1294 works there is from dendrochronology of timbers no primary sources. We can however also see this return architectural flow in the windows of Valle Crucis Abbey and the Église de St. Etienne in Moudon.
3. Dr. Adam Chapman. 2013. *Welsh Battlefields Historical and Documentary Research: Maes Moydog 5 March 1295*. Cardiff: Cadw, Welsh Government & CBHC.

4. We can translate the word *princeps* in Classical Latin as 'leader' or 'chief' – but given Madog's self-declaration of Prince of Wales, and the Worcester Annalists likely interpretation of prince as *princeps* I think we should more accurately use 'prince'.
5. Chron. Worcester, 519. '*Quinto die Martii Willelmus de Bello Camp comes Warewik commisit bellum cum Wallensibus in loco quod dicitur lingua eorum Meismeidoc; et prostravit ex illis de nobilioribus septingentos viros praeter submersos et letaliter vulneratos. Sed Madocus ap Lewelin eorum princeps cum dedecore vix evasit.*'
6. John E. Morris. 1901. *The Welsh Wars of Edward I.* Oxford: Clarendon Press. 256.
7. J. G. Edwards. 1924. 'The Battle of Maes Madog and the Welsh Campaign of 1294–5'. *The English Historical Review* 39: 10.
8. Dr. Adam Chapman. 2013. *Welsh Battlefields Historical and Documentary Research: Maes Moydog*. Cardiff: Cadw, Welsh Govdrnment & CBHC.
9. CPR Edward I vol 3 1288–1292, 506. 'To R. archbishop of Canterbury. Requests for his prayers for peace, the king having sent envoys to treat for peace with the king of France at the request of B. bishop of Albano and S. bishop of Palestrina.'
10. Mary C. L. Salt. 1929. 'List of English Embassies to France, 1272–1307'. *The English Historical Review* 44: 271. '17 November 1295, Edward sent Walter Langton, John of Berwick, and Hugh Despenser to consult with the cardinals as to a truce with France (Fœdera, p. 832). The king of the Romans was asked to send envoys to Chambéry in January 1296 (ibid., p. 834). 1 January 1296, John of Pontoise, Aymer de Valence, Walter Langton, Amadeus of Savoy, Hugh Despenser, Thomas Berkeley, Hugh de Vere, Henry of Newark, Itier d'Angouleme, William Greenfield, John of Selvesdon, John of St. Clare, the duke of Brabant, and the counts of Bar and of Holland, were appointed to treat of peace with the cardinals (ibid.)'
11. John Marrone & Charles Zuckermann. 1975. 'Cardinal Simon of Beaulieu and Relations Between Philip the Fair and Boniface VIII'. *Traditio*, Vol. 31. 216. n53. 'The legates had succeeded in arranging a meeting at Cambrai in mid-January 1296 among representatives of Edward, Philip, and the German ruler Adolf … The meeting at Cambrai must have broken up late in February or early in March, since the legate Bertrand returned to England for further discus sions with Edward on March 12.'
12. Chron. Langtoft, 238–9. '*Revynt le chardynal de Kaumbray of respouns; Et del ray de Fraunce, cum après orrouma, Sir Emery de Sauvay, quens de graunt renouns, Vynt en la compaynye, et Otes de Grauntsouns. Cil vynt hors de Cypre de ses compaynouns, Ke quant Acres fu prise, la mer as avyrouns En passaunt eschapaynt sanz altres achesouns.*'
13. Chron. Guisborough Vol 2, 69. '*Eodem anno in terra sua Vallis Anandiæ apud Loghmaban obiit nobilis ille vir dominus Robertus de Bruys quartus*' or 'In the same year [1295], that noble man Lord Robert de Bruys the fourth [actually fifth] died in his country of Annandale at Lochmaben.'
14. A. A. M. Duncan. 2002. *The Kingship of the Scots 842–1292.* Edinburgh: Edinburgh University Press. 651–2. 'the treaty must have reached Scotland, where it was confirmed at an assembly on 23 February 1296, and the Scots, knowing of Edward's muster, and made bold by French promises, summoned their host.'
15. Ibid. 652. 'He [Edward] aimed first at the richest surety, Berwick, offering peace to the burgesses.'

16. Ibid. 'He [Balliol] could not bear these, nor remain in homage and fealty, 'although [they were] extorted by your violent pressure', and therefore renounced those homages done by himself and by any of his subjects with lands in England.'
17. Ibid. 653. 'And the claim that fealty had been extorted by force may have been necessary for ecclesiastical eyes and ears but was so manifestly false that it could only be noted parenthetically. If oaths meant anything, this was a rebellion.'
18. Ibid. 'on 5 April, Edward's armies advanced in and beyond the Tweed valley, determined on suppression of that rebellion. The battle of Dunbar on 27 April 1296.'
19. Ibid. 'The battle of Dunbar on 27 April 1296, a disaster for the Scots.'
20. Hist. Anglicana, 312. '*Domini autem comes de Lenenas, prsedictus Jacobus et Johannes de Foules se ad pacem et voluntatem domini nostri regis postmodum reddiderunt, et dominus noster rex cum dominis Alba- nensi episcopo, comite Selandise, Johanne de Griliaco, Ottone de Grandissono, et exercitu suo toto apud Rokesburgh festum Pentecostale sollempnizavit.*'
21. A. A. M. Duncan. 2002. *The Kingship of the Scots 842–1292*. Edinburgh: Edinburgh University Press. 653. 'John issued a letter 'giving back' (*avons rendu*) the kingdom on 2 July at Kincardine and 10 July at Brechin, both before and after the act of resignation at Montrose (8 July), a deliberate reflection of his fealty (20 November 1292), inauguration (30 November) and homage (26 December).'
22. Ibid. 'Edward moved gradually toward a position of denying the existence of a Scottish kingdom, a position he finally took up … in 1303–04.'
23. Alain Demurger. 2018. '*Othon de Grandson et les templiers d'Épailly' in Communicating the Middle Ages: Essays in Honour of Sophia Menache*. London: Routledge. 42. '*Dans années-là, Othon de Grandson n'est donc de passage en France et plus précisément à Paris qu'au début de l'été 1296. C'est à ce moment et en ce lieu que Jacques de Molay a pu le rencontrer. Un acte atteste du passage en Bourgogne du grand maître en avril 1296: il a assisté au chapitre général de la province de France à la Saint Jean-Baptiste 1296 et c'est de Paris qu'il est allé à Arles pour tenir le chapitre général prévu, en août 1296. Deux actes attestent de cette rencontre à Paris alors. L'un est dû à Othon de Grandson: il donne aux templiers une rente perpétuelle de 200 livres tournois assise sur les biens gu'il possède à Salins, dans la comté de Bourgogne; l'acte est daté du 14 juillet 1296 à Paris. Le second est de Jacques de Molay qui concéde à Othon une rente de 2000 livres tournois à prendre sa vie durant en deux termes (Purification de la Vierge et Saint Pierre-et-Paul) sur les caisses des maisons du Temple de Paris ou de Lvon. Le document est daté de Paris (Factas in mansione nostra apud Parisius) au mois de juill le dimanche après la fête des apôtres Pierre et Paul 1287 (sic). Cette lettre du grandmaitre est interpolée dans des lettres du pape Clément V datée du 17 août 1308 à Ligugé, près de Poitiers.*' Or 'In those years, Othon de Grandson was therefore only passing through France and more precisely in Paris at the beginning of the summer of 1296. It was at this time and in this place that Jacques de Molay was able to meet him. An act attests to the grand master's visit to Burgundy in April 1296: he attended the general chapter of the province of France on Saint John the Baptist 1296, and it was from Paris that he went to Arles to hold the general chapter. expected, in August 1296. Two acts attest to this meeting in Paris then. One is due to Othon de Grandson: he gives the Templars a perpetual annuity of 200 *Livres Tournois* based on the property he owns in Salins, in the County of Burgundy; the act is dated July 14, 1296, in Paris. The second is from Jacques

de Molay who grants Othon an annuity of 2000 *Livres Tournois* to take one's life in two terms (Purification of the Virgin and Saint Peter-and-Paul) on the coffers of the houses of the Temple of Paris or Lvon. The document is dated Paris (*Factas in mansione nostra apud Parisius*) in the month of July the Sunday after the feast of the apostles Peter and Paul 1287 (sic). This letter from the great master is interpolated in letters from Pope Clement V dated August 17, 1308, to Ligugé, near Poitiers.'

24. Chron. Guisborough. Vol 2, 71. '*Eodem anno obiit Gilbertus comes Gloucestræ*' or 'In the same year [1295] died Gilbert, Earl of Gloucester'
25. Ibid. 74. '*Edmundus multos jam stipendiarios conmocamezat, mumultos thesauros exhauserat, velut homo fa cetus et largissimus, cum jam tantam militian retinere non posset, eo quod non haberet stipendia, decidit vultus ejus et infirmatus est cinta Pentecosten, et sic deficiente pecunia defecit et spiritus, et post dies paucos viam universe carnis ingressus est; præcepitque nostris ut asportarent eum secum, nec sepelirentur ossa sua nisi cum solverentur et debita, feceruntque sic. Et post treugas initas, reduxerunt secum s ad fratrem suum regem, et per eum honorifice sepulta sunt apud Westmonasterium Londoniis.*' Or 'Edmund had already discharged many soldiers, had exhausted many treasures, like a wealthy and generous man, when he was no longer able to keep such a militia, because he had no wages, his countenance fell and he became infirm around Pentecost, and thus, for want of money, his spirit failed, and after a few days he entered the way of the whole flesh; and he ordered our men to carry him away with them, and not to bury his bones unless the debts were paid, and they did so. And after the truce entered, they brought him back with them to their brother the king, and by him he was honourably buried at Westminster in London.
26. John Julius Norwich. 2011. *The Popes*. London: Chatto & Windus. 189.
27. Charles L. Kingsford. 1909. *Sir Otho de Grandison 1238?–1328.* Transactions of the Royal Historical Society 3: 153. n2.
28. J. De Sturler. 1960. *Le Paiment a Bruxelles des Allies Franc Comtois d'Edouard 1er Roi d'Angleterre* (Mai 1297). Cahiers Bruxelles V: 21. *'De son côté, Othon de Grandson a rencontré les envoyés pontificaux en France, en juillet 1296; il s'est rendu, lui aussi, à Moulins (septembre 1296), à Cambrai (fin décembre 1296), en Brabant (janvier 1297) et, probablement des cet hiver, en « Bourgogne » (entendons: en Franche-Comté de Bourgogne) et en Savoie (15). En accomplissant pareil voyage, Othon se rapprochait précisément de Grandson (16), ou s'élevait le château de ses ancêtres, où il s'était rendu en 1295, à son retour de Chypre, et d'où il n'était revenu en 1296 que pour mettre ses services à la disposition de son royal ami, Edouard Ier. Dans son pays natal, une personnalité d'envergure comme la sienne pouvait rendre d'immenses services au parti qu'elle représentait.*' Or 'For his part, Othon de Grandson met the papal envoys in France in July 1296; he also went to Moulins (September 1296), to Cambrai (end of December 1296), to Brabant (January 1297) and, probably this winter, to 'Burgundy' (meaning: to Franche-Comté de Bourgogne) and in Savoy. By making such a journey, Othon was getting closer precisely to Grandson where the castle of his ancestors stood, where he had gone in 1295, on his return from Cyprus, and from where he had not been returned in 1296 only to place his services at the disposal of his royal friend, Edward I. In his native country, a personality like his could provide immense services to the party he represented.'

29. Esther Rowland Clifford. *A Knight of Great Renown: The Life and Times of Othon de Grandson*. Chicago: University of Chicago Press, 1961. 140–41.
30. Frantz Funck-Brentano. 1888. *Philippe le Bel et la Noblesse Franc-Comtois*. Paris: La Bibliotheque de l'Arsenal .15–16.
31. *Fœdera*. 196. '*Renaud de Burgoyne, Cuens de Montbeliard, Foban de Chalun Sire d'Arlay, Johan de Burgoyne, Joban de Montbeliard, Gautier de Montfaucon – Sires de Montfaucon, Thebald Sirer de Noef Chastel, Simon de Montbeliard, Sires de Montron, Rohan Sires de Faucony, Estiephne d'Oiselier Sires de Vile Noeve, Pierres de Genvill Sires de Monay, Hymbertus Sire de Clerenaus Joban d'Oiselier, Sires de Flag, Wauter Sires de Chasteuvileyne, Oede Sires de Montferrand, Guillame Sires Cocondrai, Estiephne Sires de Vorseber, Johan Sires de Jou, Gérard Sires d'Arguel, Du Contee de Borgoigne...outre la somme de seissante mil livres de Tornoys pezytz, les queles il ont la eu & recei de nostre donn, pour la dite guerre faire, & continuer par cest An, qui finera le primer jour du mois de Juyn, dorroms & paeroms a Brussel en Brebant, chescun An apres, tant come la dite guerre durra, & fe continuer, trent mil livres de la dite monoie, de Turnois petirz, ou la valour, en autres monoies.*'
32. J. De Sturler. 1960. *Le Paiment a Bruxelles des Allies Franc Comtois d'Edouard 1er Roi d'Angleterre* (Mai 1297). Cahiers Bruxelles V: 25–27, 33. '*Sachent tuit cil qui ces lettres verront e orront que cum li noble home e senhor Johan de Chalon sire Darlay, Johan de Borgonhe, Gautier de Mont Falcon, e Symon de Montbeliard sire de Montron, en nom dels meismes principalment e comme procureor des nobles homes mestre Johan de Chalon comte Daussuerre e senhor de Rochefort, Renaud de Bor gonhe comte de Montbeliard, Johan senhor de Montfalcon. Tibaut senhor de Nuef Chastel, Eyme senhor de Fauconhi, Estiene Doiselier senhor de Vilenove. Pierre de Gienvile senhor de Marnei, Johan Doiselier senhor de Flagi, Wauthier senhor de Chastel Vilein, Hymbert senhor de Clarevaus, Odes senhor de Montferant, Guilheaumes senhor de Cocondray, Johan senhor de Joi. Estevenot senhor Doiselier, e Guilheaumes senhor Darguel, en nome des ditz nobles e nome de Girard senhor Darquel aient promis e juré à nos. Othe de Gransson e Johan de Berewik clerc, messages de nostre senhor Edward par la grace Deu roy Dengleterre e en nom du meisme roy, que li meisme quatre procureor e tuit li autre noble desus nomé, por avoir laide du dit roy Dangleterre en deniers à defendre lor droit contre le roy de France, eideront en bone foi le dit Roy Dangleterre eidantz de la guerre que li meisme Roys Dangleterre e sui eidant ont e auront contre le roy de France e contre se hoirs.*'
33. Chron. Rishanger. 416. '*Dominam Johannam de Acre, primo desponsatam Gilberto, Comiti Gloucestriæ; et postea, propria voluntate, absque consilio Domini Regis vel aliorum amicorum, contraxit matrimonium cum uno simplici, serviente suo domino Eymero; cui procuravit, ante desponsationem, arma militaria. Cum autem pervenisset ad notitiam Domini Regis de tali fatuo facto, Dominus Rex, nimio furore succensus, capi fecit eum, et incarcerari apud Bristowe: et quia legitimum matrimonium non potuit irritari, per consilium Epis- coporum et aliorum, liberatus fuit; quem Dominus Rex postea vero multum dilexit.*' Or 'Lady Joan of Acre, first betrothed to Gilbert, Earl of Gloucester; and afterwards, of her own free will, without the advice of the Lord King or of other friends, she contracted marriage with a simple man, a servant of his lord Eymer; to whom he procured, before the betrothal, military arms. But when he came to the Lord King's notice of such a foolish deed, the Lord King, inflamed with exceeding fury,

caused him to be taken and imprisoned at Bristol; whom Lord King afterwards loved very much.' Chron. Albani, 27. '*Dominam Johannam de Acra, 'quæ processutemporis tradita est Domino Gilberto, Comiti Gloucestriæ, legitimo matrimonio; quæ peperit ei duos filios; quo defuncto, assumpsit sibi quemdam militem, elegantem forma, sed tenuem substantia. Non dico quod omnes proceres terræ hoc factum gratis animis exceperunt, terræ nullus expugnavit; omnes metu vel reverentia frænarunt ora; metu, quia ex regia prosapia, quia filia Regis, reverentia, quia Comitissa præcipua regni. Atta- men aderat unus e magnatibus terræ, qui in auribus Domini Regis, patris sui, intonuit, quod ejus honori adversum foret hujusmodi matrimonium, cum nonnulli nobiles, reges, comites, et barones eam adoptabant toro legitimo. Cui illa respondit; - 'Non est ignominiosum 'neque probrosum magno Comiti, et potenti, pauper- 'culam mulierem, et tenuem, sibi legitimo matrimonio 'copulare; sic vice versa, nec Comitissæ non est repre- 'hensible, nec difficile, juvenem strenuum promovere.' Placuit responsio ejus Domino Regi, et sic sopita est indignatio ejus et optimatum.'* Or 'Lady Johanna de Acre, 'who, in course of time, was given to Lord Gilbert, Earl of Gloucester, in lawful marriage; who bore him two sons; when he died, he took to himself a certain soldier, elegant in form, but thin in stature. I do not say that all the nobles of the land did this for nothing no one conquered the earth; fear, because of the royal lineage, because the Countess was the chief of the kingdom, who was in the ears of the Lord King, she thundered that such a marriage would be against her honor, when some nobles, counts, and barons adopted her as a legitimate toro. to 'coup' a thin one with a legitimate marriage; and so vice versa, it is neither reprehensible nor difficult for the countess to promote a vigorous young man.'

34. David Kusman. 2020. '*Haute Noblesse et Profit Financier. Les Activitiés d'Othon de Grandson dans les Anciens Pays-Bas à la fin du XIII Siècle au Regard des Practiques de la Noblesse des Anciens Pays-Bas.'* In *Othon I de Grandson (vers 1240–1328).* Lausanne: Cahiers Lausannois d'Histoire Médiévale. 86-90. '*Othon de Grandson est chargé par le duc de Brabant de sonder les intentions d'Amédée. Celui-ci, après avoir consulté ses conseillers, marque son accord. Puisque Othon de Grandson est toujours censé négocier le mariage de Jeanne de Gloucester et d'Amédée V, afin de ne pas provoquer le courroux du roi d'Angleterre, des premières noces clandestines ont lieu au château ducal de Louvain au début de l'année 1297.'* Or 'Othon de Grandson was charged by the Duke of Brabant with sounding out the intentions of Amadeus V28. The latter, after consulting his advisors, gave his agreement. Since Othon de Grandson was still supposed to negotiate the marriage of Joan of Gloucester and Amadeus V, in order not to provoke the wrath of the King of England, the first clandestine wedding took place at the ducal castle of Louvain at the beginning of 1297.' In his note 28 Kusman does caution '*Dans le texte de Cabaret, Othon de Grandson devient, par exemple, Pierre de Grandson, ce qui incite à la prudence*' Or 'In Cabaret's text, Othon de Grandson becomes, for example, Pierre de Grandson, which calls for caution regarding its accuracy.' Kusman sees in the marriage a degree of independence on the part of Savoy in concluding a marriage with Brabant instead of England, and Othon de Grandson's complicity in negotiations rewarded by the castellany of Monthey. Kusman suggests that Grandson takes part in the marriage clandestinely so as not to provoke a tempestuous Edward. However, Kusman does not mention Joan of Acre's relationship and pregnancy with Ralph Monthemer which rendered a marriage with Amédée de Savoie obviously impossible and bases his thesis on the notoriously unreliable *Chronique de Savoye de*

Cabaret written more than a century (1419) after the events they purport to portray. The author finds it hard, though not impossible, to credit Grandson acting clandestinely against Edward given the better sourced overwhelming evidence we have to the contrary describing the relationship between envoy and king. Whatever the precise timeline of events the result was an outcome which strengthened the alliance against Philippe le Bel not one that compromised it.

35. Mary C. L. Salt. 1929. List of English Embassies to France, 1272-1307. *The English Historical Review* 44: 271-2. Citing Fœdera, 837–38, 843, 849, 858–59, 881, 885, 887 & CPR Edward I vol 3 1292–1301, 394.
36. George Peddy Cuttino, 1941, 'Bishop Langton's Mission for Edward I, 1296–1297'. *Journal of British Studies*: University of Iowa. 154. '*Domino Johhani de Cabilone, domino Darlay, Johaoni de Burgundia, Gualtero de Monte Falcone et Simoni de Mont Beliard domino de Montron, nomine nobilium Burgundie, confederatorum Regis Anglie, pro medictate pagamenti 60.000 li. sibi debitarum pro primo anno confederacionis predicte, per manus dominorum J., J., G. et S. predictorum, apud Bruxellam, mense Maij, anno XXV*°'
37. RG 1322, 44. No 457. '457. *Les paroles coment monseignur Ottes de Granson doit respondre au roi de Fraunce endroit de la priere qe le roi de Fraunce fist pur les Escoz e les Baiones qi demeorent en oustage en Engleterre*.'
38. British Library. Add. MSS 7965.

Chapter 13

1. N. B. Lewis. 1948. 'The English Forces in Flanders, August–November 1297' in *Studies in Medieval History* presented to F. M. Powicke. Oxford. 310–18.
2. Stanislao Cordero Pamparato. 1902. *Documenti per la storia del Piemonte (1265–1300)*. Paravia: Turin. 100.
3. H. Rothwell. 1927. 'Edward I's Case against Philip the Fair over Gascony in 1298'. *The English Historical Review* 574. 'This attempt to treat Gascony as a forfeited fief was resisted vigorously by the vassal on any one of three grounds: 1. '*Terra Vasconie*' had always been held by the kings of England as an allodial possession and never as a fief; and for reasons given the treaty of Paris of 1259 had not sufficed to alter its allodial nature, and make it a fief of the French Crown with a fief's liability to fofeiture. 2. The treaty of Paris of 1259 was a contract, and as such binding on the one party only if observed by the other. The king of France had never fulfilled his undertakings in that treaty: therefore the king of England could not be bound by his. On this ground again the king of England was no vassal of the king of France, and could not therefore be guilty of treason. 3. The feudal contract was completely reciprocal in both the nature and extent of its obligations, and the penalty for infringing them was the same for both lord and vassal: '*ita ... pro quolibet istorum vassallus feudum amitteret, sic et dominus amittit proprietatem*.' Even assuming that he had ever been lord, the king of France had long ago flagrantly transgressed his obligations, had thereby been *'in culpa'* for violating the feudal relation, and thereby forfeited his lordship.'
4. Dante Alighieri. Purgatorio, 20. 43–45. '*Io fui radice de la mala pianta, che la terra cristiana tutta aduggia, sì che buon frutto rado se ne schianta*'.

5. Frantz Kervyn de Lettenhoven. 1854. *Etudes sur l'histoire du XIII siècle. Mémoires d'académie royale de Belgique* XXII.
6. Reg. Boniface VIII. 1: No 2626 '*Dispensalio super matrimonio cumfilio etfilia. Anglic et. Francie regum. (*fol 55 1).
7. T. Wright, Ed., and trans. 1839. 'The political songs of England from the reign of John to that of Edward II'. CS, 6, 178.
8. H. Rothwell. 1927. 'Edward I's Case against Philip the Fair over Gascony in 1298'. *The English Historical Review* 42: 575. 'Neither side accepted it at first, and one of Philip's barons even tore and trampled upon it in open court.'
9. Joseph.R. Strayer. 1980. T*heReignofPhiliptheFair*. PrincetonUniversityPress: Princeton. 16.
10. Justine Firnhaber-Baker. 2024. *House of Lilies: The Dynasty that Made Medieval France*. London: Penguin Books Ltd. 205. 'It was Philip, driven by his insecurities, his stubbornness, and his grandiose idea of royal majesty, who forced Edward into a war in Gascony.'
11. CPR Edward I vol 3. 1292–1301, 394. 'Notification that the king is sending Master Raymond Arnaldi de Rama, Westminster. canon of Bazas Vasateusis), king's clerk, the bearer, as his envoy to A.[médée] count of Savoy, the king's kinsman, and Otto de Grandisono, knight, touching a treaty of peace to be entered into with the king of France.'
12. Ibid. 418.
13. Gaston Raynaud. 1885. '*Nouvelle charte de la Pais aus englois (1299)*'. *Romania* XIV. 279–80.
14. Elizabeth A. R. Brown. 1988. 'The Political Repercussions of Family Ties in the Early Fourteenth Century: The Marriage of Edward II of England and Isabelle of France'. Speculum 63: 576. 'Had it not been for the marriage and the French king's hopes to see a grandchild hold the lands, he would never have considered relinquishing them.'
15. Seymour Phillips. 2011. *Edward II*. London: Yale University Press .132.
16. *Fœdera*. 208–9.
17. CPR Edward I vol 3 1292–1301, 430. 'Pardon to Taldus Janiani and his fellows, merchants of the society of the Westminster. Friscobaldi of Florence, for receiving in their houses in London 99/. 10s. of pollards and crockards brought from beyond seas, contrary to the late ordinance that bad money should not be brought within the realm, of which trespass they were convicted before Otto de Grandisono and John de Drokenesford, specially appointed thereto by the king.'
18. A 'crockard' being a silver penny where the crown was replaced by a chaplet of roses. A 'pollard' being a variety with a bare headed bust, from the English word for a cow without horns.
19. CCR Edward I vol 4 1296–1302, 264. 'August 2 [1299], Westminster. To the keeper of the forest of Asshedon. Order to cause Otto de Grandi Sono to have in that forest six bucks of the king's gift.'
20. CChR Henry III Edward I vol 2 1257–1300, 479. 'August [1299], Westminster. Grant to Otho de Grandi Sono, and his heirs, of a weekly market Westminster on Wednesday at his manor of Acconagh, co. Tipperary, and of a yearly fair there on the vigil and the feast of St. Margaret and the thirteen days following; grant also of free warren in all his demesne lands in Acconagh and Mouscry, co. Tipperary, Isowen, co. Tipperary and co. Waterford, Estremoy and Honey, cos. Limerick and Kerry.'

21. Max Bruchet. 1900. *Inventaire partiel* du *Trésor* des *chartes* de *Chambéry. No 322. 'Litteram publicam a Johanne, domino de Cossonay et Margarita de Villars, ejas uxore emantam vendicionis facte domino Ottpni de Grandissoni de villa et toto territorio de Souchie. Datam Lausanne. Junii AD 1299.'*
22. François Forel. Ed. 1862. *Régeste soit Répertoire Chronologique de Documents Relatifs à l'Histoire de la Suisse Romande. Première Série*. Vol XIX. Lausanne. 480. Nos 2272, 2273 & 2279.
23. Francis Palgrave. 1827. The Parliamentary Writs. London. Vol 1. 642. 'Grandisono, Otto de … summoned to a Parliament or Council, held at the New Temple, London, on the feast of St. Luke the Evangelist, 18 Oct. 1299.'
24. Bernard Burke. 1866. *A Genealogical History of the Dormant, Abeyant Forfeited and Extinct Peerages of the British Empire*. London: Harrison. 242. 'GRANDISON-BARON GRANDISON. By Writ of Summons, dated 21 September 1299.'
25. François Forel. Ed. 1862. *Régeste soit Répertoire Chronologique de Documents Relatifs à l'Histoire de la Suisse Romande. Première Série*. Vol XIX. Lausanne. 480. No 2297. '*1300, 31 janvier. Conventiones inter dominum episcopum et comitem Gebennensem ac multos alios barones, que conventiones confecte sunt sub sigillis dominorum episcopi Lausannensis, Ame dei comitis Gebennensis, Humberti domini de Thoyri et de Villar, Walteri de Montefalconis domini de Vilaufens, domini Johan. de Cossonay, Petri coudomini de Stavay, domini Ottonis de Grandissono, domini Petri de Bellomonte, domini Stephani de Balmis militis pro domino Petro domino de Chanvenz, ultima die mensis januarii, anno domini MCCC.*' Or 1300, 31 January. Agreements between the lord bishop and the count of Geneva and many other barons, which agreements were concluded under the seals of the lords bishop of Lausanne, Amédée count of Geneva, Humbert the lord of Thoyri and de Villar, Walter de Montefalcon [Montfaucon], the lord of Vilaufens, lord Jean de Cossonay, Pierre Coudomini de Stavay, lord Otto de Grandisson, lord Pierre de Bellomonte, lord Stephen de Balmis, my suit for lord Pierre lord de Chanvenz [Champvent], on the last day of the month of January, in the year lord 1300.'
26. Ibid. 'Grandisono, Otto de … summoned to Parliament at London, on the second Sunday in Lent, 6 March 1300.'
27. Ibid. 'Grandisono, Otto de … summoned to perform Military Service in person against the Scots. – Muster at Carlisle, on the Nativity of St. John the Baptist, 24 June 1300.'
28. *Fœdera*. 2–3.
29. CChW 1244 – 1326, 110-1. 'June 15 [1300], Thirsk. To W. bishop of Chester, treasurer, and John de Langeton, chancellor. Mandate to send hastily to the king the letter which he formerly devised to send to the pope in answer to the news of the Holy Land which the pope sent by bull, so that the king can have the letter or the transcript at Durham on Friday next, or very early on Saturday, so that he may have advice on it before Sir Ottes de Granzon leaves him; also to send to the king Master John de Caam to be with him at Durham on Friday at vespers, or early on Saturday.'
30. Nicolas Harris Nicholas. Ed. 1828. *The Siege of Caerlaverock*. London: J. B. Nichols. 24. '*Guillelmes de Grant son palee de Argent et de asur suralee de bende rouge et trois eigleaus portoit de or fin bien fais e beaus*.'
31. Howard de Walden. 1904, trans Thomas Evelyn Scott-Ellis. *Some Feudal Lords and Their Seals MCCCJ*. London: De Walden Library. ix.

32. Ibid. xiii. '*Sane ad celsitudinem regiam potuit pervenisse, & in tuae libro memoriae nequaquam ambigimus contineri, qualiter ab antiquis temporibus regnum Scotiae pleno jure pertinuit, & adhuc pertineie dinoscitur ad ecclesiam supra dictam; quodque illud, sicut accepimus, progenitoribus tuis, regni Angliæ Regibus, sive tibi feudale non extitit, nee existit.*'
33. Ibid. ix. 'claiming on the suggestion of the French, the feudal superiority, not for the Scottish but for Pope. Boniface himself'. Esther Rowland Clifford. 1961. *A Knight of Great Renown: The Life and Times of Othon de Grandson*. Chicago: University of Chicago Press. 177. 'Boniface, egged on by the French, wrote to Edward that Scotland had never belonged either to him or to his forebears but had always been a fief of the Roman church.'
34. Michael Prestwich. 1997. *Edward I*. Yale: Yale University Press. 396.
35. CChW 1244 – 1326, 113. 'Aug 10 [1300], Gerton, To the Bishop of Vicenza. The king is grieved to learn by his letters that he has received such sad news from the court of Rome that he cannot stay in France where he is, and where his presence is very necessary for the king's business, but must presently go to that court. The king had already sent Sir Otes de Grantzon and other messengers to the parts where the bishop is, on the business there, and prays for his good offices. As requested, he has recommended the bishop to the pope by letters of which he sends a transcript.'
36. *Fœdera*. 3.
37. Howard de Walden. 1904, trans Thomas Evelyn Scott-Ellis. *Some Feudal Lords and Their Seals MCCCJ*. London: De Walden Library. ix.
38. Ibid. x.
39. Ibid. xviii. '*Scimus enim Pater Sanctissime et notorium est in partibus Angliae et nonnullis aliis non ignotum quod a prima institutione regni Angliae Reges ejusdem regni tarn temporibus Britonum quam Anglorum superius et directum dominium regni Scotise habuerunt et in possessione vel quasi superioritatis et directi dominii ipsius regni Scotiae successivis temporibus extiterunt.*'
40. E. L. G. Stones. Ed. 1970. *Anglo-Scottish Relations 1174–1328. Some Selected Documents*. Oxford: The Clarendon Press. No. 30. '*Sub temporibus itaque Ely et Samuelis prophete vir quidam strenuus et insignis, Brutus nomine, degenere Trojanorum post excidium urbis Troie multis nobilibus Trojanorum applicuit in quandam insulam tunc Albion vocatam, a gigantibus inhabitatam, quibus sua et suorum devictis potencia et occisis eam nomine suo Britanniam sociosque suos Britones appellavit. . . Arturus rex Britonum princeps famosissimus Scociam sibi rebellem subjecit, et penetotam gentem delevit et postea quemdam nomine Anguselum in regem Scocie prefecit et cum postea idem rex Arturus apud civitatem Legionum festum faceret celeberimum, interfuerunt ibidem omnes reges sibi subjecti inter quos Anguselus rex Scocie servicium pro regno Scocie exhibens debitum gladium regis Arturi detulit ante ipsum et successive omnes reges Scocie omnibus regibus Britonum fuere subjecti. Succedentibus autem regibus Anglis in predicta insula et ipsius monarchiam et dominium optinentibus subsequenter. . . Adelstanus rex Anglie Constantinum regem Scotorum sub se regnaturum constituit dicens gloriosius est regem facere quam regem esse*'. *Fœdera*. 9.
41. Glastonbury Archive. 'Marquess of Bath, Longleat'. 39, 203r (s. xiv)
42. Ibid.

43. E.L.G. Stones. Ed. 1970. *Anglo-Scottish Relations 1174–1328. Some Selected Documents.* Oxford: The Clarendon Press. No. 29. '*Certificacio magistri Willielmi de Sardene*' or 'Advice of Master William of Sardinia'.
44. Esther Rowland Clifford. 1961. *A Knight of Great Renown: The Life and Times of Othon de Grandson.* Chicago: University of Chicago Press. 183. 'Boniface was still continuing his tactics of blowing now hot, now cold à *la fie dures, à la fie moles'* as the three counts of Flanders had described his words to their father.'
45. John Julius Norwich. 2011. *The Popes.* London: Chatto & Windus. 189.
46. CPR Edward I vol 3 1292–1301, 607. '14 October [1301] Promise to Gérard [de Wippains] archdeacon of Richemund, king's clerk, to pay him by Easter out of the money of the tenth or fifteenth 309l. 3s. 4d expenses incurred by him as the king's envoy on special affairs at the court of Rome, from 15 April, 28 Edward I, to 23 June, 29 Edward I, as appears by his account before John de Drokenesford, king's clerk, keeper of the Wardrobe. By letters patent of the said John. The like to Otto de Grandisono to pay him by Easter out of the same money 332l. like expenses as envoy at the court of Rome from 21 June, 28 Edward I, to 31 May following.'
47. *Fœdera.* 7.
48. Ibid. 3.
49. CPR Edward I vol 3 1292–1301, 607. '30th September [1301] Protection with *clause volumus*, for one year, for Master Gérard de Wippayns, archdeacon of Richmond, going to the court of Rome on the king's affairs. By K.'
50. Ibid. 569. '4th February [1301] Protection with *clause volumus*, for one year, for Otto de Grandisono, gone to the court of Rome on the king's affairs.'
51. *Fœdera.* 13–14. CPR Edward I vol 4 1301–1306, 10. 'Treaty made between the men of Philip, king of France, to wit, the count of Saint Pool, the count of Drues, Monsieur Hubert de Bonville and Monsieur Piers Flote, knights of that king, and the bishop of Chester, the earl of Lincoln, the archdeacon of Richmond and John de Berewyk, canon of York, touching a truce with the Scots.'
52. CPR Edward I vol 4 1301–1307, 24. '5th March [1302] Notification to B. the Pope that, whereas before the term of St. Andrew the Apostle last, the king appointed Walter, bishop of Coventry and Lichfield, Amadeus, count of Savoy, Otto de Grandissono, knight, and Master Gérard de Wyppeyns, archdeacon of Richmond, as envoys to hear the Pope's pronouncement touching the king's compromise with the king of France, the said count and knight for many reasons have excused themselves from coming; and that, to avoid delay in the business by their absence, he appoints the two others as his proctors therein. Appointment of the bishop and archdeacon as proctors.'
53. *Fœdera.* 15.
54. Esther Rowland Clifford. 1961. *A Knight of Great Renown: The Life and Times of Othon de Grandson.* Chicago: University of Chicago Press. 187. 'But when the embassy crossed the channel on February 14 1302, Othon went with them to Paris instead of continuing on to Rome. He and Amédée had firmly refused to undertake another mission to the Curia. . .It is quite possible that both Othon and Amédée had realised the hopelessness of waiting for a papal decision and had convinced the king that their time would be better spent in negotiating directly with the French."
55. Pierre Dupuy. Ed. 1655. *Histoire du differend d'entre le pape Boniface VIII et Philippe le Bel, roy de France.* Paris. 44. '*Philippus Dei gratia Francorum Rex, Bonifacio se*

gerenti pro summo Pontifice, Salutem modicam, seu nullam. tua maxima fatuitas in temporalibus.'

56. Georges Picot. Ed. 1901. *Documents relatifs aux Etats Généraux et assemblées réunis sous Philippe le Bel.* Paris. No 5. 15.
57. CPR Edward I vol 4 1301–1307, 30. 'Appointment of Amadeus of Savoy, Henry de Lacy, earl of Lincoln, Aymer de Valencia, the king's kinsmen, Otto de Grandisono, Hugh Despenser, Amaneuus, lord of Lebret, knights, Master William de Grenefeld, dean of Chichester, and Jolin de Berewyk, dean of Wymburn, as the king's envoys to treat touching the re-establishment of peace with the king of France.' *Fœdera.* 16.
58. Giovanni Villani. *Nuovo Chronica.* Ed. Guiseppe Porta. 1997. *Tomo Secondo.* LV. '*Questo Piero era tessitore di panni povero uomo, e era piccolo di persona e sparuto, e cieco dell'uno occhio, e d'età di più di LX anni; lingua francesca né latina non sapea, ma in sua lingua fiamminga parlava meglio, e più ardito e stagliato che nullo di Fiandra e per lo suo parlare commosse tutto il paese a le grandi cose che poi seguiro.*' Or 'This Peter was a poor man, a weaver of cloth, and was small in person and gaunt, and blind in one eye, and over sixty years of age; He did not know the French or Latin language, but in him he spoke the Flemish language better, and more bold and distinguished than anything in Flanders and because of him speaking about him moved the whole country to the great things that then followed.'
59. Ann. Gandenses. 25. 'They shouted, as they had agreed before the fight, two words, namely 'shield or 'breastplate' and 'friend' for 'shield' in Flemish has an aspirate, which the French and Gauls cannot pronounce, and is written thus, 'scilt'. As soon as those who had remained in the town understood this, though previously they had supported the French, some with genuine, others with feigned, favour and goodwill, all with one accord came over to their victorious fellow-townsmen and began with them to slaughter and massacre the French, whether on guard or asleep, shouting with the newcomers, 'Shield and friend'.
60. Ibid.
61. CPR Edward I vol 4 1301–1307, 56. '15th August [1302] Appointment of Amadeus of Savoy and Henry de Lacy of Lincoln, carls, and Aymer de Valencia, the king's kinsmen, Otto de Grandisono, Amaneuus lord of Lebret, knights, Master William de Grenefeld, dean of Chichester, and Master Robert de Pykering, canon of York, as plenipotentiaries to treat of peace with Philip, king of France.' *Fœdera.* 17.
62. Ibid. '10th January [1303] Appointment of Amadeus count of Savoy, Henry de Lacy, earl of Lincoln, the king's kinsmen, and Otto de Grandisono, knight, as plenipotentiaries to make a treaty of peace with Philip, king of France. [*Fœdera.*] The like of the same to make a treaty of peace and confederation with the said Philip against all men, except the church of Rome.' *Fœdera.* 21.
63. *Fœdera.* 24–25.
64. Ibid. 54.
65. *Fœdera.* 20.
66. Bernard Andenmatten: 'Grandson, Pierre II de' in *Dictionnaire historique de la Suisse* (DHS), *version du 07.02.2006.* https://hls-dhs-dss.ch/fr/articles/017804/2006–02-07/, consulté le 27.03.2024. Marriage contract dated 27 April 1303. Between Pietro di Grançon and Bianca figlia del fu Lodovico di Savoia Signore di Vaud. State Archives, vol 102. 28. fascicule 1.

67. Esther Rowland Clifford. 1961. *A Knight of Great Renown: The Life and Times of Othon de Grandson*. Chicago: University of Chicago Press. 189. Citing. Parliament 1854. Minutes of evidence taken before the Committee for Privileges to whom the petition of Sir Henry Paston Bedingfeld of Oxborough in the county of Norfolk … to Her Majesty, praying Her Majesty to determine the abeyance of the Barony of Grandison by summoning the petitioner to Parliament as Lord Grandison; together with Her Majesty's reference thereof to this House, and the report of the Attorney General thereon, were referred. London. 99.
68. RG iii, 414. No 4589. '*Rex dilecto et fideli suo Johanni de Hastinges, senescallo suo Vasconie, salutem. Cum mittamus dilectos et fideles nostros Amedeum, comitem Sabaudie, consanguineum nostrum carissimum, et Ottonem de Grandisono ad partes ducatus predicti, ad seisinam civitatum, villarum, castrorum et alio rum locorum de eodem ducatu, juxta formam pacis inter nos et magnificum principem dominum Philippum, Dei gracia regem Ffrancorum illustrem, jam inite et firmate, ad opus nostrum nostroque mine capiendam, et ad quedam alia ibidem facienda que eis plenius duximus injungenda, vobis man damus quod eisdem comiti et Ottoni duo milia librarum chipotensium ad expensas suas pro pre missis negociis expediendis ibidem de dicti ducatus exitibus liberetis. Et nos vobis inde debitam alloca cionem fieri faciemus. Datum apud Castrum Puel larum, iij. die Junii. Et fuerunt patentes.*'
69. *Fœdera*. 22–23.

Chapter 14

1. Walter Eustace Rhodes. 1901. 'The Italian Bankers in England and their Loans to Edward I and Edward II' in *Historical Essays* 151–52. Citing Perruzi 153–54. *Ricordo per chi passa in Inghilterra: Vestir basso color, esser umile, Grosso in aspetto ed in fatti sottile: Male sia a l'Inglese se t'atterra. Fuggi le cure e chi pur ti fa guerra: Spendi con cuor e non ti mostrar vile: Pagar al giorno, a risouoter gentile, Mostrando che bisogno ti sotterra: Non far più inchiesta ch' abbi fondamento: Compera a tempo se ti metta bene, Ne t'impacciar con uomini di corte. Osserva di chi può 'l comandamento. Con tua nazione unirti t'appartiene; E far per tempo ben serrar le porte.*'
2. RG iii. 4593. '*4593. Rex dilecto clerico suo Aymerici, magistro Petro constabulario castri sui Burderale, vel ejus locum tenenti, salutem. Mandamus vobis quod de exxitibus ducatus predicti quos recipere vos continget, liberari faciatis Johanni Ballard et sociis suis, mercatoribus de societate Ballardorum', vel ipsorum attornatis, tria milia [librarum parisiensium, vel in alia moneta, que iidem mereatores nobis ad mandatum venerabilis patris W., Conventrensis et Lychfeldensis episcopi, thesaurarii nostri, ad expensas dilectorum fidelium nostrorum Amadei comitis Sabaudie, consanguinei nostri carissimi, et Ottonis de Grandissono, nuper per preceptum nos trum ad partes Vasconie pro seisina ducatus predicti recipienda ad opus nostrum proficiscenciam mutuarunt: videlicet pro expensis dicti comitis duo milia librarum parisiensis et, pro expensis prefati Ottonis, mille libras ejusdem monete. Et nos vobis inde in compoto vestro allocacionem debitam ha bere faciemus. Datum apud Kynlos' in Scocia, xvij. die Oetobris. Per billam Johannis de Drokenesford. Et fuerunt patentes.*'
3. Ibid. 4700. '*4700. Rex constabulario Burdegale qui no vel qui pro tempore faerit, salutem, Sciatis quod constituimus dilectum nobis Johannem Gytardi contrarotulatorem castri*

nostri Burdegale, et eidem vestes et stipendia concessimus, prout in litteris nostris patentibus sibi inde confectis plenius continetur. Quare vobis mandamus quatinus ipsum Johannem ad predictum contrarotalarie officium admittatis, et ei vestes et stipendia predicta, dein eeps et eciam a tempore quo dictum contrarotularie officium per dilectos et fideles nostros Henricum de Lacy, comitem Lincolnie, et Ottonem de Grandisono de mandato nostro extitit commissum, per solvatis. Et nos de hiis que sibi solveritis in vestro compoto debitam allocacionem fieri faciemus, In cujus, ete. Datum apud Westmonasterium, iij. die Aprilis. Per manns magistri Petri Aymerici.'

4. *RG iii. 4736.* '*4736. Rex dilecto et fideli suo Jacobo de Montibus*'*, judici majoris senescaleie Agenensis, salutem. Cum dilecti et fideles nostri Henricus de Lacy, comes Lincolnie, et Otto de Grandisono, miles, per nos ad partes Aquitannie destinati, de tue fide litatis industria et circumspectione provida confidentes, te ad regimen judicature predicte duxerint admittendum sub stipendiis consuetis, nos, factum ipsorum ratum habentes, mandamus omnibus sub ditis et vassallis judicature predicte ut tibi tan quam judici pareant et intendant, quamdiu nostre placuerit volantati. Volumus tamen quod dilecto et fideli nostro Johanni de Havering., militi, senes callo nostro ducatus Aquitannie, necnon senescallo majoris senescallie Agenensis sis obediens et intendens. Damus nichilominus tenore presencium in mandatis nostro thesaurario Agenensi ut tibi de stipendiis tuis faciat responderi. Nos enim quod tibi pro stipendiis tuis solverit in suis volumus compotis allocari. T. R. apad Westmonasterium, xxx. die Marcii.*'
5. Ibid. 4841. '4841. *Pro Rainfredo de Durofforti, milite, de custodia castri de Turno[ne) Rex dilecto et fideli suo Johanni de Havering., senescallo Vasconie, et magistro Ricardo de Havering., constabulario Burdegale, vel eorum loca tenentibus, salutem. Cum dilectus et fidelis noster Henricus de Lacy, co Lincolnie, et Oto de Grandisono, miles, ad partes predicti ducatus Aquitannie per nos destinati, Rainfredo de Duroforti, militi, tradiderint custodiam et castellaniam castri nostri de Turnone in Agenesio*', *ad vadia quinque solidorum tur sium parvorum per diem taxata per ipsos, vobis mandamus quatinus prefato Rainfredo vel ejus mandato castri predieti et castellanie custodiam tradatis, tamdiu tenendam per ipsum quamdiu nostre placuerit voluntati, et eidem per thesaurarium Agenensem vadia pretaxata faciatis exsolvis quod enim eidem exsolutum fuerit precipimus in prefati thesaurarii compotis allocari. Datum apud Westmonasterium, xxx. die Marcii. Et fuerunt patentes.*'
6. Ibid. 4865. '4865. *Rex senescallo suo dicti ducatus et constabulario Burdegale qui nunc sunt vel pro tempore fuerint, salutem. Mandamus vobis quod Brasco de Tarze*' *dimittatis et haberi faciatis terram et balli am de Mareneino eum juribus et pertinenciis suis pro illo precio pro quo dilecti et fideles nostri Henricas de Lacy, comes Lincolnie, et Otto de Grandi sono, miles, nuper gerentes vices nostras in dieto ducatu, dimiserunt eidem tenendam, donee heredibus domini de Tarzes et aliis loci ejusdem ex heredatis pro nobis restitui fecerimus terras suas. In cujus, etc. Datum ut supra. Eiga.*'
7. Ibid. 4732. '*4732. Rex constabulario Burdegale qui nune est et qui pro tempore fuerit, Salutem. Cum dilecti et fideles nostri Henricus de Lacy, comes Lincolnie, et Otto de Grandisono, miles, ad partes dicti ducatus Aquitannie per nos destinati, dilectum nobis Bernardum Pelleti priorem et dominum Mansi, juris utriusque doctorem, in clericum nostrum duxerint retinendum, ab ipso ipso juramento fidelitatis capto, ducentas et quinquaginta libras bonerum turonensinm parvorum, quorum quatuor valeant unum sterlingum, in feodum assignantes eidem, necnon triginta solidos bonorum turonensium*

par pro espensis suis singulis diebas quibus extra domicilium suum negociis nostris ipsum va contigerit, nosque per nostras patentes litteras factum predietorum Henrici et Ottonis ratum habuerimus et acceptum, prout in nostris litteris plenius continetur, vobis mandamus quatinus de medietate dieti feodi singulis annis in festo Pasche et de alia melietate in festo Omnium Sanctorom satisfaciatis eidem, necnon de expensis cum litteris suis in virtute juramenti per ipsum prestiti nu merum dierum quibus nostris vacaverit negociis testificantibus, quociens fuerit opportunum, sibi nichilominus de arreragiis respondentes. Quod sibi solveritis de predictis, volmns et precipimus in vestris compotis allocari. In cujus, etc. Datum ut supra.

8. Ibid. 4757. *'4757. Mandatum est [pro] magistro Rogero de Gaya quod, cum dilecti et fideles nostri Henricus de Lacy, comes Lincolnie, et Otto de Grandisono, mi es, per nos ad partes Aquitannie destinati, ipsum ad custodiam forestarum de Antrix et Lectorensi diocesis, et ad vendendum herbagia, paseua et mus mortuum forestarum predictarum, necnon ad consulendum thesaurario Agenensi cum incurrementa per ipsum vendi continget, et eciam ad revocandum alienata per gentes nostras minus juste, ipsum duxerin tpreficiendum, sub stipendiis x. librarum turonensium parvorum: no nos, de ipsius ha fidelitatis industria confidentes, faetum ratum bentes, mandamus omnibus subditis nostris in premissis sibi pareant et intendant, quamdiu nostre placuerit voluntati, Volumus tamen que quod dilecto et fideli nostro Johanni de Haveringg militi, senescallo nostro ducatus Aquitannie, neeno senescallo Agenensi, sit obediens et intendens. De mus nichilominus tenore presencium in mandatis nostro thesaurario Agenensi ut sibi de stipendiis suis faciat responderi. Nos enim quod sibi pro stipendiis suis solverit, in suis volumus compotis alo cari. Datum apud Westmonasterium.xXx. die Apri' lis.'*

9. Ibid. 4915. '4915, *Rex dilecto et fideli suo Johanni de Havering., senescallo suo dicti ducatus, salutem. Significavit nobis Gaillelmus de Cortosia, mercator quod, cum sub protectione dilecti et fidelis postri Johannis de Hasting., nuper senescalli nostri in dicto ducatu, centum tonellos vini haberet, Reymun dus Gaufridi et Petrus de Burdegala, mercatores de Burdegala, dictos tonellos maliciose ceperunt, ques reddere noluerunt ad mandatum dieti senescalli nec eciam ad ordinacionem et mandatum dilectorum et fidelium nostrorum consanguineorum Amadei et Henrici, comitum Sabaudie et Lincolnie, et Ottonis de Grandisono, nuper vices nostras gerencium in ducatu predicto, set ab ipsis ad nos frivole appellarunt ut possent evadere restitucionem predictam. Unde, cum talem malieiam sustinere minime de beamus, vobis mandamus quod, non obstante dicta appellacione, predictos tonellos cum vino, vel valorem in quantum valebant tempore recepeionis predicte, eidem mereatori, vel attornato suo presentem litteram deferenti, sine more dispendio reddi et restitui faciatis, et mandatum* predietorum *comitum et Ottonis super hoe factum teneatis, et teneri et servari ab aliis faciatis sine quacumque; ita quod ad nos non veniat iterata querela. Datum apud Westmonasterium, vi, die Aprili.'*

10. Ibid. 4828. '4828, *Rex dileeto et fideli suo senescallo Agen nensi, et aliis justiciariis et offi[ciariis] suis, salutem. Cum dilecti et fideles nostri Henricus de Lacy, comes Lincolnie, et Otto de Grandisono miles, nobili viro Bernardo de Rovynhano', domicello, nomine nostro rancores et odia aliqua, cri mina et excessus sub certis formis, prout in eorum litteris seriosius continetur, duxerint remittenda nos, dietam remissionem ratam habentes et firmam, vobis mandamus quatinus, suppletis hiis que secundum ordinacionem et remissionem restant implenda per ipsum super contentis in litteris*

remissionis predicte, ipsum seu gentes suas, quoad jus nostrum attinet, nullatenus molestetis nec permit tatis per aliquos molestari. In eujus, ete. T. ut supra.'

11. Esther Rowland Clifford. 1961. *A Knight of Great Renown: The Life and Times of Othon de Grandson.* Chicago: University of Chicago Press. 197.
12. Pierre Courroux. '*Bernard de Rovignan, sire de Buzet et bandit de grand chemin, à l'origine d'une guerre franco-anglaise*'. Retrieved 23 April 2024. https://chateau-fabriquesdebuzet.fr/bernard-de-rovignan-sire-de-buzet-et-bandit-de-grand-chemin-a-lorigine-dune-guerre-franco-anglaise/
13. RG iii. 4756. '4756. *Mandatum est senescallo Agenensi quod locum de Castilhonesio, quem cum suis pertinenciis universis vestre seneschallie Agenensi integraliter applicamus, faciat per unum dumtaxat bajulum gubernari, et hominibus ejusdem loci suos usus, consuetudines et libertates, prout justum fuerit, inviolabiliter observari. Datum apud Westmonasterium, tercio die Aprilis.*'
14. Ibid. 4599. '4599. *Rex omnibus ad quos, ete., salutem Cum dilecta consanguinea nostra Margareta, comitissa Ffaxensis et vieecomitissa Bearnensis, sheramen um fidelitatis [nobis nuper Tholose prestiterit, coram dilectis et fidelibus nostris, Amadeo Sahaudie, et Henrico, Lineolnie comitibas, consanguineis nostris karissimis, et Ottone de Grandisono, milite, procuratoribus et nunciis nostris ad hoc specialiter onstitutis: nolentes sibi ex hoe imposterum prejndiciam generari, volumus et concedimus quod prefati comitissa et beredes sui dictum juramentum fidelitatis, in loco ubi antecessores ipsius comitisse illud consueverunt facere et non alibi, nobis et he redibus nostris de cetero facere tencantur, et quod predictum juramentum Tholose* prestitum sibi vel heredibus *suis non cedat aliqualiter in prejadicium in faturum. In cujus, ete. Datum ut supra. E fuerunt iste tres littere* prescripte patentes.'
15. Esther Rowland Clifford. 1961. *A Knight of Great Renown: The Life and Times of Othon de Grandson.* Chicago: University of Chicago Press. 199. 'Philip can have had little hope that this would pacify the contentious offspring of Gaston de Béarn, and he was undoubtedly very much relieved when Marguerite did homage to Edward's three lieutenants, for it meant that she would now devote herself to plaguing the English officials instead of the French.'
16. Reg. Boniface VIII. 1: 277–80. Doc 5345. 5345 (X) '*Latran, Jeudi saint, 4 avril 1303. Repovatur processus adversas cos, etiam si imperiali sut regali fulgeant dignitate », qui venientibus ad Sedem Apostolicam impedimentum prestanl. (fol. 374.) Ad perpetuam rei memoriam. Excomunicamus et thematizamus omnes illos, qui ad Sedem Apostolicam venientes vel recedentes ab es capiunt, spoliant vel detinere presumunt, aut impedimentum aliquod exhibont, quominus ad eandem Sedem libere, cum personis et rebus suis veniant et recedant ab eadem, etiam si imperiali aut regali fulgeant dignitate.*'
17. Ch. V. Langlois. 1889. '*Documents Relatifs a Bertrand de Got (Clément V)*'. *Revue Historique* 40: 53.
18. Ibid. 52.
19. Ibid. 53. 'des *cadeaux au pape et à sa suite, à savoir: au pape lui-même, vingt tonneaux de vin, vingt bœufs, vingt porcs, vingt béliers, douze bulors, douze hérons, deux esturgeons, et une croix d'or cum crystallo et imagine aurea.*'
20. Ibid. 53–54. '*Item, dominus senescallus in civitate Burdegale existens recepit rumores xVIe die Augusti quod comes Fuxi cum maxima multitudine armatorum partes intraverat comitis Armaniaci, terram et patriam dicti comitis destruendo, homicidia, depredationes*

et incendia castro rum, villarum et ecclesiarum in dominio ipsius domini regis et ducis in contemptum regii honoris faciendo; super quo deliberatione habita cum consilio domini regis illarum parcium et etiam cum consilio domini pape et domini Othonis de Grandisono, ex unanimi eorum con silio et assensu, pro conservacione pacis et regii honoris exercitum citavit armatorum ad xxv™ diem Augusti, qui ad rebelles debellandos et predictos excessus corrigendos irent ad partes Armaniaci predictas cum ipso senescallo ad vadia consueta. Et superveniente sic dicto senescallo Vasconie cum exercitu supra dicto, prosequendo comitem Ffuxi et suos complices qui bene evadere non potuit, ut prospexit, quin captus fuisset et destructus propter sua facinora et excessus, dominum papam interim requisivit, mediantibus comitissa matre sua, comitissa Bearnie Constancia, sorore sua, et pluribus proceribus ex parte dicti comitis propter imminens periculum et intolerabile damnum vitandum quod manus ad pacem apponere dignaretur: qui precibus eorum inclinatus per consilium sui collegii guerram predictam modo qui sequitur quietavit et sedavit: videlicet quod idem comes Ffuxi omnia dampna que fecerat vel per ipsum fuerant perpetrata quoquo modo in partibus Armeniaci predictis infra certum diem secundum ordinationem dicti domini pape et senescalli faceret emendari, pro despectu namque et injuriis quos fecerat dicto domino regi et duci pacem suam infringendo, eorumdem domini pape et senes calli voluntati et ordinacioni totaliter se submisit.'

21. Ibid. 54. '*Item, dominus senescallus perpendens quod dominus papa recessu rus erat de Burdegala IIII die septembris eodem anno versus Lugdunum pro coronatione sua, ne briga seu discordia aliqua in via ipsius domini pape in tanto tumultu gencium in terra ipsius domini regis oriretur, de consilio dicti domini Othonis et aliorum consiliariorum domini regis illarum parcium, ut sic forcius Tatum dominum usque ad suum exitum de ducatu conduceret, decentem comitivam armato rum* secum duxit ad vadia consueta.'
22. *Regestum Clementis papæ V. 1885*. Rome: *The Catholic Church.* No 22. '*22. Lunelli, 19 oct. 1305. Annuens supplicationibus Othonis de Grandisono dispensat cum nepote eius super residentia. (f. 46).*' And No 44 '*44. Nemausi, 21 oct. 1305. Obtentu Othonis de Grandisono confertur eius consanguineo prioratus de Lareyo monasterio s. Benigni Divionensi ord. s. Ben. Lingonen. dioec. subiectus et ad praesens per obitum Philippi va cans. (f. 8 a).*'
23. Sophia Menache. 2003. *Clement V*. Cambridge: Cambridge University Press. 17. Chron. Guisborough. Vol 2, 241. '*murus lapideus a latere viæ, super quem multi ascenderant ut v viderent eum, et oppressit multos, inter quos mortuus est comes Britanniæ, et Carolus s frater regis Franciæ læsus est.*' or 'A stone wall collapsed on the side of the road, over which many had climbed to see him, and crushed many, among whom the count of Brittany died, and Charles, the brother of the king of France, was wounded.'
24. Esther Rowland Clifford. 1961. *A Knight of Great Renown: The Life and Times of Othon de Grandson*. Chicago: University of Chicago Press. 208–9. 'Since there is no record of new powers having been granted to him, it may be that he remained there as Edward's resident ambassador. Although the practice of appointing envoys separately for each mission and even giving them separate letters of protection for each detail of their business was to continue in general use for another century at least, 'there were semi-permanent English representatives at the courts both of France and of Rome from a time when royal requests for papal privileges and concessions came to be more than occasional demands.' Citing G. P. Cuttino. 1940. English Diplomatic Administration 1259-1339. London: Oxford University Press. 96-7.

25. *Regestum Clementis papæ V*. 1885. Rome: *The Catholic Church*. Nos 1284 & 1285. '*1284. Matiscone, 8 mart. 1306. Annuens supplicationibus Othonis de Grandissono concedit infrascriptis, ut ad ecclesias sui pa tronatus curam animarum habentes, quae hucusque clericis secularibus assignabantur, praesentare pos sint de monasterii sui canonicis, qui tamen sicut prius abbati obedire tenentur. (cap. 119, f. 39 a). Dil. filiis.. abbati et conventui mon. Lascurren. Premonstraten. ord. Lausanen. dioc. Devotorum preces ... Dat. Matiscone, VIII idus martii, anno primo.*' And '*1285. Matiscone, 8 mart. 1306. Mandat infrascriptis, ut illam concessionem fa ciant observari. (eod., f. 39a). Ven. fratri.. episcopo Lausanen. et dil. filiis.. priori de Grandissone Lausanen, dioc. ac Sansoni de Calvomonte canonico Trecen. Devotorum ... Dat. ut supra.*'
26. Ibid. No. 454. *'454.Lugduni, 20 ian. I 306. Iohanni, nato Berti de Frescobaldis de Florentia militis, canonico Saresbirien., providit Clemens Pp. V de praebenda de Hautevorth, quam Guillelmus de Sabaudia, tunc canonicus Saresbirien., obtinebat, quo ordinem Minorum ingresso, S(imon) episcopus Saresbirien. vacantem praebendam Ri chardo de Bello, canonico Saresbirien., contulit, qui etiam praebendam in dicta ecclesia obtinebat. Obtentu Othonis de Grandisono militis et ad petitionem praefati Iohannis mandat infrascriptis, quatenus episcopum et Richardum monere ac efficaciter inducere procurent, ut infra quindecim dies praebendam ipsam Iohanni restituant eique de damnis et expensis satisfaciant; quod si parere noluerint, illos citare curent, ut coram sede apostolica compareant. (f. 78 a). Dil. filiis.. Exonen. et Alvisien. Sanxonen. archidiaconis ac mag. Bartholomeo de Florentia canonico Londonien. eccl. Ad ausus malignantium ... Dat. Lugd., XIII kal. febr.'*
27. Ibid. Nos 285 & 286. '*285. Petente Guillelmo de Grandisono milite dispen sat cum eius filio, ut non obstante quod nuper quaedam beneficia eccl. obtinuerit, possit adhuc unum vel plura alia, quorum proventus trecento rum marcarum sterlingorum valorem annuum non excedant, recipere. (f. 50 a). Sedis apostolice ... Dat. (sine data).' And '286. Cum quodam alio filio supradicti Guillelmi dispensatur eodem modo, mutatis mutandis. (f. 50 a).*'
28. Steven Runciman. 1954. *A History of the Crusades: Volume III The Kingdom of Acre and the later Crusades*. Eleventh Edition. London: The Folio Society. 365. 'The Prior Hayton arrived [on Cyprus] from Avignon in May 1308 with a letter from the Pope.' Esther Rowland Clifford. 1961. *A Knight of Great Renown: The Life and Times of Othon de Grandson*. Chicago: University of Chicago Press. 'Probably before Othon left for England, he saw yet another friend, for in 1306 Hayton of Corycus, now a Premonstratensian monk, arrived from Cyprus with the report on the Mongols that caused Clement to set plans on foot for a new crusade.'
29. Antony R. Leopold. 2000. *How to Recover the Holy Land: The Crusade Proposals of the Late Thirteenth and Early Fourteenth Centuries*. Aldershot: Ashgate Publishing Ltd. 24 and 29.
30. C. Köhler, 1903–4. '*Deux projets de croisade en terre-sainte composée à la fin du xiiie siècle et au debut du xive*', *Revue de l'Orient Latin*. 420. *'Cet ensemble de constatations nous autorise assurément à prononcer ici le nom d'Othon de Grandson.*' Or 'This set of observations certainly authorises us to pronounce the name of Othon de Grandson here.'
31. Paulin Paris, 1869. '*Hayton, prince d'Arménie, historien,' Histoire littéraire de la France*, 25. Paris 499. '*Nous penchons à reconnaitre Hayton comme l'auteur.*' Or 'We are inclined to recognise Hayton as the author.' Or 'This set of observations certainly

authorises us to pronounce the name of Othon de Grandson here.' J. Delaville Le Roulx. 1886. *La France en Orient au XIVe siècle. Expéditions du Maréchal Boucicaut*, vol 1. 66. n1. '*Nous crovons que ces mémoires, qui accompagnent dans les manuscrits le texte d'Hayton, doivent lui étre attribués.*' Or 'We believe that these memoirs, which accompany Hayton's text in the manuscripts, must be attributed to him.'

32. Alan Forey. 2017. 'Otto of Grandson and the Holy Land, Cyprus and Armenia'. *Crusades* 16. Taylor & Francis.
33. C. Köhler, 1903–4.' *Deux projets de croisade en terre-sainte composée à la fin du xiiie siècle et au debut du xive*', *Revue de l'Orient Latin*. 420. '*En effet, c'est dans la première partie seulement que nous trouvons des renseignements auto biographiques précis et concordant avec ce que nous savons d'Othon de Grandson, et c'est dans la seconde partie surtout que l'on constate des analogies avec le Projet de croisade de Havton.*' Or 'Indeed, it is only in the first part that we find precise autobiographical information consistent with what we know about Othon de Grandson, and it is especially in the second part that we see analogies with the Havton Crusade Project.'
34. CPR Edward I vol 4 1391–1307, 424. 'April 7 [1306], Winchester. Grant to Edward, the king's son, whom the king caused to be decorated with the belt of knighthood last Whitsuntide, of the duchy of Aquitaine, for the maintenance of his state, to hold to him and after him to the kings of England reigning by hereditary right, on condition that he may not alienate it or any part of it, or detract from it, or diminish it in any way. By p.s. and the whole Council. The like to him of the said duchy and the Isle of Oleron. The like of the land of Agenais.'
35. Seymour Phillips. 2011. *Edward II*. London: Yale University Press. 112.
36. Ibid. 113.

Chapter 15

1. Chron. Guisborough, Vol 2, 245–46. '*Robertus de Brus, quintus filius filii illius Roberti de Brus qui, ut supradictum est, disceptavit cum Johanne de Balliolo coram rege Angliæ circa regnum Scotim, et judicialiter, ut supra patet, a sua petitione absolutus est, perverso fretus consilio ad regnum Scotin aspiravit; timensque dominum Johanem Cumyn, comitem de Badenach, qui erat homo potens in terra illa, et fidelis domino regi Anglie, cui homagium fecerat; et sciens se impediri posse per eum, misit ad eum in dolo dos ex fratribus suis, Thomam videlicet de Brus et Nigellum, rogans ut dignaretur venire ad se apad Dunfres, super quibusdam negotiis trac aturus cum eo quæ tangebant utrosque … Qui cum pacifice loqueretur et excusaret se, noluit exaudire sermonem ejus, sed, ut conspiraverat, percussit eum pede et gladio.*' Or 'Robert de Brus, the fifth son of the son of that Robert de Brus who, as aforesaid, disputed with John de Balliol before the king of England about the Scots kingdom, and judicially, as is clear above, was acquitted of his petition, aspired to the Scots kingdom, relying on a perverse counsel; and fearing Lord John Comyn, Count of Badenach, who was a powerful man in that country, and faithful to the Lord King of England, to whom he had done homage; and knowing that he could be hindered by him, he sent to him two of his brothers, namely Thomas de Brus and Nigellus, begging him to condescend to come to him at Dumfries, and to discuss with him certain matters which concerned both of them … When he

spoke peaceably and excused himself, he refused to listen to his speech, but, as he had conspired, struck him with his foot and sword.'

2. Henry Summerson. 2019. *Lanercost Priory*. English Heritage. London. 28–29.
3. Ibid. 30.
4. Chron. Lanercost. 79.
5. Chron. Guisborough. 252. '*In eadem Quadragesima tenuit dominus rex Angliæ parliamentum suum apud Carliolum*' or 'In the same Lent, the lord king of England held his parliament at Carlisle.'
6. *Rotuli Parliamentum; ut et petitiones et placita in Parliamento tempore Edward R. I.* vol 1. 210–11.
7. Chron. Guisborough. Vol 2, 253. '*biliter excommunicaverunt dominum Robertum de Brus cum fautoribus suis*,' or 'they boldly excommunicated Sir Robert de Brus with his supporters.'
8. CPR Edward I vol 4 1301–1307, 531. 'June 21 [1307], Carlisle. Protection with clause volumus, for three years in Ireland, for Otto de Grandisono, going beyond seas on the king's service. By K. on the information of the treasurer. Letters for him nominating Roger de Prestenden his attorney in Ireland. By K. on like information.'
9. Elizabeth A. R. Brown. 1988. 'The Political Repercussions of Family Ties in the Early Fourteenth Century: The Marriage of Edward II of England and Isabelle of France'. *Speculum* 63: 576. n7. 'In 1307 (that is, between Easter, 26 March, and the death of Edward I on 7 July) Philip the Fair issued a letter cancelling and remitting the fines incurred by Edward and his officials in Gascony, on condition that the terms of the peace treaty of 1303 be executed before the following Christmas. The favour was granted at the request of Clement V.'
10. CCR Edward I vol 5 1302–1307, 526. 'Feb 28 [1307], Lanercost. Memorandum, that on Sunday, 26 February, at Lanercost, the king ordained and ordered for certain reasons that immediately after three weeks from the next tournament, which will be at the quinzaine of Easter next, Sir Peter de Gavaston shall be ready to cross the sea at Dover for Gascony, and shall remain there without returning until he shall be recalled by the king and by his permission.' Seymour Phillips. 2011. *Edward II*. London: Yale University Press. 120–21. The well-known account comes from Guisborough, but its details have been plausibly doubted by the young Edwards biographer Seymour Phillips.
11. Chron. Lanercost. 179–80. 'Thomas de Brus and his brother Alexander and Sir Reginald de Crawford, who had been severely wounded in their capture by lances and arrows, he likewise took alive to the King, who pronounced sentence upon them, and caused Thomas to be drawn at the tails of horses in Carlisle on the Friday after the first Sunday in Lent,1 and then to be hanged and afterwards beheaded. Also, he commanded the other two to be hanged on the same day and afterwards beheaded; whose heads, with the heads of the four others aforesaid, were set upon the three gates of Carlisle, and the head of Thomas de Brus upon the keep of Carlisle. Nigel, the third brother of Robert, had been hanged already at Newcastle.' Chron. Guisborough. Vol 2, 252 '*In Quadragesima vero sequente misit a se cum parte exercitus sui duos fratres suos, dominum scilicet Thomaum de Brus qui Anglicos semper odio habuerat, et dominum Alexandrum clericum, qui ex improviso a nostris de nocte capti sunt, et judicialiter tracti et suspensi.*' Or 'On the following Lent he sent from himself with part of his army two of his brothers, namely Lord Thomas de Brus, who had always hated the

English, and Lord Alexander the cleric, who were taken by surprise by our men at night, and judicially drawn and hanged.'

12. Chron. Lanercost. 181–82. 'On Easter Day 4 the aforesaid Dungal was knighted by the King's hand'
13. Chron. Guisborough. Vol 2, 266. '*equitavit quasi duo milliaria; et quarta feria requievit; die autem Jovis venit apud Burch-super-Sandes, et ibi disposuit in crastino permanere; erantque sibi modus et con suetudo singulis quasi diebus in lecto jacere usque ad horam nonam; die vero Veneris cum eleyaretur a suis ut comederet, inter manus corum expiravit. Translatusque est rex ex hoc mundo die translationis Sancti Thomæ archiepiscopi et martyris. Celaveruntque sui mortem regis quousque veniret filius ejus et magnates terræ.*' Or 'he rode about two miles; and on Wednesday he rested; and on Thursday he came to Burgh-upon-Sands, and arranged to remain there on the morrow; and it was a habit and a pleasure for him to lie in bed every day until the ninth hour; but on Friday, when he had been forced by his people to eat, he expired in their hands. And the king was transferred from this world on the day of the transfer of Saint Thomas the archbishop and martyr. And they hid the king's death until his son and the great men of the land came.'
14. Chron. Lanercost. 182.
15. CPR Edward I vol 4 1301-1307, 537. 'Memorandum of the death of Edward I. at Burgh on Sands, 7 July [Fœdera.]'
16. Ibid. and Chron. Guisborough, Vol 2, 266. '*Celaveruntque sui mortem regis quousque veniret filius ejus et magnates terræ*,' or 'And they hid the king's death until his son and the great men of the land came.'
17. TNA E101/373/15. fo43. '*ab xj die julii, quo die primo constitit principi de morte regis, patris sui*' or 'from the 11th day of July, on which day he first informed the prince of the death of the king, his father.'
18. Seymour Phillips. 2011. *Edward II*. London: Yale University Press. 125. 'Despite the news with which Edward learned of his accession, the news did not reach the capital formerly until Tuesday, 25 July. Until then Edward I's chancellor, Ralph Baldock, the Bishop of London, continued to seal writs with the Great Seal 'because he had no certain knowledge of the king's death before that day.'
19. *Fœdera*. 75. *'De Morte Regis. Memorandum, quod, die veneris, videlicet, feptimo die Julii, Anno Domini 1307. jubente ipfo, cujus famulantur imperio mors & vita, inclitæ recordationis, Dominus Edwardus, Rex Angliæ, apud Burgum, fuper Sabulones extra Karliolum, In eundo verfus partes Scotiæ zelo devotionis & fidei accenfus ad vindicandum defpectum, & facrilegam contumeliam, Deo & San Etæ Ecclefiæ inhumaniter factos per Robertum de Brus, qui Do minum Johannem de Comyn de Scotia, in Ecclefiâ Fratrum Minorum de Dumfres, feditiofe interfecerat: Necnon ad hujufmodi Roberti rebellionem & pertinaciam in manu potenti falubriter reprimendam; pro eo quòd contra homagii & fidelitates fuæ Sacramenta fe in Regem Scotice proditionaliter fecerat coronari Et anno Regni ejufdem Regis tricefimo quinto, ab hac luce feliciter migravit (cujus anima in cocleftibus collocetur (Magiftro Radulfo de Baudale Epifcopo London Cancellario fuo cum magno Sigillo ipfius Regis London. tunc temporis exiftente: Qui quidem Cancellarius brevia de curfu cum eodem Sigillo, per Confilium Ottonis de Grandifono, R. de Brabazon, & aliorum de Confilio ejufdem Regis, necnon & per Confilium Dominorum Willielmi de Bliburgh Cancellarii, & Walteri Renaud Custodis Garderobæ Domini Edwardi, filii &*

hæredis ipſius Domini Regis, uſque ad diem Sancti Jacobi Apoſtoli ſequentem proximo, conſignavit; eo quod praefatus Epiſcopus, de morte ejuſdem Regis, an- te diem illum, certitudinem non habebat. Et die Sabbati, proximo ſequente, ferò idem Cancellarius Regis à dicto Domino Edwardo filio, tunc apud Karliolum exiſtente (ubi Dominus Antonius de Beck Epiſcopus Dunolm. & Patriarcha Je- roſolymitanus, Dominus H. de Lacy Comes Lincolniæ, & alii Comites & Barones Regni ſecum exiſtentes, homagia & fidelitates ſuas eidem, tanquam Regi, fecerant) per litteras ipſius Domini 2 Ed. The English translation of which is in CFR Edward I vol 1 1272–1307, 558–59. 'Be it remembered that on Friday, 7 July 1307, at the bidding of Him unto whose sovereignty minister death and life, Edward, king of England, of famous memory, departed this life in the thirty-fifth year of his reign at Burgh by Sands without Carlisle, while going towards the parts of Scotland, fired with the zeal of devotion and faith, to avenge the despite and sacrilegious contumely inhumanly done to God and Holy Church by Robert de Brus, who seditiously slew John Comyn of Scotland in the church of the Friars Minors of Dumfres, and to repress with a mighty hand the rebellion of the same Robert, because contrary to his homage and his oath of fealty he caused himself to be crowned king of Scotland; Master Ralph de Baudok, bishop of London, the king's chancellor, being then at London with the great seal, which chancellor, by the counsel of Sirs Otto de Grandissono, R. le Brabazon and others of the king's council, and by the counsel of Sirs William de Blyburgh, chancellor, and Walter Renaud, keeper of the wardrobe of Edward, the king's son and heir, sealed writs of course with the same seal until St. James the Apostle following, because he had no certain knowledge of the king's death before that day, and on Saturday following received orders from the said Edward the king's son, then at Carlisle, where Anthony de Bek, bishop of Durham, patriarch of Jerusalem, H. de Lacy, earl of Lincoln, and other earls and barons of the realm did homage and fealty to him as king, by letters of the said Edward sealed under his privy seal, to bring his said father's seal to him that he might put the same under safe keeping under his seal, which seal was afterwards sent to Carlisle under the seals of the said bishop and William de Blyburgh by Hugh de Burgo, clerk of the Chancery, and Richard de Lughteburgh and John de Munden, clerks of the bishop, on Tuesday, the morrow of St. Peter's Chains.'

20. Chron. Lanercost. 183. 'On the following day, to wit, on the festival of S. Margaret, Virgin and Martyr [20 July], he received at Carlisle Castle fealty and homage from nearly all the chief men of England.'
21. Seymour Phillips. 2011. *Edward II*. London: Yale University Press. 126. '. . . ordering the chancellor to send him his father's seal. This was duly done on Tuesday 2 August.'
22. Ibid. 126–27. Philips agrees with Chaplais that the Gaveston charter was intended to be Edward's first act as king.
23. Ibid. 129–30.
24. Ibid. 131. 'Edward I was remembered elsewhere: the news of his death on 7 July reached Pope Clement Vat Poitiers two weeks later and here the Pope performed solemn obsequies for him, exalting 'the strength of his rule, his sense of justice and clemency, his crusading fervour and his many successes against all his enemies.' This was a unique papal tribute in honour of a secular ruler.'
25. Walter Ullmann. 1955. 'The Curial Exequies for Edward I and Edward III'. *The Journal of Ecclesiastical History*. Vol 6 issue 1. 26–36.
26. Seymour Phillips. 2011. *Edward II*. London: Yale University Press .130-1.

27. CPR Edward II vol 1 1307–1313, 9 Oct. 26. Westminster. 'Protection, with *clause volumus*, for two years, for Otto de Grandisono, going beyond seas on the king's service.'
28. Chron. Edward I, 3–21.
29. Marc Morris. 2009. *A Great and Terrible King*. London: Windmill Books. 365.
30. Bernard Andenmatten. Ed. 2020. *Othon I de Grandson (vers 1240–1328)*. Lausanne: Cahiers Lausannois d'Histoire Médiévale. Andenmatten's curated study featured five contributions regarding his career in Vaud, one contribution regarding an artefact in Switzerland, two related to finance, two related to crusading and only one related to his career for the English crown of over fifty years.
31. Alain Demurger. 2002. *The Last Templar*. London: Profile Books Ltd. 158.'According to the rather fanciful rumours being spread at the time, the Templars were given to dubious and immoral practise: the denial of Christ, spitting on the Cross, obscene kisses, sodomy, secrecy of the Chapters, lack of a spirit of chastity, etc.'
32. Malcolm Barber. 2006. *The Trial of the Templars*. Cambridge: Cambridge University Press. 85.
33. Ibid. 154. Molay arrived in Marseille from the East in November or December 1306. Alain Demurger. 2002. *The Last Templar*. London: Profile Books Ltd. 164. 'Jacques de Molay was still there [Poitiers] on 9 June . . . He then went to Paris to hold the general Chapter on 24 June 1307. A letter from Molay to James II of Aragon proves that he was once more in Poitiers on 4 August and still there from 8 to 11 September.'
34. Alain Demurger. 2002. *The Last Templar*. London: Profile Books Ltd. 163. 'The king of France arrived in Poitiers on 21 April 1307 and appears to have left again after 15 May. His interviews with the pope fundamentally concerned the indictment to blacken the memory of Boniface VIII, which he wanted to set in motion quickly (although Clement V would not hear of it); he also mentioned the matter of the Templars.
35. Ibid. 155 & 170.'On 24 August 1307, Clement V wrote to the king to announce the opening of an inquiry into the Temple, specifying that it had been requested by the Templars themselves.'
36. Ibid. 171-2 'On 14 September, a royal letter denouncing the crimes of the Templars . . . and ordering their arrest, was addressed to all the bailiffs and seneschals of the kingdom, enjoining them to it secret until the day had been fixed for its execution. On 22 September, the Inquisitor of France sent instructions to his inquisitors throughout the realm, Discreetly, the royal agents kept a watch on the Templars.'
37. Ibid. 172. 'On 13 October they went into action.'
38. Ibid. 164 & 172. 'Jacques de Molay acted as pallbearer at the funeral of Catherine de Valois.' And 'On 12 October, the eve of his arrest, Jacques de Molay came to Paris to attend the funeral of Catherine de Courtenay, heiress to the throne of the Latin empire of Constantinople and wife of the king's brother Charles de Valois as a guest of honour.'
39. Alain Demurger. 2024. In telephone discussion with the author, 28 September 2024.
40. CPR Edward II vol 1 1307–1311, 31. 'Dec 26 [1307], Westminster. Appointment of Peter de Gavaston, Earl of Cornwall, to be keeper of England during the king's absence beyond the seas.'
41. Seymour Phillips. 2011. *Edward II*. London: Yale University Press .134.
42. Homage was essentially the acknowledgment of the bond of tenure that existed between Lord and vassal, while fealty was an oath of fidelity made by the vassal.

43. *Fœdera.* 110. Elizabeth A. R. Brown. 1988. 'The Political Repercussions of Family Ties in the Early Fourteenth Century: The Marriage of Edward II of England and Isabelle of France'. *Speculum* 63: 578 & 580.
44. Seymour Phillips. 2011. *Edward II.* London: Yale University Press. 140–41.
45. J. R. Maddicott. 1970. *Thomas of Lancaster, 1307–1322: A study in the reign of Edward II.* Oxford University Press: London. 83. Seymour Phillips. 2011. *Edward II.* London: Yale University Press. 136.
46. Pierre Chaplais. 1994. *Piers Gaveston: Edward II's Adoptive Brother.* Oxford: Clarendon Press. 42–43.
47. *Fœdera.* 108. Seymour Phillips. 2011. *Edward II.* London: Yale University Press. 145.
48. Seymour Phillips. 2011. *Edward II.* London: Yale University Press. 145–46.
49. Ibid.
50. Ibid. 138.
51. J. Delaville Le Roulx. 1906. *Cartulaire générale de l'Ordre des Hospitalliers vol IV.* Paris: Ernest Leroux. ed. 169. No 4792
52. Malcolm Barber, 2006. *The Trial of the Templars.* Second Edition. Cambridge: Cambridge University Press. 116.
53. Pierre Chaplais. 1951. *Réglement des conflits internationaux franco-anglais au xive siècle. pièce. just, 5: G.C.,.* No 169.
54. Seymour Phillips. 2011. *Edward II.* London: Yale University Press. 147.
55. Pierre Chaplais. 1994. *Piers Gaveston: Edward II's Adoptive Brother.* Oxford: Clarendon Press. 44. Seymour Phillips. 2011. *Edward II.* London: Yale University Press. 148.
56. Chron. Guisborough, Vol 2, 274. '*Anno Domini MCCVIII. in quindena Paschæ tenuit rex parliamentum suum Londoniis, et magna fuit altercatio inter regem et comites suos pro domino Petro, ita quod obtinuerunt comites meliorem partem, dicentes ipsum Petrum esse excommunicatum et perjurum: et assignatus est dies transfretandi in terram nativitatis suæ.*' Or 'In the year of the Lord 1308 On the fortnight of Easter the king held his parliament in London, and there was a great dispute between the king and his earls for Lord Piers, so that the earls obtained the better part, saying that Piers himself was excommunicated and perjured and he was assigned the day of crossing over to the land of his birth.'
57. Seymour Phillips. 2011. *Edward II.* London: Yale University Press. 149.
58. Reg. Clement V, vols 2–3, 137–38. no 2938. '2938. Lugudiaci, 17 aug. 1308. *Confirmatur pensio facta Ottoni per magistrum militiae Templi. (cap. 581, f. 114a). Dilecto filio nobili viro Othoni de Grandissono. Tue nobilitatis devota sinceritas, per quam te gratum nostris affectibus representas, digne nos excitat et inducit, ut personam tuam plenitudine favoris apostlici prosequentes indemnitatibus tuis paternis precaveamus affectibus teque condignis favoribus honoremus. Oblata siquidem nobis tua petitio continebat, quod ab olim magister domus militie Templi Ierosoimitani attente considerans profectus multiplices, qui ex tuis operibus virtuosis eidem ordini provenerant et sperabat imposterum provenire ac volens premissa digne retributionis premio compensare, tibi de consensu sui conventus duo milia librarum Turonen. parvorum certis locis et terminis quoad viveres per manus preceptoris Francie et thesaurarii domus Parisien. eiusdem ordinis qui essent pro tempore solvere et dare promisit, prout in patentibus litteris super hoc confectis predicti conventus sigillo plumbeo munitis plenius dicitur contineri. Nos itaque tuis supplicationibus inclinati promissionem huiusmodi ratam et gratam habentes*

illam auctoritate apostolica ex certa scientia confirmamus etc. usque communimus. Et quia ex certis impedimentis provenientibus magistro et ordini supra- dictis eiusdem pecunie summam ab eodem magistro iuxta promissionem huiusmodi ha- bere non potes, nobis humiliter supplicasti, tibi super hoc per apostolice sedis providentiam de oportuno remedio provideri. Nos igitur volentes personam tuam huiusmodi devotionis obtentu dono specialis providentie prevenire tuisque providere indempnitatibus in hac parte tibi de Turribus, de Espaillierco et de Coulours domos eiusdem ordinis Lingonen., Senonen. et Trecen. diocesium cum omnibus iuribus et pertinentiis suis per te quo ad vixeris retinendas ac earum fructus, redditus et proventus usque ad summam dictorum duorum milium librarum in usus proprios convertendos tibi auctoritate apostolica duximus concedendum. Volumus autem, quod reliquum fructuum predictorum vel pecunie percipiendum ex ipsis alicui ex generalibus per nos vel specialibus per singulos prelatos regni Francie in singulis eorum diocesibus administratoribus et gubernatoribus bonorum ipsius ordinis in eodem regno seu diocesibus consistentium deputatis annis singulis facias exhiberi. Non obstantibus quibuscunque statutis et consuetudinibus ordinis supradicti iuramento, confirmatione apostolica seu quacunque firmitate alia roboratis, et quibuslibet privilegiis et indulgentiis et litteris apostolicis generalibus vel specialibus magistro et ordini supradictis vel quibusvis aliis comuniter vel divisim sub quacunque forma verborum concessis, de quibus oporteat in presentibus fieri mentionem et per que effectus presentium impediri valeat quomodolibet vel differri. Tenorem autem predictarum litterarum presentibus inseri facientes, qui talis est: Vniversis presentes litteras visuris et audituris frater Iacobus de Mollay divina gratia magister humilis pauperis militie Templi salutem in Domino. Noverint omnes, quod nos inspicientes et considerantes et diligenter advertentes grandia bona et profectus, quos nobilis et potens vir carissimus et dilectus noster in Domino dominus Otho dominus de Grandissono fecit et facit mansioni sive domui nostre et faciet toto tempore vite sue, prout firmiter credimus et speramus, nos in recompensationem et remunerationem omnium predictorum de consilio nostro et conventus nostri donamus, concedimus et assignamus tenore presentium predicto domino Othoni duo milia librarum Turonen. parvorum solvenda et reddenda ipsi domino Othoni vel suo certo mandato quolibet anno sine aliqua dilatione toto tempore vite sue, scilicet mille libras die Purificationis Domine nostre et alias mille libras die Mercurii proxima post festum apostolorum Petri et Pauli mensis iunii et sic quolibet anno toto tempore vite sue et debemus eidem dictam monetam tradere quolibet anno apud mansionem nostram Parisien. vel Lugdunen. supra Rodanum, ubi sibi melius placuerit, et nos districte precipimus in virtute sancte obedientie. preceptori Francie et thesaurario nostre domus de Parisius, qui pro tempore fuerint, quod dictam pecuniam tradant, solvant et benigne assignent omni dilatione remota domino Othoni prefato vel suo certo mandato secundum formam predictam, et pro maiori securitate et firmitate nos dedimus dicto domino Othoni presentes litteras sigillatas bulla nostri conventus factas in mansione nostra apud Parisius anno Domini millesimo ducentesimo septuagesimo septimo mense iulii die dominica post festum apostolorum Petri et Pauli. Nulli ergo etc. nostre confirmationis, concessionis et voluntatis etc.... Dat. Lugusiaci, XVI kal. septembris, anno tertio. In eundem modum venerabilibus fratribus. archiepiscopo Senonen. et Lingonen. Ac. Trecen. episcopis.'

59. Jean-Bernard de Vaivre. 2005. *Le Commanderie d'Épailly et sa Chapelle Templière durant la Période Médiévale. Académie des Inscriptions AIBL.* 197. '*Et quia ex certis*

impedimentis provenientibus magistro et ordinis supradictis eiusdem pecunie summam ab eodem magistro iuxta promissionem huiusmodi habere non potes, nobis humiliter supplicasti, tibi super hoc apostolice sedis providentiam de oportuno remedio provideri.' Or 'And because, due to certain impediments arising from the aforesaid master and order, you cannot have the sum of the same money from the same master according to this kind of promise, you have humbly begged us, that the providence of an opportune remedy be provided to you on this apostolic seat.'

60. CPR Edward II vol 1 1307–1311, 71.
61. Pierre Chaplais. 1994. *Piers Gaveston: Edward II's Adoptive Brother*. Oxford: Clarendon Press. 45.
62. CPR Edward II vol 1 1307–1311, 80. Ibid. 46.
63. *Fœdera*. 122.
64. Ibid.
65. Ibid. 123.
66. Ibid. *'REX dile&to & fideli suo Otroni de Grandisono, salutem. . .. quâ poteritis, velitis erga dictum Dominum Summum Pontificem inftare, & aliàs modis, quibus expedire videritis, interponere par tes veftras.*' Or 'KING, greetings to Othon de Grandison, his faithful one ... As far as you are able, if you are willing to appeal to the aforesaid Lord Supreme Pontiff, and in other ways which you see expedient, you will interpose your parts.'
67. Etienne Baluze. Ed. 1921. *Vitae paparum Avenionensium*. Vol 3. 87–90.
68. Seymour Phillips. 2011. *Edward II*. London: Yale University Press. 152.
69. Ibid. 153.
70. Ibid.
71. Malcolm Barber, 2006. *The Trial of the Templars*. Second Edition. Cambridge: Cambridge University Press. 116 & 120.
72. Yvonne Lanhers. 2013. *Regestum Papae Clementum V.* Rome: *The Catholic Church*. Nos 2885, 3097, 3098, 3154, 3162–63, 3166.
73. Elisabeth Lalou, 2007. Itinéraire de Philippe IV le Bel (1285–1314), Mémoires de l'Académie des Inscriptions et Belles Lettres, 2 volumes, Paris, De Boccard, Vol 2: the presence of Philippe is confirmed at Saint-Jean au Bois, then at Fontainebleau during this period, 323 and 325.
74. ANF Série JJ 40, No. 64 Robert Fawtier (dir.), *Registres du Trésor des Chartes*, Vol 1 *Règne de Philippe le Bel.* Analytical inventory by Inventaire J. Glénisson et J. Guérout, Paris, 1958, 64-65. '*Philippus Dei gratia Francorum rex, ballivo Senonensi vel ejus locum tenenti salutem. Cum sicut accepimus, magister et fratres milicie templi retroattis temp(ori)bus ex certis dum fertur causis, dum adhuc sui status libertatem haberent, tenerentur obligati nobili viro Othoni de Grandi sono militi, in duobus milibus libris turonensium annui redditus solvendis Parisius vel Lugduni singulis annis quibus vitam duxerint in humanis, ac sanctissimus pater C. (Clemens) divina providentia summus pontifex pro illis duobus milibus libris eidem Ottoni reddendis assensu nostro super hoc requisito et ad hoc interveniente ordinaverit assignare domos de Turribus et de Espalliaco dyocesis Lingoniensis et de Coulors Senonensis et Trecensis dyocesis cum suis pertinenciis, redditibus et proventibus, exitus, obvenciones et jura eorumdem percipiendis et habendos ab ipso usque ad summam redditus supradicti residuo Templo, si quod fuerit remansuro quamdiu dictus miles vitam duxerit in humanis, in solucionem*

et satisfactionem pro duobus milibus libris turonensium. Mandamus et committimus vobis, vocatis superintendentibus ad Templariorum negocium et aliis probis viris quos ad hoc videritis evocandos, assignetis dicto militi vel procuratori suo in domibus ipsis vel illis earum que ad hoc sufficere poterunt, aut si non sufficiant in ipsis et aliis magis propinquioribus et commodioribus dicto militi dictum redditum duarum millarum librarum turonensium ad vitam ipsius tenendum omnibus certa hoc legitime estimatis que in assignacionibus predictorum radentur, prout rationabiliter fuerit faciendum. Datum Pittavis XXX die julii anno Domini m° ccc octavo. 'Or 'Philip, king of the Franks, by the grace of God, greet the bailiff of Sens or the holder of his place. When, as we have received, the master and the brothers of the militia of the temple having been withdrawn from the temp(ori)s for certain reasons, as it is said, while they still had the freedom of their state, they were bound to be bound to the noble man Othon de Grandson, a knight, paying an annual rent of two thousand *Livres Tournois* o each of Paris or Lyons in the years in which they led their lives in human life, and the most holy father C. (Clement) the divine providence of the supreme pontiff for those two thousand *Livres* to be returned to the same Othon, with our assent to this requirement and intervening for this purpose, ordered to assign the houses of the Towers and of Épailly to the diocese of Lingoniensis and the Coulors of Sens and the Diocese of Trece, with its appurtenances, rents, and revenues, receiving and holding the same issues, encumbrances, and rights, from him up to the sum of the remaining rents of the aforesaid temple, if any remain as long as the said knight leads his life in human life, in payment and satisfaction for two thousand *livres tournois* We command and entrust to you, having called the superintendents to the business of the Templars, and other honest men whom you see to be summoned for this purpose, you will assign the said soldier or his agent in the houses themselves or in those of theirs which may be sufficient for this purpose, or if they are not sufficient in themselves and in others more near and convenient to the said soldier, the rent of two thousand *Livres Tournois* to be held for his life, to be held by all those lawfully estimated, who shall be shaved in the aforesaid assignments, as was reasonably to be done. Given at Poitiers on the 30th day of July in the year of the Lord 1308.' See also Elisabeth Lalou, 2007. *Itinéraire de Philippe IV le Bel (1285–1314)*, Mémoires de l'Académie des Inscriptions et Belles Lettres, 2 volumes, Paris, De Boccard, Vol 2: the presence of Philippe is confirmed at Saint-Jean au Bois, then at Fontainebleau during this period, 323 and 325.

75. Alain Demurger. 2019. *La Prisée de la maison templière d'Épailly en 1308*. In *Bulletin archéologique et historique du Châtillonnais* Ser. 7, vol. 1.37
76. Ibid. 38.
77. Ibid.
78. Ibid. 39–41. A Corvée being a day's unpaid labour owed by a vassal to his feudal lord.
79. Alain Demurger. 2015. Trans Teresa Lavender Fagan. 2018. *The Persecution of the Templars. Éditions Paypt et Rivages: Paris.* London : Trans Profile Books. 105–6.
80. Jean-Bernard de Vaivre. 2002. *Deux commandeurs de l'ordre de l'Hôpital, d'origine fribourgeoise, dans la Bourgogne du XIVe siècle (note d'information)* in *Comptes rendus des séances de l'Académie des Inscriptions et Belles-Lettres, 146e année*, N. 2. 499–530.
81. Ibid. 499-500. David Williams. 2020. Agnès de Grandson, Dame de Montagny. *Foundations* 12: 24-30.

82. J. R. Maddicott, 2005. 'Grandson (Grandison), Sir Otto de'. *Oxford Dictionary of National Biography.* 'He took the cross again in 1307.'
83. Reg. Clement V, vols 2–3,137–38. No 2785.
84. *Receuil Diplomatque de Canton de Fribourg.* Vol 2. 1840. *Fribourg: Cantonal Imprimeu. Chez Joseph-Louis Piller*. Doc LXXXVII. 48. '*Prolongation de trève avec Louis de Savoie. . . par la main de noble baron monsire Othe segnor de Grancon de la guerre qui estoit entre le dit notre segnor monsire Lois et le siens dune part, monsire levesque de Lossanne ceans de Friburg et Guilliaume en cel tans sire de Montagnie et lour aydiour dautre part, La quel treve fu faite et donée a Viveis le jeudi après la circoncision notre segnor lant corant per Mil CCC'* And n2. '*La trève avait été concluc à Vevey le 2 Janvier 1309, qui était 1308 d'après le calcul florentin en usage au pays de Vaud.*'
85. David Williams. 2022 Pierre de Grandson Part Two. *Foundations* vol 15. 6. 'Agnès was alive in 1313,23 but the year of her death is unknown. Her obit was recorded at Humilimont on 9 December, as also in the Grandison Obits, '*Obit. dne Agnet de Gandeson dna de Wypeyns ix die decembris*', and in the Beaufort-Beauchamp Book of Hours, '*5 Id. Obit. dne Agnet de Gandeson dna de Wypeyns*' She is the only sister of Othon de Grandson to be recorded in these obits.
86. Charles L. Kingsford. 1909. *Sir Otho de Grandison 1238?–1328.* Transactions of the Royal Historical Society 3: 192–93. '*A reverent pere en dieu et son chier seignur et amy, mon seignur Jehan par la grace de Dieu, Evesque de Cycestre, Chancelier d'Angleterre, Othes de Gransson salut et li apparellie a son playsir et a sa volunte. Sire, pur ce que ie sui desirranz doir bones novelles de voustre estat, le quel Dious face touz iours bon, je vous pri sire que le plus sovant que vos porrez le me veullez mander. Endroit dou mien sire, sil vous plait a savoir, i'estoye seins et haitiez, le dieu merci, quant ceste lettre fu faite. Sire, cum aucunes genz facent grief a sire Wdry de Wyppeyns, mon clerc, et le quel est en mon servise en l'eglise de Wyrkinthone dont il est persone, je vous pri, sire, que vous ses procurours voullez avoir recommande aus besoignes qui le thocheront, et que vous, sire, pour ce qu'il est en mon service, li veuillez aydier, s'il vous plait, comant il ait la proteccion le Roy a toutes ses clauses tant que a iij anz. Et me veullez, sire, si vous plait, voustre volonte mander, la quel ie feroye a mon povoir. Sire, nostre seignur vous gard. Donees Espalli le xvj iour de Jenuier.*'
87. *Fœdera.* 136–37.
88. Seymour Phillips. 2011. *Edward II.* London: Yale University Press. 154.
89. Ibid. 155. n157. Otherwise dated 25 April 1309.
90. Ibid. 157.
91. Ibid. 161. n. 187.
92. Ibid. 152. Phillips notes Lancaster's absence from royal charter witness lists from November 1308 and throughout 1309.
93. Seymour Phillips. 2011. *Edward II.* London: Yale University Press. 161–62.
94. Ibid. 164.
95. Ibid. 165.
96. Ibid. 166.
97. Jakob. Schwalm. Ed. 1893. *Constitutiones et Acta Publica Imperatorum et Regem.* Vol 4 Part 1. *Impensis Bibliopolli Hahniani*: Hannover. Nos 390. 338–83. '*et dilecto filio Octone de Grandissono tui honoris intimo zelatore*' or 'of our beloved son Othon de Grandson, the most zealous of your honour'.

98. *Fontes rerum Bernensium*. Vol 4, 431–32. No 402. '*Heinricus, Dei gracia Romanorum rex semper augustus, universis sacri Romani imperii fidelibus ... Attendentes itaque grandia, grata et accepta servicia, que nobilis Otho de Grandissono, fidelis noster, majestati nostre hactenus prestitit, devote prestat assidue ... in hujusmodi nostri doni cer titudinem pleniorem nostrum castrum et opidum Loupen, Lausanensis dyocesis*.' Or 'Henry, by the grace of God the ever august king of the Romans, to all the faithful of the Holy Roman Empire ... Attending therefore to the great and acceptable services which the noble Othon de Grandson, our faithful one, has hitherto rendered to our majesty, and that he is constantly rendering devotedly ... in the assurance of our gift of this kind, our castle and town of Laupen, in the diocese of Lausanne'
99. Ibid. 442. No 413. '*Datum apud Aquambellam, Va die Novembris, anno domini M°CCC decimo*.'
100. Etienne Baluze. 1914. *Vitae Paparum Avenionensium*. Vol 3. Paris : Librairie Letouzey et Ane. 497. '*Per procurationem unius medici, qui tane ibi morabatur, notus postea et amicus domini O[thonis] de Grandissono, quia ipsum curavit de magna infirmitate quam tune habuit in Aquebelle*.' Or 'Through the agency of a physician who was then staying there, later known and a friend of Lord O[thon] de Grandisson, because he had treated him of a great infirmity which he had at that time in Aiguebelle.'
101. Jakob. Schwalm. Ed. 1893. *Constitutiones et Acta Publica Imperatorum et Regem*. Vol 4 Part 1. *Impensis Bibliopolli Hahniani*: Hannover. No 592. 550–51. '*Item Odoni de Grandissono*'.
102. Ibid. No. 594. 552. '*quod dominum Othonem, qui est quasi in itinere vestro*' or 'that Lord Othon, who is, as it were, on your journey.' Esther Rowland Clifford. *A Knight of Great Renown: The Life and Times of Othon de Grandson*. Chicago: University of Chicago Press, 1961. 239.
103. Seymour Phillips. 2011. *Edward II*. London: Yale University Press. 173
104. *Fœdera*. 191. '*Ad Ottonem de Grandisono, unum de Nunciis ad Generale Concilium deftinatis. dilecto & fideli suo, Ottoni de Grandisono, salutem*.' Or 'To Othon de Grandson, one of the Nuncios appointed to the General Council. Greetings to Othon de Grandson, beloved and faithful.'
105. CCW Henry III, Edward, I Edward II vol 1 1244–1326, 367.
106. Seymour Phillips, 2011. *Edward II*. London: Yale University Press. 174.
107. Ibid. 180
108. Ibid.
109. Seymour Phillips, 2011. *Edward II*. London: Yale University Press. 180.
110. CPR Edward II vol 1 1307–1313, 453. 'April 6 [1312], York. Pardon to Otto de Grandisono of £430, in which he is bound as well for a prest of the wardrobe or the late king, as for other causes, and which sum is now required of him by summons of the Exchequer.'
111. Bruno Galland. 1988. *Un Savoyard sur le siège de Lyon au XIIIe siècle: Philippe de Savoie*. Bibliothèque de l'école des chartes 146: 48.
112. Robert Kool. 2006. A Thirteenth Century Hoard of Gold Florins from the Medieval Harbour of Acre. The Numismatic Chronicle vol 166. 301-320.
113. *Regestum Clementis papæ V*. 1885. Rome: *The Catholic Church*. No 8205. '*Venerabilibus fratribus. archiepiscopo Lugdunen. et. Cabilonen. ac. Matisconen. episcopis, et aliis eiusdem archiepiscopi sutfraganeis. Enormis facinoris gravitas in*

personam dilecti filii nobilis viri Ottonis de Grandissono, militis et familiaris nostri, no viter perpetrati eo nos amplius turbavit, sicut adhuc conturbat in intimis, quo eum sue devotionis et probitatis exigentibus me ritis, affectione diligimus ampliori. Eodem siquidem milite nobis graviter conquerente, famaque publica, quin potius infamia odi bili divulgante, didicimus, quod cum ipse, qui zelo fidei et devotionis accensus, iam dudum signo vivifice crucis assumpto mense augusto proximo futuro intendebat, sicut adhuc intendit in Terre Sancte subsidium transfretare', ad presentiam nostram pro benedictione, ae licentia a nobis obti nenda, de mandato nostro veniret, seque duci faceret pro sua quiete per Rodanum, Aymo de Palude, dominus de Vnarembon, nonnullis dil. filiorum nobilium virorum Amedei comitis Sabaudie et delfini Viennensis subditis, sibi associatis in hac parte complicibus, cum militem ipsum per locum, qui Pons Durino vulgariter nominatur, infra ipsius delfini terram constitutum, transitum facere contigisset, in eum et familiam suam, sicut ad vos non ambigimus pervenisse, armata manu hostiliter irruens et eundem militem viginti milibus quingentis florenis auri et aliis bonis suis, que tunc secum faciebat deferri, spolians violenter, ac ipsum et eandem familiam, ne ad sedem apostolicam accedere possent, impediens, eos capere propria temeritate presumpsit et detinere diebus pluribus captivatos, nonnullis de dicta familia letaliter in captione huiusmodi vuloeratis et quodam ipsius Octonis armigero crudeliter interempto, alias eidem gravibus iniuriis irrogatis, quam vis prefatus miles postmodum a dicto car cere sicut Domino placuit extiterit liberatus; propter quod Aymonem et complices pradictos excomunicationis sententiam per diversos processus apostolice sedis in omnes qui venientes ad sedem predictam impedirent vel molestarent quomodolibet promul gatam, non est dubium incurrisse. Profecto dum eiusdem militis multam devotionem advertimus et consideramus opera pietatis, dum etiam actus fecundos virtutibus recen semus et attendimus diligenter, quod se miles ipse gratum omnibus et placidum exhibens, nedum quod a quorumlibet no cumentis retraheret manus suas, verum etiam omnibus complacebat, non mediocri admiramur, quod sic dure prefatum Aymonem armare potuit impietas contra eum. Nos igitur nolentes, prout etiam ne debemus tante temeritatis excessum sub dissimulatione transire, fraternitati vestre in virtute obedientie per apostolica scripta mandamus, quatenus vos et quilibet vestrum, qui super hoc pro parte nostra fuerit re quisitus, per vos vel per alium seu alios dicti Aymonis suorumque complicum de quibus vobis constiterit, presentiam adeun tes, vel ad loca ubi eorum esse habitatio consuevit, si forsan ipsorum non possetis habere presentiam, accedentes, aut si for sitan ad dicta loca vobis non pateret ac cessus, in aliquibus locis vicinis de quibus huiusmodi possit monitio ad ipsorum no titiam pervenire, publice ipsos ex parte nostra monere et efficaciter inducere stu deatis, ut infra quindecim dierum spatium post monitionem huiusmodi, militi memo rato predictam florenorum summam et bona ipsa sine qualibet diminutione restituant, et de predictis iniuriis congruam et debitam satisfactionem impendant: alioquin ex eosdem, preter dictam sententiam, excomunicationis vinculo innodantes et terras ipsius Aymonis subicientes ecclesiastico interdicto, tamdiu excomunicatos singulis diebus dominicis et festivis, pulsatis campanis et candelis accensis, in ecclesiis vestrarum ci vitatum et diocesium et aliis locis de qui bus expedire videritis publice nuntietis, et faciatis ab omnibus artius evitari, donec prefato militi summam florenorum et bona restituerint supradicta et de dictis iniuriis congruam et integram satisfactionem exhi bere curaverint et a nobis meruerint super hoc absolutionis beneficium obtinere. Dat. in prioratu de Grausello etc, V nonas iulii, anno septimo.'

114. Jean-Daniel Morerod. 2020. *Finances et Sentiments* in *Othon I de Grandson (vers 1240–1328)*. Lausanne: Cahiers Lausannois d'Histoire Médiévale. 131–33.
115. ACV C IV 166, 1678.
116. Jean-Daniel Morerod. 2020. *Finances et Sentiments* in *Othon I de Grandson (vers 1240–1328)*. Lausanne: Cahiers Lausannois d'Histoire Médiévale. 128.
117. *Fontes rerum Bernensium*, 4: 567.
118. Thomas Gray of Heton. 1836. *Scalacronica: A Chronicle of England and Scotland from 1066 to 1362*. 45
119. Elizabeth A. R. Brown & Nancy Freeman Regalado. 1994. 'La Grant Feste: Philip the Fair's Celebration of the Knighting of his sons in Paris at Pentecost of 1313' in *City and Spectacle in Medieval Europe*. 56–86.
120. TNA E101/375/8. Fol.32.
121. CCR Edward II vol 1 1307–1313, 585. 'June 26 [1313], Pontoise. The like in favour of . . . Otto de Grandisono.'

Chapter 16

1. The date is disputed. Henry Charles Lea got his date of 18 March from Chron. Nangis. 300. '*Le lundi après la fête de Saint-Grégoire*' or 18 March 1314. However, other chroniclers, such as Bernard Gui *Flores Chronicorum* have proposed the Monday before the Feast of Saint Gregory, or 11 March 1314. Alain Demurger (2018) [2015]. 'The Council of Vienne and the Burning of Jaques de Molay (1311–1314)'. *The Persecution of the Templars*: *Scandal, Torture, Trial* [*La Persécution des templiers:* journal (1305–1314)]. Translated by Teresa Lavender Fagan. Profile Books, suggests 11 March as now the likely date. Also see Elizabeth A. R. Brown (2015), 'Philip the Fair, Clement V, and the end of the Knights Templar: The execution of Jacques de Molay and Geoffroi de Charny in March'. *Viator*. 47 (1): 229–92. Abstract for the article 'and suggest that the executions occurred on 11 rather than 18 March'.
2. Henry Charles Lea. 1888. *A History of the Inquisition of the Middle Ages Vol. III*. New York: Hamper & Bros, Franklin Sq. 325.
3. Gestes de Chiprois, 331. '697. *Et fur feſte parole .j. fergant le fery de la paume fur la bouche, qu'il ne poſt plus dire, & fu trayné par les cheviaus en une chapele, & le tindrent tant là que il fu bien tart, & que le peuple fu amermé & party de la plus grant partie. Et adons le dit maiſtre & le coumandour de Gafcoigne furent mis en une barque & pafés en l'ihle, quy eſt de dens le flum, & là fu le feuc alumé, & le maiſtre lor pria qu'il y fofriffent à dire ſes oryſſons, les queles il diſt à Dieu; & puis ſe livra à faire de ſon cors lor volenté. Et enſy ſeaus le pryrent & le mirent au feuc, & fu ars, & le Dieu tout puiſſant quy ſeit & conut les choſes facrées, ſil ſeit que il fuſt innocent de ſel feit que l'on lor miſt ſus luy, & les autres quy furent ars, ſont martirs devant Dieu; & ſe il font tés quy l'ayent deſervy, il ont eſté punis, mais je puis bien dire, tant que à l'aparant, je les ay coneis pour bons creſtiens & devos en lor meſſes & en lor vie.*' In English translation Paul F. Crawford. 2003. *The Templar of Tyre: Part III of the deeds of the Cypriots*. Abingdon: Routledge. 117–18
4. Chron. Godefroy de Paris. 220.

5. Translation Dan. Jones. 2017. *The Templars*. Viking Press: New York. 308. For an alternative source of the Capetian curse see *Scalacronica.* 46, which attributes the end of the Capetian line to Philippe's cruelty in the Tour de Nesle affair.
6. Sophia Menache. 2003. Clement V. Cambridge: Cambridge University Press. 17. 34. n151. '*Fertur etiam, quod ea nocte, qua mortuus est, sic fuit desertus ab omnibus, ut ex cereorum igne supra cum delapso [sic] pars corporis sit adusta. In vita tamen multum dilexit propinquos, et divitiis ac honoribus illos auxit*' 'citing Chronicon fratris Francisci Pipini, col. 751; Agnolo di Tura, Cronaca Senese, p. 343; Notae ad vitas, pp. 69, 170.' Menache adds however, 'On the other hand, this report may suggest a tendency to attest to the fulfilment of the curse of the last master of the Temple, Jacques de Molai, on account of the pope's policy against the Templars.'
7. ElizabethA.R.Brown.2019.'PhiliptheFairofFranceandHisFamily'sDisgrace:TheAdultery Scandal of 1314 Revealed, Recounted, Reimagined, and Redated', *Mediaevistik*, vol 32. n6. The continuation of the Latin universal chronicle of Guillaume de Nangis specifies that the men confessed that the affair had lasted 'about three years'. *Chronique latine de Guillaume de Nangis de 1113 à 1300 avec les continuations de cette chronique de 1300 à 1368*, 2 vols, ed. Hercule Géraud. Publications de la Société de l'histoire de France, 33, 35. Paris: Jules Renouard, 1843, 1: 405 ('*confessi sunt hoc scelus quasi per triennium frequentasse*').
8. *Scalacronica*.46.'Itwasgenerallyreportedamongthecommonpeoplethatthisscandalwas communicated to the King of France by his daughter Isabel, Queen of England' Elizabeth A. R. Brown. 2019. 'Philip the Fair of France and His Family's Disgrace: The Adultery Scandal of 1314 Revealed, Recounted, Reimagined, and Redated', *Mediaevistik*, vol 32. 79. 'What connection Isabelle's visit had with the revelation of the adultery affair is a matter of speculation.'
9. Elizabeth A.R. Brown. 1989. 'Diplomacy, adultery and domestic politics at the court of Philip the Fair: Queen Isabella's mission to France in 1314' in J. S. Hamilton & Patricia J. Bradley, Ed. *Documenting the Past: Essays in medieval history presented to George Peddy Cuttino.* Woodbridge: The Boydell Press. 66. n61.
10. Chron. Godefroy de Paris, 228. '*D'une sentence si amère Por leur traïson et péchié, Qu'il furent vif escorchié; Puis fu lor nature copée, Aux chiens et aux bestes jetée, Et puis traïné et pendu. Tel jugement lor fut rendu De lor père et de plusor. Ainsi moururent en doulor.*' Or 'With such a bitter sentence for their treason and sin, That they were flayed alive; Then their nature was cut, thrown to dogs and beasts, and then dragged and hanged. Such judgment was given Of their father and many others. Thus, they died in pain.'
11. Chron. Nangis. 302. '*Ils furent à la vue de tous écorchés tout vivans sur la place publique. On leur coupa les parties viriles et génitales, et leur tranchant la tête, on les traîna au gibet public où, dépouillés de toute leur peau, ils fnrent pendus par les épaules et les jointures des bras.*' Or 'They were flayed alive in the public square in full view of everyone. Their virile and genital parts were cut off, and their heads were cut off, and they were dragged to the public gallows where, stripped of all their skin, they were hanged by the shoulders and the joints of the arms.'
12. Chron. Godefroy de Paris, 226. '*Mès il il n'est nul feu sans fumée. Lors est la chose ainsi alée. Le fet fu ataint et prouvé, Qui jà grant pièce avoit couvé; Et en appert fu congnéu De Phelippe.*' Or 'But there is no fire without smoke. Then the thing went thus. The deed

was reached and proved, Which had already been smoldering in a large piece; And it became apparent to Philippe.'

13. Chron. Nangis. 301. '*Afin que, dans une étroite rèèlusion, privées de toute consolation humaine, elles terminassent leur vie dans linfortune et la misère.*' Or 'So that, in narrow reclusion, deprived of all human consolation, they end their lives in misfortune and misery.' Chron. Godefroy de Paris. 244. '*Prise comme garce et meschine, Et en prison emprisonnée A Gaillart, où el fu menée.*' Or 'Taken as a slut and a slave, and imprisoned in prison In Gaillard, where she was taken.' Elizabeth A. R. Brown. 2019. 'Philip the Fair of France and His Family's Disgrace: The Adultery Scandal of 1314 Revealed, Recounted, Reimagined, and Redated', *Mediaevistik*, vol 32. 71.
14. Chron. Godefroy de Paris. 244. '*Prise comme garce et meschine, Et en prison emprisonnée A Gaillart, où el fu menée.*' Or 'Taken as a slut and a slave, and imprisoned in prison In Gaillard, where she was taken.'
15. Ibid. 302. '*Quoique Jeanne, sceur de ladite Blanche, et épouse de: Philippe, comte du Poitou, eût été dans le commencement violemment soupconnée, séparée quelque temps de son mari, et gardée dans une prison au châtcau de Dourdan, ce pendant, après une enquête faite à ce sujet, elle fut lavée desdits soupcons, déclarée tout-à- fait innocente dans un parlement tenu à Paris.*' Or 'Although Jeanne, sister of the said Blanche, and wife of: Philippe, Count of Poitou, would have been in the violently suspected beginning, separated for some time from her husband, and kept in a prison at the Château de Dourdan, this after an investigation made on this subject, she was cleansed of the said suspicions, declared quite innocent in a parliament held in Paris.'
16. *Scalacronica*. 47. 'It was judged and declared by the Commons that, because of this cruelty, neither the father nor the sons should live long.'
17. Glynn Coppack & Mark Douglas. 2014. *Mount Grace Priory*. London: *English Heritage*. 16–17.
18. The name La Lance was first mentioned in 1194 in the form "*aquam, rivum de Lancea*", the origin of which is to be found in the watercourse that crosses the estate.
19. J. Grémaud. 1879. '*Necrologe de la chartreuse de La Lance*'. Lausanne: Georges Bridel. 76–81. No 2. '*Nos vero Otho, dominus Grandissoni, laudamus et approbamus pro nobis et nostris heredibus venditionem predictam factam per dictum dominum Petrum Grandissoni, nepotem nostrum, et omnia supradicta ... Datum et actum anno domini millesimo trecentesimo decimo septimo, mense octobris*.' Or 'But we Othon, Lord of Grandson, praise and approve for us and our heirs the aforesaid sale made by the said Lord Pierre de Grandson, our nephew, and all the aforesaid ... Given and acted in the year of the Lord one thousand three hundred and seventeen, in the month of October.'
20. Ibid. 82. No. 3.
21. *Brevis historia ordinis Carthusiensis auctore anonymo. Martene et Durand. Veterum scriptorum collectio*. Vol VI. 181.
22. As discussed earlier the Florentine minted gold florin fountained 3.54 grams of gold, therefore, to ascertain today's value we can simply take an October 2024 price for gold of £67.02 per gram and multiply out.
23. Bernard Andenmatten. 2000. '*L'ancienne chartreuse de La Lance*'. *Revue historique Vaudoise*. 108. 15. '*Les motivations des seigneurs de Grandson, et plus particuliè*

rement d'Othon I', sont difficiles à cerner au-delà des classiques justifications pieuses des deux chartes de fondation.'

24. Glynn Coppack & Mark Douglas. 2014. *Mount Grace Priory*. London: *English Heritage*. 17.
25. ACV C V b 37. '*Fondation par Othon, seigneur de Grandson, chevalier, d'un autel de Saint-Georges dans l'église Notre-Dame de Lausanne et dotation de cet autel au moyen de 20 livrées de rente annuelle en faveur de deux desservants*.' Or 'Foundation by Othon, Lord of Grandson, knight, of an altar of Saint-Georges in the church of Notre-Dame de Lausanne and endowment of this altar by means of 20 liveries of annual income in favour of two priests.'
26. Julian Havet. 1876. *Série chronologique des gardiens et seigneurs des îles normandes (1198–1461). S*eigneurs des *îles normandes (1198–1461)*. Bibliothèque de l'école des chartes. Tome 37. 202.
27. CPR Edward I vol 1 1272–1281, 125. '*Rex commisit Ottoni de Grandisono insulas de Gerneseye et Gereseye cum per tinenciis custodiendas quamdiu Regi placuerit, ita quod reddat regi per annum ad scaccarium regis quingentas marcas... T. R.. apud Turrim Londòn., xxv. die Novembris*.'
28. CPR Edward I vol 1 1272–1281, 188. For full Latin text see appendix.
29. *Bibliothéque Nationale de France*. MS. Lat. 10072. Fol. 201, *'magister Gulielmus de Sancto Remigio, attornatus domini Ottonis de Grandisono domini insularum.'* 20 November 1289.
30. Alexander Kelleher. 2022. "The King's Other Islands of the Sea': The Channel Islands in the Plantagenet Realm, 1254–1341'. *History* 107: 376. 460 'The position of the Norman Church in the Islands, in which ecclesiastical jurisdiction rested with the diocese of Coutances, was respected by the kings of England in line with their efforts to reclaim Normandy, and this was reflected in the continued patronage the Norman ecclesiastical establishments received from the Islanders.'
31. Ibid. 459. 'It has been persuasively argued that John and Henry III engaged in a policy which sought to disrupt the Islands as little as possible by preserving the status quo there, particularly as regards local customary law and judicial institutions.'
32. Ibid. 473. Otto's lordship of the Islands was effectively a sinecure, 'Granted on account of his intimacy with the king.'
33. Esther Rowland Clifford. 1961. *A Knight of Great Renown: The Life and Times of Othon de Grandson.* Chicago: University of Chicago Press. 264.
34. Charles L. Kingsford. 1909. *Sir Otho de Grandison 1238?–1328*. Transactions of the Royal Historical Society 3: 192
35. TNA SC 1/26/34.
36. Julian Havet. 1876. *Série chronologique des gardiens et seigneurs des îles normandes (1198–1461*). Seigneurs des îles normandes (1198–1461). *Bibliothèque de l'école des chartes. Tome 37*. 204.
37. Ibid.
38. Ibid. 205.
39. CPR Edward I vol 1 1271–1281, 411.
40. Charles L. Kingsford. 1909. *Sir Otho de Grandison 1238?–1328*. Transactions of the Royal Historical Society 3: 192. Citing Ancient Correspondence, xxxvi. 133. '*Sire, mandez moy se vous auez mande aus pors qui les chouses des ij Royames soient comunes, si*

come il a este ordene, et veullez mander aus gardeyns des pors & aus ballifs que eus leyssent passer ma gent des ysles et leur chouses franchement.'

41. Ibid. 170. Citing Ancient Petitions, 47–49, 55–59.
42. Cartulaire de Jersey. No. 104 'Lettre d'Othon de Granson, Chevalier, en date du 31 Mars 1316, par laquelle il fait remise aux religieux du Mont St. Michel de cer- taines amendes encourues tant à Jersey qu'à Guernesey par l'abbé du Mont St. Michel et le Prieur du Valle. 1316. A louz ceus qui ces presentes lettres verront et orront. Othes de Gransson chevalier saluz en Dyeu. Comme labbey et le convent dont Mont Saynt Michiel et le priour do Wale fussent en amendes pour aucunes transgressions cest assavoir pour ce que Thomas Anquetil avoyt estey batu a la Rousse Mare e pour un mast qui avoyt estey meney au Wale sus larrest le Roy, et pour un porpoys qui avoyt estey pris sanz veue en la terre dou Wale e pour une amende de quarante libvres tauxee par les justices en Gersey: Sachent touz que je avant dit Othes en tant comme il appartient a ma persone pour la devocion que je ay au moustier dou Mont Saynt Michiel et pour lame dou bon Roy Edward que Diex assoille, les amendes des transgressions dessus dites lour ay quitey et pardoney. En tesmoyg de laquel chose jay mis mon seel a ceste letre patente: fete et donée en lan de grace mil troys cenz et seze, le derrayn jour de Marz. [Collationné à l'original existant aux archives de La Manche et revêtu du sceau d'Othon de Granson]
43. Cartulaire de Jersey. No 60. '*Chier sire, sachez que Monsieur de Grantson vint as illes au Chastel de Gersuy le premier jor deu mois de Juyn.*' Or 'Dear sir, know that Monsieur de Grandson came to you at Castle of Jersey on the first day of the month of June.'
44. Charles L. Kingsford. 1909. *Sir Otho de Grandison 1238?–1328.* Transactions of the Royal Historical Society 3: 195. Kingsford published a letter to England from d'Oron written while in Vaud 9 March 1324. Ibid. 168. Kingsford surmised that 'Otho de Grandison took the opportunity to go home in his company.'
45. E. Mallet, 1855. *La plus ancienne chronique de Genève 1303–1335.* (*Fasciculus temporis) et pièces justificatives*, Geneva, (*Mémoires et documents publiés par la Société d'histoire et d'archéologie de Genève*, 9). 306 '*Item anno a Nativitate Domini MCCCXXIII, die dominica ante festum beati Luce evangeliste, videlicet XVIIo kalendas novembris obiit bone memorie et inclite recordationis illustris vir dominus Amedeus comes Sabaudie, apud Avinionem ...; et corpus ipsius domini comitis fuit apportatum in Sabaudia, et sepultum die mercurii sequenti Altecombe anno quo supra.*' It is unlikely that the count was buried on the following Wednesday, 19 October, only three days later; the date given by the Hautecombe chronicle, i.e. Thursday of the following week, 27 October, is more likely: '*Anno Domini MCCCXXIII, septimo decimo kalendas novembris obiit illustris ac inimicis suis formidabilis vir dominus Amedeus decimus primus comes Sabaudie, qui inde fuit tumulatus ac honorifice sepultus in suo monasterio Altecombe in vigilia apostolorum Simonis et Iude. Anima eius requiescat in pace, amen', Chronica abbatiae Altaecombae,* Ed. *Monumenta Historiae Patriae, III, Scriptorum, t. I, Turin*, 1840, col. 671–678: col. 675. 4. «*Anno Domini MCCCXXIX, pridie nonas novembris, obiit illustris ac.*'
46. Giovanni Villani. *Nuovo Chronica*. Ed. Guiseppe Porta. 1997. *Tomo Secondo*. CCLXVII. '*Nel detto anno MCCCXXIIII, essendo il re Carlo re di Francia stato in grande speranza e trattato col papa e con più baroni de la Magna d'essere eletto re de' Romani per le dissensioni de' due eletti re d'Alamagna.*'

47. Pierre Dubois. 1891. Ed. Ch. V. Langlois. *De Recupertatione Terre Sancte*. Paris: Alphonse Picard. Trans, W. L. Brandt. New York. 1956. 'If the lord pope should remain long in the kingdom of the French, he will probably create so many cardinals from that kingdom that the papacy will remain with us and escape altogether the grasping hands of the Romans ... Lord Charles of Valois, when the wars of Christians obedient to the lord pope have been brought to a close, can, by the grace of God, easily seize the empire of Constantinople ... It will be a source of much honour and profit to the Lord king of the French if he can procure the kingdom and empire of Germany for his brother and nephews in perpetuity. It would be well to come to an agreement on this matter with the present king [of Germany] before he can hear of the new plan for peace. The lord king, as is said to have been agreed elsewhere, would then have for himself and his heirs the whole territory situated on this side of the Rhine at Cologne, or at all events the direct overlordship and control of the countries of Provence and Savoy.' In Brian Tierney. 1988. *The Crisis of Church and State 1050–1300*. Toronto: University of Toronto Press. 195. 'Pierre Dubois presented a much more radical thesis on the royal side in his *De Recuperatione Terrae Sanctae*. Dubois proposed the wholesale expropriation of ecclesiastical estates as a part of a general reorganisation of Europe under the hegemony of the French monarchy. According to his plan the king of France was to bribe the German electors to make him emperor, his brother was to seize Constantinople, and the pope was to reside in France and become in effect a sort of chaplain to the French royal house.'
48. Johann Carl Ludwig Gieseler. 1855. *A Text-book of Church History: A.D. 1305–1517*. New York: Harper & Brothers Publishers. 29. n13. 'The German princes were summoned to meet at Bar-sur-Aube in June 1324, to depose Lewis [Louis of Bavaria], and elect King Charles of France. But only Leopold, Duke of Austria, brother of the imprisoned Frederick, made his appearance, and received several promises in return for his engagement zealously to further Charles's design, for instance a promise of help in the reconquest of Schwyz and Unterwalden.'
49. Ferdinando Gabotta. 1903. *Asti e la Politica Sabauda in Italia*. vol VII Pinerolo. 420. n2. '*In stipendiis suis (Andree Bonixpistiani de Pisis] et dicto Balatruche, eundo apud Bar, ad dominum Otonem de Granzon, missus per Dominum; xVI sol., vIr den. gross, tur ... -L. Domino Guidoni dou Fay, eundo ad regem Buemie et comiti de Bar; xx sol. gross. tur.*'

Chapter 17

1. Jean Gremaud. Ed. 1879. *Nécrologie de la Chartreuse de la Lance. Mémoires et documents publiés par la Société d'Histoire de la Suisse romande.* Vol XXXIV. Lausanne: Georges Bridel. 43. '*Aprilis 5. Obiit dnus Hocto de Grandissono fundator huius domus, anno Dni M ° CCC XXVIII.*'
2. Jean Gremaud, Ed. 1863. *Nécrologe de l'église cathédrale de Lausanne. Mélanges. Mémoires et documents publiés par la Société d'histoire de la Suisse romande*, 1st ser., XVIII. Lausanne: Georges Bridel. 130. '*Obiit dns Octho, dns Grandissoni, miles, qui dedit multa bona jocalia pro officio in festis solennibus honorificentius faciendo, scilicet capas optimas, tres cruces nobiles et tabulas aureas, infulas, plures calices et pannos*

aureos pro reparatione magni altaris et alia plura. Item dedit pro anniuersario suo vj 'lb. Laus. De quibus celerarius distribuere debet d. can. presentibus in vigiliis et missa anniuersarii sui.' Or 'Deceased Octo, a knight of Grandson, who gave many good ornaments for his service in solemn festivals, namely, the best capes, three noble crosses and gold plates, ribbons, several cups and cloths of gold for the repair of the great altar, and many other things. Likewise, he gave for his anniversary vj' *Livre Lausannois*. Of which the speedier should distributed to those present in the vigils and mass of his anniversary.' Esther Rowland Clifford. 1961. *A Knight of Great Renown: The Life and Times of Othon de Grandson.* Chicago: University of Chicago Press. 276. 'The necrology of the cathedral of Lausanne puts his death on 1 April, but it seems more probable that this was the date of the funeral.' Bernard Andenmatten. '*La Part de Dieu et la Mémoire des Hommes*' in *Othon I de Grandson (vers 1240–1328)*. Lausanne: Cahiers Lausannois d'Histoire Médiévale, 2020. 230. '*Le décalage de sept jours entre la notice de l'obituaire de la cathédrale de Lausanne et celles des deux autres nécrologes signale que la seconde date correspond probablement au jour de l'enterrement.*' Or 'The seven-day gap between the notice in the obituary of Lausanne Cathedral and those of the two other obituaries indicates that the second date probably corresponds to the day of the burial.'

3. Clifford modified the story of Grandson's passing from that originally proposed by Maxime Reymond, a modification subsequently and recently accepted by Andenmatten, albeit with criticism of the hypothetical nature of her description of the journey. Maxime Reymond, 1920. '*Le Chevalier Othon I de Grandson.*' *Revue historique vaudoise* 28. 178. Esther Rowland Clifford. 1961. *A Knight of Great Renown: The Life and Times of Othon de Grandson.* Chicago: University of Chicago Press. 276. 'During the intervening week, the cortège must have made its slow way from Aigle to Villeneuve and thence along the shores of the Léman, past Chillon to Montreux and Vevey, through the vineyards of the Lavaux and finally to Lausanne.' Bernard Andenmatten. '*La Part de Dieu et la Mémoire des Hommes*' in *Othon I de Grandson (vers 1240–1328)*. Lausanne: Cahiers Lausannois d'Histoire Médiévale, 2020. 230. n40. '*On peut partager sur ce point l'hypothèse des causes d'Othon. . . mais sa description du cortège funèbre amenant la dépouille d'Othon à la cathédrale de Lausanne est en revaunche hautement hypothétique.*' Or 'On this point, we can share the hypothesis of Othon's causes. . . but her description of the funeral procession bringing Othon's remains to Lausanne Cathedral is, on the other hand, highly hypothetical.' Clifford shares the anglophone way in making history alive by telling a story based upon a plausible hypothesis, Andenmatten meanwhile adopts the more continental style of remaining 'scientific'. Given the lack of alternative routes from Aigle to Lausanne other than described by Clifford the author finds the criticism of her unwarranted. The reader can draw their own conclusions in matters of style.
4. ACV C V b 53. '*meum ecclesia cathedrali beatae Mariae Laus mo eligo sepultra. Item volo et ordino quod, quando corpus meum ad ecclesiam deportabitur tumu landum, duo homines armati de armis meis et quilibet vexillum meum portans de eisdem armis precedant corpus meum super duos equos, quorum quilibet sit precii centum libre lausannensium; et unus equorum coperiatur armis et alius ferreo et offerantur dicti equi [cum] armis et copertoriis predictis in ecclesia Lausannensi predicta, cui iure legati rema neant in remissionem peccatorum meorum.*'
5. Ibid. '*excepta parvum aurea crucis et imaginem beatae mariae virginis argentea*'.

6. Maxime Reymond. '*Le Chevalier Othon I de Grandson*', *Revue historique vaudoise* 28 (1920). 176. Full translation of ACV C V b 53 into French was *'J'élis sépulture dans l'église cathédrale de la B. Marie. Je veux et j'ordonne que mon corps soit porté dans la tombe par deux hommes d'armes, à mes armes, précédés de ma bannière, montés sur deux chevaux, du prix de 100 livres l'un, l'un avec une couverture à mes armes, l'autre ferré et harnaché; ces deux chevaux, armés et couverts, seront donnés à l'église de Lausanne en rémission de mes péchés. Je veux et ordonne que l'on achète pour l'église de Lausanne 20 livrées de terre, pour que deux chapelains célèbrent`à perpétuité pour le repos de mon âme; ces chapelains, constitués du consentement du chapitre, sont D. Thibaud, curé de Saint-Germain, mon chapelain, et D. Hugues de Lignerolles, prêtre. Je veux et prescris que l'on achète pour. La dite église 6. Livrées de terre pour mon anniversaire, et l'on donnera 20 sols aux clercs du cheur qui auront assisté à l'office, au jour de mon obit. Mes exécuteurs testamentaires pourront racheter ces 20 et 6 livrées de terre. Je donne et lègue à l'église de Lausanne tous mes ornements, vêtements et argenterie qui y sont maintenant déposés, à l'exception d'une petite croix d'or et d'une statue de la B. Marie Vierge, d'argent, que je porte habituellement sur moi.*' A further French translation appears in Bernard Andenmatten. 2020. *Othon I de Grandson (vers 1240–1328).* Lausanne: Cahiers Lausannois d'Histoire Médiévale. 231. '*Je veux et j'ordonne que, quand mon corps sera amené dans l'église [cathédrale] pour y être enseveli, deux hommes armés portant mes armoiries et une bannière frappée de ces mêmes armoiries précèdent mon corps; ils seront montés sur deux chevaux valant chacun 100 livres de lausannois, dont l'un sera recouvert [d'une couverture frappée] de mes armes, l'autre [d'un carapaçon] de fer. Ces deux chevaux avec les armoiries seront ensuite offerts à l'Eglise de Lausanne et resteront sa propriété en vertu de cette donation, en rémission de mes péchés.*'
7. Jean Gremaud, Ed. 1863. *Nécrologe de l'église cathédrale de Lausanne. Mélanges. Mémoires et documents publiés par la Société d'histoire de la Suisse romande*, 1st ser., XVIII. Lausanne: Georges Bridel, 130. '*Obiit dns Octho, dns Grandissoni, miles, qui dedit multa bona jocalia pro officio in festis solennibus honorificentius faciendo, scilicet capas optimas, tres cruces nobiles et tabulas aureas, infulas, plures calices et pannos aureos pro reparatione magni altaris et alia plura. Item dedit pro anniuersario suo vj 'lb. Laus. De quibus celerarius distribuere debet d. can. presentibus in vigiliis et missa anniuersarii sui.*' Or 'Deceased Octo, a knight of Grandson, who gave many good ornaments for his service in solemn festivals, namely, the best capes, three noble crosses and gold plates, ribbons, several cups and cloths of gold for the repair of the great altar, and many other things. Likewise, he gave for his anniversary vj *Livre Lausannois*. Of which the speedier should distributed to those present in the vigils and mass of his anniversary.'
8. Bernard Andenmatten. '*La Part de Dieu et la Mémoire des Hommes*' in *Othon I de Grandson (vers 1240–1328).* Lausanne: Cahiers Lausannois d'Histoire Médiévale, 2020. 235-6. '*Etant donné la disparition totale du cou- vent des franciscains de Grandson, nous ne savons pas à quoi pouvait ressembler la sépulture du coeur d'Othon. Une source du XVIIe siècle mentionne seulement que se trouvait «dans la muraille (sic) la statue d'Othon de Grandson», indication qui fait penser à un enfeu abritant un gisant, sans que l'on sache évidemment si sur ce dernier se trouvait une figure faisant référence à l'organe qu'il abritait.*' Or 'Given the complete disappearance of the Franciscan convent

of Grandson, we do not know what the burial of Othon's heart could have looked like. A 17th century source only mentions that there was 'in the wall (sic) the statue of Othon of Grandson', an indication that suggests a tomb sheltering a recumbent figure, without it being obvious whether on the latter there was a figure referring to the organ it sheltered.' And Jean Gremaud. Ed. 1879. *Nécrologie de la Chartreuse de la Lance. Mémoires et documents publiés par la Société d'Histoire de la Suisse romande.* Vol XXXIV. Lausanne: Georges Bridel. 96-7. No 13. '*Hoc adito quod in die dicti aniuersarii, post missam defunctorum solempniter celebratam, supra tumbam bone memorie domini Othonis, domini Grandissoni, ibidem existentem fiat stacio defunctorum solempniter, in qua sint omnes Cartusienses, dicti Fratres Minores et dicti monachi. Qua stacione facta, omnes ibidem existentes incipiant cantare hunc Psalmum de Profundis; quo dicto sacerdos qui magnam missam celebrauerit dicat vnam oracionem defunctorum*.' Or 'It is added that on the day of the said anniversary, after the mass of the deceased has been solemnly celebrated, over the tomb in good memory of Lord Othon, Lord Grandisson, there shall be a solemn station of the deceased, in which shall be all the Carthusians, the said Friars Minor and the said monks. Having made this station, let all those present begin to sing this Psalm for the Dead; after which the priest who has celebrated a great mass says a prayer for the dead.

9. CPR Edward I vol 2 1281–1292, 490. 'Licence for William de Grandisono to strengthen his house of Asperton, co. Hereford, with a wall of stone and lime and to crenellate it.'
10. Michael Ray. 2006. 'The Savoyard Cousins: A Comparison of the Careers and Relative Success of the Grandson (Grandison) and Champvent (Chavent) Families in England'. *The Antiquaries Journal* 86: 165. 'The Grandison ivories are on display in the British Museum and the Louvre. The Grandison Breviary is among the treasures of the British Library. Bishop John's books are in the Bibliothèque Nationale in Paris and his ring at Exeter Cathedral.'
11. The current bell bears the inscription 'EX DONO IOHANNIS GRANDISON EPISCOPI EXON GVLIELMVS EVANS FECIT 1729'.
12. J. N. Dalton. 1917. *The collegiate church of Ottery St Mary being the Ordinacio et Statuta ecclesie Sancta Marie de Otery Exon. Diocesis A.D. 1338 1339.* Cambridge: Cambridge University Press. ix.
13. https://defleague.co.uk/cups/grandisson/ retrieved 2 July 2024.
14. Michael Ray. 2006. The Savoyard Cousins: A Comparison of the Careers and Relative Success of the Grandson (Grandison) and Champvent (Chavent) Families in England. The Antiquaries Journal 86: 166 and n. 386.
15. Michael Ray. 2006. 'The Savoyard Cousins: A Comparison of the Careers and Relative Success of the Grandson (Grandison) and Champvent (Chavent) Families in England'. The *Antiquaries Journal* 86:166. 'Invisible links remain through the Grandson blood line; for instance, the present royal family is descended from the Grandsons, whose descendants produced both the Yorkist and the Tudor kings of England.'
16. John Marshall. 2023. *Peter of Savoy: The Little Charlemagne*. Barnsley: Pen & Sword Books Ltd.
17. Gestes des Chiprois. 279. '542. . . '*le dit meſſire Ote de Gualanſon que eſt j chevalier d'outremer de grant renomée.*'
18. Alain Demurger. 2018. '*Othon de Grandson et les templiers d'Épailly*' in *Communicating the Middle Ages: Essays in Honour of Sophia Menache*. London: Routledge. 47. n6. Citing *Voir*

L'Estoire de Eraclès empereur et la conqueste de la terre d'Outremer, RHC OC 2. Paris, 1859. 463: '*Et fu fait seneschal du roiaume de Jherusalem sire Johan de Grely. Revenu en Occident ce Jean de Grilly fut envoyé en Guyenne comme sénéchal en 1278; accusé de malversations il fut destitué en 1287 (Grandson siégeait dans la commission!). Il passa alors au service du roi de France qui le chargea effectivement en 1288 du com- mandement du 'régiment français' d'Acre. Othon de Grandson le retrouve à Acre en 1290.*' Or 'And Sir Jean de Grailly was made seneschal of the Kingdom of Jerusalem. Returning to the West, Jean de Grailly was sent to Gascony as seneschal in 1278; accused of embezzlement he was dismissed in 1287 (Grandson sat on the commission!). He then entered the service of the King of France who effectively charged him in 1288 with command of the 'French regiment' of Acre. Othon de Grandson found him in Acre in 1290.'

19. Charles L. Kingsford. 1909. *Sir Otho de Grandison 1238?–1328.* Transactions of the Royal Historical Society 3: 125–195. '*A sun tres cher seignur, e si le plest amy, Sire Otes de Gransun, le seon marener Thomas Salekyn de Douere saluz.*' Or 'To my very dear lord, and if it pleases, my friend, Sir Othon de Grandson, his mariner Thomas Salekyn of Dover salutes.'
20. Chron. Guisborough, Vol 2, 24. '*mutato cognomine, in congressu militari parvum sonum fecit*' or 'having changed his surname, he made little noise at the military meeting'.
21. Jean-Daniel Morerod. 2020. *Finances et Sentiments* in *Othon I de Grandson (vers 1240-1328)*. Lausanne: *Cahiers Lausannois d'Histoire Médiévale*. 125 and 131. *'Couard, je ne sais pa'*.
22. Paul F. Crawford. 2003. The Templar of Tyre: Part III of the deeds of the Cypriots. Abingdon: Routledge. 121. '542. . . This Sir Otto of Grandson, who is a Western knight of great renown.' Gestes des Chiprois.. 279. '542. . . '*le dit meſſire Ote de Gualanſon que eſt j chevalier d'outremer de grant renomée.*'
23. John Brownbill. Ed. 1914. The History of the Abbey in Ledger of Vale Royal Abbey. Manchester: Manchester Record Society. 'Now there was at that time with the King a good and holy man, and a most strenuous knight in arms, named Otto de Grandison, whose memory be blessed for ever.'
24. J. R. Maddicott, 2005. 'Grandson (Grandison), Sir Otto de'. *Oxford Dictionary of National Biography.*
25. Michael Prestwich 2020. *Othon de Grandson et la Cour d'Edouard I, Othon I de Grandson (vers 1240–1328)*. Lausanne: Cahiers Lausannois d'Histoire Médiévale. 21. Published in French '*offert loyaux services à Edouard I et à sa femme Eléonore.*' I am indebted to Michael Prestwich for providing the original English text which describes Leonor as Edward's Queen not Wife. An important distinction since Prestwich's text reinforces the relationship between Leonor his Queen and Othon, one that may well have taken Grandson to pray for her departed soul in Jerusalem. The perils of translation.
26. Charles L. Kingsford. 1909. *Sir Otho de Grandison 1238?–1328.* Transactions of the Royal Historical Society 3: 125–95. Citing 1 Chronicon S. Bertini, ap. Martene and Durand, *Thesaurus Novus Anecdotorum*, iii. 751I. John of Ypres died in 1383, but he entered the monastery in 1339 and may have heard the story not many years after Othon's death.

BIBLIOGRAPHY

Andenmatten, Bernard. 1989. *La noblesse vaudoise face à la Maison de Savoie au XIII siecle. La Maison de Savoie et le Pays de Vaud* in *Revue Historique Vaudoise* 97: 35–50.

Andenmatten, Bernard. 2000. '*L'ancienne chartreuse de La Lance*' in *Revue historique Vaudoise.*

Andenmatten, Bernard.1990. *La Maison De Savoie En Pays De Vaud.* Lausanne: Editions Payot Lausanne.

Asbridge, Thomas. 2010. *The Crusades.* London: Simon & Schuster UK Ltd.

Barraclough, G. 1940. 'Edward I and Adolf of Nassau: A Chapter of Medieval Diplomacy' in the *Cambridge Historical Journal* VI

Bartlett, Robert. 1993. *The Making of Europe: Conquest, Colonization and Cultural Change 950–1350.* London: Penguin Books Ltd.

Bernard Andenmatten (Ed.) 2020. *Othon I de Grandson (vers 1240–1328)*. Lausanne: Cahiers Lausannois d'Histoire Médiévale.

Beverley Smith, J. 2014. *Llywellyn ap Gruffudd: Prince of Wales.* Cardiff: The University of Wales Press.

Blakely, Ruth Margaret. 2005. *The Brus Family in England and Scotland, 1100–1295.* Martlesham: Boydell & Brewer. 81.

Blomquist, Thomas W. 1971. 'Commercial Association in Thirteenth-Century Lucca' in *The Business History Review* 45.

Broadhurst, Ronald. J. C., 1952. *The Travels of ibn Jubayr*. London: Jonathan Cape.

Brown, Elizabeth A. R. & Regalado, Nancy Freeman. 1994. 'La Grant Feste: Philip the Fair's Celebration of the Knighting of his sons in Paris at Pentecost of 1313' in *City and Spectacle in Medieval Europe*.

Brown, Elizabeth A. R. 1987. 'The Prince is Father of the King: The Character and Childhood of Philip the Fair of France' in *Mediaeval Studies* 49.

Brown, Elizabeth A. R. 1988. 'The Political Repercussions of Family Ties in the Early Fourteenth Century: The Marriage of Edward II of England and Isabelle of France' in *Speculum* 63.

Brown, Elizabeth A. R. 1989. *'Diplomacy, adultery and domestic politics at the court of Philip the Fair: Queen Isabella's mission to France in 1314'* in J. S. Hamilton & Patricia J. Bradley (Ed.), *Documenting the Past: Essays in medieval history presented to George Peddy Cuttino.* Woodbridge: The Boydell Press.

Brown, Elizabeth A. R. 2019. *'Philip the Fair of France and His Family's Disgrace: The Adultery Scandal of 1314 Revealed, Recounted, Reimagined, and Redated'* in *Mediaevistik* Vol 32.

Brundage, James A. 1966. '"*Cruce Signari*": The Rite for Taking the Cross in England' in *Tradito* 22.

Buathier, Henri. 1995. *Jean Ier de Grailly un chevalier européen du XIIIe siècle.*

Burnand. Aug. 1911. '*La date de la naissance d'Othon 1er, Sire de* Grandson' in *Revue Historique Vaudoise* 19: 129–135.

Burt, Caroline. 2013. *Edward I and the Governance of England, 1272–1307*. Cambridge: Cambridge University Press.
Butler, Lawrence & Knight, Jeremy K. 2004. *Dolforwyn Castle, Montgomery Castle.* Cardiff: Cadw.
Carpenter, David. 2004. *The Struggle for Mastery: Britain 1066–1284*. London: Penguin Books Ltd.
Carpenter, David. 2020. *Henry III: The Rise to Power and Personal Rule 1207–1258*. New Haven: Yale University Press.
Ch. V. Langlois. 1889. *Documents Relatifs a Bertrand de Got (Clément V). Revue Historique* 40 Roth, Charles. 1948. *Cartulaire du Chapitre de Notre-Dame de Lausanne*. Lausanne: Librairie Payot.
Chaplais, Pierre. 1994. *Piers Gaveston: Edward II's Adoptive Brother.* Oxford: Clarendon Press.
Chapuisat, Jean-Pierre. 1964. '*Au service de deux rois d'Angleterre au XIIIe siècle: Pierre de Champvent*' *in Revue Historique Vaudoise* 72: 157–75.
Chapuisat, Jean-Pierre. 1989. '*De Mont-sur-Rolle à Windsor, de la Dullive à Dumfries ... La Maison de Savoie et le Pays de* Vaud' in Bibliothèque *historique vaudoise* 97.
Charrière, M. L. 1866. *Les Dynastes de Grandson Jusqu'au XIII Siècle*. Lausanne: Georges Bridel.
Clifford, Esther Rowland 1961. *A Knight of Great Renown: The Life and Times of Othon de Grandson*. Chicago: The University of Chicago Press.
Cloak, J. 1995. *Palaces and Parks of Richmond and Kew: The Palaces of Shene and Richmond.* London: Phillimore.
Cockerill, Sara. 2014. *Eleanor of Castile: The Shadow Queen*. 2nd Edition. Stroud: Amberley Publishing.
Cox, Eugene L. 1974. *The Eagles of Savoy: The House of Savoy in Thirteenth Century Europe*. Princeton: Princeton University Press.
Crawford, Paul F. 2003. *The Templar of Tyre: Part III of the deeds of the Cypriots*. Abingdon: Routledge.
Crowley, Roger. 2019. *Accursed Tower*. New Haven: Yale University Press.
d'Orville dit Cabaret, Jean. 1995. *La Chronique de Savoie*. Montmelian: La Fontaine de Siloé.
Dalton, J. N. 1917. *The collegiate church of Ottery St Mary being the Ordinacio et Statuta ecclesie Sancta Marie de Otery Exon. Diocesis A.D. 1338 1339*. Cambridge: Cambridge University Press. ix.
Darracott, Ann. 2014. *The Grandisons: Their Built and Chivalric Legacy.* Maidenhead: Maidenhead Civic Society.
Davies, Norman. 2012. *Vanished Kingdoms: The History of Half-Forgotten Europe*. London: Penguin Books.
Davies, R. R. 1987. *The Age of Conquest: Wales 1063–1415*. Oxford: Oxford University Press.
de Pont-Wullyamoz, Marie-Louise Françoise, 1796. *Anecdotes Tirées de L'Histoire et des Chroniques Suisses*. Lausanne: Chez Henri Vincent.
Hislop, Malcolm. 2020. *James of St. George and the Castles of North Wales*. Barnsley: Pen & Sword Books Ltd.
De Sturler, J. 1960. '*Le Paiment a Bruxelles des Allies Franc Comtois d'Edouard 1er Roi d'Angleterre (Mai 1297)*' in *Cahiers Bruxelles* V.Wurstemberger, J. Ludwig. 1859. *Peter*

der Zweite, Graf von Savoyen, Markgraf in Italien, Sein Haus und Seine Lande. Berne: Stæmpfle.

Demotz, Bernard. 2000. *Le Comté de Savoie du XIe au XVe Siècle*. Genève: Editions Slatkine.

Demurger, Alain. 2018. '*Othon de Grandson et les templiers d'Épailly*' in *Communicating the Middle Ages: Essays in Honour of Sophia Menache*. London: Routledge. Demurger, Alain. 2002. *The Last Templar*. London: Profile Books Ltd.

Digard, George. 1936. *Philippe Le Bel et le Saint-Siège*. 2 Vols. Paris.

Duncan, A. A. M. 2002. The Kingship of the Scots 842–1292. Edinburgh: Edinburgh University Press.

Dupuy, Pierre. 1655. *Histoire du differend d'entre le pape Boniface VIII et Philippe le Bel, roy de France*. Paris.

Edbury, Peter W. 1994. *The Kingdom of Cyprus and the Crusades, 1191–1374*. Cambridge: Cambridge University Press.

Edwards, John Goronwy. '1944. Edward I's Castle-Building in Wales' in The Proceedings of the British Academy XXXII.

Edwards, John Goronwy. 1935. *Calendar of Ancient Correspondence Concerning Wales*. Cardiff: University Press Board Cardiff.

Firnhaber-Baker, Justine. 2024. *House of Lilies: The Dynasty that Made Medieval France*. London: Penguin Books Ltd.

Forey, Alan. 1973. *The Templars in the Corona de Aragon*. Oxford: Oxford University Press. Doc XXXVI.

Forey, Alan. 2017. 'Otto of Grandson and the Holy Land, Cyprus, and Armenia' in *Crusades*, 16. Oxford & New York: Taylor & Francis

Fryde, E. B. 1962. *Book of prests of the King's Wardrobe for 1294–5*. Oxford: Clarendon Press.

Fryde, E. B., Greenway, D. E., Porter, S. & Roy, I. 1986. *Handbook of British Chronology*. 3rd Edition. London: Offices of the Royal Historical Society.

Funck-Brentano, Frantz. 1888. *Philippe le Bel et la Noblesse Franc-Comtois*. Paris: La Bibliotheque de l'Arsenal.

Galbreath, D. L. 1927. *Les Grandson d'Angleterre*. Archives Héraldiques Suisses 41.

Galland, Bruno, 1988. '*Un Savoyard sur le siège de Lyon au XIIIe siècle: Philippe de Savoie. Bibliothèque de l'école des chartes*' 146: 31–67. Bibliothèque de l'École des chartes.

Gingins-La Sarraz, Frédéric Jean Charles de. 1842. *Annales de l'abbaye du Lac-de-Joux depuis sa fondation jusqu'a sa suppression en 1536. Mémoires et documents publiés par la Société d'histoire de la Suisse romande, 1st ser.*, 1. Lausanne: Marc Ducloux.

Goldstone, Nancy. 2010. *Four Queens: The Provençal Sisters Who Ruled Europe*. London: The Orion Publishing Group.

Gough, Henry. 1900. *Itinerary of King Edward the First throughout his reign, A.D. 1272–1307, exhibiting his movements so far as they are recorded*. Paisley: Alexander Gardner.

Gravett, Christopher. 1990. *Medieval Siege Warfare*. 16th Edition. Oxford: Osprey Publishing Ltd.

Gravett, Christopher. 2007. *The Castles of King Edward I in Wales 1277–1307*. Botley: Osprey Publishing Ltd.

Gravett, Christopher. 2009. *English Castles 1200–1300*. Botley: Osprey Publishing Ltd.

Gremaud Jean (Ed.). 1863. *Nécrologe de l'église cathédrale de Lausanne. Mélanges. Mémoires et documents publiés par la Société d'histoire de la Suisse romande*, 1st ser., XVIII. Lausanne: Georges Bridel.

Gremaud Jean (Ed.).1879. *Nécrologie de la Chartreuse de la Lance. Mémoires et documents publiés par la Société d'Histoire de la. Suisse Romande.* Vol XXXIV. Lausanne: Georges Bridel.

Hennessy, Mark. 1996. 'Manorial organisation in early thirteenth-century Tipperary' in *Irish Geography* Vol 29: 2.

Hilton, Lisa. 2008. *Queens Consorts: England's Medieval Queens*. London: Weidenfeld & Nicolson.

Hindley, Geoffrey. 2003. *A Brief History of the Crusades*. London: Constable & Robinson Ltd.

Howell, Margaret. 1998. *Eleanor of Provence*. Oxford: Blackwell Publishers Ltd.

Ibn al-Furat, 1971. *Ayyubids, Mamlukes and Crusaders*, Vol 2: Translated and edited by Jonathan Malcolm Riley-Smith, Lyons, Cameron & Lyons, Ursula. Cambridge. W. Heffer & Sons Ltd.

Jacoby, David. 2005. 'Aspects of Everyday Life in Frankish Acre' in *Crusades* 4: Nicolle, David. 2001. *The Crusades*. London: Osprey Publishing Ltd.

Jéquier, Hugues. 1971. La Chartreuse de la Lance. Imprimerie Gutenberg.

Kaeuper, Richard W. 1973. *Bankers to the Crown: The Riccardi of Lucca and Edward I.* Princeton: Princeton University Press.

Kelleher, Alexander. 2022. '"The King's Other Islands of the Sea": The Channel Islands in the Plantagenet Realm, 1254–1341' in *History*. Vol 107. Issue 376.

Kennedy, Hugh. 1994. *Crusader Castles*. Cambridge: Cambridge University Press.

King, Andy. 2016. *Edward I: A New King Arthur?* London: Allen Lane & Penguin Random House.

Kingsford, Charles L. 1909. 'Sir Otho de Grandison 1238? –1328' in *Transactions of the Royal Historical Society* 3: 125–195.

Köhler, C. 1903–04. '*Deux projets de croisade en terre-sainte composée à la fin du xiiie siècle et au debut du xive*' in *Revue de l'Orient Latin.*

Köhler, C., Hayton of Corycus. *La flor des Estoires de la Terre d'Orient.*

Leopold. Antony R. 2000. *How to Recover the Holy Land: The Crusade Proposals of the Late Thirteenth and Early Fourteenth Centuries*. Aldershot: Ashgate Publishing Ltd.

Lewis, N. B. 1948. 'The English Forces in Flanders, August–November 1297' in *Studies in Medieval History* presented to F. M. Powicke. Oxford.

Lloyd, Simon. 1988. *English Society and the Crusade, 1216–1307*. Oxford: Clarendon Press.

Luttrell, Anthony. 2015. 'Observations on the Fall of the Temple' in *Élites et Ordres Militaires au Moyen Age*. Madrid: Casa de Velasquez.

Maddicott, J. R. 1970. *Thomas of Lancaster, 1307–1322: A study in the reign of Edward II.* Oxford University Press: London.

Maddicott, J. R. 2005. 'Grandson (Grandison), Sir Otto de'. Oxford Dictionary of National Biography.

Malcolm, Barber. 2006. *The Trial of the Templars.* Cambridge: Cambridge University Press.

Marshall, Christopher 1992. *Warfare in the Latin East 1192–1291.* Cambridge: Cambridge University Press.

Menache, Sophia. 2003. *Clement V*. Cambridge: Cambridge University Press.

Michelet, Jules (Ed.). 1841–51. *Procés des Templiers. Tome* 2. Paris.

Morerod, Jean-Daniel. 2012. *La Cathédrale Notre-Dame de Lausanne: Monument européen, temple vaudois.* Lausanne: La Bibliothèque des Arts.

Morerod, Jean-Daniel. 2020. *Finances et Sentiments* in *Othon I de Grandson (vers 1240–1328)*. Lausanne: Cahiers Lausannois d'Histoire Médiévale.

Morris, John E. 1901. *The Welsh Wars of Edward I.* Oxford: Clarendon Press.

Morris, Marc. 2009. *A Great and Terrible King.* London: Windmill Books.

Nicholson, Helen. 2004. *Knights Templar 1120–1312.* 11th Edition. Oxford: Osprey Publishing Ltd.

Nicolle, David. 2005. *Crusader Castles in the Holy Land 1192–1302.* Oxford: Osprey Publishing Ltd.

Nicolle, David. 2005. *Acre 1291.* 3rd Edition. Oxford: Osprey Publishing Ltd.

Nicolle, David. 2014. *Mamluk 'Askari 1250–1517.* Oxford: Osprey Publishing Ltd.

Norwich, John Julius. 2011. *The Popes.* London: Chatto & Windus.

Norwich, John Julius. 2016. *Sicily: A Short History from the Ancient Greeks to the Cosa Nostra.* London: John Murray.

Phillips, Seymour. 2011. *Edward II.* London: Yale University Press.

Poupardin, René. 1907. *Le Royaume de Bourgogne (888–1038).* Paris: Librairie Honoré Champion.

Powicke, Sir Maurice. 1953. *The Thirteenth Century 1216–1307.* Oxford: Oxford University Press.

Prestwich, Michael. 1972. *War, Politics and Finance: The Reign of Edward I.* London: Faber & Faber Ltd.

Prestwich, Michael. 1997. *Edward I.* Yale: Yale University Press.

Prestwich, Michael. 2020. '*Othon de Grandson et la Cour d'Edouard I*' in *Othon I de Grandson (vers 1240–1328).* Lausanne: Cahiers Lausannois d'Histoire Médiévale.

Pryce, Huw. 2005. *The Acts of Welsh Rulers: 1120 to 1283.* Cardiff: University of Wales Press.

Ray, Michael. 2006. 'The Savoyard Cousins: A Comparison of the Careers and Relative Success of the Grandson (Grandison) and Champvent (Chavent) Families in England' in *The Antiquaries Journal* 86.

Raynaud, Gaston. 1887. *Les gestes des Chiprois. Recueil de chroniques françaises écrites en Orient au 13e & 14e siècles (Philippe de Navarre & Gérard de Montréal publié pour la première fois pour la Société de l'Orient latin.)*

Reeve, Matthew M. 2006. 'The Painted Chamber at Westminster, Edward I, and the Crusade' in *Viator-Medieval and Renaissance Studies* 37: 189–221.

Reymond, Annick Voirol. 2013. 'Grandson Castle 1,000 years of history'. Grandson: Artgraphic Cavin SA.

Reymond, Maxime. 1920. '*Le Chevalier Othon I de Grandson*' in Revue *Historique Vaudoise* 28.

Rothero, Christopher. 1984. *The Scottish and Welsh Wars 1250–1400.* 20th Edition. Botley: Osprey Publishing Ltd.

Rothwell, H. 1927. 'Edward's Case against Philip the Fair over Gascony in 1298' in *The English Historical Review* 42: 572–82.

Runciman, Steven. 1954. *A History of the Crusades: Volume III The Kingdom of Acre and the later Crusades.* 11th Edition. London: The Folio Society.

Runciman, Steven. 1960. *The Sicilian Vespers.* London: Penguin Books.

Salt, Mary C. L. 1929. 'List of English Embassies to France, 1272–1307' in *The English Historical Review* 44: 263–78.

Seward, Desmond 2000. *The Monks of War: The Military Orders*. London: The Folio Society.

Strayer, Joseph R. 1980. *The Reign of Philip the Fair*. Princeton: Princeton University Press

Tanquerey, Frédéric Joseph. 1916. *Recueil de Lettres Anglo-Françaises, 1265–1399*. Paris: Librairie Ancienne Honoré Champion.

Taylor, Arnold. 1974. *The King's Works in Wales 1277–1330*. London: Her Majesty's Stationery Office.

Taylor, Arnold. 1985. *Studies in Castles and Castle-Building*. London: The Hambledon Press.

Taylor, Arnold. 1986. *The Welsh Castles of King Edward I*. London: The Hambledon Press.

Taylor, Arnold. 1963. 'Some notes on the Savoyards in North Wales, 1277–1300. With special reference to the Savoyard element in the construction of Harlech Castle' in *Genava* 11: 289–315. Burnand. Aug. 1911. '*Vaudois en Angleterre au XIIIe siècle, avec Othon Ier de Grandson: (d'après M.C.-L. Kingsford)*' in *Revue Historique Vaudoise* 19: 212–218.

Taylor, Arnold.1950. 'Master James of St. George' in *The English Historical Review* 65: 433–457.

Tierney, Brian. 1988. *The Crisis of Church and State 1050–1300*. Toronto: University of Toronto Press.

Turner, Rick. 2010. 'The Life and Career of Richard the Engineer' in *The Impact of the Edwardian Castles in Wales*. Oxford: Oxbow Books. 46–58.

Tyerman, Christopher. 1996. *England and the Crusades, 1095–1588*. Chicago: University of Chicago Press. Previté-Orton, C. W. 1912. *The Early History of the House of Savoy (1000–1233)*. Cambridge: Cambridge University Press.

Ullmann, Walter. 1955. 'The Curial Exequies for Edward I and Edward III' in *The Journal of Ecclesiastical History*. Vol. 6 issue. 1. 26–36.

Voutaz, Canon Jean-Pierre & Rouyer, Pierre. 2013. *Discovering the Great Saint Bernard*. Martigny: Les Editions du Grand-Saint-Bernard.

Weir, Alison. 2020. *Queens of the Crusades: Eleanor of Aquitaine and her Successors*. London: Penguin Random House UK.

Wenner, Manfred W. 1980. 'The Arab/Muslim Presence in Medieval Central Europe' in *International Journal of Middle East Studies* 12: 59–79.

Williams, David. 2021. 'Ebal III and Ebal IV de Grandson' in *Foundations* Vol 13.

Williams, David. 2022. 'Pierre de Grandson Part I' in *Foundations* Vol 14.

Williams, David. 2022. 'Pierre de Grandson Part II' in *Foundations* Vol 15.

Wilson, Peter H. 2017. *The Holy Roman Empire*. 2nd Edition. London: Penguin.

Wright, Thomas. 1839. *The Political Songs of England from the Reign of John to that of Edward II*.

INDEX